# A Manual For The Christian Minister
## Dr. Lee Ann B. Marino, Ph.D., D.Min., D.D.

# Understanding Demonology, Spiritual Warfare, Healing, And Deliverance

# UNDERSTANDING DEMONOLOGY, SPIRITUAL WARFARE, HEALING, AND DELIVERANCE

A Manual for the Christian Minister

Dr. Lee Ann B. Marino, Ph.D., D.Min., D.D.

Published by:
APOSTOLIC UNIVERSITY PRESS
(A division of The Righteous Pen Publications Group)
www.apostolicuniversity.org

All rights reserved. Except as permitted under the U.S. Copyright Act of 1976, no part of this book may be reproduced, distributed, or transmitted in any form or by any means, electronic or mechanical, or saved in any information storage and retrieval system without written permission from the author.

**Unless otherwise noted, all Scriptures taken from The Expanded Bible.** Copyright ©2011 by Thomas Nelson. Used by permission. All rights reserved.

Scripture quotations marked **MEV** are from the **Modern English Version**. Copyright © 2014 by Military Bible Association. Used by permission. All rights reserved.

All passages marked **KJV** are taken from the **Holy Bible, Authorized King James Version,** Public Domain.

Scripture quotations marked **GNT** are from the **Good News Translation in Today's English Version- Second Edition** Copyright © 1992 by American Bible Society. Used by Permission.

Cover photo: *Michael the Archangel*, by Claudio Coello (1642-1693). All photographs throughout this book are in the Public Domain.

Book Classification: Books › Religion & Spirituality › Christian Books & Bibles › Theology › Angelology & Demonology
Books › Religion & Spirituality › Occult & Paranormal › General

Copyright © 2018, 2025 by Dr. Lee Ann B. Marino.

ISBN: 1-940197-49-X
13-Digit: 978-1-940197-49-4

Printed in the United States of America.

I'm putting on the armor of God, to start my day;
Because I know God seeks to show He loves me today.
This armor will protect me from the haunts that seek
To discourage me from His purpose and call to be meek.
So, one piece at a time, I shall place on, right here,
A long, thoughtful moment, of armor and gear.

I commit to be strong in the Lord, and His power,
Knowing He's with me, right to the last hour.
I put it on, standing against the devil's plans,
Because I know I am strong in God's hands.
My struggle is not against flesh and blood,
But the spiritual forces that seek to throw mud.
When the day of evil comes, I shall stand,
Firm and prepared, with the heavenly band.

With the belt of truth buckled around my waist,
I know that all things shall be put into place.
With my feet prepared with the Gospel of peace,
I shall run and not get tired, and all stress shall cease.
With the shield of faith in front of me, ready
For the fiery darts that seek to leave me unsteady.

With the helmet of salvation, my head is secure
From the ways that the enemy seeks to offer a lure.
With the Sword of the Spirit, the Word of God,
I am embracing His truth wherever I trod.
In the Spirit, I'll pray, on all sorts of times and days,
With all kinds of prayers and ready battle plays.
Yes, I am alert and aware, and thinking of others,
My friends in the Lord, spiritual sisters and brothers.

This spiritual battle is not for the weak,
Nor for the timid, nor for those who feel bleak.
We must stand as warriors, a fighting brigade,
Who know that our work should not be delayed.
For the battle is real, and is rough, and is made,
But with God on my side, I am never afraid.

# - TABLE OF CONTENTS -

| | | |
|---|---|---|
| | Introduction | 1 |

### Part 1: Demonology

| | | |
|---|---|---|
| 1 | The Nature and Work of Divine Powers | 7 |
| 2 | The Nature and Work of Demonic Powers | 61 |
| 3 | Identifying Spirits | 121 |
| 4 | Demonology and Mythology Around the World | 163 |
| 5 | The Occult | 191 |
| 6 | Witchcraft and Magic | 245 |
| 7 | Superstitions | 279 |

### Part 2: Spiritual Warfare

| | | |
|---|---|---|
| 8 | Preparing for Eternal Battle: Ephesians 6 | 301 |
| 9 | Getting in the Eternal Battle: The War Scroll of the Dead Sea Scrolls | 329 |
| 10 | Developing Needed Spiritual Disciplines | 369 |

### Part 3: Healing and Deliverance

| | | |
|---|---|---|
| 11 | Healing and Deliverance | 391 |
| 12 | Having the Right Attitude About Healing and Deliverance | 419 |
| 13 | Ethics in Healing and Deliverance | 449 |
| 14 | Regulating Healing and Deliverance Ministry | 483 |
| 15 | Helping Others Maintain Healing and Deliverance | 503 |

| | | |
|---|---|---|
| | References | 525 |
| | About the Author | 539 |

# - INTRODUCTION -

A few years ago, I was invited to attend a class on demonology. I was thrilled, as it was an area of study I'd been interested in learning more about for quite some time. I couldn't find much about it, outside of information direct from the occult community. In those days, that information was difficult to come by, and you had to have an "in" within the community to learn much about it. The class was not really a class, but a study that turned out to be about believer's authority and spiritual warfare. There was never a mention about demons, powers of demons, authorities and ranks of demons, or a thing about proper demonology, but lots of the same rhetoric we might hear any other day of the week in a church somewhere in the United States.

It wasn't the first time I'd been invited to something on the topic of demonology, deliverance, healing, or spiritual warfare that turned out to be a far cry from whatever it claimed to be about. It seemed like the modern-day information available on such topics was limited, to say the least, and didn't delve as deeply into the subject matter as I desired to do so. I wanted more than just a nominal Christian sermon on the subject; I wanted to study the realms and explorative nature of the issues that touch the lives of so many individuals, knowingly and unknowingly, in our world, today.

This drove me to take the leap and learn about demonology, both from the perspective of Christian history and occult instruction, and into the ways such examination relates to issues of the Christian life in terms of spiritual warfare, healing, and deliverance. I have never considered myself much of a deliverance minister, for no other reason than the work I have done in deliverance and healing over the years doesn't nearly resemble that which I've seen elsewhere. The more I studied, however, I learned that I have done extensive work in healing and deliverance, and that it is important to give a different perspective than the norm to the work. The result is this textbook, expanding and teaching on matters of demonology, spiritual warfare, healing, and deliverance from a complete and comprehensive perspective.

Demonology, spiritual warfare, healing and deliverance are all relatively hot topics nowadays. It seems we can't sign on to any semblance of social media without someone who has a word, an idea, a class, or a need to promote something about one of the aforementioned topics. If you judge by what you see, demonic possession, discomfort, illness, unhappiness, and every condition under the sun rates and represents people's desire to turn around their lives, in more ways than one. The result has been a rush of people who believe they are divinely called, appointed, and anointed to handle matters of deliverance, healing, and spiritual warfare, all with their own ideas and concepts as to how to get the job done. Now, as many pursue these so-called experts to try and find a sense of normal in their lives, the ministers and individuals who attempt to engage in this sort of ministry do so without proper training, education, and accountability to ensure the work is done properly, ethically, and with Christian integrity.

This text seeks to teach on the essential matters of cosmology, history, identity, and context of matters related to all things of the spiritual realm and the way we interact with them down here. This book is divided into three sections: Demonology, which covers divine powers, demonic powers and their operations, spirits, demonology and mythology around the world, the occult, witchcraft and magic, and superstitions; Spiritual warfare, which examines Ephesians 6, the War Scroll of the Dead Sea Scrolls, and spiritual disciplines we should all seek to adopt; and healing and deliverance, covering healing and deliverance, having the right attitude about such matters, ethics, regulating such ministries, and helping others to maintain healing and deliverance in their own lives. Each chapter includes assignments for thorough study and thought, and text is clearly designed for academic and scholarly use.

Every provision has been made to ensure that understanding this material is thorough, detailed, and clear as possible. Recognizing it is a series of big topics that are interconnected, the material presented seeks to provoke the thought of the student as they embark on their study of these topics. Included are pictures, both ancient and modern, to help with the conceptual aspects of the work and to give a visual angle to the matters discussed. Given this book is for textbook use, there is plenty of discussion, information, and material for classroom discussion.

For those who are teaching this in classroom setting, students should have a working knowledge of the Biblical apocrypha and its various divisions: pseudepigrapha, deuterocanonical, and New Testament, the concept of what it means for something to be canonical, and the various traditions that have existed throughout Jewish and Christian history as pertain to the Scriptures. Students should have a reasonable, working knowledge of Bible history and of the relevance of prophecies, apocalyptic literature, and visionary encounters. It is also wise to incorporate hands-on experience and participation with this work, in some form or another, to aid in the process of explanation and understanding. This is an advanced class, suitable for advanced degree work or seminarians, and is not advisable for use as a general text for a church Bible study or church class.

Lastly, when considering all that has been presented within this text, any and all questions, concerns, or issues as pertain to matters of a medical nature or questions of treatment or diagnosis should remain with a medical professional, and not with the contents of this book. This book is for scholarship purposes only and is not intended for the diagnosis or treatment of any disease or ailment.

It is my prayer that this text enlightens your life and enhances your understanding of all things spiritual: divine, demonic, battle-worthy, and transformational as we move through our processes of healing and deliverance.

Part 1

# DEMONOLOGY

*Heavenly ambiance*

## - CHAPTER ONE -
## The Nature and Work of Divine Powers

Through His power [In Him; or By Him] all things were created [John 1:3; Heb. 1:2]—things in heaven and on earth, things seen and unseen, all powers [or heavenly authorities; thrones], authorities [dominions; kingdoms], lords [rulers], and rulers [authorities; these four may refer to angelic hierarchies, or to earthly and heavenly rulers]. All things were created through Christ and for Christ.
(Colossians 1:16)

Demonology is one aspect of the spiritual realm often unexplored by Christian ministers. The reason for this is relatively simple: most don't study it. We know of Satan, but that's about it in terms of spiritual rank and file. Why we do not tend to study the demonic realm has all sorts of other understandings with it: some relate to superstition, some are afraid, and some do not think studying the demonic realm is appropriate for believers. Granted, there may be some truth to the latter. Studying the ins and outs of the demonic is not for everyone, and it is not something every Christian should study alone. Most believers are trying to figure out their lives, how to most effectively live their faith in the world today, and exploring the dark spiritual territory of the netherworlds may not be something every believer is prepared and ready to undertake. This, however, is not the case for a minister who is interested in or pursuing deliverance or healing ministry. If we are in ministry and we claim to have that purpose, study of the demonic realm and understanding of things such as demons, spirits, and their various operations are things we should know how to identify.

Christians often make the accusation that occultists don't know what they are getting themselves into as they explore the various realms of the demonic spiritual world. It's true there are some who dabble here and there without much thought to their actions, but when it comes to demons, ranks of demons, and different orders of demons, most serious occultists have a strong leg up over Christians in understanding the demonic. They understand different controls, powers, ranks, and powers of demons, demonic orders, and spirits, because they see such as an integrated understanding of their spiritual belief.

As a rule, we respond in fear to the spiritual realm, but I don't know how seriously we take much of it, especially from an educational or scholarly perspective. If we are to be effective in spiritual warfare, healing, and deliverance, we need to understand the power of God and the countering effects of demonism. To see this clearly, we must delve into both and see the way that both operate, clearly and properly, from the Christian perspective.

## **Heaven**

Talk of heaven often elicits misty-eyed images of a land far, far away, one on the clouds where angels play harps and look like chubby, overfed babies. Music groups have sung about it, we compare good times to it, and overall, the concept or ideal of heaven is so appealing to us, we have made heaven as something for, by, and about us. If we are to be Scriptural and understanding of the power of God, heaven is, first and foremost, the dwelling place of the throne of our omnipresent, omnipotent God. This causes great confusion, as few understand how God can be both in heaven and here, but that is a part of the presence and reality of God as outside of time and space. Heaven is something otherworldly; we cannot relate to it if we limit our understanding to what we can see and experience right now.

In the Bible, there are at least eleven different mentions of visions of God in heaven, but we do not find explanations of every vision or detailing of what they saw in terms of physicalities and things we can relate to in understanding. The most detailed explanations we find of heaven in the Bible are in Isaiah, Ezekiel, Daniel, and Revelation:

*In the year that King Uzziah died I saw the Lord sitting on a throne, high and lifted up, and His train filled the temple. Above it stood the seraphim. Each one had six wings. With two he covered his face, and with two he covered his feet, and with two he flew. One cried to another and said:*

*"Holy, holy, holy, is the Lord of Hosts; the whole earth is full of His glory."*

*The posts of the door moved at the voice of him who cried, and the house was filled with smoke.*

*And I said: "Woe is me! For I am undone because I am a man of unclean lips, and I dwell in the midst of a people of unclean lips. For my eyes have seen the King, the Lord of Hosts."*

*Then one of the seraphim flew to me with a live coal which he had taken with the tongs from off the altar in his hand. And he laid it on my mouth, and said, "This has touched your lips, and your iniquity is taken away, and your sin purged."*

*Also I heard the voice of the Lord saying, "Whom shall I send, and who will go for us?"*

*Then I said, "Here am I. Send me."*
(Isaiah 6:1-8, MEV)

*Christ Ascended into Heaven, Dome of Monastery, Mirozh, Russia*

*It was the thirtieth year, on the fifth day of the fourth month [of Ezekiel's life, or of Nabopolassar's reign, or since King Josiah's reforms]. I was by the Kebar River [canal; a branch of the Euphrates River south of Babylon] among the people who had been carried away as captives [exiles]. The sky [heavens] opened, and I saw visions of God.*

*It was the fifth day of the month of the fifth year that King Jehoiachin had been a prisoner [in exile/captivity; 593 BC; 2 Kin. 24:12, 15]. The Lord spoke his word [word of the Lord came] to Ezekiel son of Buzi in the land of the Babylonians by the Kebar River [Canal; 1:1]. There he felt the power of the Lord [the hand of the Lord was on him].*

*When I looked, I saw a stormy wind [windstorm] coming from the north [storms often represent the presence of God; Jer. 23:19]. There was a great cloud with a bright light [or lightning flashing] around it and fire flashing out of [or brightness all around] it. Something that looked like glowing metal [or amber] was in the center of the fire. Inside the cloud [or the fire; its midst] was what looked like four living creatures [Rev. 4:6-8], who were shaped like [had the appearance of] humans, but each of them had four faces and four wings. Their legs were straight. Their feet were like a calf's hoofs and ·sparkled [gleamed] like polished [burnished] bronze [Rev. 1:15]. The living creatures had human hands under their wings on their four sides. All four of them had faces and wings, and their wings touched each other. The living creatures did not turn when they moved, but each went straight ahead.*

*Their faces looked like this: Each living creature had a human face [or the face of a man] and the face of a lion on the right side and the face of an ox on the left side. And each one also had the face of an eagle. That was what their faces looked like. Their wings were spread out above. Each had two wings that touched one of the other living creatures and two wings that covered its body. Each went straight ahead. Wherever the spirit [or wind] would go, the living creatures would also go, without turning. The living creatures would also go, without turning. The living creatures looked like burning coals of fire or like torches. Fire went back and forth among the living creatures. It was bright [radiant], and lightning flashed from it. The living creatures ran [darted] back and forth like bolts [flashes] of lightning.*

*Now as I looked at the living creatures, I saw a wheel on the ground by each of the living creatures with its four faces. The wheels and the way they were made [their construction/structure] were like this [had this appearance]: They looked like sparkling chrysolite [or topaz; or beryl]. All four of them looked the same, like one wheel crossways inside [in the middle*

*OF] ANOTHER WHEEL. WHEN THEY MOVED, THEY WENT IN ANY ONE OF THE FOUR DIRECTIONS, WITHOUT TURNING AS THEY WENT. THE RIMS OF THE WHEELS WERE HIGH AND FRIGHTENING [OR AWESOME] AND WERE FULL OF EYES ALL AROUND.*

*WHEN THE LIVING CREATURES MOVED, THE WHEELS MOVED BESIDE THEM. WHEN THE LIVING CREATURES WERE LIFTED UP [ROSE] FROM THE GROUND, THE WHEELS ALSO WERE LIFTED UP [ROSE]. WHEREVER THE SPIRIT [OR WIND] WOULD GO, THE LIVING CREATURES WOULD GO. AND THE WHEELS WERE LIFTED UP [ROSE] BESIDE THEM, BECAUSE THE SPIRIT OF THE LIVING CREATURES WAS IN THE WHEELS. WHEN THE LIVING CREATURES MOVED, THE WHEELS MOVED. WHEN THE LIVING CREATURES STOPPED, THE WHEELS STOPPED. AND WHEN THE LIVING CREATURES WERE LIFTED [ROSE] FROM THE GROUND, THE WHEELS WERE LIFTED [ROSE] BESIDE THEM, BECAUSE THE SPIRIT OF THE LIVING CREATURES WAS IN THE WHEELS.*

*NOW, OVER [STRETCHED OVER] THE HEADS OF THE LIVING CREATURES WAS SOMETHING LIKE A DOME [VAULT; EXPANSE; OR PLATFORM; GEN. 1:2] THAT SPARKLED LIKE ICE [CRYSTAL] AND WAS ·FRIGHTENING [OR AWESOME]. AND UNDER THE DOME [VAULT; EXPANSE; OR PLATFORM] THE WINGS OF THE LIVING CREATURES WERE STRETCHED OUT STRAIGHT TOWARD ONE ANOTHER. EACH LIVING CREATURE ALSO HAD TWO WINGS COVERING ITS BODY. I HEARD THE SOUND OF THEIR WINGS, LIKE THE ROARING SOUND OF THE SEA [SOUND OF MANY WATERS], AS THEY MOVED. IT WAS LIKE THE VOICE OF GOD ALMIGHTY [THE ALMIGHTY], A ROARING SOUND [TUMULT] LIKE A NOISY ARMY. WHEN THE LIVING CREATURES STOPPED, THEY LOWERED THEIR WINGS.*

*A VOICE CAME FROM ABOVE THE DOME [VAULT; EXPANSE; OR PLATFORM] OVER THE HEADS OF THE LIVING CREATURES. WHEN THE LIVING CREATURES STOPPED, THEY LOWERED THEIR WINGS. NOW ABOVE THE DOME [VAULT; EXPANSE; OR PLATFORM] THERE WAS SOMETHING THAT LOOKED LIKE A THRONE. IT LOOKED LIKE A SAPPHIRE GEM [OR LAPIS LAZULI]. AND ON THE THRONE HIGH ABOVE WAS A SHAPE [FORM; FIGURE] LIKE A HUMAN [MAN]. THEN I NOTICED THAT FROM THE WAIST UP THE SHAPE LOOKED LIKE GLOWING METAL [OR AMBER] WITH FIRE INSIDE. FROM THE WAIST DOWN IT LOOKED LIKE FIRE, AND A BRIGHT LIGHT WAS ALL AROUND. THE SURROUNDING GLOW [RADIANCE; BRIGHTNESS] LOOKED LIKE THE RAINBOW IN THE CLOUDS ON A RAINY DAY. IT SEEMED TO LOOK LIKE [THIS WAS THE APPEARANCE OF THE LIKENESS OF] THE GLORY OF THE LORD [HIS MANIFEST PRESENCE]. SO WHEN I SAW IT, I BOWED [FELL] FACEDOWN ON THE GROUND AND HEARD A VOICE SPEAKING.* (Ezekiel 1:1-28)

*AS I LOOKED,*

THRONES WERE PUT IN THEIR PLACES,
  AND GOD, THE ETERNAL ONE, [THE ANCIENT OF DAYS] SAT ON HIS THRONE.
HIS CLOTHES WERE WHITE LIKE SNOW,
  AND THE HAIR ON HIS HEAD WAS LIKE WOOL [WHITE].
HIS THRONE WAS MADE FROM FIRE,
  AND THE WHEELS OF HIS THRONE WERE BLAZING WITH FIRE.
A RIVER OF FIRE WAS FLOWING
  FROM IN FRONT OF HIM.
MANY [A THOUSAND] THOUSANDS OF ANGELS WERE SERVING HIM,
  AND MILLIONS [TEN THOUSAND TIMES TEN THOUSAND; ANGELS] STOOD BEFORE HIM.
COURT WAS READY TO BEGIN [SAT IN JUDGMENT],
  AND THE BOOKS WERE OPENED. (Daniel 7:9-10)

AFTER THE VISION OF THESE THINGS I LOOKED, AND [LOOK; BEHOLD] THERE BEFORE ME WAS AN OPEN DOOR IN HEAVEN. AND THE SAME [FIRST] VOICE THAT SPOKE TO ME BEFORE, THAT SOUNDED LIKE A TRUMPET [1:8], SAID, "COME UP HERE, AND I WILL SHOW YOU WHAT MUST HAPPEN AFTER THIS." IMMEDIATELY I WAS IN THE SPIRIT [OR SPIRIT; A STATE OF DEEP SPIRITUAL COMMUNION WITH GOD; 1:10], AND [LOOK; BEHOLD] BEFORE ME WAS A THRONE IN HEAVEN, AND SOMEONE WAS SITTING ON IT. THE ONE WHO SAT ON THE THRONE LOOKED LIKE PRECIOUS STONES, LIKE JASPER AND CARNELIAN [A SYMBOL OF GREAT BEAUTY, PURITY AND VALUE]. ALL AROUND THE THRONE WAS A RAINBOW [OR HALO] THE COLOR OF [OR THAT LOOKED LIKE] AN EMERALD. AROUND THE THRONE THERE WERE TWENTY-FOUR OTHER THRONES WITH TWENTY-FOUR ELDERS SITTING ON THEM [PROBABLY ANGELIC LEADERS]. THEY WERE DRESSED IN WHITE AND HAD GOLDEN CROWNS [WREATHS SYMBOLIZING HONOR OR VICTORY; SEE 2:10] ON THEIR HEADS. LIGHTNING FLASHES AND NOISES AND THUNDER [OR THE RUMBLING OF THUNDER; PHENOMENA ASSOCIATED WITH GOD'S APPEARANCE AT MOUNT SINAI; EX. 19:16-18] CAME FROM THE THRONE. BEFORE THE THRONE SEVEN LAMPS WERE BURNING, WHICH ARE THE SEVEN SPIRITS [EITHER ANGELS OR THE "SEVENFOLD SPIRIT"—THE HOLY SPIRIT PORTRAYED IN HIS PERFECTION; 3:1] OF GOD. ALSO BEFORE THE THRONE THERE WAS SOMETHING THAT LOOKED LIKE A SEA OF GLASS, CLEAR LIKE CRYSTAL.

IN THE CENTER AND AROUND THE THRONE WERE FOUR LIVING CREATURES WITH EYES ALL OVER THEM [FULL OF EYES], IN FRONT AND IN BACK. THE FIRST LIVING CREATURE WAS LIKE A LION. THE SECOND WAS LIKE AN OX [OR CALF]. THE THIRD HAD A FACE LIKE A MAN. THE FOURTH WAS LIKE A FLYING EAGLE [EZEK. 1:10; ANGELIC BEINGS IDENTIFIED WITH THE MOST POWERFUL EXAMPLE OF VARIOUS SPECIES]. EACH OF THESE *four living creatures had six wings and was covered all over with eyes [full of eyes], inside and out. Day and night they never stop [rest from] saying:*

*"Holy, holy, holy is the Lord God Almighty [All-powerful].*
  *He was, He is, and He is coming [1:4, 8]."*

*[Whenever] These living creatures give glory, honor, and thanks to the One who sits on the throne, who lives forever and ever. Then the twenty-four elders bow down before the One Who sits on the throne, and they worship Him Who lives forever and ever. They put their crowns down [cast/lay their crowns; 4:4] before the throne and say:*

*"You are worthy, our Lord and God,*
  *to receive glory and honor and power [strength],*
*because You made all things.*
  *Everything existed and was made,*
  *because You wanted it [by Your will]."* (Revelation 4:1-11)

*Then I saw a scroll in the right hand of the One sitting on the throne. The scroll had writing on both sides and was kept closed [sealed] with seven seals [a wax stamp that sealed a document shut]. And I saw a powerful [mighty] angel calling [proclaiming] in a loud voice, "Who is worthy to break the seals and open the scroll?" But there was no one in heaven or on earth or under the earth who could open the scroll or look inside it. I cried bitterly [much] because there was no one who was worthy to open the scroll or look inside. But one of the elders said to me, "Do not cry! [Look; Behold] The Lion from the tribe of Judah [a messianic title; Gen. 49:9-10], David's descendant [the root of David; a messianic title applied to Christ; Is. 11:10], has won the victory [overcome; conquered] so that He is able to open the scroll and its seven seals."*

*Then I saw a Lamb [Jesus] standing in the center of the throne and in the middle of the four living creatures and the elders [or between the throne and the living creatures and among the elders]. The Lamb looked as if He had been killed [slaughtered; slain]. He had seven horns and seven eyes, which are the seven spirits of God [either angels or the "sevenfold Spirit"; see 1:4] that were sent into all the world. The Lamb came and took [received] the scroll from the right hand of the One sitting on the throne.*

When He took the scroll, the four living creatures and the twenty-four elders [4:4] bowed down [fell] before the Lamb. Each one of them had a harp and golden bowls full of incense, which are the prayers of God's holy people [Ps. 141:2]. And they all sang a new song [Ps. 33:3; 40:3; 98:1] to the Lamb:

"You are worthy to take the scroll
   and to open its seals,
because You were killed [slaughtered; slain],
   and with the blood of Your death [Your blood] You bought [ransomed; purchased; redeemed] people for God
   from every tribe, language, people, and nation.
You made them to be a kingdom of priests [or and priests; Ex. 19:6] for our God,
   and they will rule [reign; other manuscripts have "they reign" (present tense)] on the earth."

Then I looked, and I heard the voices of many angels around the throne, and the four living creatures, and the elders. There were thousands and thousands [myriads of myriads and thousands of thousands; a myriad can mean either ten thousand or many thousands; here means "countless"] of angels, saying in a loud voice:

"The Lamb Who was killed [slaughtered; slain] is worthy
to receive power, wealth, wisdom, and strength,
honor, glory, and praise [or blessing]!"

Then I heard all creatures in heaven and on earth and under the earth and in the sea saying:

"To the One Who sits on the throne
   and to the Lamb
be praise [or blessing] and honor and glory and power
   forever and ever."

The four living creatures said, "Amen [Hebrew for "so be it"]," and the elders bowed down [fell] and worshiped. (Revelation 5:1-14)

*When the Lamb opened the seventh seal [the final and climactic seal; 5:1], there was silence in heaven for about half an hour [a dramatic pause induced by awe]. And I saw the seven angels who stand before God and to whom were given seven trumpets [trumpets often announce God's appearance, accompanied by judgment and victory; Josh. 6].*

*Another angel came and stood at the altar, holding a golden ·pan for incense [censer; incense burner]. He was given much incense to offer with the prayers of all ·God's holy people [the saints; Ps. 141:2]. The angel put this offering on the golden altar before the throne. The smoke from the incense went up from the angel's hand to [in the presence of] God with the prayers of God's people [the saints]. Then the angel filled the ·incense pan [censer; incense burner] with fire from the altar and threw it on the earth, and there were thunder and loud noises [was rumbling thunder], flashes of lightning, and an earthquake [4:5].*

*Then the seven angels who had the seven trumpets prepared to blow them [8:2].* (Revelation 8:1-6)

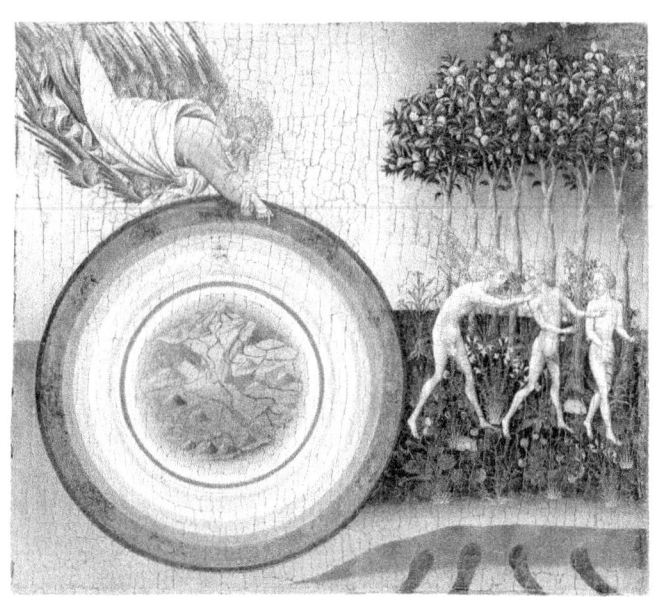

*Creation of the World and the Expulsion from Paradise, Giovanni di Paolo (1403-1482)*

The ancients understood the cosmos to be domed in shape, with heaven above the dome of the sky. Beyond what we can see (the blue of the sky) is the place where God resides. Down below was the world of the dead. In the middle was the earth, the place where people dwell. Heaven was regarded with mystery, much as we regard it today. The exact nature, form, and shape of heaven are unknown to us because we only have shades and images of what heaven is like. When we hear of heaven, it is described in terms and relations to what we know now. Much of it, we understand in a metaphorical or figurative context, because the realm of

God does not mirror, nor relate, to how we necessarily understand it here. The great prophets, mystics, and visionaries of the ages have brought us types and shadows, but as we are not present in heaven's paradise now, we do not understand everything about its majesty. Many ancient writings feature heaven in seven distinct levels (including the Ascension of Moses and The Gospel of Bartholomew), paralleling the use of the number seven to the number of God, or perfection, with each level representing different aspects of worship, purpose, and dwelling. The Book of 3 Enoch depicted heaven as having ten levels, echoing the principle of a new establishment, something new and otherworldly. The Apostle Paul speaks of experiencing the "third heaven" himself, showing the early belief that heaven was divided into different parts:

*I KNOW A MAN IN CHRIST [A BELIEVER] WHO WAS TAKEN UP [CAUGHT UP; SNATCHED AWAY] TO THE THIRD HEAVEN [THE PRESENCE OF GOD] FOURTEEN YEARS AGO [PAUL IS INDIRECTLY REFERRING TO HIMSELF]. I DO NOT KNOW WHETHER THE MAN WAS IN HIS BODY OR OUT OF HIS BODY, BUT GOD KNOWS. AND I KNOW THAT THIS MAN WAS TAKEN UP [CAUGHT UP; SNATCHED AWAY] TO PARADISE [ANOTHER NAME FOR HEAVEN; LUKE 23:43; REV. 2:7]. I DON'T KNOW IF HE WAS IN HIS BODY OR AWAY FROM HIS BODY, BUT GOD KNOWS. HE HEARD THINGS HE IS NOT ABLE TO EXPLAIN [INEXPRESSIBLE; INEFFABLE], THINGS THAT NO HUMAN IS ALLOWED TO TELL.* (2 Corinthians 12:2-4)

It is also clearly the resting place of the righteous in Christ, as a new shift from the grave, after the resurrection of Jesus. This proves there is both spiritual and physical resurrection, and spiritual resurrection is as valid a belief as physical:

*SO WE ALWAYS HAVE COURAGE. WE KNOW THAT WHILE WE LIVE [ARE AT HOME] IN THIS BODY, WE ARE AWAY [ABSENT; OR EXILES] FROM THE LORD. WE LIVE [WALK] BY WHAT WE BELIEVE [FAITH], NOT BY WHAT WE CAN SEE [SIGHT]. SO I SAY THAT WE HAVE COURAGE [OR ARE CONFIDENT]. WE REALLY WANT [WOULD PREFER] TO BE AWAY [ABSENT; OR EXILED] FROM THIS BODY AND BE AT HOME WITH THE LORD. OUR ONLY GOAL [AIM; AMBITION] IS TO PLEASE GOD [HIM] WHETHER WE LIVE HERE [ARE AT HOME] OR THERE [ARE ABSENT/EXILED], BECAUSE WE MUST ALL STAND BEFORE CHRIST TO BE JUDGED [THE BEMA/JUDGMENT SEAT OF CHRIST; THE BEMA WAS A RAISED PLATFORM FROM WHICH CIVIC LEADERS MADE PRONOUNCEMENTS AND RENDERED JUDGMENT]. [...SO THAT] EACH OF US WILL RECEIVE WHAT WE SHOULD GET—GOOD OR BAD—FOR THE THINGS WE DID IN THE EARTHLY BODY.* (2 Corinthians 5:6-10)

Heaven does not just represent paradise or an ideal world, no matter how much we try to portray it in such a way in pop culture. It also represents authority, a seat from which judgment, governance, and decisions come. This is why in the New Testament, Jesus frequently spoke of the "Kingdom of Heaven" and the "Kingdom of God" interchangeably. The Kingdom of God was God's power and presence, His heavenly governance, here on earth and throughout all space. One represented the other, and one was the other.

*As soon as Jesus was baptized, He came up out of the water. Then heaven [the sky/heavens] opened, and He saw God's Spirit coming down [descending and lighting/settling] on Him like a dove [either in the form of a dove, or in bird-like descent]. And a voice from heaven said, "This is My Son, Whom I love [dearly beloved Son; Ps. 2:7; Gen. 22:2], and I am very [well] pleased with Him [Is. 42:1]."* (Matthew 3:16-17)

*"They are blessed [or Blessed are those...; and so through v. 10] who realize their spiritual poverty [are the poor in spirit],*
*for the kingdom of heaven belongs to them [is theirs]...*

*They are blessed who are persecuted for doing good [doing what's right; the sake of righteousness],*
*for the kingdom of heaven belongs to them [is theirs]...*

*Rejoice and be glad, because you have a great reward in heaven. People did the same evil things to [They likewise persecuted] the prophets who lived before you...*

*In the same way let your light shine before others [for people to see], so that they will see the good things you do [your good deeds/works] and will praise [glorify; give honor to] your Father in heaven...*

*I tell you the truth, until heaven and earth are gone [pass away; disappear], not even the smallest letter [one jot; one iota; the smallest Greek letter] or the smallest part [stroke; tittle] of a letter will be lost [pass away; disappear] until everything has happened [is accomplished/achieved]...*

*[Therefore] Whoever refuses to obey [ignores; breaks; annuls] any command*

*[ONE OF THE LEAST OF THESE COMMANDS] AND TEACHES OTHER PEOPLE NOT TO OBEY THAT COMMAND [TO DO LIKEWISE] WILL BE THE LEAST IMPORTANT [CALLED/CONSIDERED LEAST] IN THE KINGDOM OF HEAVEN. BUT WHOEVER OBEYS [KEEPS; PRACTICES] THE COMMANDS AND TEACHES OTHER PEOPLE TO OBEY THEM WILL BE [CONSIDERED; CALLED] GREAT IN THE KINGDOM OF HEAVEN...*

*[FOR] I TELL YOU THAT IF YOU ARE NO MORE OBEDIENT THAN [UNLESS YOUR RIGHTEOUSNESS SURPASSES/EXCEEDS THAT OF] THE TEACHERS OF THE LAW [SCRIBES] AND THE PHARISEES, YOU WILL NEVER [OR CERTAINLY NOT] ENTER THE KINGDOM OF HEAVEN...*

*BUT I TELL YOU, DO NOT SWEAR AN OATH AT ALL. DON'T SWEAR AN OATH USING THE NAME OF HEAVEN [...NEITHER BY HEAVEN], BECAUSE HEAVEN IS GOD'S THRONE...IF YOU DO THIS, [...SO THAT] YOU WILL BE TRUE CHILDREN [CHILDREN; OR SONS] OF YOUR FATHER IN HEAVEN. [FOR] HE CAUSES THE [HIS] SUN TO RISE ON EVIL PEOPLE AND ON GOOD PEOPLE, AND HE SENDS RAIN TO THOSE WHO DO RIGHT AND TO THOSE WHO DO WRONG [ON THE JUST/RIGHTEOUS AND THE UNJUST/UNRIGHTEOUS]...*

*SO [THEREFORE] YOU MUST BE PERFECT, JUST AS YOUR FATHER IN HEAVEN IS PERFECT."*
(Matthew 5:3, 10, 12, 16, 18, 19, 20, 34, 45, 48)

Within our understanding of Kingdom governance, the authority of heaven reigns here among those who are willing and ready to follow God. This is a contrast to Israel, which wanted the prestige of being a nation like all others (1 Samuel 8:1-22, Ezekiel 20:32). We are here, as citizens of heaven, if we are obedient to God (Ephesians 2:12-19, Philippians 3:20).

*THE KINGS OF THE EARTH PREPARE TO FIGHT [TAKE THEIR STAND],*
  *AND THEIR LEADERS MAKE PLANS [PLOT] TOGETHER*
*AGAINST THE LORD*
  *AND HIS APPOINTED ONE [ANOINTED; MESSIAH; THE KING, ULTIMATELY JESUS; ACTS 4:25-28].*
*THEY SAY, "LET'S BREAK THE CHAINS THAT HOLD US BACK [THEIR CHAINS/BONDS]*
  *AND THROW OFF THE ROPES THAT TIE US DOWN [THEIR ROPES/CORDS FROM US]."*

*BUT THE ONE WHO SITS IN HEAVEN [GOD] LAUGHS;*
  *THE LORD MAKES FUN OF [RIDICULES; DERIDES] THEM.*
*THEN THE LORD WARNS THEM [SPEAKS TO THEM IN ANGER]*
  *AND FRIGHTENS THEM WITH HIS ANGER [FURY].*

*HE SAYS, "I HAVE APPOINTED [INSTALLED; SET] MY OWN KING OVER MY HOLY MOUNTAIN, ZION [THE LOCATION OF THE TEMPLE IN JERUSALEM; 9:11; 48:2, 11; 50:2; 1 KIN. 8:1]."* (Psalm 2:2-6)

*THE LORD LOOKS DOWN FROM HEAVEN AND SEES EVERY PERSON.* (Psalm 33:13)

*THE LORD LOOKED DOWN FROM HIS HOLY PLACE ABOVE; FROM HEAVEN HE LOOKED [GAZED] DOWN AT THE EARTH.* (Psalm 102:9)

It's obvious the relevance of heaven was prominent for the ancients, and would have been such for Christians, as well. Heaven was the seat of God, thus the voice of power and guidance for us from God, the One Who is greater than all we can conceive down here. Any word, message, or messenger sent from heaven came with the authority of God, and the power to bring healing, instruction, and change.

## Divine powers

The reference to divine powers is one by which we understand the structure of God's work within the world through different spiritual agents. In other words, divine powers are those forces or beings in this world that are otherworldly and stand in place for the work of God. Most of us understand those different forces to be different ranks of angels, or messengers of God, who operate at God's bidding. They are not God Himself but work on His behalf to ensure His will throughout the universe.

It is to the shame of Christians that we do not know as much about divine powers as occultists know about demonic ones. We know that God is the Supreme being of the universe, but there is an order by which heavenly and divine powers operate. Different angels operate different regions within the heavenly and natural realms, and in many ways, we have extended or mystified those different ranks within Christian lore and understanding.

It is impossible to study, nor properly understand, demonology and spiritual warfare without understanding some level of cosmology, or study of the cosmos. The cosmos includes the entire universe, and cosmology includes the questioning perplexities of the universe, its creation, and its fate. This means ancient man was more interested in the fate of everything rather than just the fate of human beings, and this markedly altered their perceptions of salvation and salvation history. The ancients believed the realm of being to be bigger than we understand today, and as a result, they saw things such as spirits, demons, and angels to interconnect with human experience in more than just a context of inconvenience or troubling someone's life. It was a part of a bigger problem, a symptom, if you will, a part of the bigger matrix of existence that could impact somebody's life into eternity. Human beings weren't disconnected from the disorder of the universe; they were a part of it, and being a part of this bigger issue meant humans experienced it, within themselves, in different ways.

Much of what we understand about the spiritual realm has come about over the years by mixing Biblical precept with cultural influence or teaching. We talk much about God and often about human order (which is frequently spoken of improperly), but we don't talk about divine powers or heavenly order, indicating there is a serious disconnect in the way we understand authority to intercept. If we understand heavenly order, it helps us understand natural order in a much better way. Rather than being a matter of rank and file and who does what, we can see the way structure and order interact in heaven to bring about the perfect management of spiritual matters.

There are at least eleven different ranks and files of divine powers mentioned throughout history, all of which fall back on expansions of Biblical verses which make mention of various spiritual powers:

GOD HAS PUT CHRIST OVER [FAR ABOVE] ALL RULERS, AUTHORITIES, POWERS, AND KINGS [LORDS; DOMINION], AND EVERY OTHER TITLE GIVEN [NAME THAT IS NAMED] NOT ONLY IN THIS WORLD [AGE] BUT ALSO IN THE NEXT [COMING ONE]. (Ephesians 1:21)

HIS PURPOSE WAS THAT THROUGH THE CHURCH ALL THE RULERS AND POWERS IN THE HEAVENLY WORLD [REALM; PLACES; 1:3, 20; 2:6] WILL NOW KNOW GOD'S WISDOM, WHICH HAS SO MANY FORMS [MULTI-FACETED/MULTI-DIMENSIONAL WISDOM]. (Ephesians 3:10)

THROUGH HIS POWER [IN HIM; OR BY HIM] ALL THINGS WERE CREATED [JOHN 1:3; HEB. 1:2]—THINGS IN HEAVEN AND ON EARTH, THINGS SEEN AND UNSEEN, ALL POWERS [OR HEAVENLY AUTHORITIES; THRONES], AUTHORITIES [DOMINIONS; KINGDOMS], LORDS [RULERS], AND RULERS [AUTHORITIES; THESE FOUR MAY REFER TO ANGELIC HIERARCHIES, OR TO EARTHLY AND HEAVENLY RULERS]. ALL THINGS WERE CREATED THROUGH CHRIST AND FOR CHRIST. (Colossians 1:16)

*THE LORD HIMSELF WILL COME DOWN FROM HEAVEN WITH A LOUD COMMAND [OR SHOUT], WITH [OR ACCOMPANIED BY; OR PRECEDED BY] THE VOICE OF THE ARCHANGEL [A LEADING OR RULING ANGEL; DAN. 10:13; JUDE 9], AND WITH THE TRUMPET CALL OF GOD. AND THOSE WHO HAVE DIED BELIEVING [THE DEAD] IN CHRIST WILL RISE FIRST [1 COR. 15:51-57].* (1 Thessalonians 4:16)

*NOT EVEN THE ARCHANGEL MICHAEL [A LEADER AMONG GOD'S ANGELS; DAN. 10:13, 21; 12:1; REV. 12:7], WHEN HE ARGUED [CONTENDED] WITH THE DEVIL ABOUT WHO WOULD HAVE [ABOUT] THE BODY OF MOSES, DARED TO JUDGE THE DEVIL GUILTY [BRING A SLANDEROUS/BLASPHEMOUS JUDGMENT]. INSTEAD, HE SAID, "THE LORD PUNISH [REBUKE] YOU [PROBABLY A STORY TOLD IN THE TESTAMENT OF MOSES, A JEWISH WRITING OF THE EARLY FIRST CENTURY AD]."* (Jude 1:9)

*ENOCH, THE SEVENTH DESCENDANT FROM ADAM [COUNTING ADAM FIRST; GEN. 5:18-24], SAID [PROPHESIED] ABOUT THESE PEOPLE: "LOOK [BEHOLD], THE LORD IS COMING WITH MANY THOUSANDS OF HIS HOLY ANGELS [HOLY ONES].* (Jude 1:14)

In Judaism, the list of divine powers is:

- **Chayot Hakodesh ("the holy living beings")**[1]: The highest angelic rank, known for being seated around God's throne and holding up the earth. They are the angels present in Ezekiel's vision of the four creatures (Ezekiel 1, 10), the angels present when Elijah was taken to heaven (2 Kings 2), those surrounding the throne of the Ancient of Days (Daniel 7:7-13), and the four living beings found in Revelation (Revelation 4:6-8).[2]

- **Ophanim ("thrones" or "wheels")**: Angels known for their wisdom, who guard God's throne in heaven. They are considered angels before the throne of God, described as being covered with eyes in Ezekiel 1:15-21. In Kabbalah, the ophanim are led by the archangel Raziel.[3]

- **Erelim ("great")**: Angels known for compassion and wisdom. In Kabbalah, the archangel Tzaphikel leads this group of angels.[4]

- **Chasmalim ("brilliant ones")**: Angels known for love, kindness, and grace, led by the Archangel Zadkiel. According to Jewish tradition,

Zadkiel is the angel who interferes in the sacrifice of Isaac in Genesis 22.[5]

- **_Seraphim_ ("burning ones"):** Angels known for their work for justice, led by the archangel Chamuel. They are mentioned in the Prophet Isaiah's vision (Isaiah 6:2-3) and frequently found throughout the Book of Enoch.[6]

- **_Malachim_ ("messengers" or "angels")**: Angels known for their beauty and mercy, led by the archangel Raphael. Their nature is to serve as messengers, to convey divine messages.[7]

*17th century Ethiopian manuscript of the miracles of Michael the Archangel.*

- **_Elokim_ or _Elohim_ ("godly beings"):** Warrior angels known to ensure good prevails over evil.[8]

- **_Bene Elokim_ or _Bene Elohim_ ("sons of gods")**: Angels that exist to give glory to God, focusing on the protection of God's people during the end battle of good and evil. The Archangel Michael is considered the warrior leader of this rank of angels, as is found in Daniel 12:21.[9]

- **_Cheruvim_ ("to be near," "mighty")**: Angels that deal with the separation of sin that keeps humans from God, and helps them draw closer to God. The Cheruvim are led by the archangel Gabriel. They first appear in Scripture in Genesis 3:24, when Adam and Eve were driven from the Garden of Eden and cheruvim were sent to guard the way to the tree of life (Genesis 3:24).[10]

- ***Ishim* ("protector," "guardian")**: Angels closest in level and being to humans, whose focus is the Kingdom of God here on earth. Their leader is the archangel Sandalphon.[11]

In Christianity, there are several different lists of divine powers. Many of these overlap with Jewish ideas about angels, but some are very different. The Christian tradition of angelic order comes from different medieval theologians, categorizing the angels into "choirs," divided into three groups, known as "spheres." The two most notable theologians to develop these theories were Pseudo-Dionysius and Thomas Aquinas. Their categories were:

**The First Sphere:** Seraphim, Cherubim, and Thrones

- **Seraphim**: Similar to the Jewish concept of Seraphim, they are the attendants or guardians of the throne of God. They have six wings: two cover the face, two cover the feet, and two are for mobility in the form of flying. (Isaiah 6:1-7)[12]

- **Cherubim**: Associated with the glory of God, appearing to be as people, double winged. (Revelation 4-6)[13]

- **Thrones**: These angels are not near the throne, but reside just above the universe, where heaven and the universe meet. They are considered intermediaries for the lower ranks of angels to access God.[14]

**The Second Sphere:** Dominions (Lordships), Virtues (Strongholds), Powers (Authorities)

- **Dominions (Lordships)**: Angels of leadership who maintain the duties of the angels and notify them of God's various instructions.[15]

- **Virtues (Strongholds)**: Also known as the "Spirits of motion," they are responsible to control the elements and dominate the changing seasons and natural orders of creation. They also control miracles and miraculous signs and stand to provide God's integrities to people of courage, grace, and valor.[16]

- **Powers (Authorities)**: Warrior angels defending the universe and humans against evil forces. They are also called potentates and fight evil spirits who try to bring about evil through people.[17]

**The Third Sphere:** Principalities (Rulers), Archangels, Angels

- **Principalities (Rulers)**: Principalities are spiritual beings considered hostile and intolerant to God and human beings, but they were originally created by Christ and for Him. Even though they have become hostile to Him, they still serve His purpose, just in a way many do not consider. Within this categorization of angels are also powers, cosmological powers, dominions, and thrones.[18]

- **Archangels**: Leading angels who are considered unique messengers at critical times in salvation history. They are not necessarily all the same, as the word "archangel" refers to a "chief angel," one that has some sort of lead over any group of angels or of this specific choir, such as Michael the Archangel is considered a Seraphim.[19]

*The Assumption of the Virgin, Francesco Botticini (1446-1497), depicting the different orders of angels in heaven*

- **Angels:** A general category of angel closest to human beings and the issues that affect the material world. Their primary job is to deliver prayers to God and God's messages from prayer. They can access any other rank or choir of angel at any time.[20]

## Divine powers in the Bible

Angels tend to appear as mysterious figures, coming in and out of situations as quickly as they appear. Sometimes they have a message, other times they appear to be guardians of matters or protectors of the will of God. No matter how we spin it, angels are not more important than God, nor are they stand-ins for God Himself. They are angels, His messengers, His servants, beings that give us examples of service for God as well as delivering the important messages He has for us.

Beyond general statements about the existence of angels, the work of angels in the Bible resembles that of angels seen in non-canonical works: that of messengers, guides, teachers and protectors, spiritual beings endowed with important purposes sent to earth in the work of God. Angels are mentioned approximately 290 times in the entire Bible, showing their important work and role as messengers of heaven. There are a couple of key things to keep in mind when studying divine powers:

- **The word "angel" means "messenger":** The terminology is the same in the Hebrew and the Greek, and the word can also be used to describe a person who carries a message (Job 1;14, Luke 7:24, Luke 9:52), a prophet (Isaiah 42:9), priests (Malachi 3:1), and the apostles of the church (Revelation 1:20). "Angel" was also used to refer to the pillar of cloud that surrounded the Israelites (Exodus 14:19). This does not make a person a divine power but expresses how an angel operates. They are mentioned approximately 273 times in the Protestant version of the Bible, and more in Catholic and Orthodox canons.

- **Angels are not human beings:** Angels are a separate category of being; spiritual beings that are "ministering spirits" (Hebrews 1:14), if you will. People do not become angels when they die. They do not have human bodies, although when they are on earth, they can appear in human form (Hebrews 13:2). Angels are ministering spirits, servants created by God. The Scriptures do not tell us when they were created, but being heavenly beings in their origin, they were probably a part of the creation of the heavenlies (Genesis 1:1, Nehemiah 9:6, Job 38:1-7, Psalm 148:2-5, Colossians 1:16). They do not marry, nor reproduce sexually (Matthew 22:30). Angels do not reproduce from a singular ancestor or group of ancestors (Luke 20:34-36). They are not born, nor do they die. We do not know how many angels there are, but it appears they are many. In the New Jerusalem, we will be met by many angels (Hebrews 12:22-23).

- **Angels can appear as any sort of human being:** Even though it does appear most angelic appearances were as men (Genesis 18, Daniel 10:5-6, Matthew 28:3, Luke 1:26-38), there is also evidence angels can assume female form (Zechariah 5:9).

- **Angelic abilities:** Angels are stronger than humans (Psalm 103:20), know more than we do (Daniel 9:21-13, 10:10-14), but are not omnipotent nor omnipresent. Their primary purposes are to worship and praise God (Isaiah 6:1-3, Revelation 4-5), deliver messages (Acts 7:52-53), offer guidance (Acts 8:26, Acts 10:1-8), provide for needs (Genesis 21:17-20, 1 Kings 19:6), protect (Daniel 3), deliver from danger (Acts 5, Acts 12), strengthen and encourage (Matthew 4:11, Acts 5:19-20, Acts 27:23-25), answer the prayers of God on behalf of His people (Daniel 9:20-24), care when people die (Luke 16:22), or punish sin (2 Kings 19:20-34).

One of the reasons we are limited in our experience and knowledge of spiritual powers is because much of the history and understanding of spiritual operation comes from traditions and sources not found in the Bible canons we readily embrace in modern times. Over time, the ancients came to understand different things about spirituality as they studied and sought God, and unfortunately, not all these revelations made it into Biblical canons. They are found, however, in writings known as the Pseudepigrapha and Apocrypha, found in both New and Old Testament times, sometimes seen on par with Biblical understanding, sometimes as traditions, and sometimes as things that expounded or taught on Biblical truths.

There are also groups that consider some of these books to be "canonical," on par with the rest of Scripture, according to the canons they accept as valid. These are not off-color groups, but traditional groups of Orthodox Christians and Jews alike embrace these different writings that are not so readily embraced in the west.

## Non-canonical explanations of divine powers

It is foolish for us to assume these writings have had no influence on the Bible or on the way our spiritual formation is shaped. The ancients were far more mystical in their views of the world and the cosmos and were far more interested in spiritual beings and powers than we are today. The ancients viewed the world as a cosmic chaos and saw the order of God and His operation in it as stilling that chaos, brought into the world by sin. Early creation accounts (including those found in the Bible) attempted to explain the disorder and disruption they saw around them, both in nature and in people. The New Testament is full of references to Old Testament Pseudepigrapha and Apocrypha, for no other reason than these teachings were a part of the lives of early believers. When the New Testament letters were written and circulated, believers were acquainted with understandings of angelic and other spiritual beings through Jewish contact. Formerly pagan believers understood such through their pagan mythologies, which we will discuss later in this book.

When it comes to non-canonical works, however, their views show us the evolution of understanding between the concept that the dead are gone forever and know nothing to the belief in a full afterlife, complete with paradise and eternal damnation as spiritual theory and doctrine. The way that heaven and hell came into spiritual vernacular and focus largely evolved through powerful visions of those who had amazing visions, mystical experiences, or prophetic insights into such, either writing as those who were pillars of the faith or who were individuals writing under the pen names of those individuals of faith. There are numerous writings that detail such understandings we have of heaven, and some Pseduepigraphic and Deuterocanonical writings essential to the understanding of divine powers include:

## The Book of Jubilees (also called "Lesser Genesis" or "Leptogenesis")

The Book of Jubilees is aptly called a "Lesser Genesis" because it gives a recounting of Genesis from the perspective of its traditional dictation as an oral tradition, directly given by an angel to Moses. As early as 1:26 and 2:1, the Book of Jubilees makes important mention of angels:

*AND HE SAID TO THE ANGEL OF THE PRESENCE: WRITE FOR MOSES FROM THE*

*BEGINNING OF CREATION TILL MY SANCTUARY HAS BEEN BUILT AMONG THEM FOR ALL ETERNITY.*[21]

*AND THE ANGEL OF THE PRESENCE SPAKE TO MOSES ACCORDING TO THE WORD OF THE LORD, SAYING: "WRITE THE COMPLETE HISTORY OF THE CREATION, HOW IN SIX DAYS THE LORD GOD FINISHED ALL HIS WORKS AND ALL THAT HE CREATED, AND KEPT SABBATH ON THE SEVENTH DAY AND HALLOWED IT FOR ALL AGES, AND APPOINTED IT AS A SIGN FOR ALL HIS WORKS."*[22]

The Book of Jubilees was well-known in early Christianity and is considered a canonical book by the Ethiopian Orthodox Church and Ethiopian Jews. It was also used among the Essene community, which originally penned the Dead Sea Scrolls.

The main theme of angels within Jubilees is to serve as representatives or messengers of God, with the intention of distancing humanity from God in terms of awe and reverence. It is from this tradition that "the angel of the Lord" appears, where we recognize the angel of the Lord to be such a close, accurate representation of God, that it is as if one encounters the Lord Himself. God's angelic beings were there as teachers and guides, to reveal things to humanity that were not otherwise understood, nor seen. Angels were not specifically messengers of God all the time but could also be messengers sent from Satan to counterfeit the works of one such as Moses, such as happened with the plagues of Egypt. There were angels to represent good knowledge and others evil, and one such demonic angel was Mastêmâ, who we will discuss more later.

**The Books of Enoch**

The Books of Enoch (1 Enoch [Ethiopian Enoch], 2 Enoch, [Slavonic Secrets] and 3 Enoch [Hebrew Book of Enoch]) have come into vogue the past few years because of the movie, *Noah*, which heavily drew on imagery and detailing from Enoch, versus Biblical reference. Enoch was a mysterious Biblical figure that we know little about who, in the books of Enoch, is revealed as a powerful prophet whose revelations from God include substantial understandings and revelations of the cosmos and spiritual realm. The book of Enoch frequently refers to angels as "watchers and holy ones" (also found in the Aramaic portions of the book of Daniel) and their exact nature and form is often disputed. It is in Enoch that we learn more about the "watchers" (the first 37 chapters of 1 Enoch are about the Watchers) marrying human women, and they introduced magic and witchcraft into the world by revealing the secrets of the universe to these women. The books refer to both divine and fallen angels, and mention the archangels Michael, Uriel, Gabriel, and Raphael by name as those chief angels who judge the world and other fallen angels. 1 Enoch was considered canonical by much of the early church, and was one text included, then excluded, then included, then excluded, then excluded again by early church councils. It is still considered canonical among the Ethiopian Orthodox Church and among some Eastern Orthodox groups. It is also referenced in Jude 1:14:

*ENOCH, THE SEVENTH DESCENDANT FROM ADAM [COUNTING ADAM FIRST; GEN. 5:18-24], SAID [PROPHESIED] ABOUT THESE PEOPLE: "LOOK [BEHOLD], THE LORD IS COMING WITH MANY THOUSANDS OF HIS HOLY ANGELS [HOLY ONES]."*
as a section heading found in Enoch 60:8:

*BUT THE MALE*
*IS NAMED BEHEMOTH,*
*WHO OCCUPIED*
*WITH HIS BREAST*
*A WASTE WILDERNESS*
*NAMED DUIDAIN,*
*ON THE EAST OF THE GARDEN*
*WHERE THE ELECT AND RIGHTEOUS DWELL,*
*WHERE MY GRANDFATHER WAS TAKEN UP,*
*THE SEVENTH FROM ADAM,*
*THE FIRST MAN,*
*WHOM THE LORD OF SPIRITS CREATED.*[23]

The passage continues to include the following about order, both divine and demonic:

*AND I BESOUGHT THE OTHER ANGEL*
*THAT HE SHOULD SHOW ME THE MIGHT OF THOSE MONSTERS,*
*HOW THEY WERE PARTED ON ONE DAY AND CAST,*
*THE ONE INTO THE ABYSSES OF THE SEA,*
*AND THE OTHER UNTO THE DRY LAND OF THE WILDERNESS.*

*AND HE SAID TO ME:*
*'THOU SON OF MAN, HEREIN THOU DOST SEEK TO KNOW WHAT IS HIDDEN.'*
*AND THE ANGEL OF PEACE WHO WAS WITH ME SAID TO ME:*
*'THESE TWO MONSTERS, PREPARED CONFORMABLY TO THE GREATNESS OF GOD, SHALL FEED...*
*WHEN THE PUNISHMENT OF THE LORD OF SPIRITS SHALL REST UPON THEM,*
*IT SHALL REST IN ORDER*
*THAT THE PUNISHMENT OF THE LORD OF SPIRITS MAY NOT COME, IN VAIN,*
*AND IT SHALL SLAY THE CHILDREN WITH THEIR MOTHERS AND THE CHILDREN WITH THEIR FATHERS.*
*AFTERWARDS THE JUDGMENT SHALL TAKE PLACE ACCORDING TO HIS MERCY AND HIS PATIENCE.'*

*The Archangel Uriel, as depicted on a stained-glass window in St. John's Church, Wiltshire, England.*

*AND THE OTHER ANGEL WHO WENT WITH ME AND SHOWED ME WHAT WAS HIDDEN TOLD ME WHAT IS FIRST AND LAST IN THE HEAVEN IN THE HEIGHT,*
*AND BENEATH THE EARTH IN THE DEPTH,*
*AND AT THE ENDS OF THE HEAVEN, AND ON THE FOUNDATION OF THE HEAVEN.*
*AND THE CHAMBERS OF THE WINDS,*
*AND HOW THE WINDS ARE DIVIDED,*
*AND HOW THEY ARE WEIGHTED,*

*AND (HOW) THE PORTALS OF THE WINDS ARE RECKONED, EACH ACCORDING TO THE POWER OF THE WIND,*
*AND THE POWER OF THE LIGHTS OF THE MOON, AND ACCORDING TO THE POWER THAT IS FITTING:*
*AND THE DIVISIONS OF THE STARS ACCORDING TO THEIR NAMES,*
*AND HOW ALL THE DIVISIONS ARE DIVIDED.*
*AND THE THUNDERS ACCORDING TO THE PLACES WHERE THEY FALL,*
*AND ALL THE DIVISIONS THAT ARE MADE AMONG THE*
*LIGHTNINGS THAT IT MAY LIGHTEN,*

*AND THEIR HOST THAT THEY MAY AT ONCE OBEY.*
*FOR THE THUNDER HAS PLACES OF REST (WHICH) ARE ASSIGNED (TO IT) WHILE IT IS WAITING FOR ITS PEAL;*
*AND THE THUNDER AND LIGHTNING ARE INSEPARABLE,*
*AND ALTHOUGH NOT ONE AND UNDIVIDED, THEY BOTH GO TOGETHER THROUGH THE SPIRIT*
*AND SEPARATE NOT.*
*FOR WHEN THE LIGHTNING LIGHTENS,*
*THE THUNDER UTTERS ITS VOICE,*
*AND THE SPIRIT ENFORCES A PAUSE DURING THE PEAL,*
*AND DIVIDES EQUALLY BETWEEN THEM;*
*FOR THE TREASURY OF THEIR PEALS IS LIKE THE SAND,*
*AND EACH ONE OF THEM AS IT PEALS IS HELD WITHIN A BRIDLE,*
*AND TURNED BACK BY THE POWER OF THE SPIRIT,*
*AND PUSHED FORWARD ACCORDING TO THE MANY QUARTERS OF THE EARTH.*
*AND THE SPIRIT OF THE SEA IS MASCULINE AND STRONG,*
*AND ACCORDING TO THE MIGHT OF HIS STRENGTH HE DRAWS IT BACK WITH A REIN,*
*AND IN LIKE MANNER IT IS DRIVEN FORWARD*
*AND DISPERSES AMID ALL THE MOUNTAINS OF THE EARTH.*
*AND THE SPIRIT OF THE HOAR-FROST IS HIS OWN ANGEL,*
*AND THE SPIRIT OF THE HAIL IS A GOOD ANGEL,*
*AND THE SPIRIT OF THE SNOW HAS FORSAKEN HIS CHAMBERS*
*ON ACCOUNT OF HIS STRENGTH*
*- THERE IS A SPECIAL SPIRIT THEREIN,*
*AND THAT WHICH ASCENDS FROM IT IS LIKE SMOKE,*
*AND ITS NAME IS FROST.*
*AND THE SPIRIT OF THE MIST IS NOT UNITED WITH THEM IN THEIR CHAMBERS,*
*BUT IT HAS A SPECIAL CHAMBER;*
*FOR ITS COURSE IS GLORIOUS*
*BOTH IN LIGHT AND IN DARKNESS,*
*AND IN WINTER AND IN SUMMER,*

*AND IN ITS CHAMBER IS AN ANGEL.*
*AND THE SPIRIT OF THE DEW HAS ITS DWELLING AT THE ENDS OF THE HEAVEN,*
*AND IS CONNECTED WITH THE CHAMBERS OF THE RAIN,*
*AND ITS COURSE IS IN WINTER AND SUMMER:*
*AND ITS CLOUDS AND THE CLOUDS OF THE MIDST ARE CONNECTED,*
*AND THE ONE GIVES TO THE OTHER.*

*AND WHEN THE SPIRIT OF THE RAIN GOES FORTH FROM ITS CHAMBER,*
*THE ANGELS COME AND OPEN THE CHAMBER*
*AND LEAD IT OUT,*
*AND WHEN IT IS DIFFUSED OVER THE WHOLE EARTH*
*IT UNITED WITH THE WATER ON THE EARTH.*
*AND WHENSOEVER IT UNITES WITH THE WATER ON THE EARTH...*

*FOR THE WATERS ARE FOR THOSE WHO DWELL ON THE EARTH;*
*FOR THEY ARE NOURISHMENT FOR THE EARTH FROM THE MOST HIGH*
*WHO IS IN HEAVEN:*
*THEREFORE THERE IS A MEASURE FOR THE RAIN,*
*AND THE ANGELS TAKE IT IN CHARGE.*
*AND THESE THINGS I SAW*
*TOWARDS THE GARDEN OF THE RIGHTEOUS.*
(1 Enoch 60:9-23)[24]

This singular section from 1 Enoch proves the powerful way in which Enoch's cosmology was prevalent in explanation of everything, from natural powers, to angels, to divine messages. To the author of the books of Enoch, the world was dimensional, a part of a bigger cosmos. Sorting out its explanations came forth from spiritual answers. Rather than looking, as many in modern society do, to science to solve everything, the author of Enoch recognized science does not now, nor can explain things that only a spiritual perspective can. Spirits are attributed to every visible natural force, seen as different powers that execute the operation of natural function and purpose. Sometimes, they are seen as the same function or identity as angels, because they serve to do the bidding of God. The ancients identified all as such, all having a power their own, because of the purposeful and destructive nature behind them. As the pagans did, this does not mean the ancient Hebrews saw the world in a polytheistic manner, but rather one of henotheism; they believed their God was supreme, and ultimately, the only true deity (as evolved with time), but they saw the different forces that exist as having their own powers and operations from their chief deity, Yahweh. It sounds complicated, but it is not; they identified the inherent powers present within each natural cosmological force and gave certain levels of animation to each as they considered their purpose.

## The War Scroll

The Dead Sea Scrolls do not just contain fragment scrolls from the Old Testament, as some believe. The Dead Sea Scrolls were the sacred texts of an ultra-orthodox Jewish mystical community known as the Essenes. They considered themselves to be a different people, a group with a mission, apocalyptic in nature, preparing for the coming of the Messiah. In keeping with their strict nature, they observed specified diets, conduct, and rules that were unique to their people. In addition to upholding the inspiration of many Old Testament writings, the Book of Jubilees, and 1 Enoch, the Essenes had their own writings, all of which reflect their style and beliefs about life. Most are militant in nature, including a writing known as the War with the Sons of Light with the Sons of Darkness. In it, the Sons of Light fight alongside the Sons of Darkness, people who work with Belilal, a demon. Obviously, if this is a question of battle, the angels in question have militant characteristics as warriors.

*WHO IS LIKE YOU, O GOD OF ISRAEL, IN HE[AV]EN AND ON EARTH, THAT HE CAN PERFORM IN ACCORDANCE WITH YOUR GREAT WORKS AND YOUR GREAT STRENGTH. WHO IS LIKE YOUR PEOPLE ISRAEL, WHOM YOU HAVE CHOSEN FOR YOURSELF FROM ALL THE PEOPLES OF THE LANDS; THE PEOPLE OF THE SAINTS OF THE COVENANT, LEARNED IN THE STATUTES, ENLIGHTENED IN UNDERSTAN[DING ...] THOSE WHO HEAR THE GLORIOUS VOICE AND SEE THE HOLY ANGELS, WHOSE EARS ARE OPEN; HEARING DEEP THINGS. [O GOD, YOU HAVE CREATED] THE EXPANSE OF THE SKIES, THE HOST OF LUMINARIES, THE TASK OF SPIRITS AND THE DOMINION OF HOLY ONES, THE TREASURES OF [YOUR] GL[ORY. . . ] CLOUDS. HE WHO CREATED THE EARTH AND THE LIMITS OF HER DIVISIONS INTO WILDERNESS AND PLAIN, AND ALL HER OFFSPRING, WITH THE FRU[ITS ...], THE CIRCLE OF THE SEAS, THE SOURCES OF THE RIVETS, AND THE RIFT OF THE DEEPS, WILD BEASTS AND WINGED CREATURES, THE FORM OF MAN AND THE GENER[ATIONS OF] HIS [SEE]D, THE CONFUSION OF LANGUAGE AND THE SEPARATION OF PEOPLES, THE ABODE OF CLANS AND THE INHERITANCE OF THE LANDS, [... AND] HOLY FESTIVALS, COURSES OF YEARS AND TIMES OF ETERNITY.* (Col. 10:9-16)[25]

The War Scroll takes on another depth of understanding as relates to an ancient perspective of cosmology: human beings pick sides, and those sides are either seen as good or bad. Angels also have sides to pick, as good or bad. This brings forth further revelation of angels and their power to be good or bad, and such influence can be positive or negative in our lives.

## The Book of Tobit

Tobit is a book classified as Deuterocanonical (a word meaning "second canon") among Catholics or as an Old Testament apocryphal book among Protestants. It is one of twelve books of dispute that bridge the Old and New Testaments together and were even included in the original 1611 King James Version of the Bible. They were of question during the Protestant Reformation, but were formally removed by Puritans, who desired to purify anything and everything of anything they felt might seem too Catholic. These books, unlike the others we are looking at, are easily accessible and included in some versions of the Bible widely available.

Tobit is a story of a righteous Hebrew man who lived during a time of unrighteousness in Nineveh, and the calamities and adventures of his son,

*The Angel Raphael with Bishop Domonte, Bartolome Esteban Murillo (1617-1782)*

Tobias. Through a series of demonic encounters, he is attacked for doing the right thing, becomes blind, and as a result, his marriage strains. He then comes across a woman named Sarah, who is also tormented by demons who kill every man she marries before they can consummate the relationship. The angel Raphael comes, heals Tobit's blindness, and frees Sarah from her demon. The work of the Angel Raphael then continues to guide Tobias to his future, to gather money from a relative, to handling a fish that tried to swallow his foot, to the marriage of Tobias and Sarah and the healing of Sarah's father from blindness.[26]

*As Tobit and Sarah were praying, God in heaven heard their prayers and sent his angel Raphael to help them. He was sent to remove the white film from Tobit's eyes, so that he could see again, and to arrange a marriage between Sarah and Tobit's son Tobias, who, as her cousin, had the right to marry her.*

*Raphael was also ordered to expel the demon Asmodeus from Sarah. At the very moment that Tobit went back into his house from the courtyard, Sarah, in her house in Ecbatana, was coming downstairs.* (Tobit 3:16-17, GNT)

*Tobias then went out to look for someone who knew the way to Media and would travel with him. Almost as soon as he left the house, he found himself face-to-face with Raphael. Tobias did not know that Raphael was an angel of God, so he asked him where he was from.*

*I am an Israelite, Raphael answered,*
*one of your distant relatives, and I have come here to Nineveh to find work.*

*Do you know the way to Media? Tobias asked.*

*Yes, I do, Raphael replied.*

*I have been there many times, and I know all the roads well. I used to stay with our relative Gabael, who lives there in the town of Rages. It takes at least two days to travel there from Ecbatana, the capital city, because Rages is up in the mountains.*

*Then Tobias said to Raphael,*
*Wait here for me, my friend, while I go in and tell my father. I would like for you to travel with me, and I will pay you for the journey.*

*All right, Raphael said,*
*I'll wait, but don't take too long.*

*Tobias went in and told his father,*
*I have found an Israelite to travel with me.*

*Call the man in, Tobit replied.*
*I would like to know what family and tribe he belongs to, and whether he is a reliable traveling companion for you.*

*So Tobias went out and called to Raphael,*
*My father would like to meet you. When Raphael came in, Tobit greeted him first.*

Then Raphael returned the greeting,
I hope all is well with you.

But Tobit replied,
How can all be well with me? I'm blind and can't see a thing. It's like being dead and no longer able to see the light. I might as well be dead! I can hear people talking, but I can't see them.

Cheer up! Raphael said to him.
God is going to cure you soon, so don't worry!

Tobit then said,
My son Tobias wants to go to Media. Can you go with him and show him the way? I will pay you, of course.

Raphael replied,
Certainly I can go with him. I have traveled there many times and I know all the roads in the mountains and on the plains.

Tobit questioned him further,
Tell me, my friend, what family and tribe do you belong to?
But Raphael asked,
Why do you need to know that?

Tell me the truth, said Tobit.
What is your name, and who are you?

Raphael replied,
My name is Azarias, and I am the son of the older Ananias, one of your relatives.

Then Tobit said to him,
Welcome to our home! God bless you, my son. Please don't be offended because I wanted to know the truth about you and your family. As it turns out, you are from a good family and a relative at that! I knew Ananias and Nathan, the two sons of the older Shemaiah. They were always loyal to their religion. We used to travel together to Jerusalem and worship there.

*Your relatives are fine people, and you come from good stock. Have a safe journey.*

*Tobit continued,*
*I will pay the normal daily wage plus expenses for both of you. Be a good companion to Tobias, and I will add a bonus to your wages.*

*I will go with him, Raphael said.*
*And don't worry; we will get there and back safely. The roads are not dangerous.*

*God be with you! Tobit replied. Then he called Tobias and said to him, Son, get everything ready that you need for the journey, so that the two of you can be on your way. May God and his angel watch over you both and bring you back to me safe and sound.*

*Before leaving for Media, Tobias kissed his father and mother good-bye. Tobit said again,*
*Have a safe journey!*
(Tobit 5:4-16, GNT)

*So Tobias and the angel started out toward Media, taking Tobias' dog along with them. They walked on until sunset, then camped by the Tigris River. Tobias had gone down to wash his feet in the river, when suddenly a huge fish jumped up out of the water and tried to swallow one of his feet. Tobias let out a yell, and the angel called to him,*

*Grab that fish! Don't let it get away.*

*Then Tobias grabbed the fish and dragged it up on the bank.*

*Cut the fish open, the angel instructed,*
*and take out its gall bladder, heart, and liver. Keep these with you; they can be used for medicine, but throw away the guts.*

*Tobias did as the angel had told him. Then he cooked the fish, ate part of it, and salted the rest to take along with him.*
*The two continued on together until they were near Media.*

*THEN TOBIAS ASKED,*
*AZARIAS, MY FRIEND, WHAT DISEASES CAN BE CURED BY THIS GALL BLADDER, HEART, AND LIVER?*

*THE ANGEL ANSWERED,*
*THE HEART AND LIVER CAN BE BURNED AND USED TO CHASE AWAY A DEMON OR AN EVIL SPIRIT THAT IS TORMENTING SOMEONE. THE ATTACKS WILL STOP IMMEDIATELY, AND THE PERSON WILL NEVER BE TROUBLED AGAIN. YOU CAN USE THE GALL BLADDER TO TREAT SOMEONE WHOSE EYES ARE COVERED WITH A WHITE FILM. JUST RUB IT ON HIS EYES AND BLOW ON THE FILM, AND HE WILL BE ABLE TO SEE AGAIN.*
(Tobit 6:1-8, GNT)

This look at angels shows the direct guidance of their work in the lives of humanity, maybe in a direct way many of us do not typically consider possible. Raphael's direct guidance in the life of Tobit shows a certain intimate care in the nature of God, one that cares enough to make sure that the littlest details of life and deliverance were met through the instructions of a divine messenger.

It also proves that angels follow God's direction, not their own. Raphael's work was to do as he was instructed, not as he desired or wanted to do of his own will. This shows the nature of servanthood present in the work of divine powers, those which seek to reflect the nature of the One Who sends them, rather than they, themselves.

## The Testament of Moses

The Testament of Moses was a first-century Jewish apocryphal document found in two different parts: The Testament of Moses and the Assumption of Moses. It is quoted in Jude 1:9 in the New Testament, among quotations from it in early church writings, displaying its relevance and renown among believers of the first century. Its major theme is Moses delivering the sacred writings and traditions to Joshua, as well as several prophecies about the nation of Israel to be withheld until the proper time. Most of these prophecies are histories of Israel, from the time of Moses until the period of Hellenization, including references to Herod, the destruction of the temple, persecution of the Jews, and coming punishment for the Gentiles. Some scholars speculate its authorship lies within the Essene community.[27] Much of the work is in fragments, but what we do find within its contents is another theme about the work of angels:

*AND THEN HIS KINGDOM SHALL
APPEAR THROUGHOUT ALL HIS
CREATION,
AND THEN SATAN SHALL BE NO MORE,
AND SORROW SHALL DEPART WITH
HIM.
THEN THE HANDS OF THE ANGEL
SHALL BE FILLED
WHO HAS BEEN APPOINTED CHIEF,
AND HE SHALL FORTHWITH AVENGE
THEM OF THEIR ENEMIES.
FOR THE HEAVENLY ONE WILL ARISE
FROM HIS ROYAL THRONE,
AND HE WILL GO FORTH FROM HIS
HOLY HABITATION
WITH INDIGNATION AND WRATH ON ACCOUNT OF HIS SONS.*
(The Testament of Moses, Chapter 10)[28]

*The Ascent of Yahoel and Abraham (c. 1300), featuring the angels Melchidael, Yahoel, Anafiel, and Metatron.*

The Testament of Moses pictures a chief angel, many assume to be the Archangel Michael, operating in warrior mode, fighting in apocalyptic battle much like we see reference to him in the book of Daniel. The ideas we see prevalent in Scripture have a way of coming around, of imagery rounding itself out and making a name for itself in a different way than it had before. In this instance, the writing made sense to those who received it; it made the angelic battle real for them, relevant to their situations and circumstances, as a reality of God's intervention on their behalf. It placed their day, their issue at the center of prophetic battle and encouraged readers to take hope, for God would, in the long run, intervene on their behalf.

## The Apocalypse of Abraham

The Apocalypse of Abraham is, most likely, an early first-century Pseudepigraphic Jewish work based on earlier writings brought into one document, kept, most likely, from the time when Abraham lived on the earth. It is considered as a Jewish writing, and while most don't consider it relevant today, it was a writing of great prominence in the time of the New Testament. In It, we see a detailing of key points in Abraham's life, including his life as a young man assisting his father in the creation of idols, the experience of being asked to sacrifice Isaac, and of his later vision of heaven and future judgment.[29]

In The Apocalypse of Abraham, we find an angel named Yahoel, who was sent to guide Abraham and instruct him on essential matters pertaining to sacrifice:

*AND WE WENT, THE TWO OF US TOGETHER FOR FORTY DAYS AND NIGHTS, AND I ATE NO BREAD AND DRANK NO WATER, BECAUSE MY FOOD AND MY DRINK WAS TO SEE THE ANGEL WHO WAS WITH ME, AND TO HEAR HIS SPEECH. AND WE CAME TO THE MOUNT OF GOD, MOUNT HOREB, AND I SAID TO THE ANGEL, "SINGER OF THE ETERNAL ONE! I HAVE NO SACRIFICE WITH ME, NOR AM I AWARE OF THE PLACE OF AN ALTAR ON THE MOUNTAIN; HOW CAN I BRING A SACRIFICE?" AND HE SAID TO ME, "LOOK AROUND YOU." AND WHEN I LOOKED AROUND, THERE FOLLOWING US WERE ALL THE PRESCRIBED ANIMALS, THE YOUNG HEIFER, THE SHE GOAT, THE RAM, THE TURTLE DOVE AND THE PIGEON.* (The Apocalypse of Abraham 10:1-4)[30]

*AND THE ANGEL SAID TO ME, "ABRAHAM!" AND I SAID, "HERE AM I." AND HE SAID, "SLAUGHTER ALL THESE ANIMALS, AND DIVIDE THEM INTO HALVES, THE ONE AGAINST THE OTHER, BUT DO NOT SEVER THE BIRDS. AND GIVE THESE TO THE MEN WHOM I WILL SHOW YOU, STANDING BY YOU, FOR THESE ARE THE ALTAR UPON THE MOUNTAIN, TO OFFER A SACRIFICE TO THE ETERNAL BUT THE TURTLE DOVE AND THE PIGEON GIVE TO ME, FOR I WILL ASCEND UPON THE WINGS OF THE BIRD, SO THAT YOU MAY BE ABLE TO SEE IN HEAVEN, AND UPON EARTH, AND IN THE SEA, AND IN THE ABYSS, AND IN THE UNDERWORLD, AND IN THE GARDEN OF EDEN, AND IN ITS RIVERS, AND IN THE FULLNESS OF THE WHOLE WORLD AND ITS CIRCLE - YOU SHALL GAZE INTO THEM ALL."* (The Apocalypse of Abraham 11:1-3)[31]

*AND I DID EVERYTHING ACCORDING TO THE COMMAND OF THE ANGEL, AND GAVE THE ANGELS WHO HAD COME TO US, THE DIVIDED ANIMALS, BUT THE ANGEL JAOEL TOOK THE BIRDS. AND I WAITED UNTIL THE EVENING SACRIFICE. AND THERE FLEW AN UNCLEAN BIRD DOWN UPON THE CARCASSES, AND I DROVE IT AWAY. AND THE UNCLEAN BIRD SPOKE TO ME AND SAID, "ABRAHAM, WHAT ARE YOU DOING UPON THESE HOLY HEIGHTS, WHERE NO MAN EATS OR DRINKS, NOR IS THERE UPON THEM THE FOOD OF MAN, BUT THESE HEAVENLY BEINGS CONSUME EVERYTHING WITH FIRE, AND WILL BURN YOU UP. FORSAKE THE MAN WHO IS WITH YOU AND FLEE, FOR IF YOU ASCEND INTO THE HEIGHTS*

*THEY WILL DESTROY YOU."* (The Apocalypse of Abraham 13:1-6)[32]

*AND I UTTERED THE WORDS THAT THE ANGEL TAUGHT ME. AND THEN THE ANGEL SAID TO ME, "ANSWER HIM NOT! FOR GOD HAS GIVEN HIM POWER OVER THOSE WHO ANSWER HIM." AND THE ANGEL SPOKE TO ME AGAIN SAYING, "HOWEVER MUCH HE SPEAK TO YOU, ANSWER HIM NOT, IN ORDER THAT HE MAY HAVE NO FREE ACCESS TO YOU, BECAUSE THE ETERNAL ONE HAS GIVEN HIM 'WEIGHT AND WILL' IN THIS RESPECT." AND I DID THAT WHICH WAS COMMANDED ME BY THE ANGEL, AND NO MATTER HOW MUCH HE SPOKE TO ME, I ANSWERED HIM NOTHING WHATSOEVER.* (The Apocalypse of Abraham 15:1-2)[33]

The major thing all these books have in common, especially with the book of Genesis, is the essential nature of sorting out cosmologic issues within relation to cosmology. They are commentaries and revelations on why things are the way they are, how they got this way, and how they can sort themselves out. They were not written to stand as a scientific statement or some sort of outdoing others in the nature of truth but show genuine process of how people sorted through the evil and chaos they saw as well as the good and the true experience they could have from spiritual understanding.

## **The Apocalypse of Zephaniah**

This ancient text follows the same style of the book of Zephaniah in the Bible, paralleling the apocalyptic visual imagery found therein. Its main purpose is to reveal what happens beyond death. It is the Angel of the Lord who guides Zephaniah through the vision, as various angels execute the work of carrying off the souls of the ungodly, writing down the good deeds of humans, and overseeing the maintenance of the afterlife.

*THE ANGEL OF THE LORD SAID UNTO ME, "COME, LET ME SHOW THEE THE PLACE OF RIGHTEOUSNESS."*

*THEN I SAW TWO OTHER ANGELS WEEPING OVER THE THREE SONS OF JOATHAM, THE PRIEST. I SAID, "O ANGEL, WHO ARE THESE?" HE SAID, "THESE ARE THE ANGELS OF THE LORD ALMIGHTY. THEY WRITE DOWN ALL THE GOOD DEEDS OF THE RIGHTEOUS UPON THEIR SCROLLS AS THEY WATCH AT THE GATE OF HEAVEN." AND I TAKE THEM FROM THEIR HANDS AND BRING THEM UP BEFORE THE LORD ALMIGHTY; HE WRITETH THEIR*

*NAME IN THE BOOK OF THE LIVING. ALSO THE ANGELS OF THE ACCUSER WHO IS UPON THE EARTH, THEY ALSO WRITE DOWN ALL THE SINS OF MEN UPON THEIR SCROLLS. THEY ALSO SIT AT THE GATE OF HEAVEN. THEY TELL THE ACCUSER AND HE WRITETH THEM UPON HIS SCROLL SO THAT HE MIGHT ACCUSE THEM WHEN THEY COME OUT OF THE WORLD (AND GO) DOWN THERE."* (Apocalypse of Zephaniah 3:1, 5-9)[34]

*THEN I WALKED WITH THE ANGEL OF THE LORD. I LOOKED BEFORE ME AND I SAW A PLACE THERE. THOUSANDS OF THOUSANDS AND MYRIADS OF MYRIADS OF ANGELS ENTERED THROUGH IT. THEIR FACES WERE LIKE A LEOPARD, THEIR TUSKS BEING OUTSIDE THEIR MOUTH LIKE WILD BOARS. THEIR EYES WERE MIXED WITH BLOOD. THEIR HAIR WAS LOOSE LIKE THE HAIR OF WOMEN, AND FIERY SCOURGES WERE IN THEIR HANDS. WHEN I SAW THEM, I WAS AFRAID. I SAID UNTO THAT ANGEL WHO WALKED WITH ME, "OF WHAT SORT ARE THESE?" HE SAID UNTO ME, "THESE ARE THE SERVANTS OF ALL CREATION WHO COME TO THE SOULS OF UNGODLY MEN AND BRING THEM AND LEAVE THEM IN THIS PLACE. THEY SPEND THREE DAYS GOING AROUND WITH THEM IN THE AIR BEFORE THEY BRING THEM AND CAST THEM INTO THEIR ETERNAL PUNISHMENT."* (Apocalypse of Zephaniah 4:1-7)[35]

*THEN A GREAT ANGEL CAME FORTH HAVING A GOLDEN TRUMPET IN HIS HAND, AND HE BLEW IT THREE TIMES OVER MY HEAD, SAYING, "BE COURAGEOUS! O ONE WHO HATH TRIUMPHED. PREVAIL! O ONE WHO HATH PREVAILED. FOR THOU HAST TRIUMPHED OVER THE ACCUSER, AND THOU HAST ESCAPED FROM THE ABYSS AND HADES. THOU WILT NOW CROSS OVER THE CROSSING PLACE. FOR THY NAME IS WRITTEN IN THE BOOK OF THE LIVING." I WANTED TO EMBRACE HIM, (BUT) I WAS UNABLE TO EMBRACE THE GREAT ANGEL BECAUSE HIS GLORY IS GREAT.* (Apocalypse of Zephaniah 9:1-3)[36]

*AND AGAIN THE GREAT ANGEL COMETH FORTH WITH THE GOLDEN TRUMPET IN HIS HAND BLOWING OVER THE EARTH. THEY HEAR (IT) FROM THE PLACE OF THE SUNRISE TO THE PLACE OF THE SUNSET AND FROM THE SOUTHERN REGIONS TO THE NORTHERN REGIONS. AND AGAIN HE BLOWS (IT) UP UNTO HEAVEN AND ITS SOUND IS HEARD. I SAID, "O LORD, WHY LEFT THOU ME NOT UNTIL I SAW THEM ALL?" HE SAID UNTO ME, "I HAVE NOT AUTHORITY TO SHOW THEM UNTO THEE UNTIL THE LORD ALMIGHTY RISETH UP IN HIS WRATH TO DESTROY THE EARTH AND THE HEAVENS. THEY WILL SEE AND BE DISTURBED, AND THEY WILL ALL CRY OUT, SAYING, 'ALL FLESH WHICH IS ASCRIBED TO THEE WE WILL GIVE UNTO THEE ON THE DAY OF THE LORD.' WHO WILL STAND IN HIS PRESENCE WHEN HE RISETH IN HIS WRATH <TO DESTROY> THE EARTH <AND THE HEAVENS?> EVERY TREE WHICH GROWETH UPON THE EARTH WILL BE PLUCKED UP WITH ITS ROOTS AND FALL DOWN. AND EVERY HIGH TOWER AND THE BIRDS WHICH FLY*

*WILL FALL ..."* (Apocalypse of Zephaniah 12:1-8)[37]

Zephaniah's vision shows a detailed picture of the way people viewed the afterlife during the time of the New Testament. It also shows the spiritual aspects of operation that many do not consider as pertain to the angels, as the ministering servants of heaven.

## **The Apocalypse of Baruch (2 and 3 Baruch)**

Baruch was a scribe who worked closely with the Prophet Jeremiah (Jeremiah 32:12-16, Jeremiah 36:4-32, Jeremiah 43:3-6, Jeremiah 45:1-2). As a classic obscure figure (to whom are also attributed 2 and 3 Baruch), Baruch received powerful visions, the first vision being of the fall of Jerusalem, and then apocalyptic visions about the future and the fall of the wicked and the good of the righteous, and the second vision, of the heavenly and the divine, consisting of heaven in five levels. Its main purpose was to lend spiritual understanding to the temple and the fact that it no longer stood on earth, referring to a time after 587 BC and possibly the destruction of Jerusalem in 70 AD. Instead of insisting the temple to be rebuilt on earth, it made clear that the temple was preserved in heaven, and was maintained by the angels:

AND IT CAME TO PASS ON THE MORROW THAT, LO! THE ARMY OF THE CHALDEES SURROUNDED THE CITY, AND AT THE TIME OF THE EVENING, I, BARUCH, LEFT THE PEOPLE, AND I WENT FORTH AND STOOD BY THE OAK. AND I WAS GRIEVING OVER ZION, AND LAMENTING OVER THE CAPTIVITY WHICH HAD COME UPON THE PEOPLE. AND LO! SUDDENLY A STRONG SPIRIT RAISED ME, AND BORE ME ALOFT OVER THE WALL OF JERUSALEM. AND I BEHELD, AND LO! FOUR ANGELS STANDING AT THE FOUR CORNERS OF THE CITY, EACH OF THEM HOLDING A TORCH OF FIRE IN HIS HANDS. AND ANOTHER ANGEL BEGAN TO DESCEND FROM HEAVEN. AND SAID UNTO THEM: 'HOLD YOUR LAMPS, AND DO NOT LIGHT THEM TILL I TELL YOU. FOR I AM FIRST SENT TO SPEAK A WORD TO THE EARTH, AND TO PLACE IN IT WHAT THE LORD THE MOST HIGH HAS COMMANDED ME.' AND I SAW HIM DESCEND INTO THE HOLY OF HOLIES, AND TAKE FROM THERE THE VEIL, AND HOLY ARK, AND THE MERCY-SEAT, AND THE TWO TABLES, AND THE HOLY RAIMENT OF THE PRIESTS, AND THE ALTAR OF INCENSE, AND THE FORTY-EIGHT PRECIOUS STONES, WHEREWITH THE PRIEST WAS ADORNED AND ALL THE HOLY VESSELS OF THE TABERNACLE. AND HE SPOKE TO THE EARTH WITH A LOUD VOICE:

*'Earth, earth, earth, hear the word of the mighty God,*
*And receive what I commit to you,*
*And guard them until the last times,*

*Archangel Gabriel, from somewhere during the 13th century.*

*So that, when you are ordered, you may restore them,*
*So that strangers may not get possession of them.*
*For the time comes when Jerusalem also will be delivered for a time,*
*Until it is said, that it is again restored for ever.'*
*And the earth opened its mouth and swallowed them up.*

*And after these things I heard that angel saying unto those angels who held the lamps: 'Destroy, therefore, and overthrow its wall to its foundations, lest the enemy should boast and say:*

*"We have overthrown the wall of Zion,*
*And we have burnt the place of the mighty God."'*
*And they have seized the place where I had been standing before.*

*Now the angels did as he had commanded them, and when they had broken up the corners of the walls, a voice was heard from the interior of the temple, after the wall had fall saying:*

*'Enter, you enemies,*
*And come, you adversaries;*
*For he who kept the house has forsaken (it).'*
(2 Baruch 6:1-8:2)[38]

*And as I was conversing with them, behold angels came bearing baskets full of flowers. And they gave them to Michael. And I asked the angel, Lord, who are these, and what are the things brought hither from beside them? And he said to me, These are angels (who) are over the righteous. And the archangel took the baskets, and cast them into the vessel. And the angel said to me, These flowers are the merits of the righteous. And I saw other angels bearing baskets which were (neither) empty nor full. And they began to lament, and did not venture to draw near, because they had not the prizes complete. And Michael cried and said, Come hither, also, ye angels, bring what ye have brought. And Michael was exceedingly grieved, and the angel who was with me, because they did not fill the vessel.*

*And then came in like manner other angels weeping and bewailing, and saying with fear, Behold how we are overclouded, O Lord, for we were delivered to evil men, and we wish to depart from them. And Michael said, Ye cannot depart from them, in order that the enemy may not prevail to the end; but say to me what ye ask. And they said, We pray thee, Michael our commander, transfer us from them, for we cannot abide with wicked and foolish men, for there is nothing good in them, but every kind of unrighteousness and greed. For we do not behold them entering [into Church at all, nor among spiritual fathers, nor] into any good work. But where there is murder, there also are they in the midst, and where are fornications, adulteries, thefts, slanders, perjuries, jealousies, drunkenness, strife, envy, murmurings, whispering, idolatry, divination, and such like, then are they workers of such works, and of others worse. Wherefore we entreat that we may depart from them. And Michael said to the angels, Wait till I learn from the Lord what shall come to pass.*

*And in that very hour Michael departed, and the doors were closed. And there was a sound as thunder. And I asked the angel, What is the sound? And he said to me, Michael is even now presenting the merits of men to God.*

*And in that very hour Michael descended, and the gate was opened; and he brought oil. And as for the angels which brought the baskets which were full, he filled them with oil, saying, Take it away, reward our friends an hundredfold, and those who have laboriously wrought good works. For those who sowed virtuously, also reap virtuously. And he said also to those bringing the half-empty baskets, Come hither ye also; take away the reward according as ye brought, and deliver it to the sons of men. [Then he said also to those who brought the full and to those who brought the half-empty baskets: Go and bless our friends, and say to them that thus saith the Lord, Ye are faithful over a few things, I will set you over many things; enter into*

*THE JOY OF YOUR LORD.]*

*AND TURNING HE SAID ALSO TO THOSE WHO BROUGHT NOTHING: THUS SAITH THE LORD, BE NOT SAD OF COUNTENANCE, AND WEEP NOT, NOR LET THE SONS OF MEN ALONE. BUT SINCE THEY ANGERED ME IN THEIR WORKS, GO AND MAKE THEM ENVIOUS AND ANGRY AND PROVOKED AGAINST A PEOPLE THAT IS NO PEOPLE, A PEOPLE THAT HAS NO UNDERSTANDING. FURTHER, BESIDES THESE, SEND FORTH THE CATERPILLAR AND THE UNWINGED LOCUST, AND THE MILDEW, AND THE COMMON LOCUST (AND) HAIL WITH LIGHTNINGS AND ANGER, AND PUNISH THEM SEVERELY WITH THE SWORD AND WITH DEATH, AND THEIR CHILDREN WITH DEMONS. FOR THEY DID NOT HEARKEN TO MY VOICE, NOR DID THEY OBSERVE MY COMMANDMENTS, NOR DO THEM, BUT WERE DESPISERS OF MY COMMANDMENTS, AND INSOLENT TOWARDS THE PRIESTS WHO PROCLAIMED MY WORDS TO THEM.*

*AND WHILE HE YET SPAKE, THE DOOR WAS CLOSED, AND WE WITHDREW. AND THE ANGEL TOOK ME AND RESTORED ME TO THE P/ACE WHERE I WAS AT THE BEGINNING. AND HAVING COME TO MYSELF, I GAVE GLORY TO GOD, WHO COUNTED ME WORTHY OF SUCH HONOR. WHEREFORE DO YE ALSO, BRETHREN, WHO OBTAINED SUCH A REVELATION, YOURSELVES ALSO GLORIFY GOD, SO THAT HE ALSO MAY GLORIFY YOU, NOW AND EVER, AND TO ALL ETERNITY. AMEN.* (3 Baruch 12:1-17:4)[39]

The vivid picture of heaven shows the purity therein, and the call of the angels to maintain it. As we can see from other works, it makes sense to see ministerial servants in this capacity, as those who stand as the guardians of all that is honorable and good about eternity.

## The Gospel of Bartholomew

The work of writing non-canonical books did not stop with New Testament times or Jewish authors, and the tradition of writing works under the name of relevant figures to give them credibility spanned hundreds of years after the time of Christ. The question as to the authorship of some New Testament apocryphal works is debated, but nonetheless, these works are still highly relevant into the manner of which Scripture, tradition, and non-canonical ideas about faith and spirituality permeated the lives of early believers.

Bartholomew wasn't the most notable of the twelve apostles; in fact, he may very well be one of them that most don't know or recognize by name. It is possible it is identical to two other works, The Questions of Bartholomew, or The Resurrection of Jesus Christ (by Bartholomew). The book itself takes liberties in some of its spiritual interpretations (including the fall of man), but follows heavily in inspiration of 1 Enoch. The work is an intense depiction of Jesus' descent into hell, followed by a graphic vision of hell. This means both the presence of angels and demons is contained within its contents:

*AND HE LED THEM AWAY INTO A PLACE THAT IS CALLED CHERUBIM (CHERUKT SLAV., CHAIROUDEE GR., LAT. 2 OMITS), THAT IS THE PLACE OF TRUTH.*

*AND HE BECKONED UNTO THE ANGELS OF THE WEST AND THE EARTH WAS ROLLED UP LIKE A VOLUME OF A BOOK AND THE DEEP WAS REVEALED UNTO THEM.* (The Gospel of Bartholomew 3:6-7)[40]

The Gospel of Bartholomew also refers to the creation of over 6,000 angels, several by name that are generally unfamiliar to most:

*FOR, INDEED, I WAS FORMED (AL. CALLED) THE FIRST ANGEL: FOR WHEN GOD MADE THE HEAVENS, HE TOOK A HANDFUL OF FIRE AND FORMED ME FIRST, MICHAEL SECOND [VIENNA MS. HERE HAS THESE SENTENCES: FOR HE HAD HIS SON BEFORE THE HEAVENS AND THE EARTH AND WE WERE FORMED (FOR WHEN HE TOOK THOUGHT TO CREATE ALL THINGS, HIS SON SPAKE A WORD), SO THAT WE ALSO WERE CREATED BY THE WILL OF THE SON AND THE CONSENT OF THE FATHER. HE FORMED, I SAY, FIRST ME, NEXT MICHAEL THE CHIEF CAPTAIN OF THE HOSTS THAT ARE ABOVE], GABRIEL THIRD, URIEL FOURTH, RAPHAEL FIFTH, NATHANAEL SIXTH, AND OTHER ANGELS OF WHOM I CANNOT TELL THE NAMES. [JERUSALEM MS., MICHAEL, GABRIEL, RAPHAEL, URIEL, XATHANAEL, AND OTHER 6,000 ANGELS. LAT. I, MICHAEL THE HONOUR OF POWER, THIRD RAPHAEL, FOURTH GABRIEL, AND OTHER SEVEN. LAT. 2, RAPHAEL THIRD, GABRIEL FOURTH, URIEL FIFTH, ZATHAEL SIXTH, AND OTHER SIX.] FOR THEY ARE THE ROD-BEARERS (LICTORS) OF GOD, AND THEY SMITE ME WITH THEIR RODS AND PURSUE ME SEVEN TIMES IN THE NIGHT AND SEVEN TIMES IN THE DAY, AND LEAVE ME NOT AT ALL AND BREAK IN PIECES ALL MY POWER. THESE ARE THE (TWELVE, LAT. 2) ANGELS OF VENGEANCE WHICH STAND BEFORE THE THRONE OF GOD: THESE ARE THE ANGELS THAT WERE FIRST FORMED.*
*AND AFTER THEM WERE FORMED ALL THE ANGELS. IN THE FIRST HEAVEN ARE AN HUNDRED MYRIADS, AND IN THE SECOND AN HUNDRED MYRIADS, AND IN THE THIRD AN HUNDRED MYRIADS, AND IN THE FOURTH AN HUNDRED MYRIADS, AND IN THE FIFTH AN*

*HUNDRED MYRIADS, AND IN THE SIXTH AN HUNDRED MYRIADS, AND IN THE SEVENTH (AN HUNDRED MYRIADS, AND OUTSIDE THE SEVEN HEAVENS, JERUSALEM MS.) IS THE FIRST FIRMAMENT (FLAT SURFACE) WHEREIN ARE THE POWERS WHICH WORK UPON MEN.*

*FOR THERE ARE FOUR OTHER ANGELS SET OVER THE WINDS. THE FIRST ANGEL IS OVER THE NORTH, AND HE IS CALLED CHAIROUM (. . . BROIL, JERUSALEM MS.; LAT. 2, ANGEL OF THE NORTH, MAUCH), AND HATH IN HIS HAND A ROD OF FIRE, AND RESTRAINETH THE SUPER-FLUITY OF MOISTURE THAT THE EARTH BE NOT OVERMUCH WET.*

*AND THE ANGEL THAT IS OVER THE NORTH IS CALLED OERTHA (LAT. 2, ALFATHA): HE HATH A TORCH OF FIRE AND PUTTETH IT TO HIS SIDES, AND THEY WARM THE GREAT COLDNESS OF HIM THAT HE FREEZE NOT THE WORLD.*

*AND THE ANGEL THAT IS OVER THE SOUTH IS CALLED KERKOUTHA (LAT. 2, CEDAR) AND THEY BREAK HIS FIERCENESS THAT HE SHAKE NOT THE EARTH.*

*AND THE ANGEL THAT IS OVER THE SOUTH-WEST IS CALLED NAOUTHA, AND HE HATH A ROD OF SNOW IN HIS HAND AND PUTTETH IT INTO HIS MOUTH, AND QUENCHETH THE FIRE THAT COMETH OUT OF HIS MOUTH. AND IF THE ANGEL QUENCHED IT NOT AT HIS MOUTH IT WOULD SET ALL THE WORLD ON FIRE.*

*AND THERE IS ANOTHER ANGEL OVER THE SEA WHICH MAKETH IT ROUGH WITH THE WAVES THEREOF.* (The Gospel of Bartholomew 4:28-35)[41]

The purpose in writing the Gospel of Bartholomew was to give a certain explanation in greater detail to the spirituality of the resurrection. In and of the manuscripts we find in the New Testament, we do not find great detail about Jesus' time in the tomb, His descent into the nether regions, and in what specifically transpired. This writing sought to give insight to this most spiritually relevant event, much as Jubilees sought to do the same with the early experiences connected to the Hebrew people.

## The Epistle of the Apostles (Epistula Apostolorum)

This particular writing appears to be an early church instruction given by Jesus Himself but dates a bit after the time of the New Testament, somewhere around 140-150 AD. Probably more about church politics and polarities, its main goal was to impress instruction upon its readers and warn them against rising divisions in the church. It shows evidence of changes away from New Testament patterns and thoughts in church structures, but reiterates understandings of many New Testament passages, as well as discussion of things related to levels of heaven and apocryphal references of angels:

*Now that which he revealed unto us is this, which he spake: It came to pass when I was about (minded) to come hither from the Father of all things, and passed through the heavens, then did I put on the wisdom of the Father, and I put on the power of his might. I was in heaven, and I passed by the archangels and the angels in their likeness, like as if I were one of them, among the princedoms and powers. I passed through them because I possessed the wisdom of him that had sent me. Now the chief captain of the angels, [is] Michael, and Gabriel and Uriel and Raphael followed me unto the fifth firmament (heaven), for they thought in their heart that I was one of them; such power was given me of my Father. And on that day did I adorn the archangels with a wonderful voice (so Copt.: Eth., Lat., I made them quake - amazed them), so that they should go unto the altar of the Father and serve and fulfil the ministry until I should return unto him. And so wrought I the likeness by my wisdom; for I became all things in all, that I might praise the dispensation of the Father and fulfil the glory of him that sent me (the verbs might well be transposed) and return unto him. (Here the Latin omits a considerable portion of text without notice, to near the beginning of c. 17.)*

*For ye know that the angel Gabriel brought the message unto Mary. And we answered: Yea, Lord. He answered and said unto us: Remember ye not, then, that I said unto you a little while ago: I became an angel among the angels, and I became all things in all? We said unto him: Yea, Lord. Then answered he and said unto us: On that day whereon I took the form of the angel Gabriel, I appeared unto Mary and spake with her. Her heart accepted me, and she believed (She believed and laughed, Eth.), and I formed myself and entered into her body. I became flesh, for I alone was a minister unto myself in that which concerned Mary (I was mine own messenger, Eth.) in the appearance of the shape of an angel. For so must I needs (or, was I wont to) do. Thereafter did I return to my Father (Copt. After my return to the Father, and run on). (13-14)*[42]

## The Sibylline Oracles

The Sibylline Oracles are a collection of extensive and long poetic songs, written as divine utterances from early prophetesses, received in an ecstatic state of spiritual frenzy. They reflect the beliefs of early believers, spanning different Christian and Jewish sects of the early centuries of the faith. They echo many apocalyptic themes as well as the telling of salvation history. There are approximately twelve to fourteen books, written by different sources, and exist today in many fragments.

Because their very nature was prophetic, they reveal significant mystical and spiritual revelation we do not always see prevalent in New Testament apocryphal writings. In keeping with other ancient traditions, they make reference to the angelic realm, especially those angels of pseudepigrapha tradition:

*And then shall Uriel, mighty angel, break*
*The bolts of stern and lasting adamant*
*Which, monstrous, bold the brazen gates of Hades,*
*Straight cast them down, and unto judgment lead*
*All forms that have endured much suffering,*
*Chiefly the shapes of Titans born of old,*
*And giants, and all whom the deluge whelmed,*
*And all that perished in the billowy seas,*
*And all that furnished banquet for the beasts*
*And creeping things and fowls, these in a mass*
*Shall (Uriel) summon to the judgment-seat;*
*And also those whom flesh-devouring fire*
*Destroyed in flame, even these shall he collect*
*And place before the judgment-seat of God.*
*And when the high-thundering Lord of Sabaoth*
*Making an end of fate shall raise the dead,*
*Sit on his heavenly throne, and firmly fix*
*The mighty pillar, then amid the clouds*
*Christ, who himself is incorruptible,*
*Shall come unto the Incorruptible*
*In glory with pure angels, and shall sit*
*At the right hand on the great judgment-seat*
*To judge the life of pious and the way*

*OF IMPIOUS MEN.*
(Sibylline Oracles 2:280-300)[43]

*O THOU HIGH-THUNDERING BLESSED HEAVENLY ONE,*
*WHO HAST SET IN THEIR PLACE THE CHERUBIM,*
*I, WHO HAVE UTTERED WHAT IS ALL TOO TRUE,*
*ENTREAT THEE, LET ME HAVE A LITTLE REST;*
*FOR MY HEART HAS GROWN WEARY FROM WITHIN.*
*BUT WHY AGAIN LEAPS MY HEART, AND MY SOUL*
*WITH A WHIP SMITTEN FROM WITHIN CONSTRAINED*
*TO UTTER FORTH ITS MESSAGE UNTO ALL?*
*BUT YET AGAIN WILL I PROCLAIM ALL THINGS*
*WHICH GOD COMMANDS ME TO PROCLAIM TO MEN.*
*O MEN, THAT IN YOUR IMAGE HAVE A FORM*
*FASHIONED OF GOD, WHY DO YE VAINLY STRAY?*
(Sibylline Oracles 3:1-4)[44]

The heavenlies have always been a source of song and inspiration, and in the tradition of such, the Sibylline Oracles prove the heralding of heavenly powers, teaching us the correct way to go as they echo and guide along the way.

## **The Apocalypse of Paul**

The Apocalypse of Paul is an early Christian document detailing the Apostle Paul's vision of heaven, spoken of in 2 Corinthians 12:1-10:

*DOUBTLESS IT IS NOT PROFITABLE FOR ME TO BOAST. SO I WILL MOVE ON TO VISIONS AND REVELATIONS OF THE LORD. I KNEW A MAN IN CHRIST OVER FOURTEEN YEARS AGO—WHETHER IN THE BODY OR OUT OF THE BODY I CANNOT TELL, GOD KNOWS— SUCH A ONE WAS CAUGHT UP TO THE THIRD HEAVEN. AND I KNEW THAT SUCH A MAN— WHETHER IN THE BODY OR OUT OF THE BODY I CANNOT TELL, GOD KNOWS— WAS CAUGHT UP INTO PARADISE AND HEARD INEXPRESSIBLE WORDS NOT PERMITTED FOR A MAN TO SAY. OF SUCH A PERSON, I WILL BOAST. YET OF MYSELF I WILL NOT BOAST, EXCEPT IN MY WEAKNESSES. FOR IF I DESIRE TO BOAST, I WILL NOT BE A FOOL, FOR I WILL BE SPEAKING THE TRUTH. BUT NOW I RESIST, LEST ANYONE SHOULD THINK OF ME ABOVE THAT WHICH HE SEES ME TO BE OR HEARS FROM ME. AND LEST I SHOULD BE EXALTED ABOVE MEASURE BY THE ABUNDANCE OF REVELATIONS, A THORN WAS GIVEN*

*ME IN THE FLESH, A MESSENGER OF SATAN, TO TORMENT ME, LEST I BE EXALTED ABOVE MEASURE. I ASKED THE LORD THREE TIMES THAT THIS THING MIGHT DEPART FROM ME. BUT HE SAID TO ME, "MY GRACE IS SUFFICIENT FOR YOU, FOR MY STRENGTH IS MADE PERFECT IN WEAKNESS." THEREFORE MOST GLADLY I WILL BOAST IN MY WEAKNESSES, THAT THE POWER OF CHRIST MAY REST UPON ME. SO I TAKE PLEASURE IN WEAKNESSES, IN REPROACHES, IN HARDSHIPS, IN PERSECUTIONS, AND IN DISTRESSES FOR CHRIST'S SAKE. FOR WHEN I AM WEAK, THEN I AM STRONG. (MEV)*

The Apocalypse of Paul also details a long vision of hell, as is common in such early apocalypses. As it is an entire depiction of heaven, portions of it reference the Apocalypse of Zechariah and make more references to angels than we can print here. It reveals a true guiding intimacy with them, seeing them in their element, each revealed through the Biblical references in Ephesians and Colossians, one by which they teach and reveal as they take the Apostle Paul through the intricacies of the vision:

*AT THE HOUR APPOINTED, THEREFORE, ALL THE ANGELS, EVERY ONE REJOICING, COME FORTH BEFORE GOD TOGETHER TO MEET HIM AND WORSHIP HIM AT THE HOUR THAT IS SET; AND LO, SUDDENLY AT THE SET TIME THERE WAS A MEETING, AND THE ANGELS CAME TO WORSHIP IN THE PRESENCE OF GOD, AND THE SPIRIT CAME FORTH TO MEET THEM, AND THERE WAS A VOICE, SAYING: THENCE COULD YE, OUR ANGELS, BRINGING BURDENS OF NEWS? THEY ANSWERED AND SAID: WE ARE COME FROM THEM THAT HAVE RENOUNCED THE WORLD FOR THY HOLY NAME'S SAKE, WANDERING AS STRANGERS AND IN THE CAVES OF THE ROCKS, AND WEEPING EVERY HOUR THAT THEY DWELL ON THE EARTH AND HUNGERING AND THIRSTING FOR THY NAME'S SAKE; WITH THEIR LOINS GIRT, HOLDING IN THEIR HANDS THE INCENSE OF THEIR HEART, AND PRAYING AND BLESSING AT EVERY HOUR, SUFFERING ANGUISH AND SUBDUING THEMSELVES, WEEPING AND LAMENTING MORE THAN ALL THAT DWELL ON THE EARTH. AND WE THAT ARE THEIR ANGELS DO MOURN WITH THEM, WHITHER THEREFORE IT PLEASETH THEE, COMMAND US TO GO AND MINISTER LEST THEY DO OTHERWISE, BUT THE POOR MORE THAN ALL THAT DWELL ON THE EARTH. (THE SENSE REQUIRED AS SHOWN BY GR. IS THAT THE ANGELS ASK THAT THESE GOOD MEN MAY CONTINUE IN GOODNESS.) AND THE VOICE OF GOD CAME UNTO THEM, SAYING: KNOW YE THAT FROM HENCEFORTH MY GRACE SHALL BE ESTABLISHED WITH YOU, AND MINE HELP WHICH IS MY DEARLY BELOVED SON, SHALL BE WITH THEM, RULING THEM AT ALL TIMES; AND HE SHALL MINISTER UNTO THEM AND NEVER FORSAKE THEM, FOR THEIR PLACE IS HIS HABITATION. WHEN, THEN, THESE ANGELS DEPARTED, LO, THERE CAME OTHER ANGELS TO WORSHIP IN THE PRESENCE OF THE MAJESTY, TO MEET THEREWITH, AND THEY WERE WEEPING. AND THE SPIRIT OF*

*God went forth to meet them, and the voice of God came, saying: Whence are ye come, our angels bearing burdens, ministers of the news of the world? They answered and said in the presence of God: We are come from them which have called upon Thy Name, and the snares of the world have made them wretched, devising many excuses at all times, and not making so much as one pure prayer out of their whole heart all the time of their life. Wherefore then must we be with men that are sinners? And the voice of God came unto them: Ye must minister unto them until they turn and repent; but if they return not unto Me, I will judge them. (8-10)*[45]

*And the angel answered and said unto me: What things soever I now show thee here, and whatsoever thou hearest, reveal them not unto any upon earth. And he led me and showed me: and I heard there words which it is not lawful for a man to utter; and again he said: Yet again follow me and I will show thee that which thou must relate and tell openly.*

*And He brought me down from the third heaven, and led me into the second heaven, and again he led me to the firmament, and from the firmament he led me unto the gates of heaven. And the beginning of the foundation thereof was upon the river that watereth all the earth. And I asked the angel and said: Lord, what is this river of water? And he said unto me: This is the Ocean. And suddenly I came out of heaven, and perceived that it is the light of the heaven that shineth upon all the earth (or, all that land). And there the earth (or, land) was seven times brighter than silver. And I said: Lord, what is this place? And he said unto me: This is the land of promise. Hast thou not yet heard that which is written: Blessed are the meek, for they shall inherit the earth? The souls therefore of the righteous when they are gone forth of the body are sent for the time into this place. And I said unto the angel: Shall then this land be made manifest after (Lat. before) a time? The angel answered and said unto me: When Christ Whom thou preachest cometh to reign, then by the decree of God the first earth shall be dissolved, and then shall this land of promise be shown and it shall be like dew or a cloud; and then shall the Lord Jesus Christ the eternal king be manifested and shall come with all His saints to dwell therein; and He shall reign over them a thousand years, and they shall eat of the good things which now I will show thee.*

*And I looked round about that land and saw a river flowing with milk and*

*HONEY. AND THERE WERE AT THE BRINK OF THE RIVER TREES PLANTED, FULL OF FRUITS: NOW EVERY TREE BARE TWELVE FRUITS IN THE YEAR, AND THEY HAD VARIOUS AND DIVERS FRUITS: AND I SAW THE FASHION (CREATION) OF THAT PLACE AND ALL THE WORK OF GOD, AND THERE I SAW PALM-TREES OF TWENTY CUBITS AND OTHERS OF TEN CUBITS: AND THAT LAND WAS SEVEN TIMES BRIGHTER THAN SILVER. AND THE TREES WERE FULL OF FRUITS FROM THE ROOT EVEN TO THE UPPER BRANCHES. (COPTIC. HAS: FROM THE ROOT OF EACH TREE UP TO ITS HEART THERE WERE TEN THOUSAND BRANCHES WITH TENS OF THOUSANDS OF CLUSTERS, [AND THERE WERE TEN THOUSAND CLUSTERS ON EACH BRANCH,] AND THERE WERE TEN THOUSAND DATES IN EACH CLUSTER. AND THUS WAS IT ALSO WITH THE VINES. EVERY VINE HAD TEN THOUSAND BRANCHES, AND EACH BRANCH HAD UPON IT TEN THOUSAND BUNCHES OF GRAPES, AND EVERY BUNCH HAD ON IT TEN THOUSAND GRAPES. AND THERE WERE OTHER TREES THERE, MYRIADS OF MYRIADS OF THEM, AND THEIR FRUIT WAS IN THE SAME PROPORTION.) AND I SAID UNTO THE ANGEL: WHEREFORE DOTH EVERY TREE BRING FORTH THOUSANDS OF FRUITS? THE ANGEL ANSWERED AND SAID UNTO ME: BECAUSE THE LORD GOD OF HIS BOUNTY GIVETH HIS GIFTS IN ABUNDANCE UNTO THE WORTHY; FOR THEY ALSO OF THEIR OWN WILL AFFLICTED THEMSELVES WHEN THEY WERE IN THE WORLD, DOING ALL THINGS FOR HIS HOLY NAME'S SAKE. (21-22)*[46]

The role of angels remains constant; praise, teachers, guides and instructors, showing the way of God by working as His ministerial servants.

## **The Shepherd of Hermas**

The Shepherd of Hermas is an early church document of great relevance that was considered to bear important prominence in the early church. It was penned somewhere around the end of the first century (around the same time frame as the book of Revelation) and was considered canonical among Christians of the first centuries. It consists of five visions, twelve mandates, and ten parables, most of which relate to the nature of church restoration, calling to repentance anyone who has come against it through sin. Many believe it is a vision of the same Hermas mentioned by Paul in Romans 16:14. It is serious by nature, but hopeful in its outlook. The "shepherd" of Hermas is, most likely, a reference to Jesus Christ, Who is the One responsible for this vision.

The Shepherd of Hermas mentions both good and evil powers and pays special attention to the angel referred to as the "angel of repentance." As a key theme in Hermas, repentance was not only possible, but it was also encouraged by a divine messenger:

*Be ye converted, ye that walk after the commandments of the devil, (the commandments which are so) difficult and bitter and wild and riotous; and fear not the devil, for there is no power in him against you.*

*For I will be with you, I, the angel of repentance, who have the mastery over him. The devil hath fear alone, but his fear hath no force. Fear him not therefore; and he will flee from you."*

*I say to him, "Sir, listen to a few words from me." "Say what thou wilt," saith he. "Man, Sir," I say, "is eager to keep the commandments of God, and there is no one that asketh not of the Lord that he may be strengthened in His commandments, and be subject to them; but the devil is hard and overmastereth them."*

*"He cannot," saith he, "overmaster the servants of God, who set their hope on Him with their whole heart. The devil can wrestle with them, but he cannot overthrow them. If then ye resist him, he will be vanquished and will flee from you disgraced. But as many," saith he, "as are utterly empty, fear the devil as if he had power.*

*When a man has filled amply sufficient jars with good wine, and among these jars a few are quite empty, he comes to the jars, and does not examine the full ones, for he knows that they are full; but he examineth the empty ones, fearing lest they have turned sour. For empty jars soon turn sour, and the taste of the wine is spoilt.*

*So also the devil cometh to all the servants of God tempting them. As many then as are complete in the faith, oppose him mightily, and he departeth from them, not having a place where he can find an entrance. So he cometh next to the empty ones, and finding a place goeth into them, and further he doeth what he willeth in them, and they become submissive slaves to him.*

*"But I, the angel of repentance, say unto you; Fear not the devil; for I was sent," saith he, "to be with you who repent with your whole heart, and to strengthen you in the faith.*

*BELIEVE, THEREFORE, ON GOD, YE WHO BY REASON OF YOUR SINS HAVE DESPAIRED OF YOUR LIFE, AND ARE ADDING TO YOUR SINS, AND WEIGHING DOWN YOUR LIFE; FOR IF YE TURN UNTO THE LORD WITH YOUR WHOLE HEART, AND WORK RIGHTEOUSNESS THE REMAINING DAYS OF YOUR LIFE, AND SERVE HIM RIGHTLY ACCORDING TO HIS WILL, HE WILL GIVE HEALING TO YOUR FORMER SINS, AND YE SHALL HAVE POWER TO MASTER THE WORKS OF THE DEVIL. BUT OF THE THREATENING OF THE DEVIL FEAR NOT AT ALL; FOR HE IS UNSTRUNG, LIKE THE SINEWS OF A DEAD MAN.*

*HEAR ME THEREFORE, AND FEAR HIM, WHO IS ABLE TO DO ALL THINGS, TO SAVE AND TO DESTROY, AND OBSERVE THESE COMMANDMENTS, AND YE SHALL LIVE UNTO GOD."*
(The Shepherd of Hermas Mandate 11 4[47]:6-[49]:3)[47]

Later, we find the following reference to holy angels in a parable:

*"I TOLD THEE JUST NOW," SAITH HE, "THAT THOU ART UNSCRUPULOUS AND IMPORTUNATE, IN ENQUIRING FOR THE INTERPRETATIONS OF THE PARABLES. BUT SINCE THOU ART SO OBSTINATE, I WILL INTERPRET TO THEE THE PARABLE OF THE ESTATE AND ALL THE ACCOMPANIMENTS THEREOF, THAT THOU MAYEST MAKE THEM KNOWN UNTO ALL. HEAR NOW," SAITH HE, "AND UNDERSTAND THEM.*

*THE ESTATE IS THIS WORLD, AND THE LORD OF THE ESTATE IS HE THAT CREATED ALL THINGS, AND SET THEM IN ORDER, AND ENDOWED THEM WITH POWER; AND THE SERVANT IS THE SON OF GOD, AND THE VINES ARE THIS PEOPLE WHOM HE HIMSELF PLANTED;*

*AND THE FENCES ARE THE [HOLY] ANGELS OF THE LORD WHO KEEP TOGETHER HIS PEOPLE; AND THE WEEDS, WHICH ARE PLUCKED UP FROM THE VINEYARD, ARE THE TRANSGRESSIONS OF THE SERVANTS OF GOD; AND THE DAINTIES WHICH HE SENT TO HIM FROM THE FEAST ARE THE COMMANDMENTS WHICH HE GAVE TO HIS PEOPLE THROUGH HIS SON; AND THE FRIENDS AND ADVISERS ARE THE HOLY ANGELS WHICH WERE FIRST CREATED; AND THE ABSENCE OF THE MASTER IS THE TIME WHICH REMAINETH OVER UNTIL HIS COMING."*
(Shepherd of Hermas Parable 5 5[58]:1-5[58]3)[48]

It is clear from Hermas' vision that the place of the angels was to remain with God and God's people, throughout eternity, acting as friends and advisers, from the beginning of time. Angels weren't just obscure figures, but active participants in the spiritual life and development of those who were a part of God's church.

## The Apocryphal Revelation of Saint John the Theologian

There isn't much known about this text, save it is a vision of the transformation of the heavens and the earth after Jesus returns. In the tradition of the work of apocalypses, it covers the experience of the antichrist, the trauma of tumult between worldly systems, and the ultimate paradise to follow. In it, angels are pictured as being those who shall lift all righteous off the earth to meet the Lord in the air:

*AND AGAIN I SAID: LORD, AND AFTER THAT WHAT WILT THOU DO? AND I HEARD A VOICE SAYING TO ME: HEAR, RIGHTEOUS JOHN. THEN WILL I SEND FORTH MINE ANGELS OVER THE FACE OF ALL THE EARTH, AND THEY SHALL LIFT OFF THE EARTH EVERYTHING HONOURABLE, AND EVERYTHING PRECIOUS, AND THE VENERABLE AND HOLY IMAGES, AND THE GLORIOUS AND PRECIOUS CROSSES, AND THE SACRED VESSELS OF THE CHURCHES, AND THE DIVINE AND SACRED BOOKS; AND ALL THE PRECIOUS AND HOLY THINGS SHALL BE LIFTED UP BY CLOUDS INTO THE AIR. AND THEN WILL I ORDER TO BE LIFTED UP THE GREAT AND VENERABLE SCEPTRE, ON WHICH I STRETCHED FORTH MY HANDS, AND ALL THE ORDERS OF MY ANGELS SHALL DO REVERENCE TO IT. AND THEN SHALL BE LIFTED UP ALL THE RACE OF MEN UPON CLOUDS, AS THE APOSTLE PAUL FORETOLD. ALONG WITH THEM WE SHALL BE SNATCHED UP IN CLOUDS TO MEET THE LORD IN THE AIR. AND THEN SHALL COME FORTH EVERY EVIL SPIRIT, BOTH IN THE EARTH AND IN THE ABYSS, WHEREVER THEY ARE ON THE FACE OF ALL THE EARTH, FROM THE RISING OF THE SUN EVEN TO THE SETTING, AND THEY SHALL BE UNITED TO HIM THAT IS SERVED BY THE DEVIL, THAT IS, ANTICHRIST, AND THEY SHALL BE LIFTED UP UPON THE CLOUDS...*[49]

We don't tend to think of angels as working, but here we see them working to the commands of God, right along through the most difficult of spiritual times and trials.

The New Testament apocryphal references presented here show a variance of themes in the work of divine powers, but all show a major unifying theme of ministerial service. They show angels actively, revealing their work in a deep way and offering their insights to the church that was trying to sort itself out, both in spiritual and mystical component. The church has never been a dry organization void of spiritual life or activity, and belief in spiritual powers reminds us of that. We might not understand it all, and we can see from these early writings that they certainly did not understand it all, either. They were people, having spiritual experiences, walking them out, managing them, and trying to sort them out was an essential part of the faith. Some of those experiences were so noteworthy, they were written down and shared, but it speaks to us so many others throughout history who have experienced the same and did so without knowing such visions and revelations were shared by others, once upon a time.

**Divine powers mentioned by name**

The Bible:

- Michael (Daniel 12:1, Jude 1:9, Revelation 12:7, and additional traditions)
- Gabriel (Daniel 9:21-17, Luke 1:19, and additional traditions)

The Deuterocanonicals:

- Raphael (Tobit 3, 4, 6, the Gospel of Bartholomew)
- Uriel (2 Esdras, 4 Esdras, Latin Esdras or Latin Ezra, The Apocalypse of Peter, the Gospel of Bartholomew)

The Pseudepigrapha, Apocrypha, and Jewish or Christian tradition:

- Camael (Jewish mythology)
- Jophiel (The Revelation of Moses, Jewish mythology)
- Xathanael (The Gospel of Bartholomew)
- Phanuel (1 Enoch)
- Raguel (1 Enoch)
- Sariel (Jewish mythology)
- Jerahmeel (2 Esdras, 4 Esdras, Latin Esdras or Latin Ezra)
- Eremiel (The Apocalypse of Zephaniah)
- Hanael (Jewish mythology)
- Kepharel (Jewish mythology)
- Ananiel (1 Enoch)
- Ramiel (1 Enoch, 2 Baruch)
- Selaphiel (2 Esdras, 4 Esdras, Latin Esdras or Latin Ezra)

- Jegudiel (2 Enoch)
- Barachiel (3 Enoch)
- Zadkiel (Jewish mythology)
- Samael (The Ascension of Moses)
- Ananiel (1 Enoch)
- Metatron (1 Enoch)
- Phamael (3 Baruch)
- Yahoel (The Apocalypse of Abraham)
- Chairoum (The Gospel of Bartholomew)
- Oertha (The Gospel of Bartholomew)
- Kerkoutha (The Gospel of Bartholomew)
- Naoutha (The Gospel of Bartholomew)
- Gabuthelon (2 Esdras)
- Aker (2 Esdras)
- Arphugitonos (2 Esdras)
- Beburos (2 Esdras)
- Zebyleon (2 Esdras)

Jewish Kabbalah:

- Metatron
- Raziel
- Tzaphkiel
- Tzadkiel
- Khamael
- Raphael
- Haniel
- Michael
- Gabriel
- Sandalphon

## Chapter 1 Assignments

- Create a diagram of the way the ancients viewed the universe.
- Write an essay (5-8 sentences) on the powers and work of angels between earth and heaven.

- Construct a short answer-style response (1-4 sentences) in which non-canonical works have helped shape our concepts about heaven and the afterlife.
- Take two of the angels represented in this chapter and create an infographic on each of them, explaining who they are, what they do, and where they are found.

## - CHAPTER TWO -
## THE NATURE AND WORK OF DEMONIC POWERS

*THE DEVIL WHO RULES THIS WORLD [GOD OF THIS AGE] HAS BLINDED THE MINDS OF THOSE WHO DO NOT BELIEVE [UNBELIEVERS]. [...SO THAT] THEY CANNOT SEE THE LIGHT OF THE GOOD NEWS— THE GOOD NEWS ABOUT [THAT REVEALS] THE GLORY OF CHRIST, WHO IS EXACTLY LIKE [THE IMAGE OF] GOD.*
(2 CORINTHIANS 4:4)

Now that we have a better understanding of how divine powers operate, we can better understand the demonic realm and the workings of demonic powers. Everything demonic mirrors that of everything divine and realizing this gives fresh insight into how the demonic works. God's power and realm was first, and that means Satan's attempts to mimic the realm of the spiritual falls in the category of an evil inversion or imitation of the true power and Kingdom that is essential and eternal.

The last chapter proved the true order and splendor that exists within the heavenly realms. Here on earth, our focus tends to be on the order we can see with our own eyes. We are fixated on the role of leadership in the church, figuring out how God recognizes authority, and how it is proper for us to do the same. It's a challenge if we don't recognize the powers God has put into place within His divine wisdom, especially those who follow His commands and work as His ministerial servants in the universe.

The truth is that everything under heaven is under the subjection of

God, and even in cases of evil, all things are used to bring about realization of the consequences of sin and willful human nature. This includes the demonic realm, which we often think of as the evil counterpart of God. In contrast with the various pagan mythologies present in the ancient world, Satan is not as powerful as God, just in an evil way. Satan is subordinate to God; always has been and always will be, because he started out in heaven, as an angel, just like the ones explored in the previous chapter.

To understand healing, spiritual warfare, and deliverance, we must understand the rank and order of demonic powers, how they manifest, and what they do. Just as we make the effort to understand God's order, we should also understand demonic order, because demonic activity is not, contrary to belief, haphazard. The better we understand the operation, the better we will recognize demonic activity.

## **Satan**

The word "Satan" is from the Hebrew title (denoting a being, not a personal name) *Ha-Satan*, which literally means "the opposer," "the accuser," or "the adversary." The term denoting a personal being occurs thirteen times in the Old Testament, found in Job and in Zechariah. Outside of these instances, the word Satan is found in the Old Testament not as a title, but to indicate something has the potential to be accusatory, adversarial, or contradictory.

Job, as one of the oldest existing books in the Bible (perhaps the oldest ever recorded), shows the work of a personal being whose sights served no other purpose but to antagonize Job and prove he would not withstand the pressure. Satan's ultimate goal was to pull Job away from God, proving if he was allowed to bring enough calamity into his life, Job would leave God.

*ONE DAY THE ANGELS [SONS OF GOD] CAME TO SHOW THEMSELVES [STAND] BEFORE THE LORD, AND SATAN [THE SATAN; MEANS "THE ACCUSER" OR "THE ADVERSARY"; EITHER THE DEVIL OR A MEMBER OF GOD'S HEAVENLY COURT] WAS WITH THEM. THE LORD SAID TO SATAN, "WHERE HAVE YOU COME FROM?"*

*SATAN [1:6] ANSWERED THE LORD, "I HAVE BEEN WANDERING AROUND [ROAMING] THE EARTH, ·GOING BACK AND FORTH IN [PATROLLING] IT."*

*Then the Lord said to Satan, "Have you noticed [considered; set your heart on] my servant Job? No one else on earth is like him. He is an honest and innocent man, honoring God and staying away from evil [1:1]."*

*But Satan [1:6] answered the Lord, "Job honors God for a good reason [Does Job honor/fear/respect God for no good reason?]. You have [Don't you...?] put a wall [hedge; to protect from danger] around him, his family, and everything he owns. You have blessed the things he has done [all the works of his hands]. His flocks and herds are so large they almost cover [burst forth on] the land. But reach out [stretch forth] your hand and destroy [afflict] everything he has, and [see if] he will curse you to your face."*

*The Lord said to Satan [1:6], "All right, then. Everything Job has is in your power [hand], but you must not touch Job himself [but don't send your hand against him]." Then Satan [1:6] left the Lord's presence.* (Job 1:6-12)

In the end, Job prevailed. He came against his adversary and proved there was more to him than just easy times and rewards. As a long wisdom discourse (a style of literature common to the ancient Middle East), the book of Job doesn't seek to answer the "why' of matters. His discourses with God don't tell us why bad things happen to good people, nor does it tell us why suffering exists. It leaves us not with a sense that questions are bad, but that our preconceived answers are often wrong. Still, the question remained: who was Satan, and why did he pick on Job?

Before *Lucifer* was a television show and long before it was the name of the cat in Disney's *Cinderella*, the term "Lucifer" literally meant "morning star," "shining one," or "daystar." The figure of Satan, before his fall as the enemy of God, was as the chief angel of worship in heaven, and 2 Enoch reports him as an archangel before the fall.

*And one from out the order of angels, having turned away with the order that was under him, conceived an impossible thought, to place his throne higher than the clouds above the earth, that he might become equal in rank to My power.*

*And I threw him out from the height with his angels, and he was flying in the air continuously above the bottomless.* (2 Enoch 29:3-4)[1]

Much of what we believe about the fall of Lucifer (and his transformation into Satan) comes from Isaiah 14:9-17:

*The place of the dead [or The grave; Sheol] is excited [stirred up]*
  *to meet you when you come.*
*It wakes the spirits of the dead [ghosts],*
  *the leaders [rams] of the world.*
*It makes kings of all nations*
  *stand up from their thrones to greet you [rise up from their thrones].*
*All these leaders will make fun of you [respond]*
  *and will say,*
*"Now you are weak, as we are.*
  *Now you are just like us."*
*Your pride [or pomp; splendor] has been sent down to the place of the dead [or the grave; Sheol].*
  *The music from your harps goes with it.*
*Flies [or Maggots] are spread out like your bed beneath you,*
  *and worms cover your body like a blanket.*
*How you have fallen from heaven,*
  *morning star [or day star; or shining one; still addressing the king of Babylon, though sometimes applied to Satan],*
  *even though you were as bright as the rising sun [son of the dawn]!*
*In the past all the nations on earth bowed down before you [or were laid low by you],*
  *but now you have been cut down.*
*You told yourself,*
  *"I will go up to heaven [or ascend to the sky].*
*I will put my throne*
  *above God's stars.*
*I will sit [or rule] on the mountain of the gods [assembly],*
  *on the slopes of the sacred mountain [or the north; or Mount Zaphon; known as the mountain of Baal].*
*I will go up [ascend] above the ·tops [or high places] of the clouds.*
  *I will be like God Most High."*
*But you were brought down to the grave [or the place of the dead; Sheol],*
  *to the deep places where the dead are [of the pit].*

*Those who see you stare at you.*

*They think about [ponder] what has happened to you*
*and say, "Is this the same man who caused great fear on [shook the] earth,*
  *who shook [made to tremble] the kingdoms,*
*who turned the world into a desert,*
  *who destroyed [overthrew] its cities,*
*who captured people in war*
  *and would not let them go home?"*

Study of this passage reveals a bigger prophecy about the King of Babylon, but there are questions as to its full fit within that. The king of Babylon led on earth, not in heaven, and did not have the ability to ascend from the heights and then be brought so low. Such a position would have been reserved for one with access to heaven, such as an angel. What most likely happened is the Prophet Isaiah paralleled the fall of the King of Babylon with that of the fall of Lucifer, drawing on the pride of Lucifer and seeing that same analogy present in the King of Babylon. Babylon was considered a primary enemy of Israel and of the things related to God, so it makes sense the king of Babylon would compare with Satan: he, too, was an enemy. This tendency to associate an ancient ruler with Satan or a demon happens in one other place in the Bible, in reference to the ruler of Tyre in Ezekiel 28:1-19:

*Lucifer, Cornelis Galle I (1576-1650)*

*The Lord spoke His word [word of the Lord came] to me, saying: "Human [Son of man; 2:1], say to the ruler of Tyre: 'This is what the Lord God says:*

*Because you are [your heart is] proud,*
  *you say, "I am a god.*
*I sit on the throne [seat] of a god*
  *in the middle [heart] of the seas."*
*You think you are as wise as a god,*
  *but you are a human [mortal; man], not a god.*

*[LOOK; BEHOLD] YOU THINK YOU ARE [ARE] WISER THAN DANIEL [14:14].
YOU THINK YOU CAN FIND OUT ALL SECRETS [NO SECRET IS HIDDEN FROM YOU].*

*THROUGH YOUR WISDOM AND UNDERSTANDING
   YOU HAVE MADE YOURSELF RICH.
YOU HAVE GAINED [GATHERED] GOLD AND SILVER
   AND HAVE SAVED IT IN [IN] YOUR STOREROOMS [TREASURIES].*

*THROUGH YOUR GREAT SKILL IN TRADING,
   YOU HAVE MADE YOUR RICHES GROW.
YOU ARE TOO [YOUR HEART IS] PROUD
   BECAUSE OF YOUR RICHES.*

*"'SO THIS IS WHAT THE LORD GOD SAYS:*

*[BECAUSE] YOU THINK YOU ARE WISE
LIKE A GOD,*

*BUT [THEREFORE, LOOK/BEHOLD] I WILL BRING FOREIGN PEOPLE AGAINST YOU,
   THE CRUELEST [MOST RUTHLESS] NATIONS.
THEY WILL DRAW THEIR SWORDS
   AND DESTROY ALL THAT YOUR WISDOM HAS BUILT [AGAINST YOUR BEAUTY AND WISDOM],
AND THEY WILL DISHONOR [DEFILE] YOUR GREATNESS [SPLENDOR].*

*THEY WILL KILL YOU [BRING YOU DOWN TO THE PIT];
   YOU WILL DIE A TERRIBLE [VIOLENT] DEATH
LIKE THOSE WHO ARE KILLED AT SEA [OR IN THE HEART OF THE SEA].*

*WHILE THEY ARE KILLING YOU [IN THE PRESENCE OF THOSE KILLING YOU],
   YOU WILL NOT [WILL YOU...?] BE ABLE TO SAY ANYMORE, "I AM A GOD."
YOU WILL BE ONLY A HUMAN, NOT A GOD,
   WHEN YOUR MURDERERS KILL YOU [IN THE HANDS OF THOSE WHO KILL YOU].*

*YOU WILL DIE LIKE AN UNCLEAN PERSON [THE DEATH OF THE UNCIRCUMCISED];
FOREIGNERS WILL KILL YOU [...IN THE HANDS OF STRANGERS/FOREIGNERS].
I HAVE SPOKEN, SAYS THE LORD GOD.'"*

*The Lord spoke His word [word of the Lord came] to me, saying: "Human [Son of man; 2:1], sing a funeral song [lament; dirge] for the king of Tyre. Say to him: 'This is what the Lord God says:*

*You were an example [the seal/signet] of what was perfect,*
*full of wisdom and perfect in beauty.*

*You had a wonderful life,*
*   as if you were in Eden [were in Eden], the garden of God [like Adam; Gen. 1—2].*
*Every valuable gem was on [covered] you:*
*   ruby [or carnelian], topaz [or chysolite], and emerald [or diamond],*
*   yellow quartz [or chrysolite], onyx, and jasper,*
*   sapphire [or lapis lazuli], turquoise, and chrysolite [or beryl; or emerald].*
*Your jewelry [settings and mounts] was made of gold.*
*   It was prepared on the day you were created.*

*I appointed a living creature [cherub] to guard you.*
*   I put you on the holy mountain of God.*
*You walked among the gems that shined like fire [fiery stones].*

*Your life was right and good [You were blameless in your ways]*
*   from the day you were created,*
*until evil [wickedness; unrighteousness] was found in you.*

*Because you traded with countries far away [or in abundance],*
*   you learned to be cruel [were filled with violence], and you sinned.*
*So I threw you down [banished you] in disgrace [or defilement] from the mountain of God.*
*   And the living creature [cherub] who guarded you*
*forced you out [expelled you] from among the gems that shined like fire [fiery stones].*
*You became too [Your heart was] proud*
*   because of your beauty.*
*You ruined [corrupted] your wisdom*
*   because of your greatness [splendor].*
*I threw you down to the ground.*
*   Your example taught a lesson to [or I made a spectacle of you before]*

*OTHER KINGS.*

*YOU DISHONORED [DESECRATED; PROFANED; RITUALLY] YOUR PLACES OF WORSHIP [SANCTUARIES]*
  *THROUGH YOUR MANY SINS AND DISHONEST TRADE.*
*SO I SET ON FIRE THE PLACE WHERE YOU LIVED [SENT FIRE OUT FROM YOUR MIDST],*
  *AND THE FIRE BURNED YOU UP [CONSUMED YOU].*
*I TURNED YOU INTO ASHES ON THE GROUND*
  *FOR ALL THOSE WATCHING TO SEE [BEFORE THE EYES OF ALL WHO SAW YOU].*

*ALL THE NATIONS WHO KNEW YOU*
  *ARE SHOCKED [APPALLED; AGHAST] ABOUT YOU.*
*YOUR PUNISHMENT WAS SO TERRIBLE,*
  *AND YOU ARE GONE FOREVER.'"*

Lucifer desired to be God Himself, worthy of the worship and adoration reserved only for God. What specifically brought on this desire is unknown, although the Pseudepigraphic Life of Adam and Eve has Satan refusing to bow down during the creation of humanity. Other theories have existed as related to free will and just a desire to be worshiped, and there is also the obvious question of pride, but just where the pride originated is of speculation. The result was a revolt, a battle in the heavenlies, where approximately one-third of the angels of heaven also revolted with Lucifer. They were thrown out of heaven because of the battle, with the Archangel Michael taking the lead.

*THEN THERE WAS A WAR IN HEAVEN. MICHAEL [AN ARCHANGEL AND PROTECTOR OF GOD'S PEOPLE; DAN. 10:13, 21; 12:1; JUDE 9] AND HIS ANGELS FOUGHT AGAINST THE DRAGON, AND THE DRAGON AND HIS ANGELS FOUGHT BACK. BUT THE DRAGON WAS NOT STRONG ENOUGH, AND HE AND HIS ANGELS LOST THEIR PLACE IN HEAVEN. THE GIANT [GREAT] DRAGON WAS THROWN DOWN [CAST; HURLED] OUT OF HEAVEN. (HE IS THAT OLD SNAKE [ANCIENT SERPENT] CALLED THE DEVIL OR SATAN [GEN. 3:1, 15], WHO TRICKS [DECEIVES; LEADS ASTRAY] THE WHOLE WORLD.) THE DRAGON WITH HIS ANGELS WAS THROWN DOWN [CAST; HURLED] TO THE EARTH.*

*THEN I HEARD A LOUD VOICE IN HEAVEN SAYING:*

*"THE SALVATION AND THE POWER AND THE KINGDOM OF OUR GOD*
  *AND THE AUTHORITY [POWER] OF HIS CHRIST [MESSIAH; ANOINTED ONE] HAVE NOW COME [DAN. 7:14].*

*[FOR] THE ACCUSER [THE NAME SATAN MEANS "ACCUSER" IN HEBREW; JOB 1:6-12; 2:1-6; ZECH. 3:1-2] OF OUR BROTHERS AND SISTERS,*

  *WHO ACCUSED THEM DAY AND NIGHT BEFORE OUR GOD,*
  *HAS BEEN THROWN [CAST; HURLED] DOWN.*
*AND OUR BROTHERS AND SISTERS DEFEATED [CONQUERED] HIM*
  *BY THE BLOOD OF THE LAMB'S DEATH [LAMB; BY MEANS OF CHRIST'S SACRIFICIAL DEATH]*
  *AND BY THE MESSAGE THEY PREACHED [WORD OF THEIR WITNESS/TESTIMONY].*
*[AND] THEY DID NOT LOVE THEIR LIVES SO MUCH*
  *THAT THEY WERE AFRAID OF [AVOIDED] DEATH.*
*SO REJOICE, YOU HEAVENS*
  *AND ALL WHO LIVE THERE!*
*BUT IT WILL BE TERRIBLE FOR [WOE TO] THE EARTH AND THE SEA,*
  *BECAUSE THE DEVIL HAS COME DOWN TO YOU!*
*HE IS FILLED WITH ANGER [WRATH],*
  *BECAUSE HE KNOWS HE DOES NOT HAVE MUCH TIME [HAS LITTLE TIME]."*
(Revelation 12:7-12)

Scholars do not agree on what time frame this passage in Revelation covers, but it is clear there is a parallel between the fall of Satan and his dismissal from heaven and the ultimate victory of the believers. The story is retold to give hope and comfort, and to remind believers that they have the ultimate victory. Satan may torment for a time, but he is ultimately fallen, and that fall is more relevant than the difficulties we experience with him. When exactly Satan fell is unknown, but it must have been before the creation of man, as Satan was present in the serpent, operating against Adam and Eve, in the Garden of Eden:

*NOW THE SNAKE [SERPENT] WAS THE MOST CLEVER [SHREWD; CUNNING; CRAFTY] OF ALL THE WILD ANIMALS THE LORD GOD HAD MADE. ONE DAY THE SNAKE SAID TO THE WOMAN, "DID GOD REALLY SAY THAT YOU MUST NOT EAT FRUIT FROM ANY TREE IN THE GARDEN?"*

*THE WOMAN ANSWERED THE SNAKE [3:1], "WE MAY EAT FRUIT FROM THE TREES IN THE GARDEN. BUT GOD TOLD US, 'YOU MUST NOT EAT FRUIT FROM THE TREE THAT IS IN THE MIDDLE OF THE GARDEN [THE TREE OF THE KNOWLEDGE OF GOOD AND EVIL]. YOU MUST NOT EVEN TOUCH IT [EVE WAS ADDING TO THE DIVINE COMMAND], OR YOU WILL DIE.'"*

*BUT THE SNAKE [3:1] SAID TO THE WOMAN, "YOU WILL [MOST CERTAINLY] NOT DIE. [FOR] GOD KNOWS THAT IF YOU EAT THE FRUIT FROM THAT TREE [FROM IT], [YOUR EYES WILL BE OPENED AND] YOU WILL LEARN ABOUT [EXPERIENCE; KNOW ABOUT] GOOD AND EVIL AND YOU WILL BE LIKE GOD!"*

*THE WOMAN SAW THAT THE TREE WAS BEAUTIFUL [PLEASING TO THE EYES], THAT ITS FRUIT WAS GOOD TO EAT [FOR FOOD], AND THAT IT WOULD MAKE HER WISE. SO SHE TOOK SOME OF ITS FRUIT AND ATE IT. SHE ALSO GAVE SOME OF THE FRUIT TO HER HUSBAND WHO WAS WITH HER [APPARENTLY HE WAS PRESENT BUT SILENT WHILE THE WOMAN SPOKE TO THE SNAKE], AND HE ATE IT.* (Genesis 3:1-6)

2 Enoch 31:4-5 reaffirms the presence of Satan in the Garden of Eden, as the one who beguiled Eve:

*THE DEVIL IS THE EVIL SPIRIT OF THE LOWER PLACES, AS A FUGITIVE HE MADE SOTONA FROM THE HEAVENS AS HIS NAME WAS SATANAIL (SATAN), THUS HE BECAME DIFFERENT FROM THE ANGELS, (BUT HIS NATURE) DID NOT CHANGE (HIS) INTELLIGENCE AS FAR AS (HIS) UNDERSTANDING OF RIGHTEOUS AND SINFUL (THINGS).*

*AND HE UNDERSTOOD HIS CONDEMNATION AND THE SIN WHICH HE HAD SINNED BEFORE, THEREFORE HE CONCEIVED THOUGHT AGAINST ADAM, IN SUCH FORM HE ENTERED AND SEDUCED EVA (EVE), BUT DID NOT TOUCH ADAM.* [2]

We can see from all these passages that the identity of an accuser, who we understand to be a fallen angel, is, first and foremost, the enemy of God. As a secondary point, he has become the enemy of those who follow God. He desires to be in the place of God; thus he wants the world to follow him so he can gain the ultimate control. Satan proves the ultimate lesson in futility. No matter how many follow him, he still won't be, nor have the status of God. Irrational as it may be, Satan still makes his attempts, century after century, to gain a victory he already lost through Jesus Christ's atonement.

This, however, doesn't stop him. It also doesn't stop some from finding his ways desirable. Those who follow him and his ways become, in turn, adversaries themselves, causing trouble and issues. Those angels who followed him, in turn, became his bidders – and we more commonly refer to them as demons, or dark angels.

**The work of Satan**

If Jesus is our Advocate with the Father (2 John 2:1), Satan is our adversary against everything God instructs or desires us to do. Over the past twenty-five or so years, there is a lot of talk about the work of Satan in an abstract sense: through thoughts or ideas, negativity or negative concepts, and very little is spoken of in terms of actual action or ways that Satan operates within individuals and their lives to get them away from God. This has led us to treat Satan as if he is an abstract character, something to contend with in a Hollywood-esque style fashion. We think if we use earthly methods to try and outsmart or outwit our enemy, it will work, just like it appears to work in the movies. This has led to ridiculous and fanciful deliverance ministries that resemble things done in the movies, often to disastrous and misleading results.

Our highly psychological world has a way of wanting to crawl inside the minds of every evildoer or sinful perpetrator in the hopes we will be able to understand what happened, how it happened, and what turned someone to behave in this manner. The work of Satan and his opposition to God proves that some things just happen without proper explanation. Satan's fall did not have an explanation beyond the realities that evil does exist, and it rears itself in ways we may not consider comfortable in us all; more so in some than in others.

If we carefully examine the text we looked at earlier with Adam and Eve, we can understand better the way Satan operates in our lives and his overall agenda. It is Satan's purpose to deceive, to use lies and dishonest means to make us believe things about God that are not true as he distorts God's Words to us. He is an influence; a subtle dialogue we have that we don't even recognize causes us to go against what we know God has commissioned and follow a different course. If we are as God has created us, Satan is against us.

*THIS DOES NOT SURPRISE US [AND NO WONDER, SINCE...]. EVEN SATAN CHANGES HIMSELF TO LOOK LIKE [DISGUISES HIMSELF AS; MASQUERADES AS] AN ANGEL [MESSENGER] OF LIGHT [TRYING TO FOOL PEOPLE INTO THINKING HE IS FROM GOD,*

*WHO IS PURE LIGHT]*. (2 Corinthians 11:14)

Many of us picture Satan as a red-bodied and horned devil, running around with a tail and pitchfork. We think we can easily identify Satan with grotesque or funny appearance, but the truth couldn't be further from this imagery. The inspiration behind the Apostle Paul's words are important to reveal the deceptive nature of Satan. They echo Eve's experience with Satan in the garden. There are going to be times when we have a Job experience, and everything right in front of us seems to disappear, such obviously being a case of Satan's work. Much of the time, however, Satan's work is a little more insidious than that. Satan appears as an angel of light, as a play on his experience and work as the angel Lucifer. He appears bright; good; wonderful; amazing; beyond what we could imagine. He comes as everything that seems desiring and important to us, as our innermost hopes and dreams. It is a deception; something that seems like what we want or need but has a high price behind it.

*YES, IN THE PAST YOU LIVED [WALKED] THE WAY THE WORLD LIVES [ACCORDING TO THE COURSE/WAYS/AGE OF THIS WORLD], FOLLOWING THE RULER [SATAN] OF THE EVIL POWERS THAT ARE ABOVE THE EARTH [DOMINION/AUTHORITY OF THE AIR; PROBABLY DEMONIC FORCES]. THAT SAME SPIRIT IS NOW WORKING IN THOSE WHO REFUSE TO OBEY GOD [THE CHILDREN/SONS OF DISOBEDIENCE]*. (Ephesians 2:2)

When the Bible speaks of Satan as the prince and power of the air, it is not giving Satan more power than God or speaking that the entire world is devoid of God or His presence. The earth is the Lord's, and the fullness thereof reflects Him, as the Scriptures say (Psalm 24:1). God is still God; and He is still supreme, even over Satan. The passage refers to the means for Satan's work, operating his influence and deception over this current world, working through the "sons of disobedience" (Ephesians 2:2). His power, however, is limited to what he has been allowed, and it is temporary, and shall cease in time (Romans 16:20).

The work of Satan is not so difficult to define that we need to go over a case-by-case point of its ins and outs. Let's also not get so deep into this that we think everything that happens to us in this life that is bad or difficult is as the result of Satan. We will talk more about this later in this book, but we are human; we sin of our own failing, we do things wrong, and sometimes we battle with people and concepts rather than always running to the extreme that Satan is the reason for everything that happens to us. This doesn't mean Satan does not exist, nor does it mean that we should be ignorant of his devices. It means we should keep a balanced perspective and know and recognize Satanic work by discernment. The experience of Job gives us profound insight into the ways Satan attacks individuals. Satan can operate via torment. People can be attacked in anything unique to this physical realm: our fleshly bodies (physical illness, injury, or attack), our mental states (mental calamities, anguish, mental stress, or insanity), our spiritual well-being (assurance of faith or salvation, belief systems, knowledge of truth) and remove people or things from our lives that we have learned to rely on. If there is something we have attachment to or investment in, Satan can touch it, twist it around, and bring us to a place of deceit where we do not believe in God and His love for us as we should.

## Hell

In teaching about Satan, we often hear of hell as his abode, but then we also hear about Satan as if he has an omnipresence everywhere in the entire world, always. This has led to extensive confusion about the locale of hell, as well as the locale of Satan, as well as just what hell is and what hell does.

Fiery images of a burning inferno with Satan at the helm permeate our consciousness when we think on and consider the work of hell. Many are unaware that our popular imagery of hell comes from pagan concepts that infiltrated culture and belief systems for thousands of years. We like the idea that good equals reward and bad equals punishment, and hell has become the ultimate imagery for such a concept. The concept of torture and torment for everything that people have done wrong appeals to us, especially when we stop and think about the wrong done to us. The imagery of hell with fire is not without its roots, but somewhere in here, the message about hell and its operation has been distorted, causing us to think that hell is all about fire and brimstone, with no redeeming purpose.

The Bible teaches us that Satan is not restricted to hell, nor does he do the most of his work there. The Bible teaches us that Satan prowls, seeking those whom he may devour, going to and fro in the earth. As the prince and power of the air, his true influence is right here, on earth. If Satan has power to influence and is not everywhere at every time, how does he know when to act, and how to act? The answer is simpler than you might think: he, and his demons, are on the prowl.

*The Lord said to Satan, "Where have you come from?" Satan [1:6] answered the Lord, "I have been wandering around [roaming] the earth, going back and forth in [patrolling] it."* (Job 1:7)

*Control [Discipline] yourselves and be careful [alert]! The devil, your enemy, goes around [prowls] like a roaring lion looking for someone to eat [devour].* (1 Peter 5:8)

So that leaves the question, where is hell, and what is it if Satan isn't there all the time? To understand teaching on hell, we need to go back to the original definitions and understandings as pertain to the dead and what happens after death. As with most spiritual realities, evolution of hell and the abode of the dead has its influence at different points in history, and it is not as simple to explain, nor describe, as many do when they study the Bible. Once again, it is an evident understanding that is reflected in Scripture but not always clarified there.

Whereas "paradise" typically refers to heaven or to the transformed heavens and earth at the end of time (Luke 23:43, 2 Corinthians 12:3-4, Revelation 2:7), descriptions of hell, the abode of the dead, and the afterlife, aren't always as clearly identified. Beliefs about the afterlife have changed over time, through different influences, and the identities as to where people go after death has changed.

The term "hell" was originally a reference to the place of the dead, or the abode of the dead, as was understood in an old English terminology. In ancient Hebrew religious understanding, they did not embrace a belief as pertains to the afterlife. They believed once someone was dead, they were dead, and the ultimate punishment as relates to sin was death. Through offspring, they were able to achieve immortality, thus the belief in the necessity and importance of procreation. Such would continue the family line, and some way, somehow, would help a person receive immortality through ancestral legacy.

The promise of eternal life is something that has always rested in the heart of God, but it wasn't something people always understood properly or with much insight. The concept of being able to live on eternally, without death, defies the natural mind. The ancient Hebrew word for the grave was *Sheol*, which literally meant "place of the dead." In the place of the dead, those souls were there, awaiting resurrection, as a sort of temporary holding place. No one knew how long they would be there or how it would all work out, but the understanding of the grave was that such placement therein would not be permanent.

Because God was associated with life and the grave with death, the grave was the one place where it was believed God did not dwell. Being dead indicated a separation between an individual and God, and while the ancients might have questioned the permanence of such a state at different points in time, the separation from life in death was associated with separation from God.

It's not as simple as to say everyone felt this way about the grave, or to say there was no question as to where the righteous or unrighteous went when they died. Division of *Sheol* began early in time, as is seen in 1 Enoch 22:1-14, indicating that even though there was an original belief that the fate of all was the same, distinctions between the righteous and unrighteous were made over time:

AND THENCE I WENT TO ANOTHER PLACE, AND HE SHOWED ME IN THE WEST [ANOTHER] GREAT AND HIGH MOUNTAIN [AND] OF HARD ROCK.

AND THERE WAS IN IT FOUR HOLLOW PLACES, DEEP AND WIDE AND VERY SMOOTH. HOW SMOOTH ARE THE HOLLOW PLACES AND DEEP AND DARK TO LOOK AT.

THEN RAPHAEL ANSWERED, ONE OF THE HOLY ANGELS WHO WAS WITH ME, AND SAID UNTO ME: 'THESE HOLLOW PLACES HAVE BEEN CREATED FOR THIS VERY PURPOSE, THAT THE SPIRITS OF THE SOULS OF THE DEAD SHOULD ASSEMBLE THEREIN, YEA THAT ALL THE SOULS OF THE CHILDREN OF MEN SHOULD ASSEMBLE HERE. AND THESE PLACES HAVE BEEN MADE TO RECEIVE THEM TILL THE DAY OF THEIR JUDGEMENT AND TILL THEIR APPOINTED PERIOD [TILL THE PERIOD APPOINTED], TILL THE GREAT JUDGEMENT (COMES) UPON THEM.'

I SAW THE SPIRITS OF THE CHILDREN OF MEN WHO WERE DEAD, AND THEIR VOICE WENT FORTH TO HEAVEN AND MADE SUIT. THEN I ASKED RAPHAEL THE ANGEL WHO WAS WITH ME, AND I SAID UNTO HIM: 'THIS SPIRIT--WHOSE IS IT WHOSE VOICE GOETH FORTH AND MAKETH SUIT?'

AND HE ANSWERED ME SAYING: 'THIS IS THE SPIRIT WHICH WENT FORTH FROM ABEL, WHOM HIS BROTHER CAIN SLEW, AND HE MAKES HIS SUIT AGAINST HIM TILL HIS SEED IS DESTROYED FROM THE FACE OF THE EARTH, AND HIS SEED IS ANNIHILATED FROM AMONGST THE SEED OF MEN.'

*Then I asked regarding it, and regarding all the hollow places: 'Why as one separated from the other?'*

*And he answered me and said unto me: 'These three have been made that the spirits of the dead might be separated. And such a division has been made <for> the spirits of the righteous, in which there as the bright spring of water. And such has been made for sinners when they die and are buried in the earth and judgement has not been executed on them in their lifetime. Here their spirits shall be set apart in this great pain till the great day of judgement and punishment and torment of those who curse for ever, and retribution for their spirits. There He shall bind them for ever. And such a division has been made for the spirits of those who make their suit, who make disclosures concerning their destruction, when they were slain in the days of the sinners. Such has been made for the spirits of men who were not righteous but sinners, who were complete in transgression, and of the transgressors. They shall be companions: but their spirits shall not be slain in the day of judgement nor shall they be raised from thence. Then I blessed the Lord of glory and said: 'Blessed be my Lord, the Lord of righteousness, who ruleth for ever.*[3]

By the time of the New Testament, there were many varied beliefs about the afterlife, the resurrection of the body, heaven, the righteous dead, and where people went when they died. The Sadducees were a Jewish sect that rejected any notion of the resurrection of the dead, at any point in time. They also rejected any notion of the afterlife or of otherworldly life (including divine powers or demonic spirits), and believed there was no reward, at any point in time, for righteousness outside of this life. The Pharisees believed in the resurrection of the dead, an afterlife, and the existence of divine powers and demonic spirits. Both the Sadducees and Pharisees considered themselves to be right in their approach of spiritual matters. Many believers in the first century were influenced by any number of different belief systems, including ones that were pagan or philosophical in nature. All these differing beliefs about the afterlife found their way into the traditions present in those times, and people believed many different and frequently complicated things about death, life, and the afterlife.

In the Greek Septuagint and referenced in the New Testament, *Sheol* is translated as *Hades*. The word, once again, refers to the abode of the dead. It was not as simple to assume, however, that the abode of the dead was considered one thing at this time that was the same for everyone. As people questioned the role of righteousness, unrighteousness, and separateness, more questions about where everyone went and what happened to them after death shaped the existing beliefs about the grave and death.

Over time, the righteous dead went to a place known as Abraham's Bosom, which is only mentioned in the New Testament one time as it was a later evolution of belief in life after death in Judaism:

*Jesus said, "There was a rich man who always dressed in the finest clothes [purple and fine linen] and lived in luxury [or feasted sumptuously] every day. And a very poor man named Lazarus, whose body was covered with sores, was laid at the rich man's gate. He wanted [longed] to eat only the small pieces of food that fell [what fell] from the rich man's table. And [Even] the dogs would come and lick his sores [dogs were viewed as despicable scavengers, not household pets]. Later [Now it happened that], Lazarus died, and the angels carried him to the arms of Abraham [Abraham's side/bosom; the imagery of a banquet, with Abraham as host and Lazarus as honored guest]. The rich man died, too, and was buried. In the place of the dead [Hades], he was in much pain [torment]. Looking up [Lifting up his eyes,], the rich man saw Abraham far away with Lazarus at his side [in his bosom]. He called, 'Father Abraham, have mercy on me! Send Lazarus to dip his finger in water and cool my tongue, because I am suffering [in agony] in this fire [Is. 66:24]!' But Abraham said, 'Child, remember when you were alive you had the good things in life, but bad things happened to Lazarus. Now he is comforted here, and you are suffering [in agony]. Besides [all this], there is a big pit [great gulf/chasm set in place] between you and us, so no one can cross over to you, and no one can leave there and come here [to us].' The rich man said, 'Father, then please [I ask/beg you to] send Lazarus to my father's house. [For] I have five brothers, and Lazarus could warn them so that they will not come to this place of pain [torment].' But Abraham said, 'They have the law of Moses and the writings of the prophets [Moses and the prophets]; let them learn from [listen to] them.' The rich man said, 'No, father Abraham! [But] If someone goes to them from the dead, they would believe and change their hearts and lives [repent].' But Abraham said to him, 'If they will not listen to Moses and the prophets, they will not listen to [be persuaded/convinced by] someone who comes back from the dead.'"* (Luke 16:19-31)

Abraham's Bosom was considered a "holding tank" of heaven, if you will, where the righteous dead awaited the coming Messiah to allow the way for eternity in paradise. It was a place of comfort, a section of *Sheol* that echoed the ability to remain alive and present, even after death. It appears to have emerged after the Second Temple period, and reference of which is found in the Apocalypse of Zephaniah 11:1-6:

*And I also saw multitudes. He brought them forth. As they looked at all of the torments they called out, praying before the Lord Almighty, saying, "We pray unto Thee on account of those who are in all these torments so that Thou might have mercy on all of them." And when I saw them, I said to the angel who spoke with me, "<Who are these?>" He said, "These who beseech the Lord are Abraham and Isaac and Jacob. Then at a certain hour daily they come forth with the great angel. He soundeth a trumpet up unto heaven and another soundeth upon the earth. All the righteous hear the sound. They come running, praying to the Lord Almighty daily on behalf of these who are in all these torments."*[4]

Many Christian theologians throughout the ages have made Abraham's Bosom synonymous with heaven or paradise, but this would not have correlated with the thought of the Old and New Testament times prior to the resurrection. We recognize our understanding of the resurrection does change our belief about the dead, eternal life, and the afterlife, but in the first century prior to the resurrection, such a belief would have been unknown. Abraham's Bosom was an acknowledgement that there is some life after death, in some form or another, and that the righteous and the wicked do not share the same fate. God wanted us to know what we do does matter, and though the language might sometimes be tricky, the evolution of these concepts about the afterlife does affirm these different principles for us.

*Gehenna* was a term also used to refer to the grave or hell in the New Testament, but it introduced new imagery to the picture of hell. It was a reference to the "Valley of Hinnom," a place right outside of Jerusalem that was used as a refuse dump, a place where trash was burned. Whatever was left became compost, decomposed matter for creatures that feed on deceased matter, such as maggots or worms:

*You are snakes [serpents]! A family of poisonous snakes [brood/offspring of*

*VIPERS]! HOW ARE YOU GOING TO ESCAPE GOD'S JUDGMENT [THE SENTENCE/JUDGMENT/DAMNATION OF HELL/GEHENNA; 5:22]?* (Matthew 23:33)

*IF YOUR EYE CAUSES YOU TO SIN [LOSE FAITH; STUMBLE], TAKE IT OUT. IT IS BETTER FOR YOU TO ENTER THE KINGDOM OF GOD WITH ONLY ONE EYE THAN TO HAVE TWO EYES AND BE THROWN INTO HELL [GEHENNA; V. 43]. IN HELL THE WORM DOES NOT DIE; THE FIRE IS NEVER PUT OUT.* (Mark 9:47-48)

The use of such imagery was to parallel the abode of the dead, represented by decomposition, with purification, or fire. The use of fire in hell wasn't literal, but imagery used to represent a purification of wickedness, of those who would not repent in this lifetime. Fire is used throughout the Bible to indicate purification (Palm 66:10-12, Jeremiah 4:4-7, Ezekiel 20:47-49, Malachi 3:2-3, 1 Corinthians 3:13-15, 1 Peter 1:7); even the Holy Spirit is represented by fire (Matthew 3:11, Luke 3:16, Luke 12:47-49, Acts 2:3, Hebrews 12:29). It is not used to imply punishment, but to give ear to the concept of the purification of the world and the cessation of wickedness. In hearing such, people would realize wickedness – and wicked ways – would no longer exist one day.

This reference to the "second death" is also found in Revelation, through the reference of the "lake of fire" (Revelation 20:14, 21:8), is one that does not lead to eternal life. Such individuals, due to their wickedness, shall be a part of the ultimate purification, one where they shall abide where God does not exist. The "torture" of such a place is the absence of God, the inability to walk in eternal life with God and with those who are saved, and a complete and total division that what they have done shall be remembered no more, indicating they shall not live on, even through ancestral memory.

The final reference to hell or a hell-like place in Scripture is from the Greek word *Tartarus*, found in 2 Peter 2:4:

*[FOR IF] WHEN ANGELS SINNED, GOD DID NOT LET THEM GO FREE WITHOUT PUNISHMENT [SPARE THEM]. [BUT] HE SENT THEM TO HELL [TARTARUS; A GREEK TERM FOR THE UNDERWORLD] AND PUT THEM IN CAVES OF DARKNESS WHERE THEY ARE BEING HELD FOR JUDGMENT [GEN. 6:1-4; JUDE 6].*

This particular use refers to a place of imprisonment for those demons that followed Satan, and is a paralleled reference to 1 Enoch 21:1-10:

> *AND I PROCEEDED TO WHERE THINGS WERE CHAOTIC. AND I SAW THERE SOMETHING HORRIBLE: I SAW NEITHER A HEAVEN ABOVE NOR A FIRMLY FOUNDED EARTH, BUT A PLACE CHAOTIC AND HORRIBLE. AND THERE I SAW SEVEN STARS OF THE HEAVEN BOUND TOGETHER IN IT, LIKE GREAT MOUNTAINS AND BURNING WITH FIRE. THEN I SAID: 'FOR WHAT SIN ARE THEY BOUND, AND ON WHAT ACCOUNT HAVE THEY BEEN CAST IN HITHER?' THEN SAID URIEL, ONE OF THE HOLY ANGELS, WHO WAS WITH ME, AND WAS CHIEF OVER THEM, AND SAID: 'ENOCH, WHY DOST THOU ASK, AND WHY ART THOU EAGER FOR THE TRUTH? THESE ARE OF THE NUMBER OF THE STARS [OF HEAVEN], WHICH HAVE TRANSGRESSED THE COMMANDMENT OF THE LORD, AND ARE BOUND HERE TILL TEN THOUSAND YEARS, THE TIME ENTAILED BY THEIR SINS, ARE CONSUMMATED.' AND FROM THENCE I WENT TO ANOTHER PLACE, WHICH WAS STILL MORE HORRIBLE THAN THE FORMER, AND I SAW A HORRIBLE THING: A GREAT FIRE THERE WHICH BURNT AND BLAZED, AND THE PLACE WAS CLEFT AS FAR AS THE ABYSS, BEING FULL OF GREAT DESCENDING COLUMNS OF FIRE: NEITHER ITS EXTENT OR MAGNITUDE COULD I SEE, NOR COULD I CONJECTURE. THEN I SAID: 'HOW FEARFUL IS THE PLACE AND HOW TERRIBLE TO LOOK UPON!' THEN URIEL ANSWERED ME, ONE OF THE HOLY ANGELS WHO WAS WITH ME, AND SAID UNTO ME: 'ENOCH, WHY HAST THOU SUCH FEAR AND AFFRIGHT?' AND I ANSWERED: 'BECAUSE OF THIS FEARFUL PLACE, AND BECAUSE OF THE SPECTACLE OF THE PAIN.' AND HE SAID [[UNTO ME]]: 'THIS PLACE IS THE PRISON OF THE ANGELS, AND HERE THEY WILL BE IMPRISONED FOR EVER.'* (1 Enoch 21:1-10)[5]

Neither passage makes mention of *Tartarus* as being a place for humans, but from what we have seen in other passages, the referencing is the same, for the same place and the same type of recompense for sin.

The most vivid imagery of hell is found in the Apocalypse of Peter, which is a dramatic New Testament apocryphal work that depicts a small picture of a beautiful heaven, a place for the righteous, and hell with graphic punishments for sins:

> *AND OVER AGAINST THAT PLACE I SAW ANOTHER, SQUALID, AND IT WAS THE PLACE OF PUNISHMENT; AND THOSE WHO WERE PUNISHED THERE AND THE PUNISHING ANGELS HAD THEIR RAIMENT DARK LIKE THE AIR OF THE PLACE.*

> *AND THERE WERE CERTAIN THERE HANGING BY THE TONGUE: AND THESE WERE THE BLASPHEMERS OF THE WAY OF RIGHTEOUSNESS; AND UNDER THEM LAY FIRE, BURNING AND PUNISHING THEM. AND THERE WAS A GREAT LAKE, FULL OF FLAMING MIRE, IN WHICH WERE CERTAIN MEN THAT PERVERT RIGHTEOUSNESS, AND TORMENTING ANGELS AFFLICTED THEM.*

*And there were also others, women, hanged by their hair over that mire that bubbled up: and these were they who adorned themselves for adultery; and the men who mingled with them in the defilement of adultery, were hanging by the feet and their heads in that mire. And I said: I did not believe that I should come into this place.*

*And I saw the murderers and those who conspired with them, cast into a certain strait place, full of evil snakes, and smitten by those beasts, and thus turning to and fro in that punishment; and worms, as it were clouds of darkness, afflicted them. And the souls of the murdered stood and looked upon the punishment of those murderers and said: O God, Thy judgment is just.*

*And near that place I saw another strait place into which the gore and the filth of those who were being punished ran down and became there as it were a lake: and there sat women having the gore up to their necks, and over against them sat many children who were born to them out of due time, crying; and there came forth from them sparks of fire and smote the women in the eyes: and these were the accursed who conceived and caused abortion.*

*And other men and women were burning up to the middle and were cast into a dark place and were beaten by evil spirits, and their inwards were eaten by restless worms: and these were they who persecuted the righteous and delivered them up.*

*And near those there were again women and men gnawing their own lips, and being punished and receiving a red-hot iron in their eyes: and these were they who blasphemed and slandered the way of righteousness.*

*And over against these again other men and women gnawing their tongues and having flaming fire in their mouths: and these were the false witnesses.*

*And in a certain other place there were pebbles sharper than swords or any spit, red-hot, and women and men in tattered and filthy raiment rolled about on them in punishment: and these were the rich who trusted in their riches and had no pity for orphans and widows, and despised the commandment of God.*

*AND IN ANOTHER GREAT LAKE, FULL OF PITCH AND BLOOD AND MIRE BUBBLING UP, THERE STOOD MEN AND WOMEN UP TO THEIR KNEES: AND THESE WERE THE USURERS AND THOSE WHO TAKE INTEREST ON INTEREST.*

*AND OTHER MEN AND WOMEN WERE BEING HURLED DOWN FROM A GREAT CLIFF AND REACHED THE BOTTOM, AND AGAIN WERE DRIVEN BY THOSE WHO WERE SET OVER THEM TO CLIMB UP UPON THE CLIFF, AND THENCE WERE HURLED DOWN AGAIN, AND HAD NO REST FROM THIS PUNISHMENT: AND THESE WERE THEY WHO DEFILED THEIR BODIES ACTING AS WOMEN; AND THE WOMEN WHO WERE WITH THEM WERE THOSE WHO LAY WITH ONE ANOTHER AS A MAN WITH A WOMAN.*

*AND ALONGSIDE OF THAT CLIFF THERE WAS A PLACE FULL OF MUCH FIRE, AND THERE STOOD MEN WHO WITH THEIR OWN HANDS HAD MADE FOR THEMSELVES CARVEN IMAGES INSTEAD OF GOD. AND ALONGSIDE OF THESE WERE OTHER MEN AND WOMEN, HAVING RODS AND STRIKING EACH OTHER AND NEVER CEASING FROM SUCH PUNISHMENT.*

*AND OTHERS AGAIN NEAR THEM, WOMEN AND MEN, BURNING AND TURNING THEMSELVES AND ROASTING: AND THESE WERE THEY THAT LEAVING THE WAY OF GOD.* (Verses 20-33)[6]

*The Map of Hell, Sandro Botticelli (1445-1510), depicting different levels of hell*

It's obvious from the examination of it all that the devil is associated with hell, and it has become his domain because hell was a place of death, the only place in the cosmos where God was not believed to reside. Satan, being resigned to a place within the cosmos, took on the abode of the dead. Therefore, he and his workers would have a chief place of residence with the dead and would experience the same fate as the wicked, who do his bidding, in this world.

There are different groups that believe different things about the afterlife, and all claim their positions are Biblical. In a certain sense, most of them are right. A belief in physical death awaiting physical resurrection is Biblical; a belief in physical death awaiting physical resurrection while in a place of paradise is also Biblical; as is a belief in a second death or place of complete alienation from God. All have had their place at different points in time in spiritual belief, and all these belief systems are found within the pages and history of salvation, and all reflect different ways people have viewed the afterlife. While we clearly know there is one, it's very clear that people's understandings of it have not always been the same.

Hell – both belief in it, in one form or another, and understanding of it, on some level – proves our actions have consequences, and some of those actions reap an eternal consequence. If we choose consistently to do the wrong thing, the thing that takes us away from God, we will find ourselves in a position without His presence, permanently. If we consider that we have an entire lifetime to get ourselves right with God and some do not take it, it makes the concept of hell a little more bearable and a little less unjust. If we choose to avoid God or to alienate ourselves from Him, He does not force us to spend eternity with Him.

Nowadays we argue and debate over the finer points of salvation, taking advantage of the fact that we have a printed Bible to debate over. People in ancient times did not have this luxury, and heavily relied on traditions, writings, and legends they were familiar with from their cultural exposure. To say a belief in hell is unbiblical isn't true. It is true that the way we frequently describe it and the way we use imagery of hell is not exactly accurate as to describe what may be, but there is a spiritual realm, void of God, that is reserved for the devil, his angels, and the wicked who are unable to face judgment.

## **Levels of hell**

Just as there are beliefs about various levels of heaven, there are beliefs about various levels of hell. Most are probably readily familiar with the nine levels of hell found in *Dante's Inferno*: Limbo, Lust, Gluttony, Avarice and Prodigality, Wrath and Sullenness, Heresy, Violence, Fraud, and Treachery, but these can hardly be considered theological points. They exist in Dante's writing for dramatic effect, a way to illustrate punishment for different sins. Long before Dante, however, there were beliefs about the existence of different levels in hell. Adherents of Jewish mysticism (especially Kabbalah) recognize seven different compartments or habitations of hell, to copy the seven levels of heaven:

- **Sheol** (שְׁאוֹל: "underworld", "Hades"; "grave")
- **Abaddon** (אֲבַדּוֹן: "doom", "perdition")
- **Be'er Shachat** (בְּאֵר שַׁחַת: *Be'er Shachath* — "pit of corruption")
- **Tit ha-Yaven** (טִיט הַיָוֵן: "clinging mud")
- **Sha'are Mavet** (שַׁעֲרֵי מָוֶת: *Sha'arei Maveth* — "gates of death")
- **Tzalmavet** (צַלְמָוֶת: *Tsalmaveth*:"shadow of death")
- **Gehinnom** (גֵּיהִנּוֹם: *Gehinnom* — "valley of Hinnom"; "Tartarus", Purgatory")[7]

**Order of demons**

Demons are, in essence, angels who are fallen from the place of God's throne and now dwell in the abode of Satan, doing his work and his bidding in the world. As Satan is the "prince of demons" (Matthew 12:24, Matthew 25:41), he is the leader of their work. Instead of being messengers of God's love and purpose, they come as messengers and instigators of dark trouble. Just as there is rank and order to the angels of the heavenlies, there is, too, rank and order to demonic powers, those who operate for evil rather than good.

There are several different lists of demonic classification, all of which emerged out of different time frames and paralleling different beliefs that existed at that time in history. There is no set nor standard rule as to their order, although there are a few rankings that are more common than others.

A more modern ranking completely mirrors that of Christian order:

**The first hierarchy:** Seraphim, Cherubim, Thrones[8]

- **Seraphim ("Order of the Powers"):** Demonic seraphim specialize in revenge and justice and defeating enemies via demonic means. They are the seat for teaching astrology, dark arts, and divination. Much of their work relates to guardianship and defense, and they are considered the element of fire.

- **Cherubim:** Specializing in foretelling the past, present, and future; assisting in astral projection, past life regression, and foretelling. Knowledge and rulership extend over fixed stars.

- **Thrones:** Assist in ruling the planets and issuing revenge and justice in a distorted sense. They assist in the practice of black magic.

**The second hierarchy:** Dominions, Principalities, Powers[9]

- **Dominions ("The Brilliant Ones"):** Help to access Satanic powers within each being, revealing true abilities through unity with Satan. They assist with demonic meditation, spiritual realizations, psychic ideas, and integration of material and spiritual within and individual.

- **Principalities:** Influence large groups of people in worldly events; nations, leaders, and groups of force.

- **Powers:** Territorial demons influencing and controlling territories to execute deeds and conflicts within the earth.

**Third hierarchy:** Virtues, Archdemons, Demons[10]

- **Virtues:** Bestow confidence and fearlessness; assist in magic and encouragement to "come out swinging" when in a compromised situation.

- **Archdemons:** Leaders of demonic hosts.

- **Demons (Lesser Demons):** Sometimes disguised as dark figures with glowing red eyes, wings and some fur. Many consider them to be extraterrestrial beings from other different planets, living with Satan.[11]

One of the first, and perhaps, oldest records of demonic ranking is found in the Pseudepigraphic Testament of Solomon, which has Solomon subjugating different demons and spirits in order to force them to construct the temple. The writing itself echoes of deep magic and incantation, with Solomon using their own arts to subjugate them. The order of demons as found in this work is:

**First hierarchy:**[12]

- **Leviathan:** The prince of the demonic seraphim. Tempts humans into giving into heresy.
- **Asmodeus:** Tempt people into wantonness.
- **Astaroth**: The prince of Thrones, tempting humans into laziness.
- **Berith**: The prince of the cherubim, tempting people to be argumentative and to commit murder.
- **Gressil**: The third prince of thrones, tempting humans with impurity.
- **Verrine**: Temps with impatience.
- **Sonneillon**: Fourth prince of thrones, tempting men with hatred.

**Second hierarchy:**[13]

- **Carreau:** Prince of powers, tempting people with rudeness and hardness of heart.
- **Carnivean:** Prince of powers, tempting people to shamelessness and obscenity.
- **Oeillet:** The prince of dominions, tempting people to break a vow of poverty.
- **Rosier:** Second in order of dominions, tempting people toward sexual impurity.
- **Verrier:** Prince of principalities, tempting people to disobedience.

**Third hierarchy:**[14]

- **Belias:** The prince of virtues, tempting humans with arrogance, to be bad parents, vanity, and gossip.
- **Olivier:** The prince of archdemons, tempting humans with mercilessness and cruelty toward the poor.
- **Luvart:** Prince of demons.

Other classifications of demons include:

### *The Book of Abramelin* (14th, 15th century)[15]
- Lucifer
- Leviathian
- Satan

- Belilal

**Sub-princes:**[16]
- Astaroth
- Maggot
- Asmodee
- Beelzebub
- Oriens
- Paimon
- Ariton
- Amaymon

***The Lanterne of Light* (1409-1410 Lollard tract)**[17]
- Lucifer (pride)
- Beelzebub (envy)
- Sathanus (wrath)
- Abaddon (sloth)
- Mammon (greed and covetousness)
- Belphegor (gluttony)
- Asmodeus (lust)

**Alphonso de Spina (1467)**[18]
- Demons of fate
- Goblins
- Incubui and succubi
- Wandering groups/armies of demons
- Familiars
- Drudes
- Cambions (demons born part human, part demon)
- Lying and mischievous demons
- Demons that attack the saints
- Demons that lure women into organized witchcraft

***De Occulta Philosophia* (1509-1510)**[19]
- Oriens (east)
- Paymon (west)
- Egyn (north)

- Amaymon (south)

***Sempiphorsas and Schemhamforas* (1686)**[20]
- False spirits
- Spirits of lying
- Vessels of antiquity
- Avengers of wickedness
- Jugglers
- Airy powers
- Furies sowing mischief
- Stifers or triers
- Tempters or ensnarers

***Binsfield's Classification of Demons* (1589)**[21]
- Lucifer: pride
- Mammon: greed
- Asmodeus: lust
- Leviathan: envy
- Beelzebub: gluttony
- Satan: wrath
  Belphegor: Sloth

**Barrett's *The Magus* (1801)**[22]
- **Beelzebub:** False Gods – Idolaters
- **Pythius:** Spirits of lying – liars
- **Belial:** Vessels of iniquity – invent evil things
- **Asmodeus:** Revengers of wickedness
- **Satan:** Imitators of miracles – witches and warlocks
- **Merihem:** Aerial powers – purveyors of pestilence
- **Abaddon:** Furies – sowers of discord
- **Astaroth:** Caluminators – inquisitors and fraudulent accusers
- **Mammon:** Maligenii – tempters and ensarers

## Work of demonic powers

The main purpose of demonic powers is to execute the work of evil in the world. If angels serve to deliver God's purposes and execute His will, demons exist to do the same work for Satan. As we can see from the lists above, there are many different theories about which demons are responsible for what, and most can safely agree that while there is rank and file in demonic order, nobody exactly understands it in the same way. From the Bible, we understand that demons can be involved in moral impurity (Deuteronomy 18), false doctrine (1 Timothy 4:1, Revelation 2:14), spiritual battle (Ephesians 6:12), possession (Acts 5), physical malady (Job 2:1-10, Matthew 9:32-33, Matthew 12:2, Luke 9:37-42), and mental disturbance (Mark 5:4-5).

## **Demons in the Bible**

Only a handful of demons are named in the Bible. Sometimes demons are associated with ancient pagan gods, and other times, demons seem to have their own unique identities. The Scriptures themselves tell us these gods are not always just fake deities, but are sometimes demons (Deuteronomy 32:17, Psalm 106:37). The identities of such gods with demons and demonic activity related intimately to the sacrifices, offerings, and rituals surrounding their cult of devotion. Frequently, human, and especially child sacrifice, was an identifying factor.

In the Old Testament, demons were classified in two ways: *satyrs* ("shaggy goats") (Isaiah 13:32, 34:14) and *shedim* or *daimonion* (Ps. 106-35-39, 32:17). The word "demon" appears about sixty-three times in the New Testament, although most demons are not mentioned by name. The demons mentioned by specified name in the Bible are:

- **Ashima (2 Kings 17:30):** Most likely a reference to Asmodeus, a demon mentioned in the book of Tobit. A false Syrian god made into an idol.

- **Ashtoreth (Athtar, Astarte) (2 Kings 23:13):** Fertility goddess of the ancient Phoenicians and Canaanites; revered in Egypt as a goddess of war; the equivalent of Babylon's Ishtar; referred to as the "Queen of heaven" in Jeremiah 7:19)

- **Azazel (Leviticus 16:18,10, 26):** Connected with wickedness and impurity; tradition refers to Azazel is an angel who refused to bow down to Adam at creation in the Apocalypse of Abraham.

- **Adrammalech (2 Kings 17:31):** Samaritan god to whom children were sacrificed.

- **Legion (Matthew 8:28-32, Mark 5:1-13, Luke 8:26-33):** A term for a group of demons found in the New Testament.

- **Abaddon/Apollyon (Revelation 9:11):** Also mentioned in an ancient magical text known as the *Greater Key of Solomon*. Abaddon is Greek name for Apollyon.

- **Baal-Berith (Judges 8:33, 9:4):** A god prevalent in Shechem, that the Jews entered into with Shechem.

- **Belphegor (Baal-Peor) (Numbers 25:3,5):** God of the Moabites, manifested as a phallus and praised through orgies; captured, raped, and scarified women to Ball-Peor.

- **Behemoth (Job 40:15-24):** Enormous beast of burden, bones of bronze and limbs of iron; a desert spirit, fruitless earth dweller. Also described as Leviathan's twin in 1 Enoch.

*Leviathan, Thomas Hobbes (1588-1679)*

- **Beelzebub (Lord of the flies) 2 Kings 1:2-3,6,16, Matthew 10:25, 12:24,27, Mark 3:32, Luke 11:15,18-19):** A Canaanite deity mentioned in both the Old and New Testaments as on par with Satan. In the occult, Beelzebub is considered a high-ranking demon.

- **Chemosh (Judges 11:23-24):** God of the Moabites.

- **Molech (Leviticus 18:21, 20:2-5, Judges 10:6, 1 Kings 11:5,7,33, 2 Kings 23:10,13, Isaiah 57:5,9, Jeremiah 32:35, Jeremiah 49:1,3, Zephaniah 1:5, Acts 7:43):** Canaanite god associated with child sacrifice.

- **Leviathan (Job 3:8, Job 26:13, Job 41:1,5,12, Psalm 74:14, Psalm 104:26, Psalm 148:7, Isaiah 27:1, Revelation 12:3):** A great sea creature considered a monster and associated with the west and with water, associated with the creation of chaos.

- **Lilith (Proverbs 2:18-19, Proverbs 5:3, Isaiah 34:14):** Long before Lilith was Frasier Crane's wife on *Cheers* and his ex-wife on *Frasier*, Lilith was a night demon, associated with an owl. Jewish lore from The Alphabet of Ben Sira has Lilith as the first wife of Adam, who desired equality, rather than submission. As a result, Lilith became a demon, a source of death for children. This legend was far later than most documents we are exploring in this book, emerging somewhere between 700 and 1000 AD. Prior to this time when Lilith took human form, the identity of Lilith was as a borrowed screech owl, a Mesopotamian (particularly Persian) group of night demons. References to a "strange" or "immoral" woman found in Proverbs are believed to be a reference to Lilith in Proverbs 2:18-19 and Proverbs 5:3.

    The Alphabet of Jesus ben Sirach reports the following of Lilith:

*When God created His world and created Adam, He saw that Adam was alone, and He immediately created a woman from earth, like him, for him, and named her Lilith. He brought her to Adam, and they immediately began to fight: Adam said, "You shall lie below" and Lilith said, "You shall lie below for we are equal and both of us were [created] from earth." They did not listen to each other. When Lilith saw the state of things, she uttered the Holy Name and flew into the air and fled. Adam immediately stood in prayer before God and said: "Master of the universe, see that the woman you gave me has already fled away." God immediately sent three angels and told them: "Go and fetch Lilith if she agrees to come, bring her, and if she does not, bring her by force." The three angels went immediately and caught up with her in the [Red] Sea, in the place that the Egyptians were destined to die. They seized her and told her: 'If you agree to come with us, come, and if not, we shall drown you in the sea.' She answered: 'Darlings, I know myself that God created me only to afflict babies with fatal disease when they are eight days old I shall have permission to harm*

*THEM FROM THEIR BIRTH TO THE EIGHTH DAY AND NO LONGER WHEN IT IS A MALE BABY BUT WHEN IT IS A FEMALE BABY, I SHALL HAVE PERMISSION FOR TWELVE DAYS.' THE ANGELS WOULD NOT LEAVE HER ALONE, UNTIL SHE SWORE BY GOD'S NAME THAT WHEREVER SHE WOULD SEE THEM OR THEIR NAMES IN AN AMULET, SHE WOULD NOT POSSESS THE BABY [BEARING IT]. THEY THEN LEFT HER IMMEDIATELY. THIS IS [THE STORY OF] LILITH WHO AFFLICTS BABIES WITH DISEASE."*[23]

- **Mammon (Matthew 6:24, Luke 16:19,11,13):** Aramaic god signified by greed.

- **Belilal (Without Worth) (2 Corinthians 6:15):** Identified as a name for Satan, typically associated with sex, lust, darkness, and confusion.

### Non-canonical explanations of demonic powers

The Pseudepigrapha and Apocrypha have much to say about the demonic realm, as we have already seen. In exploring the nature of the supernatural, non-canonical documents frequently reveal to us how people assessed the spiritual realm. Looking at the realm of demons is no different. Many Biblical demonic figures overlap with non-canonical ones, as well as seeing the nature of the demonic through unique figures and unique experiences had therein.

The origin of demons is considered the same as we understand from Biblical study: they were fallen angels who fell along from Satan into sin and disobedience. Some trace the origin of demons through the serpent, as a race of fallen beings from another world, but more commonly, they are associated with fallen angels. Most demons outside of canonical reference are in multiple sources of pseudepigraphic or apocryphal reference, showing their relevance and influence among believers.

### The Book of Jubilees

As a retelling of creation and the beginnings of the faith, the Book of Jubilees frequently inserts additional details into the retelling of the ancient recounts. Often detailing, such as the role of angels or demons, comes into greater play. For example, in the flood narrative of Genesis, we find the following:

> AND IN THE THIRD WEEK OF THIS JUBILEE THE UNCLEAN DEMONS BEGAN TO LEAD ASTRAY THE CHILDREN OF THE SONS OF NOAH, AND TO MAKE TO ERR AND DESTROY THEM.
>
> AND THE SONS OF NOAH CAME TO NOAH THEIR FATHER, AND THEY TOLD HIM CONCERNING THE DEMONS WHICH WERE LEADING ASTRAY AND BLINDING AND SLAYING HIS SONS' SONS.
>
> AND HE PRAYED BEFORE THE LORD HIS GOD, AND SAID:
>    'GOD OF THE SPIRITS OF ALL FLESH, WHO HAST SHOWN MERCY UNTO ME
>    AND HAST SAVED ME AND MY SONS FROM THE WATERS OF THE FLOOD,
>    AND HAST NOT CAUSED ME TO PERISH AS THOU DIDST THE SONS OF PERDITION;
>    FOR THY GRACE HAS BEEN GREAT TOWARDS ME,
>    AND GREAT HAS BEEN THY MERCY TO MY SOUL;
>
>    LET THY GRACE BE LIFT UP UPON MY SONS,
>    AND LET NOT WICKED SPIRITS RULE OVER THEM
>    LEST THEY SHOULD DESTROY THEM FROM THE EARTH.
>    (The Book of Jubilees 10:1-3)[24]

A little later on, we see mention of an individual named Mastêmâ, who shall become very relevant in many documents:

> AND THE CHIEF OF THE SPIRITS, MASTÊMÂ, CAME AND SAID: 'LORD, CREATOR, LET SOME OF THEM REMAIN BEFORE ME, AND LET THEM HARKEN TO MY VOICE, AND DO ALL THAT I SHALL SAY UNTO THEM; FOR IF SOME OF THEM ARE NOT LEFT TO ME, I SHALL NOT BE ABLE TO EXECUTE THE POWER OF MY WILL ON THE SONS OF MEN; FOR THESE ARE FOR CORRUPTION AND LEADING ASTRAY BEFORE MY JUDGMENT, FOR GREAT IS THE WICKEDNESS OF THE SONS OF MEN.'
>
> AND HE SAID: LET THE TENTH PART OF THEM REMAIN BEFORE HIM, AND LET NINE PARTS DESCEND INTO THE PLACE OF CONDEMNATION.'
>
> AND ONE OF US HE COMMANDED THAT WE SHOULD TEACH NOAH ALL THEIR MEDICINES; FOR HE KNEW THAT THEY WOULD NOT WALK IN UPRIGHTNESS, NOR STRIVE IN RIGHTEOUSNESS.

*AND WE DID ACCORDING TO ALL HIS WORDS: ALL THE MALIGNANT EVIL ONES WE BOUND IN THE PLACE OF CONDEMNATION AND A TENTH PART OF THEM WE LEFT THAT THEY MIGHT BE SUBJECT BEFORE SATAN ON THE EARTH.* (Jubilees 10:8-11)[25]

Mastêmâ is a demon frequently identified with Satan throughout various texts. He is considered the angel of disaster and the father of all evil, one noted as hostile or persecutory toward the things of God. Throughout Jubilees, Mastêmâ is found sending plagues, testing Abraham, and aiding the Egyptian priests who oppose Moses.

*AND THE PRINCE MASTÊMÂ SENT RAVENS AND BIRDS TO DEVOUR THE SEED WHICH WAS SOWN IN THE LAND, IN ORDER TO DESTROY THE LAND, AND ROB THE CHILDREN OF MEN OF THEIR LABOURS. BEFORE THEY COULD PLOUGH IN THE SEED, THE RAVENS PICKED (IT) FROM THE SURFACE OF THE GROUND.*

*AND FOR THIS REASON HE CALLED HIS NAME TERAH BECAUSE THE RAVENS AND THE BIRDS REDUCED THEM TO DESTITUTION AND DEVOURED THEIR SEED.* (The Book of Jubilees 11:10-11)[26]

*AND THE PRINCE MASTÊMÂ CAME AND SAID BEFORE GOD, 'BEHOLD, ABRAHAM LOVES ISAAC HIS SON, AND HE DELIGHTS IN HIM ABOVE ALL THINGS ELSE; BID HIM OFFER HIM AS A BURNT-OFFERING ON THE ALTAR, AND THOU WILT SEE IF HE WILL DO THIS COMMAND, AND THOU WILT KNOW IF HE IS FAITHFUL IN EVERYTHING WHEREIN THOU DOST TRY HIM.* (The Book of Jubilees 17:16)[27]

*AND IN THE SIXTH YEAR OF THE THIRD WEEK OF THE FORTY-NINTH JUBILEE THOU DIDST DEPART AND DWELL <IN [2372 A.M.] THE LAND OF MIDIAN>, FIVE WEEKS AND ONE YEAR. AND THOU DIDST RETURN INTO EGYPT IN THE SECOND WEEK IN THE SECOND YEAR IN THE FIFTIETH JUBILEE.*

*AND THOU THYSELF KNOWEST WHAT HE SPAKE UNTO THEE ON [2410 A.M.] MOUNT SINAI, AND WHAT PRINCE MASTÊMÂ DESIRED TO DO WITH THEE WHEN THOU WAST RETURNING INTO EGYPT <ON THE WAY WHEN THOU DIDST MEET HIM AT THE LODGING-PLACE>.* (The Book of Jubilees 48:1-2)[28]

*AND ON THE FOURTEENTH DAY AND ON THE FIFTEENTH AND ON THE SIXTEENTH AND ON THE SEVENTEENTH AND ON THE EIGHTEENTH THE PRINCE MASTÊMÂ WAS BOUND AND IMPRISONED BEHIND THE CHILDREN OF ISRAEL THAT HE MIGHT NOT ACCUSE THEM.*

*AND ON THE NINETEENTH WE LET THEM LOOSE THAT THEY MIGHT HELP THE EGYPTIANS AND PURSUE THE CHILDREN OF ISRAEL.* (The Book of Jubilees 48:15-16)[29]

Jubilees also makes mention of Belial:

*LET THY MERCY, O LORD, BE LIFTED UP UPON THY PEOPLE, AND CREATE IN THEM AN UPRIGHT SPIRIT, AND LET NOT THE SPIRIT OF BELIAR RULE OVER THEM TO ACCUSE THEM BEFORE THEE, AND TO ENSNARE THEM FROM ALL THE PATHS OF RIGHTEOUSNESS, SO THAT THEY MAY PERISH FROM BEFORE THY FACE.* (Jubilees 1:19)[30]

*Terror Antiquus, Leon Bakst (1866-1924)*

Most poignant about the Jubilees version of demonic activity is that it was always used for a divine purpose. Ultimately, the decisions we all make are our own, and it is our choice to follow the ways of the enemy or the ways of God. The work of demonic powers was always done within God's foresight, without a haphazard medium, and its work and operation was in no way outside of the function of God. This was done to prove God as supreme over the demons, with the full power to bind and loose, and to show that even evil teaches us an eternal lesson.

## The Books of Enoch

1 Book of Enoch, as a detailed account about spiritually related activity in the earth, is an extensive and rich source for histories and information about demons and demonic activity. Enoch identifies demons as fallen angels but identifies them in a slightly different detail than some of the other works. 1 Enoch 15:1-11 describes them as such:

*AND HE ANSWERED AND SAID TO ME, AND I HEARD HIS VOICE: 'FEAR NOT, ENOCH, THOU RIGHTEOUS MAN AND SCRIBE OF RIGHTEOUSNESS: APPROACH HITHER AND HEAR MY VOICE. AND GO, SAY TO [[THE WATCHERS OF HEAVEN]], WHO HAVE SENT THEE TO INTERCEDE [[FOR THEM: "YOU SHOULD INTERCEDE"]] FOR MEN, AND NOT MEN FOR YOU: WHEREFORE HAVE YE LEFT THE HIGH, HOLY, AND ETERNAL HEAVEN, AND LAIN WITH WOMEN, AND DEFILED YOURSELVES WITH THE DAUGHTERS OF MEN AND TAKEN TO*

*YOURSELVES WIVES, AND DONE LIKE THE CHILDREN OF EARTH, AND BEGOTTEN GIANTS (AS YOUR) SONS? AND THOUGH YE WERE HOLY, SPIRITUAL, LIVING THE ETERNAL LIFE, YOU HAVE DEFILED YOURSELVES WITH THE BLOOD OF WOMEN, AND HAVE BEGOTTEN (CHILDREN) WITH THE BLOOD OF FLESH, AND, AS THE CHILDREN OF MEN, HAVE LUSTED AFTER FLESH AND BLOOD AS THOSE [ALSO] DO WHO DIE AND PERISH. THEREFORE HAVE I GIVEN THEM WIVES ALSO THAT THEY MIGHT IMPREGNATE THEM, AND BEGET CHILDREN BY THEM, THAT THUS NOTHING MIGHT BE WANTING TO THEM ON EARTH. BUT YOU WERE [FORMERLY] SPIRITUAL, LIVING THE ETERNAL LIFE, AND IMMORTAL FOR ALL GENERATIONS OF THE WORLD. AND THEREFORE I HAVE NOT APPOINTED WIVES FOR YOU; FOR AS FOR THE SPIRITUAL ONES OF THE HEAVEN, IN HEAVEN IS THEIR DWELLING. AND NOW, THE GIANTS, WHO ARE PRODUCED FROM THE SPIRITS AND FLESH, SHALL BE CALLED EVIL SPIRITS UPON THE EARTH, AND ON THE EARTH SHALL BE THEIR DWELLING. EVIL SPIRITS HAVE PROCEEDED FROM THEIR BODIES; BECAUSE THEY ARE BORN FROM MEN, [[AND]] FROM THE HOLY WATCHERS IS THEIR BEGINNING AND PRIMAL ORIGIN; [THEY SHALL BE EVIL SPIRITS ON EARTH, AND] EVIL SPIRITS SHALL THEY BE CALLED. [AS FOR THE SPIRITS OF HEAVEN, IN HEAVEN SHALL BE THEIR DWELLING, BUT AS FOR THE SPIRITS OF THE EARTH WHICH WERE BORN UPON THE EARTH, ON THE EARTH SHALL BE THEIR DWELLING.] AND THE SPIRITS OF THE GIANTS AFFLICT, OPPRESS, DESTROY, ATTACK, DO BATTLE, AND WORK DESTRUCTION ON THE EARTH, AND CAUSE TROUBLE: THEY TAKE NO FOOD, [BUT NEVERTHELESS HUNGER] AND THIRST, AND CAUSE OFFENCES. AND THESE SPIRITS SHALL RISE UP AGAINST THE CHILDREN OF MEN AND AGAINST THE WOMEN, BECAUSE THEY HAVE PROCEEDED [FROM THEM].*[31]

In other words, Enoch associated the fallen angels with those who came to earth to mate with human women. The result of their offspring were Nephilim, or giants, and the spirits that came forth from them were evil and oppressive. It was these spirits that came forth from them upon their demise, for no other reason at all but the beings produced from such a union were not fully human and had spiritual capabilities with them. Just as angels are identified as "spirits," so, too, demons fall into that category, with the latter being identified as evil. They were angels who fell in their rebellion against God, mated with human women, and corrupted both the angelic realm and the human realm.

One of the primary ways these demons furthered their own rebellion was to teach forbidden, hidden information that was not for mankind to know. These various things, known in Enoch as "stolen mysteries," are the root of things such as alchemy, astrology, creation of medicines, weaponry, beautification, and divination methods. As a result of this information, humanity began in a long course of intense and difficult sorrows. This was taught by direct influence of Azazel, along with mention of several other demons, including Amazarak, Armers, Barkayak, Akibeel, Tamiel, Asaradel, and Samyaza:

*Moreover Azazyel taught men to make swords, knives, shields, breastplates, the fabrication of mirrors, and the workmanship of bracelets and ornaments, the use of paint, the beautifying of the eyebrows, the use of stones of every valuable and select kind, and of all sorts of dyes, so that the world became altered.*

*Impiety increased; fornication multiplied; and they transgressed and corrupted all their ways.*

*Amazarak taught all the sorcerers, and dividers of roots:*
*Armers taught the solution of sorcery;*
*Barkayal taught the observers of the stars;*
*Akibeel taught signs;*
*Tamiel taught astronomy;*
*And Asaradel taught the motion of the moon.*

*And men, being destroyed, cried out; and their voice reached to heaven.*
(1 Enoch 8:1-9)[32]

*Thou hast seen what Azazyel has done, how he has taught every species of iniquity upon earth, and has disclosed to the world all the secret things which are done in the heavens.*

*Samyaza also has taught sorcery, to whom thou hast given authority over those who are associated with him. They have gone together to the daughters of men; have lain with them; have become polluted;*

*And have discovered crimes to them.*
*The women likewise have brought forth giants.*
*Thus has the whole earth been filled with blood and with iniquity.*
*And now behold the souls of those who are dead, cry out.*
*And complain even to the gate of heaven.*

*THEIR GROANING ASCENDS; NOR CAN THEY ESCAPE FROM THE UNRIGHTEOUSNESS WHICH IS COMMITTED ON EARTH. THOU KNOWEST ALL THINGS, BEFORE THEY EXIST.*

*THOU KNOWEST THESE THINGS, AND WHAT HAS BEEN DONE BY THEM; YET THOU DOST NOT SPEAK TO US.*

*WHAT ON ACCOUNT OF THESE THINGS OUGHT WE TO DO TO THEM?*
(1 Enoch 9:5-14)[33]

The fate of Azazel, as the ringleader, along with those who follow him by implication, is also found in 1 Enoch:

*SAYING, SAY TO HIM IN MY NAME, CONCEAL THYSELF.*
*THEN EXPLAIN TO HIM THE CONSUMMATION WHICH IS ABOUT TO TAKE PLACE; FOR ALL THE EARTH SHALL PERISH; THE WATERS OF A DELUGE SHALL COME OVER THE WHOLE EARTH, AND ALL THINGS WHICH ARE IN IT SHALL BE DESTROYED.*

*AND NOW TEACH HIM HOW HE MAY ESCAPE, AND HOW HIS SEED MAY REMAIN IN ALL THE EARTH.*

*AGAIN THE LORD SAID TO RAPHAEL, BIND AZAZYEL HAND AND FOOT; CAST HIM INTO DARKNESS; AND OPENING THE DESERT WHICH IS IN DUDAEL, CAST HIM IN THERE.*

*THROW UPON HIM HURLED AND POINTED STONES, COVERING HIM WITH DARKNESS;*

*THERE SHALL HE REMAIN FOR EVER; COVER HIS FACE, THAT HE MAY NOT SEE THE LIGHT.*

*AND IN THE GREAT DAY OF JUDGMENT LET HIM BE CAST INTO THE FIRE.*
(1 Enoch 10:3-9)[34]

Enoch shows Azazel as one of three angels given chief responsibility for idolatry present in the time of Noah:

*THE IDOLATRY OF THE GENERATION OF ENOSH CAUSES GOD TO REMOVE THE SHEKINA FROM EARTH. THE IDOLATRY INSPIRED BY 'AZZA, 'UZZA AND 'AZZIEL.*
(3 Enoch 5, Introduction)[35]

## The Apocalypse of Abraham

Just as Yahoel was sent to guide Abraham and his movements, the wicked Azazel appears again, as an "unclean bird" to disturb Abraham in the process of sacrifice:

*And it came to pass, when I saw the bird speak, I said to the angel, "What is this, my lord?" And he said, "This is ungodliness; this is Azazel." And he said to it, "Disgrace upon you, Azazel! For Abraham's lot is in heaven, but yours is upon the earth. Because you have chosen and loved this for the dwelling place of your uncleanness. therefore the Eternal Mighty Lord made you to be a dweller upon the earth, and through you every evil spirit of lies, and through you wrath and trials for the generations of ungodly men; for God, the Eternal Mighty One, has not permitted that the bodies of the righteous should be in your hand, in order that thereby the life of the righteous and the destruction of the unclean may be assured. Hear this my friend, and begone with shame from me. For it has not been given to you to play the tempter in regard to all the righteous. Depart from this man! You cannot lead him astray. He is an enemy to you, and to those who follow you and love what you desire. For, behold, the vesture which in heaven was formerly yours has been set aside for him, and the mortality which was his has been transferred to you."* (The Apocalypse of Abraham 13:1-7)[36]

*And the angel said to me, "Know that from henceforth the Eternal One has chosen you. Be of good courage and use this authority so far as I bid you, against him who slanders the truth. Should I not be able to put him to shame who has scattered over the earth the secrets of heaven, and has rebelled against the Mighty One? Say to him, 'Become the burning coal of the furnace of the earth! Go, Azazel, into the inaccessible parts of the earth, for your heritage is to be over those who are with you, the ones brought forth with the stars and clouds, and with the men whose portion you are, even those who exist on account of your being. Justification shall be your enemy. Now depart from me by your perdition!* (The Apocalypse of Abraham 14:1-4)[37]

## The Dead Sea Scrolls

The apocalyptic nature of the Qumran community created a militancy within them that pertained to choosing the right or the wrong side, with

God's battle ultimately won, even during periods where it seemed as if the enemy was gaining ground. In several documents, demons play a central role, as they consider the role of spiritual influence in their identities and they examine the role of spiritual warfare.

There is more than one set of demons mentioned in the documents. One of the fragments found is known as Curses of Belial:

*The Community Council shall say together in unison, 'Amen. Amen.' Then [they] shall curse Belial and all his guilty lot, and they shall answer and say, 'Cursed be [Be]lial in his devilish (Mastematic) scheme, and damned be he in his guilty rule. Cursed be all the spir[its of] his Mot in their Evil scheme. And may they be damned in the schemes of their [un]clean pollution. Surely [they are the to]t of Darkness. Their punishment will be the eternal Pit. Amen. Amen. And cursed be the Evi[l] One [in all] of his dominions, and damned be all the sons of Bel[ial] in all their times of service until their consummation [forever. Amen. Amen.'] And [they are to repeat and say, 'Cursed be you, Angel of the Pit and Spir[it of Destruction in al[l] the schemes of [your] gu[ilty] inclination, [and in all the abominable [purposes] and counsel of [your] Wick[edness. And damned be you in [your] [sinful] d[omi]n[ion] [and in your wicked and guilty rule,] together with all the abom[inations of She]ol and [the reproach of the P]it, [and with the humiliations of destruction, with [no remnant and no forgiveness, in the fury of [God's] wrath [for]ever [and ever.] Amen. A[men.] [And cursed be al]l who perform their [Evil schemes,] who establish your Evil purposes [in their hearts against] Go[d's Covenant,] so as to [reject the words of those who see] his [Tru]th, and exchange the Judge[ments of the Torah...]* (Column 2:1-11)[38]

In another document, known as Song of the Sage, we find an extensive description for performing casting out or exorcism, specifically addressing Lilith among other unnamed demons:

*"And I, the Instructor, proclaim His glorious splendour so as to frighten and to te[rrify] all the spirits of the destroying angels, spirits of the bastards, demons, Lilith, howlers, and [desert dwellers...] and those which fall upon men without warning to lead them astray from a spirit of understanding and to make their heart and their [...] desolate during the present dominion of wickedness and predetermined time of humiliations for*

*THE SONS OF LIG[HT], BY THE GUILT OF THE AGES OF [THOSE] SMITTEN BY INIQUITY – NOT FOR ETERNAL DESTRUCTION, [BU]T FOR AN ERA OF HUMILIATION FOR TRANSGRESSION.*

*SING FOR JOY, O RIGHTEOUS ONES, FOR THE GOD OF WONDER- MY PSALMS ARE FOR THE UPRIGHT AND [LET...] ALL WHO ARE BLAMELESS EXALT HIM."* (4Q510-511)[39]

The War Scrolls, specifically the War with the Sons of Light With the Sons of Darkness, makes mention of Belial:

*FOR THE IN[STRUCTOR, THE RULE OF] THE WAR. THE FIRST ATTACK OF THE SONS OF LIGHT SHALL BE UNDERTAKEN AGAINST THE FORCES OF THE SONS OF DARKNESS, THE ARMY OF BELIAL: THE TROOPS OF EDOM, MOAB, THE SONS OF AMMON, THE [AMALEKITES]... I[SRAEL. THEN THE]RE SHALL BE A TIME OF SALVATION FOR THE PEOPLE OF GOD, AND A TIME OF DOMINION FOR ALL THE MEN OF HIS FORCES, AND ETERNAL ANNIHILATION FOR ALL THE FORCES OF BELIAL. THERE SHALL BE G[REAT] PANIC [AMONG] THE SONS OF JAPHETH, ASSYRIA SHALL FALL WITH NO ONE TO COME TO HIS AID, AND THE SUPREMACY OF THE KITTIM SHALL CEASE THAT WICKEDNESS BE OVERCOME WITHOUT A REMNANT. THERE SHALL BE NO SURVIVORS OF [ALL THE SONS OF] DARKNESS.* (Column 1:1,5-7)[40]

*[FOR G]OD AGAINST ALL THE N[ATIONS, ... JUDGM]ENT UPON ALL FLESH. THE GOD OF ISRAEL IS RAISING HIS HAND IN HIS WONDROUS [STRENG]TH [AGAINST ALL THE SPIRITS OF WICK[EDNESS ... M]IGHTY ONES OF THE GODS ARE GIRDING THEMSELVES FOR BATTL[E, AND] THE FORMATION[S OF THE H[O]LY ONES [ARE REA]DYING THEMSELVES FOR A DAY OF [VENGEANCE ...] THE GOD OF I[SRAE]L [...] TO REMOVE BEL[IAL ...]* (Column 15:13-17)[41]

*...[REMNANT AND SURVIVOR. SO] THE GOD OF ISRAEL SHALL RAISE HIS HAND AGAINST THE WHOLE MULTITUDE OF BELIAL. AT THAT TIME THE PRIESTS SHALL SOUND A SIGNAL.* (Column 18:3)[42]

The Damascus Document, which was a document of community rule, also makes mention of Belial:

*AND ON THE CONSUMMATION OF THE PERIOD [OF THE NUMBER] OF THESE YEARS THEY SHALL NO MORE JOIN THEMSELVES TO THE HOUSE OF JUDAH. BUT SHALL EVERY ONE STAND UP AGAINST HIS NET.*

*THE WALL SHALL HAVE BEEN BUILT,
THE BOUNDARY BEEN FAR REMOVED.*

*AND DURING ALL THESE YEARS BELIAL SHALL BE LET LOOSE AGAINST ISRAEL, AS GOD SPAKE THROUGH ISAIAH THE PROPHET, THE SON OF AMOS, SAYING: 'FEAR AND THE PIT AND THE SNARE ARE UPON THEE, O INHABITANT OF THE LAND.' THIS MEANS THE THREE NETS OF BELIAL, CONCERNING WHICH LEVI THE SON OF JACOB SPAKE, BY WHICH HE CAUGHT ISRAEL AND DIRECTED THEIR FACES TO THREE KINDS OF RIGHTEOUSNESS. THE FIRST IS FORNICATION, THE SECOND IS THE WEALTH (OF WICKEDNESS), THE THIRD IS THE POLLUTION OF THE SANCTUARY. HE THAT COMETH UP FROM THIS SHALL BE CAUGHT BY THAT, AND HE THAT ESCAPETH FROM THIS SHALL BE CAUGHT BY THAT.* (The Damascaus Document 6:7-12)[43]

Lastly, the Dead Sea Scrolls make mention of beings known as angels of destruction. Echoing their name, their sole purpose is to destroy the things of God and the people of God, closely connected to Belial, with a similar fate:

*AND TO RE[COUNT] YOUR WORKS OF TRUTH AND THE JUDGMENTS OF YOUR WONDROUS STRENGTH. AND YOU, [O GOD], CREATED US FOR YOURSELF AS AN ETERNAL PEOPLE, AND INTO THE LOT OF LIGHT YOU CAST US IN ACCORDANCE WITH YOUR TRUTH. YOU APPOINTED THE PRINCE OF LIGHT FROM OF OLD TO ASSIST US, FOR IN [HIS] L[OT ARE ALL SONS OF RIGHTEOUS]NESS AND ALL SPIRITS OF TRUTH ARE IN HIS DOMINION. YOU YOURSELF MADE BELIAL FOR THE PIT, AN ANGEL OF MALEVOLENCE, HIS [DOMINIO]N IS IN DARKNE[SS] AND HIS COUNSEL IS TO CONDEMN AND CONVICT. ALL THE SPIRITS OF HIS LOT -- THE ANGELS OF DESTRUCTION-- WALK IN ACCORD WITH THE RULE OF DARKNESS, FOR IT IS THEIR ONLY [DES]IRE.* (The War With the Sons of Light with the Sons of Darkness Column 13:9-12)[44]

*WHEN [BELIAL] PREPARES HIMSELF TO ASSIST THE SONS OF DARKNESS, AND THE SLAIN AMONG THE INFANTRY BEGIN TO FALL BY GOD'S MYSTERIES AND TO TEST BY THESE MYSTERIES ALL THOSE APPOINTED FOR BATTLE, THE PRIESTS SHALL BLOW THE TRUMPETS OF ASSEMBLY SO THAT ANOTHER BATTLE LINE MIGHT GO FORTH AS A BATTLE RESERVE, AND THEY SHALL TAKE UP POSITION BETWEEN THE BATTLE LINES. FOR THOSE EMPLOYED IN BATTLE THEY SHALL BLOW A SIGNAL TO RETURN. THEN THE CHIEF PRIEST SHALL APPROACH AND STAND BEFORE THE BATTLE LINE, AND SHALL ENCOURAGE THEIR HEART BY [THE WONDROUS MIGHT OF GOD AND] FORTIFY THEIR HANDS FOR HIS BATTLE.* (The War With the Sons of Light with the Sons of Darkness Column

16:11-14)⁴⁵

*AND POWER AND MIGHT AND GREAT FURY WITH FLAMES OF FIRE [THEREIN ARE ALL THE ANGELS OF DESTRUCTION]*
*FOR THEM WHO TURNED ASIDE OUT OF THE WAY,*
*AND ABHORRED THE STATUTE,*
*SO THAT THERE SHOULD BE NO REMNANT,*
*NOR ANY TO ESCAPE OF THEM.*
*FOR GOD CHOSE THEM NOT FROM THE BEGINNING OF THE WORLD,*
*AND ERE THEY WERE FORMED HE KNEW THEIR WORKS.*
*AND HE ABHORRED THEIR GENERATIONS FROM OF OLD,*
*AND HID HIS FACE FROM THEIR LAND TILL THEY WERE CONSUMED.*
(The Damascus Document 2:4-7)⁴⁶

The Dead Sea Scroll documents show the ultimate end of demons, and that is their fate in the lake of fire, where they will be no more. But it also shows us something else, and that is their true point that God is primary, in control, and even evil serves its purpose in this world. It doesn't excuse it, it doesn't make it right, and it certainly does not mean we should seek to engage with it, but it does prove that even the evil that happens in this world serves a purpose. That purpose is to illuminate the goodness of God, to contrast it with the evil that exists, and to reveal love by proving what love is not. Instead of chasing after and pursuing evil, we should be pursuing God, and battling on His side, the side of light.

## The Book of Tobit

We already saw the touching way that angelic intervention was a part of the book of Tobit. This up-close-and-personal angelic encounter is not something we are deeply in touch with in modern society, but was a clear evidence of the way people believed angels could interact with humans. As the counter of the angelic force Raphael, we see the primary demon, Asmodeus, involved in the difficulty and torment of those involved in the story. Considered the "worst of demons," Asmodeus is identified as a demon of lust:

*TOBIAS THEN SAID TO RAPHAEL,*

*AZARIAS, MY FRIEND, I HAVE ALREADY HEARD ABOUT SARAH'S SEVEN FORMER HUSBANDS, AND HOW EACH ONE DROPPED DEAD ON HIS WEDDING NIGHT, EVEN BEFORE HE COULD GET TO BED. ACCORDING TO THE STORY I HEARD, A DEMON KILLED THEM. HE DOESN'T HARM SARAH, BUT HE KILLS EVERY MAN WHO TRIES TO GET NEAR HER. I AM AFRAID OF THIS DEMON. I AM AN ONLY CHILD, AND IF I WERE TO DIE, THE SORROW WOULD SEND MY PARENTS TO THEIR GRAVES. THEY DON'T EVEN HAVE ANOTHER SON TO BURY THEM.*

*THE ANGEL REPLIED,*
*HAVE YOU ALREADY FORGOTTEN YOUR FATHER'S INSTRUCTIONS? HE TOLD YOU TO MARRY A WOMAN FROM YOUR OWN TRIBE. SO, LISTEN CAREFULLY TO WHAT I SAY. DON'T WORRY ABOUT THE DEMON. MARRY SARAH! I KNOW THAT TONIGHT RAGUEL WILL LET SARAH MARRY YOU. WHEN YOU GO INTO THE BEDROOM, TAKE THE FISH'S HEART AND LIVER WITH YOU AND PLACE THEM ON THE BURNING INCENSE, SO THAT THE ODOR WILL SPREAD THROUGHOUT THE ROOM. WHEN THE DEMON SMELLS IT, HE WILL LEAVE AND NEVER COME NEAR SARAH AGAIN. BUT BEFORE YOU CONSUMMATE THE MARRIAGE, BOTH OF YOU MUST GET UP AND PRAY FOR THE LORD IN HEAVEN TO BE MERCIFUL TO YOU AND TO PROTECT YOU. DON'T BE AFRAID. SARAH WAS MEANT TO BE YOURS FROM THE BEGINNING OF CREATION. YOU WILL RESCUE HER FROM THE DEMON, AND SHE WILL GO WITH YOU TO YOUR HOME. YOU AND SARAH WILL HAVE MANY CHILDREN, WHOM YOU WILL LOVE VERY MUCH. SO DON'T WORRY!* (Tobit 6:13-17, GNT)

Likewise, the angel following Tobias offers advice on how to handle demons:

*THEN TOBIAS ASKED,*
*AZARIAS, MY FRIEND, WHAT DISEASES CAN BE CURED BY THIS GALL BLADDER, HEART, AND LIVER?*

*THE ANGEL ANSWERED,*
*THE HEART AND LIVER CAN BE BURNED AND USED TO CHASE AWAY A DEMON OR AN EVIL SPIRIT THAT IS TORMENTING SOMEONE. THE ATTACKS WILL STOP IMMEDIATELY, AND THE PERSON WILL NEVER BE TROUBLED AGAIN. YOU CAN USE THE GALL BLADDER TO TREAT SOMEONE WHOSE EYES ARE COVERED WITH A WHITE FILM. JUST RUB IT ON HIS EYES AND BLOW ON THE FILM, AND HE WILL BE ABLE TO SEE AGAIN.* (Tobit 6:6-8, GNT)

*WHEN THEY HAD FINISHED THE MEAL, AND IT WAS TIME TO GO TO BED, SARAH'S PARENTS LED YOUNG TOBIAS TO THE BEDROOM. HE REMEMBERED RAPHAEL'S instructions, so he took the fish's liver and heart out of the bag where he had been keeping them. Then he placed them on the burning incense. The smell drove the demon away from them, and he fled to Egypt. Raphael chased after him and caught him there. At once he bound him hand and foot.* (Tobit 8:1-3, GNT)

Tobit's story shows us a torture of a demon in one of the most intimate ways imaginable, but it also shows that through true angelic guidance, any demon can be overcome.

**The Gospel of Bartholomew**

*As Bartholomew's Gospel echoed writings about angels, it also featured demons, in particular, Belilal and Satan, in contrast to the work of Michael and other holy angels:*

*And Jesus answered and said: Blessed art thou, Bartholomew, my beloved, because thou sawest this mystery, and now will I tell thee all things whatsoever thou askest Me. For when I vanished away from the cross, then went I down into Hades that I might bring up Adam and all them that were with him, according to the supplication of Michael the archangel.*

*Then said Bartholomew: Lord, what was the voice which was heard?*

*Jesus saith unto him: Hades said unto Beliar: As I perceive, a God cometh hither. [Slavonic and Latin 2 continue:] And the angels cried unto the powers, saying: Remove your gates, ye princes, remove the everlasting doors, for behold the King of glory cometh down.*

*Hades said: Who is the King of glory, that cometh down from heaven unto us?*
*And when I had descended five hundred steps, Hades was troubled, saying: I hear the breathing of the Most High, and I cannot endure it. (Latin 2. He cometh with great fragrance and I cannot bear it.) But the devil answered and said: Submit not thyself, O Hades, but be strong: for God Himself hath not descended upon the earth. But when I had descended yet five hundred steps, the angels and the powers cried out: Take hold, remove the doors, for behold the King of glory cometh down. And Hades said: O, woe unto me, for I*

*HEAR THE BREATH OF GOD.]*

*GREEK. AND BELIAR SAID UNTO HADES: LOOK CAREFULLY WHO IT IS THAT, FOR IT IS ELIAS, OR ENOCH, OR ONE OF THE PROPHETS THAT THIS MAN SEEMETH TO ME TO BE. BUT HADES ANSWERED DEATH AND SAID: NOT YET ARE SIX THOUSAND YEARS ACCOMPLISHED. AND WHENCE ARE THESE, O BELIAR; FOR THE SUM OF THE NUMBER IS IN MINE HANDS.*

*[SLAVONIC: AND THE DEVIL SAID UNTO HADES: WHY AFFRIGHTEST THOU ME, HADES? IT IS A PROPHET, AND HE HATH MADE HIMSELF LIKE UNTO GOD: THIS PROPHET WILL WE TAKE AND BRING HIM HITHER UNTO THOSE THAT THINK TO ASCEND INTO HEAVEN. AND HADES SAID: WHICH OF THE PROPHETS IS IT? SHOW ME: IS IT ENOCH THE SCRIBE OF RIGHTEOUSNESS? BUT GOD HATH NOT SUFFERED HIM TO COME DOWN UPON THE EARTH BEFORE THE END OF THE SIX THOUSAND YEARS. SAYEST THOU THAT IT IS ELIAS, THE AVENGER? BUT BEFORE HE COMETH NOT DOWN. WHAT SHALL I DO, WHEREAS THE DESTRUCTION IS OF GOD: FOR SURELY OUR END IS AT HAND? FOR I HAVE THE NUMBER (OF THE YEARS) IN MINE HANDS.]*

*BE NOT TROUBLED, MAKE SAFE THY GATES AND STRENGTHEN THY BARS: CONSIDER, GOD COMETH NOT DOWN UPON THE EARTH.* (Gospel of Bartholomew 1:8-18)[47]

*AND AS HE THUS SPAKE, JESUS RAISED HIM UP AND SAID UNTO HIM: BARTHOLOMEW, WILT THOU SEE THE ADVERSARY OF MEN? I TELL THEE THAT WHEN THOU BEHOLDEST HIM, NOT THOU ONLY BUT THE REST OF.*

*BUT THEY ALL SAID UNTO HIM: LORD, LET US BEHOLD HIM.*

*AND HE LED THEM DOWN FROM THE MOUNT OF OLIVES AND LOOKED WRATHFULLY UPON THE ANGELS THAT KEEP HELL (TARTARUS), AND BECKONED UNTO MICHAEL TO SOUND THE TRUMPET IN THE HEIGHT OF THE HEAVENS. AND MICHAEL SOUNDED, AND THE EARTH SHOOK, AND BELIAR CAME UP, BEING HELD BY 660 (560 GR., 6,064 LAT. 1, 6,060 LAT. 2) ANGELS AND BOUND WITH FIERY CHAINS. AND THE LENGTH OF HIM WAS 1,600 CUBITS AND HIS BREADTH 40 (LAT. 1, 300, SLAV. 17) CUBITS (LAT. 2, HIS LENGTH 1,900 CUBITS, HIS BREADTH 700, ONE WING OF HIM 80), AND HIS FACE WAS LIKE A LIGHTNING OF FIRE AND HIS EYES FULL OF DARKNESS (LIKE SPARKS, SLAV.). AND OUT OF HIS NOSTRILS CAME A STINKING SMOKE; AND HIS MOUTH WAS AS THE GULF OF A PRECIPICE, AND THE ONE OF HIS WINGS WAS FOUR-SCORE CUBITS.*

*And straightway when the apostles saw Him, they fell to the earth on their faces and became as dead.*

*But Jesus came near and raised the apostles and gave them a spirit of power, and He saith unto Bartholomew: Come near, Bartholomew, and trample with thy feet on his neck, and he will tell thee his work, what it is, and how he deceiveth men.*

*And Jesus stood afar off with the rest of the apostles.*

*And Barthololmew feared, and raised his voice and said: Blessed be the Name of thine immortal kingdom from henceforth even for ever. And when he had spoken, Jesus permitted him, saying: Go and tread upon the neck of Beliar: and Bartholomew ran quickly upon him and trode upon his neck: and Beliar trembled. (Vienna MS. has: And Bartholomew raised his voice and said thus: O womb more spacious than a city, wider than the spreading of the heavens, that contained him whom the seven heavens contain not, but thou without pain didst contain sanctified in thy bosom, &c.: evidently out of place. Latin 1 has only: Then did Antichrist tremble and was filled with fury.)*

*And Bartholomew was afraid, and fled, and said unto Jesus: Lord, give me an hem of Thy garments (Lat. 2, the kerchief (?) from thy shoulders) that I may have courage to draw near unto him.*

*But Jesus said unto him: Thou canst not take an hem of My garments, for these are not My garments which I wore before I was crucified.* (Gospel of Bartholomew 4:10-19)[48]

*And Bartholomew raised up Satan and said unto him: Go unto thy place, with thine angels, but the Lord hath mercy upon all his world. (50, 51, again enormously amplified in lat. 2. Satan complains that he has been tricked into telling his secrets before the time. The interpolation is to some extent dated by this sentence: 'Simon Magus and Zaroes and Arfaxir and Jannes and Mambres are my brothers.' Zaroes and Arfaxata re wizards who figure in the Latin Acts of Matthew and of Simon and Jude).*

*But the devil said: Suffer me, and I will tell thee how I was cast down into this place and how the Lord did make man.*

*I WAS GOING TO AND FRO IN THE WORLD, AND GOD SAID UNTO MICHAEL: BRING ME A CLOD FROM THE FOUR CORNERS OF THE EARTH, AND WATER OUT OF THE FOUR RIVERS OF PARADISE. AND WHEN MICHAEL BROUGHT THEM GOD FORMED ADAM IN THE REGIONS OF THE EAST, AND SHAPED THE CLOD WHICH WAS SHAPELESS, AND STRETCHED SINEWS AND VEINS UPON IT AND ESTABLISHED IT WITH JOINTS; AND HE WORSHIPPED HIM, HIMSELF FOR HIS OWN SAKE FIRST, BECAUSE HE WAS THE IMAGE OF GOD, THEREFORE HE WORSHIPPED HIM.*

*AND WHEN I CAME FROM THE ENDS OF THE EARTH MICHAEL SAID: WORSHIP THOU THE IMAGE OF GOD, WHICH HE HATH MADE ACCORDING TO HIS LIKENESS. BUT I SAID: I AM FIRE OF FIRE, I WAS THE FIRST ANGEL FORMED, AND SHALL WORSHIP CLAY AND MATTER?*

*AND MICHAEL SAITH TO ME: WORSHIP, LEST GOD BE WROTH WITH THEE. BUT I SAID TO HIM: GOD WILL NOT BE WROTH WITH ME; BUT I WILL SET MY THRONE OVER AGAINST HIS THRONE, AND I WILL BE AS HE IS. THEN WAS GOD WROTH WITH ME AND CAST ME DOWN, HAVING COMMANDED THE WINDOWS OF HEAVEN TO BE OPENED.*

*AND WHEN I WAS CAST DOWN, HE ASKED ALSO THE SIX HUNDRED THAT WERE UNDER ME, IF THEY WOULD WORSHIP: BUT THEY SAID: LIKE AS WE HAVE SEEN THE FIRST ANGEL DO, NEITHER WILL WE WORSHIP HIM THAT IS LESS THAN OURSELVES. THEN WERE THE SIX HUNDRED ALSO CAST DOWN BY HIM WITH ME.*

*AND WHEN WE WERE CAST DOWN UPON THE EARTH WE WERE SENSELESS FOR FORTY YEARS, AND WHEN THE SUN SHONE FORTH SEVEN TIMES BRIGHTER THAN FIRE, SUDDENLY I AWAKED; AND I LOOKED ABOUT AND SAW THE SIX HUNDRED THAT WERE UNDER ME SENSELESS.* (Gospel of Bartholomew 4:51-57)[49]

With the Gospel of Bartholomew expounding the "whats" of the spirituality connected to the death and resurrection of Jesus, it also answers the questions many probably had as to why Satan remains a force in this world and how he can be overcome. Bartholomew proves he has already been defeated, and that we do have victory over him, even if the complete victory of his destruction has not yet come.

## The Shepherd of Hermas

Because the Shepherd of Hermas focused so much on the powers of good and bad, on doing right and maintaining purity, it is most natural demons and evil powers come up in its works. The struggle between good and evil rages on, even in the church, thus it is most relevant it arises:

*Now see the works of the angel of wickedness also. First of all, he is quick tempered and bitter and senseless, and his works are evil, overthrowing the servants of God. Whenever then he entereth into thy heart, know him by his works."*

*"How I shall discern him, Sir," I reply, "I know not." Listen," saith he. "When a fit of angry temper or bitterness comes upon thee, know that he is in thee. Then the desire of much business and the costliness of many viands and drinking bouts and of many drunken fits and of various luxuries which are unseemly, and the desire of women, and avarice, and haughtiness and boastfulness, and whatsoever things are akin and like to these—when then these things enter into thy heart, know that the angel of wickedness is with thee.*

*Do thou therefore, recognizing his works, stand aloof from him, and trust him in nothing, for his works are evil and inexpedient for the servants of God. Here then thou hast the workings of both the angels. Understand them, and trust the angel of righteousness.*

*But from the angel of wickedness stand aloof, for his teaching is evil in every matter; for though one be a man of faith, and the desire of this angel enter into his heart, that man, or that woman, must commit some sin.*

*And if again a man or a woman be exceedingly wicked, and the works of the angel of righteousness come into that man's heart, he must of necessity do something good.*
*Thou seest then," saith he, "that it is good to follow the angel of righteousness, and to bid farewell to the angel of wickedness.*

*This commandment declareth what concerneth faith, that thou mayest trust the works of the angel of righteousness, and doing them mayest live unto God. But believe that the works of the angel of wickedness are difficult; so by not doing them thou shalt live unto God."* (Shepherd of Hermas Mandate 6 2:[36]4-2[36]10)[50]

*"Fear the Lord," saith he, "and keep His commandments. So keeping the commandments of God thou shalt be powerful in every deed, and thy doing shall be incomparable. For whilst thou fearest the Lord, thou shalt do all things well. But this is the fear wherewith thou oughtest to be afraid, and thou shalt be saved.*

*But fear not the devil; for, if thou fear the Lord, thou shalt be master over the devil, for there is no power in him. [For] in whom is no power, neither is there fear of him; but in whom power is glorious, of him is fear likewise. For every one that hath power hath fear, whereas he that hath no power is despised of all.*

*But fear thou the works of the devil, for they are evil. While then thou fearest the Lord, thou wilt fear the works of the devil, and wilt not do them, but abstain from them.*

*Fear therefore is of two kinds. If thou desire to do evil, fear the Lord, and thou shalt not do it. If again thou desire to do good, fear the Lord and thou shalt do it. Therefore the fear of the Lord is powerful and great and glorious. Fear the Lord then, and thou shalt live unto Him; yea, and as many of them that keep His commandments as shall fear Him, shall live unto God."*
(The Shepherd of Hermas, Mandate 7, 1[37]:1-1[37]4)[51]

Hermas' vision is clear: We should not fear the devil, because we should make a point to be master over him and his ways. It is our place to acknowledge his works and take note of them, and recognize the spiritual powers present behind each and every evil action. We should recognize this in others as well as ourselves, and take note, and master evil, fearing the Lord more than running wild with disobedience or superstition.

## **The Sibylline Oracles**

These early church prophecies, written in verse and song, do not just speak detailing of history or the great spiritual revelations of angelic work. They also pay special attention to Belial, spoken of as Beliar. An interesting note: they identify the work of Belial as that of the antichrist:

*Those who shall then receive the victor's crown.*

*But when this sign shall everywhere appear-*
*Children with gray hair on their temples born-*
*And human sufferings, famines, plagues, and wars,*
*And change of times, and many a tearful wail,*
*Ah! of how many parents in the lands*
*Will children mourn and piteously weep,*
*And with shrouds bury flesh and limbs in earth,*
*Mother of peoples, with the blood and dust*
*Themselves defiling. O ye wretched men*
*Of the last generation, evil doers,*
*Terrible, childish, not perceiving this,*
*That when the tribes of women do not bear*
*The harvest time of mortal men is come.*
*Near is the ruin when impostors come*
*Instead of prophets speaking on the earth.*
*And Beliar shall come and many signs*
*Perform for men. And then of holy men,*
*Elect and faithful, there shall be confusion,*
*And pillaging of them and of the Hebrews.*
(Sibylline Oracles 2:195-210)[52]

The ancients understood the Antichrist to be a figure that was a spirit running through individuals, rather than one specified individual, as we shall discuss in the next chapter. In this particular prophetic passage, it specifically identifies the root of such an individual to be Satanic, the seat of demonism.

## **The Apocalypse of Paul**

As the Apocalypse of Paul details Paul's journey through heaven and hell, it is most natural the topic of demons comes up. Perhaps the most interesting aspect of Paul's apocalypse is the fact that he is able to see what is going on within hell from his position in heaven, and the work of evil angels maintaining the demonic realm:

*And I went after the angel, and he took me into heaven, and I looked upon the firmament, and saw there the powers; and there was forgetfulness which deceiveth and draweth unto itself the hearts of men, and the spirit*

*OF SLANDER AND THE SPIRIT OF FORNICATION AND THE SPIRIT OF WRATH AND THE SPIRIT OF INSOLENCE AND THERE WERE THE PRINCES OF WICKEDNESS. THESE THINGS SAW I BENEATH THE FIRMAMENT OF THE HEAVEN.*

*AND AGAIN I LOOKED AND SAW ANGELS WITHOUT MERCY, HAVING NO PITY, WHOSE COUNTENANCES WERE FULL OF FURY, AND THEIR TEETH STICKING FORTH OUT OF THEIR MOUTH: THEIR EYES SHONE LIKE THE MORNING STAR OF THE CAST, AND OUT OF THE HAIRS OF THEIR HEAD AND OUT OF THEIR MOUTH WENT FORTH SPARKS OF FIRE. AND I ASKED THE ANGEL, SAYING: WHO ARE THESE, LORD? AND THE ANGEL ANSWERED AND SAID UNTO ME: THESE ARE THEY WHICH ARE APPOINTED UNTO THE SOULS OF SINNERS IN THE HOUR OF NECESSITY, EVEN OF THEM THAT HAVE NOT BELIEVED THAT THEY HAD THE LORD FOR THEIR HELPER AND HAVE NOT TRUSTED IN HIM.* (The Apocalypse of Paul)[53]

The polarity between angels and demons was never clearer than it is here in the Apocalypse of Paul. Angels minister unto God; demons do the work of ministering through unrepentance, handling the issues that demons themselves have taken on; namely, those of the ultimate fallen angel, Satan.

## The Acts of Andrew

A unique testimony that is the earliest recorded of the work of the Apostle Andrew. It is classified as "unique" because nobody knows exactly how old it is or which Christian sect received it. It focuses mainly on the miracles of the Apostle Andrew and his works, not discussing much of theology or the nature of the church or issues as pertain to it. This, most likely, makes it an extremely early work, one that predates many of the issues the church would start to fight and face later in time.

In its contents, Andrew sees the devil himself, and refers to him as Amael, indicating he was working through an individual:

*AND ANDREW SAW THE DEVIL, HOW HE WAS TALKING TO THE MULTITUDES; BUT THE DEVIL DID NOT SEE THE BLESSED ANDREW. THEN ANDREW ANSWERED THE DEVIL, AND SAID: O BELIAL MOST FIENDISH, WHO ART THE FOE OF EVERY CREATURE; BUT MY LORD JESUS CHRIST WILL BRING THEE DOWN TO THE ABYSS. AND THE DEVIL, HAVING HEARD THIS, SAID: I HEAR THY VOICE INDEED, AND I KNOW THY VOICE, BUT WHERE THOU ART STANDING I KNOW NOT. AND ANDREW ANSWERED AND SAID TO THE DEVIL: WHY, THEN, HAST THOU BEEN CALLED AMAEL? IS IT NOT BECAUSE THOU ART BLIND, NOT SEEING ALL*

*THE SAINTS? AND THE DEVIL, HAVING HEARD THIS, SAID TO THE CITIZENS: LOOK ROUND NOW FOR HIM SPEAKING TO ME, FOR HE IS THE MAN. AND THE CITIZENS, HAVING RUN IN DIFFERENT DIRECTIONS, SHUT THE GATES OF THE CITY, AND SEARCHED FOR THE BLESSED ONE, AND DID NOT SEE HIM. THEN THE LORD SHOWED HIMSELF TO ANDREW, AND SAID TO HIM; ANDREW, RISE UP AND SHOW THYSELF TO THEM, THAT THEY MAY LEARN MY POWER, AND THE POWERLESSNESS OF THE DEVIL WORKING IN THEM.*

*THEN ANDREW ROSE UP, AND SAID IN PRESENCE OF ALL: BEHOLD, I AM ANDREW WHOM YOU SEEK. AND THE MULTITUDES RAN UPON HIM, AND LAID HOLD OF HIM, SAYING: WHAT THOU HAST DONE TO US, WE ALSO WILL DO TO THEE. AND THEY REASONED AMONG THEMSELVES, SAYING: BY WHAT DEATH SHALL WE KILL HIM? AND THEY SAID TO EACH OTHER: IF WE TAKE OFF HIS HEAD, HIS DEATH IS NOT TORTURE; AND IF WE BURN HIM, HE WILL NOT BE FOR FOOD TO US. THEN ONE OF THEM, THE DEVIL HAVING ENTERED INTO HIM, ANSWERED AND SAID TO THE MULTITUDES: AS HE HAS DONE TO US, SO LET US ALSO DO TO HIM. LET US RISE UP, THEN, AND FASTEN A ROPE TO HIS NECK, AND DRAG HIM THROUGH ALL THE STREETS AND LANES OF THE CITY; AND WHEN HE IS DEAD, WE SHALL SHARE HIS BODY. AND THEY DID AS HE SAID TO THEM; AND HAVING FASTENED A ROPE ROUND HIS NECK, THEY DRAGGED HIM THROUGH THE STREETS AND LANES OF THE CITY, AND THE FLESH OF THE BLESSED ANDREW STUCK TO THE GROUND, AND HIS BLOOD FLOWED TO THE GROUND LIKE WATER. AND WHEN IT WAS EVENING THEY CAST HIM INTO THE PRISON, HAVING BOUND HIS HANDS BEHIND HIM; AND HE WAS IN SORE DISTRESS.*

*AND IN THE MORNING AGAIN THEY BROUGHT HIM OUT, AND HAVING FASTENED A ROPE ROUND HIS NECK, THEY DRAGGED HIM ABOUT; AND AGAIN HIS FLESH STUCK TO THE GROUND, AND HIS BLOOD FLOWED. AND THE BLESSED ONE WEPT AND PRAYED, SAYING: DO NOT FORSAKE ME, MY LORD JESUS CHRIST; FOR I KNOW THAT THOU ART NOT FAR FROM THY SERVANTS. AND AS HE WAS PRAYING, THE DEVIL WALKED BEHIND, AND SAID TO THE MULTITUDES: STRIKE HIM ON THE MOUTH, THAT HE MAY NOT SPEAK.*

*AND WHEN IT WAS EVENING THEY TOOK HIM AGAIN TO THE PRISON, HAVING BOUND HIS HANDS BEHIND HIM, AND LEFT HIM TILL THE MORROW AGAIN. AND THE DEVIL HAVING TAKEN WITH HIMSELF SEVEN DEMONS WHOM THE BLESSED ONE HAD CAST OUT OF THE COUNTRIES ROUND ABOUT, AND HAVING GONE INTO THE PRISON, THEY STOOD BEFORE HIM, WISHING TO KILL HIM. AND THE DEMONS ANSWERED AND SAID TO ANDREW: NOW HAST THOU FALLEN INTO OUR HANDS; WHERE IS THY GLORY AND THY EXULTATION, THOU THAT RAISEST THYSELF UP AGAINST US, AND DISHONOUREST US, AND TELLEST OUR DOINGS TO THE PEOPLE IN EVERY PLACE AND COUNTRY, AND HAST MADE OUR*

WORKSHOPS AND OUR TEMPLES TO BECOME DESOLATE, IN ORDER THAT SACRIFICES MAY NOT BE BROUGHT TO THEM? BECAUSE OF THIS, THEN, WE SHALL ALSO KILL TIME, LIKE THY TEACHER CALLED JESUS, AND JOHN WHOM HEROD BEHEADED.

AND THEY STOOD BEFORE ANDREW, WISHING TO KILL HIM; AND HAVING BEHELD THE SEAL UPON HIS FOREHEAD WHICH THE LORD GAVE HIM, THEY WERE AFRAID, AND DID NOT COME NEAR HIM, BUT FLED. AND THE DEVIL SAID TO THEM: WHY HAVE YOU FLED FROM HIM, MY CHILDREN, AND NOT KILLED HIM? AND THE DEMONS ANSWERED AND SAID TO THE DEVIL: WE CANNOT KILL HIM, BUT KILL HIM IF THOU ART ABLE; FOR WE KNEW HIM BEFORE HE CAME INTO THE DISTRESS OF HIS HUMILIATION. THEN ONE OF THE DEMONS ANSWERED AND SAID: WE CANNOT KILL HIM, BUT COME LET US MOCK HIM IN THE DISTRESS OF HIS HUMILIATION. AND THE DEMONS CAME AND STOOD BEFORE HIM, AND SCOFFED AT HIM. AND THE BLESSED ONE HEARING, WEPT; AND THERE CAME TO HIM A VOICE SAYING: ANDREW, WHY WEEPEST THOU? AND IT WAS THE VOICE OF THE DEVIL CHANGED. AND ANDREW ANSWERED AND SAID: I AM WEEPING BECAUSE GOD COMMANDED ME, SAYING, BE PATIENT TOWARD THEM. AND THE DEVIL SAID: IF THOU CANST DO ANYTHING, DO IT. AND ANDREW ANSWERED AND SAID: IS IT FOR THIS, THEN, THAT YOU DO THESE THINGS TO ME? BUT FORBID IT THAT I SHOULD DISOBEY THE COMMANDMENT OF MY LORD; FOR IF THE LORD SHALL MAKE FOR ME A CHARGE IN THIS CITY, I SHALL CHASTISE YOU AS YOU DESERVE. AND HAVING HEARD THIS, THEY FLED.

AND WHEN IT WAS MORNING THEY BROUGHT HIM OUT AGAIN, AND HAVING FASTENED A ROPE ABOUT HIS NECK, THEY DRAGGED HIM; AND AGAIN HIS FLESH STUCK TO THE GROUND, AND HIS BLOOD FLOWED TO THE GROUND LIKE WATER. AND THE BLESSED ONE, AS HE WAS BEING DRAGGED ALONG, WEPT, SAYING: LORD JESUS CHRIST, BE NOT DISPLEASED WITH ME; FOR THOU KNOWEST, LORD, WHAT THE FIEND HAS INFLICTED UPON ME, ALONG WITH HIS DEMONS. THESE TORTURES ARE ENOUGH, MY LORD; FOR, BEHOLD, I AM DRAGGED ABOUT FOR THREE DAYS. BUT DO THOU, LORD, REMEMBER THAT THOU WAST THREE HOURS UPON THE CROSS, AND DIDST CRY OUT TO THE FATHER, MY FATHER, WHY HAST THOU FORSAKEN ME? WHERE ARE THY WORDS, LORD, WHICH THOU SPAKEST TO US, CONFIRMING US, WHEN WE WALKED ABOUT WITH THEE, SAYING TO US, YE SHALL NOT LOSE ONE HAIR? CONSIDER, THEN, LORD, WHAT HAS BECOME OF MY FLESH, AND THE HAIRS OF MY HEAD. THEN JESUS SAID TO ANDREW: O OUR ANDREW, THE HEAVEN AND THE EARTH SHALL PASS AWAY, BUT MY WORDS SHALL NOT PASS AWAY. TURN THYSELF THEN, ANDREW, AND BEHOLD THY FLESH THAT HAS FALLEN, AND THY HAIR, WHAT HAS BECOME OF THEM. AND ANDREW TURNED, AND SAW GREAT TREES SPRINGING UP, BEARING FRUIT; AND HE GLORIFIED GOD. (The Acts of Andrew)[54]

This story echoes with us because it shows the individual's ability to overcome the work of the devil through faith in the Lord. The Acts of Andrew are reminiscent of the Acts of the Apostles, and the intense persecution and scourging they experienced in the early church due to their faith and calling out things in the spirit realm that others to not rightly see. Regardless of the difficulties, we know God is our protector, and in our most difficult hours, He works miracles, even now.

## **The Martyrdom of Bartholomew**

The Martyrdom of Bartholomew is a detailing of the trial and death of the Apostle Bartholomew. In it, there is a dialogue between the Apostle Bartholomew and the devil, much in the same style of Satan's dialogue with Jesus in the wilderness, only longer and more in-depth. It draws on the work of demons in the lives of individuals, particularly in the form of idolatry:

*Original stipple engraving of The Life of Milton: In Three Parts. To which are added, Conjectures on the origin of Paradise lost: with an appendix, William Hayley (1745-1820)*

*AND IT CAME TO PASS ON THE FOLLOWING DAY, AS THEY WERE SACRIFICING, THE DEVIL BEGAN TO CRY OUT: REFRAIN, YE WRETCHED ONES, FROM SACRIFICING TO ME, LEST YE SUFFER WORSE FOR MY SAKE; BECAUSE I AM BOUND IN FIERY CHAINS, AND KEPT IN SUBJECTION BY AN ANGEL OF THE LORD JESUS CHRIST, THE SON OF GOD, WHOM THE JEWS CRUCIFIED: FOR, BEING AFRAID OF HIM, THEY CONDEMNED HIM TO DEATH. AND HE PUT TO DEATH DEATH HIMSELF, OUR KING, AND HE BOUND OUR PRINCE IN CHAINS OF FIRE; AND ON THE THIRD DAY, HAVING CONQUERED DEATH AND THE DEVIL, ROSE IN GLORY, AND GAVE THE SIGN OF THE CROSS TO HIS APOSTLES, AND SENT THEM OUT INTO THE FOUR QUARTERS OF THE WORLD; AND ONE OF THEM IS HERE JUST NOW, WHO HAS BOUND ME, AND KEEPS ME IN SUBJECTION. I IMPLORE YOU, THEREFORE, SUPPLICATE HIM ON MY ACCOUNT, THAT HE MAY SET ME FREE TO GO INTO OTHER HABITATIONS.*

*THEN THE APOSTLE ANSWERED: CONFESS, UNCLEAN DEMON, WHO IS IT THAT HAS INJURED ALL THOSE THAT ARE LYING HERE FROM HEAVY DISEASES? THE DEMON ANSWERED: THE DEVIL, OUR RULER, HE WHO IS BOUND, HE SENDS US AGAINST MEN,*

*THAT, HAVING FIRST INJURED THEIR BODIES, WE MAY THUS ALSO MAKE AN ASSAULT UPON THEIR SOULS WHEN THEY SACRIFICE TO US. FOR THEN WE HAVE COMPLETE POWER OVER THEM, WHEN THEY BELIEVE IN US AND SACRIFICE TO US. AND WHEN, ON ACCOUNT OF THE MISCHIEF DONE TO THEM, WE RETIRE, WE APPEAR CURING THEM, AND ARE WORSHIPPED BY THEM AS GODS; BUT IN TRUTH WE ARE DEMONS, AND THE SERVANTS OF HIM WHO WAS CRUCIFIED, THE SON OF THE VIRGIN, HAVE BOUND US. FOR FROM THAT DAY ON WHICH THE APOSTLE BARTHOLOMEW CAME I AM PUNISHED, KEPT HOUND IN CHAINS OF FIRE. AND FOR THIS REASON I SPEAK, BECAUSE HE HAS COMMANDED ME. AT THE SAME TIME, I DARE NOT UTTER MORE WHEN THE APOSTLE IS PRESENT, NEITHER I NOR OUR RULERS.*

*THE APOSTLE SAYS TO HIM: WHY DOST THOU NOT SAVE ALL THAT HAVE COME TO THEE? THE DEMON SAYS TO HIM: WHEN WE INJURE THEIR BODIES, UNLESS WE FIRST INJURE THEIR SOULS, WE DO NOT LET THEIR BODIES GO. THE APOSTLE SAYS TO HIM: AND HOW DO YOU INJURE THEIR SOULS? THE DEMON ANSWERED HIM: WHEN THEY BELIEVE THAT WE ARE GODS, AND SACRIFICE TO US, GOD WITHDRAWS FROM THOSE WHO SACRIFICE, AND WE DO NOT TAKE AWAY THE SUFFERINGS OF THEIR BODIES, BUT RETIRE INTO THEIR SOULS.*

*THEN THE APOSTLE SAYS TO THE PEOPLE: BEHOLD, THE GOD WHOM YOU THOUGHT TO CURE YOU, DOES THE MORE MISCHIEF TO YOUR SOULS AND BODIES. HEAR EVEN NOW YOUR MAKER WHO DWELLS IN THE HEAVENS, AND DO NOT BELIEVE IN LIFELESS STONES AND STOCKS. AND IF YOU WISH THAT I SHOULD PRAY FOR YOU, AND THAT ALL THESE MAY RECEIVE HEALTH, TAKE DOWN THIS IDOL, AND BREAK IT TO PIECES; AND WHEN YOU HAVE DONE THIS, I WILL SANCTIFY THIS TEMPLE IN THE NAME OF OUR LORD JESUS CHRIST; AND HAVING BAPTIZED ALL OF YOU WHO ARE IN IT IN THE BAPTISM OF THE LORD, AND SANCTIFIED YOU, I WILL SAVE ALL.*

*THEN THE KING GAVE ORDERS, AND ALL THE PEOPLE BROUGHT ROPES AND CROWBARS, AND WERE NOT AT ALL AIDE TO TAKE DOWN THE IDOL. THEN THE APOSTLE SAYS TO THEM: UNFASTEN THE ROPES. AND WHEN THEY HAD UNFASTENED THEM, HE SAID TO THE DEMON DWELLING IN IT: IN THE NAME OF OUR LORD JESUS CHRIST, COME OUT OF THIS IDOL, AND GO INTO A DESERT PLACE, WHERE NEITHER WINGED CREATURE UTTERS A CRY, NOR VOICE OF MAN HAS EVER BEEN HEARD. AND STRAIGHTWAY HE AROSE AT THE WORD OF THE APOSTLE, AND LIFTED IT UP FROM ITS FOUNDATIONS; AND IN THAT SAME HOUR ALL THE IDOLS THAT WERE IN THAT PLACE WERE BROKEN TO PIECES.* (The Martyrdom of Bartholomew)[55]

It's clear that the rendering of the text is to draw on the miracles of the Apostle Bartholomew, much as the Acts of Andrew echoed the work of the Apostle Andrew. Still, the revelation on the demonic that comes through this text is clearer than we find in most. While we've already elaborated on the way that demons may torment or bother people, it shows how they can gain hold over people. The work of idolatry is no joke, even though we may not take it very seriously in our times. Whenever we place something before God, there is a spiritual realm that takes hold in our lives, and it is never positive. Calling upon the name of a false god, of a false work, or of a false leadership always allows idolatry – and demons – to take root in our lives.

## **The Gospel of Nicodemus**

The Gospel of Nicodemus is known as a "Passion narrative" in that it recounts much of the crucifixion of Jesus Christ. Taking things a step further, delving into more of a spiritual description of the work of Christ in death, the Gospel of Nicodemus details Jesus' trial, crucifixion, death, descent into hell, spiritual liberation of the righteous, and ascent into heaven. Because hell has a prominence in this work, so does Satan, who is identified as Beelzebub, prince of hell:

*THEN THE PRINCE OF HELL TOOK SATAN, AND WITH GREAT INDIGNATION SAID TO HIM, O THOU PRINCE OF DESTRUCTION, AUTHOR OF BEELZEBUB'S DEFEAT AND BANISHMENT, THE SCORN OF GOD'S ANGELS AND LOATHED BY ALL RIGHTEOUS PERSONS! WHAT INCLINED THEE TO ACT THUS?*

*THOU WOULDST CRUCIFY THE KING OF GLORY, AND BY HIS DESTRUCTION, HAST MADE US PROMISES OF VERY LARGE ADVANTAGES, BUT AS A FOOL WERT IGNORANT OF WHAT THOU WAST ABOUT.*

*FOR BEHOLD NOW THAT JESUS OF NAZARETH, WITH THE BRIGHTNESS OF HIS GLORIOUS DIVINITY, PUTS TO FLIGHT ALL THE HORRID POWERS OF DARKNESS AND DEATH;*

*HE HAS BROKE DOWN OUR PRISONS FROM TOP TO BOTTOM, DISMISSED ALL THE CAPTIVES, RELEASED ALL WHO WERE BOUND, AND ALL WHO WERE WONT FORMERLY TO GROAN UNDER THE WEIGHT OF THEIR TORMENTS HAVE NOW INSULTED US, AND WE ARE LIKE TO BE DEFEATED BY THEIR PRAYERS.*

*Our impious dominions are subdued, and no part of mankind is now left in our subjection, but on the other hand, they all boldly defy us;*

*Though, before, the dead never durst behave themselves insolently towards us, nor, being prisoners, could ever on any occasion be merry.*

*O Satan, thou prince of all the wicked, father of the impious and abandoned, why wouldest thou attempt this exploit, seeing our prisoners were hitherto*
*always without the least hopes of salvation and life?*

*But now there is not one of them does ever groan, nor is there the least appearance of a tear in any of their faces.*

*O prince Satan, thou great keeper of the infernal regions, all thy advantages which thou didst acquire by the forbidden tree, and the loss of Paradise, thou hast now lost by the wood of the cross;*

*And thy happiness all then expired, when thou didst crucify Jesus Christ the King of Glory.*

*Thou hast acted against thine own interest and mine, as thou wilt presently perceive by those large torments and infinite punishments which thou art about to suffer.*

*O Satan, prince of all evil, author of death, and source of all pride, thou shouldest first have inquired into the evil crimes of Jesus of Nazareth, and then thou wouldest have found that he was guilty of no fault worthy of death.*

*Why didst thou venture, without either reason or justice to crucify him, and hast brought down to our regions a person innocent and righteous, and thereby*

*hast lost all the sinners, impious and unrighteous persons in the whole world?*
*While the prince of hell was thus speaking to Satan, the King of Glory said to Beelzebub, the prince of hell, Satan, the prince shall he subject to*

*THY DOMINION FOR EVER, IN THE ROOM OF ADAM AND HIS RIGHTEOUS SONS, WHO ARE MINE.*
(Gospel of Nicodemus 18:1-14)[56]

Once again, we see the clear message that Christ is superior to Satan. Satan is subject to God, time and time again. No matter what happens, the enemy does not get the victory.

## Demonic powers mentioned by name

The Bible:

- **Ashima** (2 Kings 17:30)
- **Ashtoreth (Athtar, Astarte)** (2 Kings 23:13)
- **Azazel** (Leviticus 16:18,10, 26)
- **Adrammalech** (2 Kings 17:31)
- **Legion** (Matthew 8:28-32, Mark 5:1-13, Luke 8:26-33)
- **Abaddon/Apollyon** (Revelation 9:11, Greater Key of Solomon)
- **Baal-Berith** (Judges 8:33, 9:4)
- **Belphegor (Baal-Peor)** (Numbers 25:3,5)
- **Behemoth** (Job 40:15-24, 1 Enoch)
- **Beelzebub (Lord of the flies)** (2 Kings 1:2-3,6,16, Matthew 10:25, 12:24,27, Mark 3:32, Luke 11:15,18-19)
- **Chemosh** (Judges 11:23-24)
- **Molech** (Leviticus 18:21, 20:2-5, Judges 10:6, 1 Kings 11:5,7,33, 2 Kings 23:10,13, Isaiah 57:5,9, Jeremiah 32:35, Jeremiah 49:1,3, Zephaniah 1:5, Acts 7:43)
- **Leviathan** (Job 3:8, Job 26:13, Job 41:1,5,12, Psalm 74:14, Psalm 104:26, Psalm 148:7, Isaiah 27:1, Revelation 12:3)
- **Lilith** (Proverbs 2:18-19, Proverbs 5:3, Isaiah 34:14, The Alphabet of Ben Sira)
- **Mammon** (Matthew 6:24, Luke 16:19,11,13)
- **Belial (Without Worth)** (2 Corinthians 6:15, The War with the Sons of Light with the Sons of Darkness, the Gospel of Bartholomew)

The Apocrypha, Pseudepigrapha, and Jewish lore:

- **Asmodeus** (Tobit)

- **Amazarak** (1 Enoch)
- **Armers** (1 Enoch)
- **Barkayak** (1 Enoch)
- **Akibeel** (1 Enoch)
- **Tamiel** (1 Enoch)
- **Asaradel** (1 Enoch)
- **Samyaza** (1 Enoch)
- **Amaros** (1 Enoch)
- **Gadreel** (1 Enoch)
- **Baraquel** (1 Enoch)
- **Chazaquiel** (1 Enoch)
- **Bezaliel** (1 Enoch)
- **Kokabiel** (1 Enoch)
- **Penemuel** (1 Enoch)
- **Sariel** (1 Enoch)
- **Shamsiel** (1 Enoch)
- **Yeqon** (1 Enoch)
- **Amael** (The Acts of Andrew)
- **Beliar** (The Sibylline Oracles, The Gospel of Bartholomew)
- **The Antichrist** (The Apocalypse of Paul)
- **Mastêmâ** (Jubilees, Curses of Belilal)
- **Samael** (The Ascension of Moses, the Apocryphon of John)

## Chapter 2 Assignments

- Write an essay (5-8 sentences) on the four definitions of the grave and hell. How did humans come to understand the afterlife?
- Take two demons (one Biblical, one non-canonical) and create an infographic on each of them, explaining who they are, what they do, and where they are found. Which cultures adapted these demons? How did believers come to encounter them? What was their response to these demons in their spiritual lives?
- Write a short-answer prose (1-4 sentences) on why a belief in demons matter. Why do demons exist? Why is it important to recognize their activity within the world, and more immediately, in the life of the believer?

## - CHAPTER THREE -
### IDENTIFYING SPIRITS

[BY THIS] WE KNOW THAT WE LIVE [ABIDE; REMAIN] IN GOD AND HE LIVES [ABIDES; REMAINS] IN US,
BECAUSE HE GAVE US [OF; FROM; 3:24] HIS SPIRIT [WE SHARE IN HIS SPIRIT].
(1 JOHN 4:13)

If you are a churchgoer, you've probably heard certain things described as "spirits." As a group, we have been too quick to run around and label people's behavior as "spirits," identifying any number of behaviors with Jezebel, Leviathan, or maybe we've talked about the concept of resurrecting or picking up someone else's "mantle." We might think someone has a certain spirit based on a limited experience with them, or we might go as far as to declare someone to have the spirit of a deceased person (sometimes long deceased) based on casual observation.

The problem with all this is most in church today (including those classified as "deliverance ministers") have very little, if any training, in spirit identification. It sounds good, it looks impressive, and it gives a certain air of authority. It makes it sound like leaders and church members who throw the terminology around really know what they are doing, and how to do it better than the rest. The truth behind the appearance is much more sinister, or perhaps the proper word is lazy. Most likely, those who like to talk about the spirit of this or that or the mantle of this or that are repeating some trend or some idea that someone else started, somewhere in time, and they have no idea what is behind it, or if, indeed, the assessments they are making are, indeed, factual. It's just a new trend, something commonly said, and the scary part is most don't even realize the implications of what they are saying.

To handle spirits or any sense of deliverance ministry properly, we need to apply ourselves to do more than read an internet or magazine article that labels something in a specific way. The deeper questions of spiritual realities aren't answered in a social media video, no matter how well circulated it may be. We live in an era of entertainment-driven preaching, where the minister who manufactures the most sensationalism wins the admiration and respect of others, but we don't consider that many who might be entertaining know how to wow without any substance. Identifying spirits is more than just a matter of knowing how to put on a good show; it's also a matter of listening and watching, having the knowledge to go along with the claims that are made.

From what we have already learned, angels and demons qualify as "spirits." As a result, one might think it is safe to assume that when encountering a spirit, the usage of the term is either godly or ungodly, and that is the end of it. There are times when the word "spirit" is used interchangeably for an angel or a demon, and the use of it in this context is not incorrect. The term "spirit," however has a wider connotation and a wider usage, and it is our purpose to be as accurate as possible when dealing with spirits as ministers of God. Here we will explore the world of spirits and how to properly identify them in our world today.

### **Defining the words "soul" and "spirit"**

In the Bible, the words "soul" and "spirit" have more than one association. This is not uncommon with ancient language translations, as language was not as evolved in earlier times of history. There are a few different words we translate in definition, and as they overlap, it is important we look at both:

- ***Nephesh:*** A soul, living being, life, self, person, desire, passion, appetite, emotion.[1]

- ***Psuche:*** Greek counterpart to the Hebrew *nephesh*. Breath; the breath of life; of men; the soul.[2]

- ***Ruach*** : wind, spirit[3]

- ***Pneuma:*** Greek counterpart to the Hebrew *ruach*. The spirit, i.e. the vital principal by which the body is animated; a spirit, i.e. a simple essence, devoid of all or at least all grosser matter, and possessed of the power of knowing, desiring, deciding, and acting; the disposition or influence which fills and governs the soul of any one; a movement of air (a gentle blast).[4]

While we are here to look at spirit more than soul, it is important we understand the nature of the two in Bible terms. The first examples we see of life animation in the Bible is found in the world "soul," found as early as Genesis 2:7:

*AND THE LORD GOD FORMED MAN OF THE DUST OF THE GROUND, AND BREATHED INTO HIS NOSTRILS THE BREATH OF LIFE; AND MAN BECAME A LIVING SOUL.* (KJV)

Even in the beginning, before people started explaining character, personality, and various levels of morality, there was a spiritual principle placed within man, that of life animation. It couldn't be seen, and no one knew where it came from, save it came from God. With that understanding, there has always been a spiritual component to the force of life, mystery surrounding the principle of that life loss in death and trying to figure out who is what and who does what in the in-between of life, caused human beings to seek out God in a deeper and more profound way.

The ancients weren't so deep as to make the extensive divisions between soul and spirit that we make today. They started with the identifying factor of the soul, and it, overtime, became associated with the realm of the spirit. Both were invisible; both were intangible; and both seemed to give life and force without ever being seen. Today you might hear a popular minister describe the soul as the "mind, will, and emotions," but to those in Biblical times, they wouldn't have made that kind of specified distinction. Unless the spirit was referring to a specific identity (such as the Holy Spirit), they didn't make a distinction between the soul and the spirit of individuals. The soul and the spirit were the same part of a being, that same "breath of life" that came from the Almighty and animated the body, giving light to our personality and controlling our conduct. It is the essence of who we are, attributes that identify us and make us unique, and the entire being of us as people.

As we discussed earlier, people of the ancient world were trying to figure things out with the limited information they had about the world around them. By making observations, they came to a place where they noticed things in others, had various spiritual experiences or encounters, and tried their very best to describe concepts and principles that were notably abstract, with little way to verbalize them easily. In other words: the people of Bible times came to a point in their understanding where they believed in the animation and life of the soul or spirit of a being outside of the body, because of what they'd seen and experienced. Without spirit or soul, the body was nothing but a shell, with no influence or power. It might sound weird and sort of sci-fiesque, but the ancients saw life intimately connected to the soul and the spirit. Without one or the other, there was no life.

This is important for one reason: people of Bible times didn't make human nature as complex as we sometimes do. They believed that the influence of the person came from various powers, and those powers were either good or bad. They weren't as deep as to think someone could be a good human being if they were nothing but evil and rotten, and they didn't try to see the "good" in people, especially if there wasn't any to be seen. People were closely identified with what they did and how they behaved, and how someone was, is how they were assumed to be. The spirit of a person, or the deciding attributes therein, were what defined someone or something, and that nature related to the spiritual world as a connecting factor. They were either good or bad, and that behavior reflected in their nature.

"Spirit" was about more than just being spooky; it was about identifying who or what something was. The use of the word extended to the breath of God, wind, vital power, strength, life force, creative power, feelings and emotions, intelligence, personality, and purpose. This extended beyond humans because it was seen as a spiritual entity or identification. Spirit connected man to God, permanently and without question, but it also had the power to connect or draw elsewhere. The body couldn't exist without the soul or spirit's animating force, so it made sense to the ancients that the soul, or spirit, could take on a life of its own as an independent thing from the body. If spirit or soul can animate outside the body, it only makes sense that spirit can exist outside of human beings but must still represent or be connected to something in the spiritual realm.

Thus, the emergence of "spirits," or deciding attributes that were associated with a person or a thing, comes into full force to identify spiritual principles or character within beings, things, and even those we cannot easily identify. The word "spirit" extends far beyond the spooky realm of demons, ghosts, and goblins, and also relates to the way a person is, their character, their actions, and their understandings. More than anything else, spirits are attributes of something; a person, a divine being, or a demonic power.

## **The nature of a spirit**

The description of spirit as a "wind" describes its very nature in a way we can easily understand. In John 3:3-8, Jesus tells us:

*Jesus answered, "I tell you the truth [Truly, truly I say to you], unless you are born again [or from above; this may be a play on words, meaning both "again" and "from above"], you cannot be in [experience; see] God's kingdom."*

*Nicodemus said to Him, "But if a person is already old, how can he be born again [or from above; 3:3]? He cannot enter his mother's womb again. So how can a person be born a second time [Can he enter his mother's womb a second time and be born]?"*

*But Jesus answered, "I tell you the truth [Truly, truly I say to you], unless you are born from water and the Spirit [equivalent to being born again (3:3); water could symbolize physical birth, but more likely symbolizes spiritual cleansing which brings renewal; Ezek. 36:25-27], you cannot enter God's kingdom. Human life comes from human parents [That which is born of the flesh is flesh; flesh here means human nature], but spiritual life comes from the Spirit [that which is born of the Spirit is spirit]. Don't be surprised [amazed; astonished] when I tell you, 'You [plural, referring to the Jews or the Jewish leaders] must be born again [or from above; 3:3].' The wind [one word means both "wind" and "spirit" in Greek] blows where it wants to and you hear the sound of it, but you don't know where the wind comes from or where it is going. It is the same with every person who is born from the Spirit." [We cannot comprehend or control the Spirit, but we experience his effect.]*

This passage gives great insight into how people felt about the spirit (in particular, or in this specific instance, the Holy Spirit) or spirits in general:

- **They operate as the "wind":** We know the wind is there and we can see its effects, but we can't see the wind itself.

- **In and of itself, spirits and "spirit" are invisible:** We can identify spirits by their associations (character, actions, behaviors) but nothing more, because we cannot see them with the naked eye.

- **Spirits are from or associated with other spirits:** Every spirit is either an association with a human person (either the flesh, good, or bad) or a spiritual entity (God or Satan).

- **Spirit is born from spirit:** Everything in the world reproduces after its own kind, so spiritual association comes from spiritual identity, and the origin of a spirit always comes from the spiritual world.

Spirit, therefore, operates with animation and identifies the characteristics or natures of a subject. It comes from somewhere else, as a force and power, and is in many ways indescribably in and of itself. The only way a spirit can be identified is by its characteristics and attributes, and that makes the work of spirits that easy – and complicated – to understand.

## Dark spirits in the Bible

All spirits have the same basic nature (in their make-up), as we've already discussed. Their main criteria is being noted through something, because they operate on a spiritual realm we cannot see. Not all spirits are as notable as the Holy Spirit or maybe the characteristics of a person. While a spirit is a spirit is a spirit despite their characteristics and interactions with humanity, it is very clear not all spirits are the same. The Bible clearly identifies certain spirits (we might classify as dark spirits or demons) with negative attributes that exert their presence in our world.

- *Sa'iyr*: A reference to being "hairy," "covered in hair," or "shaggy" like a goat, *sa'iyr* is a reference to a devil[5], although this is not its exclusive use for its fifty-nine uses in the Old Testament. It is also used to describe someone who is hairy or shaggy, such as Esau (Genesis 27:11, Genesis 27:23) or a male goat (Genesis 37:31, Leviticus 10:16, Leviticus 16:10). Thus, the usage of the term with a demon spirit is not always the proper way it is used, but because of the use of a goat as an idol and its association as a sin offering, it became associated with demonic spirits. Its Greek companion is *satyr*, which was associated with a male being that was part human, part goat. This imagery shows a certain mythology, with the ability to transform a human life, much as a spirit can do.

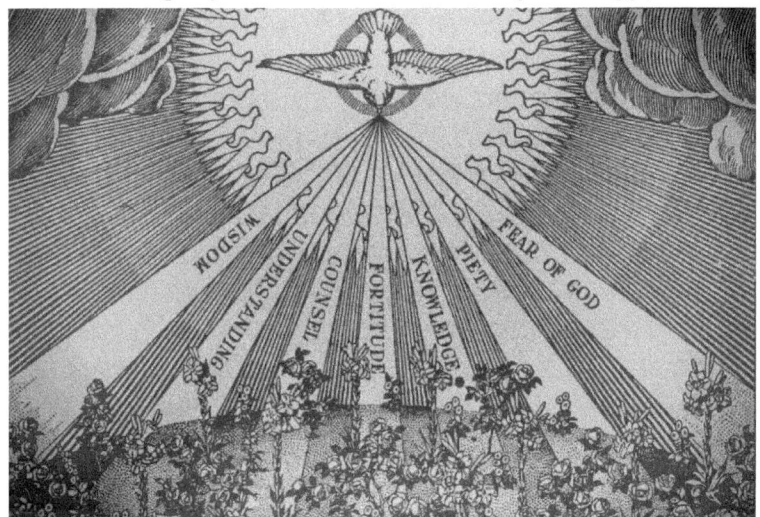
*Depiction of the seven different gifting attributes of the Spirit as found in Isaiah 11:2-3.*

- **Shuwd**: From the Hebrew word meaning "demon" or most closely what we associate with a demon, from the word that literally means "waste" or "desolation."⁶ This was probably from an association with demons and barren or dry places, as well as the nature of a demonic spirit in one's life. The word itself only has about two uses in the Old Testament: Deuteronomy 32:17 and Psalm 106:37, both of which refer to pagan gods found in the Old Testament. The equivalent of this word is *daimonion* in Greek.

## Where did spirits come from?

The concept of influencing spirits is as old as the Bible itself, as Satan took on the form of a snake to tempt Eve in the Garden of Eden. Such morphing into various forms is unique among spirits, because human beings cannot transform themselves in such a manner. If we understand a spirit to be a characteristic or an attribute, it is a force present in many varied forms. Yet the ancients still desired to sort out the truth from the false, and more than anything, explain where evil came from. We know about God because we have read about His existence and that which was from God was clearly of God, but what about the presence of evil – where did that come from?

Some people believed they were the spirits of dead humans once they departed, but that doesn't fit what we understand about those who are genuinely dead who die. 1 Enoch offers an interesting answer to the question:

*AND HE ANSWERED AND SAID TO ME, AND I HEARD HIS VOICE: 'FEAR NOT, ENOCH, THOU RIGHTEOUS MAN AND SCRIBE OF RIGHTEOUSNESS: APPROACH HITHER AND HEAR MY VOICE. AND GO, SAY TO [[THE WATCHERS OF HEAVEN]], WHO HAVE SENT THEE TO INTERCEDE [[FOR THEM: "YOU SHOULD INTERCEDE"]] FOR MEN, AND NOT MEN FOR YOU: WHEREFORE HAVE YE LEFT THE HIGH, HOLY, AND ETERNAL HEAVEN, AND LAIN WITH WOMEN, AND DEFILED YOURSELVES WITH THE DAUGHTERS OF MEN AND TAKEN TO YOURSELVES WIVES, AND DONE LIKE THE CHILDREN OF EARTH, AND BEGOTTEN GIANTS (AS YOUR) SONS? AND THOUGH YE WERE HOLY, SPIRITUAL, LIVING THE ETERNAL LIFE, YOU HAVE DEFILED YOURSELVES WITH THE BLOOD OF WOMEN, AND HAVE BEGOTTEN (CHILDREN) WITH THE BLOOD OF FLESH, AND, AS THE CHILDREN OF MEN, HAVE LUSTED AFTER FLESH AND BLOOD AS THOSE [ALSO] DO WHO DIE AND PERISH. THEREFORE HAVE I GIVEN THEM WIVES ALSO THAT THEY MIGHT IMPREGNATE THEM, AND BEGET CHILDREN BY THEM, THAT THUS NOTHING MIGHT BE WANTING TO THEM ON EARTH. BUT YOU WERE [FORMERLY] SPIRITUAL, LIVING THE ETERNAL LIFE, AND IMMORTAL FOR ALL GENERATIONS OF THE WORLD. AND THEREFORE I HAVE NOT APPOINTED WIVES FOR YOU; FOR AS FOR THE SPIRITUAL ONES OF THE HEAVEN, IN HEAVEN IS THEIR DWELLING. AND NOW, THE GIANTS, WHO ARE PRODUCED FROM THE SPIRITS AND FLESH, SHALL BE CALLED EVIL SPIRITS UPON THE EARTH, AND ON THE EARTH SHALL BE THEIR DWELLING. EVIL SPIRITS HAVE PROCEEDED FROM THEIR BODIES; BECAUSE THEY ARE BORN FROM MEN, [[AND]] FROM THE HOLY WATCHERS IS THEIR BEGINNING AND PRIMAL ORIGIN; [THEY SHALL BE EVIL SPIRITS ON EARTH, AND] EVIL SPIRITS SHALL THEY BE CALLED. [AS FOR THE SPIRITS OF HEAVEN, IN HEAVEN SHALL BE THEIR DWELLING, BUT AS FOR THE SPIRITS OF THE EARTH WHICH WERE BORN UPON THE EARTH, ON THE EARTH SHALL BE THEIR DWELLING.] 11. AND THE SPIRITS OF THE GIANTS AFFLICT, OPPRESS, DESTROY, ATTACK, DO BATTLE, AND WORK DESTRUCTION ON THE EARTH, AND CAUSE TROUBLE: THEY TAKE NO FOOD, [BUT NEVERTHELESS HUNGER] AND THIRST, AND CAUSE OFFENCES. AND THESE SPIRITS SHALL RISE UP AGAINST THE CHILDREN OF MEN AND AGAINST THE WOMEN, BECAUSE THEY HAVE PROCEEDED [FROM THEM].* (1 Enoch 15:1-11)[7]

In other words, Enoch attributes the presence of evil spirits to exist thanks to the fallen angels who dwelled on this earth and then intermarried with women, explaining the concept in that the beings to result from such a union were not human in their true origin, with the ability now to influence and damage the lives of humans. They lived among them and, therefore, know how to torment them. Whether this is a literal truth or a metaphor of some sorts is an issue many might like to debate, but it places fallen spirits in line with human beings, subjecting them to understand and know just how to get to humans most effectively, because they know what befalls humankind.

Spirits come from the spirit realm, and they are here to remind us of the presence that there is more out there than might meet the eye.

## **Heavenly spirits**

Spirits can reflect the divine as much as they can reflect the demonic, even though we tend to identify them with the dark side more than the positive side. An example of this is the seven spirits of God:

*GRACE AND PEACE TO YOU FROM THE ONE WHO IS AND [THE ONE WHO] WAS AND [THE ONE WHO] IS COMING [THESE THREE DESCRIPTIONS FUNCTION LIKE TITLES FOR GOD; EX. 3:14-15], AND FROM THE SEVEN SPIRITS [REFERRING EITHER TO ANGELS OR TO THE "SEVENFOLD SPIRIT"—THE HOLY SPIRIT PORTRAYED IN HIS PERFECTION (THE NUMBER SEVEN INDICATING COMPLETENESS)] BEFORE HIS THRONE...* (Revelation 1:4)

*WRITE THIS TO THE ANGEL [MESSENGER; SEE 1:20] OF THE CHURCH IN SARDIS [THE CAPITAL OF THE ROMAN PROVINCE OF LYDIA IN WESTERN ASIA MINOR]: "THE ONE [THE RESURRECTED JESUS] WHO HAS THE SEVEN SPIRITS [REFERRING EITHER TO ANGELS OR TO THE "SEVENFOLD SPIRIT"—THE HOLY SPIRIT PORTRAYED IN HIS PERFECTION; 1:4] AND THE SEVEN STARS [1:16] SAYS THIS [THESE THINGS]: I KNOW WHAT YOU DO [YOUR WORKS]. PEOPLE SAY [YOU HAVE A NAME/REPUTATION] THAT YOU ARE ALIVE, BUT REALLY YOU ARE DEAD."* (Revelation 3:1)

*LIGHTNING FLASHES AND NOISES AND THUNDER [OR THE RUMBLING OF THUNDER; PHENOMENA ASSOCIATED WITH GOD'S APPEARANCE AT MOUNT SINAI; EX. 19:16-18] CAME FROM THE THRONE. BEFORE THE THRONE SEVEN LAMPS WERE BURNING, WHICH ARE THE SEVEN SPIRITS [EITHER ANGELS OR THE "SEVENFOLD SPIRIT"—THE HOLY SPIRIT PORTRAYED IN HIS PERFECTION; 3:1] OF GOD.* (Revelation 4:5)

*THEN I SAW A LAMB [JESUS] STANDING IN THE CENTER OF THE THRONE AND IN THE MIDDLE OF THE FOUR LIVING CREATURES AND THE ELDERS [OR BETWEEN THE THRONE AND THE LIVING CREATURES AND AMONG THE ELDERS]. THE LAMB LOOKED AS IF HE*

*HAD BEEN KILLED [SLAUGHTERED; SLAIN]. HE HAD SEVEN HORNS AND SEVEN EYES, WHICH ARE THE SEVEN SPIRITS OF GOD [EITHER ANGELS OR THE "SEVENFOLD SPIRIT"; SEE 1:4] THAT WERE SENT INTO ALL THE WORLD.* (Revelation 5:6)

Because seven is the number of perfection, it is most relevant seven spirits are described as being the attributes, or purpose, of God. God is perfect; thus, seven spirits represent God's perfection, perfect nature, and most perfect character. There is nothing lacking or missing in God, and seven spirits draws that out. The fact that seven spirits are mentioned doesn't mean God is seven or is somehow an endorsement of polytheism but reflects the reality that the nature of God is sevenfold. This reiterates the seven different gifting attributes of the Spirit, found in Isaiah 11:2-3:

*THE SPIRIT OF THE LORD WILL REST UPON HIM [1 SAM. 16:13; MATT. 3:16].*
   *THE SPIRIT WILL GIVE HIM WISDOM AND UNDERSTANDING, GUIDANCE [COUNSEL] AND POWER.*
   *THE SPIRIT WILL TEACH HIM TO KNOW [OF KNOWLEDGE] AND RESPECT [THE FEAR OF] THE LORD.*
*THIS KING WILL BE GLAD TO [HE WILL GLADLY/WITH DELIGHT] OBEY [REVERE; FEAR] THE LORD.*
*HE WILL NOT JUDGE BY THE WAY THINGS LOOK [APPEARANCES; THE VISION OF HIS EYES]*
   *OR DECIDE BY WHAT HE HEARS [THE HEARING OF HIS EARS].*

These spirits are wisdom, understanding, guidance, power, knowledge, respect, and obedience.
   There are also seven different spiritual gifts, sometimes called the graces of God, found in Romans 12:6-8:

*WE ALL HAVE DIFFERENT GIFTS, EACH OF WHICH CAME BECAUSE OF THE GRACE GOD GAVE US. THE PERSON WHO HAS THE GIFT OF PROPHECY SHOULD USE THAT GIFT IN AGREEMENT WITH THE FAITH [OR IN PROPORTION TO THEIR FAITH]. ANYONE WHO HAS THE GIFT OF SERVING SHOULD SERVE. ANYONE WHO HAS THE GIFT OF TEACHING SHOULD TEACH. WHOEVER HAS THE GIFT OF ENCOURAGING [EXHORTING] OTHERS SHOULD ENCOURAGE [EXHORT]. WHOEVER HAS THE GIFT OF GIVING TO OTHERS SHOULD GIVE FREELY [GENEROUSLY]. ANYONE WHO HAS THE GIFT OF BEING A LEADER SHOULD TRY HARD WHEN HE LEADS [LEAD DILIGENTLY/ENTHUSIASTICALLY]. WHOEVER HAS THE GIFT OF SHOWING MERCY TO OTHERS SHOULD DO SO WITH JOY [CHEERFULNESS].*

These are prophecy, service, teaching, encouraging, giving, leadership, and mercy.

In 1 Enoch 20:1-7, there are seven spirits, seven angels who watch and guard:

*THESE ARE THE NAMES OF THE ANGELS WHO WATCH.*
*URIEL, ONE OF THE HOLY ANGELS, WHO PRESIDES OVER CLAMOUR AND TERROR.*
*RAPHAEL, ONE OF THE HOLY ANGELS, WHO PRESIDES OVER THE SPIRITS OF MEN.*
*RAGUEL, ONE OF THE HOLY ANGELS, WHO INFLICTS PUNISHMENT ON THE WORLD AND THE LUMINARIES.*
*MICHAEL, ONE OF THE HOLY ANGELS, WHO, PRESIDING OVER HUMAN VIRTUE, COMMANDS THE NATIONS.*
*SARAKIEL, ONE OF THE HOLY ANGELS, WHO PRESIDES OVER THE SPIRITS OF THE CHILDREN OF MEN THAT TRANSGRESS.*
*GABRIEL, ONE OF THE HOLY ANGELS, WHO PRESIDES OVER IKISAT, OVER PARADISE, AND OVER THE CHERUBIM.*[8]

Other spirits include:

- **The Spirit of truth** (1 John 4:6)
- **An excellent spirit** (Proverbs 17:27)
- **A humble spirit** (Proverbs 16:19)
- **The Holy Spirit** (Psalm 51:11, Isaiah 63:10-11, Matthew 1:18-20, Matthew 3:1, Matthew 12:31-32, Matthew 28:19, Mark 1:8-10, Mark 12:36, John 14:26)

These perfecting identities prove God's provision, perfection, and representation in the earth. We may not understand God down here, but as we walk out our faith, we gain a better understanding of His work. All these groups of "seven" spirits, graces, and angels impact our lives and our spiritual operations down here. They reflect the attributes, care and integrity of our God, of the One from which all these good things come. Our spiritual gifts and abilities are not from us; they come from God, for His purpose and Kingdom vision. The power of divine spirits connects us to God.

On the inverse, the Bible also states that demonic spirits can also come in multiples of seven:

*"THEN THE EVIL SPIRIT GOES OUT AND BRINGS SEVEN OTHER SPIRITS EVEN MORE ·EVIL [WICKED] THAN IT IS, AND THEY GO IN AND LIVE THERE. SO THE PERSON HAS EVEN MORE TROUBLE THAN BEFORE [THE LAST STATE OF THAT PERSON IS WORSE THAN THE FIRST]. ·IT IS THE SAME WAY [SO IT WILL BE] WITH THE EVIL PEOPLE WHO LIVE TODAY [THIS EVIL GENERATION]."* (Matthew 12:45)

*"THEN THE EVIL SPIRIT [IT] GOES OUT AND BRINGS SEVEN OTHER SPIRITS MORE EVIL THAN IT IS, AND THEY GO IN AND LIVE THERE. SO THE PERSON HAS EVEN MORE TROUBLE THAN BEFORE [THE LAST STATE OF THAT PERSON IS WORSE THAN THE FIRST]."* (Luke 11:26)

*AFTER THIS, WHILE JESUS WAS TRAVELING THROUGH SOME CITIES [OR TOWNS] AND SMALL TOWNS [VILLAGES], HE PREACHED AND TOLD [PROCLAIMED; ANNOUNCED] THE GOOD NEWS [GOSPEL] ABOUT GOD'S KINGDOM. THE TWELVE APOSTLES WERE WITH HIM, AND ALSO SOME WOMEN WHO HAD BEEN HEALED OF SICKNESSES AND EVIL [DEFILING; UNCLEAN; 4:33] SPIRITS: MARY, CALLED MAGDALENE [PROBABLY BECAUSE SHE WAS FROM THE TOWN OF MAGDALA], FROM WHOM SEVEN DEMONS HAD GONE OUT...* (Luke 8:1-2)

The use of the number seven here doesn't indicate the demons are godly, but rather that the people of said generation are so wicked, they are the embodiment or completion of evil. In the case of Mary Magdalene, seven demons left her, indicating a dual message: at one time, she was, in some way, the completion of evil, but thanks to a perfect God, she was set free. No devil in hell, no evil spirit can overcome the goodness of God.

## Discernment of spirits and testing spirits

The Scriptures, from beginning to end, make it very clear not every spirit is from God. This is in total opposition to the words we are spoken of nowadays that encourage us to embrace every system and every spirit as being the same. This is not just in the sense of religious differences (although there certainly are different spirits in different religions), but also in the sense of receiving people among us who may claim to be of the same beliefs, the same system, and similar ideas. There are many who appear to be on the "same team" who aren't, and the only way we can understand or recognize a spirit is through discernment and testing.

One gift we seldom speak about when it comes to charismatic spiritual gifts is discernment. If you are going to walk in any semblance of deliverance ministry or handle work in ministry, period, discernment is essential. If we do not operate in a gift of discernment, we can spend a lot of time chasing after the wrong things, following the wrong ideals, trusting the wrong people, and being led into all sorts of places that relate to spiritual untruth.

*So choose some men from each tribe—wise men who have understanding [discernment] and experience—and I will make them leaders over you.* (Deuteronomy 1:13)

*Because God has given me a special gift [His grace], I have something to say to everyone among you. Do not think you are better than you are. [Instead] You must decide what you really are [think sensibly; think with sober discernment] by [based on; in accordance with] the amount of faith God has given you.* (Romans 12:3)

*The Spirit gives to another person the power to do miracles [works of power], to another the ability to prophesy [prophecy]. And He gives to another the ability to know the difference between good and evil [discernment/distinguishing of] spirits. The Spirit gives one person the ability to speak in different kinds of languages [or ecstatic utterance; tongues] and to another the ability to interpret those languages [interpretation of tongues].* (1 Corinthians 12:10)

*This is my prayer for you: that your love will grow [increase; abound] more and more; that you will have knowledge and understanding [insight; discernment] with your love.* (Philippians 1:9)

Discernment of spirits is probably not as oft desired as other spiritual gifts because it's not as flashy. Having such a gift changes one's perception about the people they meet, about the spiritual manifestations that might come out of an event or might be worked in a certain situation or atmosphere, and it can quickly change the course of who one is or is not willing to work with in a ministry setting. It is the ability to sort out various spirits, spiritual identities, the spirits behind something, and spiritual manifestations as being from God or not being from God. It sounds easy enough, but discernment of spirits is a gift one gains confidence in as they study spiritual operations and allow themselves the space and time to process the spirits they see around them.

We need the gift of spiritual discernment to help establish a balance of truth in our church settings, as well as our life settings. Every day and in every way, it is possible to yearn for and desire that which is not God without realizing we are falling into the ultimate demonic trap. It is a gift that helps keep us honest and keep us aware of the fact that we can miss God. We can fall into the temptation to follow things that are not of God because they glitter bright and flashy to get our attention.

In addition to discerning spirits, we should test spirits:

*MY DEAR FRIENDS [BELOVED], MANY FALSE PROPHETS [DEUT. 13:1-5; 18:14-22; MARK 13:22] HAVE GONE OUT INTO THE WORLD. SO DO NOT BELIEVE [TRUST] EVERY SPIRIT, BUT TEST THE SPIRITS TO SEE IF THEY ARE FROM GOD [THE FALSE TEACHERS EVIDENTLY CLAIMED THAT THEIR TEACHING WAS FROM THE SPIRIT; 1 COR. 12:1-3; 14:29; 1 THESS. 5:19-21]. THIS IS HOW YOU CAN KNOW [RECOGNIZE] GOD'S SPIRIT: EVERY SPIRIT [A TEACHER/PROPHET CLAIMING INSPIRATION FROM THE SPIRIT] WHO CONFESSES [ACKNOWLEDGES] THAT JESUS CHRIST CAME TO EARTH AS A HUMAN [IN THE FLESH] IS FROM GOD. AND EVERY SPIRIT WHO REFUSES TO SAY THIS ABOUT JESUS [DOES NOT CONFESS/ACKNOWLEDGE JESUS] IS NOT FROM GOD [2 JOHN 7]. IT IS THE SPIRIT OF THE ENEMY OF CHRIST [ANTICHRIST; 2:18, 22], WHICH YOU HAVE HEARD IS COMING, AND NOW HE IS ALREADY IN THE WORLD.*

*MY DEAR CHILDREN [2:1], YOU BELONG TO [ARE FROM] GOD AND HAVE DEFEATED [CONQUERED; OVERCOME] THEM [THE ANTICHRISTS/FALSE TEACHERS]; BECAUSE GOD'S SPIRIT, WHO IS IN YOU, IS GREATER THAN THE DEVIL, WHO IS IN THE WORLD [THAT WHICH IS IN YOU IS GREATER THAN THAT WHICH IS IN THE WORLD]. AND THEY BELONG TO [ARE FROM] THE WORLD, SO WHAT THEY SAY IS FROM THE WORLD, AND THE WORLD LISTENS TO [HEARS; OBEYS] THEM. BUT WE BELONG TO [ARE FROM] GOD, AND THOSE WHO KNOW GOD LISTEN TO [HEAR; OBEY] US. BUT THOSE WHO ARE NOT FROM GOD DO NOT LISTEN TO [HEAR; OBEY] US. THAT IS HOW WE KNOW [RECOGNIZE] THE SPIRIT THAT IS TRUE AND THE SPIRIT THAT IS FALSE [DECEIVES; ERRS].* (1 John 4:1-6)

Testing spirits isn't the most fun job any of us can have, but it is important. As human beings, and especially as human beings following God, we want to rely on the idea that we can trust people and take them at face value. When it comes to the spiritual realm, we like to do the same with spirits, whether those spirits come to us on their own as a presence or in the form of a person. The Bible tells us we can't approach the spiritual realm this simply, but we need to aware ourselves of the fact that we do have an enemy and that enemy is not working for our good. Spirits can be good or bad, and therefore, we test them:

- **Is it a spirit you can believe?:** If the Bible warns against not believing every spirit, this must mean some are simply unbelievable. If it sounds that outlandish, it probably is, and probably not someone speaking by the Spirit.

- **Do they acknowledge Jesus Christ as come in the flesh?:** There are many spiritual movements that reject the notion of Jesus as ever having been among us in human form. Even from the earliest of Christian times there have been those who debate the ability of Christ to inhabit human flesh, telling us that His fleshly body was an illusion. If someone is encouraging the belief that Jesus was never here as a human being, that is a sign of a false spirit because it is denying the entire presence and work of Jesus Christ in this world.

- **Are they against the very spirit of Christ?:** Antichrist is "against Christ," and yes, this does literally indicate being against Jesus Christ in His very being. It represents more than this, however. Being anti-Christ means being against the anointing of Christ, which can refer to being against the work of Christ as the Messiah, against those who follow Christ, or against those whom Christ has anointed to do His work in the world. Obviously, there are many complex ways a spirit can manifest in a false way as an "antichrist."

- **Are they deceivers?:** Deceivers are those who desire you to think one thing about them or about what they are doing but have an alternate or underlying motive behind their agenda. For example, a deceiver is one who might make it look as if they have a huge, thriving ministry, but only have a few followers. Someone might appear to have a deliverance ministry, and testify to many who are healed, but in reality, no one is healed. Deceit is against the truth, and those who engage in deceit have no part with the Lord.

- **Who do they speak by?:** Some things sound great to us as people. They appeal to our flesh, to the concepts we hold dear in this world, and they make us feel right at home, right where we are. There is no challenge to grow or change with such thoughts. If a message is that easy to swallow, doesn't challenge one at all or doesn't seem to offer any counterpoint to the flesh, it's most likely not a spirit from God.

- **Who is listening to the message?:** I want to be careful in what I say here because a rejected message or messenger does not necessarily mean someone is speaking from God. We've come to associate small crowds and ministries that are not following the trends of megachurches with accuracy, and this is not always the case. It's not how many people are following a message as much as who is following it, and if a person cannot receive the correction of truly established apostles and prophets, chances are very good there is a bad spirit behind that work.

## Spirits mentioned in the Bible

For all the "spirits" we throw out left and right, there is a limited list of things identified specifically as spirits in the Bible. In addition to demons and angels, there are the following:[9]

- **Heaviness** (Isaiah 61:3 and Proverbs 16:2)
- **Infirmity** (Luke 13:11)
- **Fear** (2 Timothy 1:7)
- **Wounded/crushed** (Proverbs 18:14)
- **Evil** (1 Samuel 16:14)
- **Unclean** (Matthew 12:43, Zechariah 13:2, Mark 5:2-20)
- **Stupor** (Romans 11:8)
- **Anti-Christ** (1 John 4:3)
- **Error** (1 John 4:6)
- **Brokenness** (Proverbs 17:22)
- **Disobedience** (Ephesians 2:2)
- **Lying** (1 Kings 22:21-23)
- **Prostitution** (Hosea 4:12)
- **Divination** (Acts 16:16)

- **Deceiving** (1 Timothy 4:1)
- **Perversity:** (Isaiah. 19:14)
- **Jealousy:** (Numbers 5:14)
- **Haughtiness** (Proverbs 16:18)

To be honest, I can't remember the last time someone mentioned anything on this list when they spoke about spirits. Because of the nature of the things on this list, they don't make for a big, dramatic show or an intense message that will bring anyone and everyone out to hear about it. None of us like to hear that the spirits of the Bible are things we all must address within ourselves, so preachers focus on perceived "big things" that can get attention and judgment out of finger-pointing at others. When spirits come up, they are grand and dramatic (and we shall address some of this next), but unfortunately, those viewpoints of spirits are not supported anywhere in Scripture. These are things that, in keeping with our previously spoken concept, are attributes or characteristics that people might display. They are believed to be spiritual in nature, something that says something about the guiding forces and influences in one's life.

It's not completely incorrect to attribute a character issue within someone as a "spirit," but that is different from saying something is a spirit with a spiritual origin or identification. We have become very comfortable labeling everything we see or everything we like to identify as a "spirit" or a spiritual issue, but this is not always the case. Sometimes people emanate certain things from their personalities or behaviors that are reflections of them and where they are and are characteristics of the flesh more than the spirit. Being properly trained in spirits and spirit identification helps us to recognize the difference, and that's one of the major reasons why it is so important to raise up Biblical lists and identifications for spirits. Some relate to problems, some relate to woundedness, some relate to downright spiritual issues, but more than anything, recognizing criteria for Biblical spirits helps us to sort out the true from the false. These specific identified spirits tell us a few things about the way that spirits, whether positive or negative, work in our lives:

- **Through our emotional states:** Many speak on emotions and controlling our emotions. Most speak of them abstractly, in a way that is confusing to apply emotional discipline. In a non-abstract, more practical application, we must monitor our emotional states to make sure we do not run wild with our feelings into realms where we can, as people, quickly get out of control. Emotions are funny things; we can feel many ways about something in a short period of time. Our moods can zoom from zero to a thousand in the blink of an eye. Emotions are good indicators of things around us; what vexes us, causes us happiness or joy, what causes sorrow, and how we are feeling about life in general, but they can change as fast as we first experience them. Gaining insight into why we feel as we do and persevering through no matter how we feel will give us an edge up over spirits that seek to cause confusion and issue within us.

- **Through our countenance:** Our countenance is our general temperament, most often expressed through our body language, face, or facial expressions. We could define, by extension, our countenance to be our own personal "spirit," the way are by our nature and conditioning, and how we respond to situations and others. If by our nature we are given to anger or to a nasty disposition, such will invite issues within our character to arise. It is important we learn to temper ourselves accordingly, inviting the fruit of the Spirit (Galatians 5:22-23) to enter our lives and to transform our countenances from the worldly being to a spiritual one.

- **Through our perception of ourselves:** How we carry ourselves is evident to others. Over the past fifty years or so, we've attempted to explain behaviors such as deceit, lying, disobedience, jealousy, and haughtiness as insecurity. We teach that such things emerge because people do not feel good about themselves, but this is not what the Scriptures indicate about such behaviors. If we think more of ourselves than we ought, we're going to believe we have the right to mistreat others and exalt ourselves above other people. Such opens the door to poor behavior and character and failing to honor our neighbor as we honor ourselves.

- **Through our beliefs:** What we believe makes a difference. There are so many things to believe, ideas to follow, concepts to embrace, and belief systems to follow, we can be easily swayed. There are many systems that present themselves far better and more professional than Christianity, and such can make the deceptions they bury beneath the surface an appealing shock when the time comes for their unveiling. We will never believe perfectly, but we should ascribe to believe as accurately as possible. This means being connected to good people, good leadership, and devoting ourselves to the instruction of the Lord.

- **Through our understanding:** The way we process information and what we perceive in the world can vary greatly from person to person. This can be a good thing, or it can be a negative thing. If the enemy can distort how we understand things, we can easily be swayed toward the wrong things in our interactions with others.

- **Through our integrity:** If we do not operate by a compass of right character, we won't act properly. Operating without integrity swings the door wide open to be known for spiritual activity that is not only demonic, it is unbecoming and hurtful to others.

- **Through our desire to know more:** There's nothing wrong with learning, curiosity, or expanding our individual worlds beyond what we might know or see in the immediate. Growth is an important part of the spiritual life, and walking with God means we should want to know more about ourselves, where we came from, and what He desires of us. The problem with wanting to know more is what we want to know about and our drive to turn our knowledge into something competitive or envious of others. Knowledge should edify, not puff up.

Note the following things are not found on the list of Biblical spirits:

- Any form of same-gender loving relationships
- Being transgender, nonbinary, or anywhere on the queer spectrum
- Gender non-conformity
- Alcoholism or drug addiction
- Overspending
- Dating
- Using technology
- Television
- Offense

- Infertility
- Critical
- Inflexible
- Divorce
- Abortion
- Birth control

...or any of the other diverse things we label as spirits, that have absolutely nothing to do with spirits, whatsoever. The list we have here proves to us that we should be very careful with what we label as a spirit, what we are quick to say someone has or does not have in terms of the spiritual realm, and maintain a true sense of discernment when it comes to something as important as spiritual identification.

## **Spirits in the pseudepigrapha and apocrypha**

The major difference between the Bible's explanation of spirits and those found in the Pseudepigrapha and Apocrypha is the latter focuses more on the origin of spirits and why they are there rather than on their mere presence or existence. We have already explored this aspect of spirits in the Apocrypha, quite in depth in previous chapters. The image of spirits as attributes and characteristics continues in the apocrypha and pseudepigrapha, following much of the same imagery and nature as found in the Bible. Some are good, and some are bad, and many more are mentioned by name than we frequently see in the Bible.

A unique point is found in the way that God is specifically identified as "Lord of the spirits," in reference to the heavenly spirits that do His work in heaven and the world, as well as the "spirits" of flesh, referring to man:

*GOD OF THE SPIRITS OF ALL FLESH, WHO HAST SHOWN MERCY UNTO ME*
*AND HAST SAVED ME AND MY SONS FROM THE WATERS OF THE FLOOD,*
*AND HAST NOT CAUSED ME TO PERISH AS THOU DIDST THE SONS OF PERDITION;*

*FOR THY GRACE HAS BEEN GREAT TOWARDS ME,*
*AND GREAT HAS BEEN THY MERCY TO MY SOUL;*

*LET THY GRACE BE LIFT UP UPON MY SONS,*
*AND LET NOT WICKED SPIRITS RULE OVER THEM*

*LEST THEY SHOULD DESTROY THEM FROM THE EARTH.*
(The Book of Jubilees 10:3)[10]

Inversely, Mastêmâ is referred to as the chief of demonic spirits, and comes forth to answer to the true Chief of all spirits:

*AND THE CHIEF OF THE SPIRITS, MASTÊMÂ, CAME AND SAID: 'LORD, CREATOR, LET SOME OF THEM REMAIN BEFORE ME, AND LET THEM HARKEN TO MY VOICE, AND DO ALL THAT I SHALL SAY UNTO THEM; FOR IF SOME OF THEM ARE NOT LEFT TO ME, I SHALL NOT BE ABLE TO EXECUTE THE POWER OF MY WILL ON THE SONS OF MEN; FOR THESE ARE FOR CORRUPTION AND LEADING ASTRAY BEFORE MY JUDGMENT, FOR GREAT IS THE WICKEDNESS OF THE SONS OF MEN.'*

*AND HE SAID: LET THE TENTH PART OF THEM REMAIN BEFORE HIM, AND LET NINE PARTS DESCEND INTO THE PLACE OF CONDEMNATION.'* (The Book of Jubilees 10:8-9)[11]

Clearly, God is shown as the seat and primacy of all things, including those that are in rebellion, and that try to sway the hearts of men.

## Pop culture spirits

Calling certain things out as spirits tends to operate or move in trends. At one point in time, we heard a lot about the "spirit of Mammon," or a reference to greed, or love of money. Mammon can be classified as a spirit since it is identified as a demon in the Bible, but this is an exception to the rule rather than the standard. When many "spirits" are called out, especially in trends, they are either exaggerated, are improperly identified, or are not really spirits. For this reason, any time a spiritual "trend" emerges, we should be quick to check the veracity of it and assess whether what we are hearing about is factual.

- **"Python spirit":** I had never heard of a "python spirit" until a couple of years ago, when it was suddenly everywhere. It was spoken of in the context of everything from peer pressure to bad relationships, but closer inspection reveals the translation – and identity of it as a special sort of unique snakelike spirit – is incorrect. "Python" is the literal rendering of the Greek in Acts 16:16, usually translated properly as a "spirit of divination." The use of the python was in connection with the god Apollo, meaning the girl was possessed with the spirit of divination as a medium for that specific Greek god. It has nothing to do with the colloquial context with which it has come to be associated.

- **The "Spirit of Jezebel":** There is nothing in the Bible that identifies Jezebel as a transferrable spirit. Jezebel was a human being, wife of Ahab, who was an extremely wicked king in Israel's history (1 Kings 16:30, 1 Kings 21:25-26). The Bible tells us Ahab deliberately sought out Jezebel because he was so wicked, and we learn she was of the royal house of Ethbaal, king of the Sidonians, known for its pagan ways (1 Kings 16:29-34). That should tell us right then and there that the story of Jezebel is a lot more complex than we make it out to be, and many of our associations with Jezebel have been written in and amended by cultural associations. Jezebel was not a prostitute, a morally loose woman, an adulterer, or a seducer. In fact, the dynamics of Ahab and Jezebel were meant to be a reflection on the wickedness of Ahab's leadership, not Jezebel. The story is not one of a weak man or a weak leadership, but by a king who knew how to rebel against God in the most relevant way possible…and unfortunately, as we tend to do in society, our entire focus has been on the woman instead of the man. She did persecute the prophets, particularly Elijah, under the auspices of Ahab, who was comfortable having her do the dirty work (1 Kings 18:4, 9-15, 1 Kings 19:1-3). Despite this fact, there is not a single verse where it ever says Elijah was sent to Jezebel (1 Kings 18:1-3, 16-19). They represent a sense of codependency with each other, knowing that certain responses will illicit things in the other (1 Kings 21:1-29), and as Ahab desired to be wicked by pursuing Jezebel in the first place, he was successful as we can see from her reign as queen. Some feel that the reference to a woman named Jezebel in Revelation 2:20 proves there is a "spirit of Jezebel," but close examination of the text indicates such was either the woman's name or is a reference to someone being an idolater in a Jezebel pattern (the followers of the church brought her in and followed her wicked ways), but nothing indicates that there was a spirit of Jezebel present in that woman. None of this identifies Jezebel as a "spirit," and there is no such thing as a "spirit of Jezebel." Moreover, many of the characteristics associated with her "spirit," such as a desire for control (she didn't have to desire power; she had it) disunity (she and Ahab were perfectly united against the things and people of God), usurping authority (Jezebel never once usurped any authority; she did everything she did with the auspice and approval of Ahab; plus, she was queen so that meant she had authority); or of sexual promiscuity (we discussed this already). The characteristics we have attributed to a "Jezebel spirit" were not within Jezebel. It's not to say that Jezebel was not wicked or was not a follower of God, because both statements are true, and she certainly had her own issues as pertain to good leadership and integrity. This trend of labeling everyone and everything we don't like as Jezebel, however, proves we lack true Biblical understanding of spirits and Bible figures.

- **The "Pharisee spirit":** There's no question if we read the Scriptures that the Pharisees were often something else. They were among the most learned men in Biblical law, both written and oral traditions, and were the sought-out individuals by the common man to explain the finer points of the law to those who brought inquiries, wanted to discover spiritually legal loopholes, or wanted greater explanation of the law in their society. Jesus discussed extensively with the Pharisees, on more than one occasion, and addressed their ways, the ways they were rebelling against God, and more than anything else, the way they deceived others with their false piety (Matthew 23:1-36). If we study the words of Jesus, the Pharisees had many issues; they didn't just have one spirit present among all of them. This also doesn't mean there is a singular spirit known as a "Pharisee spirit." Never once did Jesus accuse them of having such a specific spirit, and it is evident not all of them had such vehemently negative characteristics, as Gamaliel in the book of Acts was sympathetic to the issues of the early church (Acts 5:34-39. Acts 22:3).

- **The "spirit of insecurity":** I attribute this oft-referenced imaginary spirit to a play on modern psychology that often credits poor behavior to insecurity or low self-esteem, identifying it as a root cause of all misdoings in the world today. I don't deny that insecurity exists, but the characteristics of insecurity are far different than those of arrogance or deliberate sin against others, and there is no indication anywhere in the Scriptures that there is such a thing as a spirit of insecurity or one of low self-esteem.

- **The "spirit of offense":** Nowadays we try to force unity without the Spirit in a blind hope we can keep everyone together, even in the face of something seriously wrong or sinful. The Bible does not encourage connection with others at all costs, and while it gives us the perfect system for handling offense (taking it to the person, taking a witness, and taking it before the church, Matthew 5:23-26), the Bible does allow for the fact that offense happens. When the Bible speaks of offense, it is not in the same way as we understand it today. In Bible times, people understood sin to be interconnected, and offense happened when one person sinned against someone and, in some way, their sin caused someone else to sin. The original word for "offense" translates as "trap" or "snare," and it implies someone else has set a snare or a trap for someone else, causing them to be in trouble, in a bad place, to sin, or to do something to hurt someone else. The Bible is not blind to the fact that offense does occur between people because of sin, but that doesn't mean being offended is a sin, nor does it mean that offense is a spirit. Offense is a response to an offender's actions, a condition that can lead to other issues and spirits, such as woundedness or brokenness, but offense is not, anywhere, a spirit. For this reason, it is essential we, as believers, make every effort to avoid being people who cause offense and conduct ourselves with the love of the Lord.

*The Deeds of the Antichrist, Luca Signorelli (c. 1445-1523)*

- **A "critical or judgmental spirit":** We are warned against being judgmental in multiple places in the Bible (Matthew 7:1-6, Matthew 12:7, Mark 4:24, Luke 6:37, John 8:15, Romans 2:1-3). We are told it is reserved for God (not that it stops anyone), but nowhere is judgment ever spoken of as being a spirit. Being critical wasn't a Biblical designation, and the closest thing we might see in Scripture is the idea of being contentious (Proverbs 21:19, Proverbs 26:21, Proverbs 27:15, Romans 2:8, 1 Corinthians 11:16), or a difficult, nagging person. This is nowhere identified, however, as a spirit in proper translation of the Word. In more modern paraphrases, judgment is sometimes called a "critical spirit," but this is not a proper rendering of the passage.

- **A "religious spirit":** If there is one thing you do not want to be labeled as in this day and age, it is being "religious." Being religious is associated with being legalistic, traditional, into rules, and a catch-all term for someone who says things others don't want to hear. It has become a slur, something to indicate an individual doesn't know God except through religion, and that they have no real relationship with Him. I strongly dislike the way we use the word, as if it's some sort of derogatory identity, because such detracts from our ancestors, who would have all identified themselves as religious people in a positive light. For thousands of years, religion identified those systems that sought to follow God and those who were identified with it were those who made their best efforts to do His will. Creating religion as a "spirit" to be rebuked or combatted defies James 1:27:

    *RELIGION THAT GOD THE FATHER ACCEPTS AS PURE AND WITHOUT FAULT [UNDEFILED] IS THIS: CARING FOR ORPHANS AND WIDOWS [2:1-13, 15-16; EX. 22:22; DEUT. 14:29] WHO NEED HELP [IN THEIR TROUBLE/DISTRESS/PERSECUTION], AND KEEPING YOURSELF FREE FROM THE WORLD'S EVIL INFLUENCE [UNSTAINED/UNPOLLUTED BY THE WORLD; 4:4-10].*
    If we are truly people of God, truly those identified with the values of religion, we should push ourselves to good works.

- **"Mantles":** When people speak of mantles and putting on mantles, it is never connected to spirits or to spiritual divination, but it is often exactly what it is. Let us understand that mantling is a legitimate

Biblical practice and is done in combination with the ordination of a prophet (1 Kings 19:19, 2 Kings 2:9-14). It signified a passing of the ministry from a teacher to a student, from one prophet with authority who recognized the authority of a new prophet, and there is nothing wrong with the practice in a Biblical context. This is not how it is being used, however, as we often hear it spoken of in the context of putting on the mantle of another minister, usually deceased, or wondering where the person is to take up that "mantle." The principle of spooky mantling is often heralded by people who express great dissatisfaction with the modern church and feel things were more spiritual or more exciting in the signs and wonders department in a different time, believing therefore that those of old had a stronger mantling, or ministry purpose, than we have today. There is nothing to suggest such is Biblical, and if anything, people into this concept are calling up the spirits of deceased people and attempting to put on their characteristics, thus calling into play the principles of mediums, possession, and divination.

- **The Antichrist:** The antichrist is often not spoken of as a spirit, but as a literal being, one who is to enter the picture of world history at just the right time to incite his reign of terror. Many point to the beast of Revelation as the antichrist, but the word "antichrist" is not found anywhere in Revelation's prophecy. The teaching on the antichrist is found in the writings of 1 and 2 John:

*My dear children [2:1], these are the last days [it is the last hour; suggesting urgency, though not claiming the end was near]. [Just as] you have heard that the enemy of Christ [antichrist] is coming, and now many enemies of Christ [antichrists; false teachers; 2:22; 2 John 7] are already here. This is how we know that these are the last days [it is the last hour]. These enemies of Christ were in our fellowship, but they left us [they went out from us; probably to form a rival fellowship]. They never really belonged to us [but they were not of us]; [for] if they had been a part of us, they would have stayed [remained; abided] with us. But they left, and this shows [or so that it would be shown] that none of them really belonged to us.*

*You have the gift [anointing; probably the Holy Spirit and/or the spiritual gift of the Word of God applied to their hearts; v. 24; 1 Sam. 16:13; Is. 61:1; John 16:13; 2 Cor. 1:21-22] that the Holy One gave you [from the Holy One; a reference to God the Father (Ps. 71:22) or more likely Jesus Christ (Mark 1:24; John 6:69)], so you all know the truth [or have knowledge; know]. I do not write to you because you do not know the truth but because you do know the truth. And you know that no lie comes from the truth.*

*Who is the liar? It is the person who does not accept [denies; repudiates] Jesus as the Christ [Messiah; Anointed One]. This is the enemy of Christ [antichrist]: the person who does not accept [denies; repudiates] the Father and His [the] Son. Whoever does not accept [denies; repudiates] the Son does not have the Father. But whoever confesses [acknowledges; accepts] the Son has the Father, too.* (1 John 2:18-23)

*This is how you can know [recognize] God's Spirit: Every spirit [a teacher/prophet claiming inspiration from the Spirit] who confesses [acknowledges] that Jesus Christ came to earth as a human [in the flesh] is from God. And every spirit who refuses to say this about Jesus [does not confess/acknowledge Jesus] is not from God [2 John 7]. It is the spirit of the enemy of Christ [antichrist; 2:18, 22], which you have heard is coming, and now he is already in the world.* (1 John 4:2-3)

*[For] Many false teachers [deceivers] are in [have gone out into] the world now [Mark 13:5-6, 22] who do not confess that Jesus Christ came to earth as a human [in the flesh]. Anyone who does not confess this is a false teacher [the deceiver] and an enemy of Christ [the antichrist; one who radically opposes Christ; 1 John 2:18, 22; 4:3].* (2 John 1:7)

The antichrist is also seen in the apocryphal Revelation of John the Theologian. In this apocryphal work, the antichrist imagery parallels that of Daniel's prophecy:

*And again I said: Lord, reveal to me what he is like. And I heard a voice saying to me: The appearance of his face is dusky; the hairs of*

*HIS HEAD ARE SHARP, LIKE DARTS; HIS EYEBROWS LIKE A WILD BEAST'S; HIS RIGHT EYE LIKE THE STAR WHICH RISES IN THE MORNING, AND THE OTHER LIKE A LION'S; HIS MOUTH ABOUT ONE CUBIT; HIS TEETH SPAN LONG; HIS FINGERS LIKE SCYTHES; THE PRINT OF HIS FEET OF TWO SPANS; AND ON HIS FACE AN INSCRIPTION, ANTICHRIST; HE SHALL BE EXALTED EVEN TO HEAVEN, AND SHALL BE CAST DOWN EVEN TO HADES, MAKING FALSE DISPLAYS. AND THEN WILL I MAKE THE HEAVEN BRAZEN, SO THAT IT SHALL NOT GIVE MOISTURE UPON THE EARTH; AND I WILL HIDE THE CLOUDS IN SECRET PLACES, SO THAT THEY SHALL NOT BRING MOISTURE UPON THE EARTH; AND I WILL COMMAND THE HORNS OF THE WIND, SO THAT THE WIND SHALL NOT BLOW UPON THE EARTH.* (The Apocryphal Revelation of Saint John the Theologian)[12]

This passage, along with those of 1 and 2 John, affirm the concept that the power of the antichrist is a spirit, one that manifests in more than one person in this world for a specified period of time (three years, or possibly up to three thousand years in prophetic understanding) through idolatry, power, violence, and might, and is against that of Christ, and against the anointing of those who follow after Christ, rather than one specific person to arise at a specified point in history.

## **Familiar spirits**

Familiar spirits are a category of spirit all their own, mentioned in multiple places throughout the Old Testament. We can identify their purpose and their work as a lesser demon by their title: they are familiar, or around all of us, with knowledge of our lives and what makes us "tick." The term "familiar spirit" is an old European term used to describe close spirits, reflecting the origins of the word "familiar" as the concept of one who was in a household. The familiar spirit, therefore, reflects to this kind of imagery.

*16th century image of a witch feeding her familiar spirits.*

They know about us, they know what we do, they know what is important to us, and they know just how to handle things so we will buy into their deception. This term was used to describe an *obe* in Hebrew, which referred to a vessel or a container (such as a medium was a "vessel" of a familiar spirit) and *pytho* in the Greek, associated with the god, Apollo.

Passages about familiar spirits include:

*DO NOT GO [TURN] TO MEDIUMS OR FORTUNE-TELLERS [WIZARDS] FOR ADVICE [AND DO NOT SEEK THEM], OR YOU WILL BECOME UNCLEAN [IN A RITUAL SENSE]. I AM THE LORD YOUR GOD.* (Leviticus 19:31)

*I WILL BE [SET MY FACE] AGAINST ANYONE WHO GOES [TURNS] TO MEDIUMS AND FORTUNE-TELLERS [WIZARDS] FOR ADVICE, BECAUSE THAT PERSON IS BEING UNFAITHFUL TO [PROSTITUTING HIMSELF AGAINST] ME. SO I WILL CUT HIM OFF FROM HIS PEOPLE.* (Leviticus 20:6)

*A MAN OR WOMAN WHO IS A MEDIUM OR A FORTUNE-TELLER [WIZARD] MUST BE PUT TO DEATH. YOU MUST STONE THEM TO DEATH; THEY HAVE BROUGHT IT [BLOOD] ON THEMSELVES [19:31; 20:6].* (Leviticus 20:27)

*WHEN YOU ENTER THE LAND THE LORD YOUR GOD IS GIVING YOU, DON'T LEARN TO DO THE HATEFUL [DETESTABLE; ABHORRENT; ABOMINABLE] THINGS THE OTHER NATIONS DO. DON'T LET ANYONE AMONG YOU OFFER A SON OR DAUGHTER AS A SACRIFICE IN THE FIRE [12:30-31]. DON'T LET ANYONE USE MAGIC [DIVINATION; EX. 7:11; EZEK. 21:21] OR WITCHCRAFT, OR TRY TO EXPLAIN THE MEANING OF SIGNS [AUGURY OR SORCERY]. DON'T LET ANYONE TRY TO CONTROL OTHERS WITH MAGIC [CAST SPELLS], AND DON'T LET THEM BE MEDIUMS [CONSULT/INQUIRE OF GHOSTS OR SPIRITS] OR TRY TO TALK WITH THE SPIRITS OF [CONSULT] DEAD PEOPLE [1 SAM. 28]. THE LORD HATES [DETESTS] ANYONE WHO DOES THESE THINGS. BECAUSE THE OTHER NATIONS DO THESE THINGS, THE LORD YOUR GOD WILL FORCE [DISPOSSESS] THEM OUT OF THE LAND AHEAD OF YOU. BUT YOU MUST BE INNOCENT [BLAMELESS] IN THE PRESENCE OF THE LORD YOUR GOD. THE NATIONS YOU WILL FORCE OUT [DISPOSSESS] LISTEN TO PEOPLE WHO USE MAGIC [DIVINATION] AND WITCHCRAFT, BUT THE LORD YOUR GOD WILL NOT LET YOU DO THOSE THINGS.* (Deuteronomy 18:9-13)

*THEN SAUL SAID TO HIS SERVANTS [ADVISERS; ATTENDANTS], "FIND ME A WOMAN WHO IS A MEDIUM [IS A NECROMANCER; HAS A FAMILIAR SPIRIT] SO I MAY GO AND ASK HER*

*WHAT WILL HAPPEN [INQUIRE OF/CONSULT HER]." HIS SERVANTS ANSWERED, "THERE IS A MEDIUM [A NECROMANCER; WOMAN WITH A FAMILIAR SPIRIT] IN ENDOR."* (1 Samuel 28:7)

*JOSIAH DESTROYED [REMOVED; GOT RID OF] THE MEDIUMS, FORTUNE-TELLERS [SPIRITUALISTS], HOUSE GODS, AND IDOLS. HE ALSO DESTROYED [REMOVED; GOT RID OF] ALL THE HATED GODS [DETESTABLE/ABOMINABLE PRACTICES] SEEN IN THE LAND OF JUDAH AND JERUSALEM. THIS WAS TO OBEY [FULFILL; CONFIRM] THE WORDS OF THE TEACHINGS [LAW; TORAH] WRITTEN IN THE BOOK [SCROLL] HILKIAH THE PRIEST HAD FOUND IN THE TEMPLE [HOUSE] OF THE LORD.* (2 Kings 23:24)

*SAUL DIED BECAUSE HE WAS NOT FAITHFUL TO THE LORD AND DID NOT OBEY [ACTED UNFAITHFULLY AGAINST THE WORD OF] THE LORD. HE EVEN WENT TO A MEDIUM AND ASKED HER FOR ADVICE [COUNSEL].* (1 Chronicles 10:13)

*HE MADE HIS CHILDREN PASS THROUGH [SACRIFICED HIS CHILDREN IN THE] FIRE IN THE VALLEY OF BEN HINNOM. HE PRACTICED MAGIC AND WITCHCRAFT AND TOLD THE FUTURE BY EXPLAINING SIGNS AND DREAMS [DIVINATION; AUGERY]. HE GOT ADVICE FROM [DEALT WITH] MEDIUMS AND FORTUNE-TELLERS [SPIRITUALISTS; SPIRITISTS; DEUT. 18:9-13]. HE DID MANY THINGS THE LORD SAID WERE WRONG [MUCH EVIL IN THE LORD'S SIGHT/EYES], WHICH MADE THE LORD ANGRY.* (2 Chronicles 33:6)

*SOME PEOPLE SAY, "ASK THE MEDIUMS AND FORTUNE-TELLERS [NECROMANCERS; SPIRITISTS], WHO WHISPER [OR CHIRP] AND MUTTER [USING INCANTATIONS TO CALL UP SPIRITS; 1 SAM. 28:8-11], WHAT TO DO." BUT I TELL YOU THAT PEOPLE SHOULD ASK THEIR GOD FOR HELP. WHY SHOULD PEOPLE WHO ARE STILL ALIVE ASK SOMETHING FROM THE DEAD? [OR "SHOULD NOT A NATION CONSULT THEIR GODS, ASKING THE DEAD ON BEHALF OF THE LIVING?"; IN THIS INTERPRETATION THE QUOTATION CONTINUES TO THE END OF THE VERSE].* (Isaiah 8:19)

*THE EGYPTIANS WILL BE AFRAID [LOSE HEART],*
  *AND I WILL RUIN THEIR PLANS [CONFUSE THEIR COUNSEL].*
*THEY WILL ASK ADVICE FROM [CONSULT] THEIR IDOLS AND SPIRITS OF THE DEAD,*
  *FROM THEIR MEDIUMS AND FORTUNE-TELLERS [MAGICIANS; NECROMANCERS].*
(Isaiah 19:3)

Historically speaking, familiar spirits were considered spirits that would assist with the practice of magic because they were close to humanity and to those who engaged in the practice of magic. This was an intimate part of divination, fortune-telling, and work as a psychic or medium, because familiar spirits would aid practitioners in the information and statements used in magical practice. As a rule, modern practitioners of neopagan witchcraft (Wicca, for example) don't talk about familiar spirits like they did in ancient times in Europe, where identification of familiar spirits was common, but this does not mean such a spirit no longer exists.

Have you ever watched programs with psychics or mediums, such as *Long Island Medium*, *Crossing Over with John Edwards*, or read books by people such as Edgar Cayce or James Van Praagh? If you have, one of the first questions you probably have, as a believer, is where do they get their information from? Often it appears they are getting some of the information right at least some of the time, and if you know about the Biblical prohibitions on such, the question is, how do they get it right if it's not of God? The answer is through familiar spirits.

It should be said that many individuals who claim to operate as psychics, mediums, or who operate in divination (we shall speak of these individuals and what they specifically do in our chapter on witchcraft and magic) are clever deceivers who know how to create an atmosphere prime for stealing people's money. The spirit of brokenness many feel in the time of grief or loss can lead people to do desperate things, and there are many who hope for and seek the assistance of such people to try and bring grief. Careful observation shows psychics and mediums are quick to give vague and leading information about a distant loved one, information that can apply to anyone, and then in the emotional state of a distraught person, they are fast to provide supplementary information to the psychic or medium who is quick to fill-in the blanks. It's not always as spiritual as it might sound; sometimes it is nothing more than a clever and deceptive mind game.

This is not always the case, however, and when correct information appears to exist, it is from the work of a familiar spirit, one assisting the psychic or medium in their practice of witchcraft. The Bible makes it clear that whether we believe in the resurrection of the dead, or not, the dead are not in the realm of the living, giving information to those who are alive:

*Therefore we are always confident, knowing that while we are at home in the body, we are absent from the Lord. For we walk by faith, not by sight. Instead, I say that we are confident and willing to be absent from the body*

*AND TO BE PRESENT WITH THE LORD.* (2 Corinthians 5:6-8, MEV)

*THE LIVING KNOW THEY WILL DIE,*
  *BUT THE DEAD KNOW NOTHING.*
*DEAD PEOPLE HAVE NO MORE REWARD,*
  *AND PEOPLE FORGET THEM [THE MEMORY OF THEM IS FORGOTTEN].* (Ecclesiastes 9:5)

*YOU WILL TURN BACK INTO THE DUST OF THE EARTH AGAIN [THE DUST WILL RETURN TO THE EARTH AS IT WAS],*
  *BUT YOUR [AND THE] SPIRIT WILL RETURN TO GOD WHO GAVE IT [3:21; GEN. 2:7; 3:19].*
(Ecclesiastes 12:7)

Is it possible to have a spiritual experience where you see a deceased individual glorified with the Father (perhaps in a vision or a dream)? Yes, because this is a spiritual vision that is not playing a divine guessing-game with information. Such can bring comfort and assurance and has a radically different purpose. That individual is seen where they are now – with the Lord – not busying themselves with parlor tricks. The difference is the spirit behind the work, and the purpose is the result.

## **The spirits of cultural lore**

Every culture in the world has specific traditions and mythologies that relate to the spirits that help, hurt, bother, or sometimes torture the inhabitants of a society. Let us understand that people of history were not always well-cultured or educated, and societies did not always have a proper understanding of medicine, ailment, or science behind issues and illnesses people may have had. Superstition was common, and people genuinely believed problems and issues had supernatural causes. There are dozens and dozens of lists of spirits and demons that inflicted people in various ways, everything from playing tricks to causing death. They are a fascinating look into the mentality of people long ago, and in some ways, not that different from where we are, today.

The most fascinating aspect of cultural spirits and folklore tradition around spirits is the way that many overlap. Even though the traditions of these creatures and beings are found in completely different parts of the world, they often hold similar characteristics to other spirits in other places. This tells us a few things about the ancients and their spiritual understandings: most had fears that overlap, many people had experiences that were much like those in other parts of the world, and humanity has always had the same questions about life, death, and the spiritual world. Recognizing these things helps us to sort through some of the information about these different spirits and come to a better understanding of what is real from what is exaggerated.

It is not possible to cover every cultural spirit present the world over, but here are some common ones that we do find reference to in our modern world and in modern reference:

- **Boogeyman:** A non-specific monster who is used in different cultures to scare children into behaving well. Because he is not identified with any specified characteristics, the Boogeyman is often associated within the minds of each child who sees it. It is from an old term meaning "hobgoblin." Which is considered a mischievous, trouble-making spirit. The concept of the Boogeyman is worldwide, and in different cultures is known as the Sack Man, El Coco, Babau, Butzemann, Bala, Newanay Mama, Talasam, babaroga, Bonhomme Sept-Heures, Old Hag, Quankus, Awd Goggie, Der Schwarze Mann, Jumbi, Ou-wu, Tonton Macoute, Marabecca, L'Uomo Nero, and Papa Doc.[13]

- **Cambion:** The term for the offspring of an incubus or a succubus and a human. Also known as a changeling, anunnaki, Grendel, mooncalf, Merlin, or Nephilim.[14]

- **The demons of King James:** In 1591, King James set out to write his *Daemonologie* and identified four categories of spirits: Spectra (spirits that trouble houses and solitary places), obsession (spirits that haunt people and trouble them at specific times of the day), possession (spirits that enter a person and trouble them), and faeries (spirits that prophesy, consort, and transport).[15]

- **Drude:** A demonic night spirit associated with nightmares. Common in German folklore.[16]

- **Dwarf:** A mythical creature that lives in the mountains of the earth, working in the various forms of smithing, mining, and crafting. They are associated with wisdom and work as wise beings. In modern times, they are portrayed as very short and unattractive.[17]

- **Elves:** Supernatural beings found in European and Asian cultural folklore, especially Germanic countries. At one time in history, they were associated with demons. They were associated with an assortment of things, including illness, sexual pranks, misfortune, or good fortune. In other cultures, they are known as Yokai, Ayakashi, Mononoke, or Mamono.[18]

- **Fairy:** A mythical being with metaphysical and supernatural characteristics. It has been used to describe all magical creatures and also a specific classification of them, with an unknown origin. According to the King James *Daemonologie*, they were beings of magical powers that functioned much as familiar spirits do. They were known to sometimes play pranks and giving them sweets or other goods was believed to keep them happy and content. An example of a type of fairy is a leprechaun.[19] Pixies are often associated with fairies or sprites, but in the traditional folklore, they were regarded as a separate race and at warring odds with one another.[20]

- **Ghost:** A spirit believed to be the soul or spirit of a dead person that is now haunting, infiltrating, or appearing in some form to the living. A belief in ghosts is found worldwide, from the most ancient times, and has been a common subject and theme among cultural and religious practice of magic, present on every continent. They are also known as apparitions, haunts, phantoms, poltergeists, shades, specters, spirits, spooks, and wraiths.[21]

- **Ghoul:** An evil monster or spirit found in Arabic mythology. They are believed to inhabit burial grounds or graveyards and eat human flesh. Worldwide, they are also known as aswang, ghola, or jinn.[22]

- **Gnome:** A spirit present in magic and alchemy, originating in the Renaissance period. They live underground, in the earth. We most typically see gnomes as garden statues or small figurines, representing the principle of a household deity used to bring good luck or ward off evil spirits. Gnome-like creatures are found all over the world as dwarfs, chalybes, telchines, dactyls, Wroclaw's dwarfs, tomtes, and elementals.[23]

- **Goblin:** A monster, found most often in European folklore, but also found in equivalent forms worldwide. Pictured as small and hideous in appearance, mischievous or downright evil, and greedy with magical powers. They are like brownies, dwarves, gnomes, imps, and kobolds and are known in other parts of the world as dokkaebi, pukwudgie, kallikantzaros, and hobogoblins.[24]

- **Gremlin:** A mythological creature like an imp, interested in making trouble and working machinery or mechanics.[25]

- **Imp:** A being used in the context of a familiar spirit for a witch, often thought of as like a fairy or gnome in folklore.[26]

*Incubus, 1870*

- **Incubus and succubus:** Even though angels and demons are believed to exist without sex, an incubus is a demon in male form who seek to engage in sexual activity with women. A succubus is the female version of an incubus, seeking to seduce men. The purpose is to alter the genetic experience of humanity by introducing demons therein. The mythologies of both incubus and succubus date back thousands of years to prehistoric times and are present in Genesis (the flood myth), Arabia, Egypt, India, Brazil, Germany, Zanzibar, Chile, Sweden, and Turkey. Some demons with these same characteristics, known by different names, include Batibat, Gancanagh, Krampus, Al Basti, Huli jing, revenant, spirit spouse, Xana, Pontianak, and Moura Encantada.[27,28]

- **Revenant:** A visible ghost or a living corpse that is believed to be revived from death to haunt or bother the living. In the 1100s, it was believed a revenant was someone who died and did not receive a Christian rite of burial, and in the 1700s, the Greeks believed a revenant was the body of a deceased excommunicant. Also, like draugr, dybbuk, and gjenganger.[29]

- **Sprite:** A fairy-like, supernatural being, usually used for elves and fairies. A water sprite is a spirit associated with the water, such as a water nymph.[30]

- **Troll:** Beings isolated to mountains, rocks, or caves that live in small family dwellings and are generally old and ugly in appearance. They are from Norse and Scandinavian mythologies and folklore.[31]

- **Vampire:** An otherworldly being identified from ancient times as present in Slavic, Mesopotamian, Hebrew, Greek, and Roman cultures for thousands of years. They subsist by feeding on the life of the living, usually in the form of blood. Historically speaking, they were usually considered revenants of evil beings, the deceased spirits of suicide victims or witches, a corpse with a bad spirit, or someone living who was bitten by a vampire. The imagery we use to describe vampires today is more modern, emerging in the 1700s. This is like the Irish dwarf legend of Abhartach and the German Nachzehrer.[32]

- **Werewolf:** A mythological human being with the ability to transform into a wolf or wolf-like being originating in Europe and transforming throughout time. This echoes of ancient mythologies where people could change into wolves, especially in ancient Greek and Latin writings. Similar mythologies are found throughout the world, including werecats, werebears, Damarchus, kitsune, and nagual.[33]

- **Zombie:** Similar to a revenant, a zombie is a part of the realm of the "undead" existing as a human corpse without a soul. They are raised from the dead through witchcraft or magic in Haitian Voodoo understanding. It does not play a part in the traditional or formal aspects of the religion but is a part of the superstition of the belief system.[34]

## **Regional spirits**

When it comes to identifying spirits in areas, we find the specific nature of spirits and the mannerisms and character we often see in people present in an area or region. It's not to say that such is always a negative thing, nor is it meant in a sense of judgment. It's an awareness, as something we may specifically have to deal with or encounter in a ministry situation when we go into an area or region.

*THEN JESUS ASKED HIM, "WHAT IS YOUR NAME?"*

*HE ANSWERED, "MY NAME IS LEGION [A LEGION WAS ABOUT 5,000 SOLDIERS IN THE ROMAN ARMY], BECAUSE WE ARE MANY SPIRITS." HE BEGGED JESUS AGAIN AND AGAIN NOT TO SEND THEM OUT OF THAT AREA [LAND; REGION].* (Mark 5:9-10)

Legion is an example of a regional spirit, one that inhabits a specific area or specific region. On the surface, they might seem like customs, interactions, or cultural ways of life that have been somewhere for ages, but those ages have come into practice through different spiritual accesses throughout history. How they get there depends on the spiritual history as well as secular history, different governments involved in the interactions with that nation, occupations, slavery, politics, and social customs.

For example, I have dealt with people from nations that are, very clearly, out of touch with the fact that they lie. It's not one person, or two, or a few, but every interaction I have had with an individual in those countries consist of lies. They can range from the severe or very serious to the sublime, but underneath all of them, the major commonality is a singular thread of dishonesty. When confronted, the individuals who lie don't see it as lying. They see it as their unique interaction, their way of communication, and many feel it is very rude of me to point out their dishonesty. They feel that I should be forbearing with it, view it as a part of who they are, and overlook the fact they have spoken outright lies.

This made me curious about the root causes of such prevalent behaviors. It's one thing when you meet a dishonest person or two, but seeing it so commonplace, over and over again, with the same responses each time made me curious where such a custom could evolve. In researching the history of the nations, I was able to see how the lying spirit took root in their people. It became a way of life, a custom, a manner of dealing with others and interaction in such a way that nobody thinks of it as lying; it's just how they live and handle one another.

Understanding regional spirits and how they operate requires time and effort to see the realities present where people live. It is easy to think we can go somewhere and just lay hands on people to see spirits depart, but when we recognize the influence of regional spirits, it explains to us one of the reasons why spirits don't always "let go" so easily.

*When an evil [defiling; unclean] spirit comes out of a person, it travels through dry [waterless; arid] places, looking for a place to rest, but it doesn't find it. So the spirit says, "I will go back to the house [the person] I left." When the spirit comes back, it finds the house still empty, swept clean, and made neat [put in order; fixed up]. Then the evil spirit goes out and brings seven other spirits even more evil [wicked] than it is, and they go in and live there. So the person has even more trouble than before [the last state of that person is worse than the first]. It is the same way [So it will be] with ·the evil people who live today [this evil generation]."* (Matthew 12:43-45)

If there is nothing there to help deliver the spirits over regions, deliverance for individuals will be difficult to maintain. It's not impossible, but it takes that much more effort, support, and personal discipline to keep a person connected to a place of deliverance and future victory in their lives. When a spirit is a part of who they understand themselves to be as people, in a cultural, regional, or identifying sense, it takes practical understanding to bring forth needed deliverance. Before anything else, however, we must take the time to properly define and recognize them.

## Caution in recognizing spirits

If spirits are attributes or characteristics, that means they are recognized by their actions, or their "fruit," if you will.

*You will know these people by what they do [their fruit]. Grapes don't come [Can you pick grapes...?] from thornbushes, and figs don't come from [and figs from...?] thorny weeds [thistles]. In the same way, every good [healthy; sound] tree produces good fruit, but a bad [rotten; diseased] tree produces bad fruit. A good [healthy; sound] tree cannot produce bad fruit, and a bad [rotten; diseased] tree cannot produce good fruit. Every tree that does not produce good fruit is cut down and thrown into the fire. In the same way, you will know these false prophets [them] by what they do [their fruit].* (Matthew 7:16-20)

The words of Matthew 7 are speaking on recognizing false prophets, but they apply across the board when it comes to the realm of recognizing any type of spirit. The "fruit" spoken of is not those things that we often associate with successes or failures; they are products, the results of something that is done. It is about quality over quantity, and the principle that the foundations of what we do or have make a difference in the result.

For example, I was approached not long ago by a pastor in Kenya whose second question to me was, "How many churches have you planted?" He was quick and excited to list the six churches he'd been involved in planting and wore that number as if it was a badge of pride. I answered his question, but I also stated that I was more interested in quality rather than quantity. We can plant as many churches as we like, but if those churches don't have the proper infrastructure, they won't be able to meet the needs that exist, and they will eventually fall apart as they attempt to expand without right foundations. This is an example of the way that we tend to chase after earthly ideals as pertain to ministry expansions without considering the proper nature of spiritual preparation and identification. On the surface, in the flesh, the fact that he was a part of six church plantings was something we'd find noble and spiritual. We don't have enough information, however, to make that assessment. Those churches could be unraveling or falling apart at the seams because they don't have the right foundations to bear fruit.

The same is true when it comes to identifying spirits. If we are given to look at things in a fleshly way rather than a spiritual foundation manner, we can easily get lost and miss the spirits present in something, be it an activity, a person, a project, or an issue. Thus, we must train ourselves to observe fruit, or product, rather than mere human expansions and expressions of being active or busy.

To be foundational, we should acquaint ourselves with Scriptural spirits: angels, demons, and spirits in the form of attributes and characteristics. The second thing we should do is understand how deliverance works, which we will see later in this book. Not every spirit is called to be cast out in the same manner. For example, the Bible speaks of binding those who are broken and casting out unclean spirits (Isaiah 61:1-3, Matthew 8:16, 8:31, Mark 1:39. Mark 6:13, Mark 16:17, Luke 9:1). The manner and way of healing still leads to freedom, but the method is most relevant to the product of spiritual fruit that must come forth from the process.

We should also realize not everything is classified, nor should be classified, as a "spirit." We are quick to label everything and anything we notice in people as a spirit today, and we consider that to be spiritual discernment. In contrast, however, what we see in the Scriptures about spirits proves labelling everything as a spirit to be a sign one doesn't have proper spiritual discernment. If discernment indicates one can sort through things and recognize differences, that means not everything is a spirit and not everything is a good spirit or a bad spirit. True deliverance ministry as well as true healing ministry requires the ability to tell things apart and know what is behind what might manifest on the surface.

Maintaining a position of non-judgment is also essential. While we sit on social media and argue over whether Christians can judge, that we judge things everyday or how far we can go in our positions about judgment, God still tells us we shouldn't judge, but we don't ever talk about why we shouldn't judge others. The reason is simple but creates spiritual complexities if we ignore its principle. Judgment is not just deciding for others what they should or shouldn't do but also assessing people from a worldly or fleshly perspective. Judgment assumes that things are the way they are based on surface appearances and on the product of quantity over quality instead of looking at what's there spiritually. For example, judgment would say a man dating a woman is a great catch because he's a church pastor, and for no other reason. Judgment says that woman is lucky to have that man, because he's a pastor, and he is going to be a great, spiritual catch for that woman. Why is it a judgment? Because it is making the assumption that these people aren't any more than they seem on the surface. There are plenty of pastors in this world who are abusive, mistreat their spouses, use drugs, or use the pulpit for personal gain. To just say a man is a great catch because he is a pastor is a judgment. It doesn't consider his personal character, why he is a pastor, what motivates him, or yes, the spirits that are a part of his life that might have weight over him. It makes assumptions; and if we are making judgments, we don't have room for the Spirit to speak to us about the realities in a situation. If we want to be truly discerning, we have to put down the judgments about people, things, and situations and start listening to what God reveals to us about the foundations behind them.

Recognizing spirits for what they are, what is behind them, and what may very well be behind things is not easy. It comes as we learn, as we grow, and as we understand the very fundamentals of spiritual foundation in our cosmos as well as our world. The only way we can do that is as we apply ourselves to the learning of these things, dedicating ourselves to understanding all spiritual things in deeper and more profound ways.

## **Chapter 3 Assignments**

- Write an essay (5-8 sentences) on the nature of spirits, what they are, and how they operate.
- There are numerous stories, legends, and fairy tales surrounding the list of cultural spirits that we find in this chapter. Research two stories or legends that contain one or more of these creatures and create a slideshow presentation on each story or legend and the way the cultural spirits are presented therein.
- Examining the different mythological spirits, you can see different parallels within the superstitions and beliefs of the cultures from which they emerged and the symptoms or actions they displayed. Looking at the church today, identify a new spirit – give it a name, identify its characteristics, and the circumstances from which it emerges.

*Ceiling painted dome Cupola angels fighting demons in Vatican Museums*

# - CHAPTER FOUR -
## Demonology and Mythology Around the World

He made us able [adequate; competent] to be servants of a new agreement from Himself to His people [covenant; Jer. 31:31–34; Luke 22:20]. This new agreement [covenant] is not a written law [of the letter], but it is of the Spirit. The written law [letter] brings death, but the Spirit gives life.
(2 Corinthians 3:6)

Traditions as relate to demons are found all over the world. Many different belief systems embrace different theories about demons and mythologies of demons, depending on the beliefs and principles taught therein. No matter where you go in the world, there has always been some belief system that relates to demons, the afterlife, and the role of the supernatural overlapping and coming to greet us, right where we are, with a message from heaven or from demons.

Mythology refers to the different histories and stories collected by different groups of people and then passed down, usually in the form of an oral tradition, for centuries. Mythologies are not "myths" in the sense we use the term today (referring to something as false or untrue), but as histories, things that remind people of where they came from and how they, as a people, fit into the greater scheme of creation and destiny. Mythologies are very revealing as to how people view themselves, what they think of who they are, how they got there, and most relevant to our discussion, what they believe about supernatural realms and interactions.

While angels do not exist worldwide in all belief systems, demons certainly do. There are also differing beliefs in different groups about the demonic and the way they believe interaction with the demonic changes or influences their ways of being. From the scary to the sublime, to those who believe engaging with the demonic can gain them influence or power, various mythologies and constructs give us insight into the different ways thoughts about the demonic influence the world we live in and the way we believe.

## Satan as a concept

Not everyone in the world acknowledges Satan as a personified spirit, fallen angel, or a being. One of the major distinctions between indigenous religion and later emerging religious strains is the idea, or concept, of a chief enemy in the being of Satan (or a larger, demonic adversarial being). Ancient pagan strains do acknowledge evil spirits, or demons, but they do not recognize the being, of an enemy, in Satan.

The being of Satan is recognized differently, if at all, around the world. It is even safe to say the being of Satan is recognized differently within different Christian groups. There are those who think Satan is more of a war against ourselves, against the bigger picture, or a general term for any enemy we might encounter.

## Modern Judaism

*Jews in Vienna, Austria, sometime in the last century.*

Modern-day Judaism is a mixed bag on spirituality and spiritual understandings, in general. If one has had limited exposure to modern Judaism, it is understandable to make the assumption that Judaism today looks just like it did in Bible times, but this is incorrect. After the temple was destroyed in 70 AD, the face of Judaism became very different. The sacrifices were abolished and the teachings of the Rabbis became front and center in the definitions and understandings of what it meant to be a Jew. Down through the ages, Judaism today does not even remotely resemble Biblical Judaism.

We have already looked at traditional Jewish notions, Scriptures, and writings as pertain to angels and demons, most in-depth, and we will not be reiterating those listings here, in this chapter. More of what we will look at pertains to Judaism in connection to those beliefs today, and ways those beliefs have changed.

Judaism today is, in many ways, different from it was even 100 or 50 years ago. The modern Jewish community faces a trauma-based identity, resulting from the Holocaust. As the staple of the heart of Judaism, the question is of the Jewish people and their call to stand as a set-apart spiritual people for God in this world. As we can see from the Old Testament, the ancestors of the Jewish people didn't always have the best of luck in discerning the answers to this question. The Jews of today are no different, although there are many who are still trying, especially to examine the issues from an ethical perspective.

Judaism is the modern-day product of the religion that evolved from tribal henotheism among the Hebrews to monotheism, starting with Abraham somewhere around 2,000 B.C. The keys of Jewish observance have always been keeping the Sabbath, observing the Old Testament festivals established in the Torah, study of the law of God as found in the Torah, and understanding the law within the context of life and society.

There are three main strains of Judaism: Orthodox, Conservative, and Reform. Messianic Judaism is considered a branch of Evangelical Christianity and is not considered to be valid Judaism. Orthodox is the most conservative, interpreting the Bible through the various traditions of the Rabbis throughout the ages; Conservative is in the middle, more interested in modern understandings of the law and more political involvements, and Reform is the most liberal of all groups, and most socially minded. The three branches of Judaism range from the seriously theological (almost to the point of being grave) among Orthodox Jews to, in some instances, denying the existence of God or adapting New Age or pagan principles in their spirituality. The various extremes in Judaism mean there isn't one singular position on the existence of demons and the demonic realm in Jewish thought. It depends on the Jew and their sect of Judaism, and sometimes even their own personal understandings, updates, and ideas about the spiritual realm.

The Orthodox, obviously, embrace the spiritual realms in full, both divine and demonic, as is evident from their strong understandings of the Old Testament and Pseudepigraphical documents. Their powerful interest in the mystical realms of spirituality have led to many different rabbis and instructors, all drawing on such commentaries, to expound on their understandings. Conservative Judaism is generally theistic in tone, embracing angels, as a general rule, within tradition. Some believe in Satan and evil, and some do not. Reform Judaism does embrace angels, but the way in which it is done may vary, or their existence may be rejected, all together, as may demons, as well.

Overall, it is safe to say that many Jews do believe in the existence of demons, but their concept of the realm of Satan and demons is radically different from the Christian concepts many of us have of them. They see them as opposers, as spiritual forces against God and against the people of God, without seeing the demonic realm as an impassioned source of temptation and wrong that often goes on in life. They believe strongly in the will of the individual, in the decision to make personal choices that are right or wrong, and attribute much of what happens to individuals as the result of their own decisions.

This emphasis on personal will has influenced other Jews away from the concept of Satan and demons, especially in a literal sense. They may believe in nothing; they may believe in everything; they may respect the decisions of others to believe as they do; and still, there are those who scoff at everything. When it comes to the afterlife, demons, and Satan, it is best to ask a Jewish person how they feel about such things.

*Zoroaster, founder of Zoroastrianism*

## Zoroastrianism

If you have never heard of Zoroastrianism, you are not alone. It was never the most popular religion in the world, as it is very ethnically driven. Because they do not receive converts, it is safe to say they are certainly not the most populated group today. That doesn't nullify its relevance in history, however. This group and its history reveal many primitive ideas about Satan, hell, and demons that have absorbed into religions with more religious prominence, down the ages.

Zoroastrianism is more properly asserted among adherents as *Mazdayasna* and as *Parsees* in India. The group was founded by its prophet, Zoroaster, sometime in the sixth century, B.C. It is one of the world's oldest monotheistic religions, originally present in Persia (modern-day Iran), with most of its modern-day followers in India. There are four modern strains, all of which vary slightly in their understanding of creation, the call of Zoroaster, and of the way in which the dualism of the world takes shape, but they all hold specific foundations that illuminate their purpose. It follows the belief of one deity, known as Ahura Mazda, who has an evil counterpart, though not equally as powerful, named Aura Mainyu This gives the religion a strong dualistic quality, describing the world and spiritual things through the viewpoints of good versus evil. Aura Mainyu is responsible for evil in this world, and human beings are caught up in the middle of this cosmic tumult as they come to a place of utilizing their free will and free choice for good or evil. Zarathustra received the message, as Ahura Mazda's messenger, to invite all human beings to choose between good and evil in the beings of Ahura Mazda and Aura Mainyu. Those who did more good than bad found their way into heaven, while those who had more bad deeds than good went to hell, with corresponding levels to match the wicked deeds done.[1]

The demons of Zoroastrianism contained six or seven archdemons, known as daevas:[2]

- **Aka Manah:** Demon of sensual desire (especially evil thought), sent to seduce Zoroaster.
- **Indra:** Also found in Vedic Hinduism, god of war and weather
- **Sauru:** The destroyer
- **Taurvi:** Opposer of wholeness
- **Zairitsha:** Poisons plants, keeping from immortality
- **Naonhaithya:** Discontentment
- **Aeshma:** – Wrath

Others include:[3]

- **Xeshm:** Additional wrath, specifically, wrath in opposition to obedience
- **Amesha Spenta:** Freezes the minds of creatures so they are unable to practice righteousness
- **Gannag Menog:** "Stinking spirit"
- **Akatash:** Perversion
- **Anashitih:** Strife
- **Anast:** Falsehood
- **Apaush** and **Spenjaghra:** Cause drought
- **Araska:** Vengeance
- **Ashmogh:** Apostasy
- **Az:** Greed
- **Buht:** Idolatry
- **Bushasp:** Sloth
- **Diwzhat:** Deception, hypocrisy
- **Eshm:** Wrath
- **Freptar:** Distraction and deception
- **Jeh:** Prostitution
- **Mitokht:** Skepticism, falsehood
- **Nang:** Disgrace, dishonor
- **Nas:** Pollution, contamination
- **Niyaz:** Gluttony, greed
- **Pinih:** Stinginess, hoarding
- **Rashk:** Envy
- **Sij:** Destruction
- **Sitoj:** Denies doctrine
- **Spazg:** Slander
- **Spuzgar:** Negligence
- **Taromaiti:** Scorn
- **Varun:** Unnatural lust
- **Astiwihad:** Demon of death
- **Aghash:** Evil eye
- **Dahak:** Serpent-like monster king
- **Cheshima:** Opposes clouds; source of earthquakes and whirlwinds
- **Kunda:** Carries sorcerers
- **Uta:** Brings about sickness found through ingestion
- **Vizaresh:** Fights for souls of the dead

## **Hinduism**

Hinduism is a complicated, albeit ancient, pagan religion, that may very well be the oldest existing religion in the world. Its emergence is a syncretism of ancient Indian cultures, traditions, and practices, and there is no one founder of Hinduism. While the merging of everything started somewhere around 500 BC, its origins go back more than six thousand years in time.

Because Hindu understanding of religion and religious system is so ancient, it consists of thousands of strains and different ideas about spiritual matters. There is not one singular perspective, nor one singular strain of tradition. As Hinduism also embraces the validity of any spiritual path, Hinduism also tends to absorb traditions and ideas wherever it is present. This can make Hinduism difficult to define, explain, and understand within a western construct.

*Vishnu as the Cosmic Man (Visharupa) (c. 1800)*

We can explain Hinduism as a pagan worship system involving polytheism, or the worship of many deities. Most Hindus explain their polytheism as emanations of one supreme deity (333,333,333 to be exact), and while this may be at the center of what they are trying to depict, their basic worship pattern is polytheistic, recognizing the emanations as different entities or deities. Hindus may practice forms of henotheism (worship one deity in primacy but not believe it is the supreme deity) or may worship different deities. The chief "trinity" (called trimurti) of deities in Hinduism are Brahma (creator), Shiva (destroyer), and Vishnu (protector). There are six different philosophies and two schools, known as Vedanta and Yoga. There are five modern Hindu trends that surround deities that are worshipped, and those deities include Vishnu, Shiva, Devi, and Smartism, where five different deities are worshiped and honored in the same way. There is no formalized hierarchy or governing body or specified holy scriptures. While there are many writings held in esteem, they are not considered on the same level of inspiration as the Bible is in Christianity. Many of their writings contain extensive mythologies, philosophical thought, and spiritual knowledge.

In the devotional walk of a Hindu, there are many rituals observed at home and include worship after bathing, singing, meditations, chants, and reciting scriptures. Many are vegetarian in desire to remain in keeping with their four aims of human life: *dharma* (righteousness), *artha* (wealth), *kama* (pleasure), and *moksa* (freedom from rebirth). Ceremonies, festivals or holidays, and sacrificial offerings are done at temples (considered the house of the gods), overseen by priests. Many Hindus stop at their temples daily or regularly to perform devotional offerings.

Hindus don't believe in heaven or hell, as we speak of in western religion. Instead, they believe in reincarnation, where they work on various spiritual issues over a period of several lives. Karma, or a register of the good or bad a person does, determines one's position in the cycle of rebirth and reincarnation. The ultimate liberation is to no longer incarnate, the state of *moksa*, spoken of earlier, which is seen as total detachment from all things in this world. The exact nature of this state is not always clearly defined and can also be seen as the ultimate spiritual enlightenment, a union with the divine or the gods, unselfishness, knowledge of self, or a sense of unity found throughout all existence.[4]

Even though heaven and hell aren't principles of Hinduism, Hindus do still recognize demons, similar in concept and duty to those found in Christianity at times, and at other times, more like ancient pagan spirits and demons we see in various international cultures. Sometimes these demons are worshiped, sacrificed to, or honored to keep them happy or content (thus not harming or tormenting anyone). There are many of them, including:[5]

- **Bhuta:** A deceased human being with a bad soul who died in tragedy. Also used to describe the five elements (ether, wind, fire, earth, and water).

- **Kali:** An angry form of the goddess Shakti, considered a mother and connected to Shiva. Operations serve to be fierce and aggressive to purge the desires of the ego from human beings.

- **Kali Yuga:** As with many things in Hinduism, Kali represents a duality, both a goddess and a demon, in one being. Kali Yuga is the more aggressive, evil-seeking demonic counterpart to the goddess of Kali.

- **Koka and Vikoka:** Kali's twins that instigate war and evil actions.

- **Panis:** A class of demons that watches over stolen cows, as the cow is seen as sacred in Hinduism.

- **Pishacha:** Carnivorous demons.

- **Rakshasas:** A race of evil beings found in Hindu mythology that seek to live in abandoned or lonely places that seek to eat human beings.

- **Vetala:** A vampire-like demon that exist as spirits inhabiting dead bodies.

- **Vinayakas:** Four different demons that seek to create difficulties and obstacles in life. They have since been merged into one deity, named Vinyaka, that is appointed by Shiva as Leader of the Ganas.

- **Vipracitti:** The chief of Danavas, which is a race of giants at war with the gods.

- **Virabhadra:** The patron of occult practices, created to fight Daksha.

## Buddhism

Buddhism is the religion that follows the teachings and principles of the Buddha, Siddhartha Gautama, a prince in India, who desired to discover true enlightenment as pertains to the suffering of humanity. Around 500 BC, he set out to find the answers he sought. Siddhartha Gautama left his world of privilege to meditate and contemplate the essential questions of life. The result of his search is what we now call Buddhism, which focuses on the individual's ability to attain enlightenment as they take steps to find the ultimate liberation from suffering.

Buddhism originated from within Hinduism and Hindu culture, which means many of the same base themes are found in Buddhism. Buddhism varies from Hinduism as it is non-theistic or does not acknowledge the existence of a god. There are some references to gods or goddesses here and there, but the understanding of them is different from both a pagan and theistic viewpoint. They are seen more as spirits of nature or having a supernatural presence that affect us here on earth. The religion is individual based, believing an individual can find the ultimate answer and source of enlightenment within themselves. Buddhism's central concept is that of *dukkha*, which relates to its principle of Four Noble Truths. *Dukkha* relates to dissatisfaction in life, or suffering, which we, in this life, cling to, even though we will not find what we seek in temporary, fleeting things that are not eternal. The Four Noble Truths revolve around *dukkha*: its existence, its rising up within an individual, finding ways to cease *dukkha*, and the path that leads to its ultimate end. It is this eternal path that sends people seeking, and that Buddhists seek to resolve throughout this life. The endless cycle of dissatisfaction keeps people returning life after life in the form of rebirth, suffering, and then dying again. *Karma* is produced as humans seek after things we should not, and keep us coming back, repeatedly, to resolve unresolved issues from our last life. When we are finally able to control *dukkha*, causing it to cease or at least be contained, we will attain nirvana, which is where one finds moksha, or liberation.

*Buddha in the Sky*

Buddhists believe in "the Middle Way," finding the middle path between extremes of nothing and constant hedonism. To this end, they follow The Noble Eightfold Path, which consists of Right Understanding, Right Thought, Right Speech, Right Action, Right Livelihood, Right Effort, Right Mindfulness, and Right Concentration.

Lay devotees follow the five precepts, which include abstinence from killing, stealing, sensual misconduct, lying, and intoxicants. Monks abstain from sex, eating before noon, jewelry, perfume, and entertainment, sleeping on high beds, dancing, singing, and receiving money. There is no scriptural canon, and every Buddhist tradition has its own unique texts.

There are approximately eighteen different schools of Buddhist thought, and all vary slightly in their understandings of Buddhism and the teachings of the Buddha. Many details are eschewed on his life and practices, and that means everyone understands the execution a little differently. Most focus on *dhyana*, or meditation, meant to focus the mind on something specific (such as breathing or a saying or mantra) to avoid disturbances in one's mental state by things around them. Some visualize, some practice thoughts on specific ideas or sayings that don't have simple answers, and some focus on the principle of being empty, or without underlying nature. They are also big on ritual devotions, such as prayer, prostration, offerings, pilgrimage, and chanting.[6]

Buddhists do not believe in angels, much because they do not believe in a central, theistic deity. This does not mean, however, that they have no teachings on demons. The Buddhist sutras teach on four types of demons: three internal, known as afflictions, illness, and death, and the external strain, which are considered demons from the spiritual world. Internal demons, such as negative mental actions (hatred, jealousy, greed) are psychological aspects that relate to the demonic. External demons tend to reflect cultural demons or concepts of cultural demons, present in India, Tibet, and other nations where Buddhism has historical ties.[7] Some external demons include:[8]

- **Yama**: Lord of death

- **Mara:** Evil king of demons who tempts Buddha

- **Yakshas** and **Rakshasas:** Devour people whole and eat human flesh

- **Khumbhandas:** Consume human spirits to sustain themselves

- **Hayagriva:** Demon protector of Tibetan horse dealers, with a horse head; chases Avalokiteshvara (the deity of compassion)

- **Alavaka:** Cannibal demon who destroyed an entire kingdom before the intervention of Buddha

- **Oni:** Horned demons with three fingers, three toes, who appear in many different colors. Torturers and jailers in the Buddhist afterlife

- **Preta:** Hungry ghosts that are insatiable, unsatisfiable, reborn beings or spirits trapped by the evil deeds they have done

## Islam

Islam is a religion that we hear about frequently in the news media, especially the past twenty or so years. Before this time, Islam was seldom discussed, and was certainly not a newsworthy story, without a prominent face in the international news scene. Due to media attention, it is safe to say that Islam is not always accurately portrayed, nor is it always fairly examined from a thorough angle. While we might see programs about Buddhism and Judaism that clarify not all Buddhists and Jews see things exactly the same way, the same is not done for Islam. For this reason, the average person knows little about Islam, except a view the media portrays that is frequently inaccurate.

Islam is the Arabic word for "submission" and describes the way a Muslim, or follower of Allah, desires to live their life. It is a monotheistic religion started in the seventh century A.D. by its founder, known as the Prophet Mohammed, in Saudi Arabia. Mohammed is regarded as the last and final prophet, the true apostle of the message, in a long line of prophets (those who have taught monotheism) sent to proclaim

*Pilgrims at Mecca*

the message of Islam to the world. Other acknowledged prophets include Adam, Enoch, Noah, Abraham, Isaac, Lot, Jacob, Moses, Aaron, Ezekiel, David, Solomon, Elijah, Jonah, John the Baptist, and Jesus. While the basic tenants of Islam are simple to understand, the way they are understood differ, depending on the school of Islam one follows. Muslims adhere to the Qur'an, which they believe contains the literal word of Allah. Muslims practice the Five Pillars of Islam: *shahadah* (the Islamic creed, "There is no god but Allah and Mohammed is his prophet;" faith), *salat* (prayer, done five times per day, in Arabic), *sawm* (fasting), *Hajj* (pilgrimage to Mecca), and *zakat* (almsgiving, charity; $1/40^{th}$ of one's income). Muslims believe a person's deeds will render them *Jannah* (eternal paradise) or *Jahannam* (hell) after the day of resurrection, where all of mankind will be judged.

Outside of these basics, the exact way the Qur'an is interpreted and the way an individual displays their faith varies, as dependent upon the school of Islam one follows. Each school of Islam holds to its own understandings of etiquette, social interaction, diet, social duty, and morality, with some ardently stricter than others. There are two main divisions of Islam: Shi'ite and Sunni and now two other divisions that are smaller, but prominent in world events, Ahmadiyya and Khawarij. Sunni Muslims comprise about 80% of the Muslim population worldwide and are known for their emphasis on traditions of the actual teachings and words of the Prophet Mohammed. They are an average Muslim you may encounter, with some variations of their schools of law. Shi'ite Islam is most popular in the Middle East, comprising about 10% of Islam worldwide. They claim their succession through the Prophet Mohammed's son-in-law and believe only some of his descendants can claim the right to scholarship and leadership authority in Islam. They do not believe Sunni Muslims are truly Muslim and trace themselves through different leaders. They are more extreme, more radical, and less mainline than Sunni Muslims. The Ahmadiyya Muslim community is a restoration movement within Islam, believing it needs to be returned to its true focus, lost over the centuries. They follow the lead of Mirza Ghulam Ahmad and are similar in doctrine to Sunni Islam. Khawarji are set apart from Shi'ite and Sunni Muslims, and are more radical in their understanding, with a long history of physical violence and political revolt.[9]

The more spiritual aspects of Islam are outlined in the six articles of faith. According to the Qur'an and the Hadith (traditions of Mohammed's teachings), every Muslim must believe:[10]

- In Allah as the only god
- Angels
- The holy books (*Taurat* – Torah, first five books of the Bible, Gospel – New Testament, and Qur'an)
- The prophets
- The day of judgment
- God's predestination

As Muslims embrace angels as the workers of Allah (they believe it was the Angel Gabriel who gave Mohammed the Qur'an), they believe they seek to execute judgment, provide messages, assist in the work of Allah, control the elements, and guardian angels, who protect the believe throughout their lives. Islam is also where the concept of a guardian angel comes from. Nine angels are mentioned by name in the Qur'an:

- *Jibreel* (Gabriel)
- *Mikaaeel* (Michael)
- *Izraaeel* (Ariel)
- *Israffeel* (Raphael)
- *Munkar Nakeer*
- *Kiraman Katibeen/Raqeeb Ateed*
- *Ridhwan*
- *Maalik*
- *Hafadha*

With an understanding of angels, Islam also embraces a belief in the demonic. Muslims do not see demons as fallen angels, as they do not believe they have the free will to disobey Allah. Instead, they believe they are unseen beings with free choice, known as *jinn*, or spirits.

The best-known *jinn* is *Iblis*, also known as *Shaytan*, or Satan, who refused to bow in the presence of Adam at creation. This belief, as are some of those related to angels, is found in Pseudepigraphic writings, thus proving their presence in Mohammed's culture.[12]

Muslim demons, or *jinn*, are often well-known through culture, such as ghouls and genies. Belief as to the exact nature of *jinn* does vary among Muslim communities, and some consider them a literal means of temptation for sin, as metaphors for issues, and maybe even an ancient concept for bacteria![13]

## **Christianity**

The belief in angels and demons is core to most Christians, and it is safe to say that most Christians who believe in the Scriptures in any context probably believe in the existence of angels and demons, although the way they believe in them frequently varies.

*Holy Bible on a church pew*

Demons are decidedly more controversial in Christianity than angels. Most like the idea of angels, and over the past 20 years, New Age trends in the nature and ideas as pertain to angels have renewed interest in them in many Christian circles. Demons, however, aren't quite that popular. In fact, the only time you hear many messages on demons is in the case of a message specifically about demons or about deliverance. Otherwise, the topic of demons tends to remain mute.

Demonology is not well-studied in many Christian circles today because it is not widely respected by academics and intellectuals. The reason for this is simple: many Christian groups have taken demonology to a level that is cartoonish and ridiculous, and movies, such as the *Exorcist* and *The Omen* tend to fancify demonic activity to a point where we do not take such matters seriously anymore. There are those who believe Biblical demons represent ideas about ailments and illnesses that aren't supported in the face of modern medicine, and Christian groups who encourage elaborate and dangerous exorcisms without any evidence to their validity cause more skepticism in the face of such issues. Coupled with the idea that demonology and exorcism are aspects of Middle Age Catholicism, many Christians are distancing themselves from the concept of demonology because they don't properly understand it.

The best-established records of demonology are found in high-church settings, such as Roman Catholicism, Orthodox Catholicism, Anglicanism, and some higher church Protestants, such as Lutherans and Presbyterians.

The way they understand demons, however, is not always rooted in the Scriptures or the traditional writings of Bible times, but often from cultural lore and ideals throughout the ages or from their founding. For example, Puritans were particularly interested in maintaining spiritual purity and were quick to accuse people of witchcraft or working with demons based on accusations and hallucinations that, very well, may not have been real. This led to innocent women and men burned at the stake or hanged, and a true misconception of demons and how demons operate.

Higher church ideas about demons usually forms through influence or possession, causing individuals to experience torment or torture, usually in four stages, according to traditional Catholic concept of demonic possession: oppression, obsession, possession, and integration. Individuals who are experiencing this kind of demonic encounter can pray, receive exorcism as done by a trained priest or minister, and have the demon exorcised, or removed, from the person's body and life.[14]

There are also those Christians who reject the idea of literal demons as fallen angels and feel demons reflect the temptations we face as people. Still, there are some who feel they do not exist at all, as nothing more than mere imaginations of people's conjuring and things we should not embrace, nor take seriously, in this day and time.

Some Christians are, still, the exact opposite: they feel everything is a demon, almost in a cartoonish "the devil made me do it!" kind of way. In many circles such as Pentecostalism, Charismatic, or neo-Charismatic groups, anything that is seen as negative is identified as spiritual or demonic. This has been taken to an extreme in many who now label anyone and anything they dislike as a "spirit" of some sort, such as Jezebel, Leviathan, or other behaviors, such as drug abuse, alcoholism, pornography, sexual abuse, power, control, and sometimes even dislike of someone else. Without a proper understanding of the nature of the flesh, everything has become a spirit.

The result of such has been exorcisms and deliverance ministries that are often untrained and knowledgeable in demonology and traditional concepts of demons as found throughout history. While it is safe to say that history has not always understood demonology clearly and properly and yes, some elements of culture and lack of understanding have always infiltrated their explanation of spiritual things, we still must understand the role demonology has played and recognize spiritual concepts throughout history. Relying too much on one individual's concept of what is demonic has led to many confusing and strange versions of exorcism and deliverance.

## **Indigenous religion**

Indigenous religion is any religious group that is native, or founding, to a specific region. Everywhere in the world, you find examples of indigenous religion, even though not all of them have survived to the present day. There are two types of indigenous religion: those tribal groups that have maintained their culture and way of life from the earliest of times, and those groups that are from another place in origin but have found themselves at the seat of a culture, for long periods of time. Indigenous religion may be found in syncretic form (such as alongside Christianity) or may be maintained as its own unique religious source, but the role of indigenous religion sheds light on the style and form of religion, sometimes in its most primitive form.

Indigenous religious groups do vary from culture to culture, but they usually have a few things in common. The first is their positioning within certain environmental characteristics, thus leading them to explain the world around them within the specific construct of their atmospheric experience. Their goal is to develop the mythologies that shape their understanding of their existence, their position in the world, and adapting to their environment. They do not typically have written scriptures or books, but rely on the traditions of their ancestors, notable by dance, costuming, rituals, and different artifacts that they believe hold power or relevance, connecting them to the past.

*Native American girl somewhere in the late nineteenth century*

Indigenous theologies are varied, usually evolving over time and echoing a great and mighty spirit, maybe a god or goddess, who is responsible for creation. Many are polytheistic in the Buddhist sense, believing the different spirits to be emanations of nature or natural forces.

These spirits control the weather, blight, illness, drought, and other powerful forces that nobody can seemingly explain. Shamans, witchdoctors, priests or priestesses have special powers that enable them to see the spiritual realm and, by so doing, they can offer insight into the natural order of things, to help others, right where they are. Most desire to instill good morals and beliefs in their people, although they may vary from what those of non-indigenous culture may consider good or moral. Many also embrace various forms of magic, used to try and control the elements or the spiritual realm. Some are more forceful in their use of magic than others, and the result is a host of spiritual experiences, from the seemingly sublime to downright scary, within the culture and experience of indigenous religion.

Believing in the power of spirits means indigenous groups acknowledge beings like angels and demons, believing the dead live on and can visit human beings from the "underworld" or through a form of incarnation in an animal or through a natural force. They believe such shows the interconnectedness of all beings.

Some believe in an evil counterpart to the Great Spirit, who controlled their own lesser spirits, which worked to tempt people away from the work of the Great Spirit, and many recognize such spirits within their own belief systems. Demons in indigenous religion tend to take the form of animals, and are associated in character with those beings, such as wolves or birds.[15] Examples of indigenous religions include:

- Native Americanism (Iroquois, Dakota, Sioux, Apache, Cherokee, Navaho, First Nation, Metis, Inuit)
- Shamanism
- Voodoo
- Santeria
- Native African religions (Yoruba, Okuyi, Serer, Aka, Dahomean, Edo, Hausa, Odinani, Vodun, Dogon, Berber, ancient Egyptian)
- Aboriginal religion
- Shintoism
- Bon

## **Unique groups**

This last section looking at specific beliefs of religious groups as pertain to demons is a general overview of some off-the-beaten-track religious groups that have particularly strong views on demonology.

- **Gnosticism:** A group not properly defined in modern culture (as Gnosticism is a modern designation, and not how they identified themselves), Gnosticism was a Christian and Jewish offshoot, a subgroup, if you will, based on a belief that secret, hidden, and obtained knowledge by the believer could lead to spiritual enlightenment and freedom. It was unique enough to be classified as its own thing, and adapted its own system of scriptures, rituals, and rites. Gnostics sought liberation from ignorance, seeking knowledge, in all things, pursuing spiritual things rather than being earthbound as materialistic beings (hyletics). Gnosticism evolved out of the understanding of the ancients as a cosmos in chaos, and that chaos was ordered or sorted through Gnostic understanding, exercised through various rites and rituals, exclusive only to the group. The Gnostics believed the world existed in dualities: light and dark, good and evil, spirit and matter, and never the twain shall meet, as the saying goes. The true god was unknowable, and the God of the Old Testament was regarded as a demigod, the creator, who desired to take worship from the true god, who was considered the true father, especially of Jesus. In between earth and the true god were *Aeons*, deity-like beings that are also identified as some angels. One of the most important of these was Sophia, or "wisdom," a *Demiurgos*, or half-maker, of creation. Another prominent name was Armozel, the first light-aeon.[16]

*Hermes Mercurius Trismegistus, from the book The Divine Pymander, John Everard (1650)*

An archon was a servant of the Demiurge, or creator god standing in between believers and the true god. Across the different schools of Gnostic thought, we find the following names of archons:[17]

- Yaldabaoth/Saklas/Samael
- Iao
- Sabaoth
- Astaphanos/Astaphaios
- Adonaios
- Elaios/Ailoaios/Ailoein
- Horaios
- Seth
- David
- Eloiein
- Paraplex
- Hekate
- Ariouth
- Typhon
- Iachtanabas

Without getting into the expansive – and complicated – definitions of Gnosticism, it is important to acknowledge many of the more modern groups that refer to themselves as such do not reflect an accurate history of Gnosticism in its original form. They reflect modern concepts of what we believe we know about Gnosticism, but the reality is we know very little about this group from its own perspective. Much of the knowledge we have of it is from detractors or opposers, and some of that information has proven exaggerated or false.

*New Age meditation as an abstract illustration*

- **New Age:** Describing the New Age Movement in a paragraph or two is virtually impossible, because there are multiple strains and beliefs present within its identity. That is what makes it a movement, foundationally rooted in the belief that with the switch from the astrological sign of Pisces to the sign of

Aquarius, a new age, a new era, shall usher in, without the dominances of religion (particularly Christianity). The projected result is believed to be a coming era of world harmony and peace, absent of conflict and marked by intellectual and spiritual enlightenment. The New Age Movement reflects strains of virtually every world religion (particularly the aspects that are more esoteric or mystical), removes them from their constructs, and creates an entirely new sense of what it means to be in terms of beliefs and supernatural powers. New Agers have a particular interest in angels as messengers, and many believe they serve to provide direct messages and guidance to New Agers through channeling, magic, spiritual revelation, protection, and important wisdoms for the age in which we live. Demons are not often as well defined, although many do believe in what they call "dark forces" that seek to keep people unenlightened and under the control of conventional religion and society. In a certain sense, the New Age Movement could be described as "white Hinduism," taking some key spiritual concepts from Hinduism, mixing them with other traditions, and changing the foundational ways such was, and is, practiced.

*Angel Moroni on the Reno, Nevada Temple*

- **Mormonism:** Mormonism is a relatively new religion, especially in light of what we have discussed in this chapter. Started in 1830 by a man named Joseph Smith, its core tenant of foundation rests on the angelic visit of the Angel Moroni (a fallen Native American warrior) to Joseph Smith, bringing a set of golden plates from heaven that contained an ancient record of people descended from the Israelites in the Americas. As a result, he, and those who follow him to this day, believe the Native Americans are descendants of the ancient Israelites.

For the sake of space, we aren't going to get into the evidence against this claim. The accuracy of Joseph Smith's visions has been questioned (there are anywhere from three to eight different versions of the initial experience), as have the accuracy of the Book of Mormon's details, as the Native Americans do not have the same DNA ancestors as those from the Middle East. Regardless, Joseph Smith's religion, known as the Church of Jesus Christ of Latter-Day Saints, has long had a spiritual edge that involves divine revelation, messages from angels, and in the process, the restoration of the "true church" lost through thousands of years of apostasy, dating back to Adam and Eve in the garden. Mormonism contains complex doctrines of the world, rituals, performing rites, and a belief in the secret realm of ritual. Much of their rite and spiritual understanding comes from Freemasonry, which we shall discuss in an upcoming chapter.

Mormons believe Jesus and Satan are spirit brothers, both of whom were brought before the Grand Council in heaven at the beginning of time. They were given a requirement: to come to earth, in human form, to participate in the salvation of mankind. Satan was not willing to do so, and he and a third of the spirit brothers rebelled with him.

Mormons speak of spirit brothers because they believe in many gods in the universe, all polygamous, with an infinite number of spirit children. Thus, Jesus and Satan are seen as having the same spiritual parentage.

Mormon mythology relies heavily on concepts of infinite spirits and polygamy. This leads to an additional emphasis on angels. There's little talk of demons. They do believe they exist, but they are not the focus. Demons are spirits sent to earth that never received a physical body. They can interfere with human experience but aren't the primary focus of the group.[18]

- **The Baha'i Faith:** If you have never heard of the Baha'i Faith, it is not surprising. It is a Persian-originated religion that focuses on spiritual unity: the unity of God, humanity, and religion. It was founded by Baha'u'llah in 1863, opposed by Islamic clergy in different countries to this very day.

    *The Baha'i House of Worship in Ashgabad, Turkmenistan (1919)*

    Its purpose is, by emphasizing certain virtues as divine, that each "prophet" has brought forth a message needed in a specific time, such as Buddha, Jesus, Mohammed, and now, in the end time, the Bab and Baha'u'llah. Adherents of the faith accept science and religion as harmonious and have unique beliefs as pertain to the existence of angels and demons. The Baha'i Faith rejects the existence of both, believing neither has been created, and that evil and Satan are a part of the lower aspects of humanity. An "angel," in the sense of Baha'i, refers to a selfless person who works to be positive in this world.[19]

## The demons of mythology

Most of us studied Greek and Roman mythology in school without studying the other pagan mythologies that dominated the world. Few, if ever, did we speak much about those outside of European culture. If you think back to many of those stories, they provide insight into the world of more ancient cultures and the way in which they saw the world. Much like the work of indigenous religion, mythologies served the purpose to explain purpose in the world and make sense of those things and circumstances that could not be easily controlled.

There are ten main headings as pertain to mythology: Biblical, Celtic (Gaulish, Irish, Scottish), Egyptian, Greek, Japanese, Mayan, Mesopotamian, Norse, Roman, and Zoroastrian. Within each heading we find specific subheadings, and within those subheadings we find specific legends, ideas, and concepts about the way the ancients viewed the world.

The demons of mythology often run parallel to each other, with specific gods and demons taking center stage, all equivalents of one another. We have already discussed some of these creatures in cultural demons and also in different explanations of cosmology and demonology. This shows common source and experience among the ancients in their view of the world, and while some do deviate from one another, they reveal the spiritual issues many of the ancient world faced. Here we will look at some lists we haven't examined.[20]

Mesopotamian:[21]

- Utukku
- Lamassu/Shedu
- Asakku
- Edimmu
- Siris
- Anzû
- Humbaba
- Asag
- Hanbi
- Kur
- Lamashtu
- Pazuzu
- Rabisu

Finnish:[22]

- Ajatar
- Hiisi
- Naaki
- Perkele

Hungarian:[23]

- Baba
- Boszorkany

- Fene
- Guta
- Szepasszony
- Vadleany

Slavic:[24]

- Domovoi
- Likho
- Vilas
- Vodyanoy
- Rusalkas

Egyptian:[25]

- Ammit
- Apophis
- El Naddaha
- Qed-her
- Set

Celtic:[26]
- Fomorians (Fomoria)
- Dullahan

Greek:[27]
- Daemons
- Agathodaemon
- Cacodemon
- Eudaemon
- Daemones Ceramici (Asbestos, Omodamos, Sabaktes, Smaragos, Syntribos)
- Vampire Daemons (Empousa, Mormo, Mormolukeia)
- Three-Bodied or Triple-Bodied Daemon

Norse:[28]

- Muspelheim
- Troll cross

Roman:[29]

- Manes
- Lares
- Lemures
- Genii
- Di Penates

Japanese[30]

- Yokai
- Ayakashi
- Mononoke
- Tengu
- Kuchisake-onna
- Chochin-oiwa
- Kidomary
- Nekomata
- Tsuchigumo
- Gama Yokai
- Narikama
- Oni

Mayan[31]

- Xiquiripat ("Flying Scab")
- Cuchumaquic ("Gathered Blood")
- Ahalpuh ("Puss Demon")
- Ahalgana ("Jaundice Demon")
- Chamiabac ("Bone Staff")
- Chamiaholom ("Skull Staff")
- Ahalmez ("Sweepings Demon")

- Ahaltocob ("Stabbing Demon")
- Xic ("Wing")
- Patan ("Packstrap")

**Demonology and construct**

What we can see from our extensive look at demons around the world is the way in which demonology often relates to the construct of where it is found. People encounter the demonic much in the same way they encounter the divine, or what they perceive to be divine: through experience. At some point in time, someone first had an angelic encounter, spoke of it, and someone else believed in it enough to share it with the next generation. The same is true with record of the demonic. Someone had an experience, they saw it in keeping with something that was not in alignment with the divine, and they created a verbal record that was later written.

Demonology, like all spiritual things, falls within a greater construct, or form or assembly, as is found within a religious context. Trying to understand the demons of a group without understanding something about the group (and often the culture associated with such) doesn't readily make sense. There is a certain concept, or foundational group of ideas, that echoes the principles of demons and demonic activity that is found rooted in something else. Most often, we see it in the form of good and evil, and try to sort the two out within the greater scheme of society, nature, and uncontrollable forces as all three collide and create an environment where people seek answers. The answers they seek are not always easily found, and thus, supernatural explanation is a part of that construct.

Reflections of demons are reflections of the ideas of a culture and their environmental, emotional, spiritual, and cultural concepts about evil, folklore, and the ways people believed evil could influence their lives. It is evident that while we may not see the world in quite the same way others have, we can all agree upon the fact that evil has a way of damaging the way people perceive their experiences with life and spiritual things. When someone was sick or ill, they saw it as demonic, because it was a counter to life. When a group of people experienced the complexities of a drought or natural disaster, they saw it as demonic, because it brought devastation. Strange things seen in the night, missing bodies from graveyards, hearing strange voices, or seeing things that just didn't fit right with a situation all were attributed to the demonic realm, causing people fear and fright what they do not recognize, understand, or perceive properly.

As long as humanity continues, we will have supernatural experiences and encounters with the divine and the demonic, until the time when the demonic is no longer a part of spiritual existence. Until that time, we must strive for understanding, both historical and current, to realize and recognize the spiritual ills and difficulties of humanity so we can offer education, hope, and healing as ministers of God.

**Chapter 4 Assignment**

- Examining the role of demons in religion and mythology worldwide, write an essay (5-8 sentences) on why demons seem to be such a universal facet. Using examples of demons as found in different religions, expound on why you believe these conceptual demons came into being among the different cultures?

## - CHAPTER FIVE -
### The Occult

[Nothing in all the world [Nothing in all creation; *or* No creature] can be hidden from God.
Everything is clear [naked] and lies open before Him [exposed to His eyes],
and to Him we must explain the way we have lived [give an account; answer].
(Hebrews 4:13)

It's impossible to discuss the realms of the demonic and not discuss the intricate and complex world of the occult. Often confused with cults (which are different, although sometimes they overlap), the occult is a world many do not dare to go and even more do not understand. The concept of the occult, what goes on there, much of the ritual rumors we hear about, and the fear many have about the powers people claim to have as pertain to the occult leads many away from insight and study as relates to it, giving those who practice it an even greater illusion of power.

Make no mistake: studying and reading about the occult is not for everyone, and it takes a very strong faith and personal ability - the gifting and anointing of God - to handle delving into its contents without temptation to participate. The concept and allure of having the ability to solve one's problems through magic, occult connection, control, and the illusion of the power to manipulate elements and participate in something open to only a select few has appealed to many people throughout history.

The realm of the occult is not quite as simple, however, as it might seem on the surface. It's not just someone knowing how to pull a rabbit out of a hat or membership within an organization that doesn't reveal all its details to the rest of the world. Being a part of the occult means embracing a hidden realm of understanding that many feel is only exclusive to a few people. It is, indeed, an illusion of power, but the spiritual impact of such power on a person can impact their lives in very complex ways.

It is not possible to explain every single intricacy of the occult in this chapter, but we will do our best to explore foundational basics that help clarify its existence, purpose, and realities to recognize it properly for deliverance ministry.

## What is the occult?

The word "occult" means "hidden." It refers to the realm of the supernatural, of coming to an understanding which operates the natural world, "behind the scenes," in a systematic approach. There are many different aspects of the occult, including magic, astrology, witchcraft, sorcery, divination, and even Satanism. As with anything, there are different perceptions of the occult, different ways one might be involved in its activities, and different levels of involvement.

It is so-called "hidden" because it is believed to be information that is not readily available to everyone, but only to a select few who become enlightened enough to receive the revelations it contains. Most occult groups operate by levels of knowledge, followed by initiations that relate to the information or secret purposes they will obtain as they advance within that organization or group.

## The difference between the occult and indigenous religion

All religion, the world over, from beginning to end, has some form of occult strains within its ranks. It is never the mainline form of the group (as in something studied and practiced by every member therein), but every single religious group holds specific strains of secret knowledge that is not available to everyone, and only open to a select few. This means even within indigenous religious groups, there are occult strains, whether it is through medicine men, shamans, or other individuals who are believed to have access to alternate spiritual realms, states of consciousness, and most essentially, hidden or secret insights.

Indigenous religion in its general existence, however, is not all occult. It is indigenous, which means it reflects early religious trends that became foundations for cultural trends and religious understandings within regions at an early point in human history. Much of indigenous religion relates to unseen spiritual forces seen through natural ones, or animated through them, but they do not believe the spiritual world is, overall, hidden from general knowledge or that understanding natural forces is impossible. Rather, indigenous religion tries to obtain a sense of harmony and balance with the natural forces they can see, and to understand a sense of what is behind them.

The occult functions on a less primitive plain, one that seeks to understand the behind-the-scenes nature of all things natural and supernatural, and how to harness and channel those powers in an effort to apply such principles to one's life. The goal of such lies in obtaining the secret, esoteric (or hidden) principles that are not accessible to everyone. When one is a part of the occult in any form, they are trying to access this information to foretell the future, make major life decisions, contact those from the spiritual realm or from the dead, control the elements, make certain things happen for them in this life, or maintain a certain standing or feeling of understanding over the universe.

The occult is more than just a sense of spiritual worship or belief system. It is technically classified as a form of a science, because it is based on a practice of investigation into the realms of the paranormal, or that which is outside of normal experience and cannot be readily explained. In many ways, and as uncomfortable as it may cause us to be, the occult and its realms are the very foundation of our modern sources of science and medicine.

## **The principles of esotericism**

Every one of us has had an experience that we can't easily explain, simply because they are simply unexplainable. That might seem like a simplistic explanation, but the experiences are beyond the average, normal experience. We don't have the proper language or foresight to figure them out, let alone explain them to others. The vision of a fleeting creature before one's eyes, the ability to perceive an experience before it happens, a profound dream that leaves us with the impression of a message, having the sense of something in the spiritual realm that one cannot see, or the presence or sense of another's feelings or thoughts without aforementioned knowledge of them are all "unexplained" experiences. These unexplained experiences are not uncommon, but don't happen to the average person often enough to rate them an ordinary occurrence. Because they are lesser experiences, they are frequently sought after, fascinating to people, and considered of intrigue...and the rarer, the more intriguing.

Throughout the history of mankind, people have always sought to understand the unexplainable. Those unspoken (or sometimes debated) coincidences merit exploration and explanation, and it became general consensus that not everyone had ample access to the reasonings for such. If everyone understood it, then it would be obvious and easily explained. Thus, information as pertains to these issues was perceived to be hidden – forbidden – unknowable – unless someone had the secret knowledge about it.

This information, therefore, became exclusive to those who were "initiated," or who had received certain rites associated with different groups. These different rites were believed to open an individual to new worlds and new connections, so they could function on a higher plane of awareness and information than the average person. Those who received these rites and this hidden knowledge were forced to keep it secret, discussing it only among others who, likewise, were a part of the inner circle of hidden rite and knowledge. It was not to be shared with those outside the group. To do so could incur punishment, exile from the group, or, in some instances, death.

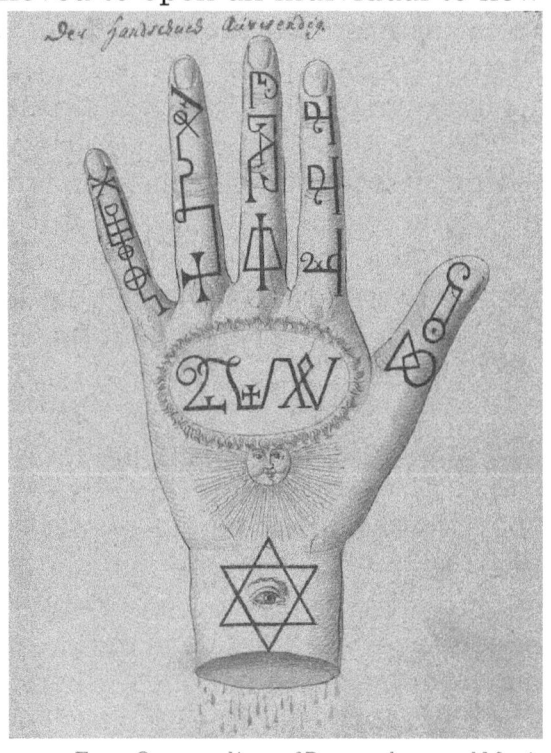

*From Compendium of Demonology and Magic (c. 1775)*

That is how seriously occultists treat the knowledge they feel they have. Even though elements of it are quite pseudoscientific (meaning false science), occultists believe firmly in their experience and information. It is a position and a reality of vital importance to those who believe in it, life-changing, life-altering, perceptiveness that they do not feel is accessible to all.

The way occultists view the world, and their work, is not as simple as saying it is a set of beliefs about the way supernatural occurrences work.

Occultists are interested in the dynamics of a thing as much as the cause, and while they very well may acknowledge supernatural powers, they are equally interested in the construct, or the way a thing happens, and seek to study that. By studying the way things work, they discover more about them, and find ways to bring about those same results and same powers in their own innerworkings.

## **Occult foundations**

As with all things that relate to a spiritual or paranormal nature, there are different strains of occultism that have their own variations and unique themes and governing principles. There are a few foundational principles that govern most, if not all, occult belief systems: alchemy, magic, extra-sensory perception, astrology, spiritualism, religion, and divination.

- **Alchemy:** Alchemy is considered, by modern standards, to be pseudoscience, but we could classify it as a primitive form of chemistry. The goal of alchemy is to mix various chemical or elemental things together to cast a spell, bring about something spiritual, say certain words when certain elements mix, or more relevantly, change base metals into gold. Alchemy was also used to find cures for disease and find a way to live eternally.

- **Magic:** We will be exploring magic specifically in the next chapter, but as it is a foundational aspect of occultism, we must discuss it here, in brief. Magic is the use of various spiritual forces over natural ones via the means of spellcasting. By invoking a spell, mixing certain elements together, doing things at certain times of the cycle of the moon or in certain periods during a month, year, or day, or exerting force over certain natural elements via a perceived spiritual means.

- **Extra-sensory perception:** There are many ways people describe extra-sensory perception, but it is the ability to perceive something without the use of the natural five senses found in human biology. It can include telepathy (transferring thoughts between people without speech), precognition (knowing the future), clairvoyance (perception of beings or objects that are not visible to others or known by others who may be present), clairaudience (the ability to hear beings or objects not visible to others), and empathy (the ability to perceive beings or objects by feelings or emotional perceptions). An individual who utilizes one or any assortment of these different abilities is known as a psychic.

- **Astrology:** Astrology could be described as a primitive astronomy, although the goal and outcome are markedly different. Astrology is the study of the way different celestial objects (planets, stars, constellations) move and the belief that the movement of those different objects impacts on human issues, personalities, and interactions. The ancient world understood the interpretations of astrology to be divine communications from the gods. It has been found in different forms in most ancient cultures in different parts of the world. While modern-day applications have proven it false, it was considered a legitimate study and science in ancient times. There are still many who rely on its reports, in the form of horoscopes, to make major-life decisions.

- **Spiritualism:** Spiritualism is the belief that those who have died can still communicate and interact with the living, because those spirits are believed to intermingle with the world of the departed. The belief in seeking deceased spirits for guidance, direction, or words from the beyond is from ancient times, as can be seen in Biblical and archaeological texts. Deceased spirits communicate with the living through a medium, or an individual who believes they can serve as a conduit of that deceased or otherworldly being. Mediums either work as the spirit overtakes their bodies and they enter a trance, or as one where different things happen around them, because the spirits are making their presence known to this individual in the room. The work of spiritualism became an entire movement in 1800s America, beginning with the work of the Fox sisters, who believed they had the ability to communicate through the dead through a series of raps and taps, thus creating a code. These women were later proved fraudulent, but by that point in time, the movement had taken off. Originally, the work of spiritualism had a religious quality to it, but as with most things, it has a secular component to it now, as well. The motivating factor is question of the human soul in the picture of eternity, life after death, and what happens after we die.

- **Religion:** Religion is the spiritual quest of humanity to find God, the afterlife, immortality, culture, ethics, and spiritual purpose in a systematic package. The occult is fascinated with religion and spiritual understandings, although they do not generally accept every aspect of a religion that exists. Most often, they receive certain parts of it and embrace those as the foundation for more esoteric or supernatural beliefs.

- **Divination:** Divination is any attempt by a portentous method to try and predict the future. In divination, an object is used to make the process seem more "random," if you will, thus leaving the results up to the gods or spirits of fate. It is found in virtually every culture worldwide. Different forms of divination include looking for signs through documentation, casting lots, using different methods to distinguish between different possibilities, and unrestricted forms that are meant to bring an off-the-cuff answer to any possible issue. We shall discuss divination more in-depth in the next chapter.

## Occult science

The concepts of "science" and the occult might seem worlds apart, especially because modern science has frequently disproven occult theories and their major foundations. This has not stopped the occult from identifying itself as "scientific," and from believing it is a set of specifically applied principles that fit the construct of their hidden or secret knowledge. The word "science" is used in the same context of Religious Science or Christian Science, which is applying a systematic set of research principles to discover what they desire to learn about natural and spiritual order.

Occult science is that specific, systematic research dedicated to proving occult ideas and theories. It grew in popularity through a religious group known as Theosophy. Theosophy is an openly occult movement with a name that literally means "god wisdom," emphasizing occult experiences in the spiritual realm through intuition, meditation, revelation, or transcending human consciousness. They also emphasize the esoteric, or hidden teachings, known only among themselves. They are dedicated to finding hidden understanding in international sacred books, the mystery of nature, and achieving psychic powers.[1]

The three main proponents of occult science all belonged to Theosophy. they were Helena Blavatsky, the founder of the Theosophical religion; Rudolf Steiner, who went on to break with Theosophy and start the Anthroposophical Society, and Alice Bailey, who was one of the first writers to identify a "new age."

Some keys of occult science include:

- Secrets of nature
- Extra-sensory perception abilities
- Spiritual evolution of the human person
- The cosmos from the occult perspective (astral world order)
- Attainment of hidden or secretive knowledge
- Palmistry
- Face reading
- Numerology
- Karma
- Reincarnation
- Astrology, particularly from the perspective of the passing from one age to another and in determining personalities based on astrological charting
- Magic
- Alchemy
- Meditation

## Bible passages of interest among occultists

Contrary to popular belief, the Bible is used by occultists. It is considered a sacred text and is used by many occultists as a source of spell casting or to cast spells by using its words. Some use it by opening it up to a random passage, asking a question, and then reading the text that falls below a person's finger as an answer to the question. Obviously, the way occultists interpret it is different from the way Christians interpret it, focusing on more secretive or elusive understandings of the wording. Some texts considered of importance include:

*THE CUP YOU HAVE STOLEN IS THE ONE [IS THIS NOT WHAT...?] MY MASTER [LORD] USES FOR DRINKING AND FOR EXPLAINING DREAMS [DIVINATION; PERHAPS BY POURING OIL IN WATER AS A MEANS OF TELLING THE FUTURE (CALLED LECANOMANCY)]. YOU [IS NOT*

*WHAT YOU...?] HAVE DONE A VERY WICKED THING!* (Genesis 44:5)

- Use of an ancient occult method to answer questions, using liquid poured into a cup and gazed at to find shapes, words, or messages.

*HE MUST STAND BEFORE ELEAZAR THE PRIEST, AND ELEAZAR WILL GET ADVICE FROM THE LORD BY USING THE URIM [EX. 28:30]. AT HIS COMMAND ALL THE ISRAELITES [SONS/CHILDREN OF ISRAEL, THE WHOLE COMMUNITY/ASSEMBLY/CONGREGATION] WILL GO OUT, AND AT HIS COMMAND THEY WILL ALL COME IN.* (Numbers 27:21)

*HE PRAYED TO [INQUIRED OF] THE LORD, BUT THE LORD DID NOT ANSWER HIM THROUGH DREAMS, URIM [DEVICES CARRIED BY THE HIGH PRIEST TO INQUIRE OF GOD; EX. 28:30], OR PROPHETS.* (1 Samuel 28:6)

- These verses mention of the Urim and Thummim, which were two objects used to discern the will of God by the high priest. What exactly they were is of extreme debate, but they were used to foretell the will of God, using a method of chance.[2]

*GOD SAYS, "BE STILL AND KNOW THAT I AM GOD.*
 *I WILL BE PRAISED [EXALTED] IN ALL THE NATIONS;*
*I WILL BE PRAISED [EXALTED] THROUGHOUT THE EARTH."*
(Psalm 46:10)

- Used for principles of meditation and occult focus.

*THE PHILISTINES CAME TOGETHER [ASSEMBLED; MOBILIZED] AND MADE CAMP AT SHUNEM. SAUL GATHERED ALL THE ISRAELITES AND MADE CAMP AT GILBOA. WHEN HE SAW THE PHILISTINE ARMY, HE WAS AFRAID, AND HIS HEART POUNDED WITH FEAR [TREMBLED VIOLENTLY]. HE PRAYED TO [INQUIRED OF] THE LORD, BUT THE LORD DID NOT ANSWER HIM THROUGH DREAMS, URIM [DEVICES CARRIED BY THE HIGH PRIEST TO INQUIRE OF GOD; EX. 28:30], OR PROPHETS. THEN SAUL SAID TO HIS SERVANTS [ADVISERS; ATTENDANTS], "FIND ME A WOMAN WHO IS A MEDIUM [IS A NECROMANCER; HAS A FAMILIAR SPIRIT] SO I MAY GO AND ASK HER WHAT WILL HAPPEN [INQUIRE OF/CONSULT HER]."*

*HIS SERVANTS ANSWERED, "THERE IS A MEDIUM [A NECROMANCER; WOMAN WITH A FAMILIAR SPIRIT] IN ENDOR."*

*THEN SAUL PUT ON OTHER CLOTHES TO DISGUISE HIMSELF, AND AT NIGHT HE AND TWO OF HIS MEN WENT TO SEE THE WOMAN. SAUL SAID TO HER, "TALK TO [CONSULT] A SPIRIT FOR ME. BRING [CONJURE] UP THE PERSON I NAME."* (1 Samuel 28:4-8)

- Used to defend the occult practice.

*I TELL YOU THE TRUTH, ALL THESE THINGS WILL HAPPEN WHILE THE PEOPLE OF THIS TIME ARE STILL LIVING [BEFORE THIS GENERATION PASSES AWAY; EITHER THE GENERATION THAT SEES THE DESTRUCTION OF JERUSALEM (AD 70), OR A FUTURE GENERATION OF THE END TIMES].* (Matthew 24:34)

- Used to defend belief in reincarnation.

*THE SMELL [SCENT] OF YOUR PERFUME [COLOGNE; OIL] IS PLEASANT [WONDERFUL],*
  *AND YOUR NAME [REPUTATION] IS PLEASANT LIKE EXPENSIVE [OR POURED OUT] PERFUME [COLOGNE; OIL].*
  *THAT'S WHY THE YOUNG WOMEN LOVE YOU.*
(Song of Solomon 1:3)

- Used as a spell to arouse love in another.

*TAKE AWAY MY SIN [REMOVE MY SIN WITH HYSSOP; EX. 12:22; A PLANT USED IN PURIFICATION RITUALS; LEV. 14:4, 6, 49–51; NUM. 19:18], AND I WILL BE CLEAN.*
  *WASH ME, AND I WILL BE WHITER THAN SNOW [IS. 1:18].*
(Psalm 51:7)

- Frequently used to purify the circle or magician working a spell.

*MY SORES STINK AND BECOME INFECTED*
  *BECAUSE I WAS FOOLISH.*
*I AM BENT OVER AND BOWED DOWN;*
  *I AM SAD [WALK AROUND MOURNING] ALL DAY LONG.*
*I AM BURNING WITH FEVER [MY LOINS ARE BURNED WITH FEVER],*
  *AND MY WHOLE BODY [FLESH] IS SORE [NOT SOUND].*
(Psalm 38:5-7)

*I AM LIKE THE DEAF; I CANNOT HEAR.*
  *LIKE THE MUTE, I CANNOT SPEAK [OPEN MY MOUTH].*

*I AM LIKE THOSE WHO DO NOT HEAR,*
  *WHO HAVE NO ANSWER [REPROOF] TO GIVE [IN THEIR MOUTH].*
(Psalm 38:13-14)

*THE LORD LOOKED DOWN FROM HIS HOLY PLACE ABOVE;*
  *FROM HEAVEN HE LOOKED [GAZED] DOWN AT THE EARTH.*
*HE HEARD THE MOANS [GROANS] OF THE PRISONERS,*
  *AND HE FREED [RELEASED] THOSE SENTENCED TO DIE.*
(Psalm 102:19-20)

- Used to establish belief that the dead are among the living on earth.

## Occult texts

There are literally thousands of occult writings and texts, each unique to different eras or points in times as relate to magic, spellcasting, and information obtained or important to occultists in that time period. There are a few, however, that stand out above the rest and are frequently cited as foundational when it comes to occult practice.

- ***The Key of Solomon:*** Also called *Clavicula Salomonis* or *Mafetah Shelomoh*, it is a spellcasting text attributed to King Solomon (although no such attribution is factual). Its standard style of magic that echoes the Renaissance era. It is divided into two different books, with the first containing different words and precepts to conjure and invoke spirits as well as curses and methods to find lost items, become invisible, and gain favor. The second book contains purification rites and ways in which spells and incantations should be executed. According to the legend, the book was recorded by Solomon for Rehoboam.[3]
- ***The Lesser Key of Solomon:*** Also called *Clavicula Salmonis Regis* or *Lemegeton*. The text is an anonymous spell book on demonology, written somewhere around the mid-1600s from texts spanning a few centuries earlier. Most of its contents are replicas or taken from older works, all of which relate to witchcraft and spells. It is divided into five different books – *Ars Goetia, Ars Theurgia-Goetia, Ars Paulina, Ars Almadel,* and *Ars Notoria*. The *Ars Goetia* lists seventy-two different demons, the *Ars Theurgia Goetia* speaks on ways to

summon and control spirits, the *Ars Paulina* contains writings from the 1500s on magic and on different magical spells (attributed to the Apostle Paul) and different angels and spirits of the degrees of the Zodiac (360 in all), the *Ars Almadel* talk about scrying and creating a wax tablet, and the *Ars Notoria* contains different prayers to help magicians retain the information they need in order to cast spells.[4]

- **The Book of the Dead:** There are two different *Books of the Dead*, both of relate to magic: *The Tibetan Book of the Dead* and *The Egyptian Book Of The Dead*. *The Tibetan Book of the Dead*, also called *Bardo Thodol* (meaning after death liberation by hearing) was designed to be a guidebook for those who have died to transition to a new form of existence. It is believed to have been an eighth century work by Padma-Sambhava, an Indian Buddhist who introduced Buddhism to Tibet. *The Egyptian Book of the Dead* is a translation of the *Papyrus of Ani* and provides the roots of Hermeticism. Its purpose is to provide different magical spells designed to assist those who have died in their journey through the underworld.[5,6]

- **The works of Hermes Mercurius Trismegistus:** There are a few different works by Hermes Trismegistus, especially the work *Corpus Hermeticium*, which includes *The Divine Pymander* and *The Virgin of the World*. These works create a bridge between Greek spiritual theories that laid the foundations for Gnosticism to ancient Egyptian deities, magic, and ideals.[7]

- ***Dogme et Rituel de la Haute Magie*:** Translated as *Dogma and Ritual of High Magic,* it was occultist Eliphas Levi's text on ritual magic.

- ***La Clef de la Magie Noire*:** *The Key of Black Magic*, written by Stanislas de Guaita, who founded the Cabalastic Order of the Rosicrucian. Considered an inspirational text in modern Satanism.[8]

## Occult religions

Even though there are groups that maintain their identity within mainline religious denominations while holding to occult ideals (we shall discuss them next), there are religious groups in existence that are strictly occult in their understanding – and are very upfront about that fact.

The difference between an occult religion and a secret society is one foundation: in most occult groups, the pursuit within its identity is spiritual religious identity, which transcends religion and cultural perception. Membership with any mainline organization is permitted, as long as one remains devoted to the occult. Secret societies are not specifically religious in nature and are not designed to provide a spiritual identity of a group. Some secret societies require a group to hold a specified set of religious beliefs, while others do not espouse any special religious understanding. Even though the beliefs of secret societies are often found within occult foundations, the rules, regulations, and governing concepts (especially as pertains to membership) are often different.

- **Gnosticism:** We discussed Gnosticism in its basic elements in our last chapter, and let us understand that Gnosticism, as you might hear about it in your own community or even in the United States, for that matter, is probably not authentic. Let's be upfront in saying that authentic Gnosticism is very rare, existing in limited communities in a few places worldwide (particularly Iraq and Iran). If you hear about modern-day revivals of Gnosticism, they are just that – modern concepts, most often mixed with other forms of belief from different religious strains – to form a newer

*The Emerald Tablet of Hermes Trismegistus, translated by Isaac Newton (c. 1680)*

concept of what someone believes their understanding of Gnosticism has to offer the world today. Discoveries of information on Gnostics in the late 1800s and early 1900s about these different groups led occultists to incorporate some of the beliefs and ideas contained therein into their traditions, and the result is many different "Gnostic churches," all of which embrace different aspects of Gnosticism with various traditions and faith beliefs. Such include the Celtic Gnostic

Church, the French Gnostic Church, Ecclesia Gnostica, Apostolic Johannite Church, and Ecclesia Gnostica Catholica.

- **Hermeticism:** An occult spiritual tradition based on the writings of Hermes Trismegistus that center on magic and wisdom. Hermes Trismegistus was believed to be a syncretism of the Greek god, Hermes, and the Egyptian god, Thoth, incorporated by Greek culture as a polytheistic being in one, "thrice great."

- **Theosophy:** We spoke of Theosophy a bit earlier, as it was a modern-day founding organization to the concept of occult science. Theosophy is a mixture of different occult strains founded by Helena Blavatsky in New York City in 1875. Influenced by many different international strains of esoterism and religion, the society moved its headquarters to Adyar, India in 1878. It considers itself to be the "inner life in every religion," reflecting the hidden beliefs and understandings of life beyond that which may appear to be obvious. The fundamental works of Theosophy include *Isis Unveiled* and *The Secret Doctrine*.[9]

    *Theosophical Society seal*

- **Thelema:** Thelema is both a religious belief and a strain of magic, formulated in the twentieth century by Aleister Crowley, who we will speak more on later in this chapter. Thelema is a word that means "will" and is frequently summarized as "Do what thou wilt shall be the whole of the law." Adherents of Thelema believe their purpose in life is to discover and act upon their true will, their innermost nature. In order to achieve this, Thelemites practice their unique form of magik.

    *Aleister Crowley, founder of Thelema*

    Most Thelemites follow the writings, politics, and ethics of Crowley, but not all feel the same way about the prominence of his work. Thelema incorporates Egyptian paganism and mysticism with various forms of hedonism, which is seeking personal pleasure as the highest goal in life, along with ritual and structure to form a religious identity.[10]

- **Modern paganism:** Much like Gnosticism, modern pagan strains are based on information we have about ancient religions that is often incomplete or lacking in detail. As a result, modern pagan groups are piecing together things we know about the different ancient pagan systems and mixing them with modern values and ideals, all to become the modern pagan systems we recognize today. Most modern pagan groups mix polytheism (worship of many gods), animism and pantheism (the belief that spiritual deity manifests in all things, and that all things are identical with the divine, thus everything is god). Such groups typically follow a strain of polytheism and magic present in the ancient world, either Egyptian, Celtic, Germanic, Roman, Greek, Kemetic, Slavic, or Norse. Their rituals are devised by older traditions and are done surrounding new moons, feasts, festivals, and other ancient ideals mixed with goddess theologies, ecology, and nature worship. These groups include modern druids, witches, Wicca, Heathenism, Druidism, and goddess worship.

*Black Wiccan pentagram*

- **New Age Movement:** We spoke of the origins of the New Age Movement earlier, and in description, the New Age Movement is difficult to describe. It is best described as a culmination of most, if not all, the religions and spiritual movements of the era incorporated with a modern twist. New Agers believe that with the ushering in of the age of Aquarius, the entire world will find itself in a place of peace and harmony. By reconciling different world religions and beliefs into one system (piecing different parts of them together), they are preparing for this great ushering in. Theosophy is

*Woman practicing yoga*

often credited as the forerunner for the modern New Age Movement, which rose to particular prominence in the 1970s. It does not have a standard statement of belief, but most adherents reject evil, Satan, and sin as existing, believing that if they realize the god that is within them, they will no longer fall into the mistakes and evil of their past lives. The more one comes to know their god, which is considered an impersonal, general life force, the less they will continue on their current courses of action. Most believe in reincarnation, pantheism, karma, meditation, and an assortment of other beliefs that they take from various religions, paganism, and culture and put together in one generalized – and personalized – belief system.

- **Mormonism:** In writing this book, where exactly to place Mormonism became a question, because most assume it to be a sect of Christianity. This identity comes from those in the church itself who identify themselves as such, but the truth of their history is a different story. In the early years of Mormonism, nobody desired to identify themselves as Christian. Even though the religion has tried to clean itself up over the years, it still holds to its main

*Joseph Smith, founder of Mormonism*

purposes and ties, all of which extend back to the occult. The roots of Mormonism come from Freemasonry, of which all the early founders were members. The initiation rites, temple rites, and rituals are all exact copies of those found in Freemasonry, done in the same way, with similar requirements.

- **Jehovah's Witnesses:** Most of us wouldn't easily believe that the group we see going door-to-door that seems so literal and austere on matters has occult origins, but it, in fact, does. The founder of the organization which would become Jehovah's Witnesses was Charles Taze Russell, a man who, like Joseph Smith, was a

*Charles Taze Russell, founder of the International Bible Students Association, (later to become Jehovah's Witnesses)*

Freemason. There is no question of the connection in foundations to the occult, as the very theology and foundation of the Watchtower organization was pyramidology, a belief that a special message, especially the message of salvation, is contained within the different dimensions and chambers present in the pyramids of Egypt. Jehovah's Witnesses imagery from its early days are loaded with occult symbolism, including those from ancient Egypt and from Freemasonry. Even though it is no longer found in their Bible version today, the chart "of the ages," complete with the pyramid, was found in their Bibles for many years and in copies of early Watchtower works.

## **Mystical and occult groups/orders found in mainline religions**

As was said earlier, all mainline religions have either mystical, occult, or more esoteric, forms of belief as offshoots of their different central theologies and tenants of faith. While adhering to the exteriors – and often fundamental foundations – of faith, these different groups seek to understand deeper, less obvious facets of belief and spirituality. The result are groups that often take their foundational precepts and add various magical or hidden components to them, to take them beyond the level of belief and thought to which they frequently abide and appeal to the common man or woman.

It should be said that not everything taught in more esoteric or occult groups off mainline religions is always a blasphemy. Some of it is simply a look at more of a mystical side of the religion or beliefs, and much of it focuses on deeper aspects of things taught in general scripture or doctrine. Much of the mystical aspects of religion focus on the nature of the person in relation to the greater picture, as the divine deity worshiped or honored is so relevant, and the individual sees themselves as a part of the creation of that deity rather than as superior to the rest of it. Not all mystical aspects of mainline religion are into things as heavily as general occultists, and many still maintain their own beliefs, without adapting the extremism or the witchcraft of the occult. These groups are classified as mystical because of their emphasis on divine experience or spiritual experience, or "occult," because they emphasize a hidden side to their belief systems and sometimes initiation rites, all of which are not readily understood by everyone. Determining the level of occultism in practice depends on the group, often the person practicing the specifics of the religion, and the understandings therein of the evolution of such.

Many times, what often makes a mystical group take on an occult quality is the removal of it from its construct, i.e., trying to apply it without its basic theology or religious roots. The occult has a way of taking little bits of different pieces of different religions and then putting them back together outside of their construct, thus turning it into something other than what it is. Most of these movements started as general mystical movements, but once the occult started piecing parts of them together, many of their pieces have become other things together, entirely.

- **Kabbalah:** The realm of Jewish esotericism. Literally translated, it means "that which is received." It is divided into three different categories: theoretical (inner dimensions that relate to reality), spiritual worlds (souls, angels, meditation, elevating states of consciousness), and magical (altering and influencing nature). Many of the magical aspects of Kabbalah have never been published, because it was recognized such could be dangerous in the wrong hands. As a result, there are theories about it, but much of the magical aspects of Kabbalah have gone into extinction. As a discipline, those who practice it are trying to discover a greater relationship with eternity and God's creation. The foundational understanding of Torah study is on four levels: *Peshat* (direct interpretation), *remez* (allegoric meaning), *derash*

    *Tree of Life, Rodrigo Tebani (1987)*

    (Rabbinic interpretations), and *sod* (the inner, esoteric meaning). It has surfaced in different periods of Jewish history, although Kabbalists believe it originated in Eden, revealed only to an elect few throughout history. In modern times, the tradition of Kabbalah is found in the theologies present in Hasidic Judaism and some offshoots of Orthodox Judaism. Modern-day groups, such as the main one that refers to itself as Kabbalah, does use the central text, the Zohar, but incorporates additional New Age elements within its understandings, thus rendering it no longer genuine Kabbalah.[11,12]

- **Sufi:** Sufism is the esoteric branch of Islam. The word "Sufi" is from the Arabic word for a mystic, drawn from the word for "wool," as describes the woolen garments worn by early Islamic mystics. Although many did believe Sufism derived from non-Muslim sources, the movement is now believed to have originated in communities of Muslims who disagreed with the worldliness of the Islamic communities, beginning in the late seventh and early eighth centuries. Much like the monastic movements of early Christianity, Sufism did not seek to escape the world to avoid the guidelines of their belief system; they did it to gain better insight and adherence to Islamic law.

  *Whirling dervishes posing for a photo outside Galata Mevlevihanesi (1870)*

  They would be known for constantly meditating on the Qur'an and focus on the end of the world, to the point where it would cause them grief and sorrow. They were also known for night prayers and acts of charity. Around 801, a woman named Rabi'ah al-Adawiyah began teaching on divine love as a central aspect of Sufism. Sufi Islam is best known for its poetry, which expresses intense, mystical ideas about the divine as expressed through symbolism. The best-known Sufi poet was Jalal al-Din al Rumi, whose mystical love poems are used in poetry classes worldwide. In the thirteenth century, fraternal orders of Sufism began to emerge, and through Sufism, their ideas and expansion wrought extensive international presence throughout the ages. It is a discipline without magic, brought about through intense spiritual seeking, study, and revelation, and asceticism. Sufism has experienced a fate like Kabbalah in that its practices have been absorbed by New Age communities and outsiders who practice it in part, thus rendering much of what we see called "Sufism" today to be no longer genuine Sufi Islam.[13]

- **Tantra:** Much of Hindu mythology already has an esoteric air to it, thus Hinduism doesn't have one specific strain of esotericism, like many other religions do. There are many different aspects of Hinduism that might be considered more esoteric, especially by western standards. Tantra is one such esoteric tradition, found within Hindu and Buddhist systems. The word literally means "loom" or "weave" and relates to interweaving different traditions into a practice or a text, like the weaving done on a loom. It is used to apply to many different things, including life, spirituality, and even construction. The focus for tantra is found in several texts known as *Tantras*, *Agamas*, or *Samhitas*, and include the *Rig Veda*, *Harshacharita*, *Dashakumaracharita*, and *Atharvaveda*. It developed somewhere in the first millennium AD, beginning with the Kapalikas, or "skull men," who we know little about. Around the fifth century, we start seeing traditions that reflect what is now understood to be Tantra. Even though tantra is often associated in the west with sexual positions and sexual practice, it is far more than just about sex in its originating context. It focuses on rituals around deity worship, mantras, visualization and identification with a deity, initiation, esotericism, secrecy, gurus, ritual mandalas, reevaluation of the body, women and their status, analogical thinking, and rethinking negative thoughts.[14]

*Buddhist mandala*

- **Monasticism:** Monasticism is yet another movement that has gained modern-day popularity, without its proper construct to anchor its understanding. The monastic movement of Christianity took place at the end of the third century, when groups of Christians decided to leave the politics and complications they saw infiltrating the church, and retreat to the desert to discover deeper ways of living and understanding their faith. The result was an entire movement devoted to living simply and strictly, without

*Syncletia of Alexandria, Desert Mother*

worldly distractions, so as to focus on prayer, Scripture, and the deeper things of God. These early monastics became the Desert Fathers and Mothers; individuals whose writings and ways of life became a source of inspiration and emulation for many others whose desires were also to attain Christian perfection. Christian monastics were and are focused on attaining spiritual perfection and seek it out through hesychasm (tradition of prayer that includes meditation, specific postures, and development of inner stillness), struggling for perfection, illumination, divinization, and prayer and obedience. They focus on living in solitary states or with others who live with the same desire for perfection.[15]

- **New Thought:** New Thought is a philosophical movement that arose in the nineteenth and early twentieth centuries that centers on metaphysical ideals about thought and the mind as foundational to the things that happen to a person in their lives. It emerged in contrast to empiricism and religious skepticism, both of which were pervasive in that period of history.

    *Positive attitude*

    Scientific advancements still left many questions, and New Thought emerged as a more positive outlook as people looked to the idea of changing their lives with answers that were not so much tangible as thought-based and more spiritualized in nature. There are many different divisions of New Thought, some which are more occult than others, and it is, in many ways, the foundation of the "Name it, claim it" and "Word-Faith" divisions of non-denominational Christianity. It is also the foundation of positive thinking and visualization seminars, Religious Science, the Unity Movement, Christian Science, and the International New Thought Alliance. Within New Thought, Jesus is regarded as a healer and teacher or omitted all together, with a prominent focus on overcoming illness, disease, sin, and improper thoughts as a matter of wrong approach that can be overcome by thinking differently about any and all situations.[16]

- **Swedenborgianism:** More properly identified as the Church of the New Jerusalem, Swedenborgianism was the work of Emmanuel Swedenborg (1688-1772), a Swedish scientist and philosopher who spent the final thirty years of his life writing theological books based on a series of spiritual experiences he had. The basic premise of Swedenborgianism is that of the spiritual realm establishing a new church, something present in those who believe Jesus is the one God of heaven and earth, and that the spiritual meaning behind the Scriptures is how we come to the revealed truth of the Second Coming. Swedenborg claimed his writings to be inspired, and the Church of the New Jerusalem upholds them as such. The doctrine of the church as pertains to its universal nature and belief in any believer as a part of salvation's experience, is not that unique. The metaphysical nature of Swedenborgian, however, is a little more unique. Swedenborgians believe before creation, there was no space and time, and that is where the spiritual world resides. It is divided into heaven and hell, where the realities of the soul's internal being become reality. The retainment of memories from the spirit world are commonly understood in past life regression, although the church denies reincarnation. They reject Trinitarianism, ancient church councils, many standard church forms and traditions, creeds, and believe in the progressive advance of the church. In summary, it mixes and alters more common elements found in different Christian traditions, but gives them a more esoteric edge, accentuated by Swedenborgian's writings and belief in the need to test all earlier teachings.[17,18]

*Emmanuel Swedenborg, Carl Frederik Von Breda (1759-1818)*

## Secret societies

The concept of a "secret society" is intriguing to many, and problematic for many more, as people seek to understand what goes on in such a group. Many attempt to explain away the secret nature of the groups in modern society, in effort to try and gain modern acceptance. With the advance of the internet, the concept of secret societies has gained a whole new momentum, new ideals and new concepts about what they do and why they exist.

In keeping with our examination of the occult in this chapter, secret societies always, without a doubt, meet the definition of being in line with the occult. While sometimes their activities may vary from the standards of reincarnation, alchemy, magic, astrology, extra-sensory perception, spiritualism, religion, and divination, secret societies always hold to certain esoteric sub-principles and also embrace high ideals of secrecy, believing only those within the group can understand it properly, and the levels of knowledge one achieves increases with each level of initiation.

It is also worth saying that most, if not all, people, somewhere in the world, have a relative or a connection to someone who belongs to a secret society. Many believe – and join – different secret organizations with the intent to do charitable works, create a sense of brotherhood or belonging, be active in the community, or network with the hope and purpose of pursuing a better job or creating better job opportunities. Just because someone is involved in a secret society doesn't mean someone is inherently evil, or bad, or understands everything we are going to talk about today. There are many who are a part of secret societies who know little to nothing of the origins of their groups, believe they are Christian, about the betterment of humanity, or about changing the world, for the better. Even though there is no question that secret societies aren't of spiritual benefit, there are many who are in them without such understanding. There is no reason to cut people off from your life, stop speaking with them, or treat them as are sub-human. Rather, we are here to learn, to explore, and to develop a better understanding of these groups so we know how to recognize and work with individuals who are in them.

**Freemasonry**

It is difficult to summarize Freemasonry in a paragraph or two. It is a complex system of rites, initiations, and memberships that are known the world over and connected with any number of different conspiracy theories. As the world's largest secret society, freemasonry (known as Free and Accepted Masons or Antient Free and Accepted Masons) started somewhere in the late sixteenth or early seventeenth centuries in Scotland and England. There are different lineages of masonry, but their practices are almost identical. Freemasons trace their ancestry much further than their history, however, to believe they are the spiritual descendants of stonemasons involved in the construction of King Solomon's temple. Masons embrace different degrees of initiation, going to a Master Mason, all of which reveal different levels of knowledge and ritual among the membership. To qualify for study beyond the third level (Entered Apprentice, Fellow Craft, and Master Mason), an individual in the Scottish rite must complete those first three levels, to move up from four to 33. The different levels of initiation are known as degrees, and in training for such, masons learn about their interactions with others, the Supreme Being (or Grand Architect), Freemasonic principles and ideals, and history. Masonic rites are ritualized, with each jurisdiction setting up their own rituals. They believe the universe has been created – and designed – by the Grand Architect, using the square and compass to emphasize these aspects of symmetry, order, and craftsmanship within creation – and the need for each Mason to embody such principles in their own lives. Masonry is a maze of different signs, called gestures, and grips, called tokens, and words to gain admission to meetings, identify visitors, and degree levels of involvement. Masons are also obligated to maintain secrecy of the order by oath, associated with the gestures, tokens, and words of each degree.

*Freemasons assembling for a picture*

Historically speaking, exposure of such secrets could render an individual death, but now, most are just suspended from the order.

To be a member, a man (no women allowed; organizations that admit women are not traditional or regular organizations exclusive to men) must petition the lodge in his community through the support of an existing member. Members study for initiation, are approved by a vote of the membership, and pay the expense of dues annually. Masons must come of their own will, believe in a Supreme Being (which one is left to the individual), be at least 18-25 years old, be of good morals, reputation, and sound mind and body, free-born and provide character references. Masonry does not classify itself as a religion; however, in the western world, the King James Version of the Bible is always displayed as "the Volume of the Sacred Law" in every open lodge. The two main bodies of Masonry, one through the York Rite and the other through the Scottish Rite, do not require members to be Christians, although they prohibit atheists and agnostics from membership. Other lesser-known rites, such as the Swedish Rite and some other smaller groups, only allow Christian members, and still others allow atheists and agnostics. Lodges are where Masons meet for rituals, ceremony, and meetings, led by a Worshipful Master. Each lodge is issued a charter or warrant by a Grand Lodge, that governs Masonic lodges in a specified region. Masons are typically noted by charitable community service, exclusion of women (although there are some non-traditional orders that do receive them now) and being considered "free thinkers."

Masonry has been tied to all sorts of world events, from the Holocaust to different political elections, to the founding of the United States, and the Constitution of the United States, which does uphold Masonic principles. There are many religious denominations, including Roman Catholicism, some branches of Islam, and many of Evangelical (especially Pentecostal) and Protestant Christianity that deem membership with Masonry as grounds for excommunication, disfellowship, or disassociation. There are many reasons for this, but the foundational element is the theology of Masonry coupled with its secretive nature. In modern times, we must be careful what we listen to when we learn about such things as Masonry. Some of what we hear about Freemasonry is speculative, some of it is foundational, and some of it is nothing more than absurd. To say Masons are running the world is an exaggeration of the truth, and it is better to learn facts rather than trying to create chaos.[19]

*Image of a Prince Hall Military Lodge*

## Prince Hall Masonry

Historically speaking, Freemasonry was open exclusively to white males, because one of the major points of membership was living as a free citizen, rather than as a slave.

Before the American Revolution, fifteen free black men (one of them being Prince Hall) petitioned to join St. John's Lodge, in Boston. They were denied, and most lodges remained segregated until the 1960s. It remains as such in some Masonic jurisdictions, to this day. Instead, these men were initiated into Masonry through the Grand Lodge of Ireland in 1775. Due to the segregation present in the lodges, the men had a difficult time obtaining a charter and fought all the way to the Grand Master of the Mother Grand Lodge of England for membership. They received a charter for African Lodge No. 1 in 1784 and became the first African Lodge. Prince Hall, as leader, became a Provincial Grand Master. After his death, the members formed a Grand Lodge and was later named the Prince Hall Grand Lodge. There are two sets of organizations within Prince Hall Masonry: the Prince Hall National Grand Lodge, and Prince Hall Affiliation. Prince Hall Masonry is not acknowledged as a legitimate Masonic organization by all Freemasons.[20]

## **Shriners**

The Shriners, also known as Shriners International and formerly known as Ancient Arabic Order of the Nobles of the Mystic Shrine (was changed in 2010), is a branch of Freemasonry for those who are Master Masons. The order was founded in 1870 in New York City, by those who desired an additional fraternity because they felt the traditional work of masonry was too focused on ritual. They uphold Masonic principles and believe in fun, fellowship, and in charitable work, which usually takes the form of Shriners Hospitals for children, which connects 22 different hospitals together for care of sick or ill children at no cost to their families.[21,22]

*Shriner's emblem*

## **Order of the Eastern Star**

A Masonic entity open to men and women but typically associated with ritual and participation for women. It was started in 1850 and approved by the Masonic Fraternity in 1873. To participate, one must be a Master Mason or related to or connected to a Mason. The order

*Order of the Eastern Star emblem*

follows character-building principles from the Bible, modeling after different Bible women, although it is open to women of any religion. Order of the Eastern Star has, through the years, given to different charitable causes, including Alzheimer's Disease, juvenile diabetes, and juvenile asthma research.[23]

## Order of the Amaranth

A Masonic-based organization for Master Masons and their wives or other female family members, dating back to 1873. It is based on the Amarante Order, a fraternal order for Swedish knights, founded by Queen Christina of Sweden in 1653. Their major philanthropic work is the Amaranth Diabetes Foundation.[24,25]

*Order of the Amaranth emblem*

## White Shrine of Jerusalem

An order for women connected to men involved with Freemasonry and for Master Masons, founded in 1895 in the state of Illinois. Their purpose is to be spiritual, charitable, and fraternal. Unlike in many Masonic organizations, members must attest to a belief in Jesus Christ as Savior. Their charitable work is the Supreme Material Objective Fund, which assists in the payment of medical bills for those who are unable to cover their own expenses.[26]

*White Shrine of Jerusalem emblem*

## The Knights Templar

The Knights Templar gained interest and legendary status when it was referenced in the book *The DaVinci Code*, by Dan Brown. While there is no question the book was a fascinating and exciting read, the lines between fact and fiction were blurred by enthusiastic readers who took legends about the Knights Templar seriously and believed the fiction of the book transcended fact. The Knights Templar (also called Templars) were a religious and military order of knighthood during the

*Seal of the Knights Templar*

crusades, existing somewhere around the 1100s. They were very successful and known for excessive influence and wealth. As a result, garnered a lot of enemies.

They were destroyed by King Philip IV of France. They followed Benedictine Rule as is in place by the Cistercians, swearing poverty, chastity, and obedience, just as monks did. As devoted Catholics, they had a particular devotion to Mary, lived communally, and were not allowed to gamble, swear, or drink to intoxication. They participated in battles, built buildings, and fought against Muslim armies. There have been many legends woven about the Templars, mostly from the fact that Freemasonry introduced a special line of secret knowledge possessed by the Templars starting somewhere around the eighteenth century. Much of the legends around the Templars, such as preserving the bloodline of Christ or worshiping the head of Christ, are fanciful legends that don't have much basis in fact.

The modern-day Knights Templar Order is not, in reality, a reflection of the true Templars of old, and is an interfaith, non-denominational organization that is an "order," of sorts, and does have reflections of Secret Society structure, but does not classify as one in quite the same way. They, in fact, reject the principle of a secret society and the rules and governances therein. It appears to be another esoteric organization and order that exemplifies the lineages of Gnosticism that arose in the nineteenth and twentieth centuries. The Grand Encampment Knights Templar order is a division of Freemasonry, with membership prerequisite on membership in a Masonic Lodge.[27,28]

## Social Order of Beauceant

An order of consisting of women connected to men who are a part of the Knights Templar division of Freemasonry. They were founded in Denver, Colorado in 1890 as an assistance to help the Templars with a Conclave to be held in the city. The Commandery's Knights Templar Eye Foundation is their official charity.[29]

*Social Order of Beauceant emblem*

## Daughters of the Nile

An organization for women eighteen years or older who are related by birth or marriage to a Shriner, Master Mason, Masonic related order for girls or women, other Daughter of the Nile member, or was a patient at a Shriner's Hospital as a child. They were founded in Seattle, Washington in 1913, and their predominant purpose is to raise funds for Shriner's Hospitals for Children.[30]

*Daughters of the Nile emblem*

**Job's Daughters International**

Formerly known as the International Order of Job's Daughters, founded in Omaha, Nebraska in 1920. A Masonic-sponsored girls' organization for participants ages 10-20. It is a preparatory agency to prepare girls for membership within Order of the Eastern Star or Order of Amaranth upon aging out of the program. It adheres to similar requirements found elsewhere in Masonry and must be sponsored by a Majority Member and Master Mason if she is not related to either. Each level above the local level (local levels are known as Bethels) sponsor different philanthropic work, and the supreme project is the Hearing Impaired Kids Endowment Foundation.[31]

*Job's Daughters International emblem*

**International Order of the Rainbow for Girls**

Another Masonic-sponsored youth service organization, it focuses on community service for girls aged 11-21. Unlike some Masonic groups, the International Order of the Rainbow does not require relation to a Master Mason. Interested girls submit applications and the assembly decides if she is eligible to receive the different degrees of the order. Members are expected to be service-minded, law-abiding, acknowledge the authority present in the order, and show loyalty. Majority members of this group may become members of the Order of the Eastern Star, when they become old enough.[32]

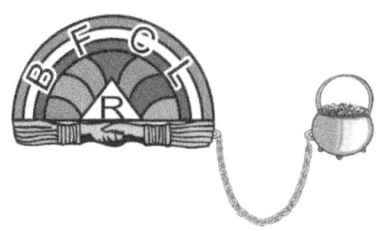

*International Order of the Rainbow for Girls*

## Rosicrucianism

Also known as the Fraternity of the Rose Cross, Rosicrucianism falls much as Freemasonry does within the principle of an "ancient revival" of older principles pieced together somewhere around the early 1600s. It was built on ancient principles of Kabbalah, Hermeticism, and more mystical traditions found in Christianity. The origins of the group are found in a writing circulated in the early 1600s about a German doctor and philosopher known as Frater C.R.C. or Christian Rosenkreuz, born in 1378, who lived 106 years. He supposedly gained great knowledge from working with mystics and masters in the Middle East, and

*Rosicrucian rose*

started the Rosicrucian Order, sometime around 1407. The first eight members, all men, made agreements to profess to be healers and receive no payment, wear no habit or uniform, meet once a year at the Spiritus Sanctus headquarters, find someone to be their successor, the letters C.R. would be their seal and mark, and their group would remain secret for a hundred years. These writings were considered allegorical or fraudulent and were not taken particularly seriously. The longer the work was around, however, the more they gained curiosity, and individuals who desired to learn the revealed truths promised in the writings. There have been many groups since that tie back to Rosicrucianism and its values. It is considered an influential figure in the formation of Freemasonry (including two rites that emerged around the end of the eighteenth century) and countless other secret societies that all use the image of the rose and cross, red cross, or "rosy cross" as part of their foundation. The more modern Rosicrucian groups are the Order of the Golden Dawn and Ancient Mystical Order Rosae Crucis, and The Rosicrucian Fellowship. Much like other secret societies, the foundations echo those of occult principles and foundations, tying them back to Egyptian, Hindu, Persian, Pythagorean, and Middle Eastern occultism. The modern Rosicrucians are, much like we have seen, similar to other modern groups that attempt to revive or continue older organizations.[33,34]

## Order of the Skull and Bones

There is much speculation about the Order of the Skull and Bones, which is an undergraduate senior secret society exclusive to Yale University in New Haven, Connecticut. It first came into the limelight when it was discovered former president George W. Bush had been a member while at Yale. It was founded in 1832 after a dispute among other Yale societies by William Huntington Russell and Alphonso Taft. Members are selected by invitation, and women are also allowed to join (since the 1990s). Membership is selected by those who have the potential for leadership. Members are known as "Bonesmen" and the society is known among members as "Bones." Their existing hall, known as the "Tomb," was completed in 1912. The society also owns Deer Island on the St. Lawrence River. The order has a reputation as a foundation for the power elite that run the world, and has long been associated with Protestant, white males (although other ethnic and religious groups have been admitted for about 80 years). Because of its secrecy and so many of its members have gone on to hold positions in the CIA, the United States government, and other places of power, it is considered of great question and interest among conspiracy theorists.[35]

*Order of Skull and Bones emblem*

## Orange Order

Also known as The Loyal Orange Institution, the Orange Order is a Protestant fraternal order located in Northern Ireland, Scotland, and the United States. It was founded in 1795 in response to Protestant and Catholic conflict in the nation, and is Masonic in style, sworn to defend the Protestant Ascendancy. They are a conservative British unionist organization and are exclusive in their membership, requiring members to be Protestant (non-Trinitarians are banned), observe Sabbatarian rules (not allowed to work) on Sundays, guardians of history and historic wars of Ireland, and cannot be of mixed marriages (Protestant and Catholic). Their affiliate organizations are Association of Loyal Orangewomen of Ireland,

*Emblem of the Orange Order*

Independent Orange Institution, Royal Black Institution, and the Apprentice Boys of Derry. Many of their marches and public displays have become violent throughout history.[36]

## Knights of Pythias

A fraternal organization and secret society founded in 1864 in Washington, D.C by Justus H. Rathbone. The organization focuses on the story of Damon and Pythias, a legend that expounds the Greek Pythagorean concepts that relate to friendship. When Pythias was accused of creating a plot against Dionysius I of Syracuse, he made a request for Dionysius to settle his affairs on the condition that he leaves his friend, Damon, a hostage. If he did not return, Damon would be killed. Pythias returned to face his own execution, and Dionysius was so taken with Pythias' love and

*Knights of Pythias emblem*

friendship to Damon, he set both free. The Knights of Pythias believe in the embodiment of these principles, loyalty, honor, and friendship, expounding these as ancient Greek philosophical principles. The organization embodies three degrees of Knighthood (Page, Esquire, Knight), and meet in a lodge, or castle. Their national structure is known as the Supreme Lodge. Their side degree, the Dramatic Order of the Knights of Khorassan, like the Masonic Shriners. Their auxiliaries include the Pythian Sisters for women and the Pythian Sunshine Girls and Junior order of Princes of Syracuse. Members must be male, in good health, who believe in a Supreme Being.[37,38]

## Independent Order of Odd Fellows

Older than Freemasonry, the international fraternity of Odd Fellows or Oddfellows date back to London in 1730. It is presupposed to have emerged from various trade alliances without union representation in Britain. Their history is largely undocumented, and no one is exactly sure where its

*Independent Order of Odd Fellows emblem*

origins lie. Their purpose is to promote friendship, love, truth, faith, hope, charity, and universal justice through charitable projects, promote good will and harmony, and avoid discrimination in fraternal experience. There are three levels of Lodge: the Lodge, the Encampment, and the Patriarchs Militant, and four lodge degrees: Initiatory, Friendship, Brotherly/Sisterly Love, and Truth. Each lodge holds nineteen different positions to maintain meetings, initiations, and the specifications of lodge rites. There are three encampment degrees: Patriarch, Golden Rule, and Royal Purple, and one lodge of the Patriarch Militants: Chevalier. Within the Odd Fellows there are different units of orders: Odd Fellows Lodge, Rebekahs Lodge, Encampment, Ladies Encampment Auxiliary, Patriarchs Militant, Ladies Auxiliary Patriarchs Militant, Junior Odd Fellows Lodge, Theta Rho Girls Club, United Youth Groups, Zeta Lambda Tau, and The Ancient Mystic Order of Samaritans. They were the first fraternity to establish homes for the elderly and orphans in the United States.[39]

## **Knights of Columbus**

As a general rule, the Roman Catholic Church has issued decrees and declarations against fraternal memberships for their members. In the same vain, Catholics were ofiten denied entry into fraternal orders. In response, the Knights of Columbus were started to offer a fraternal order and experience in a mutual benefit society for Catholic workers and immigrants in the United States. It was founded by Father Michael J. McGivney in New Haven, Connecticut in 1882. They had an entire insurance system, assisting even the sickest or most elderly of patrons. Their order is dedicated to the ideals of patriotism, charity, unity, and fraternity. There are four degrees, and a man becomes a full member at the third degree. The fourth degree serves to instill active patriotism and citizenship within a Catholic male. As an organization, they focus heavily on charity, including giving to Habitat for Humanity, Special Olympics, and disaster relief. They also promote Catholicism through the Catholic Information Service and are active in American politics. Women are not admitted as members, but participate in women's auxiliaries, such as the Daughters of Isabella, Catholic Daughters of the Americas, and the Columbiettes. Their junior organization is the

*Knights of Columbus logo*

Columbian Squires and their youth sorority is the Squire Roses.⁴⁰

## B'nai B'rith

Just as Catholics were frequently excluded from fraternal organizations, so too were Jews. Not only were Jews forbidden, but many organizations also espoused anti-Semitic sentiments at different points in their histories. B'nai B'rith has grown to become the oldest Jewish service-based organization in the world, with emphasis on uniting Jewish people and enhance Jewish identity through family life and service. It was founded by Henry Jones in New York City, 1843. Like most organizations of its time, it is fraternal in nature and structure, but unlike most other organizations, it has expanded to include political and social advocacy for Jewish people worldwide. Most of its work in modern times relates to advocacy and charitable work, including elderly and infirm, health care reform, Social Security and Medicare protection, scholarships, and disaster relief.⁴¹

*B'nai B'rith logo*

## Fraternities and Sororities

Fraternities and sororities are a mixed bag when it comes to their work and presentation, and there is no singular universal consensus as to Christian involvement or participation with them. With news of fraternal and sorority hazing over the past few years, however, there is growing concern over participation with them on college campuses. Fraternities and sororities, as a general rule, are found on different college and university campuses that exist as social organizations in the United States, the Philippines, France, the United Kingdom, Canada, Germany, and in some other nations, worldwide. Most sororities and fraternities require membership while one is an undergraduate student and then maintain their membership throughout life, post-graduation. Most are "Greek organizations," indicating their name and identity is found in Greek letters. Their requirements are usually single-sex membership, secrecy, selection of new members based on rushing (membership drive) and pledging (proving one's desire to be a member), ownership and occupancy of a property that is specifically where the sorority or fraternity belongs, and the use of different identification symbols, such as Greek letters, badges, grips, handshakes, hand signs, passwords, flowers, and colors. Many require "finishing" training as part of the pledge process, including social etiquettes, attire, and networking for new members. Their original purpose was a bridge introduction to more advanced secret societies, such as Freemasonry.

As with all societies, their histories are complicated, and most include prohibition on members of certain social standing, race, religion, or culture. The first fraternity in the United States was Phi Beta Kappa, dating back to 1775. The first sorority was Alpha Delta Pi in 1851. In addition to many standards that are considered secretive or exclusive today, fraternities and sororities are under fire for issues of alcoholism, sexism, sexual assault, and drug use and hazing today. Hazing is a practice some fraternities and sororities employ during the pledge process, inducing physical and mental torture upon pledges. Some common hazing methods include sleep deprivation, paddling, busy work, mind games, branding, enemas, or eating decaying food. There have been reports of pledges dying, thus creating an outcry against hazing and some fraternities and sororities losing their status because of such practices.

*Assorted Greek letters for different organizations*

There are hundreds of sororities and fraternities in existence. Within the past forty or so years, the idea of Christian fraternities and sororities has risen in different places, all with different membership requirements, to offer a Christian alternative to standard fraternities and sororities. These organizations are different from the more traditional Christian organizations that date back far earlier. Rather than focusing on the secrecy of traditional fraternities and sororities, many of these more modern organizations are fraternal-based ministries, employing Greek letters and other traditional aspects of fraternities and sororities, but eliminating hazing, alcohol, academic requirements, and focusing instead on discipleship, service, and charity.[42]

## Ordo Templi Orientis

Also called the OTO, "Order of the Temple of the East" or "Order of Oriental Templars" the Ordo Templi Orientis is a secret, fraternal-based occult organization founded sometime between 1895 and 1906 by Carl Kellner. Its most notable leader is the one who shaped and formed what it became, such being Aleister Crowley, who became a member in 1904. As with all other organizations of this sort, it is based on different initiations that are much like what is found in Freemasonry. There are thirteen different degrees falling under four main headings: the Man of Earth Triad, Outside all Triads, The Lover Triad, and The Hermit Triad. It is divided up into two types of rituals: the initiation into the different mysteries and the

*Ordo Templi Orientis logo*

celebration of what they call the Gnostic Mass (headed under the Ecclesia Gnostica Catholica). Its foundation is the Law of Thelema, found in the Book of the Law (written by Crowley himself). The summary of this law is: "Do what thou wilt shall be the whole of the law." They espouse a belief in a universal brotherhood and the need for universal religion. Throughout its history, there have been many who challenged the legitimacy of the organization.[43,44]

## The Hermetic Order of the Golden Dawn

Also known as Ordo Hermeticus Aurorae Aureae or The Golden Dawn. This order existed between the late 1880s (founded in Britain) and 1970s, with a few modern revivals, all of which are offshoots of the

*Golden Dawn Enochian Sigillum Dei Aemeth*

original inspiration of the work. Similar to Masonry, its major difference was the admittance of women along with men. There were three different orders, the "Golden Dawn" as the first, teaching the ideals of Hermetic Kabbalah, four classical elements, astrology, tarot, divination, and geomancy. The second order was the Ruby Rose and Cross of Gold, taught magic. The third order was the "Secret Chiefs," who were highly skilled and directed those in the other two orders. The foundation of the order were the

Cipher Manuscripts, a group of sixty different folios that explain magical initiation rituals as correspond to natural elements and classical theories of magic and symbolism. The order also contains elements of Rosicrucianism.[45,46]

## The Illuminati

*The back of the dollar bill, displaying Illuminati symbols*

If you spend time on YouTube or on social media outlets, the odds are high you have heard mention of an organization by the name of the Illuminati. As with many things related to secret societies, some of what we hear is true, and some of it is fictionalized. The term "Illuminati" means "enlightened," and was first referenced by a group founded in Bavaria in 1776. It was founded by Adam Weishaupt. In this original state, the order only existed until 1785, when it was outlawed, as the Catholic Church and Bavarian government worried about its possible influence. Its documents were both confiscated and published by the government, driving the movement more underground. Even before its prohibition, the Illuminati suffered from great internal strife and numerous divisions, including conflict with the Rosicrucians. Ever since, different groups (including the Ordo Templi Orientis) have claimed to be direct descendants of this original Illuminati group, although no claims have ever been substantiated. There were three tiers of initiation: the Nursery (Noviciate, Minerval, Illuminatus minor), The Masonic Grades (Apprentice, Companion, Master) and The Mysteries (Priest, Prince, Mage, and King).

The major link between the Illuminati and the United States government is rooted in the fact that the Illuminati was formed right before the signing of the Declaration of Independence, and it is no secret many of the Founding Fathers had ties to various occult groups and secret fraternal organizations. In fact, many of the principles found in the formation of the United States government reflect those values found in secret societies. As a result, many suggest the very founding of the United States of America relates to the Illuminati. Such theories are furthered by the use of various occult symbolism present in many national and state symbols, as well as on United States currency.

If you listen to conspiracy sources, the Illuminati as exists today controls the media, Hollywood, all major news outlets, big business, world governments, and all the banks. While the organization was founded to be non-religious, people have theorized members to include major entertainers, religious figures, and politicians – everyone from the pope to Barak Obama – judging membership by supposed hand symbols and imagery. Some believe the Illuminati has ties to Satanism or Satanic ritual. Others believe the illuminati is tied to different wealthy and prominent world families.

The role or nature of the Illuminati is veiled in secrecy, with question as to their exact nature and what they do, if anything, in modern times. There are testimonials online of individuals who claim to have experienced a modern-day form of the Illuminati, but the stories are unverified, because the details they provide are often heinous, and no organization doing such things would, in its right mind, would account for them.[47,48,49]

## **Christians and secret societies**

The major issue many raise when it comes to issues of secret societies is the level of participation a Christian may have with one (or multiple ones) and still maintain their Christian identity. There are also many deliverance ministries who feel involvement with a secret society, even if it is done by a close relative, can invite certain spirits into the life of the believer. There is no question that belonging to such societies can pose severe questions to the devout or serious believer. The entire premise of such groups as secretive, seeking different levels of secret knowledge, and the mandatory nature of keeping such as a secret contrasts with Gospel principles of honesty. There is the issue of the spirituality introduced, the idea that one is obtaining some sort of secret or otherworldly knowledge that puts them on a different spiritual plane, and the concept that one can obtain these contents only within the group. There is also the question, obviously, of what goes on in many of these organizations. Whether it's practicing magic, an outlet for vice, the attempt to network or advance socially, or dying to belong (sometimes literally) to maintain one's membership, belonging to these groups can certainly conjure spirits through their practices of magic and foundational philosophies that are rooted in revivals of ancient magical concepts.

I believe we need to examine the realities as to why membership with these groups is often appealing in the first place. By doing so, we should maintain our own personal examinations of how we behave toward others as believers, and of what our churches are offering our communities. There are reasons people may be intrigued by the appeal of a secret society, if for no other reason than just about all of them are community involved and active in charity work. They appear to have things "together," and while church boards and groups can't seem to get past go in terms of ideas and concepts, secret societies have been functioning and active for hundreds of years without the obvious conflicts many church groups have. Rank and file is clear, and those who have achieved higher levels of understanding within the organization compose its senior membership. The clarity of these ideas, purposes, and functions can make someone curious who doesn't see things working together within their spiritual communities. People like a sense of belonging, and they like the idea of belonging to an organization that at least appears to have it all together and functions well, especially within its own ranks.

No matter the spiritual foundations of such groups, their charitable work, community spirit, and ability to work with one another is notable and commendable, especially given that most churches today are less involved in such work than these organizations. There should be no question that if the church doesn't fulfill the need that many people seek, they will look for it somewhere else, and membership in some of these groups may look appealing. We are quick to condemn secret societies, but we aren't fast enough to examine ourselves and the things we do are wrong or drive people away from where they need to be.

All this having been said, there are many aspects of these organizations that are not altruistic, nor do they reflect good character. Many offer outlets and connections for vices, no matter what those vices may be. They promote a sense of partiality and favoritism. Many have, and some still, espouse racism in varied forms, and many of them promote sexism and sexist ideals. Several have been cited in riots or violence throughout history. While the work of charity and community involvement may be commendable, there is a darker side of such organizations that does not reflect Christian values, no matter what doctrine the group may espouse. There are many who join for altruistic reasons and who may maintain those goals, but there are many more who have joined for one reason, adopted another entirely, and maintained their membership for reasons far different than charity work or community involvement.

Membership within a secret society is not as simple as the issue of going to heaven or hell when someone dies (although there may be that issue the higher up one goes), but one of the Christian life and of embodying the principles of Jesus within one's purpose. It's perfectly possible to do charitable work or be involved in one's community without membership in a secret organization. If it doesn't feel like one's church has it together in the way one might desire, then be a volunteer for something on one's own. There are many ways people can be involved without having to participate in these organizations, especially as counterfeit spiritualities become involved. There are options, as one looks, and as the church, it is advisable to keep a list of different agencies and causes available for interested members who desire to be more involved in their community.

Having said all the above, being involved in a secret society can certainly open up an individual to different spirits, in many different ways, and can leave one open to counterfeit understandings of important theological and spiritual matters. It's not worth it when one can volunteer on their own for a project or event. That having been said, yes, involvement with such an organization can raise spiritual issues, and deliverance ministers need to approach such with wisdom and understanding of the occult and the beliefs therein. At the same time, it is not a special deliverance situation that transfers between family members and generations when nobody even belongs to the organization anymore. It's not special; it's not unique; and it is a situation that needs to be examined for what it is, addressed for what it is, and treated as its own unique experience and spiritual rendering therein.

## **Satanism**

Although Satanism would technically fall into the category of an occult group that is openly occult, Satanism is a religious identity and world all its own, with its unique complexities. We frequently label any group that is Christian or falls into the category of being pagan or occult as "satanic," but such a general blanket approach to labeling is, indeed, incorrect. While I do not question the underlying spiritual realities behind things we should not engage in, there are groups that do not identify with Satan, nor even believe Satan is a legitimate personification or being. Associating groups, such as Wicca, with Satanism, is considered an insult, and incorrect according to their own theology.

Satanism, as an entity, is its own religious identity, separate from other organizations. That is where the simplicity of what Satanism is begins and ends. There are many variations within Satanism, all of which cause those who practice Satanism to have different understandings and beliefs about just what it means to be a Satanist.

There are two main types of Satanism: theistic and atheistic. Theistic Satanism identifies Satan as a being, as the major deity, as more or less a father figure within the religious sentiment. Atheistic Satanists do not believe in the personalized being of Satan but believe in Satan as an identity factor within human traits, mostly linked to hedonism, or pleasure-seeking as the highest form of personal fulfillment. In atheistic Satanism, Satan is chosen as a main identity point to contrast the values and ideals present within Christianity.

*Anton LaVey, founder of the Church of Satan*

Satanism as an existing practice has a spurious history, even though accusations of such practices have existed through much of Christianity. Where exactly Satanism started nobody knows, but groups that identify as Satanic or Satan-worshiping have existed since the nineteenth century. This means that Satanism as a religious identity is relatively new, and most likely arose in rebellion to Christian standards of morality and faith present in more modern times. There is no question that Satanism represents a highly controversial belief system and, often, even more controversial religious practice.

There are all sorts of reports about animal or human sacrifices, Satanists breaking the law, rampant child abuse, torture, or other horrific occurrences directly tied to Satanists or Satanic activity. As with all things related to the occult, such things have happened at points in history, but they are not necessarily something that happens today or that was done by every Satanist throughout history. Most modern Satanists are strong adherents of the separation of church and state, advocate for human rights issues, and believe strongly in their legal right to practice their religion. They strongly believe in personal identity, independence, individualism, and freedom.

Because of the controversial nature of Satanism, most Satanic groups are underground, avoiding public scrutiny. There is little known about everything underground Satanists do, although there are plenty of rumors. Satanists believe they cooperate with Satan (whether metaphorical, literal, or in an abstract sense) to develop the powers of their being, their spiritual identities, and their minds in the form of Satanic magic. Satanic magic is classified as the "black arts," and Satanists do employ their own unique magical system in order to produce their own specified desired results. Local Satanic groups are classified as grottos, pylons, or temples. As they have set themselves apart from much of the occult community, Satanists are frequently at odds with other occult practitioners, especially those found in Wicca. They are highly critical of different religious traditions, especially Christianity. A practitioner of Satanism may meet with a group or may practice Satanism as an individual.

There is one major public body of Satanism, known as the Church of Satan. It is within the bounds of atheistic Satanism, espousing a sort of self-worship and acknowledgement. It should be said that the Church of Satan is not regarded as authentic Satanism by all Satanists, and many feel it takes on a cartoonish or insincere nature when it comes to Satanic identity. The Church of Satan was founded in 1966 by Anton LaVey, who spent his previous life as a circus performer. The Church of Satan was the first public, above-ground Satanic religious movement, giving Satanism a uniquely American identity as well as its core textbook. *The Satanic Bible*, written by LaVey himself, is considered the primary textbook of Satanism in the world today. Satanism's basic principles can be summarized in ideals from the Satanic Bible, and include:

The Nine Satanic Statements:[50]

- Satan represents indulgence instead of abstinence!
- Satan represents vital existence instead of spiritual pipe dreams!
- Satan represents undefiled wisdom instead of hypocritical self-deceit!
- Satan represents kindness to those who deserve it instead of love wasted on ingrates!
- Satan represents vengeance instead of turning the other cheek!
- Satan represents responsibility to the responsible instead of concern for psychic vampires!

- Satan represents man as just another animal, sometimes better, more often worse than those that walk on all-fours, who, because of his "divine spiritual and intellectual development," has become the most vicious animal of all!
- Satan represents all of the so-called sins, as they all lead to physical, mental, or emotional gratification!
- Satan has been the best friend the Church has ever had, as He has kept it in business all these years!

Eleven Satanic Rules of the Earth:[51]

- Do not give opinions or advice unless you are asked.
- Do not tell your troubles to others unless you are sure they want to hear them.
- When in another's lair, show him respect or else do not go there.
- If a guest in your lair annoys you, treat him cruelly and without mercy.
- Do not make sexual advances unless you are given the mating signal.
- Do not take that which does not belong to you unless it is a burden to the other person and he cries out to be relieved.
- Acknowledge the power of magic if you have employed it successfully to obtain your desires. If you deny the power of magic after having called upon it with success, you will lose all you have obtained.
- Do not complain about anything to which you need not subject yourself.
- Do not harm little children.
- Do not kill non-human animals unless you are attacked or for your food.
- When walking in open territory, bother no one. If someone bothers you, ask him to stop. If he does not stop, destroy him.

The Nine Satanic Sins:[52]

- Stupidity
- Pretentiousness
- Solipsism
- Self-deceit

- Herd conformity
- Lack of perspective
- Forgetful of past orthodoxies
- Counterproductive pride
- Lack of aesthetics

The Church of Satan rejects any other Satanic organization as legitimate, and functions via different networks of individuals who espouse the different theories of Satanism as put forth by the church. The church is headed by a High Priest, and the rituals of Satanism center around the practice of the Black Mass, one that has been specifically designed for use within the Church of Satan.

The Black Mass is a specific and deliberate inversion of the Roman Catholic mass, which is regarded as the highest form of worship in the Catholic Church. It is typically in Latin and recites the mass itself, as well as the Lord's Prayer backwards. More modern versions of the Black Mass are inversions of the Catholic mass with Satanic elements included therein.[53] The major holidays of Satanism include Walpurgisnacht (April 30, a feast for witches), Halloween, the summer and winter solstices, and the spring and fall equinox. Satanists also acknowledge their own birthdays as holidays.[54]

The Church of Satan has suffered many divisions in leadership over the years, and smaller sects of Satanism related to the Church of Satan include The Temple of Set, Order of the Left Hand Path, Order of the Trapezoid, First Satanic Church, and Our Lady of Endor Coven (Ophite Cultus Satanas).[55]

Those who are a part of Satanism, whether theistic or atheistic, no matter how they consider the role of Satan, do not believe they are loved by Satan or feel any affection from him. They are open about acknowledging their purposes for following Satan have nothing to do with his allegiance or alliance with them, and they do not believe he cares about them. They follow Satan for the power and pleasures he offers, and they enjoy having the power to be adversarial, to exercise control or magic, or to have their way in different aspects of their lives.

**Occult symbolism**

Occult symbolism is usually drawn from standard religious sources and gives a bit of an esoteric twist to make it unique. It is common to see symbols we see in religious settings: crosses, crowns, circles, triangles, chalices, flowers, and even the Name of God in different, varied forms. Many symbols echo back to those of ancient pagan religions, found in Babylon, Egypt, or Greece. As a virtual melding of many different strains of thought, occult symbolism represents itself with its melding of ideas.

A word of note: many people use some of these symbols in a non-occult context, such as the Star of David in Judaism or the Cross in Christianity. There are also many Christians who use these different elements without understanding their origin or context, so someone using these symbols does not necessarily mean someone is an occult practitioner. At the same time, the use of such symbols in churches, on hymnals or Bibles, on stained-glass windows, or other symbolism often reveals the truth about the founding members of churches or prominent donors and their not-so-public beliefs.

It is impossible to post every single occult symbol in existence in this book, but the ones we present here represent some of the base ideas or common foundational imagery used in the occult, and can be, therefore, useful in identifying it and adherents of it.

## **The Tree of life (Kabbalah)**

Originating in Kabbalah but with usage across most occult denominations and affiliations (of which the understanding of the tree is slightly different) the Tree of Life is known as the *Etz Chaim* in Hebrew. It is designed to depict the ten sephirot, or emanations, which are attributed to God and manifest through the will of God. It relates to the physical and the spiritual worlds, to one's own soul, state of being, level of wisdom and knowledge, and understanding. The unfolding will of God descends through the tree from left to right.

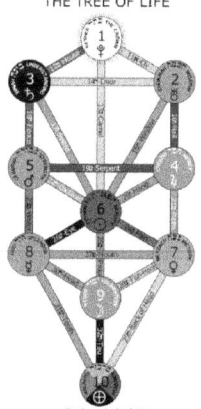

*Tree of Life*

## **Tetragrammation (Kabbalah, Magic, Christian occultism)**

In Old Testament history, pronouncing the Name of God was regarded as the ultimate blasphemy, because it was believed to speak the Name of God was to take it in vain. The letters, YHVH (sometimes translated as JVHV, or Yahweh or Jehovah) were all that remained of the Name of God, without vowel sounds, because anywhere it was found in the Old Testament, pious scribes were quick to change the name from "YHVH" to *Adonai* (which means "My Lord"). Occultists of all sorts, from Kabbalah to those of Christian occult roots, consider any title or name of God to be sacred, but believe the tetragrammation (the four letters of God's Name) to be the most powerful way to call upon God, especially because it was hidden for so many years and, therefore, unknowable today.

*Tetragrammation*

## Shem HaMephorash (72-fold name) (Kabbalah)

By tradition, the actual pronunciation for the tetragrammation was *Shem haMephorash*, as revealed by God to Moses in the burning bush. Only the high priest could speak this sacred name on Yom Kippur (the Day of Atonement) in the Jerusalem Temple in the Holy of Holies. If anyone else was to pronounce it, they would die, because they would say it wrong. It was supposedly lost when the second temple was destroyed in 70 AD. Thirteenth-century Kabbalists used the Gematria (use of Hebrew letters to create a numerical decoding system) to decode the numerical value of the Name of God, and they came out with seventy-two. They created 72 different names of God, angelic suffixes to create 72 angels, and also 72 different spirits, associated with a zodiac sign.[58]

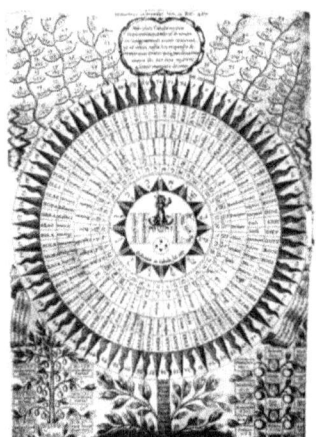
*72-Fold Name of God*

## Baphomet, the Goat of Mendes (Magic, Satanic Gnosticism, Satanism)

Originally found in Eliphas Levi's book, *Dogme et Rituel de la Haute Magie* (1854), Baphomet is a corruption of the name of Mohammed, the founder of Islam. It exists to display the world in male and female energy, central to the understanding of occultism in the 1800s. Much of the imagery relates to ancient Greek ideas,

*Statue of Baphomet*

including elemental forces (fish scales – water, semi-circle – air, feet on earth – earth, burning crown – fire) and Pan, the fertility Greek god with goat-like features. The image points upward to express the Hermetic idea, "As above, so below." Chesed and Geburah are two sephirot on the Tree of Life, displaying male and female attributes of existence. Solve and coagula on Baphomet's arms are opposing alchemical processes, meaning "dissolve" and "coagulate." Levi himself described Baphomet as the "sphinx of occult sciences." Satanists use Baphomet as a representation of Satan.[59]

## Pentagram (Paganism, Magic, Satanic Gnosticism, Satanism)

The pentagram is a five-pointed star, made using five straight strokes for its creation. It is an ancient symbol and has been used throughout history, both in pagan and Christian circles. In ancient Judaism, it represented the Torah, and the first important of the Seven Seals. In ancient Christianity, it was used to describe the five wounds of Christ (2 wrist, 2 ankle and 1 side). It has also been called the three Kings' star, believed to represent the star which led the Wise Men to the infant Jesus. In modern paganism, it represents the five elements: earth, air, fire, water, and spirit.

*Pentagram*

*Inverted pentagram*

An inverted pentagram, often with a Baphomet head, is called the Sigil of Baphomet. It is considered a modern symbol of Satanism.[60]

## Rosy Cross (Rosicrucianism, Freemasonry, Thelema magic, magic)

Associated primarily with Rosicrucianism, the Rosy Cross is found throughout the occult as a popular symbol. Every group interprets the symbolism differently, although its origins are from Christian symbolism. It is considered a symbol of immortality, sacrifice, and death. The colors yellow, blue, black and red signify air, water, earth, and fire, and white represents spirits. It is considered a union of male and female, and the rose is used in a complex fashion as a symbol of magic. The three

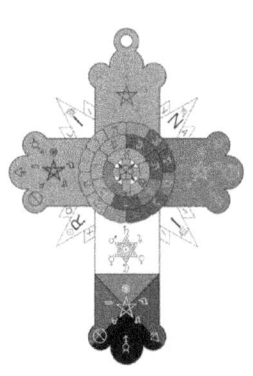
*Rosy Cross*

tiers of petals each represent different things: the first (three petals), the basic alchemical elements of salt, mercury, and sulfur; the second tier (seven petals), the seven classical planets (Sun, Moon, Mercury, Venus, Mars, Jupiter, and Saturn), the third tier (twelve petals) represents the astrological zodiac, and the total number of petals represents the number of letters in the Hebrew alphabet and twenty-two paths on the Tree of Life. Pentagrams are displayed at the end of each cross. The hexagram, or Star of David, represents the merging of two opposites (male and female). The number of alchemical and zodiac signs around the remainder of the Rosy Cross display the alchemical nature of the occult.[61]

## **Hamsa (Kabbalah)**

Hamsa literally means "five" and represents the fifth letter of the Hebrew alphabet (Heh) which is found in the Name of God. Five also represents the Torah, and the five senses, all of which should praise God. Also called the Hand of Miriam. Believed to represent the hand of God. It can be worn up or down, and is believed to ward off evil spirits, the "evil eye," and offer happiness, peace, and prosperity.[62]

*Hamsa*

## **All-seeing eye (Kabbalah, Gnostic, Satanic Gnostic, Satanism, magic, Thelema, Freemasonry, Rosicrucianism)**

The imagery of the all-seeing eye is predominately associated with Freemasonry, although it is used across the occult. It dates to the "eye of Horus," the ancient Egyptian sky god. It represents protection, royalty, health, power and vision, and in modern times, the concept of divine providence. This image is best-known as it is featured on the back of the dollar bill, as part of the Great Seal of the United States.[63]

*All-seeing eye*

## **Templar crown with cross (Freemasonry, Orange Order)**

*Templar crown with cross*

The symbol of Templar Freemasonry. In

Freemasonry, it is known as the Knights Templar Blood-Red Passion Cross and Crown. It is a common symbol on stained-glass windows and as church logos. It is most commonly used by the International Bible Students Association, the group that served as the foundation for the Watch Tower Bible and Tract Society, or better known as Jehovah's Witnesses.[64]

## Square and compass (Freemasonry)

There are dozens of symbols that relate to Freemasonry, but the best known is the square and compass. The square is an emblem of virtue, designed to remind Masons to "square their actions" by the square virtue of all mankind, and the compass exemplify wisdom of conduct and design. They are placed together with a "G" or focal point at the center, a reminder of the Grand Architect, the great creator. When the Grand Architect is at the center, peace and harmony result.[65]

*Square and compass*

## Sigillum Dei Aemaeth (magic, Rosicrucianism, general magic)

First designed by John Dee, a 16th century occultist and astrologer who worked in the court of Queen Elizabeth I. It is also known as the Seal of the Truth of God. There were earlier examples of the Sigillum Dei Aemaeth in texts John Dee would have been familiar with, he was not happy with those that exist and sought to design his own. John Dee constructed the image through angelic vision, seeking to diagram the ritual space for communication with angels.[66]

*Sigillum Dei Aemaeth*

## Star of David (Kabbalah, Rosicrucianism, Thelema magic, general magic)

Also called the hexagram or Magden David (shield of David), the Star of David is a six-pointed star created by two triangles: one upright and one inverted. No one is exactly sure where the Star of David comes from, but it

does not show up in Rabbinical literature until the

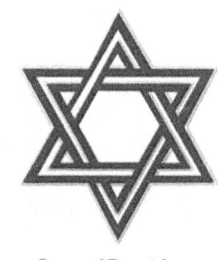
*Star of David*

Middle Ages. Around that time, Kabbalists started using it to reflect different, deeper meanings. Like other religious symbols, it has also been used by Christians and Muslims. It has many references and meanings, including the rule of God over the six points of the universe (north, south, east, west, up, down), dual nature (good and evil, male and female), and the twelve sides on the triangle relating to the twelve tribes of Israel.[67]

## **Major occult figures**

As with all things occult, there is not one singular occult figure that defines the movement. There are so many figures who, throughout history, have tried to shape and form different aspects of occult practice. This means trying to define the occult by people, one singular practice, or one singular identity is virtually impossible. Here is a list of major occult figures, of notable prominence, throughout occult history.

*Albert Pike*

- **Moses of Alexandria (1st and 2nd centuries AD):** Wrote Greek alchemical texts with Jewish influence; known as "Moses the thrice happy."

- **Mary the Jewess (1st and 3rd centuries AD):** Believed to be the first alchemist, as found in the Gnostic works of Zosimos of Panopolis.

- **Zosimos of Panopolis (300 AD):** alchemist and Gnostic mystic.

- **Paphnutia the Virgin (300 AD):** Referred to in the letters of Zosimos of Panopolis and Theosebia, who was uneducated in the things of alchemy (or possibly of a competing school).

- **Paraelsus (1493-1541):** Swiss physician, alchemist, lay theologian, and philosopher in the German Renaissance.

- **Nostradamus (1503-1566):** French scientist and seer who produced many written predictions in his book, *Les Propheties*.

- **John Dee (1527-1609):** English mathematician, astronomer, teacher, occultist, and alchemist.

- **Soulmother of Kussnacht (d. 1577):** Swiss medium.

- **Marie-Anne de La Ville (1680-1725):** French occultist.

- **Count Saint Germain (1696-1784):** An "ascended" master popular in occult theory.

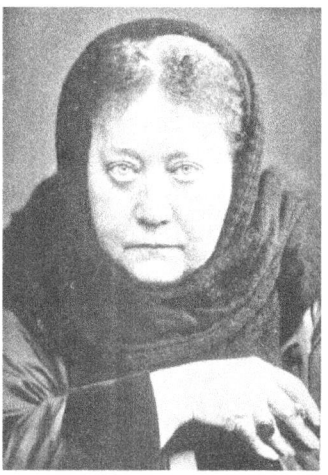
*Helena Petrovna Blavatsky*

- **Albert Pike (1809-1891):** 33rd degree Mason, Grand Master of the Order of the Palladium (a Satanic organization), and leader in the Ku Klux Klan. One of the founders of the Ancient Accepted Scottish Rite of Freemasonry.

- **Eliaphas Levi (1810-1875):** Occult author whose works included *Dogme et Rituel de la Haute Magie* and *La Clef des Grands Mysteres*.

- **Helena Petrovna Blavatsky (1831-1891):** Founder of Theosophy.

- **Kate (1837-1892), Maggie (1833-1893), and Leah Fox (1814-1900):** Founders of the Spiritualist Movement.

- **Samuel L. MacGregor Mathers (1854-1918):** Founder of the Hermetic Order of the Golden Dawn.

- **Charles Webster Leadbeater (1854-1934):** Occult writer and influential member of the Theosophical Society Adyar.

- **Albert Karl Theodor Reuss (1855-1923):** Founder of the Ordo Templi Orientis.

- **Gerald Brosseau Gardner (1884-1964):** Founder of modern witchcraft, better known as Wicca.

- **Rudolph Steiner (1861-1925):** Founder of Anthrophosophy.

- **Evangeline Adams (1868-1932):** Celebrity astrologer.

- **Alice Bailey (1880-1949):** Founder of Lucis Trust, a publishing company designed to publish her writings on Theosophical topics. Became the one of the first authors to use the term "New Age."

- **Henry Steel Olcott (1832-1907):** Co-founder of Theosophical Society.

- **Annie Besant (1847-1933):** Prominent member of the Theosophical Society; prominent author.

- **William Butler Yeats (1865-1939):** Irish occultist, poet, writer, and member of the Hermetic Order of the Golden Dawn.

- **Grigori Rasputin (1869-1916):** Russian occultist

- **Aleister Crowley (1875-1947):** Shaper of the Ordo Templi Orientis

*Alice Bailey*

- **Wilfred Talbot Smith (1885-1957):** English occultist and ceremonial magician.

- **Dion Fortune (1890-1946):** Founder of the Fraternity of the Inner Light.

- **Manly P. Hall (1901-1990):** Occult writer and teacher.

- **Doreen Valiente (1922-1999):** Pagan priestess and author.

- **Anton LaVey (1930-1997):** Founder of the Church of Satan.

- **Peter Carroll (1953- ):** Occultist, writer, and founder of chaos magic.

## **Chapter 5 Assignments**

- Write an essay (5-8 sentences) on the foundational components of the occult.
- Create a presentation on occult religions.
- Create an infographic on occult symbols.

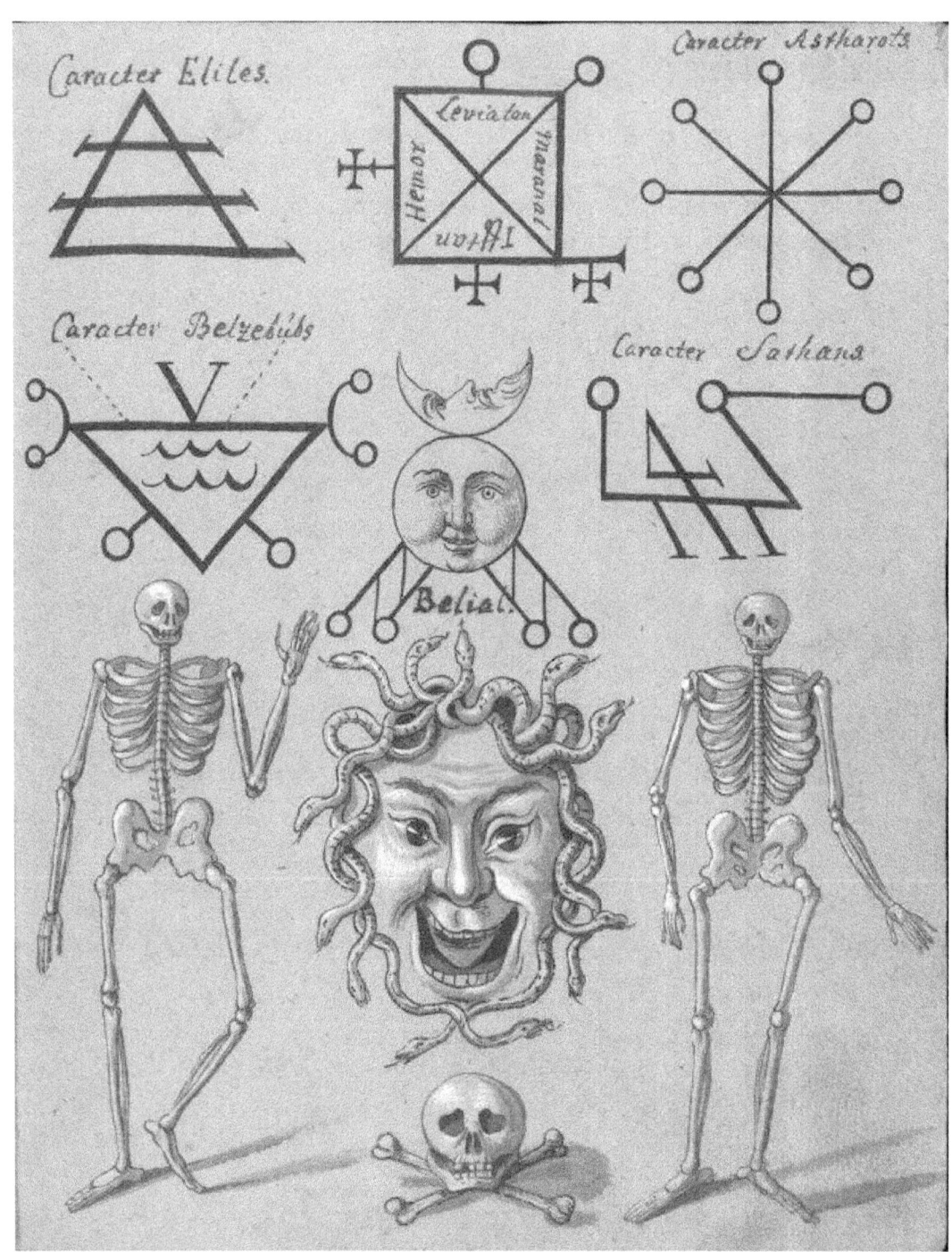

*From an 18th century demonology book*

# - CHAPTER SIX -
## Witchcraft and Magic

BUT COWARDS, THOSE WHO REFUSE TO BELIEVE [WITHOUT FAITH], WHO DO EVIL [VILE; DETESTABLE]
THINGS, WHO KILL, WHO SIN SEXUALLY, WHO DO EVIL MAGIC [SORCERY], WHO WORSHIP IDOLS,
AND WHO TELL LIES—ALL THESE WILL HAVE A PLACE [THEIR PART] IN THE LAKE OF BURNING SULFUR.
THIS IS THE SECOND DEATH [20:6]."
(REVELATION 21:8)

Witchcraft and magic are one of the edgiest and most controversial aspects of the occult and different sects of neo-paganism. The idea that someone can change and alter the course of their lives, of others, maybe even history, intrigues people who seek change or results faster than waiting or prayer can generate. Throughout the ages, magic has been a way that people have tried to understand the spiritual realm through the use of natural means, reactions, and contact with the elements that someone has never had before.

Witchcraft and magic are loaded topics, Biblically forbidden and, therefore, seldom discussed in an educational way among Christians. We often hear about common things spoken of as being witchcraft or magic, but are such things true? The question as to what exactly defines witchcraft - and magic - lie in their definitions, and in the complex world that defines them.

Just as with most of what we have studied in this book so far, magic and witchcraft fall into many different constructs, expressions, and understandings, and how magic is practiced has varied throughout the ages. Much of what is practiced today is not as ancient as you might think, but originated in the 1400s and 1500s in Europe. Its elaborate and complicated world can be explained with a few basic principles, all of which we will examine here as we seek to learn more about the ways people attempt to control their world.

## **Magic**

Most often, when people speak about witchcraft, they are speaking about a specified form of it, or what people practice when they study witchcraft, and that is magic. Magic is far from the illusions we see on stage where people pull rabbits out of hats or saw someone in half. Magic is the literal manipulation of spiritual means to bring about a desired result, using nature or natural forces. Magic can take the form of divination, channeling, spellcasting, predicting the future, or alchemy. Magic is most often studied and executed through the work of witchcraft. It is practiced by a magician, a sorcerer, a sorceress, a wizard, or a witch. A warlock is a term for an oath breaker and represents someone who would reveal the secrets and rites of the coven, and is not, under any terms, language to describe a "male witch." Witch is a neutral term and is frequently used for a modern practitioner of witchcraft, whether male or female.

The work of magic is quite ancient. As we can see from the book of 1 Enoch, it dates back at least to the time of Noah:

*And all the others together with them took unto themselves wives, and each chose for himself one, and they began to go in unto them and to defile themselves with them, and they taught them charms and enchantments, and the cutting of roots, and made them acquainted with plants. And they became pregnant, and they bare great giants, whose height was three thousand ells: Who consumed all the acquisitions of men. And when men could no longer sustain them, the giants turned against them and devoured mankind. And they began to sin against birds, and beasts, and reptiles, and fish, and to devour one another's flesh, and drink the blood. Then the earth laid accusation against the lawless ones.*

*And Azâzêl taught men to make swords, and knives, and shields, and breastplates, and made known to them the metals (of the earth) and the*

*ART OF WORKING THEM, AND BRACELETS, AND ORNAMENTS, AND THE USE OF ANTIMONY, AND THE BEAUTIFYING OF THE EYELIDS, AND ALL KINDS OF COSTLY STONES, AND ALL COLOURING TINCTURES. AND THERE AROSE MUCH GODLESSNESS, AND THEY COMMITTED FORNICATION, AND THEY WERE LED ASTRAY, AND BECAME CORRUPT IN ALL THEIR WAYS. SEMJÂZÂ TAUGHT ENCHANTMENTS, AND ROOT-CUTTINGS, ARMÂRÔS THE RESOLVING OF ENCHANTMENTS, BARÂQÎJÂL, (TAUGHT) ASTROLOGY, KÔKABÊL THE CONSTELLATIONS, EZÊQÊÊL THE KNOWLEDGE OF THE CLOUDS, ⟨ARAQIÊL THE SIGNS OF THE EARTH, SHAMSIÊL THE SIGNS OF THE SUN⟩, AND SARIÊL THE COURSE OF THE MOON. AND AS MEN PERISHED, THEY CRIED, AND THEIR CRY WENT UP TO HEAVEN . . .* (1 Enoch 7:1-8:2)[1]

## **Witchcraft**

When we think of witchcraft, we think of childhood images of little girls dressing up as old, ugly women in black outfits, who rode around on broomsticks with pointy hats. Witchcraft was something fanciful and imaginative, a way that creativity was expressed. Spells looked like things done by fairy godmothers out of Disney movies, and the entire experience and perception of witchcraft was that it was all a game. Around Halloween, we might have known someone who participated in Ouija boards, fortune telling, palmistry, tea leaves, reading cards, or a game of abnormal lift or levitation…or maybe you yourself did one of these things, at an earlier time. They were games we saw at Halloween parties, slumber parties, and group gatherings, and we treated them just like we did any other game we saw or played.

The reality behind many of these things is that they are not games, nor have they been regarded as such by practitioners of such things throughout history. Witchcraft has always been something taken with grave severity, a manner by which individuals believed they were able to garner control by combining both natural and spiritual experience.

*DISOBEDIENCE [REBELLION] IS AS BAD AS THE SIN OF SORCERY [WITCHCRAFT; DIVINATION]. PRIDE [STUBBORNNESS; ARROGANCE; PRESUMPTION; INSUBORDINATION] IS AS BAD AS THE SIN OF WORSHIPING IDOLS [IDOLATRY].* (1 Samuel 15:23)

Witchcraft is, and of itself, the practice of magic. The goal or purpose of such, as is clarified in the Scriptures, is the obtainment of control: taking things into one's own hands, operating and manipulating different things for a desired result, and bringing about the end product of a desired result. Witchcraft is the entire study, application, and use of it in an individual's life. It seldom applies on its own but is a part of a bigger religious understanding and worldview. Desiring to practice magic comes from the way an individual views the world, views spiritual things, and it should not come as a big surprise to learn it is quite different from what we find in Christianity.

## **The principles of pagan spirituality**

To understand witchcraft, we must understand where it first came from. Witchcraft, in theory and in practice, is as old as time itself. Examinations of many different Bible passages show us just how common witchcraft was, and how seriously people believed in it. Since the Bible has a clear prohibition on magic and witchcraft, have you ever wondered why there was so much record of different magical applications and spells found throughout the Scriptures?

- Abraham practiced a pagan sacrificial ritual (Genesis 1517-21)
- Joseph practiced divination using a cup (Genesis 44:3-5)
- Saul consulted a medium (1 Samuel 28:7)
- Lots were used to determine God's will (Numbers 26:55, Proverbs 16:33, Proverbs 18:18)
- Lots were used to select the replacement for Judas, Matthias (Acts 1:12-26)

On the other hand, practices of magic and witchcraft were not always so clearly "cut and dry." It's not as simple to say that people who practiced witchcraft in the Bible went without consequence. Saul was punished by God for consulting a medium, for example. The casting of lots was used to prove God was able to make the decision. The Bible makes it clear that witches and sorcerers were not to live (Exodus 22:18), and no one was to consult a medium or engage in certain spiritual practices of the pagans: namely, passing through the fire, divination, observing times (pagan holidays and feasts), enchanters, witches, charmers, consulting with familiar spirits, a wizard, or a necromancer.

*WHEN YOU ENTER THE LAND THE LORD YOUR GOD IS GIVING YOU, DON'T LEARN TO DO THE HATEFUL [DETESTABLE; ABHORRENT; ABOMINABLE] THINGS THE OTHER NATIONS DO. DON'T LET ANYONE AMONG YOU OFFER A SON OR DAUGHTER AS A SACRIFICE IN THE FIRE [12:30-31]. DON'T LET ANYONE USE MAGIC [DIVINATION; EX. 7:11; EZEK. 21:21] OR WITCHCRAFT, OR TRY TO EXPLAIN THE MEANING OF SIGNS [AUGURY OR SORCERY]. DON'T LET ANYONE TRY TO CONTROL OTHERS WITH MAGIC [CAST SPELLS], AND DON'T LET THEM BE MEDIUMS [CONSULT/INQUIRE OF GHOSTS OR SPIRITS] OR TRY TO TALK WITH THE SPIRITS OF [CONSULT] DEAD PEOPLE [1 SAM. 28]. THE LORD HATES [DETESTS] ANYONE WHO DOES THESE THINGS. BECAUSE THE OTHER NATIONS DO THESE THINGS, THE LORD YOUR GOD WILL FORCE [DISPOSSESS] THEM OUT OF THE LAND AHEAD OF YOU. BUT YOU MUST BE INNOCENT [BLAMELESS] IN THE PRESENCE OF THE LORD YOUR GOD.* (Deuteronomy 18:9-13)

This clarifies the following prohibitions:[2]

- **Yid'oni:** Channeling, contacting a dead spirit
- **Sho'el'ov** – Spiritism, using a medium to contact the dead
- **Quosem q'samim:** Casting lots to predict the future (using sticks, stones, rocks, runes, etc.) or by a similar method
- **M'onen:** Foretelling the future using nature as a source (groundhog seeing his shadow, determining the length of winter by the colored bands on a caterpillar, etc.)
- **M'nachesh:** Enchanting or charming, perhaps in the context of snake charming
- **Chover chavar:** Casting evil spells while tying knots
- **M'khaspeh:** Reciting evil spells with the intent to injure someone else
- **Doresh 'el hametim:** Any various methods to contact the dead

The question as to why these things are prohibitive is answered in the worldview present within paganism, and prevalent in parts of the world and ideologies, to this very day.

*I HAVE A DUTY [OBLIGATION; DEBT] TO ALL PEOPLE—GREEKS AND THOSE WHO ARE NOT GREEKS [OR BARBARIANS; THIS PAIRING COULD MEAN (1) ETHNIC GREEKS AND OTHER GENTILES; (2) GREEK SPEAKERS (PEOPLE IN THE ROMAN EMPIRE) AND NON-GREEK SPEAKERS (THOSE OUTSIDE THE ROMAN EMPIRE); OR (3) CULTURED PEOPLE AND UNCULTURED PEOPLE], THE WISE AND THE FOOLISH [PERHAPS CONTRASTING EDUCATED WITH UNEDUCATED, OR PHILOSOPHICALLY SOPHISTICATED (1 COR. 1:18-31) WITH* simple-minded]. That is why I want so much [am so eager] to preach the ·Good News [Gospel] to you in Rome.

[For] I am not ashamed of the Good News [Gospel], because it is the power God uses to save everyone who believes—to save the Jews first, and then to save Gentiles [the Greeks; here meaning anyone who is not Jewish; contrast v. 14]. The Good News [Gospel] shows how God makes people right with Himself [or God's righteous character; the righteousness of/from God]—that it begins and ends with faith [or that advances from one believing person to the next; or that begins with God's faithfulness and results in people's faith; from faith to faith]. As the Scripture says, "But those who are right with God will live by faith [or those made righteous through faith will live (eternally); Hab. 2:4]."

[For] God's anger [wrath; retribution] is shown [being revealed] from heaven against all the evil [ungodly] and wrong [wicked; unrighteous] things people do. By their own evil lives [wickedness; unrighteousness] they hide [suppress] the truth. God shows [reveals] His anger [wrath; retribution] because some knowledge of [what can be known about] Him has been made clear [plain; evident] to them. Yes, God has shown Himself [revealed/disclosed it] to them. For since the creation of the world, God's invisible qualities—His eternal power and all the things that make Him God [His divine nature]—have been clearly seen [perceived], understood through what God has made. So people have no excuse. They knew God, but they did not give glory to God or thank Him. Their thinking became useless [futile; pointless]. Their foolish [ignorant; uncomprehending] minds [hearts] were filled with darkness [darkened]. They claimed to be wise, but they became fools. They traded [exchanged] the glory of God Who lives forever [the immortal/imperishable God] for the worship of idols [images] made to look like earthly [mortal; perishable] people, birds, animals, and reptiles.

Because they did these things, God abandoned them to [allowed them to pursue; gave them over to] their sinful desires [the desires of their hearts], resulting in sexual impurity [uncleanness; impurity] and the dishonoring of their bodies with one another. They traded [exchanged] the truth of God for a lie [or the lie; see Gen. 3:4-5] and worshiped and served the creation

*[OR THE CREATURE; OR CREATED THINGS] INSTEAD OF THE CREATOR, WHO SHOULD BE PRAISED [OR IS BLESSED] FOREVER. AMEN.*

*BECAUSE PEOPLE DID THOSE THINGS, GOD ABANDONED THEM TO [ALLOWED THEM TO PURSUE; GAVE THEM OVER TO] SHAMEFUL [DISHONORABLE; DEGRADING] LUSTS [PASSIONS]. [THEIR] WOMEN STOPPED HAVING NATURAL SEX AND STARTED HAVING SEX WITH OTHER WOMEN [EXCHANGED NATURAL (HETEROSEXUAL) RELATIONS FOR UNNATURAL ONES]. IN THE SAME WAY, MEN STOPPED HAVING [ABANDONED] NATURAL SEX [RELATIONS WITH WOMEN] AND BEGAN WANTING [WERE INFLAMED IN THEIR LUST FOR] EACH OTHER. MEN DID SHAMEFUL THINGS WITH OTHER MEN, AND IN THEIR BODIES [THEMSELVES] THEY RECEIVED THE PUNISHMENT [RECOMPENSE; DUE PENALTY] FOR THOSE WRONGS [THEIR ERROR].*

*[AND SINCE/JUST AS] PEOPLE DID NOT THINK IT WAS IMPORTANT [CONSIDER IT WORTHWHILE; SEE FIT] TO HAVE A TRUE KNOWLEDGE OF [OR ACKNOWLEDGE] GOD. SO GOD ABANDONED THEM TO [ALLOWED THEM TO PURSUE; GAVE THEM OVER TO] THEIR OWN WORTHLESS THINKING [A DEPRAVED/CORRUPTED MIND] TO DO THINGS THEY SHOULD NOT DO. THEY ARE FILLED WITH EVERY KIND OF SIN [UNRIGHTEOUSNESS; INJUSTICE], EVIL [WICKEDNESS], SELFISHNESS [GREED], AND HATRED [EVIL; MALICE; DEPRAVITY]. THEY ARE FULL OF JEALOUSY [ENVY], MURDER, FIGHTING [STRIFE; QUARRELING], LYING [DECEIT; TREACHERY], AND THINKING THE WORST ABOUT EACH OTHER [SPITE; MALICIOUSNESS]. THEY ARE GOSSIPS AND SAY EVIL THINGS ABOUT EACH OTHER [SLANDERERS; BACKSTABBERS]. THEY HATE GOD. THEY ARE RUDE [INSOLENT; HAUGHTY] AND CONCEITED [PROUD; ARROGANT] AND BRAG ABOUT THEMSELVES [BOASTFUL]. THEY INVENT WAYS OF DOING EVIL. THEY DO NOT OBEY [RESPECT] THEIR PARENTS. THEY ARE FOOLISH [SENSELESS; UNDISCERNING], THEY DO NOT KEEP THEIR PROMISES [OR ARE COVENANT-BREAKERS], AND THEY SHOW NO KINDNESS [LOVE; AFFECTION] OR MERCY [PITY] TO OTHERS. THEY KNOW GOD'S LAW SAYS [RIGHTEOUS DECREE; JUST REQUIREMENT] THAT THOSE WHO LIVE LIKE THIS SHOULD DIE. BUT THEY THEMSELVES NOT ONLY CONTINUE TO DO THESE EVIL THINGS, THEY APPLAUD [APPROVE OF; ENCOURAGE] OTHERS WHO DO THEM.* (Romans 1:14-32)

I have taught on Romans 1 for several years, because I feel that it is a passage we do not take the proper time to understand. We are quick to use it as a weapon to argue against certain sexual orientations instead of truly seeing it for what it says, and for what it is trying to teach us. Romans was written to the church at Rome, and that means many of its members were Christian converts from paganism, rather than Judaism. Romans 1 is about including those people in the plan of God, helping them to see their own spiritual need for God and help others in evangelism, rather than criticizing sexuality. In short, the purpose of Romans 1 is to show the pagan's knowledge of God and ways they experienced Him in types and shadows before they came to a knowledge of Christ. They were able to see the work of God in nature, in times and seasons, and in the general operation of the world, as they operated in an agrarian society. Instead of worshiping God, they worshiped the creature rather than the Creator and engaged in all sorts of rites that relate to magic, sexual magic, and trying to influence the spiritual world with the material.

This is, therefore, the very foundation we need to attend to in order to properly understand the work of witchcraft and, ultimately, magic, in the spiritual realm. The pagan worldview of the divine and the spiritual is not the same as the Christian's, and trying to fit it into a Christian perspective does not work.

As we have discussed earlier, pagans view the world as a mix of polytheism, animism and pantheism. If all things are spiritual and the spiritual realm is all things, that means the material world becomes a conduit – a medium or a meeting place – for the spiritual. If all things are divine, then nature becomes a manipulating place to operate and control the spiritual.

*"I AM ALLOWED TO DO ALL THINGS [ALL THINGS ARE LAWFUL/PERMISSIBLE FOR ME; PROBABLY A SLOGAN THE CORINTHIANS WERE USING; SEE ALSO 7:1; 8:1, 4; 10:23]," BUT NOT ALL THINGS ARE GOOD FOR ME TO DO [PROFITABLE; BENEFICIAL]. "I AM ALLOWED TO DO ALL THINGS [ALL THINGS ARE LAWFUL/PERMISSIBLE FOR ME]," BUT I WILL NOT LET ANYTHING MAKE ME ITS SLAVE. "FOOD IS FOR THE STOMACH, AND THE STOMACH FOR FOOD, BUT GOD WILL DESTROY [DO AWAY WITH] THEM BOTH [PROBABLY ANOTHER CORINTHIAN SLOGAN (V. 12), MEANING ONLY THE SPIRIT MATTERS, NOT WHAT WE DO WITH OUR PHYSICAL BODIES; PAUL DISAGREES]." THE BODY IS NOT FOR SEXUAL SIN BUT FOR THE LORD, AND THE LORD IS FOR THE BODY. BY HIS POWER GOD HAS RAISED THE LORD FROM THE DEAD AND WILL ALSO RAISE US FROM THE DEAD. SURELY [DON'T...?] YOU KNOW THAT YOUR BODIES ARE PARTS [MEMBERS] OF CHRIST HIMSELF. SHOULD I TAKE THE PARTS [MEMBERS] OF CHRIST AND JOIN THEM TO A PROSTITUTE? NEVER [ABSOLUTELY NOT; MAY IT NEVER BE]! DON'T YOU KNOW THAT ANYONE WHO JOINS WITH A PROSTITUTE [IN A SEXUAL RELATIONSHIP] BECOMES ONE BODY WITH THE PROSTITUTE? FOR IT IS WRITTEN IN THE SCRIPTURES, "THE TWO WILL BECOME ONE*

*BODY [FLESH; GEN. 2:24]." BUT THE ONE WHO JOINS WITH THE LORD [IN SPIRITUAL UNION] IS ONE SPIRIT WITH THE LORD.*

*SO RUN AWAY FROM [FLEE; STAY AWAY FROM] SEXUAL SIN. EVERY OTHER SIN PEOPLE DO IS OUTSIDE THEIR BODIES, BUT THOSE WHO SIN SEXUALLY SIN AGAINST THEIR OWN BODIES. YOU SHOULD [DON'T YOU...?] KNOW THAT YOUR BODY IS A TEMPLE FOR THE HOLY SPIRIT WHO IS IN YOU AND WAS GIVEN TO YOU BY GOD. SO YOU DO NOT BELONG TO YOURSELVES, BECAUSE YOU WERE BOUGHT BY GOD [BOUGHT] FOR A PRICE. SO HONOR GOD WITH YOUR BODIES.* (1 Corinthians 6:12-20)

The Apostle Paul wasn't just speaking of a man frequenting a brothel or getting a little on the side (although that can certainly have its own spiritual implications). He was speaking about the principle of magic, of working a spell using a sexual rite with a temple prostitute, for a desired result. By becoming one with that temple prostitute, that person was becoming one with the magic she espoused, with the spirituality she represented, and in many ways, one with the demonic realm that she did not understand and did not properly discern. The Apostle Paul was cautioning believers against magic, against engaging in witchcraft, and against taking on spiritual realms they were simply unprepared to handle.

*The pagan calendar wheel of the year*

In doing so, the Apostle Paul was affirming a few things. He wasn't debating the reality or imagination of magic, as some do, but affirming that there are spiritual forces in this world and taking on the position of power and control, attempting to control nature and forces with actions, gestures, or by manipulating natural methods, is to step in the place of God and try to orchestrate things on one's own. It's not so much a question as to whether anyone really has such an ability, but the concept that one feels they have the right to try and work such manipulation, by attempting to play God.

## **The pagan year**

The best way to see the viewpoint of the pagan cycle of life is through observation of the pagan year. Cycles are essential to the understanding of paganism, because rather than see life as a singular timeline, life and the way in which spirituality and spiritual understanding moves is cyclical. The roll of the year, the repeating of different cosmic and spiritual dramas, the seeing of things change, move, shift, and come back again, are all essential to the way in which the pagan world works. With each event, each holiday (known as a sabbat), and each observance, certain principles of magic and witchcraft associate each understanding. Throughout the pagan year, certain gods and goddesses die, are reborn, fight for power, and take prominence, all in an annual cycle. Ritual and rite go along with the different sabbats and theologies of the annual calendar. The pagan year is standard among the different modern pagan groups, although the names for the festivals and the deities might change, depending on the part of the world one is in or the specific strain of witchcraft one practices.

**Eve of February 2: Imbolc, Lupercalia, Disablot, Festa candelarum, Liichtmessdag, Groundhog Day, Solmonath, Oimeaig, Candlemas**
- The corn god moves and stirs within the earth
- First fire festival of the year
- Third-degree initiations performed[3]

**Between March 21-23: Ostara, Oester, Liberalia, Anjana, Nowruz, Easter, Spring Equinox**
- The sun god defeats the dark god, who is his twin
- Enthroning of the sun god
- Solar festival[4]

**Eve before May 1: Beltane, Floralia, festival of Flora, Whitsuntide, Walpurgis Night, May Crowning, Spring Day, Calendimaggio, cantar Maggio, Mugwort Day, Os Maios, Los Mayos, May Day**
- The oak king claims the may queen as his mate
- Tradition of the Maypole[5]

**Between June 21-23: Litha, Festa Juninia, Ukon juhla, Jaan's Day, Sommersonnenwende, Klidonas, Tiregan, Saint Ivan's Night, St. John's Day, St. Hans Day, Midsummer Solstice**
- The holly king defeats the oak king
- Sun god and oak king are at the height of their power[6]

**Eve before August 1 – Lughnasadh, Lammas, Lammos, Calan Awst, Cross Quarter Day**
- The corn god dies
- Harvest festival[7]

**Between September 21-23: Mabon, Harvest Home, the Feast of the Ingathering, Mean Fromhair, Alban Elfed, Autumn Equinox**
- The dark god defeats the sun god
- Festival of light[8]

**Eve before November 1 : Samhain, Calan Gaeaf, Kalan Gwav, Hop-tu-Naa, Allantide, Halloween, All Hollow's Eve, All Souls**
- The goddess mourns the defeat and death of the oak king
- Fire festival[9]

**Between December 21-25: Yule, Yuletide, Midwinter, Yalda Night, Modranicht, Brumalia, Christmas, Boxing Day, Saturnalia, Winter Solstice**
- The oak king defeats the holly king
- Birth of the sun god (Tammuz, Harpocrates, Llew)[10]

## How witchcraft works

Witchcraft, as the practice of magic, is practiced by a witch, either as an individual, or in a coven. Magic, spells, and the like are regarded as conduits for the spiritual realm, and as one performs various magical rites, they are either seeking spiritual guidance or are getting the process started themselves. For example, an individual writing a love spell, obtaining a potion, and carving the writing into a candle (which they will burn as they cast the spell and put together the potion) is considered putting things into action, starting the process to drawing that individual to fall in love and bring them to you, as you desire.

Practitioners of magic swear by their results, believe them to work, and anticipate their results. There are tons of books, websites, and information available for those who desire to practice magic. Many modern applications of witchcraft also try to incorporate things into the mix that sound much like any religious group might offer: relationship advice, better communication, success, better health, love, and yes, even prosperity in one's life as they apply the precepts of magic within their own lives. Whether it's contacting a psychic to foretell the future, consulting a horoscope to divine the stars, casting a direct spell for a desired result, or some other form of divination, witchcraft believes it pulls on the stars, manipulates the spiritual realm through the natural, and gets everything aligned and in place for the desired results.

**Forms of magic**

There are three main forms of magic, each of which delves into the different elements and formats one seeks to manipulate through magical formulation. They are elemental, mental, and arcane:[11]

- **Elemental:** Command the forces of nature. Examples include pyrokinesis (mastery over fire), aquakinesis (mastery over water), geokinesis (mastery over earth), aerokinesis (mastery over air), and fulgurkinesis (mastery over lightning).

- **Mental:** Magic of the will, that manifests in different ways, depending on the mental will and capacity of the user. Examples include telekinesis (moving objects with one's mind), projection (transmit ideas and feelings to others), therinology (commanding animals), harmonizing (arranging one's atmosphere to convey a specific feeling or mood), and elenchus (distinguishing lies from truth).

- **Arcane:** The practice of magic that works or operates outside the realm of normal, or typical, reality. Examples include enerkinesis (mastery over magnetic energy), summoning (manifestation of creatures), animating (give life to inanimate objects), and binding (the ability to bind or fuse something in the arcane realm with a human host; the result is giving the human host a supernatural power or ability).

**Types of magic**

There are many different strains of magic in existence, as magic has been around since virtually the beginning of time. While it is not possible to list every source or type of magic in existence, in this section, we will examine some more common categories of magic by which many others fall into.

- **Neo-pagan:** Strains of modern-day witchcraft that are based on ancient concepts of various pagan understandings to concoct a modern application, therein. Neo-paganism draws on different sources and ancient theologies for inspiration and can take on many different forms. Neo-pagan magic groups include Wicca, neo-druidism, Romvua, Heathenry, Adonism, the Goddess Movement, Faery magic, and eclectic forms of Paganism.

- **Ancestral:** Calling upon the spirits and energy of dead ancestors in a certain location, especially those of the practitioner, so as the ancestors can use the practitioner of the magic in any way they see fit.[12]

- **Enochian:** A form of magic based on invocation and commanding

- of different spirits as found in the sixteenth-century writings of John Dee and Edward Kelley. Additions to the system were founded by Samuel Liddell, MacGregor Mathers, and Aleister Crowley. They claimed their system revealed an Enochian language and script, personally dictated by an angel, with the additional claim to have secret knowledge and revelation on the contents of the Book of Enoch. It is ceremonial in approach and is considered very difficult to practice by modern standards.[13]

- **Chaos:** A modern strain of magic that rejects the structure and disciplines of other forms of magic to create a form and theory of magic that relies on whatever thoughts, beliefs, and ideas a practitioner may have to help the execution and purpose of magic in the moment.[14]

- **Circle:** Used to keep something out or keep something in; creation of a barrier to magical forces, done by drawing a circle on the floor or ground and investing with will.[15]

- **Deity:** Receiving power through magical forces from a being deemed divine, such as a god or goddess.[16]

- **Renaissance:** A division of ceremonial magic devised in the 1400s and 1500s. There are seven areas of practice: nigromancy (black magic, or demonology), geomancy, hydromancy, aeromancy, pyromancy, chiromancy (palmistry), and scapulimancy (divination method using the shoulder blades).[17]

- **White:** Magic that is used for an altruistic purpose, such as to heal, help other people, and follow the laws of nature in a better manner. Also called light magic.[18]

- **Spirit:** The use of spirits to produce a desired result, either through the control or operation of the practitioner, or for the practitioner to call upon such spirits to produce whatever result is desired.

- **Black:** Frequently employed by Satanists, its purpose is to call upon evil spirits or the devil for the purpose of obtaining one's desired interest.[19]

- **Ceremonial:** A generalized term for ritual or high magic, as it relates to the different complex rituals associated with magic.[20]

- **Traditional:** Drawing spiritual energy from the forces of nature (as well as using items from nature for said purpose) to be used however the practitioner sees fit.[21]

- **Sex:** Sex magic is the use of any form of sexual activity in a magical rite, whether private or ceremonial. Sex is used to transcend reality, bring about creative visualization, fertility, agricultural success, or general creativity.[22]

- **Folk:** Folk magic is marked by primitive views of witchcraft, spiritism, and indigenous religious beliefs. Much of these folk magic methods are in the category of sorcery, fetishes, magical spells, curses, and local deities (sometimes mixed with Christian deities).

Examples of folk magic include voodoo, Santeria, Stregheria, hoodoo, and pow-wow.

## **Spells**

Whenever we read fairy tales or watch Disney movies, odds are good that nine times out of ten, those stories integrate a spell or two in them. Spells are one of the most common practices within witchcraft. In a simple definition, a spell is a charm, a hex, a blessing, or a curse consisting of words that are believed to have magical powers, especially when spoken or thought together. Spells can accomplish different things: calling forth a spirit or demon, controlling a person's actions, preventing or causing harm, or causing a certain desired result. When someone is under a "spell," it is believed they are outside of their own controls and their own powers and are under the power of the individual who cast the spell.

Spells take on all sorts of forms. Much like the history of magic, spells have been around for thousands of years, for virtually everything under the sun, expressing the full drama of the human condition. There are spells for need, want, desire, hope, and dreams. To cast a spell, a few conditions must be met:[23]

- State the intention of the spell
- Properly timing the spell (the right phase of the moon, the right season for the spell)
- Proper use of spiritual tools to cast the spell
- Understanding the power and purpose of magic
- Write down the words to be spoken (rhyming is considered of particular importance to make the spell more powerful and easier to remember)
- Remember the spiritual laws and morals of witchcraft.

Spells can be personally written by a witch, or they can be from a book or an exterior magical tradition.

## **Examples of spells**

Casting a money spell:

Add to a red candle power in your name and then call forth the elements of the Earth. Invoke the element of fire and speak the following words aloud:

Fire, I appeal to your heat,
To help me in this magical feat,
Bring me what I ask,
As will be seen, as can be!

Sit in front of the candle flame to see her dance for a while. Speak the following words aloud three times:

*Allow the flow of passion in me,*
*and above all,*
*Allow me to completely fill its tides, inside and everywhere.*
*Enthusiasm and new Fellowship force for*
*whatever comes my way,*
*And make me eagerly seize every new day.*

Allow the candle to burn completely.

Take a shoe and put it around a red candle. Place the candle in a dark room in the center of a table. Write what do you want on a piece of paper with a quill pen dipped in black ink.

*Altar for casting spells*

Speak the following aloud:

*What I write here,*
*Please take my dream and bring about,*
*What I want is what you should get,*
*That all my dreams come true now.*

Now take the paper and fold it into a square of four quarters. Expect more of the candle with a pair of tweezers and let it burn. Imagine yourself with your wish fulfilled as burns the paper.

Sitting in a circle, each directional quarter needs to speak the following words aloud:

*West edge: Obey these words of power!*
*East edge: Watchers of the threshold, observers in the door!*
*North edge: Remove the bar of the guarded gate!*
*South edge: Obey this command of this servant of power!*

Repeat this aloud three times and summon the spirits.[24]

Casting a spell to stop oncoming rain:

When the sky begins to darken, speak aloud with feeling the following words:

*The gods of power, the gods of force,*
*I ask you now, stop this plight,*
*Stop the rain, do not need more,*
*Be dropped it, never again.*[25]

Casting a spell to protect an object:

Hold the object to be protected in your hands and repeat the following incantation:

*Wise guardian soft and strong,*
*Maintains that (I, he / she/they) when (I, he / she/they) belongs,*
*Insurance within your charge and care,*
*the current problem of the tariff,*
*There is no harm to come to happen or worse,*
*Secure and safe through it all!*[26]

## Grimoire

A grimoire is a magical textbook that covers the basics of witchcraft, magic, the creation of different magical objects, spells, charms, and how to practice different forms of divination and summon spirits. Grimoires were usually constructed using different magical symbols, and practitioners would put those symbols together to construct sentence-form spells and other conjurings. An example of a grimoire is *The Book of Shadows*, some of which can be purchased, and some of which are more the personal journals of witches and spells or practices they find successful in their own work of witchcraft. In some ways, a grimoire is a very personal account of one's experimentation and experiences within the magical realm.[27]

## **Divination**

There are countless forms of divination worldwide, all with the hope and intent to discover answers to the things that are unknown. In this section, I will attempt to discuss some of the better-known forms that are simple in application, and in subsequent sections, we shall discuss those that require more explanation.

Divination is a broad category of magic that relates to foretelling the future, answering questions, or leaving matters up to the gods of fate, in one form or another. At the root of divination are the essential questions that surround important life choices and changes, with the underlying intent to discover that which is unknown. Individuals who practice divination do so with the intent to discover the answers to their questions, hoping that by leaving things up to abstract signs, they will receive essential communication that will resolve their issue.

The basics of understanding divination, despite the differences in an object or objects used, is interpreting the position, number, form, or style of an object after it has been drenched, thrown, repositioned, unusual, or somehow altered. Divination may also come through a notable change in a human being. There are four main categories of divination:[28,29]

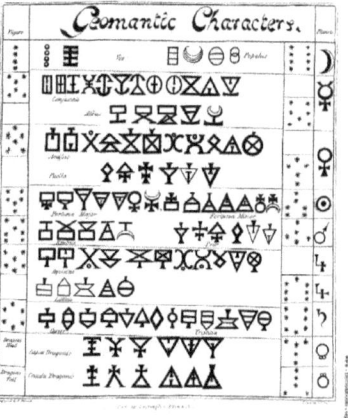
*Geomantic characters*

**Omens and omen texts**: Interpreting signs, especially those that are odd or unusual.

- **Aeromancy:** Interpreting the future by natural phenomenon, including wind, clouds, lighting, and astral phenomena.

- **Amniomancy:** Foretelling a child as a prophet, seer, or psychic due to a caul covering one's head at birth.

- **Cledonomancy:** Interpreting strange, chance, or unusual events or things overheard in conversation for foretelling or answering questions.

- **Cryptomancy:** Interpreting omens or signs.

- **Geomancy:** Interpreting markings or patterns on the ground or using objects from earth (rocks, dirt) tossed aside to form different patterns. The patterns, once cast, are interpreted.

**Sortilege:** Also known as cleromancy, done by casting lots with different items.

- **Runes:** Imprinting letters of the runic alphabet (Germanic language characters used before the introduction of Latin alphabet characters to write different Germanic languages) on stones or tiles, then selected one by one or thrown around at random for interpretive purpose in one's reading.

- **Casting lots:** Using different items, such as stones, sticks, coins, or dice (kind of like flipping a coin) to make a decision by leaving it up to divine chance.

- **Astragalomancy:** Using thrown dice with special symbols to answer questions.

*Bag of runes*

- **Favomancy:** Throwing beans on the ground and divining messages through the patterns by which they fall.

- **Shufflemancy:** Using a playlist or iPod to shuffle song. Wherever the shuffle stops, the lyrics of that song are the answer to the diviner's question.

**Augury:** Uses a rank for a set of given possibilities. May use shapes, distances, or changes in form to determine the future or the answer to a desired question.

- **Tasseography:** More commonly called "reading tea leaves," tasseography can be done with coffee grounds, tea leaves, or wine sediments. It is noting the pattern left after water is removed and grounds or sediments remain within the cup, and interpreting the signs or patterns that one finds.

*Reading tea leaves*

- **Chiromancy:** More commonly known as palmistry, completed as one studies the lines found on the palm and foretells one's future.

- **Arithmancy:** Assigning numerical values to words or phrases, studying divination through numbers. A form of numerology.

- **Cartomancy:** Using a deck of cards (either a standard deck or tarot) to determine one's future or answer one's questions. Each suit and rank is associated with a certain interpretive answer to the question.

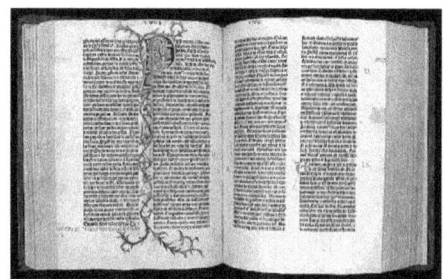

*Old Bible*

- **Dowsing:** Using a rod, stick, or a "dowsing rod" to locate items found underground, such as water, gems, metals, oil, or gravesites, without the use of digging or any scientific equipment.

**Spontaneous:** The answer comes forth from whatever the diviner sees or hear, such as a random text in a book that one happens to view in response to a question.

- **Stichomancy:** Completed as one asks a question and then opens up to a random passage in any book (usually the *I Ching*) to discover the answer.

- **Bibliomancy:** Completed as one asks a question and then opens a random passage in a sacred book (such as the Bible or Qur'an) to discover the answer.

- **Dictiomancy:** Completed as one asks a question and then opens up to a random word definition in the dictionary to discover the answer.

## Tarot

The use of tarot cards to answer questions and divine the future is a part of cartomancy, but because tarot cards are so frequently mentioned on their own, they are worthy of a section. In magic, the use of tarot cards for divining is specifically known as tarotology. The tarot card deck as we know it now originated in Europe in the 1400s as a playing card deck. To this very day, Europeans use tarot cards as they would like any other playing card deck. It wasn't until the late 1700s that the deck was used for divination purposes.

*Reading old tarot cards*

Like other cards, the tarot deck has four suits. These do vary by region: Northern Europe has French suits, Southern Europe has Latin suits, and Central Europe has German suits. Each suit has fourteen cards, numbering one to ten, and then four face cards: jack, knight, king, and queen. The tarot also has a separate twenty-one card trump suit, and one card in each deck known as the fool. There are a variety of tarot card designs, all of which reflect regional identities. There are also special tarot card decks for the occult: the Major Arcana and Minor Arcana, with symbolism unique to occult ideals and purposes.

When an individual seeks out answers from a tarot deck, the person selects a specific number of cards (usually six) at random, as guided by spiritual forces, to bring forth the answers to one's questions or to provide insight into one's future. The cards are then interpreted, usually according to the practitioner, either individually, collectively, or in pairs.[30]

## **Scrying**

The use of crystals for the purpose of divining isn't particularly special, but it is a generally large heading that has gained intense popularity over the past twenty years. Also known as seeing or peeping, scrying (as it is properly noted) is done by gazing into a specific stone (usually quartz, crystal, a crystal ball, or some other clear stone) for meditative focus in order to see or receive vision or insight into a specific situation. Scrying can also be done without the aid of a crystal or seer stone, such as with intense focus, meditation, or use of hallucinogenic drugs.

*Crystal used in scrying*

Scrying doesn't have one simple method of explanation or approach and is usually done via any method or means a person desires. Some may stare into the crystal-like substance and then stare into pure darkness, such as a dark room or hat, and interpret the different shadows or fractions of light they see as messages for interpretations. Some stare into glowing coals, mirrors, and others close their eyes.

Scrying has led to the belief that certain stones hold special revelatory powers and has generated great interest among the New Age Movement about the use of special stones, using stones as a source of power, or believing that different stones generate different energy, like the concept of a talisman or amulet.[31]

## *I Ching*

The *I Ching* is also known as the *Book of Changes* and is a Chinese divination book dating back to somewhere between the tenth and fourth centuries B.C. Its purpose was to provide a divination method easier than casting lots for those who sought to understand their futures from the perspective of Taoist and Confucist moral guidance. It produces random numbers for the practitioner to apply in hexagrams, either broken or unbroken. There are 64 possible hexagrams as well as the hexagram's name, a statement for each, and six line statements. The arrangements of the hexagrams are known as the King Wen sequence after the king who reformed the method of *I Ching* divination interpretation.[32]

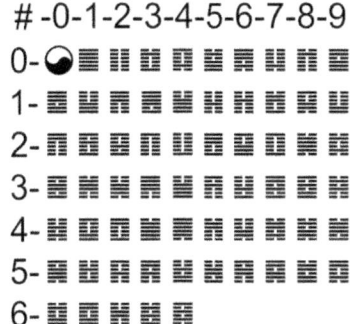

*King Wen sequence of the I Ching*

## **Numerology**

Numerology is the belief that there is a divine connection between numbers and events, as well as the nature of numbers to reveal personality traits, futures, and purposes in individuals. The father of modern numerology is Pythagoras, a Greek Mathematician. He, as did others of his time, believed that mathematical ideas were more practical than physical concepts, because they had greater accuracy.

In numerology, numbers are assigned values to letters, moving from one to nine. The value of each number is then added together, to create different meanings. Each number represents a certain significance or importance, and reveals something about the nature of the individual or question at hand. Most numerological chartings of individuals are done using their full name, their first name and/or their date of birth.

- 1 – A,J,S
- 2 – B,K,T
- 3 – C,L,U
- 4 – D,M,V
- 5 – E,N,W
- 6 – F,O,X
- 7 – G,P,Y
- 8 – H,Q,Z

*Gematria chart*

- 9 – I, R

The use of numerology can be seen in Kabbalah, Arab countries, India, Chinese culture, and in Christianity, as many cathedrals and other prominent features and buildings reflect the principles of numerology in their architecture and design. The relevance of numbers as having significance are found throughout the Bible and throughout different traditions spanning Biblical culture:[33]

- 1 – Unity
- 2 – Duality; male and female; sex; duplicity
- 3 – Holiness; perfection; manifestation
- 4 – Totality, materialization, teaching
- 5 – Human life; grace
- 6 – Man; the imperfection of humanity, sin, evil
- 7 – the "God" number; indicates perfection
- 8 – New life; resurrection
- 9 – High evolution; spiritual awareness; cosmology; coming of the antichrist
- 12 – The heavens; divine structure and placement; life, good fortune
- 1,000 – Measure of immenseness or fullness of number

A side note of understanding numbers from a spiritual perspective lies in the principle of gematria. Gematria is an Assyro-Babylonian-Greek system of applying numerical values to words or phrases, understanding the two to be identical to one another. Gematria is constructed using the Hebrew alphabet, as can be seen in the image to the right.

There are a few different ways to handle gematria, and it is most frequently used in the Talmud and Midrash. Perhaps the most famous example of gematria, however, is the use of the number 666 to denote the Beast of Revelation.[34,35]

| The Signs and Their Rulers | |
|---|---|
| Sign | Planetary Ruler |
| ♈ Aries | ♂ Mars |
| ♉ Taurus | ♀ Venus |
| ♊ Gemini | ☿ Mercury |
| ♋ Cancer | ☽ Moon |
| ♌ Leo | ☉ Sun |
| ♍ Virgo | ☿ Mercury |
| ♎ Libra | ♀ Venus |
| ♏ Scorpio | ♇ Pluto |
| ♐ Sagittarius | ♃ Jupiter |
| ♑ Capricorn | ♄ Saturn |
| ♒ Aquarius | ♅ Uranus |
| ♓ Pisces | ♆ Neptune |

*Zodiac signs and their ruling planets*

**Astrology**

We already discussed astrology in the last chapter and the foundations of what it is and how it works, but we did not delve much into the way astrology is used as a magical outlet, and how people understand it as a source of divination. Astrology, as a form of divination, finds its analysis in the production of horoscopes. Horoscopes are charts that document different astrological data of the positions and unique angles (first house – ascendant, tenth house – midheaven, seventh house – descendant, and fourth house – imum coeli) of the planets. Most horoscopes are based on sun sign astrology, which considers the position of the sun at one's birth, thus placing each person in one of twelve different zodiac signs. The zodiac is a star belt in space by which the planets move, all of which are compared to animals or other celestial beings. Each zodiac sign is in one of twelve houses, each one 30 degrees each. Coupled with this foundation, all the current movements of the planets to one another are intertwined to create one's future events. Even though astrology is quite ancient and there are many different forms of astrology (even the twelve tribes of Israel share the same symbols as the zodiac), sun astrology has only existed since 1930. For the sake of space, we are going to examine sun astrology by signs and details but will speak a bit on other zodiacs for informative purposes.

When one believes in astrology, they believe being under a certain zodiac sign inclines an individual to certain personality traits, abilities, interests, strengths, and weaknesses. Given any position of the planets (at least the classical planets), any combination of these things can influence an individual's day, month, or year. For example, someone's ability to fall in love, have a successful time on the job, get a promotion, or even experience relationship stress or discord can be based on the positioning of the planets at that time. Different signs are believed to be more compatible than others, and each sign is associated with different elements, symbols, and aspects of interpersonal relationships.

*Zodiac sign chart*

Other zodiac systems include Babylonian, Egyptian, Dendera, Hindu, and Chinese. The one used most often today has traces and traditions back to ancient Babylon, even though it is newer in its application and in the way we understand it. For at least four thousand years, people have sought answers via the stars, and the zodiac is one of the most prominent forms of divination in existence worldwide.[36,37]

## Shamanism

Shamanism is a little different than what we have discussed thus far, but because it is found in so many different spiritual systems worldwide and now have components found in the New Age Movement, it is worth an examination. Shamanism is a spiritual practice that seeks altered states of consciousness to interact with the spiritual realm, thus influencing or transmitting some of the vital information back to us in this realm. Shamanism is practiced by a shaman, who is an individual believed to have access to the spirit world, both spirits that are good and spirits that are evil. Through entering a trance state via a ritual, the shaman practices their unique form of divination and offers healing. The premise by which they travel through different spiritual planes and worlds is known as astral projection and is sometimes practiced on its own in different New Age and occultist circles. As they travel through different spiritual realms, they are guided by their spirit guides, which may take the form of supernatural or angelic beings or animals.

*Yakut Shaman (1902)*

Shamanism is found in many cultures worldwide and is not associated with any one specific spiritual or indigenous religious group, although it is a part of the construct of several of them. A shaman receives their call to practice through a dream or a vision, which draws them into their work. They work as mediators between the living and the dead within their culture, and may perform different works, such as ritual sacrifices, healing, storytelling and cultural preservation, cultural dancing or singing, fortune telling, and guide of souls, interpreting omens or symbols, sort of as a minister of their specified cultural beliefs.[38]

**Necromancy**

The forms of divination we have examined have all had one thing in common: they use objects outside of an individual person to determine and divine the future or answer needed questions. Not all forms of divination use outside, or secondary, objects. There are plenty of instances where an individual may use themselves as the personal conduit for the spirit or being they seek guidance from or with which they seek to align. In such instances, divination may hold a slightly different feeling, concept, or appearance. These next examples of divination all use a person, or individual practitioner, as the means by which the spirit world finds its way to communicate with the living.

Necromancy is, in the simplest possible definition, communicating with the dead. It is often done to provide information about the future but is also done in more modern times for other reasons, especially to provide comfort for the living about the presence of and relationship with deceased loved ones. It is classified as a black art, if not the highest of all black arts, because it is believed to do it, one must consort with demons.

*A séance with medium William Hope (c. 1920)*

Necromancy, in all its varied forms, was prohibited in the Bible, because doing so was associated with demonic activity. As individuals in the Bible went from understanding the dead to knowing nothing (Ecclesiastes 9:5) to believing in the afterlife (Job 19:25-27, Isaiah 26:19, Daniel 12:1-3), it did not change that a man could not experience resurrection without the power of God. Anything else and any other understanding indicated coersion with demons and with different demonic powers that had the potential to be deadly, as well as against the life of God. This having been said, some of the most relevant necromancers in history have, unfortunately, been members of the clergy who had access to information about astral magic, exorcism, astrology, and demonism. Today, there is an entire denominational subset devoted to necromancy, often embracing individuals of all religious beliefs in its approach to the dark arts.

An individual who practices necromancy is usually known as a medium, because they allow their own bodies to serve as a conduit for the deceased spirit or being in this realm. A medium may hear from a spirit (such as in clairaudience), may see a spirit (such as in clairvoyance), or may feel the presence of a spirit (such as an empath). At other times, an individual may literally house the spirit, with it being in their body, as the spirit speaks, acts, and interacts through them, in a spiritual practice known as channeling. With channeling, an individual may write, deliver a message, practice any number of spiritual or natural arts, or engage in any other practice to get across the point that the spirit or spirits are there, and they have something to accomplish. Modern necromancers might also use the practice of a séance or the religious aspect of it, known as Spiritualism. In a séance, the dead contacts the living through a series of knocks, supernatural movements (moving objects, making noise, removing objects). Spiritualism is the religious movement founded by the Fox sisters that exclusively devotes itself to contact with the dead and other paranormal methods of spiritual depth. Lastly, necromancers may also use any form of magic they so desire to bring about their practice of necromancy, for all purposes.

Necromancy is approached in different ways, even among practitioners of magic and among occultists. Some regard it as such a dangerous and dark work, they do not advocate it, nor do they practice it. Others believe it is necessary work, something that can bring comfort, resolve issues, or just work as powerful proof of the afterlife and of the messages one can deliver from the other side. If we understand it properly, necromancy is a form of possession, no matter how you want to spin it.[39]

## **Conjuring of spirits**

We could classify necromancy as a form of conjuring spirits (or evocation), but in necromancy, the spirit is channeled through an individual, rather than just stirring them up or bringing them "back to life" among the land of the living. The purpose of conjuring spirits is to perform a rite or cast a spell. Conjuring may also be used to bind or control

*Hand-made Ouija board*

a spirit or spirits. Some conjure spirits for the entertainment or shock value of it, to "see what happens."

Spirits can be conjured by any number of magical means: gemstones, herbs, geometrical objects, seances, specific spells found in various occult traditions, and best known, Ouija boards. Ouija is thought to be a parlor game but has a long history of divining and calling up spirits. Originally known as "talking boards" (Ouija is a brand name), they were used by spiritualists to communicate with the dead and deliver messages. Ouija boards contain the letters of the alphabet, numbers 0-9, various symbols and graphics, and the words "yes," "no," "hello," and "goodbye." The user asks a question (those deemed improper by society, such as about religion death, illness, or politics), and by using the board, the "spirits" answer. (Yes or no questions much be properly framed for the spirit to answer). By using a planchette (which is a magnifying glass), individuals hold on to the magnifier and spell different words as guided by spirits, for the purpose of receiving messages from the deceased.[40]

Ouija boards were marketed as toys, stemming from the Spiritualist movement of the 1800s. They've surged and waned in popularity over the years, becoming associated with demonic possession after the release of the movie, *The Exorcist*. From a scientific perspective, it's unlikely a talking board contacts the dead. Most believe they work through the ideomotor effect, where users make unconscious movements that cause the planchette to move and spell out words. When blindfolded, users concoct nonsense terms. While the danger in such things may be nonexistent, the intention to conjure spirits is very real, and very much against the things of God.

## **Psychic**

A psychic is an individual who claims to use methods of extra-sensory perception (also known as ESP) to recognize and explain things that are not ordinarily perceived with regular senses. Psychics typically display their abilities as a part of a stage act or as, in modern times, a part of a counseling session or advisement (to police or detectives). A psychic medium, as is a frequent term, is a psychic who obtains their information by acting as a medium and channeling spirits.[41] Psychics might

*Psychic storefront*

channel their information through extrasensory perception (ESP), telepathy, clairvoyance or clairaudience, psychokinesis, teleportation, or precognition.

In ancient times, psychics weren't used for entertainment venues. They were considered respected powers in politics, religion, and other ancient institutions. They were often used to determine outcomes, the will of the gods, moral issues, and spiritual guidance. Kings, emperors, and pharaohs would consult psychics on matters of major decisions, such as battles, expansion, or changes in governmental occupation. On a community level, they were essential in matters of major life shifts or needed emotional direction.

Today, psychics aren't seen in the same light. Societal shifts to science and rational ideas meant the world of psychics transitioned to private entertainment. They are seen more for "fun" than legitimate guidance or knowledge. While there are some who put a great deal of faith in a psychic's abilities or a psychic reading, most see the practice as more of a game then a legitimate profession or undertaking.

A psychic operates through what is known as a psychic reading, by which the psychic puts into use their different perceptions and abilities. They may use any of the different forms of magic common and available, such as palmistry, aural reading (discerning the color of a person's private energy), astrological or horoscope readings, cartomancy, fortune telling, scrying, or casting lots. Readings can be done from a distance or in person. Psychic readings usually come with a cost and are designed to bring people back to the psychic, repeatedly, over time.[42]

There are two major types of psychic reading: a cold reading and a hot reading. A cold reading is a technique used to provide information about someone without any prior knowledge of them. Psychic mediums might say the information comes through spirits or other extrasensory means, but they are often analyzing specific things about people, such as body language, age, clothing or fashion, gender, orientation, ethnicity, or manner of speech. They are high-probability guesses, often somewhat general in nature, that are confirmed or denied. A hot reading is a technique when a psychic uses information previously gathered about an individual, such as through research, overheard conversation, or some other means. Obviously, a hot reading strikes audiences or individuals as accurate, but has no sort of spiritual method involved, whatsoever. It is a deception.

## **Why are there prohibitions on witchcraft and magic?**

As we already have stated, different forms of divination and magic are found in the Bible, and not just in the form of prohibitions. This causes confusion among many, especially those who desire to practice it within their own lives. If we are understanding magic and witchcraft from a deliverance perspective, what do we need to understand to properly act as agents of faith?

The first thing we need to understand is that everyone has witchcraft in their lineage, because at some point in time, everyone practiced witchcraft or magic. It is impossible to get away from, and impossible to pretend that it never existed. This is part of why it appears in the Bible, especially in situations where people wanted to discern the will of God for themselves quickly, and without delay. The way individuals from these varied cultures would handle such situations was by casting lots (throwing rocks or some other option, akin to drawing straws), or by attempting to somehow figure out God's will with things that were around them (usually using nature or some sort of natural element). It was primitive; it was fast; and it is in the Bible to show us an honest representation of where the people were at that point in history.

The accuracy of some of these methods, however, isn't easily measured. We don't have a tested indicator of how many times in history these methods worked well, versus how many times they didn't indicate much, if anything at all, or misled with their results. The reason for this is simple: the Bible's contents exist to provide stories of faith, not scientific data. These actions reflect the level of faith people had, ways they sorted out problems, and how they discerned the will of God in their lives. It's not to say we should do things in the same way, but to recognize the reality of such things for context of time and place.

There are other things we need to consider, including the realities of where they were in their faith. The Holy Spirit did not come to live within believers until after the resurrection, and better yet, until after Pentecost. It is not accidental to note that things did start to shift after that point in time, because more primitive uses of divination and attempts to explain and understand the will of God were no longer necessary. We can see, therefore, the way that the faith of the believers evolved and became something more than it was in times past; they started to understand the way that God desired to communicate and guide them Himself; and the old ways of interacting had passed away.

It also shows us the importance of worship in Spirit and in truth (John 4:24). It is literally not possible to follow any sort of religious system without there being some leftover trace of witchcraft or magic – stemming from earlier times – if we look to worldly systems. Everything, including the Bible, shows the remnants of these precepts, because it is just the way it was for so long, and spiritualities have a way of overlapping and infiltrating one another. The prohibition on such things can only be accomplished if we understand history, truth, tradition, and the importance of Spirit and truth, which is only found in the Spirit of Truth, Who leads us into all truth (John 16:13). It is God's deepest desire that we seek Him rather than a system or method of divination to figure out our course in life. While following Him closely might venture a longer discernment process, it is more important we draw to God Himself than methods that can deceive or deny over time.

We can't deny that magic is the foundation of many of our board games and other social activities. Magic is a common element in most children's stories (which puts in perspective much of the hype about Harry Potter books – it's not any worse than any other fairy tale or story of that nature) and movies. We even use many magical terms in casual, ordinary conversation with others, and they have no aforethought or purpose other than colloquial usage. Looking at the reality of origins means we can take much of this in stride. We do not have to stop living, watching movies, listening to music, reading books to our children, playing beloved games, or enjoying life, because something may or may not have had its roots in witchcraft or magic. We use these things as teaching moments, as points to explain to children what makes us, as believers different from others, and to examine our own selves as to where we are on spiritual matters. If watching a movie or reading a book drives us to run out and begin to engage in magic or witchcraft, that is a sign our faith is not where it should be, and the weakness lies in us, rather than in whatever it is that we saw or heard.

Witchcraft and magic are Biblically prohibited, because they compose a different worldview, spiritual construct, and understanding than that of the believer. One practices magic, as a discipline, with the intent of manipulating the spiritual realm into doing whatever is most advantageous or desirable. To serve as a medium or to conjure spirits, whether deceased or demonic, we must be filled with something other than the Spirit to do it. We must be filled with a spirit, but we cannot be Spirit-filled and have room for alternate spirits to run through our lives and our beings. It also reflects a preoccupation with things we cannot know about, such as the future, end results, and a lack of faith, as we do not trust God with tomorrow enough to allow Him to guide us as we walk along. There are constructs to things; there is understanding to different perceptions of spiritual and natural reality; and participating in direct magic and witchcraft is incompatible with the worldview and spirituality we are to espouse as believers.

On a final note, witchcraft and magic take a prominent seat in many of our belief systems, even as Christians. The whole concept of taking on the "mantle" of a deceased minister or a Biblical character; constructing certain words to "claim" them spiritually; accusing people of witchcraft because we don't like them or don't agree with something about them; sabotaging reputations; deliberately attempting to put ourselves into trances to have visions or dreams; embracing altered states of consciousness; even our extreme hypes and fear methods about different occult groups all relates to witchcraft because it leads us into a place where we feel the need to take on something else in order to gain control over our right now. As believers, especially those who seek to lead the way in healing and deliverance ministry, we must step back and take a deep breath to examine the principles of Spirit and truth in our own lives and our own ministries. If we have the Spirit, we will be led into all truth. That is the ultimate reason why we do not need all these external methods of divination and magic to guide us. If we are to be effective, we must be Spirit-filled. Then, and only then, will the temptations to divine the future and divine in church fully cease.

## **Chapter 6 Assignments**

- Write an essay (5-8 sentences) on magic in the Bible, both in examples of its practice and its prohibitions.
- Create a presentation on the pagan year.
- Study two of the different forms of magic in depth and create a presentation on each.

*Superstitions and Taboos, from Weird Tales (November 1941, Vol. 36, No. 2, Pages 43-44)*

## - CHAPTER SEVEN -
### Superstitions

BUT REFUSE PROFANE AND OLD WIVES' FABLES, AND EXERCISE THYSELF [RATHER] UNTO GODLINESS.
(1 TIMOTHY 4:7, KJV)

There are many different ways that principles of the occult, magic, and witchcraft infiltrate our lives through culture. We are otherwise unaware that such things relate to their original origins, because they have been so infiltrated into our cultural traditions, interests, hobbies, and general ways of living that we have no idea what they are, or where they came from. One of the most permeating ways people engage in magic without properly understanding just what it is, is through superstitions.

Most Biblical anthropologists, with any proper understanding of the culture present during Biblical times, recognize the superstitious nature of the people in the eras spanning Biblical history and construction. Being an agricultural people, the people of Bible times took note of changes in their environment, atmosphere, climatic or weather abnormalities, and general abnormalities as present in life, death, and birth. This led to people interpreting such things as omens, and taking their cue from such oddities or abnormalities, accordingly.

What many fail to recognize is our modern-day cultures are often superstitious as well, just in different ways and with different things. We often consider ourselves superior to people of Biblical times, but in many ways, human nature embodies its same forms, over and over again, throughout history, even in us and in our present day and time. Even though we might not lose our minds over the sight of a specific type of bird, there are plenty of ways we embody good luck charms, arrangement of furniture in an environment, associate certain items with bad luck, and still carry on the long-held traditions of superstitions as relate to crossing the path of a black cat or believing the number thirteen to be unlucky.

In the principle of superstition, acting upon such is a guard against bad luck, witchcraft, evil, ensure good things happen or performance in something is on the money, or to somehow ensure that bad things do not happen to someone. At some point in time, all of us have engaged in superstition, if for no other reason than we did not know any better or thought such engagement was a game, something for fun. Over time, the principle of superstitions – based in chance, luck, good, evil, and magic – became cultural patterns and ways of life.

## **The work of superstition**

Superstition is any belief or way of living that revolves around the fear of the unknown. That unknown can take several different forms, but superstitions are almost always cultural fears that center on avoiding harm or bringing luck into a situation. They play upon any number of possibilities of chance that could happen to us in a day, and our desire to avoid negative things and bring good things into our lives.

There is nothing wrong with wanting to bring good things into one's life and avoid bad things, but the concept of a superstition is that one can ward off evil and bring good through repetitious actions that have, in and of themselves, no power to do anything. They stem from a belief in luck, which is the belief that things happen to a person by chance, without any divine plan or purpose behind them. The concept of luck speaks to a disordered universe by which things happen randomly or possibly, and if one upholds the principles of superstition, they can ward off chance and bring forth luck.

As a rule, science considers the principles behind superstitions to be irrational, without foundation, and in many ways, reflecting of a primitive culture. In most religious groups, the concept of superstition has become sinful or reflecting of a lack of faith in our modern era. Regardless, many casually watch people knock wood, cross their fingers for good luck, avoid black cats, or adapt their own good luck superstitions to pass tests, succeed at work, excel at sporting events, or just to get through a day and avoid something bad from happening.

## Folk magic and superstitions

Superstitions are an extension of folk magic, because they arise out of the unique issues and circumstances a specific body of people encounter as a culture. Throughout most of human history, every culture has employed its own unique set of superstitions to match the witchcraft, magic, environmental issues, demons, and unusual circumstances each has seen and adapted to examine or encounter one situation at a time. They have been passed down from generation to generation, as one individual tells another to do something for good luck and something else to avoid back luck.

## The psychology in superstitions

No matter how absurd the origins of a superstition may sound in the ears of one who hears it today, there is a psychology in why people persist in superstitions, even in the face of everything to the contrary, stating that following a superstition hasn't any basis in reality or fact. Over time, the more they are practiced, superstitions become a ritual. The repetition of doing the same thing over and over, with no visible result, instills a drive within someone to continue doing it even more, especially as they gain a deeper sense of resolve. If every now and then there seems to be a correlation between the action and the result, that gives further encouragement. No matter how we might like to spin it, the work of superstition in someone gives them an outlet, a work of participation, to make it seem as if one is curbing their anxiety and doing something purposeful to bring positive spirits into one's life.[1]

## Amulets, good luck charms, and talisman

An amulet is a good luck charm, an object that for some reason has a power within it that can protect its owner from danger, bad luck, misfortune, or harm. Throughout the world, amulets have been worn, carried, written, kept in houses, or on doorposts to ward off evil spirits. Examples of amulets include:[2]

- **China:** Calligraphy designed to ward off spirits
- **Judaism:** Mezuzah, tefillin, Hand of Miriam, Star of David, Chai symbol
- **Catholicism:** Sign of the Cross, crucifix, holy water, devotional scapular, Sacred Heart of Jesus image
- **Islam:** Packages with Qur'an verses, kilims, hamsa
- **Italy:** Italian horn
- **India, Nepal, and Sri Lanka:** Jackal's horn
- **Ancient Rome:** Green jasper, heliotrope, chalcedony, amethyst

A good luck charm is a charm, or another name for an amulet, that is specifically around to bring good luck, rather than protecting from harm. Any object can be used as a charm and are usually worn on the body.[3]

A talisman is like an amulet but differs in that it is believed to have magical properties that can draw good luck to an individual or can also protect from evil or harm. Most magical schools recommend a talisman be specifically designed for the individual who intends to use it, as certain symbolism familiar to those practicing magic or to the purpose of such a creation. They typically feature geomantic signs related to planets and symbols of divination and/or alchemy. Examples of talisman include:[4]

- **Star of David:** Judaism, India, China, Japan, Egypt, Christianity
- **Talismanic scroll:** Islam
- **Swastika (with arms turned to the left and the right):** Worldwide

## Feng Shui

One of the more enduring superstitions (that is now a design trend) is the principle of feng shui. Feng shui is an ancient philosophical understanding originating in China over 3,000 years ago. Its purpose is to balance different energies in a space, whether inside or outside, to assure good fortune for those who inhabit that space.

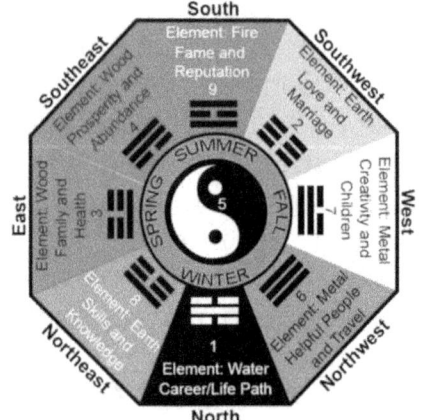

*The Feng Shui bagua*

Feng shui works through an analysis using a feng shui compass (*Luo Pan*) and a *bagua*, or feng shui energy map. The *bagua* is an octagonal grid that has the symbols of the *I Ching*, which is the foundation of feng shui.

The feng shui compass is used to access information about a building. The center contains a magnetic needle, and the different rings, bands, and symbols are all arranged around that needle, looking for the center point of the yin-yang point. Feng shui compass readings start at the front door, and one moves forward until they discover the center point, so the mapping, or design of the floor plan can begin.

The goal of feng shui is to arrange objects in a manner that allows the proper flow of energy throughout a room, as well as offering different cures for different problems. Aquariums are used to attract prosperity, Buddha statues to invite calm and peace into an atmosphere, and different colors are used to balance different harmonious elements in a space and attract and invite the proper energies. Objects or images are also selected for health benefits, energy, and balances.[5,6]

## **Household gods**

Remember the passage in Genesis where Rachel refused to stand up in her father's presence, blaming it on her period, all because she was trying to steal some of his idols?

*So Laban caught up with Jacob. Now Jacob had made his camp [pitched his tent] in the mountains, so Laban and his relatives [brothers] set up their camp [pitched] in the mountains of Gilead. Laban said to Jacob, "What have you done? You cheated me [deceived me; stole my heart] and took [carried away] my daughters as if you had captured them in a war [with a sword]. Why did you run away secretly [sneak off] and trick [deceive; steal from] me? Why didn't you tell me? Then I could have sent you away with joy and singing and with the music of tambourines and harps [lyres]. You did not even let me kiss my grandchildren [sons] and my daughters good-bye. You were very foolish to do this! I have the power to harm you, but last night the God of your father spoke to me and warned me not to say anything to you, good or bad. I know you want to go back to your home [the house of your father], but why did you steal my idols [gods; 31:19]?"*

*Jacob answered [and said to] Laban, "I left without telling you, because I was afraid you would take [forcibly remove] your daughters away from me. If you find anyone here who has taken your idols [gods], that person will be killed [not live]! Your [Our] relatives [brothers] will be my witnesses. You may look for anything that belongs to you and take anything that is yours." (Now Jacob did not know that Rachel had stolen Laban's idols.)*

*So Laban looked [went] in Jacob's tent, in Leah's tent, and in the tent where the two slave women stayed, but he did not find his idols. When he left Leah's tent, he went into Rachel's tent. Rachel had hidden the idols [teraphim; 31:19] inside her camel's saddle and was sitting on them. Although Laban looked through the whole tent, he did not find them.*

*Rachel said to her father, "Father, don't be angry with me. I am not able to stand up before you because I am having my monthly period [the way of women is on me]." So Laban looked through the camp [searched], but he did not find his idols [the teraphim].* (Genesis 31:25-35)

The items Rachel attempted to steal were household gods, or household deities. The concept of a household deity is that having a statue of a specific deity will protect the house, bringing good luck and defense against evil spirits to a specific person in the household or to the household, in general. Household deities were worshiped within the home and were represented by those small statues, amulets, or paintings, called *teraphim* in the Bible. When a family would eat, they would offer food to their personal deities. They are found in other cultures as well and were also found on objects that would be found in a home. Some homes, depending on the level of means, might have a small shrine to their specific household deity or deities. Today, we might compare this to the concept of a household patron saint, or a guardian angel, in that the being is worshiped and adored by the household. The tradition of gnomes, figurines, and embodied spirits in statue form are also in the tradition of a household deity.[7]

*The Household Gods, John William Waterhouse (1849-1917)*

Some examples of household deities include:[8]

- Brighid
- Brownie
- Frigg
- Kobold
- Lutin
- Vesta
- Bes
- Anito
- Hearth god
- Kitsune
- Chantico

## **Evil eye**

There is no more easily recognized and understood curse than the evil eye. The evil eye is believed to be a human look, intended to cause harm, ill ease, or literal illness, by which the recipient gets sick. There is also the belief that the evil eye can cast its evil on items of particular envy or note, such as if one gives the evil eye to a tree, it might wither and die, or with a car, it might permanently break down and be beyond repair, or a house might experience a broken window.

The evil eye is so prevalent in so many different cultures (especially those ancient), it is referenced in the Bible, in Proverbs 23:6:

*EAT THOU NOT THE BREAD OF HIM THAT HATH AN EVIL EYE, NEITHER DESIRE THOU HIS DAINTY MEATS.* (KJV)

It is not a worldwide superstition, although it is considered very widespread. About 36% of cultures worldwide believe in the evil eye. People have been killed and cited as witches or sorcerers with accusations of casting an evil eye in someone's direction. Historically speaking,

*Nazar amulet*

anything that goes wrong can and often was blamed on the evil eye. It was so avoided, people would even go as far as to avoid public compliments of children, for fear it might draw the ire of someone with the evil eye, in Greece, Romania, and India. In Lebanon, a woman believes it could render another woman unable to breastfeed her child, or to illness or blindness for the infant!

To remove the curse of the evil eye, one may seek out a medicine man or woman, shaman, witch, psychic, or other "spiritual healer." Most often, removal of the evil eye curse comes with a fee. To repel the evil eye, one may wear a charm decorated with an eye (called a *nazar*), a hamsa, the Italian horn, the fig sign (a fist with thumb pressed between the index and middle fingers), or the horned sign (pinky and index fingers are extended while other fingers and thumb are in a fist-like position).[9,10]

## **Lucky symbols**

Over the years, in accordance with superstition, the following symbols have become deemed as "lucky," or bringing a greater chance of benefit into one's life. Each symbol has its origins in folklore, magic, religion, tradition, or their ultimate cultural combinations:

- **The number 7:** Associated with perfection, the ultimate completion, and "the God number." Also, lucky because it is the sum of 3 (triangle) and 4 (square), both perfect forms in ancient Greek mathematics. Seven is considered a winning roll in games of chance, there are seven planets visible by our naked eye, seven colors in the rainbow, and seven days in a week.[11]

- **The number 8:** In China, the word for "fortune" sounds like the word for the number eight.[12]

- **Acorns:** According to Norse legend, they represent oak trees, which are symbols of growth, longevity, and fertility.

*Amanita muscaria mushroom*

- **Albatross:** A bird that is considered a sign of good luck for sailors.[13]

- **Amanita muscaria:** A mushroom with a red cap. Akin to finding a four-leaf clover within German lore.

- **Bamboo:** Bamboo is not the proper term for this lucky plant, but it is a relative of bamboo known as dracaena. It is hardy and lives for a long time and thus has been associated with luck. The more stalks a lucky bamboo plant has (at least three), the more luck it brings.[14]

- **Barnstar:** Originally painted on the barn by the Amish as a hex symbol to bring good luck.[15]

- **Coins:** We've all heard the expression, "See a penny, pick it up, and all day long, you'll have good luck." In the *I-Ching*, coins are also considered lucky. Special coins are those with holes, those minted the year you were born or in a year that is special to you, and those that are bent, damaged, or crooked.[16]

- **Dice:** Dice are used frequently in games of chance, and thus, are a symbol of good luck.[17]

- **Horseshoe:** Lucky when turned upwards. Horseshoes are made of iron, which was believed to have the power to ward off evil spirits, and were held in place with seven nails.[18]

- **Chimney sweep:** Believed to bring good luck when touched, especially at weddings and on New Year's.[19]

- **Dream catcher:** A Native American Ojibwe tradition that one hangs in the window to catch negative, or bad dreams, inspired by bad spirits.[20]

*Maneki-neko*

- **Four-leaf clover:** Believed by Celts to help them see fairies and avoid fairy mischief. Four leaves stand for faith, hope, love, and luck or fame, wealth, health, and faithful love. The odds of finding a four-leaf clover is about one in 10,000.[21]

- **Fish:** Considered good luck in numerous cultures because the image of a fish has been frequently used throughout religions to represent their different deities (such as the ichthus symbol in Christianity).[22]

- **Jade:** A stone used to create harmony and balance, protection, and good luck for a variety of things, including wealth and popularity.[23]

- **Ladybugs:** Stemming from a Middle Age belief that ladybugs were a symbol of protection, and now are also considered a symbol of love, joy, and prosperity.[24]

- ***Maneki-neko:*** The Japanese "beckoning cat" figurine that heralds the principles of ancient temple cats who were messengers and agents of good luck or fortune to Japanese feudal lords, monks, or who acted as heroes in different legends.[25]

- **Pig:** An old German belief states that pics absorb cast-out demons, so it was good to have them around. Having many pigs was a sign of prosperity in the Middle Ages.[26]

*Four-leaf clover*

- **Rabbit's foot:** Old belief from hoodoo magic that states the left hind foot of a rabbit captured in a cemetery at night can ward off evil magic.[27]

- **Wishbone:** An old Etruscan tradition from about 2,400 years ago stemming from a belief that birds could predict the future. When a chicken was killed, it was believed their collarbones were sacred, so they were not touched and left out in the sun. People would hold the unbroken collar bone and make a wish, hoping it would come true.[28]

- **Sarimanok:** A brightly colored bird based in the legend of the Maranao people in the Philippines.[29]

- **White elephant:** A good luck symbol in India as the white elephant, Airavata, is the personal elephant of Indra. Indra resides in Svarga, a place surrounding Mount Meru. Mount Meru is a golden mountain where the most prominent of all Hindu deities have their own kingdoms, and devotees join them there while they await their next incarnation.[30]

*Sarimanok*

- **White rat:** Within Roman society, a white rat was considered a sign of favor. Inversely, a black rat was seen as a sign of bad luck.

## Unlucky symbols

- **A black cat crossing one's path:** Black cats were associated with witchcraft, as their owners were frequently witches. They came to be considered unlucky because people believed witches could assume animal form, and that black cats were witches in disguise.[31]

- **The number 4:** The number four is considered unlucky in China, Japan, Korea, Taiwan, and other East Asian cultures because the word for the number four sounds like the word for death.[32]

- **The number 9:** In Japanese culture, the word for nine sounds like the word for torture.[33]

- **The number 17:** In Italian culture, the number seventeen is considered unlucky because the Roman numerals for seventeen (XVII) can be arranged to "VIXI," which in Latin, is a euphemism for "I am dead."[34]

- **The number 13:** The number thirteen as unlucky has a spurious history, in contrast with other histories of unlucky things. Some think it was because the thirteenth person to take their seat at the Last Supper was Judas, others think it's because Biblical references to the number 13 weren't positive (the Israelites complained thirteen times against God in the wilderness), there were thirteen steps to the gallows, the Knights Templar raid and arrest began on Friday the 13th, women have approximately thirteen periods per year, witches' covens typically have thirteen members, and so on and so forth.[35]

*Woman crossing her fingers as she walks under a ladder*

- **Opening an umbrella inside:** Umbrellas used to be for shielding one from the sun, so to open an umbrella inside (or even in the shade) would be considered an offence to the sun god. Some also believe that it is due to large umbrellas popularized in London back in the eighteenth century, which opening inside could cause injury to property or people.[36]

- **Walking under a ladder:** In medieval times, ladders symbolized the gallows, and to walk under a ladder was to mark one's own fate in a death by hanging. Spirits were also believed to inhabit the triangle shape under a ladder, so it was considered a haunted area. The triangular shape of the ladder has led to other supposed origins of the superstition, including the comparison between it and the pyramids of Egypt, and walking under it means the power of the pyramid was broken, or the use of the triangle as a Trinity symbol, thus walking under the ladder was a blasphemy that would invite the devil into one's life.[37]

- **Breaking a mirror:** It is an age-old idea that the mirror is not just a reflection of our appearances, it is also a reflection of one's soul. If the mirror is broken, it causes the soul to break, and the soul can't protect the owner from bad luck. Some think the soul avenges the one who broke the mirror (either the death of someone in the household or a close friend), and the general consensus is that one will have bad luck for seven years.[38]

- **Stepping on a crack:** Stepping on cracks is an old aspect of superstition. They are imperfections in nature or other established things, and as we learned from oddities in nature found in divination practices, cracks were regarded as bad signs. We best know the line, "Step on a crack, break your mother's back," but there are other things that are believed to happen if you step on a crack: bad luck or not get a surprise at home.[39]

*Cracks in a sidewalk*

- **Shoes on the table:** This superstition is found in the coal mining industry of North England. When a miner died in a colliery accident, his shoes were placed on a table, out of respect. Doing so when not in this situation was seen as tempting fate or calling out one's death.[40]
- **Bad luck comes in threes/people die in threes:** This origin is found in the principle of the "rule of three," or a triad, that things found in threes indicate perfection, or a set. We see this principle evident in

stories such as *The Three Little Pigs* or *The Three Musketeers*, in slogans and poetry, advertising, stories, and films. It is reflected of a belief in patterns.[41]

*Raven on a cliff*

- **Giving a clock as a gift:** In China, the words for "to give a clock" sounds like a term that means "tending to a wake or a funeral."[42]

- **Stepping on a grave:** Stepping on a grave is considered disrespectful and is considered a sacrilege, and in keeping with this tradition, it was believed you could contract a fatal disease for stepping on a grave.[43]

- **A hanging picture falling off the wall:** Some believe it forecasts someone dying. It's also a bad omen for a picture to hang on the wall crooked.[44]

- **Crows, ravens, and magpies:** These birds are associated with death, and are often used to represent death in literature.

- **Spilling salt:** Salt was, throughout much of history, considered of great worth and expense. Spilling salt, therefore, was seen as wasteful and as throwing away or losing money.[45]

- **Giving a pocket knife as a gift:** In lore, a knife is seen as symbolic of severing a relationship.[46]

- **Pointing at a rainbow:** Navaho Indians believe it is bad luck to point at a rainbow because there is such power within it.

- **Black rats:** Rats are believed to have a sixth sense regarding death and impending disaster, and in different cultures, they are considered to have powers to communicate with the other side.[47]

- **Spitting in public:** In Eastern cultures, spitting in public might land on invisible spirits who may in turn curse the spitter.[48]

- **Menstruating woman has the power to kill fields or crops:** In earlier times, people believed menstrual blood was material the fetus was made from, and the expulsion of it, was therefore, matter that didn't belong where it was going, and was something dangerous. Because women could bleed for so many days and not die, it was regarded as something both powerful and magical. Women who had their period were believed to have the power to kill crops, brighten the color of flowers, wilt trees, and even carry a fictitious substance within their bodies known as "menotoxin."[49,50]

## Everyday superstitions

There are things we often do within polite society or having fun that we don't realize are rooted in superstition. The origins of some of these are laughable, rooted in different levels of tradition and cultural superstition and identity, and all of them reveal origins to things we might otherwise never even think about.

*Knocking on wood*

- **Saying "God bless you" when someone sneezes:** – In days gone by, people believed the habitation of the soul was in the nose. When one sneezed, therefore, they could sneeze their soul out of their bodies, for it to never return. The phrase, "God bless you" is the shortened form of "God bless ya, may the devil never get ya!" which was the expression designed to protect those who sneezed from losing their souls.

- **Crossing your fingers:** Any symbolism associated with the cross was considered sacred, and crossing one's fingers is considered lucky or is associated with luck and protection because it is a way of making a cross with one's fingers.

- **Wishing upon a star:** In ancient Greece, people believed the gods would occasionally look down at earth from between the spheres, and a shooting star was a visible way the gods would accidentally drop out of this gap. Because the gods were looking down already, people believed they would be more likely to meet with any request.[51]

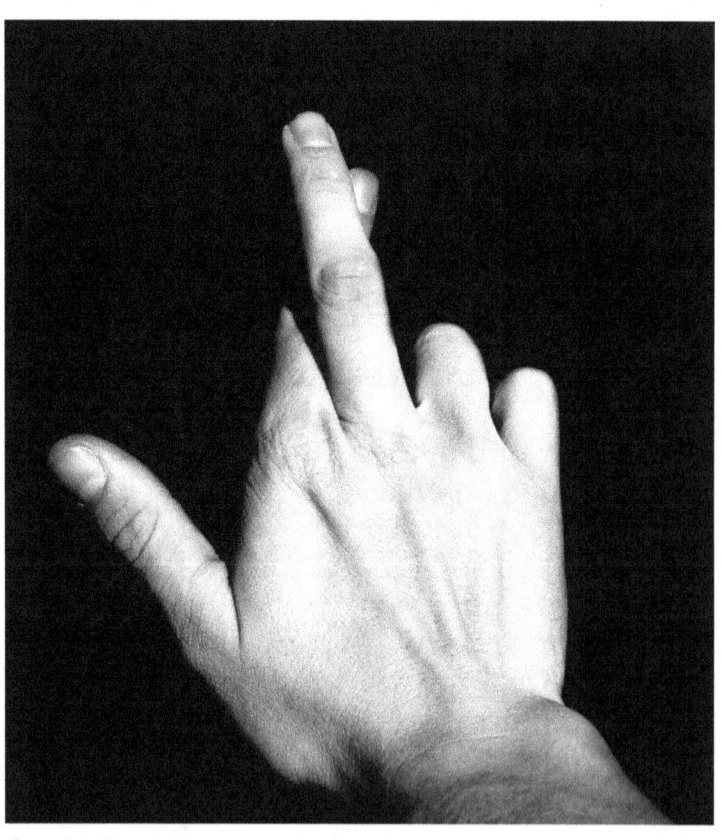
*Crossing fingers*

- **Knocking on wood:** There are two different theories as to why knocking on wood has become a way of hoping something would work out. The first is that spirits inhabited trees, and to knock wood was to gain their attention, and the second is that in the Middle Ages, churches were sites of sanctuary for criminals, so when they knocked on the church door, they knew they were safe and secure.

- **Throwing salt over your shoulder:** Generally seen as a way to ward off bad luck, throwing salt over one's shoulder is a way to blind Satan and render him helpless, as it is believed he hangs around the left shoulder.[52]

- **Saying, "Break a leg!":** This superstition ties back to the evil eye, and the belief that saying "good luck" to someone would invoke the evil eye upon them. Instead, offering the opposite of good luck verbally became a way to wish someone good luck without saying it outright.[53]

## **Be not afraid**

When the Scriptures command us to refrain from fear, we often understand it exclusively through the lens by which we see the world. We think about being afraid of a terrorist attack, or getting in a car accident, or something happening to our children or our families. We are afraid of a seeable unknown, something that we've seen happen to other people enough times that we are afraid of it now, for ourselves. In the ancient world, life wasn't always so obvious, and the realm of fear wasn't always so visible. Sure, people encountered disasters and saw things happening to others around them, but it wasn't so cut and dry when it came to fear and enemies. In a superstitious world where people had limited knowledge of how the universe works, people were afraid of what they couldn't see as much as what they could see. They were afraid of sideways glances, of hexes and spells, of witches and cauldrons that nobody could identify in common society and wanted to do everything they could to try and ward off such unseen evil.

People have always been afraid, and they felt the enemies they fought were just as valid as those things we see visible today. Fear is fear is fear is fear, and fear of the unknown, of things they never saw coming and couldn't imagine in a million years, were just as real and alive in their imaginations as things that pertain to fear are, today.

*BUT MOSES ANSWERED, "DON'T BE AFRAID! STAND STILL AND YOU WILL SEE THE LORD SAVE YOU TODAY. YOU WILL NEVER SEE THESE EGYPTIANS AGAIN AFTER TODAY.* (Exodus 14:13)

*THE LORD IS MY LIGHT [18:28; 43:3; IS. 9:2; JOHN 1:4, 9; 8:12; 1 JOHN 1:5] AND THE*

*One Who saves me [my salvation]. So why should I fear anyone [Whom should I fear]? The Lord protects [is the stronghold/refuge of] my life. So why [Of whom] should I be afraid?* (Psalm 27:1)

*Why should I be afraid of [fear] bad [evil] days? Why should I fear when evil people [...when the guilt of deceivers/the treacherous] surround me?* (Psalm 49:5)

*So don't be afraid of those people, because everything that is hidden [concealed; covered up] will be shown [revealed; uncovered; disclosed]. Everything that is secret [hidden] will be made known [clear].* (Matthew 10:26)

*[For] God did not give us a spirit [or the Spirit] that makes us afraid [timid] but a spirit [or the Spirit] of power and love and self-control [self-discipline; or good judgment].* (2 Timothy 1:7)

*Where God's love is, there is no fear [There is no fear in love], because God's perfect love drives out fear [perfect love casts out fear]. It is punishment that makes a person fear, so love is not made perfect [complete] in the person who fears [fear of punishment, not an appropriate fear of God; compare Prov. 1:7; 2 Cor. 7:15; Phil. 2:12].* (1 John 4:18)

That means when God told people in the Bible to "be not afraid," He was talking about superstition as much as He was talking about anything else. He was speaking to the fears people had, rooted in the unknown. When God told people to love their neighbor, He was tearing down the intense construct of fear of others that has been created by superstition. Instead of looking around at neighbors, friends, maybe the creepy old lady who lives on the hill as suspect, as if they had a bad motive, everyone was to be esteemed as important as everyone else. It wasn't about fighting for survival; it was about comforting fears, becoming a part of a Kingdom that is greater than anyone that we might see in this world, and stop fearing our neighbor. In our call to love our neighbor, that is an aspect of it we frequently do not hear. We are so busy thinking it must be "us or them," we don't realize we have to stop fearing them to love them.

Superstitions help us keep pagan worldviews alive, disguised as cute, cultural quirks, things that we don't connect to the intricate and intimate world of fear of others that often lie at the base. There is no question there are real, true spiritual enemies in the world and that things do happen that are outside of our control, but it is our choice, or most inward thought, as to whether we are going to allow such things to touch us in such a personal and life-altering way.

*YET WE KNOW THAT A PERSON IS MADE RIGHT WITH GOD [JUSTIFIED; DECLARED RIGHTEOUS] NOT BY FOLLOWING [THE WORKS OF] THE LAW, BUT BY TRUSTING IN [FAITH IN; OR THE FAITHFULNESS OF] JESUS CHRIST. SO WE, TOO, HAVE PUT OUR FAITH IN CHRIST JESUS, THAT WE MIGHT BE MADE RIGHT WITH GOD [JUSTIFIED; DECLARED RIGHTEOUS] BECAUSE WE TRUSTED IN [THROUGH FAITH IN; OR BECAUSE OF THE FAITHFULNESS OF] CHRIST. IT IS NOT BECAUSE WE FOLLOWED [BY THE WORKS OF] THE LAW, BECAUSE NO ONE [HUMAN BEING; FLESH] CAN BE MADE RIGHT WITH GOD [JUSTIFIED; DECLARED RIGHTEOUS] BY FOLLOWING [THE WORKS OF] THE LAW.* (Galatians 2:16)

Superstitions are an example of working our faith, trying to bring about our own results and our own protections instead of trusting in God. At the base of every person who thinks they can work their way into heaven is someone who is afraid someone else might outdo them and what they have to offer won't stand up. They are people who fear being jinxed and who, much like with superstitions, don't find what they need because they root themselves in fear that turns to pride and superiority.

In the long run, none of us can control forces greater than ourselves, especially those that seem to bring about favorable or unfavorable situations. It might seem like it due to the practice of superstitious ritual, but none of it does any actual good. Superstitions don't save us, keep us from harm, or accomplish anything purposeful or productive but give us the feeling that we are doing something to achieve our own abilities of protection against harm. In the end, whether it's nature, disaster, man's inhumanity to man, misfortune, a bad day or bad time, or just life, these things find us all the same, no matter how many times we may try to perform rituals to avoid them.

## **Chapter 7 Assignment**

- Write an essay (5-8 sentences) about superstitions, where they come from, and how you feel about them. What do they say about an individual's faith? Why do you believe people adhere to them? How can someone who is very superstitious adopt a new perspective?

# Part 2

# SPIRITUAL WARFARE

*Whole armor of God*

## - CHAPTER EIGHT -
### Preparing for Eternal Battle: Ephesians 6

YOU GAVE ME [ARMED/GIRDED ME WITH] STRENGTH IN [FOR] BATTLE.
YOU MADE MY ENEMIES BOW [HUMBLED/SUBDUED MY ENEMIES] BEFORE ME [*OR* UNDER MY FEET].
(PSALM 18:39)

This book would not be complete without a few chapters on issues that pertain to spiritual warfare and spiritual battle. We understand these things from the perspective of a drama, of a warrior-like approach that has acquired a dramatic flair for stomping on the devil's head. There's no response like a good warrior response and having this type of attitude about spiritual warfare has led us into a maze of complex and confusing messages about spiritual battle for believers. We love a good message that stirs us, makes us feel better about our struggles. We love the allure and promise that all our situations will be answered, that we will find what we are hoping for and looking for in the great beyond of faith, and that our battles will cease. We hear messages constructed in this same way, time and time again, and we respond in the same manner, believing that somehow, everything will work out.

Then we go home and resume our normal lives, wrought with the same issues, problems, challenges, and struggles, time and time again. In many, if not most cases, things don't seem to get better. They might not always get worse, but they really don't improve. At most, many people settle for a holding pattern: one where they hold on to the random promises they hear from the pulpit but maintain where they are instead of improving.

One of the major reasons why our congregations and ministers alike deal with so much spiritual attack is due to lack of proper teaching in matters of spiritual battle. We like the idea of God fighting our battles or of things getting better on their own if we just believe hard enough, so we don't do anything but wait for things to resolve themselves. Spiritual warfare, and its precepts, teach us the need to be proactive and involved in the precepts of spiritual battle.

We need to understand the essentials of spiritual warfare, particularly arming ourselves for spiritual battle, so we can teach them to our ministers and congregations, as well as live and embrace them ourselves. We need to know about our proper role as spiritual warriors, and how we can best overcome the forces of evil as we live and do good in our own personal lives and preparations. If we approach our spiritual lives with the right attitudes and mentality, we will avoid a lot of the hassle and difficulties we see in the lives of believers today.

## **Spiritual warfare**

Spiritual warfare is the basic principle that there are spiritual forces for good and evil, and both have the power to influence the believer. The spiritual realm is in constant conflict, in the greater fight between the forces of good and evil. As part of the spiritual realm (we are believers), sometimes we get caught up in the middle of this eternal battle.

Spiritual warfare conceptualizes the reality that there is an enemy, he is interested in fighting to get us away from God, and that enemy manifests in different ways in our lives.

Even if you are not big on the literal concept of Satan as a being with a pointy fork and a long tail, we encounter many trials, temptations, people, and persuasions that attempt to draw us away from the things of God – that is of no doubt. When one is a believer, there is opposition. Spiritual warfare relates to the preparations and tactical steps needed to handle the opposition that arises when one is a believer.

## **Is the battle yours, or is it God's?**

One of the biggest drawbacks to spiritual battle is the number of contradicting messages we receive today about spiritual warfare and battle. We're told that we should let God fight all our battles or that the battle is God's, so He will fight for us, but then we spend all our time battling the devil, talking to the devil, worrying about haters, focusing on our enemies, and looking to fight with people about different ways we feel we've been offended. We hear that things will get better after this struggle, or after this problem is resolved, then we are told, "new level, new devil." It doesn't help that sometimes we are told to be on the offensive, sometimes we are told to be on the defensive, and much of what we say addresses the way that we should handle people who have hurt, offended, or angered us. So much of what we discuss in church today relates to interpersonal human interactions, and we have come to focus so much on the negative aspects of those, we've gotten the idea that spiritual warfare is something God does for us, and if anything isn't going our way, we should take over and do God's job.

The problem with this mentality is that it creates a spiritual dichotomy in just what to do, and when. Any military personnel can tell you the secret to effective battle is strategy. When we fail to teach proper strategy, we leave the people open to doing whatever seems right to them in their eyes. The result is just what I described: sometimes they go on the premise God is going to do it, sometimes they think they should do it, sometimes they retaliate against their enemies, and other times, they are fighting spiritual things themselves. The combination of all these things, done at different times, has led to a flesh-dominated battle instead of Spirit-dominated strategy. There's no question that sometimes we must use different tactics to overcome the enemy but doing whatever...whenever...is one of the surest ways to be defeated.

Is the battle ours, or is it God's? The Scriptures tell us:

*So God led them through the desert [wilderness] toward the ·Red [or Reed; 10:19] Sea. The Israelites were dressed for fighting [prepared for battle] when they left the land of Egypt.* (Exodus 13:18)

*When the Ark left the camp, Moses said, "Rise up, Lord! Scatter Your enemies: make those who hate You run from You [the wilderness journey was seen as a march into battle]."* (Numbers 10:35)

*So Moses told them, "You must do these things. You must go before the Lord into battle..."But we, our servants, will prepare for battle. We will go over*

*AND FIGHT FOR THE LORD, AS YOU, OUR MASTER [LORD], HAVE SAID.* (Numbers 32:20,27)

*THE LORD HANDED THEM OVER TO [GAVE THEM INTO THE HAND OF] ISRAEL. THEY CHASED THEM TO GREATER SIDON, MISREPHOTH MAIM, AND THE VALLEY OF MIZPAH IN THE EAST [LOCATIONS NORTH AND WEST OF THE BATTLE]. ISRAEL FOUGHT UNTIL NONE OF THE ENEMY WAS LEFT ALIVE.* (Joshua 11:8)

*SO THE LORD SAVED [RESCUED; DELIVERED] THE ISRAELITES THAT DAY, AND THE BATTLE MOVED ON PAST [SPREAD BEYOND] BETH AVEN.* (1 Samuel 14:23)

*"EVERYONE GATHERED HERE [IN THIS ASSEMBLY/CROWD] WILL KNOW THE LORD DOES NOT NEED SWORDS OR SPEARS TO SAVE [RESCUE; DELIVER] PEOPLE [PS. 46:9]. THE BATTLE BELONGS TO HIM [IS THE LORD'S], AND HE WILL HAND YOU OVER TO US [GIVE YOU INTO OUR HANDS]." AS GOLIATH [THE PHILISTINE] CAME NEAR [CLOSER] TO ATTACK HIM, DAVID RAN QUICKLY [TOWARD THE BATTLE LINE] TO MEET HIM.* (1 Samuel 17:47-48)

*SAUL SAID TO DAVID, "HERE IS MY OLDER DAUGHTER MERAB. I WILL LET YOU MARRY HER [GIVE HER TO YOU AS A WIFE]. ALL I ASK IS THAT YOU REMAIN [OR BUT FIRST YOU MUST SHOW YOURSELF] BRAVE [FOR ME] AND FIGHT THE LORD'S BATTLES." SAUL THOUGHT, "I WON'T HAVE TO KILL DAVID [RAISE A HAND AGAINST HIM]. THE PHILISTINES WILL DO THAT."* (1 Samuel 18:17)

*GOD WILL BUY YOU BACK [REDEEM/RANSOM YOU] FROM DEATH IN TIMES OF HUNGER [FAMINE], AND IN BATTLE [WAR] HE WILL SAVE YOU FROM THE SWORD.* (Job 5:20)

*HE TRAINS MY HANDS FOR BATTLE SO MY ARMS CAN BEND A BRONZE BOW... YOU GAVE ME [ARMED/GIRDED ME WITH] STRENGTH IN [FOR] BATTLE. YOU MADE MY ENEMIES BOW [HUMBLED/SUBDUED MY ENEMIES] BEFORE ME [OR UNDER MY FEET].* (Psalm 18:34,39)

*WHO IS THIS GLORIOUS KING [KING OF GLORY]? THE LORD, STRONG AND MIGHTY. THE LORD, THE POWERFUL WARRIOR [MIGHTY IN BATTLE].* (Psalm 24:8)

*LORD GOD, MY MIGHTY [STRONG] SAVIOR [VICTOR], YOU PROTECT ME IN [COVER MY HEAD IN THE DAY OF] BATTLE.* (Psalm 140:7)

*PRAISE [BLESSED BE] THE LORD, MY ROCK [61:2], WHO TRAINS ME [MY HANDS] FOR*

*WAR, WHO TRAINS ME [MY FINGERS] FOR BATTLE.* (Psalm 144:1)

*YOU CAN GET THE HORSES READY FOR THE DAY OF BATTLE, BUT IT IS THE LORD WHO GIVES THE VICTORY [PS. 33:16-17].* (Proverbs 21:31)

*YOU ARE MY WAR CLUB, MY BATTLE WEAPON. I USE YOU TO SMASH [SHATTER; AND SO THROUGHOUT THIS PASSAGE] NATIONS. I USE YOU TO DESTROY KINGDOMS...LIFT UP A BANNER [A BATTLE STANDARD] IN THE LAND! BLOW THE TRUMPET [RAM'S HORN] AMONG THE NATIONS! GET THE NATIONS READY FOR BATTLE AGAINST BABYLON [CONSECRATE THE NATIONS AGAINST IT]. CALL THESE KINGDOMS OF ARARAT, MINNI, AND ASHKENAZ [NEAR LAKE URMIA AND LAKE VAN TO THE NORTHWEST OF BABYLON, AND PART OF THE COALITION AGAINST IT] AGAINST HER [TO FIGHT]. CHOOSE A COMMANDER TO LEAD THE ARMY AGAINST BABYLON [AGAINST IT]. SEND [BRING UP] SO MANY HORSES THAT THEY ARE LIKE A SWARM OF LOCUSTS.* (Jeremiah 51:20,27)

*THEN THE LORD WILL GO TO WAR AGAINST THOSE NATIONS; HE WILL FIGHT AS IN A DAY OF BATTLE.* (Zechariah 14:3)

*BE ALERT [WATCHFUL; ON YOUR GUARD]. CONTINUE STRONG [STAND FIRM] IN THE FAITH. HAVE COURAGE [OR ACT LIKE MEN (READY FOR BATTLE)], AND BE STRONG.* (1 Corinthians 16:13)

*[FOR] THESE EVIL SPIRITS ARE THE SPIRITS OF DEMONS, WHICH HAVE POWER TO DO MIRACLES [THAT PERFORM SIGNS]. THEY GO OUT TO THE KINGS OF THE WHOLE WORLD TO GATHER THEM TOGETHER FOR THE BATTLE ON THE GREAT DAY OF GOD ALMIGHTY [ALL-POWERFUL].* (Revelation 20:8)

The answer is that it is both ours and God's. It is ultimately a battle that belongs to God because it is a spiritual battle, and we know God has the ultimate victory over the enemy. It is also our battle, however, because we are ones who fight in this battle on God's side. Any soldier who has been in battle will tell you at a certain point in time, the battle became personal to them. They stood in that war, on that battleground, not just for their country, but also for the protection of their family and friends back home. They were there to guard something because they recognized the interest of protecting and defending was not just about something bigger than them; it was about them, too. The battle was theirs because they were a part of it. The same is true for us when we are in spiritual battle, as well. If we aren't willing to take on the battle as our own, as something that is so important, we will not do what needs to be done to protect ourselves and to stand for the Kingdom, and the battle is going to always be lost, and we are always going to stand defeated.

It's also important we realize that battles aren't won because soldiers do whatever they desire to do, or because they rely on higher-positioned leadership to do the work for them. If we consider spiritual warfare in light of people saying, "It's God's battle, let God fight it for you," that's exactly what we are hoping God will do. Instead of taking the direction God has provided to us for the battle, we are hoping we can do anything that we want and that God will do the fighting for us. It is God's position to provide guidance and ours to do the work He has commissioned us to do through the work and purpose of battle.

The sooner we get this, the better equipped we will be to follow the commands of God in this spiritual battle. God's commands to us aren't to be mean or a gigantic task master in the sky, but to provide valuable instructions to us so we can have the victory. This is not one of those situations that is easier said than done, because while specific situations may demand we are still and wait, and others that we are more disciplined and purposed, we can never go wrong if we allow God to minister unto us in every situation we find ourselves in.

## **Everything is not the devil**

Let's take a deep breath and realize that while it's tempting to assign everything in the world that happens (especially those things we do not like) to the devil, not everything that comes our way is demonic. One of the primary mistakes people make in spiritual warfare is assuming everything that happens to them is from the devil. There are a host of causes that very well may be behind a situation that has nothing to do with the devil. Germs, biochemical issues, a bad day, wild emotions, carelessness, and even the flesh are all things that can influence a situation.

*I USE THIS EXAMPLE [OR AN ANALOGY FROM EVERYDAY LIFE; OR AN INADEQUATE HUMAN ILLUSTRATION (LIKE SLAVERY)] BECAUSE THIS IS HARD FOR YOU TO UNDERSTAND [OF THE LIMITATIONS/WEAKNESS OF YOUR HUMAN NATURE/FLESH]. IN THE PAST YOU OFFERED THE PARTS OF YOUR BODY [OR YOURSELVES; YOUR PARTS/MEMBERS] TO BE SLAVES TO SIN [IMPURITY; DEFILEMENT] AND EVIL [LAWLESSNESS; WICKEDNESS]; YOU*

*LIVED ONLY FOR EVIL [OR ...LEADING TO EVEN MORE LAWLESSNESS/WICKEDNESS]. IN THE SAME WAY NOW YOU MUST OFFER YOURSELVES [YOUR PARTS/MEMBERS] TO BE SLAVES OF GOODNESS [RIGHTEOUSNESS]. THEN YOU WILL LIVE ONLY FOR GOD [...LEADING TO HOLINESS/SANCTIFICATION].* (Romans 6:19)

*[FOR] WE KNOW THAT THE LAW IS SPIRITUAL, BUT I AM NOT SPIRITUAL [FLESHLY; CARNAL] SINCE SIN RULES ME AS IF I WERE ITS SLAVE [SOLD TO SIN; AS A SLAVE]. [FOR] I DO NOT UNDERSTAND THE THINGS I DO. [FOR] I DO NOT DO WHAT I WANT TO DO, AND I DO THE THINGS I HATE. AND IF I DO WHAT I DO NOT WANT TO DO, THAT MEANS I AGREE THAT THE LAW IS GOOD [PAUL'S ACKNOWLEDGEMENT THAT HIS BEHAVIOR IS WRONG CONFIRMS THE LAW'S RIGHTEOUS STANDARDS]. BUT [NOW] I AM NOT REALLY THE ONE WHO IS DOING THESE HATED THINGS; IT IS SIN LIVING IN ME THAT DOES THEM. YES [FOR...], I KNOW THAT NOTHING GOOD LIVES IN ME—I MEAN NOTHING GOOD LIVES IN THE PART OF ME THAT IS EARTHLY AND SINFUL [MY SINFUL SELF; MY SINFUL NATURE; MY FLESH]. [FOR] I WANT TO DO THE THINGS THAT ARE GOOD, BUT I DO NOT [OR CANNOT] DO THEM. [FOR] I DO NOT DO THE GOOD THINGS I WANT TO DO, BUT I DO THE BAD [EVIL] THINGS I DO NOT WANT TO DO. SO IF I DO THINGS I DO NOT WANT TO DO, THEN I AM NOT THE ONE DOING THEM. IT IS SIN LIVING IN ME THAT DOES THOSE THINGS.*

*SO I HAVE LEARNED THIS RULE [OR FIND THIS PRINCIPLE/LAW AT WORK]: WHEN I WANT TO DO GOOD, EVIL IS THERE WITH ME [PRESENT WITHIN ME; CLOSE AT HAND]. [FOR] IN MY MIND [MY INMOST SELF; THE PERSON WITHIN], I AM HAPPY WITH [DELIGHT IN] GOD'S LAW. BUT I SEE ANOTHER LAW [A DIFFERENT STANDARD; OR ANOTHER POWER] WORKING IN MY BODY [OR OUTWARD ACTIONS; MEMBERS; PARTS], WHICH MAKES WAR AGAINST THE LAW [STANDARDS] THAT MY MIND ACCEPTS. THAT OTHER LAW [STANDARD; OR POWER] WORKING IN MY BODY [OR OUTWARD ACTIONS; MEMBERS; PARTS] IS THE LAW OF SIN, AND IT MAKES ME ITS PRISONER. WHAT A MISERABLE [WRETCHED] MAN I AM! WHO WILL SAVE [FREE; RESCUE; DELIVER] ME FROM THIS BODY THAT BRINGS ME DEATH [BODY DOOMED TO DIE; OR BURDEN OF DEATH]? I THANK GOD FOR SAVING ME [THANKS BE TO GOD!] THROUGH JESUS CHRIST OUR LORD!*

*SO [THEN] IN MY MIND I AM A SLAVE TO GOD'S LAW, BUT IN MY SINFUL SELF [SINFUL NATURE; FLESH] I AM A SLAVE TO THE LAW [PRINCIPLE; OR POWER] OF SIN.* (Romans 7:14-25)

The reason the Bible doesn't talk so much about people and things not being the devil is simple: the Bible is trying to show us the origins, and the realities, of spiritual things unseen. The Bible's purpose wasn't to crawl inside the minds of human beings and discern human behavior; it was to provide us the needed spiritual recognitions to understand the spiritual realm.

While the Bible is certainly not a psychology textbook, that does not mean we cannot garner a few things about human behavior from reading the Bible. Revealing the spiritual reveals realities about human nature, and the reality that as good as we might try to be, we never quite measure up:

- We are created in God's image (Genesis 1:27) but are fallen in our humanity due to sin (Romans 1:18).

- All of us have sinned and fallen short of the glory of God (Romans 3:9-18). Simply put, this means none of us are perfect.

- Humanity is a complicated ball of conditioning, due to many circumstances and conditions. We are influenced by our culture, we are influenced by our surroundings, we are influenced by our upbringing, and we are influenced by our general life conditions (Deuteronomy 13:6-18, 1 Corinthians 15:33).

- The flesh is a problem for humanity, because it is the human aspect of us that perceives the natural world and influences the spiritual aspect of us. We can be perfectly resolved in how we regard something by the Spirit, but it can easily become different when it is approached or perceived through the flesh (Romans 7:18, 1 John 1:8).

- The flesh can easily lead us into sin, no matter how much we may want to do spiritual things (Matthew 26:41, Mark 14:38).

- We always have choices in this life, even though it might not seem like we have easy answers all the time. We are influenced by our flesh and good or evil may not be our motivating factor, but what we do ultimately decides for one side or another (Psalm 37:27, Amos 5:14-15).

These facts should cause us to step back and realize some basics when interacting with others. The first is that the people we deal with are largely influenced by factors we can't always see. We tend to be angry and upset when we see obvious influencing factors (such as women in Muslim *burquahs* or men dressed as if they are from another country), but we don't realize that influencing factors are found all around us, even if we don't see them. The second is that the most influencing aspect of anyone's life is the flesh, that aspect of our nature that, no matter how much we might try, doesn't easily get redeemed. Our flesh isn't just some abstract concept in the way we see the world or that we selfishly deal with others. It is something that has been carefully formed throughout our lives and influenced by all the factors we've spoken of before. It has learned how to survive in trial, how to get what is best from everything around it, and has learned what it wants and what it doesn't want. Throughout history, people have tried to deal with the flesh in different ways. Some have attempted to mortify it physically, such as through beatings or mutilation; some have tried to starve it; still, others have tried any number of mental attempts to get the flesh to do exactly what the flesh should do, by the Spirit. No one has ever been completely successful in their endeavors, which means we should be gaining something else from the nature of the flesh and dealing with it, both within ourselves and others.

Sometimes people are just acting out of who they are, and nothing more, and nothing else. Cultural conditioning, the way someone was brought up, the values someone has, the attitudes and morals of a person, and yes, even spiritual understandings all change the way that people interact with one another. It's easy to get frustrated and start thinking every way that someone acts is from the devil, but life is really not that simple. We can sit around and curse the devil from here to eternity and back, but some things are more complicated than being that simple. Some of the issues may originate with evil forces (that's the behind-the-scenes aspect of it all), but they aren't necessarily understood as being evil or problematic in and of themselves. They are just the way people live, they are patterns of behavior, and those patterns have a complex start place and end place.

This is also one of the reasons why spiritual warfare doesn't work for a believer, and why deliverance and healing don't always take hold like they should. Many Christians find themselves constantly frustrated in their walk with God because they don't feel like they are moving forward. When, in many ways, we conveniently make God fit our cultural norms and values, we don't hear or understand His voice at work within us. If we don't learn to rightly hear from God, we will never discern His voice from that of our cultural values, and deliverance and healing easily become impossible.

Spiritual warfare, deliverance, and healing all flow together and accomplish their specific, unique purposes within us. If we are somehow otherwise influenced, living like we always have, and doing things as we always have, we won't find what we need from God.

Spiritual warfare is, therefore, a complicated concept for us, as believers, to employ for ourselves. It hits us at the very root of all that is familiar, fleshly, and comfortable. Spiritual warfare calls us out of our comfort zone, into a place where we are aware of ourselves, of our temptations, our faults and failings, of who we are, where we have come from, and open ourselves up to be shown any area of our lives that we are holding back from God. Spiritual warfare begins and ends with us, and our ability to overcome the flesh and see the realities that are often motivating us behind it.

## **Do weapons formed against us prosper?**

We love to sing songs that say no weapon formed against us will prosper, because it gives us an automatic sense of victory in battle, especially when we haven't had to do anything. Is this genuinely what the passage is saying?

*"SEE, I MADE THE BLACKSMITH.*
   *HE FANS THE FIRE TO MAKE IT HOTTER,*
      *AND HE MAKES THE KIND OF TOOL HE WANTS [FORGES A WEAPON FOR HIS PURPOSE].*
*IN THE SAME WAY I HAVE MADE THE DESTROYER TO DESTROY.*

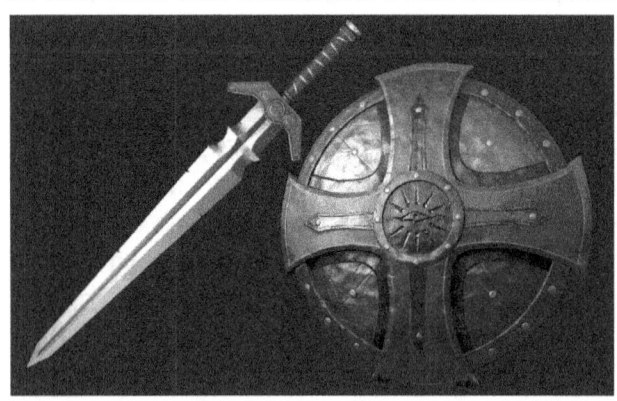

*Sword and shield*

*SO NO WEAPON THAT IS USED [FORGED] AGAINST YOU WILL DEFEAT YOU [SUCCEED].*
   *YOU WILL SHOW THAT THOSE WHO SPEAK AGAINST YOU ARE WRONG [REFUTE EVERY ACCUSATION AGAINST YOU; REFUTE EVERY TONGUE THAT RISES AGAINST YOU IN JUDGMENT].*
*THESE ARE THE GOOD THINGS [HERITAGE] MY SERVANTS RECEIVE.*
   *THEIR VICTORY [VINDICATION; RIGHTEOUSNESS] COMES FROM ME," SAYS THE LORD.*
(Isaiah 54:16-17)

The reason we are examining verse 16 as well as 17 in this passage is because it is often left out of the equation when we quote the passage. The entire chapter is speaking on the return to Jerusalem from exile, and most of us in the New Covenant would understand the chapter to be about the reign of Christ after the Second Coming. The entire chapter is about a period of peace, prosperity, and literal spiritual and life perfection at this point in history. It's not speaking about spiritual warfare, or problems with warfare, or that any issue that comes up in our lives. Rather, God is trying to reveal that in this time, there will be no issues that arise against believers that He will not be able to handle. These include false accusations, judgments, and vindictive actions.

In Biblical times, weaponry was used as an image of accusation, because Israel dealt with literal battle in Old Testament eras. Israel was a literal nation, with borders to defend, and battles to fight. Weaponry was a common facet of the life of the believer and readily understood in both a literal and metaphorical sense. This passage doesn't mean there is no battle, however, and certainly does not indicate that weapons won't be formed against us. It says, outright, that weapons will be formed. They will exist, people will plot, and others will seek to do us harm. There are things that, if we are on this side of the Second Coming and this side of heaven, we will have to deal with. That is probably one of the most primary and relevant aspects of spiritual battle we will have to face, as we delve into it for ourselves.

## **Remaining strong in the Lord**

Whenever we study spiritual warfare, we often forget the first admonition of the Apostle Paul as pertains to spiritual warfare:

FINALLY, BE STRONG IN THE LORD AND IN HIS GREAT [STRONG; MIGHTY] POWER. (Ephesians 6:10)

Being strong isn't an attribute we expound in many Christian circles. We like the principle of weakness, of being malleable by those who suggest they are leaders, and the perceived glory of following around popular leaders and those who are quick to give or receive a "word." We talk about "running to the throne, not the phone," but encourage a dependency on preachers who say what we long to hear. The simple human element in here is the flesh, longing for the hope that things will work out without us making changes or handling things differently.

This is where strength comes into our understanding of warfare: resolve. The Apostle Paul urges us to be strong in the Lord, not of our own might, but His. Because God is strong, we, too, can be strong. We can draw on His power and might to bring us to a place of resolve in our own lives.

We seldom think of God as a place to run for strength; we usually think He will be strong, and He will do all our bidding for us. Fortunately or unfortunately (depending on how you look at it), God doesn't do everything for us. God, in fact, does not do for us what He has equipped us to do ourselves, or better yet, do for Him. In spiritual battle, God provides us strength and strategy. He sends us good leadership to help us fight the battle when we are weary, and prayer warriors when we need reinforcements. It is not God's place to fight our specific battles for us; it is ours to stand and fight the battle on His behalf, with what He has equipped us to do so.

In seeing spiritual warfare through this lens, it is something we go through as believers. Despite the myths that tell us we are going through because something better is happening or because we are deeply anointed with a great purpose, warfare is something that happens to each believer. The key, or catch, is how we encounter it. So often, we are so weakened by battle, we run after every single distraction that comes our way. It is, therefore, that much more important that we come to rely on the strength of the Lord through the following:

- **Prayer:** We've started speaking on prayer in such abstract terms, almost as if it is a cure-all for everything, I don't believe we recognize the power in communication with God, especially that which operates without ceasing (1 Thessalonians 5:17). We try to make prayer deep, or demanding, or any number of things that get lost in confessions and affirmations, but if we do not find some way to communicate with God, on some level that is comfortable for us and effective, we will never find ourselves victorious in spiritual battle.

- **People to pray for us:** "Prayer partners" is a nice concept, but I haven't met many people who make it work on a regular basis. I think rather than having one main prayer partner in life, it is better to aspire to have a few friends, spiritual leaders, or mentors who are willing and able to pray for you on a regular basis. It is wise to know who prays for us, especially for very personal things. We should never hesitate to ask for prayer if we need it, even if it is in a general sense, but when it comes to personal issues, we should have a few regular people we can rely on for prayer in an intense pinch.

- **Friends who encourage us in the Lord:** Encouragement in our faith, whether it comes through church friends, friends on our job, spiritual leadership, or prayer partners, is essential to our spiritual battle and getting through the things we must go through. As we've already discussed, there are plenty of things that seek to distract or take us away from our spiritual lives. Faith is something that can be strong or fragile and often switches back and forth between the two throughout one's spiritual walk. All of us need friends who are willing to be there to rejoice when we rejoice, mourn when we mourn, and take regular steps with us - and us with them - as we figure out our faith (Romans 12:15-16).

- **Solid leadership:** Leaders can either be catalysts for where we need to be or hinder where we need to be. There are many stories of leaders who are either uninterested, unprepared, or so controlling, they are unable to be what is needed for those who are seeking assistance in the spiritual battle. The right leaders help direct us in battle, giving us the guidance of the Lord that sometimes we are unable to hear and properly receive ourselves.

- **Fellowship:** Akin to friends is fellowship, but we require more than just having people around us all the time that we like. In this spiritual walk, we never know who the most effective person may be to pray for us or to walk us through a spiritual crisis. Sometimes our friends and our family aren't the most effective people to pray us - or walk with us - through something. That's where fellowship comes in, and why fellowship is so vital to the Christian experience. Fellowship reminds us that our walk with God is about more than just us and Jesus, and how easy it is to go off on our own, without proper support, and wind up in a spiritual ditch somewhere. Fellowship makes our faith bigger than we are, and helps us be stronger, together, so we can do more as a battled unit.

- **Unity:** The best armies work as unified fronts, not as everyone going off and doing their own thing. One of the biggest reasons we face opposition is because we avoid unity with others and, instead, run off ahead of God and out on our own. Soldiers who do this in battle don't live through battle, or at best, succumb to serious, severe injuries. If we don't learn how our operations fit into the bigger scheme of battle (Kingdom work), we are going to experience chronic spiritual battles that we are unprepared to work.

- **Know ourselves:** The enemy knows just how to get us off course with the best of distractions. He knows what will rile us up, cause us to be upset or sad, what will depress us, and most relevantly, what will knock us completely off course. In the name of distractions, it happens every time, as we try to spend all our time fixing the distraction and then saying we'll resume normalcy, which never happens to the full. Some other distraction inevitably comes along and serves its same, evil purpose. We need to know distractions when we see them, know how we tick, what we can do better and how we can better serve, and how distractions effect us when they come along.

- **Recognizing our weaknesses and issues:** Satan has a way of manipulating us through the weaknesses we have. Whether it's due to mental episodes, poor self-care, emotional states, or other means, Satan has a way of manipulating our thoughts, feelings, and weak states to his advantage. Taking care of self in diverse ways goes a long way in managing spiritual warfare.

- **Desire to know, love, and serve God:** If we are serving God out of a sense of obligation, familial tradition, or just because we think it's something we have to do, we aren't going to withstand spiritual issues as they arise in a good manner. We'll resent spiritual battle, the issues that arise from it, and the complications it causes in our lives, thus causing sweeping loss in battle rather than a victory.

All these different components will help us to rest better in the strength of the Lord and be strong, ourselves. The Lord gives strength, so we can endure this battle, and something good can come out of it. It's not God's will that we spend our lives distracted and relying on a few people who help sponsor our feelings of battle over and over again. It is God's desire our strategy starts with strength and learning to discover and embrace His strength within and through us, to make that lasting difference as soldiers of the Lord.

## The best defense is a good offense

*PUT ON THE FULL ARMOR OF GOD SO THAT YOU CAN FIGHT AGAINST THE DEVIL'S EVIL TRICKS [SCHEMES].* (Ephesians 6:11)

The armor of God is a spiritual warfare weapon that is offensive in nature. There is nothing within its contents that prepares us for spiritual battle in times of retreat, covering that we did the wrong thing, or avoiding the need for prepared warfare in our lives. We must put it on in its entirety, from head to toe, to make sure we are equipped for everything that comes our way.

It's important to realize that things come our way all the time, even when we aren't suspecting them. That's why the armor of God is so complete. God has thought about the ways the enemy may easily come at us, at all our viable weaknesses, and how we can best be prepared for our lives of faith.

It's not an accident that the armor of the Lord, as we see described in Ephesians, reflects that of battle gear and attire worn by soldiers (particularly Roman soldiers) in New Testament times. By looking at the natural realm and seeing the way battle occurred, strategies were formed, and wars were won or lost, the Apostle Paul was able to see important spiritual values that are of benefit to us, even today. In natural battle, we see strategy, purpose, vision, and discipline; in spiritual battle, we see the same values, plus some. Looking at natural precepts of battle doesn't mean the values of natural battle are always proper or godly, but that the ideas behind strategy and discipline most definitely are of value for us as believers.

The Apostle Paul urges us to put on the full armor of God, not just part of it. Sometimes we are tempted to over-emphasize different pieces of armor, due to our training. It might be easy to adjust our thinking and our defenses (helmet) or defend our heart (breastplate) or walk in peace (shoes of peace), but we don't often take the full armor of God into consideration. It's fine to meditate upon the different precepts of armor and add each one to our regular repertoire of battle preparedness, but if we dare to enter out into battle with only one piece of armor or missing any piece, we are setting ourselves up for attack.

Years ago, someone told me: "You don't bring a knife to a gunfight." In other words, don't show up for battle inappropriately prepared and hope for a favorable outcome. In addition to the right mindsets and preparedness for battle, we must come wearing the right outfit. Setting things off on the right foot tells us that first impressions do matter. It's not impossible to undo them, but if we are in a battle and we show up with the wrong attire, we are going to leave ourselves exposed and unprepared for what lies ahead.

The purpose of the full armor – emphasizing completion, wholeness, and purpose – is so we can fight against any evil trick the enemy may throw our way. We cannot, and should not, ever bring a knife to a gunfight with the enemy. The whole concept of Satan as an enemy means that he knows how to get to us. In regular battle, the war is won by knowing – and understanding – just how to get to one's enemy. If we desire to exemplify this success in our own spiritual battle, we need to know our enemy and know that our enemy knows how to get to us.

Sometimes this means not being so noticeable. When soldiers are in uniform, parts of their bodies aren't recognizable from the outside. Everyone looks the same; one consistent, marching army, rather than individual people. The second armor is removed or pieces of armor change, that makes an individual stand out and stand out to be noticed by the enemy for attack. As people of God, we need to make the active commitment to making sure we know the enemy's operations and his schemes, and that we know how we can best avoid his tactics. In every action of spiritual warfare, being prepared is always our best defense.

## **Spiritual realities behind the scenes**

*[FOR] OUR FIGHT [CONFLICT; STRUGGLE] IS NOT AGAINST PEOPLE ON EARTH [FLESH AND BLOOD] BUT AGAINST THE RULERS AND AUTHORITIES AND THE POWERS [OR COSMIC POWERS/RULERS] OF THIS WORLD'S DARKNESS [DARKNESS], AGAINST THE SPIRITUAL POWERS OF EVIL IN THE HEAVENLY WORLD [REALM; PLACES].* (Ephesians 6:12)

We already briefly tapped on the fact that the Bible's purpose is to reveal what is going on behind the scenes. Despite how it is used today, the Bible was never intended to become a science textbook, a political weapon, the shaper of secular public policy, or something to hammer over people's heads unto submission. It is a record of God and people, of those who were supposed to be His own, and how they did – or as was often the case – did not measure up to where they were supposed to be. The purpose of the Bible wasn't to fix everybody else; it was to fix ourselves. From the beginning of time, God has only ever had an active remnant to work with, because most of the world has made itself content doing whatever and however it desires. The Bible stands as this specific record of how God has dealt with these people, they have dealt with God, and how God has, through His people, blessed the world.

*Marguerite in the Church with the Evil Spirits, Eugene Delacroix (1798-1863)*

So, when the Bible clarifies who our struggle is with, it is doing so to point out the spiritual realities behind the scenes. It doesn't mean to indicate that human flesh and will are of no consequence, or that every time we have a problem with someone, we should go and start cussing out the devil. The Bible is trying to remind us that in all things, our decisions and actions are either for right or wrong, for God or the devil, and that behind those actions lie a point for either side. It is the Bible's hope, and reminder, that we might be on the right side.

There's nothing wrong with acknowledging the person in the battle and the way they may behave, especially if it is, in some way, challenging, unseemly, or inappropriate. What Ephesians 6 is trying to acknowledge, however, is not so much the person or the personality as they are the strategy. When people act out, they often do so without realizing the spiritual consequences of their behavior. Their behavior, however vexing, annoying, hurtful, infuriating, damaging, or frustrating has been sent from the enemy, who desires to see you lose the spiritual battle long-term. It's not just the person who wants to get your goad, or just a matter of handling a person and what a person did to you – it is also about the Kingdom of darkness and addressing that fact in our spiritual lives.

The rulers, authorities, and powers of darkness refer to the workers of the demonic Kingdom, those we looked at in detail at the beginning of this book. They are those fallen beings, those spirits, who work the minions of the evil one in our everyday lives and our spiritual experiences. When it comes to spiritual battle, they are there, rank and file, ready to upset, frustrate, and stress each one of us out. Behind every battle we fight, every person who irks us, and every individual we just can't stand, nor stomach lies a very active and happy demon who loves to see us upset, thrown off course, and ready to give in and throw in the towel.

We talk often about emotions and emotional states and that we can't live by our feelings. Such statements are true. If we constantly go by how we feel about everyone and everything, we won't focus well and good enough on the spiritual battles at hand. We'll chase every single distraction, because of how we feel about those issues. It is out of balance, however, to suggest that we should never give credibility to how we feel about things or how something may be making us feel in each situation. Our feelings stand as indicators of right and wrong, of when something is off or doesn't feel right to us as human beings, and when we may need to draw battle lines, set boundaries, and walk away from things that are not good for us.

These facts all combine with the humanity of people in one way: if we recognize spiritual activity as the catalyst behind things, we need to respond accordingly in our lives. If someone is working as a medium for the enemy, some decisions need to be made as to the exact role they will play in our lives, how we will interact with them, if we want to remain in contact with them, and if we want, perhaps, to handle things an entirely different way.

The last major point the passage reveals to us about spiritual battle is the concept of the world. The physical world, the earth, belongs to God. It always has and always will, because God is the One Who created it. When the Bible speaks of the "world," it is using old terminology to explain the precept of the current age, or era, of time. The "world" refers to a greater system of things that is against God, that follows Satan, because the world follows its flesh, its pleasures, its desires, unto that end, whether it, and those in it, realize it.

When we talk about the world, we're not talking about specifics in the world that denominations and ministers like to pick on. It's not about music, or fashion, or make-up, or friends, or any of the specifics we try to address that may seem "worldly" to someone. Talk of the world is the general system by which the world operates, because Satan is the "prince and power of the air" (Ephesians 2:2). All this means is that Satan holds weight, and influence in this world, right now, under this present system. It doesn't mean everything that everyone does is evil or is geared for evil things, but it does mean that sometimes we have to sift through what we find – and see – to make sure the battle is ours, and we are not following ungodly or questionable influences.

*THAT IS WHY YOU NEED TO [FOR THIS REASON,] PUT ON GOD'S FULL ARMOR. THEN ON THE DAY OF EVIL [PERSECUTION GENERALLY OR END-TIME TRIBULATION] YOU WILL BE ABLE TO STAND STRONG [KEEP YOUR GROUND; RESIST THE ENEMY]. AND WHEN YOU HAVE FINISHED THE WHOLE FIGHT [AFTER YOU HAVE DONE/ACCOMPLISHED EVERYTHING], YOU WILL STILL BE STANDING.* (Ephesians 6:13)

Persecution is a part of the Christian life. We often think of persecution as having to do things we don't like or dealing with people who don't necessarily agree with us, but neither is persecution. It's not persecution when we must be forced to do the right thing or treat people right, because we can't find it within ourselves to do it without outside intervention. The concept of persecution is not accountability for our personal wrongdoing. Persecution is the outside, unwarranted attack on a person for no other reason than a specific thing, such as race or religion. Persecution is persecution because people hate the concept of something else, feel superior to it, or desire to see it die out. Persecution can come from ideals, upbringing, tensions between groups, or more notably, and more in the sense of invisible forces unseen, evil powers or spirits.

The reason God has provided us full armor – from head to toe – is to be able to stand strong, resist, and sustain the ground we have already gained. It is never God's prerogative to place us in any sort of situation that will cause us to recede, and in gaining our victories, we must maintain ourselves to keep them, no matter what. What this means is simple. It doesn't mean we never lose our tempers or get into situations that we feel we can't handle. What it does mean is that instead of being repeatedly subject to fall back or fall away from the progress we have made every time something difficult comes up, we should be able to maintain where we are and continue to move forward. The spiritual walk, the battle, is outright described as a fight in verse thirteen, because that's just what it often is. It's a fight, something we must position ourselves for, train for, and maintain ourselves through. We need to be quick to never give up, never give in, and fight to the end.

The most basic way we prepare is by putting on our spiritual armor, because it gives us the best chance to remain standing after the battle is done. For the battle, we should all be prepared. We should expect adversities, persecutions, evil, enemy forces to come at us, and in the end, that we will not lose our ground and we should continue to stand.

## The belt of truth and breastplate of righteousness

*SO STAND STRONG [OR READY], WITH THE BELT OF TRUTH TIED AROUND YOUR WAIST AND THE BODY ARMOR [BREASTPLATE] OF RIGHT LIVING [A RIGHTEOUS LIFE; OR GOD'S OWN RIGHTEOUSNESS/JUSTICE; RIGHTEOUSNESS].* (Ephesians 6:14)

*Roman soldier's belt*

Now that we have looked at the general reasons why it is important to have the whole armor, the Apostle Paul starts looking at every piece of armor and the importance it has. In standing strong and ready, we are to know just what we are wearing – and why – to identify how it protects us.

The belt of truth tied around the waist reminds us of belts we wear today. They serve to keep us standing upright, to keep pants or a skirt up, our shirt or blouse tucked in, and our appearance all-around together. In Biblical times, it was where a soldier would wear their military insignia, a specific badge signifying their rank and file. It gave some protection to the groin area, as well. The belt of truth gives us the ability to stand without shame or embarrassment, protecting that which is most delicate and private and proudly displaying who you are in Christ and all you are called to be in the process. If we keep ourselves tucked in, rank and file obvious, and our appearance together, we know we can stand firm and upright, without shame or embarrassment to go before us.

The breastplate of righteousness protects the chest area, especially the innards of the heart, lungs, and other essential internal organs. The

Scriptures specifically mention having the body armor of right living, or a righteous life, in place, and it is identified as having to do with more than just putting something on arbitrarily to make sure our outfits look right. If we allow righteousness, or a sense of doing right, to guide our lives, it will eliminate a lot of problems in battle.

Sometimes we give the enemy a foothold by what we choose to do, the habits we have, or being so emotionally needy that we trust the wrong people and walk into traps. We must guard our hearts (Proverbs 4:23), trust in the ways of the Lord, and He will give us the desires of our heart (Psalm 37:4). If we breathe in the breath of the Spirit with every breath (Job 32:8, Job 33:4), the sacredness of that breath shall protect our lungs, our speech, our very intimate connection with the work of God's image within us. If we allow righteousness to protect us, we will see our inward witness directed and our inward man renewed day by day, with God in our most intimate thoughts (2 Corinthians 4:16). When the breastplate of righteousness is on right, our direction will never be lost and the most poignant centers of desire and guidance in our lives will stand sealed.

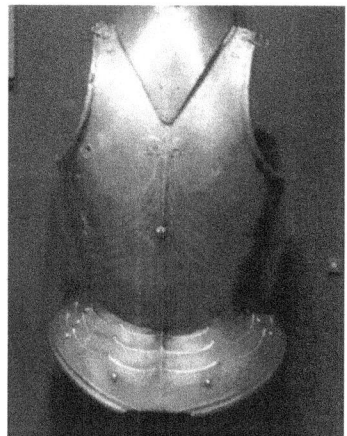
*Breastplate*

## **The shoes of peace**

*ON YOUR FEET WEAR THE GOOD NEWS [GOSPEL] OF PEACE TO HELP YOU STAND STRONG [FOR FIRM FOOTING; OR TO BE FULLY PREPARED].* (Ephesians 6:15)

Many shoe enthusiasts will tell you the right shoes make the outfit. Nobody shows up in a dress suit with a pair of sneakers on or in a workout outfit with pumps. We make sure our shoes go with our attire, because having the right – or wrong – footwear can change the entire course of what we have on, how we are

*Roman-era shoes from the Roman Army Museum*

perceived, and how well we can stand or fall. With the shoes of peace, our footing, the very thing we are grounded in, is the peace of God which passes all understanding (Philippians 4:7). We don't speak nearly enough about peace in our day, which is a shame, because peace is a grounding aspect to spiritual warfare. If we are grounded in peace, we will find ourselves more apt to walk in peace, respond with peace, and interact with peace in our lives. We should be the first to move with the Spirit as He guides us, rather than moving in hostility and anger. Such leads us to better judgment, rather than intense impulsiveness. God has provided to us the right preparation in all things, as we exercise our preparation. When we show we are willing to walk in peace and move in peace, that proves we are ready to do more in our walk with God, answering our calling and greater life purpose. Movement in peace is a lifestyle, something we are properly fitted for, something that fits us right, is not too tight or too loose, and has us ready for every experience of this life.

## **The shield of faith**

*AND ALSO [IN ADDITION TO ALL THIS; OR IN ALL CIRCUMSTANCES] USE THE SHIELD OF FAITH WITH WHICH YOU CAN STOP [EXTINGUISH] ALL THE BURNING ARROWS [FIERY DARTS] OF THE EVIL ONE.* (Ephesians 6:16)

We all know the enemy doesn't play fair. That's why he is described as an enemy, and why he has his victories against us. The work of the enemy is designed to take us out, down, wound, injure, and blight us in the battle, hitting us where it hurts the most. He allures us with what we want most, to get us away from where we need to be and attacking us right at the time we suspect or need it the least.

*Roman gladiator shield*

The shield of faith exists to handle these problems, by halting the work of those unfair, fiery darts the enemy throws at us. A body shield is held slightly out in front of the body to defend against anything thrown, or darted, in the direction of the chest and abdominal area of the body. Flaming arrows, or arrows lit on fire and then shot at a soldier or soldiers on the opposing side, were a primary and effective weapon of defense. Having a hot, fiery arrow flying at one's body required the opposing force to extinguish them as quickly as possible before they hit the body. Thus was the evolution of the shield, to quench and stop those darts from hitting the target. If faith is considered our first defense, something we hold against ourselves to prevent anything from coming at us in such a manner, it means our trust and confidence in God is the first thing we should keep out in front of us. We must remain consistent and persistent in faith in God to make sure our ultimate weapons and work of the enemy don't come at us and take us down when we are not looking.

## **The helmet of salvation and the sword of the Spirit**

*ACCEPT [RECEIVE; OR TAKE] THE HELMET OF SALVATION, AND TAKE THE SWORD OF THE SPIRIT, WHICH IS THE WORD [MESSAGE] OF GOD.* (Ephesians 6:17)

The helmet of salvation proves to us just how important our heads are in spiritual life.

*Roman soldier's helmet*

One of the biggest side jokes among people who don't play contact sports is the number of years it took contact sport players to realize they needed helmets to protect their heads. (They realized the need for a protective cup before they recognized the relevance of a helmet!) When it came to ancient battle, helmets were a common part of battle armor, because even then, soldiers could recognize the need for head protection out on the battlefield. Helmets protect heads from unwanted contact, from injuries related to striking or piercing, and overall, from any sort of jarring or stress that could seriously damage the head. There are no words to explain the importance of the helmet, because our brains control the functions of our entire body.

The helmet of salvation, therefore, reminds us of the importance in protecting our heads, and what is within them, as the believer. We should pay attention to our thoughts, our specific processes of information, the different images, ideas, and concepts we take into our minds, because all of these make a difference when we are approached and moving in spiritual battle. Anything that hits us in the head or comes into our head off the cuff can derail us off course, seriously wound us, or impact our function.

The sword of the Spirit is said to be the word of God. We learn more about the sword of the Spirit in Hebrews 4:12:

*[FOR] GOD'S WORD IS ALIVE AND WORKING [ACTIVE; POWERFUL; EFFECTIVE] AND IS SHARPER THAN A DOUBLE-EDGED SWORD. IT CUTS ALL THE WAY INTO US, WHERE THE SOUL AND THE SPIRIT ARE JOINED, TO THE CENTER OF OUR JOINTS AND BONES [PENETRATES UNTIL IT DIVIDES EVEN SOUL AND SPIRIT, JOINTS AND MARROW]. AND IT JUDGES [DISCERNS] THE THOUGHTS [IDEAS] AND FEELINGS [ATTITUDES; INTENTIONS] IN OUR HEARTS.*

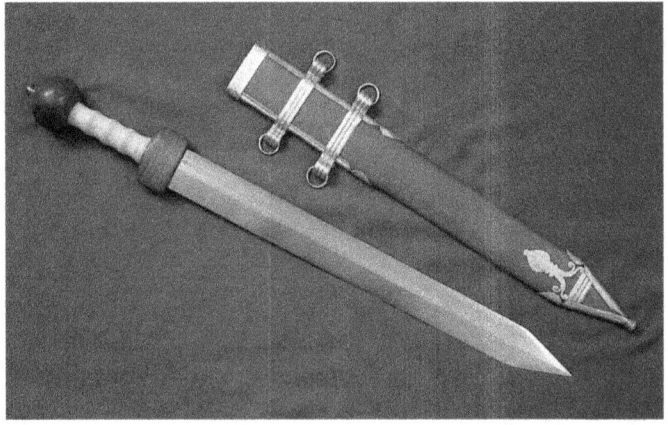

*Roman sword*

The word "word" in the Greek is the word, *rhema*, which refers to any spoken word. In the example of this passage, it is any word that is spoken from the mouth of God. The sword of the Spirit is, therefore, any word that God speaks to us. It is the proper use of Scripture, but it is more than that. It is also properly hearing from God and understanding His word to us in our lives, recognizing the benefit of both God's spoken revelation, as well as the written one. Sometimes we can so overly emphasize the written word, we forget about God's revelation to us, and that it is a vital part of our spiritual warfare. If we are unable to hear from God, we are going to be unable to follow direction, and hear that important, often overlooked spiritual guidance to help us experience a more victorious purpose in battle. Spiritual warfare isn't just done by tactical prayers or by trying to be aggressive in spirit. What we should realize as we have gone through these different stages of spiritual armor is that much of spiritual warfare rests in our character and becoming more insightful, more spiritual people at every turn. We need to hear God calling us to behave differently, handle situations differently, approach things with newness of mind and voice, and to grow as people. This is how we recognize what God is doing in season and out of season.

## The power of prayer

*PRAY IN [OR IN DEPENDENCE ON] THE SPIRIT AT ALL TIMES WITH ALL KINDS OF PRAYERS [PRAYERS AND REQUESTS], ASKING FOR EVERYTHING YOU NEED. TO DO THIS YOU MUST ALWAYS BE READY [ALERT] AND NEVER GIVE UP [WITH ALL PERSEVERANCE]. ALWAYS PRAY FOR ALL GOD'S PEOPLE [THE SAINTS].* (Ephesians 6:18)

The last aspect the Apostle Paul mentions in connection with spiritual warfare is prayer. We spoke earlier about the importance of prayer in terms of preparation for spiritual battle, and now we learn that it is an aspect of our spiritual armor, of being able to form a proper defense against the enemy. It's not just any prayer that is spoken of as being

*Praying*

powerful in battle, however. Praying in the Spirit is spoken of as the specific way we can battle in spiritual warfare through prayer, so what is prayer in the Spirit? Praying in the Spirit is more than just speaking in tongues. Often when people talk about praying in the Spirit, they start prattling off in their prayer language, and speaking in tongues can, and is definitely a form of it. To pray in the Spirit means to be in touch with the intercession of the Spirit (Romans 8:26-27), knowing what to pray for, and when. There are different ways we can pray, and we often need to pray, and we should make sure we know how to pray in different ways and to familiarize ourselves with different types of prayers. This way, we will be ready to pray in all situations and communicate exactly what needs to be voiced in each time, no matter what the specific situation at hand may be.

As soldiers, we must remain alert at all times. Being alert means being watchful and prepared, engaged and ready to go whenever we must. In that state of alertness, we aren't falling asleep on the job. We don't ignore the things that are going on around us, and we are alert to what is going on in the spiritual realm. Being a soldier on duty doesn't mean we adopt some of the exteriors we see others take on that often go nowhere. We don't have to be a miracle chaser or spend twenty-three hours a day in a prayer closet, or even a demon chaser. What God calls us to do is focus on where He desires us to be and what He desires us to become, that middle ground between awareness and obsession with things that easily lead us in one spiritual ditch or another. Not only should we be aware of ourselves, but we should be thinking about the different needs of the saints. We should pray for all our fellow soldiers, those we know, those we don't know, those we have met, will meet, or may never meet this side of heaven, our leaders and friends, and our brothers and sisters in Christ, no matter where they may be in the world.

**Spiritual warfare for you and those you lead or help**

Taking in all these precepts may seem like a lot, especially given spiritual warfare is spoken of as an aggressive form of spirituality that goes looking for trouble and seeks to steal, or take something back, from the enemy. Spiritual warfare doesn't look a lot like we portray it, because what we are taught is the need to get things right and maintain them within ourselves. The work of spiritual warfare is seldom the loud, dramatic method we used to see the old church mothers handle at the altar. It doesn't look like the loud, dramatic casting outs or exorcisms we see done in formal church services. Spiritual warfare is learning how to handle demonic forces in a quiet manner: through right living and right preparedness. We can all scream until we are hoarse, jump up and down, sweat and spit, and exhaust the living daylights out of ourselves only to wake up to the same issues and problems the next day. The only way we will ever defeat the enemy is if we will pull ourselves together and learn to apply our faith (every area of it) to our lives. Then we will start to see the victory we desire.

Making spiritual warfare practical means we live right, we teach right (if we are in ministry), and we instruct others in the ways of God, those that are clear to understand, and those that involve more study and discipline on a deeper level. We need to see God's precepts work across the board. In a deeper sense, we need to be there for those who have been indoctrinated in ways that are unproductive for spiritual battle as well as those who don't know enough about spiritual battle to engage in effective warfare. To be good at spiritual battle, we must take up our armor, take up our sword, equip ourselves with faith, and work together as one Kingdom, fighting for the battle of right throughout this world.

## **Chapter 8 Assignment**

- Write an essay (5-8 sentences) about spiritual battle and the importance of putting on the full armor of God. Include detailing on each piece of armor and its relevance.

*The cave in Qumran, West Bank, where the Dead Sea Scrolls were found*

# - CHAPTER NINE -
## Getting in the Eternal Battle: The War Scroll of the Dead Sea Scrolls

But in all these things we are completely victorious through God [*or* Christ; the One] who showed His love for us.
(Romans 8:37)

The militant nature of spiritual warfare often takes on the character of being an aggressive, forceful person. As we examined in the last chapter, that's not necessarily what God was aiming for when the topic of spiritual warfare came up in the Scriptures. It would have been contradictory to the characteristics God desired His people to have to suddenly become an aggressive war monger in the name of spiritual battle. It's not a secret that worldly war and battle don't always bring out the best in people. The repercussions of fighting for worldly things with worldly means doesn't often enhance people's lives, and this should tell us that adopting such negative behaviors is not what God desires us to do in the spiritual realm.

The militancy of spiritual battle and the way in which it is approached relates to strategy, rather than character. It is God's desire that we would not treat spiritual warfare as something haphazard, crazy, or unpredictable. The best keys to battle can be found in successful armies and in successful training, and we are able to recognize important tactics by watching the different approaches to battle found throughout Scripture and Scriptural references.

The War Scroll of the Dead Sea Scrolls is one of the most detailed examples of battle lines, preparations, formations, and orders that we can find among believers in history. They show us the importance of battle lines, structured and ordered, effective warfare. Within the War Scroll, individual battles went back and forth, with the ultimate victory going to God, and those who fought for Him, the sons of light.

Looking at the War Scroll should make us realize how important structure and order is in spiritual warfare. Written by a group who believed their predicated war would become a reality, we are able to see powerful spiritual battle lines, and why we need to take a more structurally militant approach to how we handle spiritual matters.

## The Dead Sea Scrolls

We spoke a little about the Dead Sea Scrolls earlier in this book, but we will speak a little clearer on them here to understand why the War Scroll came to be in the first place. In 1947, a goat herder was looking for a missing goat in a remote cave area of Judea when he stumbled upon several scrolls in an abandoned cave. The scrolls were found in clay jars (an ancient preservation method) in twelve different caves. Many were in fragments, but many were kept intact well enough to read their commentary and discover much about those who preserved them.

The Dead Sea Scrolls appear to have been written by an ultra-Orthodox Jewish group known as the Essenes, which we shall speak on next. The scrolls reflected the community themselves, as well as their spiritual beliefs. The spirituality of this group overlapped with their communal rule, and such is evident in that 40% are from the Hebrew Scriptures, 30% are pseudepigraphal writings (The Book of Enoch, the Book of Jubilees, the Book of Tobit, etc.), and 30% are manuscripts that relate to their specific sect, their unique beliefs, and their community guidelines. One such writing that is unique to the Dead Sea Scroll community was The War Scroll, also called the War of the Sons of Light With the Sons of Darkness, the War Rule, and the Rule of War.

The writings found among the Dead Sea Scrolls reflect a Second Temple Period influence, and are believed to be written between 520 BC and 70 AD. There's some disagreement on where the scrolls originated and how they made their way to Qumran, but there's no disagreement on the relevance of the scrolls and what an incredible find they are for anyone interested in Biblical, spiritual, or Middle Eastern history.[1]

## About the authors of the War Scroll

The Dead Sea Scroll community is a continuing revelation for those of us in our modern times. We spoke on them a little earlier, but the work of the Dead Sea Scrolls and their contents are most relevant to those who wrote them. Just as with any book that has ever been considered authoritative by a group, the collection of writings incorporated therein reflect their beliefs, what is most important to them, and what they believed would happen in their lifetimes.

The Essene community is of some debate today, but there are things we do know about them that help us to understand the writings, and especially why war was such a central facet to their spiritual interests:[2]

- They were a Jewish sect, extreme and ultra-orthodox in their approach.
- Their interpretations of Torah were attributed to a mysterious feature known as the Teacher of Righteousness. There are theories about who it might have been, but no one knows for certain. They were likely descendants of the Zadokite priesthood.
- They held initiation ceremonies for new members of the community.
- They operated by a community rule, which governed the interactions, rules, and guidelines for one another.
- They were extremely militant in their worldview, believing they would see the end of the world in their lifetime, in which the Messiah would return and overthrow the occupying Roman government in battle.
- At the same time, they were very mystical in their spiritual understanding.
- They observed strict dietary guidelines.
- They were desert dwellers, retreating from the hustle of city and sociable life to live as they desired, and maintain their strict lifestyle, until the Messiah came for them.
- They were highly prophetic.

- It is believed that John the Baptist and possibly Jesus Christ were involved with the Essene community, or at least interacted with them, based on their lifestyles and their teachings.

The Essene community disappeared sometime after the First Jewish-Roman War, which caused destruction to Qumran. It's believed, however, that some of their ideas likely influenced other groups, including Christianity. Their destruction appears to have come through war, albeit not the one they envisioned.

It's no wonder, with such a central apocalyptic theme, that the Essenes were interested in spiritual warfare as manifesting in physical battle. When we read Revelation today and we read about the battle to take place at Armageddon, we don't always think of ourselves in the battle. The War Scroll presents an up-close-and-personal approach to spiritual battle in a physical sense, one we can all understand and relate to. It gives us a visual for just what we are suiting up for in our spiritual armor and that the forces we fight in this battle. The War Scroll makes battle real and personal in a way that it was for the Essenes themselves, as they awaited the time when the battle would become alive to them.

## **Why the Roman army?**

Most believe the *Kittim*, those identified as being of darkness, were probably a reference to the Roman army, and used them as a personification of the evil sons, of dark forces, that sought to overtake and destroy those who were seen as being good within themselves.

Given the obvious disdain the Essenes, the Jews, and the church often had for the Romans in New Testament times, why was the Roman army the model for spiritual battle? Why wasn't it the Hebrew army, or maybe another historical army? We all know the Hebrews were overcome by different nations throughout history, so how did Rome become the focal inspiration for spiritual battle?

There's no question the intense Roman influence in the Apostle Paul's imagery of spiritual armor, nor is there question of influence in New Testament battles, especially those found in Revelation, as in relation to that of Rome. The Roman army was not a force to be reckoned with, as can be seen from their hundreds of years' worth of conquering and maintaining an empire beyond anything we can imagine today. As a brutal force, the

Roman army gained its historical prestige by properly training its soldiers and equipping them to move as a unified body.

The Roman army was also one that those nations overtaken and conquered by Rome dreamed of toppling one day. Rome might have been organized, they might have been militant, and they might have been one to emulate if you wanted to win, but they were also seen as the army to beat. Nobody felt they could compare to the Roman army, so that made them seem like that much more of an evil force that could not be beaten without divine intervention.

To beat your enemy, you must know your enemy, and seeing the Roman army as an evil catalyst meant learning their tactics was the best way to try and take them down. The more they saw the Roman army as a seat of evil, the better it was to learn how to operate like them. In the process, spiritual writers were able to see their methods and realize they were victorious in the world because of how they handled themselves in battle. Rather than try to overcome with force, the training them became spiritual, for the time when God Himself would have the ability to crush any and all evil, including the mighty Roman Empire.

## A word about reading the text of the War Scroll

As with much of the Dead Sea Scrolls, what we have are fragments of text that are, in some spots, left off or nonexistent. These scrolls haven't existed long enough to develop traditions about their contents, and that means segments of the text is cut off in spots. As a commentator, we are looking at the strategic nature of these scrolls, rather than at the specifics of a verse-by-verse commentary. Below is a legend on how to follow the text of this writing:[3]

- **[...]** - Lost text
- **{Text}** - Suggestion for improvement
- **(Text)** - Words not contained in the original text, but added to the translation for better understanding.
- **(?)** - uncertain reading
- **[Text]** - Added text

## Strategically prepared for battle

*For the In[structor, the Rule of] the War. The first attack of the Sons of Light shall be undertaken against the forces of the Sons of Darkness, the army of Belial: the troops of Edom, Moab, the sons of Ammon, the [Amalekites], Philistia, and the troops of the Kittim of Asshur. Supporting them are those who have violated the covenant. The sons of Levi, the sons of Judah, and the sons of Benjamin, those exiled to the wilderness, shall fight against them with [...] against all their troops, when the exiles of the Sons of Light return from the Wilderness of the Peoples to camp in the Wilderness of Jerusalem.*

*Then after the battle they shall go up from that place a[nd tile king of; the Kittim [shall enter] into Egypt. In his time he shall go forth with great wrath to do battle against the kings of the north, and in his anger he shall set out to destroy and eliminate the strength of I[srael. Then the]re shall be a time of salvation for the People of God, and a time of dominion for all the men of His forces, and eternal annihilation for all the forces of Belial. There shall be g[reat] panic [among] the sons of Japheth, Assyria shall fall with no one to come to his aid, and the supremacy of the Kittim shall cease that wickedness be overcome without a remnant. There shall be no survivors of [all the Sons of] Darkness.*

*Then [the Sons of Rig]hteousness shall shine to all ends of the world continuing to shine forth until end of the appointed seasons of darkness. Then at the time appointed by God, His great excellence shall shine for all the times of e[ternity;] for peace and blessing, glory and joy, and long life for all Sons of Light. On the day when the Kittim fall there shall be a battle and horrible carnage before the God of Israel, for it is a day appointed by Him from ancient times as a battle of annihilation for the Sons of Darkness. On that day the congregation of the gods and the congregation of men shall engage one another, resulting in great carnage.*

*The Sons of Light and the forces of Darkness shall fight together to show the strength of God with the roar of a great multitude and the shout of gods and men; a day of disaster. It is a time of distress fo[r al]l the people who are redeemed by God. In all their afflictions none exists that is like it,*

*HASTENING TO ITS COMPLETION AS AN ETERNAL REDEMPTION. ON THE DAY OF THEIR BATTLE AGAINST THE KITTIM, THEY SHALL G[O FORTH FOR] CARNAGE IN BATTLE. IN THREE LOTS THE SONS OF LIGHT SHALL STAND FIRM SO AS TO STRIKE A BLOW AT WICKEDNESS, AND IN THREE THE ARMY OF BELIAL SHALL STRENGTHEN THEMSELVES SO AS TO FORCE THE RETREAT OF THE FORCES [OF LIGHT. AND WHEN THE] BANNERS OF THE INFANTRY CAUSE THEIR HEARTS TO MELT, THEN THE STRENGTH OF GOD WILL STRENGTHEN THE HE[ARTS OF THE SONS OF LIGHT.] IN THE SEVENTH LOT: THE GREAT HAND OF GOD SHALL OVERCOME [BELIAL AND AL]L THE ANGELS OF HIS DOMINION, AND ALL THE MEN OF [HIS FORCES SHALL BE DESTROYED FOREVER].*

*THE ANNIHILATION OF THE SONS OF DARKNESS AND SERVICE TO GOD DURING THE WAR YEARS. [....] THE HOLY ONES SHALL SHINE FORTH IN SUPPORT OF [...] THE TRUTH FOR THE ANNIHILATION OF THE SONS OF DARKNESS. THEN [...] [...] A GREAT [R]OAR [...] THEY TOOK HOLD OF THE IMPLEMENT[S OF WAR.] [...] [... CHIEFS OF THE TRIBES ... AND THE PRIESTS, [THE LEVITES, THE CHIEFS OF THE TRIBES, THE FATHERS OF THE CONGREGATION ... THE PRIESTS AND THUS FOR THE LEVITES AND THE COURSES OF THE HEADS OF] THE CONGREGATION'S CLANS, FIFTY-TWO.* (Column 1:1-20)[4]

*Tryptych: The Last Judgment, Fra Angelico (1395-1455)*

The passage sets up the scene as the battle comes to ensue. The dark forces come out of their way and find the people of God, for that's what dark forces are about. They are motivated by Belial, or the evil one, and the result is complete and total panic. This is here to alert the Sons of Light, however, to the time for salvation is approaching. The following is clearly outlined as a strategic approach for the battle:

- The people are prepared. This isn't a surprise attack, but they have been prepared and ready for this fight, and now that the day has come, they know what to do and how to do it.

- There was no panic among the Sons of Light. Even though everyone else might have panicked, they did not.

- They were ready to make sure wickedness no longer existed. The battle was the battle and meant they had to do what they were prepared to do.

- They believed in showing the strength of God as a multitude. The worst thing any of us can think about doing when it comes to spiritual warfare is each do what is right in our own eyes. Such leads to messy, endless anarchy that is not easily rectified. A unified army is one that cannot easily be overcome.

- They knew the battle signal (a roar) and where their weapons were. There was no running around wondering what to do or where equipment was. Instead, they were prepared and ready.

- There was no doubt they would be victorious over the Sons of Darkness and, ultimately Belial, the motivating enemy. It was not a question as to whether they would win, but no matter how the battle might have looked, the end victory would be theirs.

## **Assembling for the battle**

*THEY SHALL RANK THE CHIEFS OF THE PRIESTS AFTER THE CHIEF PRIEST AND HIS DEPUTY; TWELVE CHIEF PRIESTS TO SERVE IN THE REGULAR OFFERING BEFORE GOD. THE CHIEFS OF THE COURSES, TWENTY-SIX, SHALL SERVE IN THEIR COURSES. AFTER THEM THE CHIEFS OF THE LEVITES SERVE CONTINUALLY, TWELVE IN ALL, ONE TO A TRIBE. THE CHIEFS OF THEIR COURSES SHALL SERVE EACH MAN IN HIS OFFICE. THE CHIEFS OF THE TRIBES AND FATHERS OF THE CONGREGATION SHALL SUPPORT THEM, TAKING THEIR STAND CONTINUALLY AT THE GATES OF THE SANCTUARY.*

*THE CHIEFS OF THEIR COURSES, FROM THE AGE OF FIFTY UPWARDS, SHALL TAKE THEIR STAND WITH THEIR COMMISSIONERS ON THEIR FESTIVALS, NEW MOONS AND SABBATHS, AND ON EVERY DAY OF THE YEAR.*

*THESE SHALL TAKE THEIR STAND AT THE BURNT OFFERINGS AND SACRIFICES, TO ARRANGE THE SWEET SMELLING INCENSE ACCORDING TO THE WILL OF GOD, TO ATONE*

*FOR ALL HIS CONGREGATION, AND TO SATISFY THEMSELVES BEFORE HIM CONTINUALLY AT THE TABLE OF GLORY. ALL OF THESE THEY SHALL ARRANGE AT THE TIME OF THE YEAR OF REMISSION. DURING THE REMAINING THIRTY-THREE YEARS OF THE WAR THE MEN OF RENOWN, THOSE CALLED OF THE CONGREGATION, AND ALL THE HEADS OF THE CONGREGATION'S CLANS SHALL CHOOSE FOR THEMSELVES MEN OF WAR FOR ALL THE LANDS OF THE NATIONS. FROM AIL TRIBES OF ISRAEL THEY SHALL PREPARE CAPABLE MEN FOR THEMSELVES TO GO OUT FOR BATTLE ACCORDING TO THE SUMMONS OF THE WAR, YEAR BY YEAR. BUT DURING THE YEARS OF REMISSION THEY SHALL NOT READY MEN TO GO OUT FOR BATTLE, FOR IT IS A SABBATH OF REST FOR ISRAEL. DURING THE THIRTY-FIVE YEARS OF SERVICE THE WAR SHALL BE WAGED. FOR SIX YEARS THE WHOLE CONGREGATION SHALL WAGE IT TOGETHER, AND A WAR OF DIVISIONS SHALL BE WAGED DURING THE TWENTY-NINE REMAINING YEARS. IN THE FIRST YEAR THEY SHALL FIGHT AGAINST MESOPOTAMIA, IN THE SECOND AGAINST THE SONS OF LUD, IN THE THIRD THEY SHALL FIGHT AGAINST THE REST OF THE SONS OF ARAM: UZ, HUL, TOGAR, AND MESHA, WHO ARE BEYOND THE EUPHRATES. IN THE FOURTH AND FIFTH THEY SHALL FIGHT AGAINST THE SONS OF ARPACHSHAD, IN THE SIXTH AND SEVENTH THEY SHALL FIGHT AGAINST ALL THE SONS OF ASSYRIA AND PERSIA AND THE EASTERNERS UP TO THE GREAT DESERT. IN THE EIGHTH YEAR THEY SHALL FIGHT AGAINST THE SONS OF ELAM, IN THE NINTH YEAR THEY SHALL FIGHT AGAINST THE SONS OF ISHMAEL AND KETURAH, AND DURING THE FOLLOWING TEN YEARS THE WAR SHALL BE DIVIDED AGAINST ALL THE SONS OF HAM ACCORDING TO [THEIR] C[LANS AND] THEIR [TERRI]TORIES. DURING THE REMAINING TEN YEARS THE WAR SHALL BE DIVIDED AGAINST ALL [SONS OF JAPHE]TH ACCORDING TO THEIR TERRITORIES.* (Column 2:1-14)[5]

One of the most impressive aspects of the War Scroll is the assembly lines for battle. Each group was ranked, specifically with numbers, and sent forth for the battle, row by row and group by group. Even though it might seem like a long and boring detail, the level of detailing every row, of every position, and the sheer number of people needed to accomplish this battle proves its divine origin. Battle must be ordered to be effective, and there is no way we can deny this point, even reiterating it multiple times. When you are taking on the entire world as a small remnant, there must be a structure to the fighting power.

This particular aspect of the scroll is most interesting. It emphasizes the spiritual, rather than practical nature of the fight in a way that most wouldn't readily notice. While the *kittim* has already been mentioned, the battle is shown as taking place over a period of seventy years, indicating the completion of two jubilee cycles, ending in a year of perfection. Not only will the *kittim* be fought, but all the forces of evil, personified by different nations, who were the enemies of Israel throughout the Old Testament. It wasn't just about the fall of one occupying army, but about the fall of everything evil, everything that sought to take out the righteous. While they might have appeared to have been victorious, in the end, God is the ultimate avenger. No enemy wins forever, and that motivates us to continue the battle as the cycles continue, and the soldiers believe.

We also see the armies continuing to practice their spiritual disciplines (sacrifices, offerings, burnings, etc.) during the battle. The battle wasn't an excuse to stop attending service, to stop being spiritual, to stop doing what was required from them, and to stop living right. In looking at it this way, it is no wonder we slip in spiritual battle and start falling in other places of our lives. A hard battle, a difficult time, unfortunate spiritual encounters, unfortunate experiences, and things not going one's way are not an excuse to become less spiritual or to pull away from spiritual things. Through our battles, we are responsible to do the work of God, to maintain our spiritual lives and do what God has asked us to do.

## **Sound the trumpet!**

*[THE RULE OF THE TRUMPETS: THE TRUMPETS] OF ALARM FOR ALL THEIR SERVICE FOR THE [...] FOR THEIR COMMISSIONED MEN, [BY TENS OF THOUSANDS AND THOUSANDS AND HUNDREDS AND FIFTIES] AND TENS. UPON THE T[RUMPETS ...][...][...][...][... THEY SHALL WRITE ... THE TRUMPETS OF] THE BATTLE FORMATIONS, AND THE TRUMPETS FOR ASSEMBLING THEM WHEN THE GATES OF THE WAR ARE OPENED SO THAT THE INFANTRY MIGHT ADVANCE, THE TRUMPETS FOR THE SIGNAL OF THE SLAIN, THE TRUMPETS OF THE AMBUSH, THE TRUMPETS OF PURSUIT WHEN THE ENEMY IS DEFEATED, AND THE TRUMPETS OF REASSEMBLY WHEN THE BATTLE RETURNS.*

*ON THE TRUMPETS FOR THE ASSEMBLY OF THE CONGREGATION THEY SHALL WRITE, "THE CALLED OF GOD."*

*Person blowing a Biblical trumpet*

*On the trumpets for the assembly of the chiefs they shall write, "The princes of God."*

*On the trumpets of the formations they shall write, "The rule of God."*

*On the trumpets of the men of renown [they shall write], "The heads of the congregation's clans." Then when they are assembled at the house of meeting, they shall write, "The testimonies of God for a holy congregation."*

*On the trumpets of the camps they shall write, "The peace of God in the camps of His saints."*

*On the trumpets for their campaigns they shall write, "The mighty deeds of God to scatter the enemy and to put all those who hate justice to flight and a withdrawal of mercy from all who hate God."*

*On the trumpets of the battle formations they shall write, "Formations of the divisions of God to avenge His anger on all Sons of Darkness."*

*On the trumpets for assembling the infantry when the gates of war open that they might go out against the battle line of the enemy, they shall write, "A remembrance of requital at the appointed time of God."*

*On the trumpets of the slain they shall write, "The hand of the might of God in battle so as to bring down all the slain because of unfaithfulness."*

*On the trumpets of ambush they shall write, "Mysteries of God to wipe out wickedness."*

*On the trumpets of pursuit they shall write, "God has struck all Sons of Darkness, He shall not abate His anger until they are annihilated."*

*When they return from battle to enter the formation, they shall write on the trumpets of retreat, "God has gathered."*

*On the trumpets for the way of return from battle with the enemy to enter the congregation in Jerusalem, they shall write, "Rejoicings of God in a*

*PEACEFUL RETURN."* (Column 2:15-3:11)[6]

In Biblical times, trumpets were used as a sign of battle alarm. At the sound of the trumpet, the soldiers knew it was time to assemble, and the advance was coming. Trumpets were not just used to indicate the start of battle, however. They were also used to indicate advance, that there were many wounded or dead soldiers, of ambush, enemy defeat, and reassembly when the battle returns. Through the trumpet, soldiers recognized it as a part of the work and call of God. On each trumpet, for each assembly and division, was a specific identity and message from the Most High. Every time that trumpet was sounded, those words were heard by those people. Those trumpets echoed the encouragement needed, words, and spiritual confessions needed to continue on to victory. Every time the trumpets were heard, people heard they were called by God, the princes of God, ruled by God, the testimonies of God, the holy congregation of God, the peace of God is present among His people, the deeds of God are mighty, and the enemy shall be scattered, God shall avenge His people. By the sound of trumpets, those who had fallen were always remembered, the mysteries of God were remembered, and the reminder that God was still God and the people should rejoice was remembered.

The trumpets associated sound with a need to pay attention and remember who they were. They were the Sons of Light, battling against the Sons of Darkness, aware and ready for what was coming next. They were the people of God, the warriors of God, and their individual problems no longer existed. They knew what being in battle meant, and they weren't afraid to step up and do what needed to be done.

Perhaps this is one of the primary reasons we are lost every time the trumpet sounds. We don't hear God call our name, our being, our purpose with that blast of the alarm. We allow our battle cry and our battle identity to be lost in our lives, our losses and hurts, and we are so easily distracted, the enemy hears the battle cry and finds us unprepared and off duty. When God blasts that trumpet, we need to hear that call tell us who we are and what we are supposed to be doing. So much was said to the Essene community in the blast of a trumpet, and we need to hear that said to us, as well. We should be listening for God's purposes when we are called to prayer, go through intense trials, or have difficult times. Our warrior stance should never be lost or questioned, because there is an enemy to defeat. God needs His active soldiers so the day can come when the enemy falls and we can all stand there, ready to rejoice.

## **Banners for the Lord's battle**

*Rule of the banners of the whole congregation according to their formations. On the grand banner which is at the head of all the people they shall write, "People of God," the names "Israel" and "Aaron," and the names of the twelve tribes of Israel according to their order of birth.*

*On the banners of the heads of the "camps" of three tribes they shall write, "The Spirit [of God," and the names of three tribes.*

*O]n the banner of each tribe they shall write, "Standard of God," and the name of the leader of the t[ribe] of its clans. [... and] the name of the leader of the ten thousand and the names of the chief[s of ...] [...] his hundreds.*

*On the banner [...] [...] [...] [...]*

*On the banner of Merari they shall write, "The Offering of God," and the name of the leader of Merari and the names of the chiefs of his thousands.*

*On the banner of the tho[us]and they shall write, "The Anger of God is loosed against Belial and all the men of his forces without remnant," and the name of the chief of the thousand and the names of the chiefs of his hundreds.*

*And on the banner of the hundred they shall write, "Hundred of God, the power of war against a sinful flesh," arid the name of the chief of the hundred and the names of the chiefs of his tens.*

*And on the banner of the fifty they shall write, "Ended is the stand of the wicked [by] the might of God," and the name of the chief of the fifty and the names of the chiefs of his tens.*

*And on the banner of the ten they shall write, "Songs of joy for God on the ten-stringed harp," and the name of the chief of the ten and the names of the nine men in his command.*

*When they go to battle they shall write on their banners, "The truth of God," "The righteousness of God," "The glory of God," "The justice of God," and after these the list of their names in full.*

*When they draw near for battle they shall write on their banners, "The right hand of God," "The appointed time of God," "The tumult of God," "The slain of God"; after these their names in full.*

*When they return from battle they shall write on their banners, "The exaltation of God," "The greatness of God," "The praise of God," "The glory of God," with their names in full.*

*The Rule of the banners of the congregation: When they set out to battle they shall write on the first banner, "The congregation of God," on the second banner, "The camps of God," on the third, "The tribes of God," on the fourth, "The clans of God," on the fifth, "The divisions of God," on the sixth, "The congregation of God," on the seventh, "Those called by God," and on the eighth, "The army of God." They shall write their names in full with all their order.*

*When they draw near for battle they shall write on their banners, "The battle of God," "The recompense of God," "The cause of God," "The reprisal of God," "The power of God," "The retribution of God," "The might of God," "The annihilation by God of all the vainglorious nations." And their names in full they shall write upon them.*

*When they return from battle they shall write on their banners, "The deliverance of God," "The*

Soldiers of the 114th infantry in Paris, using the French flag as a battle banner

*victory of God," "The help of God," "The support of God," "The joy of God," "The thanksgivings of God," "The praise of God," and "The peace of God."*

*[The Length of the Bann]ers. The banner of the whole congregation shall be fourteen cubits long; the banner of th[ree tribes' thir]teen cubits [long;] [the banner of a tribe,] twelve cubits; the banner of ten thousand, eleve[n cubits; the banner of a thousand, ten cubits; the banner of a hu]ndred, [n]ine cubits; [the banner of a fifty, ei]ght cubits; the banner of a ten, sev[en cubits . . . ]. [...][...][...]* (Column 3:13-4:1-20)⁷

Banners were used in Biblical times as signals and markers to be noticed, frequently in battle or as some sort of proclamation. Families and tribes also had unique banners that displayed family emblems or insignia that was unique to represent them. In the instance of spiritual warfare, the banners mentioned herein represent both specific groups within the Sons of Light and as heralds of the righteousness in battle. Much like the trumpets, each banner contained words of praise and heralds of God, but after the words of God came the names of each group identified within that banner. Such proves just how important being within the honor and power of God was to the Essenes, and why it should be important to us, as well. Being a part of the army of God is a privilege. It is something God has extended to us as His people. We have the unique honor of fighting on the side of right, the side of God Himself, in the battle of right and wrong. We are more than conquerors (Romans 8:37) not because of our individual abilities, but because we move under the mighty power of God. Everything we do is done, every move we make, because we are under the banner of the Lord, the Lord by which we are able to make offering, sing the song of joy, stand under His truth and righteousness, operate under His justice, and honor that justice, however it comes. We have the power to honor those who have died in His service, recognizing our cloud of witnesses (Hebrews 12:1). We are the clans of God, the camps of God, the divisions of God, and ultimately, the congregation of God. There is nothing higher or more powerful than being a part of His Kingdom, and a worthy servant in His army, worthy to fly His banner over your name.

## Shields and swords for those arranging and deploying for battle

*And on the sh[ie]ld of the Leader of the whole nation they shall write his name, the names "Israel," "Levi," and "Aaron," and the names of the twelve tribes of Israel according to their order of birth, and the names of the twelve chiefs of their tribes.*

*The rule for arranging the divisions for war when their army is complete to make a forward battle line: the battle line shall be formed of one thousand men. There shall be seven forward rows to each battle line, arranged in order; the stahon of each man behind his fellow.*

*All of them shall bear shields of bronze, polished like a face mirror. The shield shall be bound with a border of plaited work and a design of loops, the work of a skillful workman; gold, silver, and bronze bound together and jewels; a multicolored brocade. It is the work of a skillful workman, artistically done. The length of the shield shall be two and a half cubits, and its breadth a cubit and a half.*

*In their hands they hold a lance and a sword. The length of the lance shall be seven cubits, of which the socket and the blade constitute half a cubit. On the socket there she be three bands engraved as a border of plaited work; of gold, silver, and Copper bound together like an artistically designed work. And in the loops of the de sign, on both sides of the band all around, shall be precious stones, a multicolored brocade, the work of a skillful workman, artistically done, and an ear of grain. The socket shall be grooved between the bands like a column, artistically done. The blade shall be of shining white iron, the work of a skillful workman, artistically done, and an ear of grain of pure gold inlaid in the blade; tapered towards the point. The swords shall be of refined iron, purified in the furnace and polished like a face mirror, the work of a skillful workman, artistically done, with figures of ears of grain of pure gold embossed on both sides. The borders*

*Irish shield of faith*

*SHALL GO STRAIGHT TO THE POINT, TWO ON EACH SIDE. THE LENGTH OF THE SWORD SHALL BE A CUBIT AND A HALF AND ITS WIDTH FOUR FINGERS. THE SCABBARD SHALL BE FOUR THUMBS WIDE AND FOUR HANDBREADTHS UP TO THE SCABBARD. THE SCABBARD SHALL BE TIED ON EITHER SIDE WITH THONGS OF FIVE HANDBREADTHS. THE HANDLE OF THE SWORD SHALL BE OF CHOICE HORN, THE WORK OF A SKILLFUL WORKMAN, A VARICOLORED DESIGN WITH GOLD AND SILVER AND PRECIOUS STONES.*

*AND WHEN THE [... TAKE THEIR] STAND, THEY SHALL ARRANGE EVEN BATTLE LINES, ONE BEHIND THE OTHER [...] AND THERE SHALL BE A SPACE [BETWEEN ... T]HIRTY CUBITS, WHERE THE INFAN[TRY] SHALL STAND [...] FORWARD [...][...][ . . . THEY SHALL SLING] SEVEN TIMES, AND RETURN TO THEIR POSITION. AFTER THEM, THREE DIVISIONS OF INFANTRY SHALL ADVANCE AND STAND BETWEEN THE BATTLE LINES.*

*THE FIRST DIVISION SHALL HEAVE INTO THE ENEMY BATTLE LINE SEVEN BATTLE DARTS. ON THE BLADE OF THE FIRST DART THEY SHALL WRITE, "FLASH OF A SPEAR FOR THE STRENGTH OF GOD." ON THE SECOND WEAPON THEY SHALL WRITE, "MISSILES OF BLOOD TO FELL THE SLAIN BY THE WRATH OF GOD." ON THE THIRD DART THEY SHALL WRITE, "THE BLADE OF A SWORD DEVOURS THE SLAIN OF WICKEDNESS BY THE JUDGMENT OF GOD." EACH OF THESE THEY SHALL THROW SEVEN TIMES AND THEN RETURN TO THEIR POSITION.*

*AFTER THESE, TWO DIVISIONS OF INFANTRY SHALL MARCH FORTH AND STAND BETWEEN THE TWO BATTLE LINES, THE FIRST DIVISION EQUIPPED WITH A SPEAR AND A SHIELD AND THE SECOND DIVISION WITH A SHIELD AND A SWORD; TO BRING DOWN THE SLAIN BY THE JUDGMENT OF GOD, TO SUBDUE THE BATTLE LINE OF THE ENEMY BY THE POWER OF GOD, AND TO RENDER RECOMPENSE FOR THEIR EVIL FOR ALL THE VAINGLORIOUS NATIONS. SO THE KINGSHIP SHALL BELONG TO THE GOD OF ISRAEL, AND BY THE HOLY ONES OF HIS PEOPLE HE SHALL ACT POWERFULLY.* (Column 5:1-6:6)[8]

We spoke on the relevance of shields in the last chapter. As a representation of faith in our lives, they stand as an important defense against the work of the enemy in our lives. Faith, all by itself, is spoken of as something that transcends so many different aspects of our spiritual lives. It is spoken of as a spiritual gift (1 Corinthians 12:9), an aspect of spiritual warfare (Ephesians 6:16), and above all, something that proves itself as a substance (something hoped for) and an essence (the proof of what is unseen) (Hebrews 11:1). Now we can see that the shields of those in spiritual battle also have writing on them, proving how powerful the word of God and the reminders of God are in different aspects of battle. We hear reminders with the blast of a trumpet, we are under the reminders of God with banners, and now the shields also remind us of God's command and purpose in spiritual battle. Holding the shield of faith in the battle, remembering we fight for God and while it is His battle, we are His soldiers, reminds us we can't do this without Him. So often we take the posture of spiritual warfare as being our own personal agenda, something we are going to use to get something out of a fight or out of our desires, and we forget that spiritual battle isn't about us. We should never try to manipulate the spiritual realm under the guise of spiritual battle. It's not spiritual battle to get everyone in your life to change the way you want them to be, or to get your spouse to be the person you want (rather than that God wants) or even to get what you always want out of your life. It's not about you claiming your family, speaking against attacks on people, or getting everyone to align where you want them. There is a fine line between praying, believing, and manipulating things to be so, and as believers, the battle line is where we see the difference. If we don't find ourselves positioned to hear His command, under His banner, and recognizing our position with His faith out front of us, we are leaving ourselves unprotected and subjecting ourselves to manipulating others in our lives. Just because we invoke the Name of God to do things doesn't mean He knows us, or we are operating in faith (Matthew 7:15-23). How we handle ourselves in the spiritual battle is the ultimate test: do we do the will of our Father, Who is in heaven? Is our shield of faith there to go before us, defend us, and protect us – and are we ready to act powerfully? If every time you try to stand on faith and you find yourself void, it is time to check who – or what – you have your faith in, and on whose side you find yourself fighting. Spiritual battle isn't about us or our petty issues; it's about God. It proves, once and for all, where our priorities are, and if we love God for God, or we are in this for ourselves.

Once we have taken up our shield, we see the additional weapons of faith, specifically designed and equipped for their purpose. Once we take up faith, we are equipped to fight with the spiritual sword, emboldened with beautiful handiwork, precious jewels, and perfectly shined. This makes us think twice about swinging it carelessly or using it for just any purpose. If we come out with our weapon, we should be prepared to use it properly, with thought. This reminds us that spiritual battle should never, ever be done for fleshly purposes. We should never use spiritual things to try and deliberately hurt or wound others, because this is a gross misuse of the tools given to us for spiritual purposes. Spiritual warfare is about defeat of the enemy, the true spiritual enemy we have, instead of focusing on the little battles and frustrations we experience. The bigger picture – the eloquent stones, the beautiful handiwork, and the ability to see ourselves first in the reflection of our swords should forever leave us mindful and ready to remember the real reason we battle instead of being distracted by the people and issues of our lives we simply do not like.

## **Deploying the cavalry**

*SEVEN ROWS OF HORSEMEN SHALL ALSO TAKE POSITION AT THE RIGHT AND AT THE 1EFT OF THE BATTLE LINE. THEIR RANKS SHALL BE POSITIONED ON BOTH SIDES, SEVEN HUNDRED HORSEMEN ON ONE SIDE AND SEVEN HUNDRED ON THE OTHER. TWO HUNDRED HORSEMEN SHALL GO OUT WITH ONE THOUSAND MEN OF THE BATTLE LINE OF THE INFANTRY, AND THUS THEY SHALL TAKE POSITION ON ALL SIDES OF THE CAMP. THE TOTAL BEING FOUR THOUSAND SIX HUNDRED MEN, AND ONE THOUSAND FOUR HUNDRED CAVALRY FOR THE ENTIRE ARMY ARRANGED FOR THE BATTLE LINE; FIFTY FOR EACH BATTLE LINE. THE HORSEMEN WITH THE CAVALRY OF THE MEN OF THE ENTIRE ARMY, WILL BE SIX THOUSAND; FIVE HUNDRED TO A TRIBE. ALL THE CAVALRY THAT GO OUT TO BATTLE WITH THE INFANTRY SHALL RIDE STALLIONS; SWIFT, RESPONSIVE, UNRELENTING, MATURE, TRAINED FOR BATTLE, AND ACCUSTOMED TO HEARING NOISES AND SEEING ALL KINDS OF SCENES.*

*THOSE WHO RIDE THEM SHALL BE MEN CAPABLE IN BATTLE, TRAINED IN HORSEMANSHIP, THE RANGE OF THEIR AGE FROM THIRTY TO FORTY-FIVE YEARS. THE HORSEMEN OF THE ARMY SHALL BE FROM FORTY TO FIFTY YEARS OLD, AND THEY [...], HELMETS AND GREAVES, CARRYING IN THEIR HANDS ROUND SHIELDS AND A LANCE EIG[HT CUBITS LONG, ...][...] AND A BOW AND ARROWS AND BATTLE DARTS, ALL OF THEM PREPARED IN [...][...] AND TO SHED THE BLOOD OF THEIR GUILTY SLAIN. THESE ARE THE [...][...][...][...]* (Column 6:8-20)[9]

Even though this particular section is short, given in part because we only have a fragment of its contents, the deployment of the cavalry emphasizes the training and preparation of those involved. Those involved had to be prepared for battle, used to the more up-close-and-personal details of battle that could cause anxiety. Even the animals trained for battle had to maintain their composure, used to certain sounds and actions that might ordinarily spook a horse. Spiritual battle is not for the faint of heart, nor is it for those who don't know how to employ different things around them for a victorious battle. It's not a big secret that the enemy would come into ancient battles and try and damage, injure, scare, or confuse the animals used as part of battle to cripple their opposing army. Here and now, there are so many things around us that can be used to cripple or wound us indefinitely and keep us from moving. We need to watch those who are around us; those who pray for us and the company we keep that is closest to us. Sometimes we ride in like a cavalry to handle spiritual business and we do so without the proper backing to reign in effective in battle. The distractions and chaos we see aren't always our own, but they take us in, just like they take in the one who is knocked out of the battle. Reinforcements are important; equipment and equipping are important; and we must be aware of who is fighting for and with us, in every sense of the principle, always.

## **Recruitment**

*AND THE MEN OF THE ARMY SHALL BE FROM FORTY TO FIFTY YEARS OLD. THE COMMISSIONERS OF THE CAMPS SHALL BE FROM FIFTY TO SIXTY YEARS OLD. THE OFFICERS SHALL ALSO BE FROM FORTY TO FIFTY YEARS OLD. ALL THOSE WHO STRIP THE SLAIN, PLUNDER THE SPOIL, CLEANSE THE LAND, GUARD THE ARMS, AND HE WHO PREPARES THE PROVISIONS, ALL THESE SHALL BE FROM TWENTY-FIVE TO THIRTY YEARS OLD. NO YOUTH NOR WOMAN SHALL ENTER THEIR ENCAMPMENTS FROM THE TIME THEY LEAVE JERUSALEM TO GO TO BATTLE UNTIL THEIR RETURN. NO ONE CRIPPLED, BLIND, OR LAME, NOR A MAN WHO HAS A PERMANENT BLEMISH ON HIS SKIN, OR A MAN AFFECTED WITH RITUAL UNCLEANNESS OF HIS FLESH; NONE OF THESE SHALL GO WITH THEM TO BATTLE. ALL OF THEM SHALL BE VOLUNTEERS FOR BATTLE, PURE OF SPIRIT AND FLESH, AND PREPARED FOR THE DAY OF VENGEANCE. ANY MAN WHO IS NOT RITUALLY CLEAN IN RESPECT TO HIS GENITALS ON THE DAY OF BATTLE SHALL NOT GO DOWN WITH THEM INTO BATTLE, FOR HOLY ANGELS ARE PRESENT WITH THEIR ARMY. THERE SHALL BE A DISTANCE BETWEEN ALL THEIR CAMPS AND THE LATRINE OF ABOUT TWO THOUSAND CUBITS, AND NO SHAMEFUL NAKEDNESS SHALL BE SEEN IN THE ENVIRONS OF ALL THEIR CAMPS.* (Column 7:1-7)[10]

Qualifications for soldiers have long been a staple of military battle throughout history. The basic reasons for qualifications were simple: battle is hard work. To be a soldier, one must be the epitome of physical condition. Soldiers must have the ability to carry equipment, which means they must be of certain physical stature. They must be able to run and hike, all the while carrying their heavy equipment. They must have the competency to understand directions and know how to best implement commands and orders given to them. None of these things can be done by the very young, the very infirm, or the very weak, within the physical realm. The same is true when we operate in the realm of the Spirit, only we are talking about different things. We can't be spiritually sick or spiritually weak if we are going to be in battle. If handling faith is too much for someone, if it's too much to endure battle, if one cannot follow commands and directives or balks at the idea of obedience or self-motivated execution therein, then one is not going to be successful in battle. Oftentimes our successes in spiritual warfare – or our failures – are directly related to our spiritual maturity.

There's no age limit on recruitment for God's army like there was in the Essene community, but they are still teaching us something vital and important as relates to us, now. Just as we condition our physical bodies for earthly battle, we must condition ourselves spiritually for spiritual battle. The Christian life is a training ground. We are here to learn and to develop, and that means we go through spiritual basic training, we go through the regular maintenance to keep ourselves fit and perfected for battle, and we continue to grow and take time to learn specific maneuvers, tactics, weaponry, and new aspects of warfare.

## Ministry in the midst of war

*When the battle lines are arrayed against the enemy, battle line against battle line, there shall go forth from the middle opening into the gap between the battle lines seven priests of the sons of Aaron, dressed in fine white linen garments: a linen tunic and linen breeches, and girded with a linen sash of twined fine linen, violet, purple, and crimson, and a varicolored design, the work of a skillful workman, and decorated caps on their heads; the garments for battle, and they shall not take them into the sanctuary.*

*The one priest shall walk before all the men of the battle line to encourage them for battle. In the hands of the remaining six shall be the trumpets of assembly, the trumpets of memorial, the trumpets of the alarm,*

*The trumpets of pursuit, and the trumpets of reassembly. When the priests go out into the gap between the battle lines, seven Levites shall go out with them. In their hands shall be seven trumpets of rams' horns. Three officers from among the Levites shall walk before the priests and the Levites. The priests shall blow the two trumpets of assem[bly ... of ba]ttle upon fifty shields, and fifty infantrymen shall go out from the one gate and [...] Levites, officers. With each battle line they shall go out according to all [this] o[rder.... men of the] infantry from the gates [and they shall take positi]on between the two battle lines, and [...] the bat[tle ][...][...]*

*The trumpets shall blow continually to direct the slingmen until they have completed hurling seven times. Afterwards the priests shall blow on the trumpets of return, and they shall go along the side of the first battle line to take their position. The priests shall blow on the trumpets of assembly, and the three divisions of infantry shall go out from the gates and stand between the battle lines, and beside them the cavalrymen, at the right and at the left. The priests shall blow on their trumpets a level note, signals for the order of battle.*

*And the columns shall be deployed into their formations, each to his position. When they have positioned themselves in three formations, the priests shall blow for them a second signal, a low legato note, signals for advance, until they draw near to the battle line of the enemy and take hold of their weapons. Then the priests shall blow on the six trumpets of the slain a sharp staccato note to direct the battle, and the Levites and all the people with rams' horns shall blow a great battle alarm together in order to melt the heart of the enemy. With the sound of the alarm, the battle darts shall fly out to bring down the slain. Then the sound of the rams' horns shall quiet, but on the tru[m]pets the priests shall continue to blow a sharp staccato note to direct the signals of battle until they have hurled into the battle line of the enemy seven times. Afterwards, the priests shall blow for them the trumpets of retreat, a low note, level and legato. According to this rule the [pr]iests shall blow for the three divisions. When the first division throws, the [priests and the Levites and all the people with rams'] horns shall blow a great alarm to direct the bat[tle until they have hurled seven times. Afterwards,] the priests [shall blow] for them on the trumpe[ts of retreat ... and they shall take their stan]d in their positions in the battle line, [...] and shall take up position [... the sl]ain,*

*[AND ALL THE PEOPLE WITH RAMS' HORNS SHALL BLOW A VERY LOUD BATTLE ALARM, AND AS THE SOUND GOES OUT] THEIR HANDS SHALL BEGIN TO BRING DOWN THE SLAIN, AND ALL THE PEOPLE SHALL QUIET THE SOUND OF ALARM, BUT THE PRIESTS SHALL CONTINUE SOUNDING ON THE TRUMPETS OF THE SLAIN TO DIRECT THE FIGHTING, UNTIL THE ENEMY IS DEFEATED AND TURNS IN RETREAT. THE PRIESTS SHALL BLOW THE ALARM TO DIRECT THE BATTLE, AND WHEN THEY HAVE BEEN DEFEATED BEFORE THEM, THE PRIESTS SHALL BLOW THE TRUMPETS OF ASSEMBLY, AND ALL THE INFANTRY SHALL GO OUT TO THEM FROM THE MIDST OF THE FRONT BATTLE LINES AND STAND, SIX DIVISIONS IN ADDITION TO THE DIVISION WHICH IS ENGAGED IN BATTLE: ALTOGETHER, SEVEN BATTLE LINES, TWENTY-EIGHT THOUSAND SOLDIERS, AND SIX THOUSAND HORSEMEN. ALL THESE SHALL PURSUE IN ORDER TO DESTROY THE ENEMY IN GOD'S BATTLE; A TOTAL ANNIHILATION.*

*THE PRIESTS SHALL BLOW FOR THEM THE TRUMPETS OF PURSUIT, AND THEY SHALL DIVIDE THEMSELVES FOR A PURSUIT OF ANNIHILATION AGAINST ALL THE ENEMY. THE CAVALRY SHALL PUSH THE ENEMY BACK AT THE FLANKS OF THE BATTLE UNTIL THEY ARE DESTROYED. WHEN THE SLAIN HAVE FALLEN, THE PRIESTS SHALL CONTINUE BLOWING FROM AFAR AND SHALL NOT ENTER INTO THE MIDST OF THE SLAIN SO AS TO BE DEFILED BY THEIR UNCLEAN BLOOD, FOR THEY ARE HOLY. THEY SHALL NOT ALLOW THE OIL OF THEIR PRIESTLY ANOINTMENT TO BE PROFANED WITH THE BLOOD OF THE VAINGLORIOUS NATIONS.* (Column 7:9-8:9)[11]

*Depiction of a Levite, High Priest, and Priest*

So far, this section about the work of the ministers (the priests and the Levites) is the longest we've found within the War Scroll. Even given we have fragments of the scroll existing today, it's obvious that the spiritual component of this battle is given a hefty priority, especially when it comes to the work of spiritual leaders in connection with spiritual warfare. This only makes sense, and it gives spiritual leaders something to think about when surveying the scene of spiritual battle. In modern times, spiritual warfare often has an overly personal edge to it. Our focus is on what's happening to us, instead of the bigger spiritual perspective of spiritual warfare. Part of this is due to leadership that has sat down on the job and attempted to personalize warfare so much so, we've lost sight of what it is all about and of focusing on and trusting in God.

Part of why the focus specifically on the ministers of God is so intriguing is because the work of the priests and Levites wasn't that different from what many of them might done on an ordinary day. The only unique thing they did was blow the trumpets of battle, putting them on the front lines of the work, as in a leadership position. This means they had to know the operations of battle themselves and recognize their own position among the living and the dead.

It is the primary job of spiritual leadership to focus the spiritual aspect of battle for those who have decided to fight in God's army. We, too, must know strategy and recognize how to lead others through spiritual battle. More than just being there as a figurehead, leaders should take the forefront of instruction on how to maneuver in spiritual battle. They should understand how to sound the alarm, such as is identified with the words of God, and the people who follow leadership should know how to assemble in formation. If leaders aren't proactive, the people who follow will ineffectively follow and each will go their own desired way.

## **Maneuvers of battle**

*Rule for changing the order of the battle divisions, in order to arrange their position against [...] a pincer movement and towers, lien arc and towers, and as it draws slowly forward, then the columns and the flanks go out from the [t]wo sides of the battle line [that] the enemy might become discouraged.*

*The shields of the soldiers of the towers shall be three cubits long, and their lances eight cubits l[on]g. The towers shall go out from the battle line with one hundred shields on a side. F[or] they shall surround the tower on the three frontal sides, three hundred shields in all.*

*There shall be three gates to a tower, one on [the right and] one on the left. Upon all the shields of the tower soldiers they shall write: on the*

*FIRST, "MI[CHAE]L," [ON THE SECOND, "GABRIEL," ON THE THIRD,] "SARIEL," AND ON THE FOURTH "RAPHAEL." "MICHAEL" AND "GABRIEL" ON [THE RIGHT, AND "RAPHAEL" AND "RAPHAEL" ON THE LEFT.*

*AND [...] FOR TO THE FOUR [... THEY] SHALL ESTABLISH AN AMBUSH FOR THE [BATTLE LINE] OF [...] AND [... THEY SHALL FAL]L ON THE S[LAIN ...][...][...]* (Column 9:10-20)[12]

Before talking about the address of the chief priest, the War Scroll attends to the different description of maneuvers. Unfortunately, we don't have all of these, but we can see the way the spiritual incorporated with the natural. Sometimes we've heard it said, "First the natural, and then the spiritual," but the realities of spiritual warfare prove this wrong, all together. The spiritual realm is the origin of it all; the origin of everything; of the behind-the-scenes operation of life itself. Whenever we attempt to step out in spiritual battle, we are never stepping out alone, on our own, without the angels of battle there, with us. The enemy should be rightly discouraged and intimidated, because they are not able to stand in the presence of spiritual light. Here, go before us, with us, remain the love of God, which sustains, and marches on in all protective forms before us.

## The chief priest addresses the warriors

*OF OUR CAMPS, AND TO KEEP OURSELVES FROM ANY SHAMEFUL NAKEDNESS, AND HE (MOSES) TOLD US THAT YOU ARE IN OUR MIDST, A GREAT AND AWESOME GOD, PLUNDERING ALL OF OUR ENEMIES BEFO[RE U]S. HE TAUGHT US FROM OF OLD THROUGH OUR GENERATIONS, SAYING, WHEN YOU APPROACH THE BATTLE, THE PRIEST SHALL STAND AND SPEAK UNTO THE PEOPLE, SAYING, "HEAR O ISRAEL, YOU ARE APPROACHING THE BATTLE AGAINST YOUR ENEMIES TODAY. DO NOT BE AFRAID NOR FAINTHEARTED. DO NOT TREM[BLE, NO]R BE TERRIFIED BECAUSE OF THEM, FOR YOUR GOD GOES WITH YOU, TO FIGHT FOR YOU AGAINST YOUR ENEMIES, AND TO SAVE YOU" (DEUTERONOMY 20:2-4). OUR [OFFICERS SHALL SPEAK TO ALL THOSE PREPARED FOR BATTLE, THOSE WILLING OF HEART, TO STRENGTHEN THEM BY THE MIGHT OF GOD, TO TURN BACK ALL WHO HAVE WHO HAVE LOST HEART, AND TO STRENGTHEN ALL THE VALIANT WARRIORS TOGETHER. THEY SHALL RECOUNT THAT WHICH YOU SPOKE] BY THE HAND OF MOSES, SAYING: "AND WHEN THERE IS A WAR IN YOUR LAND AGAINST THE ADVERSARY WHO ATTACKS YOU, THEN YO[U] SHALL SOUND AN ALARM WITH THE TRUMPETS THAT YOU MIGHT BE REMEMBERED BEFORE YOUR GOD AND BE SAVED FROM YOUR ENEMIES (NUMBERS 10:9).* (Column 10:1-8)[13]

The address of the chief priest, once again, shows the relevance of leadership in the action of battle. Sometimes, as leaders, those entrusted to our care need to hear our voice of encouragement to push them on to greater abilities to succeed in battle. They need to hear from us, not from a random leader on television or someone on the internet. They need to hear leadership provide solid strategy to them and inspire trust and hope within them. Battle isn't always all about aggression; in fact, little of it is about that. We've made it about aggression and use of force, but in the end, that is never what wins the battle. What wins the battle is learning how to outsmart the enemy through strategy. We must remain fearless, prepared, valiant, and stick to the proper course, responding when we hear the trumpet sound.

## **The prayer of the chief priest before the warriors**

*Who is like You, O God of Israel, in he[av]en and on earth, that he can perform in accordance with Your great works and Your great strength. Who is like Your people Israel, whom You have chosen for Yourself from all the peoples of the lands; the people of the saints of the covenant, learned in the statutes, enlightened in understan[ding ...] those who hear the glorious voice and see the holy angels, whose ears are open; hearing deep things.*

*[O God, You have created] the expanse of the skies, the host of luminaries, the task of spirits and the dominion of holy ones, the treasures of [Your] gl[ory ...] clouds. He who created the earth and the limits of her divisions into wilderness and plain, and all her offspring, with fhe fru[its ...], the circle of the seas, the sources of the rivets, and the rift of the deeps, wild beasts and winged creatures, the form of man and the gener[ations of] his [see]d, the confusion of language and the separation of peoples, the abode of clans and the inheritance of the lands, [... and] holy festivals, courses of years and times of eternity. [...] these we know from Your understanding which [...] [...] Your [ears] to our cry, for [...] [...] his house [...] [...] [...]*

*Truly the battle is Yours, and by the strength of Your hand their corpses have been broken to pieces, without anyone to bury them.*

*Indeed, Goliath the Gittite, a mighty man of valor, You delivered into the*

HAND OF DAVID, YOUR SERVANT, BECAUSE HE TRUSTED IN YOUR GREAT NAME AND NOT IN SWORD AND SPEAR. FOR THE BATTLE IS YOURS. HE SUBDUED THE PHILISTINES MANY TIMES BY YOUR HOLY NAME.

ALSO BY THE HAND OF OUR KINGS YOU RESCUED US MANY TIMES BECAUSE OF YOUR MERCY; NOT ACCORDING TO OUR WORKS, FOR WE HAVE ACTED WICKEDLY, NOR FOR THE ACTS OF OUR REBELLIOUSNESS.

THE BATTLE IS YOURS, THE STRENGTH IS FROM YOU, IT IS NOT OUR OWN. NEITHER OUR POWER NOR THE STRENGTH OF OUR HAND HAVE DONE VALIANTLY, BUT RATHER BY YOUR POWER AND THE STRENGTH OF YOUR GREAT VALOR.

JUS[T AS YOU TOLD US IN TIME PAST, SAYING: "THERE SHALL COME FORTH A STAR OUT OF JACOB, A SCEPTER SHALL RISE OUT OF ISRAEL, AND SHALL CRUSH THE FOREHEAD OF MOAB AND TEAR DOWN ALL SONS OF SHETH, AND HE SHALL DESCEND OF JACOB AND SHALL DESTROY THE REMNANT FROM THE CITY, AND THE ENEMY SHALL BE A POSSESSION, AND ISRAEL SHALL DO VALIANTLY (NUMBERS 24:17-19).

BY THE HAND OF YOUR ANOINTED ONES, SEERS OF THINGS APPOINTED, YOU HAVE TOLD US ABOUT THE TI[MES] OF THE WARS OF YOUR HANDS IN ORDER THAT YOU MAY GLORIFY YOURSELF {FIGHT} AMONG OUR ENEMIES, TO BRING DOWN THE HORDES OF BELIAL, THE SEVEN VAINGLORIOUS NATIONS, AT THE HAND OF THE OPPRESSED WHOM YOU HAVE REDEEMED [WITH POWE]R AND RETRIBUTION; A WONDROUS STRENGTH. A HEART THAT MELTS SHALL BE AS A DOOR OF HOPE. YOU WILL DO TO THEM AS YOU DID TO PHARAOH AND THE OFFICERS OF HIS CHARIOTS IN THE RED SEA. YOU WILL IGNITE THE HUMBLE OF SPIRIT LIKE A FIERY TORCH OF FIRE IN A SHEAF, CONSUMING THE WICKED. YOU SHALL NOT TURN BACK UNTIL THE ANNIHILATION OF THE GUILTY. IN TIME PAST YOU FORETOLD [THE APP]OINTED TIME FOR YOUR HAND IS POWERFUL WORK AGAINST THE KITTIM, SAYING: AND ASSYRIA SHALL FALL BY A SWORD NOT OF MAN, AND A SWORD, NOT OF MEN, SHALL CONSUME HIM (ISAIAH 31: 8).

FOR INTO THE HAND OF THE OPPRESSED YOU WILL DELIVER THE [ENE]MIES OF ALL THE LANDS; INTO THE HANDS OF THOSE WHO ARE PROSTRATE IN THE DUST, IN ORDER TO BRING DOWN ALL MIGHTY MEN OF THE PEOPLES, TO RETURN THE RECOMPENSE OF THE WICKED ON THE HEAD OF [...], TO PRONOUNCE THE JUST JUDGMENT OF YOUR TRUTH ON ALL SONS OF MAN, AND TO MAKE FOR YOURSELF AN EVERLASTING NAME AMONG THE PEOPLE.

*[...] the wars, and to show Yourself great and holy before the remnant of the nations, so that [they] may know [that] [You are God ... when You] carry out judgments on Gog and on all his company that are as[semb]led [abou]t [us ...][...], for You will do battle against them from the heave[ns ...][...] upon them for confusion [...][...][...]*

*For You have a multitude of holy ones in the heavens and hosts of angels in Your exalted dwelling to pr[aise] Your [Name]. The chosen ones of the holy people You have established for Yourself in a [community]. The nu]mber (or The b]ook) of the names of all their host is with You in Your holy dwelling, and the n[umber of the holy one]s is in the abode of Your glory.*

*Mercies of blessing [...] and Your covenant of peace You engraved for them with a stylus of life in order to reign o[ver them]: for all time, commissioning the hos[ts of] Your [e]lect by their thousands and tens of thousands together with Your holy ones [and] Your angels, and directing them in battle [so as to condemn] the earthly adversaries by trial with Your judgments. With the elect of heaven [they] shall prev[ail].*

*And You, O God, are awe[some] in the glory of Your dominion, and the company of Your holy ones is in our midst for etern[al] support. We [shall direct our contempt at kings, derision and disdain at mighty men. For the Lord is holy, and the King of Glory is with us together with the holy ones. Migh[ty men and] a host of angels are with our commissioned forces.*

*The Hero of Wa[r] is with our company, and the host of His spirits is with our steps. Our horsemen are [as] the clouds and as the mist covering the earth, and as a steady downpour shedding judgment on all her offspring. Rise up, O Hero, take Your captives, O Glorious One, take Your plunder, O You who do valiantly. Lay Your hand upon the neck of Your enemies, and Your foot upon the backs of the slain. Crush the nations, Your adversaries, and may Your sword devour guilty flesh.*

*Fill Your land with glory, and Your heritage with blessing. An abundance of cattle in Your fields; silver and gold and precious stones in Your palaces. O Zion, rejoice greatly, and shine with joyful songs, O Jerusalem. Rejoice, all you cities of Judah, open your gate[s] forever that the wealth of the nations might be brought to you, and their kings shall serve you. All they*

*THAT OPPRESSED YOU SHALL BOW DOWN TO YOU, AND THE DUST [OF YOUR FEET THEY SHALL LICK. O DAUGHTER]S OF MY PEOPLE SHOUT OUT WITH A VOICE OF JOY, ADORN YOURSELVES WITH ORNAMENTS OF GLORY. RULE OVER THE KI[NGDOM OF THE ], [... AND I]SRAEL TO REIGN ETERNALLY.*

*[...] THEM THE MIGHTY MEN OF WAR, O JERUSALEM [...] THE EXALT]ED ABOVE THE HEAVENS, O LORD, [AND LET YOUR GLORY BE ABOVE ALL THE EARTH ...] [...]* (Column 10:8-12:19)[14]

The chief priest then goes on to pray, reiterating a history of victory when one sticks with God. His role was to remind them Whose battle this was and that God was the One Who would devise and direct in battle. The beautiful words show confidence in God's ability to move things forward, taking over the enemies and shower blessings on the righteous. There wasn't a question within his sights that God could do this. We see assurance and confidence here that rings with resolve and comfort. The battle is God's, and He shall have the victory. We shall be victorious because we stand with God, and He is here, with us.

Sometimes we need to focus on the praise of God and remembrance of His deeds throughout history. Remembering that God has always been good to His own through their history of battle is something every soldier must remember, no matter how difficult things may seem to get. That's why praise songs in the Bible often detail great events of spiritual history: they served to remind the person who sang them of how great God is and how the promise to remain and stand victorious will always go to Him. As the spiritual Sons of Light, we will never lose if we stay on the winning side.

## **The blessings of war**

*[... AND THEN THE CHIEF PRIEST SHALL STAND] AND HIS BROTHERS THE [PR]IESTS, THE LEVITES, AND ALL THE ELDERS OF THE ARMY WITH HIM.*

*THEY SHALL BLESS FROM THEIR POSITION, THE GOD OF ISRAEL AND ALL HIS WORKS OF TRUTH, AND THEY SHALL CURSE [BELI]AL THERE AND ALL THE SPIRITS OF HIS FORCES. AND THEY SHALL SAY RESPONSE:*

*"BLESSED IS THE GOD OF ISRAEL FOR ALL HIS HOLY PURPOSE AND HIS WORKS OF TRUTH. AND BLESSED ARE THOSE WHO SERVE HIM RIGHTEOUSLY, WHO KNOW HIM BY FAITH.*

*AND CURSED IS BELIAL FOR HIS CONTENTIOUS PURPOSE, AND ACCURSED FOR HIS REPREHENSIBLE RULE. AND CURSED ARE ALL THE SPIRITS OF HIS LOT FOR THEIR WICKED PURPOSE. ACCURSED ARE THEY FOR ALL THEIR FILTHY DIRTY SERVICE. FOR THEY ARE THE LOT OF DARKNESS, BUT THE LOT OF GOD IS LIGHT [ETERNA]L.*

*Y[O]U ARE THE GOD OF OUR FATHERS. WE BLESS YOUR NAME FOREVER, FOR WE ARE AN [ETER]NA[L] PEOPLE. YOU MADE A COVENANT WITH OUR FATHERS, AND WILL ESTABLISH IT FOR THEIR SEED THROUGHOUT THE AGES OF ETERNITY. IN ALL THE TESTIMONIES OF YOUR GLORY THERE HAS BEEN REMEMBRANCE OF YOUR [KINDNESS] IN OUR MIDST AS AN ASSISTANCE TO THE REMNANT AND THE SURVIVORS FOR THE SAKE OF YOUR COVENANT AND TO RE[COUNT] YOUR WORKS OF TRUTH AND THE JUDGMENTS OF YOUR WONDROUS STRENGTH. AND YOU, [O GOD], CREATED US FOR YOURSELF AS AN ETERNAL PEOPLE, AND INTO THE LOT OF LIGHT YOU CAST US IN ACCORDANCE WITH YOUR TRUTH. YOU APPOINTED THE PRINCE OF LIGHT FROM OF OLD TO ASSIST US, FOR IN [HIS] L[OT ARE ALL SONS OF RIGHTEOUS]NESS AND ALL SPIRITS OF TRUTH ARE IN HIS DOMINION.*

*YOU YOURSELF MADE BELIAL FOR THE PIT, AN ANGEL OF MALEVOLENCE, HIS [DOMINIO]N IS IN DARKNE[SS] AND HIS COUNSEL IS TO CONDEMN AND CONVICT. ALL THE SPIRITS OF HIS LOT -- THE ANGELS OF DESTRUCTION-- WALK IN ACCORD WITH THE RULE OF DARKNESS, FOR IT IS THEIR ONLY [DES]IRE.*

*BUT WE, IN THE LOT OF YOUR TRUTH, REJOICE IN YOUR MIGHTY HAND. WE REJOICE IN YOUR SALVATION, AND REVEL IN [YOUR] HEL[P AND] YOUR [P]EACE. WHO IS LIKE YOU IN STRENGTH, O GOD OF ISRAEL, AND YET YOUR MIGHTY HAND IS WITH THE OPPRESSED. WHAT ANGEL OR PRINCE IS LIKE YOU FOR [YOUR] EFFE[CTUAL] SUPPORT, [FO]R OF OLD YOU APPOINTED FOR YOURSELF A DAY OF GRE[AT BATTLE ...][...] TO [SUP]PORT TRUTH AND TO DESTROY INIQUITY, TO BRING DARKNESS LOW AND TO LEND MIGHT TO LIGHT, AND TO [...][...] FOR AN ETERNAL STAND, AND TO ANNIHILATE ALL THE SONS OF DARKNESS AND BRING JOY TO [AL]L [THE SONS OF LIGHT ...][...][... FOR YOU YOURSELF DESIGNATED US FOR AN APP[OINTED TIME ...][...][...] LIKE THE FIRE OF HIS FURY AGAINST THE IDOLS OF EGYPT.*

*AFTER THEY HAVE WITHDRAWN FROM THE SLAIN TO ENTER THE CAMP, ALL OF THEM SHALL SING THE HYMN OF RETURN. IN THE MORNING THEY SHALL WASH THEIR CLOTHES, CLEANSE THEMSELVES OF THE BLOOD OF THE SINFUL BODIES, AND RETURN TO THE PLACE WHERE THEY HAD STOOD, WHERE THEY HAD FORMED THE BATTLE LINE BEFORE THE SLAIN OF THE ENEMY FELL. THERE THEY SHALL ALL BLESS THE GOD OF*

Israel and joyously exalt His name together. They shall say in response:

"Blessed is the God of Israel, who guards loving-kindness for His covenant and the appointed times of salvation for the people He redeems. He has called those who stumble unto wondrous [accomplishment]s, and He has gathered a congregation of nations for annihilation without remnant in order to raise up in judgment he whose heart has melted, to open a mouth for the dumb to sing [God's] mighty deeds, and to teach feeble [hands] warfare. He gives those whose knees shake strength to stand, and strengthens those who have been smitten from the hips to the shoulder.

Among the poor in spirit [...] a hard heart, and by those whose way is perfect shall all wicked nations come to an end; there will be no place for all their mighty men. But we are the remn[ant of Your people. Blessed is] Your Name, O God of loving-kindness, the One who kept the covenant for our forefathers. Throughout all our generations You have made Your mercies wondrous for the rem[nant of the people] during the dominion of Belial. With all the mysteries of his hatred they have not led us astray from Your covenant. His spirits of destruction You have driven [away from us. And when the me]n of his dominion [condemned themselves], You have preserved the lives of Your redeemed.

You raised up the fallen by Your strength, but those who are great in height You will cut dow[n to humble them. And] there is no rescuer for all their mighty men, and no place of refuge for their swift ones. To their honored men You will return shame, and all [their] vain existence [shall be as not]hing. But we, Your holy people, shall praise Your name for Your works of truth.

Because of Your mighty deeds we shall exalt [Your splendor in] epochs and appointed times of eternity, at the beginning of day, at night and at dawn and dusk. For Your [glorio]us p[urpose] is great and Your wondrous mysteries are in [Your] high heavens, to [raise u]p those for Yourself from the dust and to humble those of the gods.

Rise up, rise up, O God of gods, and raise Yourself in power, [O King of Kings ...] let all the Sons of Darkness [scatter from before You.] Let the light of Your majesty shi[ne forever upon gods and men, as a fire burning in the dark

*PLACES OF THE DAMNED] LET IT BURN [THE DAMNED OF SH]EOL, AS AN [ETERNAL] BURNING [AMONG THE TRANSGRESSORS ... IN ALL THE APPOINTED TIMES OF ETERNITY.] [THEY SHALL REPEAT ALL THE THANKSGIVING HYMNS OF BATTLE THERE AND THEN RETURN TO THEIR CAMPS] [...]*

*FOR IT IS A TIME OF DISTRESS FOR ISRA[EL, A FIXED T]IME OF BATTLE AGAINST ALL THE NATIONS. THE PURPOSE OF GOD IS ETERNAL REDEMPTION, BUT ANNIHILATION FOR ALL NATIONS OF WICKEDNESS. ALL THOSE PR[EPARED] FOR BATTLE SHALL SET OUT AND CAMP OPPOSITE THE KING OF THE KITTIM AND ALL THE FORCES OF BELIAL THAT ARE ASSEMBLED WITH HIM FOR A DAY [OF VENGEANCE] BY THE SWORD OF GOD.* (Column 12:20-15:3)[15]

The concept of a blessing found in war sounds alien to most of us living today. We see the horrors of war firsthand on the news and all around us lies the remnants of war: Syrian refugees, Holocaust survivors, Vietnam veterans, war widows, and parents who had to bury their children too young and too soon. It doesn't seem possible that there can be a blessing in war, but spiritual battle isn't the same as natural battle. It doesn't hold the same desires, nor aspirations. Spiritual battle is about overcoming the root of things that aren't right in this world; it is about overcoming and defeating evil, once and for all. There is a blessing in overcoming evil and defeating everything that may be wrong within ourselves as well as wrong on a larger spiritual scale. There is a blessing in battle, in having the physical, mental, and spiritual ability to go through it. It changes us, but it does so for the better. Spiritual battle matures us, prepares us for greater things, and hands us greater responsibility.

    Spiritual warfare also gives us the grace to be a part of something bigger than ourselves, something deeper than just our everyday, ordinary lives. It is disturbing to note that modern trends disguised as spirituality tend to be all about ourselves and the things in our immediate circles. The advice we receive overwhelms us with the responsibilities we have on a regular basis tends to over scream every call to the bigger, deeper spiritual life that is there for every true soldier of the Lord. We aren't in this to protect our children or families, but to advocate for the Lord Himself, to fight for the bigger issue that extends love and care to all families of the earth. True warriors in spiritual battle prove that love is bigger than just one clan or group, because those who join the spiritual army care enough to fight against all wrong by doing what is right.

We should remember the blessing of battle, the way it matures and expands our lives, every time we experience the intensity of spiritual warfare for ourselves. We should rejoice in the way that God takes people who might otherwise be unprepared and unready to do much in life and turns them into great, mighty warriors, steadying anxieties and bringing forth miracles. Great miracles come from great battles, because in battle, we see the need for something deeper than just a remedy of symptoms. In spiritual battle, we see the hand of God Himself, showing interest and salvation unto His people in a way that we don't in the calm of our lives.

The leaders of God should be the first to recite, to sing, to herald the blessings of battle to anyone who is willing and ready to hear our song. We should lead the chorus because we know what God has done and what He will do, yet, even if we are in the throws of battle and don't know how the outcome will be. We've seen and we've heard, and we know how to sing the song of the spiritual battle redeemed.

## **The final battle**

*THEN THE CHIEF PRIEST SHALL STAND, AND WITH HIM HIS BROTHERS THE P[RIESTS], THE LEVITES, AND ALL THE MEN OF THE ARMY. HE SHALL READ ALOUD THE PRAYER FOR THE APPOINTED TIME OF BATTLE, AS IS WRITTEN IN THE BOO]K SEREKH ITTO (THE RULE OF HIS TIME), INCLUDING ALL THE WORDS OF THEIR THANKSGIVINGS. THEN HE SHALL FORM THERE ALL THE BATTLE LINES, AS WRIT[TEN IN THE BOOK OF THE WAR. THEN THE PRIEST APPOINTED FOR THE TIME OF VENGEANCE BY ALL HIS BROTHERS SHALL WALK ABOUT AND ENCOURAGE [THEM FOR THE BATTL]E, AND HE SHALL SAY IN RESPONSE: "BE STRONG AND COURAGEOUS AS WARRIORS. FEAR NOT, NOR BE DISCOURA[GED AND LET NOT Y]OUR [HEART BE FAINT.] DO NOT PANIC, NEITHER BE ALARMED BECAUSE OF THEM. DO NOT TURN BACK NOR [FLEE FROM THE]M. FOR THEY ARE A WICKED CONGREGATION, ALL THEIR DEEDS ARE IN DARKNESS; IT IS [THEIR] DESIRE. [THEY HAVE ESTABLISHED AL]L THEIR REFUGE [IN A LIE], THEIR STRENGTH IS AS SMOKE THAT VANISHES, AND ALL THEIR VAST ASSEMBLY [IS AS CHAFF WHICH BLOWS AWAY ... DE]SOLATION, AND SHALL NOT BE FOUND. EVERY CREATURE OF GREED SHALL WITHER QUICKLY AWAY [LIKE A FLOW]ER AT HA[RVEST TIME ... COME,] STRENGTHEN YOURSELVES FOR THE BATTLE OF GOD, FOR THIS DAY IS AN APPOINTED TIME OF BATTLE [FOR G]OD AGAINST ALL THE N[ATIONS, ... JUDGM]ENT UPON ALL FLESH. THE GOD OF ISRAEL IS RAISING HIS HAND IN HIS WONDROUS [STRENG]TH [AGAINST ALL THE SPIRITS OF WICK[EDNESS ... M]IGHTY ONES OF THE GODS ARE GIRDING THEMSELVES FOR BATTL[E, AND] THE FORMATION[S OF THE H[O]LY ONES [ARE REA]DYING THEMSELVES*

FOR A DAY OF [VENGEANCE ...] THE GOD OF I[SRAE]L [...] TO REMOVE BEL[IAL ...] IN HIS HELL [...][...][...] UNTIL EVERY SOURCE [OF ...] IS COME TO AN END. FOR] THE GOD OF ISRAEL HAS CALLED OUT A SWORD AGAINST ALL THE NATIONS, AND BY THE HOLY ONES OF HIS PEOPLE HE WILL DO MIGHTILY."

THEY SHALL CARRY OUT ALL THIS RULE [ON] THAT [DAY] AT THE PLACE WHERE THEY STAND OPPOSITE THE CAMPS OF THE KITTIM. THEN THE PRIESTS SHALL BLOW FOR THEM THE TRUMPETS OF REMEMBRANCE. THE GATES OF W[AR] SHALL OPEN, [AND] THE INFANTRY SHALL GO OUT AND STAND IN COLUMNS BETWEEN THE BATTLE LINES. THE PRIESTS SHALL BLOW FOR THEM A SIGNAL FOR THE FORMATION AND THE COLUMNS [SHALL DEPLO]Y AT THE SOUND OF THE TRUMPETS UNTIL EACH MAN HAS TAKEN HIS STATION. THEN THE PRIESTS SHALL BLOW FOR THEM A SECOND SIGNAL: [SIGNS FOR CONFRON]TATION.

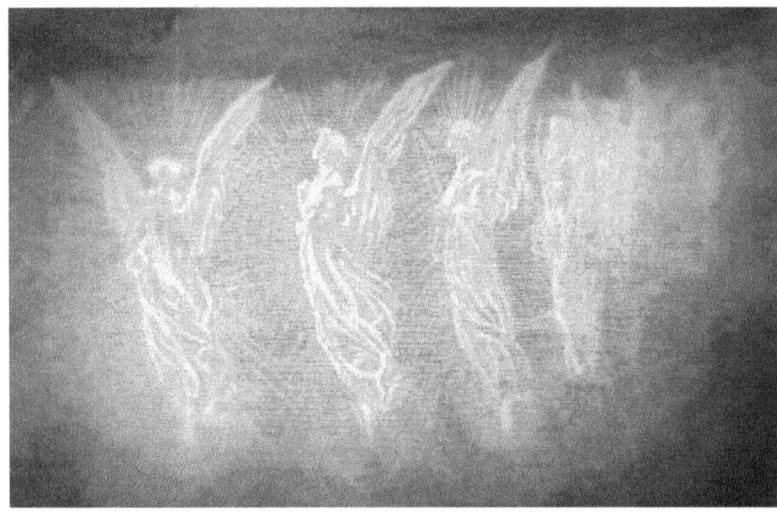
*Angels*

WHEN THEY STAND NEAR THE BATTLE LINE OF THE KITTIM, WITHIN THROWING RANGE, EACH MAN SHALL RAISE HIS HAND WITH HIS WEAPON OF WAR. THEN THE SIX [PRIESTS SHALL BLOW ON THE TR]UMPETS OF THE SLAIN A SHARP STACCATO NOTE TO DIRECT THE FIGHTING. THE LEVITES AND THE ALL THE PEOPLE WITH RAMS' HORNS SHALL BLOW [A BATTLE SIGNA]L, A LOUD NOISE. AS THE SOUND GOES FORTH, THE INFANTRY SHALL BEGIN TO BRING DOWN THE SLAIN OF THE KITTIM, AND ALL THE PEOPLE SHALL CEASE THE SIGNAL, [BUT THE PRIEST]S SHALL CONTINUE BLOWING ON THE TRUMPETS OF THE SLAIN AND THE BATTLE SHALL PREVAIL AGAINST THE KITTIM.

WHEN [BELIAL] PREPARES HIMSELF TO ASSIST THE SONS OF DARKNESS, AND THE SLAIN AMONG THE INFANTRY BEGIN TO FALL BY GOD'S MYSTERIES AND TO TEST BY THESE MYSTERIES ALL THOSE APPOINTED FOR BATTLE, THE PRIESTS SHALL BLOW THE TRUMPETS OF ASSEMBLY SO THAT ANOTHER BATTLE LINE MIGHT GO FORTH AS A BATTLE reserve, and they shall take up position between the battle lines. For those employed in battle they shall blow a signal to return. Then the Chief Priest shall approach and stand before the battle line, and shall encourage their heart by [the wondrous might of God and] fortify their hands for His battle. And he shall say in response: ["Blessed is God, for] He tests the he[ar]t of His people in the crucible. And not [...] have our slain [...]. For you have obeyed from of old the mysteries of God. [Now as for you, take courage and stand in the gap, do not fear when God strengthens...][...][...][...][...]

And He shall appoint their retribution with burning [...] those tested by the crucible. He shall sharpen the implements of war, and they shall not become blunt until [all the nations of] wickedness [come to an end].

But, as for you, remember the judgment [of Nadab and Abi]hu, the sons of Aaron, by whose judgment God showed Himself holy before [all the people. But Eleazar] and Ithamar He preserved for Himself for an eternal covenant [of priesthood]. But, as for you, take courage and do not fear them [... for] their end is emptine and their desire is for the void. Their support is without st[rength] and they do not [know that from the God] of Israel is all that is and that will be. He [...] in all which exists for eternity. Today is His appointed time to subdue and to humiliate the prince of the realm of wickedness. He will send eternal support to the company of His redeemed by the power of the majestic angel of the authority of Michael. By eternal light He shall joyfully light up the covenant of Israel peace and blessing for the lot of God, to exalt the authority of Michael among the gods and the dominion of Israel among all flesh. Righteousness shall rejoice on high, and all sons of His truth shall rejoice in eternal knowledge. But as for you, O sons of His covenant, take courage in God's crucible, until He shall wave His hand and complete His fiery trials; His mysteries concerning your existence."

And after these words the priests shall blow for them a signal to form the divisions of the battle line. The columns shall be deployed at the sound of the trumpets, until each man has taken his station. Then the priests shall blow another signal on the trumpets, signs for confrontation. When the infa[ntry] has approached [the battle] line of the Kitt[im], within throwing range, each man shall raise his hand with his weapon. Then the priests shall blow on the trumpets of the slain [and the Levites and the al]l

*THE PEOPLE WITH RAMS' HORNS SHALL SOUND A SIGNAL FOR BATTLE. THE INFANTRY SHALL ATTACK THE ARMY OF THE KITTIM, [AND AS THE SOUN]D [OF THE SI]GNAL [GOES FORTH], THEY SHALL BEGIN TO BRING DOWN THEIR SLAIN. THEN ALL THE PEOPLE SHALL STILL THE SOUND OF THE SIGNAL, WHILE THE PRIESTS CONTINUOUSLY BLOW ON [THE TRUMPETS OF THE SLAIN], AND THE BAT[TL]E P[REVAIL]S AGAINST THE K[ITTIM, AND THE TROOPS OF BELIA]L ARE DEFEATED BEFORE THEM. THUS IN THE TH[IRD] LOT [...] TO FALL SLAIN [...]*

*[AND IN THE SEVEN]TH [LOG, WHEN THE GREAT HAND OF GOD SHALL BE LIFTED UP AGAINST BELIAL AND AGAINST ALL THE FO[RC]ES OF HIS DOMINION FOR AN ETERNAL SLAUGHTER [...] AND THE SHOUT OF THE HOLY ONES WHEN THEY PURSUE ASSYRIA. THEN THE SONS OF JAPHETH SHALL FALL, NEVER TO RISE AGAIN, AND THE KITUM SHALL BE CRUSHED WITHOUT [REMNANT AND SURVIVOR. SO] THE GOD OF ISRAEL SHALL RAISE HIS HAND AGAINST THE WHOLE MULTITUDE OF BELIAL.*

*AT THAT TIME THE PRIESTS SHALL SOUND A SIGNAL [ON THE SIX TRUMPETS OF REMEMBRANCE, AND ALL THE BATTLE FORMATIONS SHALL BE GATHERED TO THEM AND DIVIDE AGAINST ALL THE CA[MPS OF THE KI]TTIM TO COMPLETELY DESTROY THEM. [AND] WHEN THE SUN HASTENS TO SET ON THAT DAY, THE CHIEF PRIEST AND THE PRIESTS AND THE [LEVITES] WHO ARE WITH HIM, AND THE CHIEFS [OF THE BATTLE LINES AND THE MEN] OF THE ARMY SHALL BLESS THE GOD OF ISRAEL THERE.*

*THEY SHALL SAY IN RESPONSE: BLESSED IS YOUR NAME, O GOD [OF GOD]S, FOR YOU HAVE DONE WONDROUS THINGS FOR YOUR PEOPLE, AND HAVE KEPT YOUR COVENANT FOR US FROM OF OLD. MANY TIMES YOU HAVE OPENED THE GATES OF SALVATION FOR US FOR THE SAK[E OF YOUR CO]VENANT. [AND YOU PROVIDED FOR OUR AFFLICTION IN ACCORD WITH YOUR GOODNESS TOWARD US. YOU, O GOD OF RIGHTEOUSNESS, HAVE ACTED FOR THE SAKE OF YOUR NAME.* (Column 15:4-18:8)[16]

The War Scroll depicts the great war of good and evil to have seven different engagements, thus representing perfection and completion within its assignment. Unlike many stories we like to hear in church, the battle doesn't go to God's side every single time. Some of the time, it appears that God's people win; at other times, the enemy has the upper hand. This reflects real life, and real time spiritual battle. The work of the enemy sometimes does get to God's people. It's not a 100% all-the-time victory. The War Scroll proves that ultimately, God does win the battle and does have the ultimate victory, but this is not always the case with us as His soldiers. We fall, we succumb, we feel the sting that we give into, and we lose the fight.

What do we do when this happens? We must remember that the victory goes to God in the bigger picture. If we are a part of spiritual warfare in a sense of battle that's bigger than we are. Our failings only matter in view of eternity if we never get back up and carry on. That's what earthly soldiers do when they fail, as well. They pick themselves up, they receive the care they need, and they move themselves on to the next battle, the next strategy, and the next set of instructions. They don't have time to stay where they are and feel bad about things, because there is another attack, another fight, another chance to do what needs to be done.

In spiritual battle, we always have another chance to do the right thing and do what's needed. That's another side blessing of battle; we don't have to get everything right the first time. The battle is God's. We walk by faith, and we trust His omnipresence and omniscience to guide us to the best battle possible. He knows our failings and fallings, and He knows what we will do before it even happens. Despite our missteps, the battle is still God's.

## **Thanksgiving and ceremony in honor of the final victory**

*[...] YOU HAVE DONE W]ONDERS UPON WONDERS WITH US, BUT FROM OF OLD THERE HAS BEEN NOTHING LIKE IT, FOR YOU HAVE KNOWN OUR APPOINTED TIME. TODAY [YOUR] POWER HAS SHINED FORTH FOR US, [AND] YOU [HAVE SHOWN] US THE HAND OF YOUR MERCIES WITH US IN ETERNAL REDEMPTION, IN ORDER TO REMOVE THE DOMINION OF THE ENEMY, THAT IT MIGHT BE NO MORE; THE HAND OF YOUR STRENGTH.*

*IN BAT[TLE YOU SHALL SHOW YOURSELF STRONG AGA]INST OUR ENEMIES FOR AN ABSOLUTE SLAUGHTER. NOW THE DAY IS PRESSING UPON US [TO] PURSUE THEIR MULTITUDE, FOR YOU [...] AND THE HEART OF WARRIORS YOU HAVE BROKEN SO THAT NO ONE IS ABLE TO STAND. YOURS IS THE MIGHT, AND THE BATTLE IS IN YOUR HAND, AND THERE IS NO [GOD LIKE YOU ...] YOUR [...] AND THE APPOINTED TIMES OF YOUR WILL, AND REPRISAL [...] YOUR [ENEMIE]S, AND YOU WILL CUT OF FROM [...] IS [...][...][...][...][...]*

*[...AND WE SHALL DIRECT OUR CONTEMPT AT KINGS,] [DERISION AND DISDAIN AT MI]GHTY MEN. FOR OUR MAJESTIC ONE IS HOLY. THE KING OF GLORY IS WITH US AND THE H[OST OF HIS SPIRITS IS WITH OUR STEPS. OUR HORSEMEN ARE] [AS THE CLOUDS*

*and as the mis[t covering the earth; as a steady downpour shedding judgment on all her offspring.*

*Rise up, O Hero,] [Take Your captives, O Glorious One, and ta]ke Your plunder, O You Who do valiantly. Lay Your hand upon the neck of Your enemies, and Your fo[o]t [upon the backs of [the slain. Crush the nations, Yo]ur [adversaries,] and let Your sword devour flesh. Fill Your land with glory, and Your inheritance with blessing.*

*An ab[undance of cattle is] s[in Your fields, silver and gold] in Your palaces. O Zion, rejoice greatly, and rejoice, all you cities of Ju[dah. Open] [Your gates forever, so that the wealth of the nations [might be brought to You, and their kings shall serve You. All they that oppressed] you shall bow down to You, [and they shall lick the dust of your feet.*

*O dau]ghters of my [peo]ple, burst out with a voice of joy. Adorn yourselves with ornaments of glory, and r[ule] over the ki[ngdom of the ...][...] Your [...] and Israel for an [eternal dominion.*

*[Then they shall gather] in the camp that n[ig]ht for rest until the morning. In the morning they shall come to the p[la]ce of the battle line, [where the mi]ghty men of the Kittim [fell], as well as the multitude of Assyria, and the forces of all the nations that were assembled unto them, to see whether [the mu]ltitude of slain [are dead] [with none to bury them; those who] fell there by the sword of God.*

*And the Hi[gh] Priest shall approach there [with] his [depu]ty, his brothers [the priests,] [and the Levites with the Leader] of the battle, and all the chiefs of the battle lines and [their officers ...] [... together. When they stand before the s]lain of the Kitt[im, they shall pr]aise there the God [of Israel. And they shall say in response: ...] [... to God Most High and ...]* (Column 18:10-19:14)[17]

The end of spiritual battle is always thanksgiving. We are thankful to God, Who has deemed us worthy to stand on His side of the winning battle. We celebrate with thanksgiving and with worship ceremony, honoring those we have lost, those who have gone before us, and praising God that evil cannot stand in the presence of our Holy God, Who is our Creator,

Sustainer, Redeemer, and yes, Vindicator forever, in Jesus' Name.

**Lessons on spiritual battle from the Essenes**

The Essenes saw, by prophecy, a battle they wouldn't survive to fight (at least not in their lifetime). They saw themselves at the crux of change, the paradigm shift between a grossly immoral and wayward world and the glory of a world to come. While they might not have understood all the details, it sounds much like the experience of Christians, even in our time. We know that a day is to come, ushering in the final battle between good and evil. Whether it's in our lifetime or a time to come, it's a reality that shall bring the evil world, as we know it, to an end.

In the meantime, we fight a smaller version of this battle on a regular basis. We find ourselves in predicaments spawned by evil realities we'd rather pretend don't exist. Choices abound that force us to decide whose side we are on, often flaunting our weaknesses before our eyes. It wouldn't seem like the bigger, greater eternal battle would have much to offer us in these smaller instances…but yet somehow, it does.

From the Essenes we learn the importance of structure and order in our spiritual lives. Order matters as much as training, insights, awareness, guidance, and proper equipment. Not everything about faith is fun or interesting; much of it is about discipline. We discipline ourselves to pray when we don't feel like it. We structure our lives to include periods of rest and self-care as much as we do activity and productivity. They show us a bigger picture; something we are part of that transcends the smallness we often feel. We are part of an eternal picture, learning as we go.

Whenever we go through spiritual battles, we must remember the bigger picture. If we do, we will remember the essential steps to find our way to spiritual purpose, regardless of how minor things might seem. Every step we take has the power to be influential for victory, no matter what it is.

**Chapter 9 Assignments**

- Write an essay (5-8 sentences) about the Essenes.
- Create a presentation on the War Scroll, its general contents, and what it teaches us about spiritual warfare.

*By The Rivers of Babylon, Gebhard Fugel (1863-1939)*

# - CHAPTER TEN -
## Developing Needed Spiritual Disciplines

Respect [Fear] for the Lord will teach you wisdom [is wise instruction/discipline].
If you want to be honored, you must be humble [Humility comes before glory].
(Proverbs 15:33)

Spirituality and spiritual life are not as simple as attending church on a Saturday or Sunday and reading the Bible occasionally. In the Christian culture we often find ourselves in, we associate spiritual discipline with Bible reading and church attendance and believe these two things will create within us the needed understandings to live a life that is structured according to God's precepts. This is a great idea, and there is no question that being a part of a good church and reading the Scriptures can help one to grow and develop in different areas of life. These two things aren't enough, in and of themselves, to become spiritually disciplined, however. We talk about these two things because they are obvious and easy, and it is the hope of many leaders that the average believer in their congregation or fellowship won't go through any sort of warfare that will require more than these two facets can handle. The obvious problem with this is that believers are going through more than this, and when we tell them to fall back on and rely on these different things, it winds up leaving them empty, looking for more, because what we have offered is just not enough.

Being a believer is about more than just church attendance and Bible reading. Both are wonderful, excellent building blocks, but they are not ends of the road in and of themselves. The Christian life is one of many facets and depths, and it should be each and every believer's prerogative to explore the whole of Christian depth throughout their lives.

Delving into the Christian life comes about through spiritual disciplines that we learn through spiritual warfare. In our lives, there are things around us that constantly beg for and demand our attention. Focusing on any one thing, especially spiritual things, is an aspect of warfare we do not often consider. The world around us is full of distractions. Being serious about God and following His commands in the battle means we learn how to hear from Him, adopting ourselves in a serious posture to gain a heart for His purpose.

If, as a minister, you desire to engage in deliverance and healing ministry, you are going to have to maintain your own sense of spiritual discipline throughout the ups and downs others go through. We need to have better answers for individuals when they go through things than to just tell them to attend more church, pray harder, or read the Bible all the time. In exploring the world of spiritual disciplines, we are going to look at some behind-the-scenes things all believers can do in order to up their spiritual warfare game and understand better what will help them to find their way to spiritual victory.

## **The problem with doing what seems right to each person**

One of the major reasons why we, as believers, often find ourselves ineffective is because we do what seems right to us instead of doing what seems right in the bigger picture. We are so busy trying to alleviate discomfort, pain, frustration, or suffering, we base our decision-making process on being temporarily uncomfortable instead of what is the right thing to do, period.

The work of spiritual warfare teaches us about being a part of something bigger than ourselves, which is what the whole of the Christian life is, in and of itself. If we look back over the concept of cosmology that we studied earlier in this book, the point the ancients were trying to make was that the realm of existence, of being, and most definitely, of spirituality, was bigger than what we could see with our own eyes. In ancient times, a person's entire world was as far as their eye could see, in each direction, from their front porch. The average person didn't travel beyond where they were born or lived throughout their lives. As a result, people's life views were narrow and small, and the concept of bigger things wasn't on their horizon.

It is amazing how many of us live blinded to the bigger picture, because we are obsessed and fixated on alleviating discomfort or distraction. We'll do what we say we are going to do when...or if...or when this happens...and when whenever our condition is met, there is something else to take its place. Spiritual warfare gives us a chance to be a part of something bigger than our immediate lives, problems, and issues. Yet if we are unwilling to yield ourselves to a higher power and do what is right in a bigger sense, we will never advance into a different spiritual place.

*IN THOSE DAYS ISRAEL DID NOT HAVE A KING. ALL THE PEOPLE DID WHATEVER SEEMED RIGHT IN THEIR OWN EYES [17:6; 18:1; 19:1].* (Judges 21:25)

In Israel's history, such behavior was a sign of disorder; that the nation didn't have proper leadership or infrastructure. It was evident of a time without proper guidance and training. The result was chaos. It was the way Israel lived until something came along and changed the course, and things were able to get back on track and follow the proper way of reasoning to solve problems and handle difficulties. It was not unlike we often see ourselves in church, today. Even though we may say we believe in certain things, most believers don't have the right training to see through their difficulty or discomfort to the right thing to do, period.

The goal of the Christian life is to transform from glory to glory and faith to faith, becoming more Christlike in our character as we grow with God. It's about more than just avoiding hell; Christianity is about adopting a new outlook and becoming something other than the destiny one had prior. This sounds simple enough, but it means that we are never done learning about the depths of spiritual disciplines. There is always more to learn and to achieve, and we should never tire of things to explore and learn about in the spiritual realm.

*HE MUST BECOME GREATER [INCREASE], AND I MUST BECOME LESS IMPORTANT [DECREASE].* (John 3:30)

*[FOR] WE KNOW THAT THE LAW IS SPIRITUAL, BUT I AM NOT SPIRITUAL [FLESHLY; CARNAL] SINCE SIN RULES ME AS IF I WERE ITS SLAVE [SOLD TO SIN; AS A SLAVE]. [FOR] I*

*DO NOT UNDERSTAND THE THINGS I DO. [FOR] I DO NOT DO WHAT I WANT TO DO, AND I DO THE THINGS I HATE. AND IF I DO WHAT I DO NOT WANT TO DO, THAT MEANS I AGREE THAT THE LAW IS GOOD [PAUL'S ACKNOWLEDGEMENT THAT HIS BEHAVIOR IS WRONG CONFIRMS THE LAW'S RIGHTEOUS STANDARDS]. BUT [NOW] I AM NOT REALLY THE ONE WHO IS DOING THESE HATED THINGS; IT IS SIN LIVING IN ME THAT DOES THEM. YES [FOR...], I KNOW THAT NOTHING GOOD LIVES IN ME—I MEAN NOTHING GOOD LIVES IN THE PART OF ME THAT IS EARTHLY AND SINFUL [MY SINFUL SELF; MY SINFUL NATURE; MY FLESH]. [FOR] I WANT TO DO THE THINGS THAT ARE GOOD, BUT I DO NOT [OR CANNOT] DO THEM. [FOR] I DO NOT DO THE GOOD THINGS I WANT TO DO, BUT I DO THE BAD [EVIL] THINGS I DO NOT WANT TO DO. SO IF I DO THINGS I DO NOT WANT TO DO, THEN I AM NOT THE ONE DOING THEM. IT IS SIN LIVING IN ME THAT DOES THOSE THINGS.* (Romans 7:14-20)

Human nature is tricky and often deceptive, and that is part of why we fall in spiritual warfare. We think we are doing what is best, we think we are doing what might feel right at the time, but we aren't seeking out God's voice in each situation to help us discern what truly is right. It might come in the form of counsel, of wise leadership, of a word of wisdom or knowledge, or maybe even a direct word from God in some way. We need to be open to this, to avoid doing what seems right, or is right in our own personal opinion, but may very well be misleading. That little bit of self-doubt which always reminds us we might need to reconsider something that we haven't heard from God about helps to ground us, keep us humble, and walking the right path.

Giving up our desire to do everything that seems right, but often is not, is a part of this process. It is, perhaps, the most intimate of all processes we deal with when we walk with God. We love our headstrong independence, and it is almost natural for us to desire to avoid accountability and instruction from others. Spiritual warfare doesn't come out successful if we all go our own way.

## **Preparation and training**

If you've ever been a fan of superhero movies, you will notice that most devote part of at least one movie to the training and preparation needed to be a great superhero. Great superheroes are made, not born that way. Even though they might be different from the time they are born and there might be things about them that always seem different from others, being a superhero that is able to do things for others merits the right kind of training. There's a big difference between being born with superhero abilities and being a great superhero that changes the world.

The same is true for spiritual warriors. We can rely on our natural abilities to get us through and hopefully get by, or we can become a great spiritual warrior because we allow ourselves the proper preparation and training. In the long run, training is a lot more effective than trying to go one's own way, because doing such prepares us for the unseen enemy and unseen circumstances that arise to confuse and derail us.

*ALL THOSE WHO COMPETE IN THE GAMES USE SELF-CONTROL [TRAIN WITH STRICT DISCIPLINE] SO THEY CAN WIN A CROWN [VICTOR'S WREATH]. THAT CROWN [VICTOR'S WREATH] IS AN EARTHLY THING THAT LASTS ONLY A SHORT TIME [PERISHABLE], BUT OUR CROWN WILL NEVER BE DESTROYED [IS IMPERISHABLE].* (1 Corinthians 9:25)

*TRAINING YOUR BODY [PHYSICAL EXERCISE] HELPS YOU IN SOME [OR SMALL] WAYS, BUT SERVING GOD [GODLINESS] HELPS YOU IN EVERY WAY BY BRINGING YOU BLESSINGS [SINCE IT HOLDS PROMISE] IN THIS LIFE AND IN THE FUTURE LIFE, TOO.* (1 Timothy 4:8)

*ALL SCRIPTURE IS INSPIRED BY GOD [BREATHED OUT BY GOD; GOD-BREATHED] AND IS USEFUL FOR TEACHING, FOR SHOWING PEOPLE WHAT IS WRONG IN THEIR LIVES [REFUTING ERROR; REBUKING], FOR CORRECTING FAULTS, AND FOR TEACHING HOW TO LIVE RIGHT [TRAINING IN RIGHTEOUSNESS].* (2 Timothy 3:16)

*Soldiers in a training exercise*

One of the biggest problems seen in the modern-day church is we do not train our people properly for any aspect of their lives, whether it is ministry, day-to-day Christian living, or general spiritual operation. What we are doing is hoping people's gifts, talents, and abilities will carry them through difficulties or things they are otherwise not expecting, and that they will come out on the other side. Unfortunately, what we are seeing instead is a rush of individuals who have no idea what to do because they never received the right training.

In spiritual warfare, we should be given proper teaching and instruction to help us handle life. This might sound simplistic, but spiritual discipline is something that is taught. We should all be in situations that encourage us to do the following:

- Challenge our levels of obedience to God
- Experience our unique gifts of the Spirit and spiritual functions
- Instruct us in the proper exercise of the Scriptures and developing a greater Scriptural understanding
- Experience the challenge of growing deeper in God, rather than just being comfortable
- Trying new things and taking on new challenges
- Training in how to hear from the Spirit as different seasons come and go in one's life
- Encouragement in exploration of worship arts, such as dance, painting, songwriting, singing, poetry, writing, and the like.
- Articulating one's encounters and experiences with God
- Sharing the revelations of God
- Adapting visions as they expand, grow, or change

The best way to continue preparing and training is to never stop. Instead of looking at spiritual life as a never-ending struggle, we must see ourselves as increasing our understanding to become more and more aware of our place within eternity. Considering eternity, training is nothing because what we learn will last forever. This helps us balance our spiritual warfare experiences because in light of eternity, we will only struggle for a short period of time.

## **Experiencing God**

The debates about the will of God and the activity or presence of the Spirit abound in different Christian circles today. It doesn't make sense to believe that we can experience the enemy but not experience God in our times. If one believes spiritual warfare is real and the enemy is after believers, how can one not believe that God is just as real and as active? If we can experience the sting of the enemy, we can experience the protection and joys of God, as real as our next breath, even more intently and powerfully than we can experience the sting of the enemy. We either believe God is greater than the enemy, or we do not, and it is that simple. If God is real, then we can experience Him, and we can embrace the full expanse of His Spirit extended to us, as believers.

*Now, brothers and sisters, I don't want you to misunderstand [be uninformed] about [concerning; or in regard to your question about; see 7:1; 8:1; 16:1] spiritual gifts. You know the way you lived before you were believers [when you were pagans/Gentiles]. You let yourselves be influenced and led away to worship idols—things that could not speak. So I want you to understand that no one who is speaking ·with the help of [by means of; in the power of] God's Spirit says, "Jesus be cursed." And no one can say, "Jesus is Lord," without the help of [except by means of/in the power of] the Holy Spirit.*

*There are different kinds of gifts, but they are all from the same Spirit. There are different ways to serve [ministries] but the same Lord to serve. And there are different ways that God works through people [kinds of action; activities] but the same God works in all of us in everything we do [all things in all people]. Something from the Spirit can be seen in [The manifestation/disclosure of the Spirit is given to] each person, for the common good. The Spirit gives one person the ability to speak with wisdom [message/word of wisdom], and the same Spirit gives another the ability to speak with knowledge [message/word of knowledge]. The same Spirit gives faith to one person. And, to another, that one Spirit gives gifts of healing. The Spirit gives to another person the power to do miracles [works of power], to another the ability to prophesy [prophecy]. And He gives to another the ability to know the difference between good and evil [discernment/distinguishing of] spirits. The Spirit gives one person the ability to speak in different kinds of languages [or ecstatic utterance; tongues] and to another the ability to interpret those languages [interpretation of tongues]. One Spirit, the same Spirit, does all these things, and the Spirit decides what to give [distributes just as he wishes to] each person.* (1 Corinthians 12:1-11)

The activity of the Spirit has not ceased. It is not an accident to note that when we start drifting further away from the Spirit, we get led into all sorts of weird and strange places from a spiritual perspective. If we want to remain prepared, we must know the Holy Spirit, the Spirit of God, and embrace that specific work of God in our experience. As we go through our different trials and times, the spiritual gifts, our relationship with God, and the insights we have developed carry us through to a better, deeper place.

It probably sounds simplistic to say we need to maintain our experience with God in the long-term of our Christian experience, but it is an overlooked aspect of our spiritual lives. We take for granted that we'll grow spiritually and stay close to God, but the truth is that we go through many different phases in our Christian life that frequently change how we feel about our spiritual experience with God. Spiritual gifts may lose their luster and the fact that so many false leaders come and go who seem to prosper and flourish can become disheartening. It is imperative the believer maintain their relationship with God and experience God, even if it doesn't always feel like it once did, to get through those times and move toward a new understanding of all things. Our experience with God is a passing from private revelation to seeing how we fit in the bigger picture of the church, the Kingdom, and within God's plan.

## **Change**

Change is one of those loaded words that we avoid in services, because as much as we might say we love the idea of new seasons and of new things in our lives, we spend a lot of time trying to avoid change. We avoid change for the simple reason that we avoid discomfort, and change is, often, extremely uncomfortable. We like our status quo, and the concept of major change is scary and different for us. It is in those places where we avoid discomfort that spiritual warfare is often the most prevalent, because we know it is time to move on and it's time to do something different, but we want to hold fast to where we are and what we know.

No relationship survives if it is unable to adapt to change, and the same is true with our spiritual relationship with God. It is not that God abandons us, but we are unable to grow with Him and endure through difficult periods if we are unwilling to embrace change in our lives.

*LOOK AT THE NEW THING I AM GOING TO DO.*

*IT IS ALREADY HAPPENING [SPROUTING/SPRINGING UP]. DON'T YOU SEE IT?*
*I WILL MAKE A ROAD [PATH; WAY] IN THE DESERT [WILDERNESS; THE RETURN FROM BABYLON IS PORTRAYED AS A NEW EXODUS]*
   *AND RIVERS [STREAMS] IN THE DRY LAND [DESERT; WASTELAND].*
(Isaiah 43:19)

*I THE LORD DO NOT CHANGE. SO YOU DESCENDANTS OF JACOB HAVE NOT BEEN DESTROYED [CONSUMED].* (Malachi 3:6)

*Learning*

God doesn't change because He doesn't need to; as He is change. We change because we are imperfect and we do need to. We have not arrived at perfection, and, therefore, must adapt to the principle of change in our lives, through all different seasons and times, in order to discover a greater sense of ourselves and our purpose in our spiritual lives.

## **Hanging up our lyres**

Psalm 137:1-6 says:

*BY THE RIVERS IN BABYLON WE SAT AND CRIED [WEPT; DURING THE BABYLONIAN EXILE]*
   *WHEN WE REMEMBERED JERUSALEM [ZION; THE LOCATION OF THE TEMPLE].*
*ON THE POPLAR [OR WILLOW] TREES NEARBY*
   *WE HUNG OUR HARPS.*
*THOSE WHO CAPTURED US [OUR CAPTORS] ASKED US TO SING;*
   *OUR ENEMIES [OPPRESSORS] WANTED HAPPY SONGS.*
*THEY SAID, "SING US A SONG ABOUT JERUSALEM [ZION; THE LOCATION OF THE TEMPLE]!"*
*BUT WE CANNOT SING SONGS ABOUT THE LORD*
   *WHILE WE ARE IN THIS FOREIGN COUNTRY [LAND]!*
*JERUSALEM, IF I FORGET YOU,*
   *LET MY RIGHT HAND LOSE ITS SKILL [FORGET; ITS SKILL OF PLAYING A MUSICAL INSTRUMENT].*

*LET MY TONGUE STICK TO THE ROOF OF MY MOUTH*
  *IF I DO NOT REMEMBER YOU,*
*IF I DO NOT THINK ABOUT JERUSALEM*
  *AS MY GREATEST JOY [OR GO UP TO JERUSALEM WITH JOY ON MY HEAD].*

The Old Testament occupations of Israel are one of the most unexplored aspects of Old Testament experience, especially in a theological context. When it is explored, it is from the angle of history, rather than the plain old fact that Israel wound up occupied because they disobeyed God. Israel wanted to be like everyone else and have the same feelings and experiences that everyone else had, and didn't want to deal with their call to change and transform as human beings. God expected a standard of Israel, and they didn't meet with it, and instead of rising to the standard, they tried even harder to be like everyone else. The result was occupation, by which God turned them over to the very people they desired to be like, to emulate, and to embody. It was never long before Israel desired to be free from the occupation, only to fall into the same patterns, all over again.

This is a type of human nature: we don't measure up, we want to be like everyone else, God calls us to be different, and we still desire to fit in better with other people, rather than be ourselves and who God has called us to be. Our spiritual desire is to keep this type of approach without challenging us to be different, with things relatively the same from week to week.

If you think about our church experiences in modern times, this is what they often sound like. The average churchgoer picks their church and attends every week with a certain expectation in mind. Services are supposed to be fun, entertaining, and certain regular displays of spirituality are encouraged. We take it as a compliment when someone runs around the room or jumps up and down. Dancing and stomping all over the altar and excessive crying are all considered spiritual displays to emulate. We assume people are really "right with God" or getting "right with God" if they do any of these things.

*THIS IS ANOTHER THING YOU DO. YOU COVER THE LORD'S ALTAR WITH YOUR TEARS. YOU CRY [WEEP] AND MOAN, BECAUSE HE DOES NOT ACCEPT [LOOK WITH FAVOR ON] YOUR OFFERINGS AND IS NOT PLEASED WITH WHAT YOU BRING.* (Malachi 2:13)

*YOU HAVE TIRED [WEARIED] THE LORD WITH YOUR WORDS.*
*YOU ASK, "HOW HAVE WE TIRED [WEARIED] HIM?"*

*YOU DID IT BY SAYING, "THE LORD THINKS [IN THE LORD'S EYES] ANYONE WHO DOES EVIL IS GOOD, AND HE IS PLEASED WITH THEM." OR YOU ASKED, "WHERE IS THE GOD WHO IS FAIR [OF JUSTICE]?"* (Malachi 2:17)

The problem is that we have associated these things with spiritual insight, when they are often nothing more than learned behaviors, conditioned responses to proper stages of church entertainment. We don't accept the idea that people need to learn, because they are not as spiritual as they claim to be. As a result, at one point or another, we do not hear from God, we keep running around the room, and we find ourselves in a place of spiritual and emotional exile.

Psalm 137, which talks about exile from a spiritual perspective, gives us a great insight into the reality of what happens when we receive realization of where we are and what we are doing. God expects that we will reach a place of maturity in Him where we stop expecting constant entertainment and outrageous displays. A part of discipline is learning, and the ability to be taught and properly influenced as He would desire us to be. We must all put up our lyres and weep over the spiritual realities that have infiltrated or manipulated us, and that often gain hold over the church. The sins of this world (including our own) should cause is to weep, then pick ourselves up and make the thoughts and ideas of the Lord our own as we meditate upon them night and day.

## **Spiritual renewal**

Spiritual renewal is a concept that gets thrown around from time to time, but it is a very important and essential aspect of Christian living. The concept of spiritual renewal is that we go through periods where our faith becomes stagnant, ho-hum, and needs an invigoration. Every generation or so, the people of God need to examine themselves, and at least once every two generations, overall spiritual renewal should take front and center stage.

*CREATE IN ME A PURE [CLEAN] HEART, GOD, AND MAKE MY SPIRIT RIGHT AGAIN [RENEW A RIGHT/STEADFAST SPIRIT IN ME].* (Psalm 51:10)

*GOD OUR SAVIOR, BRING US BACK AGAIN [RESTORE US AGAIN].*
  *STOP BEING ANGRY WITH US.*

*WILL YOU BE ANGRY WITH US FOREVER?*
  *WILL YOU STAY ANGRY [DRAW OUT YOUR ANGER AGAINST US] FROM NOW ON?*
*WON'T YOU GIVE US LIFE AGAIN?*
  *YOUR PEOPLE WOULD REJOICE IN YOU.*
*LORD, SHOW US YOUR LOVE [LOYALTY],*
  *AND SAVE US [GIVE TO US YOUR SALVATION/VICTORY].*
(Psalm 85:4-7)

*IN [AFTER] TWO DAYS HE WILL PUT NEW LIFE IN [REVIVE; RESTORE] US; ON THE THIRD DAY HE WILL RAISE US UP [IN A SHORT TIME] SO THAT WE MAY LIVE IN HIS PRESENCE.* (Hosea 6:2)

*LORD, I HAVE HEARD THE NEWS [REPORT] ABOUT YOU;*
  *I AM AMAZED [IN AWE; AFRAID] AT WHAT YOU HAVE DONE.*
*LORD, DO GREAT THINGS ONCE AGAIN IN OUR TIME [THE MIDST OF THE YEARS];*
  *MAKE THOSE THINGS HAPPEN AGAIN [THEM KNOWN] IN OUR OWN DAYS [THE MIDST OF THE YEARS].*
*EVEN WHEN YOU ARE ANGRY,*
  *REMEMBER TO BE KIND [COMPASSIONATE].*
(Habakkuk 3:2)

Spiritual renewal on the larger scale reflects the inner spiritual renewal we should do regularly. Every day, we should take some time and aware ourselves to the process of the inward self, which is renewed by the Spirit of God daily.

*YOU HAVE BEGUN TO LIVE THE NEW LIFE [PUT ON THE NEW PERSON/MAN], IN WHICH YOU ARE BEING MADE NEW [RENEWED] IN THE TRUE KNOWLEDGE OF GOD [KNOWLEDGE] AND ARE BECOMING LIKE [ACCORDING TO THE IMAGE OF] THE ONE WHO CREATED YOU [GEN. 1:26–27].* (Colossians 3:10)

*SO WE DO NOT GIVE UP [DESPAIR; LOSE HEART]. THOUGH OUR PHYSICAL BODY [OUTER PERSON] IS BECOMING OLDER AND WEAKER [DECAYING; BEING DESTROYED], OUR ·SPIRIT INSIDE US [INNER (PERSON)] IS MADE NEW [BEING RENEWED] EVERY DAY. WE HAVE SMALL TROUBLES FOR A WHILE NOW, BUT THEY [FOR OUR BRIEF AND INSIGNIFICANT TRIALS/TRIBULATIONS] ARE HELPING US GAIN [OR PRODUCING IN US] AN ETERNAL GLORY [BURDEN/WEIGHT OF GLORY] THAT IS MUCH GREATER THAN [OVERWHELMINGLY EXCEEDS] THE TROUBLES. WE SET OUR EYES NOT ON WHAT WE SEE*

*BUT ON WHAT WE CANNOT SEE. [FOR; BECAUSE] WHAT WE SEE WILL LAST ONLY A SHORT TIME [IS TEMPORARY/TRANSITORY], BUT WHAT WE CANNOT SEE WILL LAST FOREVER [IS ETERNAL].* (2 Corinthians 4:16-18)

I once heard an expression: "No man steps in the same river twice, for it's not the same river, and he's not the same man." The same is true for us in our relationship with God. The Bible is clear to educate us in the realization that what we go through, in the end, should bring us to a place of personal benefit. It's not that everything we go through is that great or personally edifying, but that coming through things to the other side should bring us to a place of empowerment and healing. The process is analogous to salvation: from the mire to a place of power. Our renewal reminds us that the power of the resurrection is present within our lives even now. The resurrection is not just about death, or what happens after death, but is also about what we do, and live through, right now. We should never be who we used to be and that means we need to take inventory and steps to renew where we are at and grow in our understanding of where we need to be.

## **Letting go**

We talk about freedom, but with freedom, we have two options: we either let go and embrace freedom, or we stay bound. That's it. It's that simple, and that difficult. The reason these are the only options is because if we don't let go, we remain stuck and bound to all the things that keep us where we are, right now. We can have it one way or the other, but we can't have it both ways.

The issues we have, especially with outcome or attack, usually arise because we want it all: we want to be free, but we still want to hold on. We want the feeling of control we have when we hold on to the things that bind us, and the way we use those things to behave inappropriately or mistreat others, but we still don't want the repercussions of feeling bound by them. For example, you can't complain about taking care of your grown children's issues if you are unwilling to tell them they need to find solutions to the issues on their own. You can't complain about mental anguish from memories if you are unwilling to release those memories, and usher in a place of forgiveness for those hurts. You can't complain about being sick if you enjoy the attention that comes with being sick. For everything we complain about, there is often a reason why we hold onto whatever it is, and that holding on is because we get something from it that we know we will not be able to hold onto if we truly get free.

*LATER [AFTER THESE THINGS] JESUS WENT [UP] TO JERUSALEM FOR A SPECIAL FEAST [FEAST/FESTIVAL OF THE JEWS]. IN JERUSALEM THERE IS A POOL WITH FIVE COVERED PORCHES, WHICH IS CALLED BETHESDA [A POOL OF WATER NORTH OF THE TEMPLE THOUGHT TO HAVE CURATIVE POWERS] IN THE HEBREW LANGUAGE [REFERRING TO ARAMAIC, THE NATIVE LANGUAGE OF THE JEWS AT THE TIME]. THIS POOL IS NEAR THE SHEEP GATE. MANY SICK PEOPLE WERE LYING ON THE PORCHES BESIDE THE POOL. SOME WERE BLIND, SOME WERE CRIPPLED, AND SOME WERE PARALYZED |, AND THEY WAITED FOR THE WATER TO MOVE. SOMETIMES [AT A CERTAIN TIME; FROM TIME TO TIME] AN ANGEL OF THE LORD CAME DOWN TO THE POOL AND STIRRED UP THE WATER. AFTER THE ANGEL DID THIS, THE FIRST PERSON TO GO INTO THE POOL WAS HEALED FROM ANY SICKNESS HE HAD. A MAN WAS LYING THERE WHO HAD BEEN SICK [AN INVALID; DISABLED] FOR THIRTY-EIGHT YEARS. WHEN JESUS SAW THE MAN AND KNEW THAT HE HAD BEEN SICK [AN INVALID; DISABLED] FOR SUCH A LONG TIME, JESUS ASKED HIM, "DO YOU WANT TO BE WELL?"*

*THE SICK MAN [INVALID] ANSWERED [HIM], "SIR, THERE IS NO ONE TO HELP ME GET INTO THE POOL WHEN THE WATER STARTS MOVING [IS STIRRED UP]. WHILE I AM COMING TO THE WATER, SOMEONE ELSE ALWAYS GETS IN [GOES DOWN] BEFORE ME."*

*THEN JESUS SAID TO HIM, "STAND UP [RISE]. PICK UP YOUR MAT [BED; COT] AND WALK." AND IMMEDIATELY THE MAN WAS WELL [WAS HEALED; BECAME WHOLE]; HE PICKED UP HIS MAT [BED; COT] AND BEGAN TO WALK.* (John 5:1-9)

Sometimes we pay so much attention to the miracles of Jesus as recorded in the New Testament, we overlook some of the very important details that surround the miracles. In this instance, what we often overlook is the way in which the man totally overlooked Jesus' question in favor of explaining all the reasons why he was not healed. Jesus asked the man if he wanted to get well, not why he was still sitting there or why he wasn't healed yet. Instead of just being direct and telling Jesus whether he wanted to be set free, he got long-winded and wordy. This should tell us something about his desire to be healed, or set free from his ailment, and that some part of him was not quite so eager, when confronted with healing, to embrace it. Embracing it meant leaving behind the people who looked upon him with pity, those who saw him as pathetic, and the ways his infirmity gained him attention. He stood there, face-to-face with the One Who not only could, but did heal Him, and he wasn't quite sure what he wanted at that moment.

Some of us are holding onto things because giving them up means letting them go, the people go who perpetrated them, the way they make us feel, and the way we use them for attention, control, or to manipulate others in our lives. Thus, Jesus asks us the same question He asked the man at the pool: Do you want to be set free?

## **Fasting**

Fasting is often a loaded topic because it's one of those things we take within the literal context of its writing, without applying it in a modern context for today. In Biblical times, fasting from food represented a real sacrifice on the part of those who would fast. There weren't many luxuries in ancient times and eating well wasn't something available to most people. The little food someone had was all they had to get through days of long physical labor, thus sacrificing food for spiritual gain was something everyone could do and could stand as a needed sacrifice to gain insight.

A "fast" is the principle of giving something up to make room for something else, usually of a spiritual nature. It is based in the classic spiritual concept of detachment: to get closer to God, one must forsake things that distract or potentially keep one from God. The traditional object for a fast was food and/or water, in which an individual would give up food or water (or both) to gain a deeper spiritual insight. The idea of fasting is found throughout the world and is acknowledged by some as having great health benefits. Many now take on fasting because they think it will be beneficial to them in their health or weight loss, but this is not the true reason why someone should undertake fasting for spiritual purposes. As fasting has become secular, it is even more important we understand it from a spiritual perspective for ourselves and our own spiritual growth, discipline, and warfare. If we only fast for superficial reasons, we will only get superficial results out of the process.

*WHEN YOU FAST [GIVING UP EATING FOR SPIRITUAL PURPOSES], DON'T PUT ON A SAD [GLOOMY; SOMBER] FACE LIKE THE HYPOCRITES. THEY MAKE THEIR FACES LOOK SAD [DISHEVELED; DISFIGURED; UNATTRACTIVE] TO SHOW PEOPLE THEY ARE FASTING. I TELL YOU THE TRUTH, THOSE HYPOCRITES ALREADY HAVE THEIR FULL REWARD [V. 2]. SO WHEN YOU FAST [V. 16], COMB YOUR HAIR [PUT OIL ON/ANOINT YOUR HEAD; TYPICAL*

FIRST CENTURY GROOMING] AND WASH YOUR FACE. THEN PEOPLE WILL NOT KNOW THAT YOU ARE FASTING, BUT YOUR FATHER, WHOM YOU CANNOT SEE [WHO IS HIDDEN/IN SECRET], WILL SEE YOU. YOUR FATHER SEES WHAT IS DONE IN SECRET [PRIVATE], AND HE WILL REWARD YOU. (Matthew 6:15-18)

WHEN JESUS AND HIS FOLLOWERS [DISCIPLES] CAME BACK TO THE CROWD, A MAN CAME TO JESUS AND BOWED [KNELT] BEFORE HIM. THE MAN SAID, "LORD, HAVE MERCY ON MY SON. HE ·HAS EPILEPSY [HAS SEIZURES; OR IS DEMENTED/A LUNATIC; THE WORD FOR EPILEPSY COULD ALSO MEAN "MOONSTRUCK" OR DEMENTED; MARK 9:17 SAYS THE BOY WAS DEMON POSSESSED] AND IS SUFFERING VERY MUCH [TERRIBLY], BECAUSE HE OFTEN FALLS INTO THE FIRE OR INTO THE WATER. I BROUGHT HIM TO YOUR ·FOLLOWERS [DISCIPLES], BUT THEY COULD NOT CURE [HEAL] HIM."

JESUS ANSWERED, "YOU PEOPLE HAVE NO FAITH, AND YOUR LIVES ARE ALL WRONG [O FAITHLESS/UNBELIEVING AND PERVERSE/CORRUPT GENERATION]. HOW LONG MUST I PUT UP [STAY; BE] WITH YOU? HOW LONG MUST I CONTINUE TO BE PATIENT [PUT UP] WITH YOU? BRING THE BOY HERE TO ME." JESUS COMMANDED [REPRIMANDED; REBUKED] THE DEMON AND IT CAME OUT OF HIM, AND THE BOY WAS HEALED FROM THAT TIME ON [MOMENT; HOUR].

*Jesus Tempted in the Wilderness, James Tissot (1836-1902)*

THE FOLLOWERS [DISCIPLES] CAME TO JESUS WHEN HE WAS ALONE AND ASKED, "WHY COULDN'T WE FORCE [DRIVE; CAST] THE DEMON OUT?"

JESUS ANSWERED, "BECAUSE YOUR FAITH IS TOO SMALL [YOU HAVE SO LITTLE FAITH]. I TELL YOU THE TRUTH, IF YOUR FAITH IS AS BIG AS [AS SMALL AS; THE SIZE OF; AS; LIKE] A MUSTARD SEED,

*YOU CAN SAY TO THIS MOUNTAIN, 'MOVE FROM HERE TO THERE,' AND IT WILL MOVE. ALL THINGS WILL BE POSSIBLE [NOTHING WOULD BE IMPOSSIBLE] FOR YOU. THAT KIND OF SPIRIT COMES OUT ONLY IF YOU USE PRAYER AND FASTING."* (Matthew 17:14-21)

Food isn't such a rarity in many parts of the world today, and there are times when we can go without eating or drinking all day, for several hours, because we are on a diet, or because we just don't feel hungry. Having a "take it or leave it" relationship with food has changed the concept of a fast, and has, in some ways, turned it into something else, entirely. If giving up food isn't a sacrifice, that defeats the purpose in fasting from it. Thus, when we are approaching a fast or feel a call to fast, we should always examine whatever it is that is taking us away from God or impeding our ability to hear from Him and select that as our choice for a fast. This means you can fast from anything that you need to fast from:

- Social media/internet usage
- Television
- Overspending/undisciplined spending
- Video games or computerized games
- Working too many hours beyond what you need
- Buying things you don't really need
- Eating out
- Pursuing destructive relationships/friendships
- Sexual activity

On the inverse, we can go on a "fast" and engage in productive behaviors that help address some of these issues:

- Addressing one's physical or mental health
- Giving usable, unwanted items to charity
- Volunteering to assist with community aid
- Visiting an elderly shut-in or family member
- Spending quality time with God in prayer and devotion
- Being quiet by turning off the large amount of noise frequently in our lives

Fasting is often done for success in an event (such as a conference or convocation), or in anticipation of something, such as a revival or ordination. While there's nothing wrong with fasting for these reasons, this shows that we don't understand fasting properly. The reason we fast is not to have a successful event or a good outcome of something, but to seek the guidance of God. By fasting, we prove we are willing to make room for Him in our lives and sacrifice whatever is in our way so we can hear from Him and do His will. It is the principle that we clutter our lives with things that keep us from God, and by fasting, we are removing those things, one by one, to replace poor habits with ones that increase our spiritual lives and interest.

All of us will be called to fast, at least for a period, in our lives. It is important, however, that we pay attention to the way God asks us to fast, because our insights and victory often lie in our attentiveness to obedience.

## **Self-discipline**

Spiritual disciplines only work if we are self-disciplined, and this is the last piece of the puzzle for us to examine in this chapter of this book. It's great to like the idea of being disciplined spiritually, but we must attune ourselves to hearing from God and obeying God for ourselves, whether anyone else is around.

Self-discipline means one has attuned themselves to necessary obedience and Christian disciplines, whether anyone knows about them or pays attention to them. Every one of us will find ourselves in situations where we're faced with questions as to what we should or shouldn't do and how we can best handle it.

HE SPOKE TO YOU FROM HEAVEN TO TEACH [INSTRUCT; OR DISCIPLINE] YOU. HE SHOWED [REVEALED TO] YOU HIS GREAT FIRE ON EARTH, AND YOU HEARD HIM SPEAK FROM THE FIRE. (Deuteronomy 4:36)

LORD, THOSE YOU CORRECT [INSTRUCT; DISCIPLINE] ARE HAPPY [BLESSED]; YOU TEACH THEM FROM YOUR LAW [INSTRUCTION; TEACHING]. (Psalm 94:12)

THESE ARE THE WISE WORDS [PROVERBS] OF SOLOMON SON OF DAVID, KING OF ISRAEL. THEY TEACH WISDOM AND SELF-CONTROL [DISCIPLINE; INSTRUCTION];
   THEY WILL HELP YOU UNDERSTAND WISE WORDS [INSIGHTFUL SAYINGS].
THEY WILL TEACH YOU HOW TO BE WISE [INSIGHTFUL] AND SELF-CONTROLLED [DISCIPLINED]

*AND WILL TEACH YOU TO DO WHAT IS HONEST [RIGHTEOUS] AND FAIR [JUST] AND RIGHT [VIRTUOUS].*
(Proverbs 1:1-3)

*WE DO NOT ENJOY BEING DISCIPLINED. IT IS PAINFUL AT THE TIME, BUT LATER, AFTER WE HAVE LEARNED FROM [BEEN TRAINED BY] IT, WE HAVE PEACE [IT PRODUCES/BEARS THE FRUIT OF PEACE], BECAUSE WE START LIVING IN THE RIGHT WAY [OR ...AND RIGHTEOUSNESS].* (Hebrews 12:11)

Self-discipline begins when we make the commitment to obey God and to do this thing called the Christian life for ourselves: not for our parents, our pastors or leaders, our children, our spouse, or to stay in a certain social circle. When faith is for us, that means we have decided we believe in Christ enough to walk this thing out in love and devotion for God and we're going to see it through. It makes us aware that even though people don't always see us, God does, and we do what we do for God, rather than to be seen of other people.

It's wonderful to have great counsel we can rely on. I encourage everyone to have at least one person they can go to for that in their lives, but it's unreasonable to think our spiritual leader or mentors can live our Christian faith for us. Your pastor or leader can't be there every second of the day to help you through every problem or make all your decisions easy for you, as many hope and believe will happen. There are going to be those times, more often than not, in fact, where you are going to have to handle things on your own, without any consultation with anyone else. We should be quick to recognize when we have caused offense, to apologize and repent in the face of wrongdoing, to ask for forgiveness when we need it, and quick to forgive when others have offended us. Our spiritual lives should display our progress as we walk greater in the fruit of the Spirit (Galatians 5:22-23) and as mature believers in our faith. Our progress should be notable to others, rather than something we measure by how many times we go to church or whether or not we get everything we want. The fruit of our walk is evident in our level of self-discipline, our ability to interact with others and make it clear this relationship with God is what we desire for ourselves.

Spiritual warfare and battles become a lot easier when we are willing to commit ourselves to everything God commands us to handle. If we desire to be good soldiers and call ourselves a part of the army of the Lord, we have to be able to be trusted with the difficult things as well as the smaller, little things. While many believers may not tarry with what we classify as "big issues," many struggle with smaller, disciplinary issues that cause them to lose focus and ultimately lose the battle. Whether big or small, much of what affects us can be handled with a good dose of spiritual disciplining, beginning with a desire to do what is right no matter what and ending with our own personal drive toward self-discipline. We may not always do it perfectly, but with God, we can certainly achieve more than we ever thought possible alone and gain far more spiritual ground.

## **Chapter 10 Assignment**

- Doing some reflection, write a few sentences (minimum 3-5) about some areas of self-discipline you could benefit from developing in a deeper way.

# Part 3

# HEALING AND DELIVERANCE

*Healing of the Blind Man by Jesus Christ, Carl Bloch (1834-1890)*

# - CHAPTER ELEVEN -
## Healing and Deliverance

AND THOSE WHO BELIEVE WILL BE ABLE TO DO THESE THINGS AS PROOF [SIGNS]: THEY WILL USE MY NAME TO FORCE [DRIVE; CAST] OUT DEMONS. THEY WILL SPEAK IN NEW LANGUAGES [TONGUES]. THEY WILL PICK UP SNAKES AND DRINK POISON WITHOUT BEING HURT. THEY WILL TOUCH [LAY HANDS ON] THE SICK, AND THE SICK WILL BE HEALED [RECOVER].
(MARK 16:17-18)

The world of healing and deliverance is a wonderful, and often complicated, state of ultimate freedom from issues, problems, ailments, and situations people find themselves in within the confines of this life. Because we live in a fallen, sinful world, we will find ourselves in need of healing at some point in time. It is not only wise, but theologically necessary, to admit that healing is an aspect of everyone's life that is never done. We may find ourselves fortunate enough to be healed from something we consider major or essential in our lives, but there will always be something within us that can be healed, if we are walking in this world. Whether big or small, healing is a powerful, eternal victory, something that transforms and changes us for the better. It is liberation, freedom, and empowerment, all wrapped up into one.

Deliverance is related to healing, and we could say it is a form of healing, but it has one major difference: deliverance liberates us from anything that may be standing in our way to work out our salvation with fear and trembling. Healing may hinder our progress, but it doesn't necessarily stop our salvation experience. In deliverance, those hindrances are removed, and healing is finally allowed to flow and take place. Deliverance is a spiritual process, one that changes a person's entire spiritual outlook, and invites anything that might block the presence of God back into one's power.

As with healing, all of us need deliverance, even if the only thing we need deliverance from is ourselves. To be effective in both, we must have the humbling realization that it's something we all need, even if it isn't as obvious in one as it is from the other. The deliverance and healing minister must maintain this outlook, submitting themselves to the deliverance and healing of God rather than thinking they are the one who is offering something to others that they themselves are above needing.

The work of healing and deliverance is essential to today's church and the many difficult and trying things people bring to the altar, needing more than just a simple prayer or momentary word to pull them through. If we aspire to be ministers who work in healing and deliverance, we must know how both work, we must aspire to be thoroughly equipped for cases that require more than just altar work, and able to identify what is needed, and when, as such arises.

## A Scriptural outlook on healing and deliverance

In Biblical times, people believed that everything had a spiritual cause. They did not have the knowledge of modern medicine that we do today, and they felt that any ailment a person had must have been the result of supernatural, spiritual, demonic possession, or the cursing of God. The evolution of superstition and lore came from this culture: if something was wrong, it must have been because someone was punished for sin, or they were tormented by the devil. Either way, ailment was something nobody wanted anything to do with, and patience and care for the sick was something nobody was very interested in doing. Because no one understood the root cause of various issues, there were no concrete cures beyond folk medicines that may or may not have helped with symptoms people had. There were no social systems in those days, and care for the sick fell back on the families of the ill, which meant the sick were often left to care for themselves. Being sick or ill was considered bad luck, and because the sick were unable to work, they were left to their own devices as beggars or paupers.

Hearing God's call to care for the sick, therefore, was a healing action, all its own. To offer the work as a spiritual balm was an important part of the healing process, whether a person's symptoms alleviated. Being there, caring, proving that one wasn't afraid of a sick person provided moral and emotional support, that society was often not generally willing to extend to those who had problems. Even in Bible times, God noted the connection between the soul, spirit, emotions, and body: those who feel better often heal faster or improve their general well-being in some way because they have been encouraged. God recognized there are different levels and ways in which people experience healing, and we can play a part in someone else's healing, even if we don't have a formal gift of laying hands and seeing people healed or the ability to counsel them long-term.

*AS A TREE GIVES FRUIT, HEALING WORDS GIVE LIFE [A HEALTHY/HEALING TONGUE IS A TREE OF LIFE], BUT DISHONEST [DECEITFUL; PERVERSE] WORDS CRUSH THE SPIRIT.* (Proverbs 15:4)

*JESUS TRAVELED THROUGH ALL THE TOWNS AND VILLAGES, TEACHING IN THEIR SYNAGOGUES, PREACHING [PROCLAIMING] THE GOOD NEWS [GOSPEL] ABOUT THE KINGDOM, AND HEALING ALL KINDS OF DISEASES AND SICKNESSES.* (Matthew 9:35)

*ALL THE PEOPLE WERE TRYING TO TOUCH JESUS, BECAUSE POWER WAS COMING FROM HIM AND HEALING THEM ALL.* (Luke 6:19)

*SO THE APOSTLES WENT OUT AND TRAVELED THROUGH ALL THE TOWNS [FROM TOWN TO TOWN], PREACHING [PROCLAIMING] THE GOOD NEWS [GOSPEL] AND HEALING PEOPLE EVERYWHERE.* (Luke 9:6)

*THE SAME SPIRIT GIVES FAITH TO ONE PERSON. AND, TO ANOTHER, THAT ONE SPIRIT GIVES GIFTS OF HEALING.* (1 Corinthians 12:9)

*IN THE CHURCH GOD HAS GIVEN A PLACE FIRST TO [APPOINTED/PLACED FIRST] APOSTLES, SECOND TO PROPHETS, AND THIRD TO TEACHERS, THEN THOSE WHO DO MIRACLES [ACTS OF POWERS], THOSE WHO HAVE GIFTS OF HEALING, THOSE WHO CAN HELP OTHERS, THOSE WHO ARE ABLE TO GOVERN [LEAD], AND THOSE WHO CAN SPEAK IN DIFFERENT LANGUAGES [OR WITH ECSTATIC UTTERANCE; DIFFERENT KINDS OF TONGUES; V. 10].* (1 Corinthians 12:28)

If we call ourselves believers, working with the sick, or those who are somehow in need of healing and deliverance, is a part of our call. That becomes especially relevant when we take on the role of ministers, or servants, in the Kingdom. Working with people who have issues is a part of what we do; it is a part of the very life and concept of the church. The heart of the church is offering salvation to a sin-sick world, one that has been clouded not just by one's personal sins, but also by the sins of others inflicted upon an unsuspecting individual. If sin is the root problem of healing and deliverance, then God is the answer, and the church is here to serve as the catalyst for that situation and all that comes along with it.

We should never forget that the reason Jesus has left us here in this world is to do His work, and that work is often dirty, messy, and uncomfortable. We often pray God will use us to do His work and we pray that He will put us on the front line of battle, but we avoid the realities of what goes along with that, once we get there. The front lines of battle aren't cushy television programs or mega-churches that are a mill for large collections and looking all churchy for the cameras; they are spiritual battles fought and won in churches that are willing to work with addicts, alcoholics, the abused, the grief-stricken, the offended, the lost and forgotten, those who have been abandoned by their families, the lonely, the "untouchable," and the ignored. The front lines of ministry are healing and deliverance, dealing with the issues that others do not desire to pay attention to and find too complex, too messy, and too intense to handle.

## **Healing and deliverance as acts of divine love**

God doesn't have to heal us; He doesn't have to deliver us. If it was God's choice to leave us as we are, in our sins, that would be within His right. Before anyone protests, we are talking about what is within His right to do, not what He does do, or should do. Human beings desire their independence; they desire to go their own way; and God is within His right to let us follow our own course, because that's what we desire. Salvation is the ultimate act that God cares about us, and along with salvation, we find healing and deliverance. Even though we are this side of heaven, God still cares enough to liberate us from the confines of sin that can bind and hamper our relationship with Him.

*I WILL PRAISE [EXALT] YOU, LORD, BECAUSE YOU RESCUED ME [BROUGHT ME UP]. YOU DID NOT LET MY ENEMIES LAUGH AT [REJOICE OVER] ME.* (Psalm 30:1)

*BUT THEN I WILL BRING HEALTH [RECOVERY] AND HEALING TO THE PEOPLE THERE. I WILL HEAL THEM AND LET THEM ENJOY [REVEAL TO THEM] GREAT [AN ABUNDANCE OF] PEACE AND SAFETY [SECURITY].* (Jeremiah 33:6)

*BUT FOR YOU WHO HONOR ME [FEAR/REVERE MY NAME], GOODNESS WILL SHINE ON YOU LIKE THE SUN [THE SUN OF RIGHTEOUSNESS WILL RISE], WITH HEALING IN ITS RAYS [WINGS]. YOU WILL JUMP AROUND [GO OUT LEAPING], LIKE WELL-FED CALVES [CALVES FROM THE STALL].* (Malachi 4:2)

Healing and deliverance are signs that God loves us, right where we are, and right in every situation we face. Let us never mistake healing and deliverance for a mere erasing of symptoms as the sign He loves us, however. Ailments are more than their symptoms and healing and deliverance are more than just hoping symptoms will go away. In healing and deliverance, we gain; we overcome; we accept our own limitations and receive the divine transformation, necessary in every situation, to accept what is and press on to what will be, that which is greater than anything we can ever imagine.

*Healing of Tobit, Matthias Stom (c. 1600-1652)*

When we are agents of healing and deliverance, (however we are called to do that), we are partakers of God's divine love to someone else. When we receive healing or deliverance, we receive that divine love ourselves. We always say the love of God has the power to change the world, and it does, as can be seen through healing and deliverance. We should be the forerunners of giving it and receiving it, and proving to others that God's love is real, He does care, and His love does transform.

## Healing as a spiritual gift

Healing is mentioned as one of the gifts of the Spirit in 1 Corinthians 12:9. This tells us:

- Healing is one of the charismatic gifts of the church, meaning it is the work of the Spirit within believers.

- Healing is open to anyone in the Body of Christ at any time, which means it is not something that should be so elusive, we go running from faith healer to faith healer, or big name to big name, who claims to have that gift. We should never treat healing as if it is a commodity, because if it is a part of the charismatic gifts, we should all know someone who walks in it, whether they are in ministry, or not.

- Healing comes from God, not from us. The gift is not a sign that someone is special or more purposed than someone else, but that God is working healing through them.

- A healing gift should never be a source of contention, nor self-aggrandizement, in the Body. Healing is not greater than other spiritual gifts, nor lesser. We should never worship healers, nor encourage others to do so. It is as important as all other gifts available to the Body by the Spirit.

- Healing, along with the other charismatic gifts, helps to bring us to perfect unity, ensuring that there is nothing lacking within the Body.

When we look at healing through this lens, it helps us to maintain a healthy balance as pertains to it. Healing isn't something anyone should be chasing after, like a groupie. We should never get it in our minds that someone with a gift of healing is better than someone else, or that we must flock to someone specific to be healed. Healing is available to whomever it is for, whenever it is needed, through whomever is given the gift to deliver it.

## Deliverance in connection with spiritual gifts

Deliverance is not specifically mentioned anywhere in the Bible as a spiritual gift. The Bible mentions the word "deliverance" 16 times in the King James Version (14 in the Old Testament, twice in the New Testament), 12 times in the Expanded Bible (nine in the Old Testament, three times in the New Testament), and 25 times in the New International Version (24 times in the Old Testament, once in the New Testament). The way the term is used is in connection with physical deliverance, most often from earthly trials, battles, or difficulties. People were literally seeking the Lord's help for escape. The way the word is used in the Bible is rarely used in the way we use it today – in terms of a spiritual deliverance – and this makes it even more important we understand a proper context of the terminology and how it can, or should, apply today.

Deliverance indicates rescuing. When one is "delivered," it is understood there is something holding one captive or encircling them beyond all natural reason or control to escape. When one cries out for the deliverance of the Lord, be it in a natural situation or a spiritual one, that individual is recognizing there is nothing – not in heaven nor on earth – that can redeem the situation or change where it's at – save the hand of God.

In Bible terms, people were delivered from enemies in battle, from those who sought to do harm, from suffering, or from sin, as in the context of salvation. When one was delivered, it was from the power of one being to the freedom, as released by an outside force.

The terminology we use to indicate "deliverance" ministry is associated with demonic possession or spiritual invasion, from which an individual needs to be "released" or "rescued." The understanding of deliverance, especially in years prior to where we are now, was enforced for all sorts of ailments, from mental illness to physical ailment, in place of medical intervention or judgment. It has only been in more recent times that we've come to understand the root cause of many ailments, and understanding everything as having a spiritual origin stems from very ancient times. The work of deliverance ministries is often spurious, without a lot of medical substance or ability, and almost no training whatsoever.

This should alert all of us to a deeper need in proper training for deliverance and healing ministry, alike. Our goal in healing is not to become doctors or diagnosticians, but to recognize spiritual issues and pains in people that manifest themselves physically, emotionally, mentally, or spiritually. It doesn't mean everything we see is a demon or a sign of demonic possession but recognizes that sin is a root cause of ailment and we can offer something deeper and more spiritual to those who seek it.

This should not cause us to believe spirits cannot bother or torture people, or that deliverance does not come to those who need spiritual release. What it demands of us is to learn that much more about the spiritual realm and learn to identify it properly, rather than as a substitute for medical advice or intervention. Any minister or individual who operates deliverance ministry should see themselves first as someone with a healing gift, and second as someone who is able to offer deliverance as a part of that healing gift. It should not be seen as some sort of distant, mystical thing, but as a rooting of healing ministry and purpose as found in the Scriptures. It says within its covers that Jesus healed those tormented with spirits, restoring them to health and wholeness:

JESUS LEFT THAT PLACE AND WENT TO THE AREA [DISTRICT; REGION] OF TYRE AND SIDON [CITIES ON THE COAST NORTH OF ISRAEL]. A CANAANITE [A NON-JEWISH (GENTILE) RESIDENT OF PALESTINE (CANAAN WAS THE ANCIENT NAME FOR PALESTINE)] WOMAN FROM THAT AREA CAME TO JESUS AND CRIED OUT, "LORD, SON OF DAVID [A TITLE FOR THE MESSIAH], HAVE MERCY ON ME! MY DAUGHTER HAS A DEMON, AND SHE IS SUFFERING VERY MUCH [IS TORMENTED; IS SEVERELY DEMON-POSSESSED]."

BUT JESUS DID NOT ANSWER THE WOMAN [ANSWER HER A WORD]. SO HIS FOLLOWERS [DISCIPLES] CAME TO JESUS AND BEGGED [ASKED; URGED] HIM, "TELL THE WOMAN TO GO AWAY. [BECAUSE] SHE IS FOLLOWING US AND SHOUTING [CRYING OUT]."

JESUS ANSWERED, "GOD SENT ME [I WAS SENT] ONLY TO THE LOST SHEEP, THE PEOPLE [HOUSE] OF ISRAEL."

THEN THE WOMAN CAME TO JESUS AGAIN AND BOWED BEFORE HIM AND SAID, "LORD, HELP ME!"

JESUS ANSWERED, "IT IS NOT RIGHT TO TAKE THE CHILDREN'S BREAD AND GIVE [THROW] IT TO THE DOGS." ["CHILDREN" REFERS TO ISRAEL; "DOGS" TO THE GENTILES.]

THE WOMAN SAID, "YES, LORD, BUT EVEN THE DOGS EAT THE CRUMBS THAT FALL FROM THEIR MASTERS' TABLE."

THEN JESUS ANSWERED, "[O] WOMAN, YOU HAVE GREAT FAITH! I WILL DO WHAT YOU ASKED [LET IT BE DONE FOR YOU AS YOU WISH]." AND AT THAT MOMENT [FROM THAT

*HOUR] THE WOMAN'S DAUGHTER WAS HEALED.* (Matthew 15:21-28)

*JESUS AND HIS FOLLOWERS [THEY] WENT TO THE OTHER SIDE OF THE LAKE TO THE AREA [LAND; REGION] OF THE GERASENE PEOPLE [GERASA WAS SOUTHEAST OF LAKE GALILEE; THE EXACT LOCATION IS UNCERTAIN]. WHEN JESUS GOT OUT OF THE BOAT, IMMEDIATELY A MAN WITH AN EVIL [DEFILING; UNCLEAN] SPIRIT CAME TO HIM FROM THE BURIAL CAVES [TOMBS; CEMETERY]. THIS MAN LIVED IN THE CAVES [TOMBS], AND NO ONE COULD TIE HIM UP [ANY MORE], NOT EVEN WITH A CHAIN. [FOR] MANY TIMES PEOPLE HAD USED [SHACKLES AND] CHAINS TO TIE THE MAN'S HANDS AND FEET, BUT HE ALWAYS BROKE THEM OFF [TORE APART THE CHAINS AND SMASHED THE SHACKLES]. NO ONE WAS STRONG ENOUGH TO CONTROL [SUBDUE] HIM. DAY AND NIGHT HE WOULD WANDER AROUND THE BURIAL CAVES [TOMBS] AND ON THE HILLS, SCREAMING AND CUTTING [BRUISING] HIMSELF WITH STONES. WHILE JESUS WAS STILL FAR AWAY, THE MAN SAW HIM, RAN TO HIM, AND FELL [BOWED] DOWN BEFORE HIM.*

*THE MAN SHOUTED IN A LOUD VOICE, "WHAT DO YOU WANT WITH ME [LET ME ALONE; WHAT BUSINESS DO WE HAVE WITH EACH OTHER; WHAT TO ME AND TO YOU; SEE 1:24], JESUS, SON OF THE MOST HIGH GOD? I COMMAND [BEG; IMPLORE; SWEAR TO] YOU IN GOD'S NAME NOT TO TORTURE [TORMENT] ME!" HE SAID THIS BECAUSE JESUS WAS SAYING TO HIM, "YOU EVIL [DEFILING; UNCLEAN] SPIRIT, COME OUT OF THE MAN."*

*...AS JESUS WAS GETTING BACK INTO THE BOAT, THE MAN WHO WAS FREED FROM THE DEMONS [HAD BEEN DEMON-POSSESSED] BEGGED TO GO WITH HIM.*

*BUT JESUS WOULD NOT LET HIM. HE SAID, "GO HOME TO YOUR FAMILY AND TELL THEM HOW MUCH THE LORD HAS DONE FOR YOU AND HOW HE HAS HAD MERCY ON YOU." SO THE MAN LEFT AND BEGAN TO TELL [PROCLAIM/PREACH TO] THE PEOPLE IN THE TEN TOWNS [OR DECAPOLIS; A LEAGUE OF TEN CITIES EAST OF LAKE GALILEE] ABOUT WHAT JESUS HAD DONE FOR HIM. AND EVERYONE WAS AMAZED.* (Mark 5:1-8, 18-20)

*THE NEXT DAY, WHEN THEY CAME DOWN FROM THE MOUNTAIN, A LARGE CROWD MET JESUS. A MAN IN THE CROWD SHOUTED [CRIED OUT] TO HIM, "TEACHER, PLEASE [I BEG YOU TO] COME AND LOOK AT MY SON, BECAUSE HE IS MY ONLY CHILD. [AND LOOK/BEHOLD] AN EVIL SPIRIT [A SPIRIT] SEIZES MY SON, AND SUDDENLY HE [OR IT] SCREAMS. IT CAUSES HIM TO LOSE CONTROL OF HIMSELF [HAVE CONVULSIONS] AND FOAM AT THE MOUTH. THE EVIL SPIRIT KEEPS ON HURTING [BATTERS; MAULS] HIM AND ALMOST NEVER LEAVES HIM. I BEGGED YOUR FOLLOWERS [DISCIPLES] TO FORCE [DRIVE; CAST] THE EVIL SPIRIT OUT, BUT THEY COULD NOT DO IT."*

*JESUS ANSWERED, "YOU PEOPLE HAVE NO FAITH, AND YOUR LIVES ARE ALL WRONG [O UNBELIEVING AND CORRUPT/PERVERSE GENERATION]. HOW LONG MUST I STAY WITH YOU AND PUT UP WITH [ENDURE; BEAR WITH] YOU? BRING YOUR SON HERE."*

*WHILE THE BOY WAS COMING, THE DEMON THREW HIM ON THE GROUND AND MADE HIM LOSE CONTROL OF HIMSELF [IN CONVULSIONS]. BUT JESUS GAVE A STRONG COMMAND TO [REBUKED] THE EVIL [DEFILING; UNCLEAN; 4:33] SPIRIT AND HEALED THE BOY AND GAVE HIM BACK TO HIS FATHER. ALL THE PEOPLE WERE AMAZED [ASTONISHED; AWESTRUCK] AT THE GREAT POWER [MAJESTY; GREATNESS] OF GOD.* (Mark 9:37-43)

This brings deliverance ministry back to its spiritual and healing origins and roots it deeply in a Biblical understanding of the ministerial work rather than as a newer invention of church sensationalism. In the Bible, the concept of "deliverance" as we use it today would have been understood as being a part of healing ministry, as healing individuals who suffered from an ailment. Deliverance, therefore, is a work of the spiritual gift of healing; it involves faith; and it involves the ability to walk out God's love in the context of helping another move from the grip of one thing to something else.

## Counterfeit and pseudoscientific healing

As Christians, we should be uniquely aware of spiritual activity in the demonic realm, and the different ways the enemy works to manipulate and deceive people. Within New Age, occult, and even general modern society, are many different aspects of pseudo-scientific or counterfeit works classified as "healing" that often accomplish nothing at all. Some of these different works are found within varying religious systems, some are from the occult, and many incorporate various energy practices into whatever it is they are doing. There are those who swear by many of these practices and insist they work, being superior to western medical techniques, and many preferring them to principles of faith healing. It is important to recognize none of these techniques have scientific backing, and none of them have been proven to be effective or to work, especially in the context they are being used. While those in the first group may work as part of existing spiritual practices within their religions of origin, taking them out of that context is not proven to be effective. We can categorize them in the following groups:

- **Removed from a religious construct** (they are a part of an existing religious system, but have been removed from it, thus taking on a counterfeit nature in that they are not being practiced as part of what they were founded to be a part of, but rather, subsisting for a specified purpose that is not their intended nature): Yoga, reiki, Ayurveda, Shamanistic medicine, acupuncture, acupressure.

- **A part of occult construct** (they are a part of occult mindset and understanding, although they are not often clearly defined as such to an onlooker): Therapeutic touch, psychic surgery, magnet therapy, orgone, energy medicine, spiritual healing, chiropractic medicine, neuro-linguistic programming.

- **Alternative medical/scientific treatments** (they are not spiritually rooted but are often believed to be cure-alls for different aliments): Homeopathy, natropathy, bioresonance therapy, Dianetics, applied kinesiology, craniosacral therapy, cannabis.

Let us never judge these different systems, because there are just as many counterfeit healing techniques present within different Christian systems, claiming to heal, but never producing such. There are Christian groups who advocate beatings, whippings, starvation, enemas, burning people's skin, tying people up, sado-masochistic style deliverance sessions, mind control, and telling people to stop seeing doctors or take medication who then killed themselves, their children, or someone else that they know. The concept of pseudoscientific healing can crop up anywhere, and it is our place to identify when someone is not being properly helped to heal, whether it comes from a Christian source or a non-Christian one.

## The limitations of medicine to heal and deliver

There are those who feel we are "healed" by medicine and "delivered" by medical care. This is an interesting proposition, but one that defies the existence of God in our lives. The appropriate perspective to have as pertains to medicine and God is that God sometimes uses medicine as the means by which He heals individuals. Sometimes we are better for medical intervention; sometimes we are not. No matter what our ailment, it should always be the first priority to seek God and to pray about whatever is going on within us or our lives. That doesn't mean we shouldn't seek out medical intervention or that we should never go to the doctor, nor does it mean we should dawdle in emergency situations, especially if we are unsure of what is going on.

*He said, "You must obey [or listen to the voice of] the Lord your God and do what He says is right [is right in His eyes/sight]. If you obey all His commands [statutes; ordinances; requirements] and keep His rules, I will not bring on you any of the sicknesses [diseases] I brought on the Egyptians. I am the Lord Who heals you [your physician]."* (Exodus 15:26)

*He forgives all my [or your] sins [iniquity]*
  *and heals all my [or your] diseases [ills].*
(Psalm 103:3)

*But He took [bore] our suffering on Him*
  *and felt our pain for us [carried our sorrows/sickness].*
*We saw His suffering*
  *and thought God was punishing Him [...stricken and afflicted by Him; God].*
*But He was wounded for the wrong we did [our transgressions];*
  *He was crushed for the evil we did [our iniquities].*
*The punishment, which made us well [brought us wholeness/peace], was given to Him,*
  *and we are healed because of His wounds [lacerations; stripes; 1 Pet. 2:24].*
(Isaiah 53:4-5)

As people who know God for ourselves, we should always keep God at the primary seat of healing and purposes of healing and deliverance, both for ourselves and others. Even though this is not a substitution for medical care, we should always be sure to pray for those who need healing or deliverance, whether someone is receiving medical care for their ailment, or not. If someone requests the laying on of hands, we should be quick, rather than resistant, to offer that spiritual balm to them, trusting God will extend His grace to them in healing and deliverance in their lives.

We should also keep in mind that science and medicine may know some things, but they do not know everything. There is no question it is difficult to have an unknown or undiagnosed ailment, but there are many, even professing Christians, who idolize medicine, the medical profession, doctors, and science, putting it all above the Word spoken by God to His people, even them, in their hour of need. As practitioners of healing and deliverance, we should be the first to recognize science and medicine have their limitations because they are industries of human beings who do not know everything. Whenever we claim to believe in divine healing, we are putting our faith in the well-being of our bodies, minds, emotions, and souls back into the hands of the Father, Who can transform any life by His power and grace.

Healing takes place in many forms, and it is essential to remember that there is always faith behind healing. It doesn't just happen in a church, when someone lays hands on us. It doesn't just happen within the confines of a limited experience, or that of traditionally understood examples of faith healing in western culture. Healing is healing is healing, and God can use anyone He desires to execute healing, however is needed, in all contexts.

## **The long history of true – and false – faith healing**

It's not a secret that the history of faith healing has been both flattering and unflattering. We could say this is just a problem of our modern times, but that would not be true, nor fair. Many of the most prevalent faith healers in history had notable, questionable flaws within their character and personality. This does prove that healing is a gift (and the gifts and call of God are irrevocable), but it also proves that people were so star-struck by the concept of healing as a means of fame, the needed influence to curtail negative behaviors was often not present. The result, as people have chased after fame and notoriety

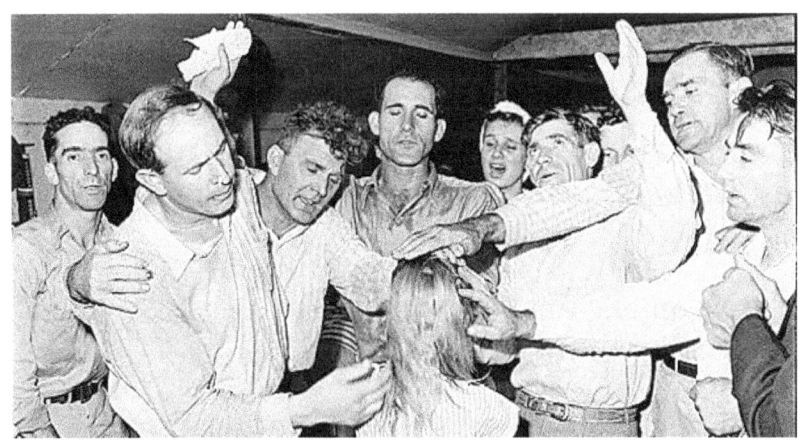

*Members of the Pentecostal Church of God (Lejunior, Kentucky) pray for a girl's healing in 1946*

through faith healing are both good and bad faith healers, legitimate and illegitimate claims, and long histories of people competing for a gift that seems to garner a great amount of attention. Even in modern times, with the variety of different tests, group testers, media researchers, and internet protests, claims of faith healers are not always legitimate, and there is an impressed need for careful observation, discernment, and tests of accuracy in the church today.

The negatives of faith healing do not detract from the positives, however. No matter how crazy some people might be or how false some claims of faith healing are, there have been genuine people who believed in the power of faith to heal and were either agents of divine healing or were recipients of it. Healing, as a sign of God's love for us, has been prevalent in every existing era since the New Testament, and shall continue to prevail, even through doubts, fears, and false claims. Some examples of faith healing throughout the ages include:

- The ability to heal the sick was a requirement for Christian leadership in the first two centuries of Christianity.[1]

- The first hospitals in history were started by Christians, those who desired to heal the sick. The first one in western civilization was established in Caesarea, Asia Minor, by Basil the Great around 370 AD.[2]

- Mentally ill patients have traditionally been treated by the church, in monasteries or institutions. While there is no question they often received subpar care, the Quakers established the first mental hospital in the United States in 1817, focusing on treating patients with moral care. This became the model for care of the mentally ill for over 150 years.[3]

- The first nurses were among the Daughters of Charity of St. Vincent de Paul, dating back to Europe in the 1600s.[4]

- Smith Wigglesworth, one of the best known ministers of the early 1900s, was completely focused on faith healing. He believed God had healed him of many ailments and stated that no knife would ever touch his body, even in life or death. As did many of his time, he believed illness was of Satanic origin and would "heal" people through hitting, slapping, or punching the part of the body that was afflicted.[5]

- John G. Lake, a faith healer who is often considered foundational to the movement, was accused of staging miracles and healings. He later started the Divine Healing Institute, along with different healing rooms.[6]

- Aimee Semple MacPherson, as flawed as she was, had a recommend from the American Medical Association, because so many of her healings had been affirmed genuine, and confirmed her healings were real.[7]

- Peter Popoff claimed to receive information from God about names and ailments in his audience, but it was discovered he would obtain his information as his staff mingled with the audience before the shows and then fed the information through a wireless system during shows in his ear. It is believed the character Jonas Nightingale in the movie *Leap of Faith* was based on Peter Popoff.[8]

- Many claimed faith healers, such as Oral Roberts and Benny Hinn, have found themselves in legal trouble for improper use of finances or fundraising practices.

- A study of 406 anxiety and depressive cases were given either intercessory prayer or no prayer, with prayer offered for 15 minutes daily for twelve weeks. Both sets of patients experienced an improvement in their cases, with no difference between the two groups.[9]

- A six-month study of forty advanced AIDS patient exposed to ten weeks of "distant healing" in intercessory prayer groups reported fewer new illnesses, physician visits, and hospitalizations.[10]

- Studies have found that churchgoers tend to be healthier and live longer than non-churchgoers.[11]

## **Why are some healed, and others not?**

Looking over the history of faith healing makes it appear spurious. It seems like it works sometimes, but not at other times. With the advance of modern science, Faith healing appears spurious; it seems like it works sometimes, and not others. It does not appear to help the case of faith healing to discern that sometimes there are alternate, scientific explanations as why faith healing works, those which appear to have nothing to do with faith, or healing.

To understand faith healing, we must first understand faith healing is not a science, and not necessarily to proof, nor evidence, via scientific method or theory. This doesn't mean science cannot enforce faith healing, or that we should throw out all scientific theory when assessing whether a person has (or has not) received healing for an ailment. It means that faith healing comes by faith, and that it is a process that is not as simple, nor as scientific, as we might like to make it out to be. Faith does not play by the rules of science, and that means faith healing might appear like any sort of contradiction of scientific understanding when it is put into play.

This does not mean we should accept pure quackery when it comes to faith healing. Some methods bear scientific rebuke, and not only do they bear rebuke from science, but they should also bear rebuke from the church. Recipients should be aware of any methods that seem to induce physical, mental, or emotional harm, are in any way unsafe or questionable in approach, or do anything that could in some way hamper treatments or existing diagnosis.

When understanding the process of faith healing, we must understand faith on the most basic level. Faith is, first and foremost, to accept the will of God for our lives. It's more than living out what we want under the guise of having God do things for us; it is truly accepting that what we want, or what we think is best, is not always that way for us. While no one suggests that people are destined to be sick, there are things we can learn through illness or ailment that we can't as easily learn when we are well. When it comes to illness or difficulty, it is often one of the most difficult things to accept in one's life. We must reach a part where we are willing to overcome our denial of diagnosis, where we insist we don't admit we have what we have and act like it doesn't exist. For even the possibility of healing to exist, we must admit there is something wrong, rather than rejecting and fighting diagnosis. We need to be real about the state of our fallen world and our bodies, minds, and emotions in this fallen world, and accept that sometimes things do happen – to good people, to bad people, to in-between people – and that sometimes the ailments we have don't go away by faith like we might want them to.

In this is learning to have faith beyond getting what we want from God. Sometimes, through illness, we learn about hearing from God. We learn to accept our limitations, to take each day as it comes, and to accept the things we cannot change. Through illness or ailment, humility often comes that won't develop in our lives through any other means.

In the concept of faith healing, there are many simpler reasons that we often overlook that may hamper the process of faith. Some people really, deep down, don't want to get healed, because it means they won't receive the same level of attention if they do. Some don't understand the precept of receiving or feel they can't receive healing for themselves.

These things happen, there aren't good answers for them, and it's not as simple as saying people do or don't have enough faith to make things happen. Sometimes people assume they were sick, but they never were, or they misdiagnosed themselves (for example, saying they had a cancer biopsy and start praying for healing before the results come back). In other instances, sometimes those who claim to have the gift of healing really don't, some don't believe in what they are doing, and some faith healers are so much about themselves, rather than God, thus running interference in the experience.

Beyond some of these more immediate reasons, sometimes people aren't healed because they have pushed their bodies beyond the reasonable limits, and their ailment remains to remind them not to push it further (such as Type 2 Diabetes). Sometimes people are healed and don't realize they are, because the manifestation of their healing isn't what they expected it to be. Sometimes reception of healing is incompatible with the precepts God has put into place through natural law or precept, and still there are those who claim to be healed who, in fact, are not.

Here is the point where faith and science overlap, and often complement one another, although we are unwilling to heed the information given because it's not what we desire to hear. God has given us every ability to be healthy, through His creation, and has put everything here to help us accomplish that means. That means God has already done His part, and He is not obligated to issue a long list of miracles for things we could do if we were only willing to put in the time and work to be healthy.

God is not going to give us miracles to help enable us to be lazy. Many of the so-called healings and miracles people are believing for could be easily "cured" through proper diet and exercise, lifestyle changes, replacing bad habits with good ones, and making the effort to live life fuller and better. This is an aspect of healing we overlook, because it doesn't make for a great show at church, but it is the reality, nonetheless.

If we are individuals who operate the gift of healing in our ministries, we must be willing to open our mouths and tell people the truth about their situations as are found within divine precept. Sometimes people aren't going to get what they desire because what they are looking for is, simply put, out of the will of God. It is not that God desires His people to be sick, but that God does not enable His people to be lazy. God also values His relationship with us first – that we might prosper even as our souls prosper – and that means if a major miraculous transformation is going to change things, the intent and purpose of the soul must come first.

Much of the success of faith healing comes down to the intangible realm that science does not account for: motives, intentions, thoughts, and reasonings of those who exercise it. If we want to see healing flow, we need to have ready hearts, ready faith, and willing ears to stand as vessels for God in delivering His message, even in difficult circumstances.

## Test every spirit

We discussed testing spirits earlier in this book in the context of learning to identify them. Testing spirits as apply to healing and healing gifts just as much as learning to identify them in a general sense. The Scriptures encourage us to test every spirit, when they come along, as pertains to all matters of faith.

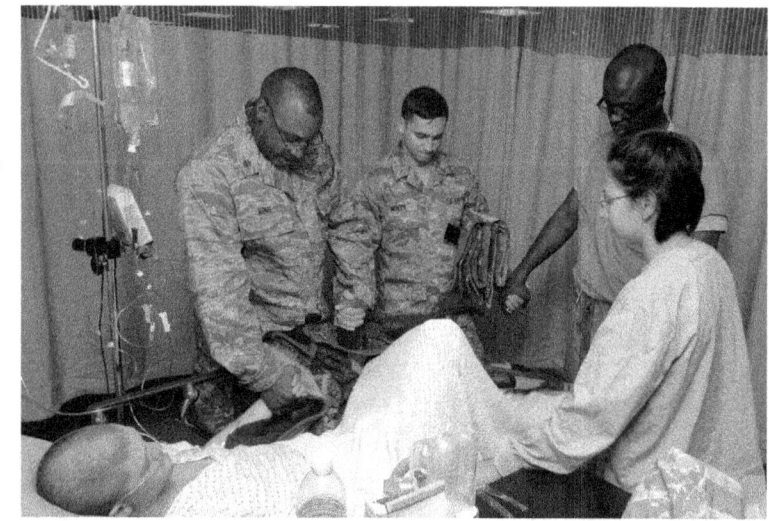

*Religious support teams pray for the healing of a patient*

The Bible does this to remind us of the "behind the scenes"

operations of the spirit realm, and that not every spirit that goes forth is of God. Things can look great, sound great, even appear to be good, but aren't always from God. Those who discern know the difference.

*My dear friends [Beloved], many false prophets [Deut. 13:1-5; 18:14-22; Mark 13:22] have gone out into the world. So do not believe [trust] every spirit, but test the spirits to see if they are from God [the false teachers evidently claimed that their teaching was from the Spirit; 1 Cor. 12:1-3; 14:29; 1 Thess. 5:19-21]. This is how you can know [recognize] God's Spirit: Every spirit [a teacher/prophet claiming inspiration from the Spirit] who confesses [acknowledges] that Jesus Christ came to earth as a human [in the flesh] is from God. And every spirit who refuses to say this about Jesus [does not confess/acknowledge Jesus] is not from God [2 John 7]. It is the spirit of the enemy of Christ [antichrist; 2:18, 22], which you have heard is coming, and now he is already in the world.*

*My dear children [2:1], you belong to [are from] God and have defeated [conquered; overcome] them [the antichrists/false teachers]; because God's Spirit, Who is in you, is greater than the devil, who is in the world [that which is in you is greater than that which is in the world]. And they belong to [are from] the world, so what they say is from the world, and the world listens to [hears; obeys] them. But we belong to [are from] God, and those who know God listen to [hear; obey] us. But those who are not from God do not listen to [hear; obey] us. That is how we know [recognize] the Spirit that is true and the spirit that is false [deceives; errs].* (1 John 4:1-6)

*Be careful of [Beware of; Watch out for] false prophets. They come to you looking gentle like sheep [disguised like sheep; in sheep's clothing], but they are really dangerous like wolves [underneath/inwardly they are ravenous/vicious/ferocious wolves]. You will know these people by what they do [their fruit]. Grapes don't come [Can you pick grapes...?] from thornbushes, and figs don't come from [and figs from...?] thorny weeds [thistles]. In the same way, every good [healthy; sound] tree produces good fruit, but a bad [rotten; diseased] tree produces bad fruit. A good [healthy; sound] tree cannot produce bad fruit, and a bad [rotten; diseased] tree cannot produce good fruit. Every tree that does not produce good fruit is cut down and thrown into the fire. In the same way, you will know these false prophets [them] by what they do [their fruit].*

*NOT ALL THOSE WHO SAY [TO ME] "YOU ARE OUR LORD" ["LORD! LORD!"] WILL ENTER THE KINGDOM OF HEAVEN, BUT ONLY THOSE WHO DO WHAT MY FATHER IN HEAVEN WANTS [THE WILL OF MY FATHER IN HEAVEN]. ON THE LAST DAY [JUDGMENT DAY; THAT DAY] MANY PEOPLE WILL SAY TO ME, "LORD, LORD, WE SPOKE FOR YOU [DID WE NOT PROPHESY IN YOUR NAME...?], AND THROUGH YOU WE FORCED OUT DEMONS [CAST OUT DEMONS IN YOUR NAME...?] AND DID MANY MIRACLES [MIGHTY WORKS IN YOUR NAME...?]." THEN I WILL TELL THEM CLEARLY [DECLARE TO THEM; PUBLICLY ANNOUNCE TO THEM], "I NEVER KNEW YOU. GET AWAY [DEPART] FROM ME, YOU WHO DO EVIL [BREAK GOD'S LAW; PRACTICE LAWLESSNESS; PS. 6:8]."* (Matthew 7:15-23)

The true test of any spiritual gift is its fruit. In the context of healing, it is whether people are healed because of that gift. The fruit of the gift starts earlier than this, however, and that is rooted in the faith of the individual who does the healing. If a person's faith is not right, spiritually grounded and focused on Jesus Christ, then that faith is going to exhibit counterfeit nature or fail to produce anything, at all.

If one claims to have a gift of healing and there is no record, anywhere, ever, of any healings, that should be cause for note and concern. It is possible the individual has chased after a long line of sensationalism and thinks they should have a healing gift because everyone else has one, or because it will get them the most attention. This displays profound immaturity and should cause a leader to desire to handle this situation behind the scenes, with love, and without a long period of waiting to address it.

Humility should also accompany a healing gift, as well as a balance of good Christian character. We should never get so caught up in a gifting ability that we forget about the need for general Christian character development. No one should ever receive special treatment because of a spiritual gift from God. All gifts come from God; all abilities come from God; and all as such return to Him. Testing spirits is about more than just determining if someone can heal someone else, although there should always be evidence of the gift of healing, if, indeed, one has this gift. Testing spirits is about seeing what is behind something, what is behind someone's character or ability, and what is the overall driving spirit behind what someone does. Instead of just looking at what might be on the surface, it is our place to test fruit, to see the root of why one does what they done, and the motivating factors therein.

## The principles of healing

Healing is, within its definition, a process of restoration, transformation, and completion to wholeness, as found within an individual. Healing is a spiritual process, freeing an individual from a manifestation of the power of sin within their lives, and liberating them to experience true freedom. Healing is more than just erasing symptoms or making it so someone doesn't experience discomfort or pain in some form. It is about moving from the power of this world to the Kingdom of God, gaining more ground for God, and gaining more insight for each healed person.

Within healing, there are four different aspects of the healing process and experience: Restoration, transformation, completion, and wholeness.

- **Restoration:** Through sin, humanity lost. We lost in more ways than we are aware, especially as we go through our lives thinking we've got it far more together than we do. There are many little issues and little examples in our lives of how far we are from God, but we fail to recognize them in the way we should. Illness, malady, physical discomforts, emotional and mental issues, and spiritual anguishes all erode at our wholeness, our completion, and our relationship with God, even if they do not come because of what we, ourselves, do directly, and even if they are unintentional or unnoticed. Healing is a part of restoration; of undoing what was done, that which we have done, and that which has damaged us, in ways we cannot and do not understand, to find a place of spiritual fullness once again (Acts 3:21).

- **Transformation:** Healing restoration does not come about without transformation, better known as change. The concept of repentance is recognizing we need a change, and in healing, it is God Who reaches out to further us in that change, in that process as we move from sin to faith (2 Corinthians 3:18).

- **Completion:** In healing, we find our completion, of the restorative change that needs to make us whole. We recognize God is the One Who makes us complete, and that oneness with Him is what changes us. We recognize our healing has come, we are now different, and that we find the answer to our needs in God, rather than in the world (Deuteronomy 28:1-14).

- **Wholeness:** Wholeness is receiving the product of healing. Thanks to God, we are whole; complete; nothing lacking. We may never find complete wholeness this side of heaven, but we can experience it in types and shadows, in small bits and pieces, as we seek God for deeper insight as to how to become more healed, more complete, and more one with Him (Psalm 34:2).

## The evidence of healing

Whenever we think about healing, we typically remember the times of the "good old days" and tent revivals, where people in wheelchairs suddenly walked, and people on crutches needed them no more, thanks to prayer and intervention at the altar. We all know there were many shysters who used these displays to defraud and steal from people, and that such still exist today. Still, the question remains, what is true evidence of healing? What happens if someone is healed, and it's not in the form of something obvious, like getting out of a wheelchair, or no longer needing crutches? What about healing from something that requires medical evidence, such as cancer or HIV? How do we measure different standards of healing, and what does it mean when someone says someone else is "healed?"

Over the past twenty-five years, we have seen a switch in the things people tend to call out when it comes to healing and deliverance lines, altar calls, and sessions. It used to be that when someone talked about being healed, they were relating healing as pertains to physical ailments. Nobody thought much about healing mental issues or emotional ones, because issues like those were not easily seen and easily and clearly designated as being healed right away, at the altar. We have now switched to talking more about mental, emotional, and spiritual problems than physical ones when it comes to healing, and the question in many minds beg, why? Why would ministers shift from physical healings that can be seen at the altar to ones that cannot be easily seen?

The answer to the question lies within the question: mental, emotional, and spiritual issues are not easily seen, nor easily detected, and it is easier to say that someone is healed from something intangible rather than something tangible. No one can really prove if someone has been healed or not if the issue afflicting them is intangible, thus it makes it easier for claims of healing to seem persuasive and real, even if they are not. Such healing enters the realm of "nobody really knows," and people may genuinely seem better for a period in their lives, possibly even months, making the claim look genuine (even if it is not). This is not to say that every time a leader calls out healing in a spiritual, emotional, or mental capacity that they are false or such is false, but it is to say that it's a lot harder to tell if such is real or fake when the ailment is not visibly seen by others.

The second reason is because mental, emotional, and spiritual health have all taken more of a front seat in modern society than they did in years' past. Mental health was never a popular topic for discussion, and emotional and spiritual disturbances were not considered a real priority of people in times where their basic goal was survival. Now we live in a very cerebral culture, where people are analyzing others without proper training and where we quickly judge the motives and mental or emotional states of other people, based on their statements, thoughts, or actions. If we lack proper training, it's very possible we are incorrect in our assessments, but making such generalizations and rash judgments has become a sweeping part of Christian culture. Whether it's social media, ministers with no psychological training, or pop culture church gods who have been deemed "experts" on absolutely everything, we have been endowed with improper or inadequate knowledge of human behavior in church, and we are easily assessing people's behaviors in a wrong or demeaning manner. It is deeply disturbing that we are quick to assess everyone else, but we do not see the unhealed, undelivered issues we, ourselves carry, and condemn others while refusing to seek the healing and deliverance we need. The "armchair psychologist" approach we see in church is often damaging and unhelpful, and it exalts the issues of others while avoiding the truth about ourselves and often those closes to us. Thus, we might say people have issues they, in actuality do not, or we might see people healed, but refuse to acknowledge it, all because we are judging them.

*THEN JESUS SAID TO HIM, "DON'T TELL ANYONE ABOUT THIS. BUT GO AND SHOW YOURSELF TO THE PRIEST AND OFFER THE GIFT [OFFERING; SACRIFICE] MOSES COMMANDED FOR PEOPLE WHO ARE MADE WELL [LEV. 14:1-32]. THIS WILL SHOW THE PEOPLE [BE A PUBLIC TESTIMONY TO; BE EVIDENCE FOR] WHAT I HAVE DONE."* (Matthew 8:4)

So just how do we measure true healing, if healing, as we can understand it, takes both tangible and intangible forms? The answer is that sometimes we can't always see it with the naked eye, but we can, if we are truly as spiritual as we like to believe, can recognize other signs:

- Transformation in the spirit of a person; in their attitude, their ability to handle and endure, in their life outlook, and in a change in their thinking and their way of viewing life.

- Alleviation of symptoms that were related to an existing diagnosis or issue.

- A state of acceptance for one's personal state, drawing them closer to God in the process and seeking Him out in a deeper way.

- Reaching a personal state of forgiveness and release, truly eliminating resentment, anger, hostility, and other complex, damaging emotions from one's mental and emotional states.

- Growing into a place of maturity; no longer seeking to obsess over one's past or what one did or did not have but understanding and accepting realities unto a place of true serenity.

- No longer seeking things from people they cannot get them from.

- Growing in spiritual maturity to the point where one can receive correction and spiritual discipline with a proper outlook and attitude.

- Making better choices that are not based on the emotional wounds of the past.

Healing doesn't always take place quickly, or at an altar call, or anything of that nature. Sometimes

*St. Paul At His Writing Desk, Rembrandt Harmenszoon van Rijn (1606-1669)*

the work of healing takes place over time, and requires us, as believers, and agents of faith, to put in the time to help people long-term, through what they go through, and express an interest in love, rather than showmanship, in the work of healing.

## **The thorn in the flesh**

No matter how many times we stand in a healing line, no matter how many times we want deliverance, and no matter how many hours a day we pray, none of us will ever be completely, 100% healed or delivered from everything that ails us. We might receive healing and deliverance for big things, for things we come to recognize as a problem or a disturbance, but there are other things in our lives that we don't receive healing or deliverance from. There are other times when things may very well cause disruption for us, and we do not receive deliverance or healing from them. This is where the "thorn in the flesh," the principle of going through, whether we are healed or not, comes into play.

*I MUST CONTINUE TO BRAG [BOAST]. IT WILL DO NO GOOD, BUT I WILL TALK NOW ABOUT VISIONS AND REVELATIONS FROM THE LORD. I KNOW A MAN IN CHRIST [A BELIEVER] WHO WAS TAKEN UP [CAUGHT UP; SNATCHED AWAY] TO THE THIRD HEAVEN [THE PRESENCE OF GOD] FOURTEEN YEARS AGO [PAUL IS INDIRECTLY REFERRING TO HIMSELF]. I DO NOT KNOW WHETHER THE MAN WAS IN HIS BODY OR OUT OF HIS BODY, BUT GOD KNOWS. AND I KNOW THAT THIS MAN WAS TAKEN UP [CAUGHT UP; SNATCHED AWAY] TO PARADISE [ANOTHER NAME FOR HEAVEN; LUKE 23:43; REV. 2:7]. I DON'T KNOW IF HE WAS IN HIS BODY OR AWAY FROM HIS BODY, BUT GOD KNOWS. HE HEARD THINGS HE IS NOT ABLE TO EXPLAIN [INEXPRESSIBLE; INEFFABLE], THINGS THAT NO HUMAN IS ALLOWED TO TELL. I WILL BRAG [BOAST] ABOUT A MAN LIKE THAT, BUT I WILL NOT BRAG [BOAST] ABOUT MYSELF, EXCEPT ABOUT MY WEAKNESSES. BUT IF I WANTED TO BRAG [BOAST] ABOUT MYSELF, I WOULD NOT BE A FOOL, BECAUSE I WOULD BE TELLING THE TRUTH. BUT I WILL NOT BRAG ABOUT MYSELF [SPARE YOU; REFRAIN FROM THIS] BECAUSE I DO NOT WANT PEOPLE TO THINK MORE OF ME THAN WHAT THEY SEE ME DO OR HEAR ME SAY [OR SAY, OR BECAUSE OF THESE EXTRAORDINARY REVELATIONS; THIS PHRASE MAY GO HERE OR WITH THE NEXT SENTENCE].*

*SO THAT I WOULD NOT BECOME TOO PROUD OF THE WONDERFUL THINGS THAT WERE SHOWN TO ME [OR BECAUSE OF THESE EXTRAORDINARY REVELATIONS; THIS PHRASE MAY BE PART OF THE PREVIOUS SENTENCE], A PAINFUL PHYSICAL PROBLEM [THORN IN THE*

*FLESH] WAS GIVEN TO ME. THIS PROBLEM WAS A MESSENGER FROM SATAN, SENT TO BEAT [TORMENT; HARASS; TROUBLE] ME AND KEEP ME FROM BEING TOO PROUD. I BEGGED [PLEADED WITH] THE LORD THREE TIMES TO TAKE THIS PROBLEM AWAY FROM [THAT IT MIGHT LEAVE] ME. BUT HE SAID TO ME, "MY GRACE IS ENOUGH FOR YOU [SUFFICIENT FOR YOU; ALL YOU NEED]. WHEN YOU ARE WEAK, MY POWER IS MADE PERFECT IN YOU [FOR (MY) POWER IS PERFECTED IN WEAKNESS]." SO I AM VERY HAPPY TO BRAG [BOAST] ABOUT MY WEAKNESSES. THEN CHRIST'S POWER CAN LIVE [RESIDE; OR REST] IN ME. FOR THIS REASON I AM HAPPY [PLEASED; CONTENT] WHEN I HAVE WEAKNESSES, INSULTS, HARD TIMES [TIMES OF NEED], SUFFERINGS [PERSECUTIONS], AND ALL KINDS OF TROUBLES [DISTRESS] FOR [FOR THE SAKE OF] CHRIST. BECAUSE WHEN I AM WEAK, THEN I AM TRULY STRONG.* (1 Corinthians 12:1-10)

The Apostle Paul's thorn in the flesh begs the question: what role does sickness, illness, disease, or discomfort play in our lives of faith when we aren't healed? There are many who get so caught up in the concept of healing and in being healed as the only possible manifestation of God's love or concern in their lives that they come to believe the only purpose illness or discomfort plays in our lives is through punishment. This is a very dark, not to mention inaccurate, view of healing and deliverance, not to mention illness or discomfort. If all we do is see punishment or penalization in illness, we are depriving ourselves of the value of healing therein and the spiritual redemption that sometimes comes through it.

We don't know today what the apostle's "thorn in the flesh" was specifically (although there are many theories about just what it might have been, including physical ailment, personal relationship or identity struggle, disease, or poor eyesight), but we see that he came to see it through a sense of grace, a redemptive measure, even though it wasn't something that was there to save him, because it wasn't Christ Himself. The apostle recognizes it was sent from Satan, but as with all things spiritual, He points out that what was intended for evil can still serve a good, divine purpose. In the thorn in the flesh, the Apostle Paul found that perfected strength, God's ability to work through him, even though he had an ailment. The power of Christ, that power to endure suffering, was within Him in a powerful way, training Him for the purpose of the Gospel. In his weakness, the apostle was made strong.

There is something to be said for those who endure intense illness, strife, or difficulty, and still overcome, despite such odds. We love the stories of the underdog who doesn't come from ideal circumstances but is still able to stand up and do something incredible. We love this theme, because it is a spiritual principle of power perfected in weakness; that God can take something that seems insurmountable and turn it into something else.

As healers, we should encourage people to approach the work of healing in their own lives, whether they are healed instantaneously at the altar, or not, or if their instance of healing is acceptance of a situation as God turns it around and gives someone an overcoming spirit to transform and change from weakness to power. No matter what someone goes through, there are many ways we can heal, we can stand as people who work to transform lives, and in the process, find what we seek from God for ourselves.

**Chapter 11 Assignments**

- Having read through the chapter, write an essay (5-8 sentences) about healing from a Biblical perspective.
- There are many claims of divine healing today. Research a current news story about healing (something that has developed within the past year) and using the Biblical examinations therein, write out your perspective on whether the claim is valid.

*Christ Healing the Bleeding Woman (Catacombs of Rome)*

# - CHAPTER TWELVE -
## Having the Right Attitude About Healing and Deliverance

Because I know this trouble [this] will bring my [result in] freedom [deliverance; or salvation], through your prayers and the help of [support from] the Spirit of Jesus Christ.
(Philippians 1:19)

Healing and deliverance (as an aspect of healing) are important aspects of the Christian life and ministry. They aren't more important than any other aspect of ministry and Christian life, but they consist of a component of Christian living that cannot be denied, nor ignored. We should never stand in the way of healing, nor should we create barriers to any individual finding the healing and deliverance they seek. This starts when we are willing to examine every idea and concept we have about healing, and start erasing the barriers that stand between us, those we love and work with, and those who come to us in the name of healing and deliverance.

Too often, we assume the worst of people when it comes to healing or their ability to heal in any given situation. We write them off as too far gone, hopeless, impossible, or even undeserving of healing. Sometimes we approach healing and deliverance with such a natural eye, we forget to acknowledge and recognize the true spirituality that is often needed to bring healing to a situation. If we walk into a situation of healing with a bad attitude, the wrong theories, feelings, thoughts, or approach, that is going to change the way healing and deliverance are available and possible within a given situation.

As believers, healing and deliverance belong to God, not us. God heals, delivers, saves, bestows, gives, and loves as He will, not as we will. When we have faith for healing, we are having faith for God to do anything beyond that which we can conceive or understand, because we are agreeing and recognizing all things are possible with God (Matthew 19:26). Healing makes the impossible possible and recognizes God can do and does do anything, outside of our limitations and our concepts of Him, because that is Who God is.

Here we will look at just what constructs a right attitude when it comes to healing and the many barriers that block and hinder us from having right concepts about healing and the manner in which God desires to do anything and everything possible to bring His people closer to Him through the work of healing and deliverance.

## The prospering soul

Prosperity might be a common topic for conferences, events, and sermons, but it is often taught incorrectly. We most commonly associate prosperity with money, and that is often where teaching on prosperity begins and ends. It is unfortunate that we have come to only associate prosperity with money, because that shows we have a lack of fullness when it comes to the understanding of the prosperous life. A better term for the concept is living a blessed life, which is found in multiple places throughout the Scriptures.

*HAPPY [BLESSED] ARE THOSE WHO DON'T LISTEN TO [WALK IN THE COUNSEL OF] THE WICKED,*
  *WHO DON'T GO WHERE SINNERS GO [STAND IN THE WAY OF SINNERS],*
  *WHO DON'T DO WHAT EVIL PEOPLE DO [SIT IN THE SEAT OF MOCKERS].*
*THEY LOVE [DELIGHT IN] THE LORD'S TEACHINGS [LAWS; INSTRUCTIONS],*
  *AND THEY THINK ABOUT [MEDITATE ON] THOSE TEACHINGS [LAWS; INSTRUCTIONS] DAY AND NIGHT.*
*THEY ARE LIKE A TREE PLANTED BY A RIVER [STREAMS OF WATER; FULL OF LIFE, STRONG, VIBRANT].*
  *THE TREE PRODUCES FRUIT IN SEASON,*
  *AND ITS LEAVES DON'T DIE [WITHER].*
*EVERYTHING THEY DO WILL SUCCEED [PROSPER].*

*But wicked people are not like that.*
   *They are like chaff that the wind blows away [dead, unstable].*
*So the wicked will not escape God's punishment [stand in the judgment].*
   *Sinners will not worship with God's people [be in the assembly of the righteous].*
*This is because the Lord takes care of His people [knows the way of the righteous],*
   *but the way of the wicked will be destroyed.*
(Psalm 1:1-6)

*Happy [Blessed] are those who respect [fear] the Lord [Prov. 1:7] and obey Him [walk in His ways].*
*You will enjoy what you work for [eat the labor of your hands],*
   *and you will be blessed [happy] with good things [prosperity].*
*Your wife will be like a fruitful vine [produce many children] in your house [Prov. 31:10–31].*
   *Your children will be like olive branches [bringing much good] around your table [Mic. 4:4; Zech. 3:10].*
*This is how the man who respects [fears] the Lord [Prov. 1:7]*
   *will be blessed.*
*May the Lord bless you from Mount Zion [the location of the Temple];*
   *may you enjoy [experience; see] the good things [prosperity] of Jerusalem all the days of your life.*
*May you see your grandchildren.*
*Let there be peace in Israel.*
(Psalm 128:1-6)

*Happy [Blessed] are those [the people] who are like this;*
*happy [blessed] are the people whose God is the Lord.*
(Psalm 144:15)

*But the person who trusts [has confidence] in the Lord will be blessed. The Lord will show him that He can be trusted [… whose trust/confidence is in Him].* (Jeremiah 17:7)

The Old Testament concept of *shalom* was more than just what we associate with peace and a lack of fighting. It was a word associated with "wholeness" or "completeness." In the place of *shalom*, one found a meaning and a value in life that was not obtainable outside of one's spiritual relationship with God. This might sound simplistic, especially when we consider the cares of life, but the blessed life – or prospering life – was directly related to one's spiritual life.

In other words, if your spiritual life wasn't right, things in your natural realm weren't going to be right, either. We're not talking about having a few disturbances, bad days, or things being completely and totally perfect, but an overall sense of wholeness and completion when it comes to the work and realm of one's life. If a person couldn't look over their lives and say that, overall, they felt blessed by God, then something, somewhere was wrong, and the ancients believed firmly whatever was wrong started with something in one's spiritual life. Whether it was idolatry, bad influences, greed, sin, or something underlying within the surface, a person's spirituality – deemed as something at the center, or grounding, of one's being – was lacking if something was consistently going awry or wrong.

To prosper in health and life, one had to prosper spiritually. First things came first, in all things, and whether it was a natural disaster, personal crisis, or issue among people, the prophets were often quick to point out areas where the people fell away from God, that they had obviously missed, and connected those back to the lack of blessing in other areas of their lives.

*THE LORD SAYS, "EVEN NOW, COME BACK TO ME WITH ALL YOUR HEART.*
*FAST, CRY [WEEP], AND BE SAD [MOURN]."*
*TEARING YOUR CLOTHES IS NOT ENOUGH TO SHOW YOU ARE SAD;*
  *LET YOUR HEART BE BROKEN [TEAR/REND YOUR HEARTS AND NOT YOUR GARMENTS;*
*TRUE REPENTANCE, NOT JUST A SHOW OF GRIEF].*
*COME BACK TO THE LORD YOUR GOD,*
  *BECAUSE HE IS KIND [GRACIOUS; MERCIFUL] AND SHOWS MERCY [COMPASSIONATE].*
*HE DOESN'T BECOME ANGRY QUICKLY [...SLOW TO ANGER],*
  *AND HE HAS GREAT LOVE [LOYALTY; MERCY; LOVINGKINDNESS].*
  *HE CAN CHANGE HIS MIND ABOUT [RELENTS FROM] DOING HARM.*
*WHO KNOWS? MAYBE HE WILL TURN BACK TO YOU [GRANT A REPRIEVE; TURN AND RELENT]*
  *AND LEAVE BEHIND A BLESSING FOR YOU.*
*GRAIN [GIFT; TRIBUTE; LEV. 2:1] AND DRINK OFFERINGS BELONG TO [OR FOR] THE LORD YOUR GOD.*
*BLOW THE TRUMPET IN JERUSALEM [ZION; 2:1];*
  *CALL FOR [DECLARE; APPOINT; CONSECRATE] A DAY WHEN EVERYONE FASTS [FAST;*

*1:14].*
*   TELL EVERYONE TO STOP WORK [CALL A SACRED ASSEMBLY]!*
*BRING THE PEOPLE TOGETHER [ASSEMBLE/GATHER THE PEOPLE]*
*   AND MAKE THE MEETING HOLY FOR THE LORD [CONSECRATE/SANCTIFY THE CONGREGATION/ASSEMBLY].*
*BRING TOGETHER THE ELDERS,*
*   AS WELL AS THE CHILDREN,*
*   AND EVEN BABIES THAT STILL FEED AT THEIR MOTHERS' BREASTS.*
*THE BRIDEGROOM SHOULD [LET THE BRIDEGROOM] COME FROM HIS ROOM [INDICATING URGENCY; NEWLY MARRIED MEN WERE EXEMPT FROM MILITARY SERVICE; DEUT. 20:7; 24:5],*
*   THE BRIDE FROM HER BEDROOM [CHAMBER].*
*THE [LET THE] PRIESTS, THE LORD'S SERVANTS [WHO MINISTER BEFORE THE LORD], SHOULD CRY [WEEP]*
*   BETWEEN THE ALTAR AND THE ENTRANCE TO THE TEMPLE [PORTICO; VESTIBULE].*
*THEY SHOULD [LET THEM] SAY, "LORD, HAVE MERCY ON [SPARE] YOUR PEOPLE.*
*   DON'T LET THEM [YOUR INHERITANCE/POSSESSION] BE PUT TO SHAME [MOCKED; A REPROACH];*
*   DON'T LET OTHER NATIONS MAKE FUN OF THEM [THEM A BYWORD].*
*DON'T LET [WHY SHOULD THE] PEOPLE IN OTHER NATIONS ASK,*
*   'WHERE IS THEIR GOD?'"*
(Joel 2:12-17)

It should be our most basic desire to see people right with God. We can't say we believe in healing and deliverance if we are unwilling to work and labor for this end goal, in and of itself. Healing and deliverance starts when we are willing to teach the faith, the truth of the faith that will help people come into a greater spiritual place with God and transform their lives, even if they have already belonged to a chain of churches prior and been saved, on the books, for twenty-plus years. If it is God's will that we prosper and be in good health, even as our soul is in good health, it takes a lifetime of teaching and blessing to walk in that truth and grow into all God would have us to become.

*MY DEAR FRIEND [BELOVED], I PRAY THAT YOU ARE DOING WELL [PROSPERING] IN EVERY WAY [ALL RESPECTS] AND THAT YOUR HEALTH IS GOOD, JUST AS YOUR SOUL IS DOING FINE [IT IS WELL WITH YOUR SOUL; YOUR SOUL IS PROSPERING]. [FOR] I WAS VERY HAPPY WHEN SOME BROTHERS AND SISTERS CAME AND TOLD ME [TESTIFIED] ABOUT THE*

*TRUTH IN YOUR LIFE AND HOW YOU ARE FOLLOWING [WALKING IN] THE WAY OF TRUTH [2 JOHN 4]. NOTHING GIVES ME GREATER JOY THAN TO HEAR THAT MY CHILDREN [MEMBERS OF THE CHURCH UNDER HIS SPIRITUAL CARE] ARE FOLLOWING THE WAY OF TRUTH [WALKING IN THE TRUTH]*. (3 John 2-4)

Our bodies follow our spirits; the natural follows the spiritual; the growth and change we desire first rests in our desire to get right with God. Our healing rests in our faith, which means we must believe in God's power to transform, and we will only believe that if we are taught that. As we tap into God's grace, into the fullness therein, and realize what we need to learn and teach in the faith to pass it on and promote healing in the lives of those we reach.

Essentials we should always teach for the prospering of the soul include:

- The nature of God
- Relationship with God
- Hearing from God
- The redemptive work of Christ
- Salvation
- The work of the Holy Spirit
- Spiritual gifts
- Faith
- Grace
- Divine love
- Christian living
- Kingdom purpose
- Understanding the Scriptures

## **Beliefs that keep our souls – and beings – from prospering**

Spiritual warfare, healing, and deliverance aren't exactly unheard-of topics in many Christian circles today. In many circles, these issues might be too relevant and, in the forefront, causing believers to almost develop a paranoid sense of their reality. We are often running from different enemies we can't see and clearly identify, and one of the biggest reasons we find ourselves running is because the enemies we often embrace as real are somehow, in some way, within us.

There are many false theories about things that don't really exist as pertain to healing and deliverance, but are blamed for any number of issues, ailments, or problems in one's life. We will call these things "deliverance junk" because they sound good, they sound spiritual and deep, but there is no substance or reality behind them. Because many Christians feel threatened by the issues of the day and the problems of the modern world, there is almost an attempt to over spiritualize things and make everything a spiritual problem or of a spiritual origin when no such thing may, in actuality, be real.

An example of this was during the 2016 presidential run. The Donald Trump-Hillary Clinton face-off was, no doubt, a media frenzy, and many Americans were mortified at the direction the campaign took, overall. Yet Christian camps didn't do what they could to die down the commotion – they fed it, and thrived on it, as they turned the American presidential debate into a spiritual battle.

*Sosthenes, Apollo, Cephas, Tychius, Epaphroditus, Caesar, and Onesiphorus of Seventy Disciples (10th-11th Century)*

Donald Trump was compared to all sorts of Biblical figures, such as Abraham, Moses, and the Prophet Elijah, said to come and take down "Jezebel." There are a host of reasons why this comparison simply doesn't fit. For one, the United States government is not a monarchy. There was no female ruler to "take down," because Hillary Clinton was not in office at the time of the election. There was no way anyone could possibly compare Donald Trump with Elijah, because he was not a prophet, and had not been told by God to do anything. Elijah was never sent to take down Jezebel; in fact, he was never sent to Jezebel, period (1 Kings 18:1-3, 16-19).

These are glaring examples of spiritual deliverance junk, propaganda that was taught to see a spiritual rescuer or shaping in a bigger battle for the American culture, but it had absolutely no Biblical substance behind it. Anyone who desired to take the time and read the story of Elijah and Ahab could have discovered this for themselves and seen the gaping holes in the formulated theory and drama that was behind it. The overwhelming evidence that those who are most at the helm of shaping Christian thought and public opinion are clearly Biblically illiterate, in the name of being super-spiritual, was both disheartening and frustrating to watch, but they give us a great insight into why our souls are not prospering. The more we follow people who promote deliverance junk, the more we are going to find ourselves empty. We cannot find God in dramatic spiritual stories, or constant political bickering, and the more that's all we want...the more we will not find ourselves healed, delivered, or prospering spiritually.

It's an unfortunate fact that our world is sensationalistic and we reward people for being outrageous, doing dangerous or unseemly stunts, behaving in an unseemly manner, acting aggressively, loudly, and inappropriately. This behavior is not just rewarded in the world; it is also rewarded in the church. We love preachers who entertain us the most, and the ante for entertainment keeps increasing with each passing year. We now think the key to deliverance is in spiritual intimidation: we'll be more outrageous, louder, bigger, and bolder than the "spirits" we think we see in people, and we'll intimidate others through it. That is exactly the attitude we saw prevalent in the 2016 election: a victory wrought by bullying, outrageous behavior, and intimidation that we have now deemed as "spiritual warfare." This is not, in any sense of concept, how any of this works. Nobody in the Bible ever went "demon hunting," chasing down problems and issues within people and their situations. Rather, they learned how to properly identify things and handle them when they recognized their presence. Jesus never screamed and yelled at demons, and neither did any of the apostles or early disciples. They spoke and addressed issues with authority, but their purpose was not to demean or intimidate to get an entertainment factor out of what was going on.

Too many in Christianity are trying to make a name for themselves through fancy deliverance messages and healing words that aren't healing or delivering in the least. We aren't asking the hard questions of healing and deliverance, and too many are having the opportunity to claim to be this or that because we get caught up in the spiritual messes they create, thinking them to be valid spiritual battles. If you listen to the wrong people, there are battles everywhere: in the government, between Christians and Muslims everywhere in the world, between religion and spirituality, between family members, and hostilities everywhere you look. Yes, there are disagreements. Yes, as we learned from subsequent chapters, spiritual warfare is real. Many of these hostilities, however, are created in the minds of people who want to sell books and CDs and stories to make you think things are far worse than they may, in reality, be. These things are distractions to real help, to real issues, and to real outlooks we need to have to stand as believers today.

*A THIEF COMES [ONLY] TO STEAL AND KILL AND DESTROY, BUT I CAME TO GIVE LIFE [THAT THEY MIGHT HAVE LIFE]—LIFE IN ALL ITS FULLNESS [ABUNDANCE].* (John 10:10)

*GLORY BE TO GOD, WHO CAN [NOW TO THE ONE WHO IS ABLE TO] DO MUCH, MUCH MORE THAN ANYTHING WE CAN ASK OR IMAGINE THROUGH HIS POWER WORKING IN US.* (Ephesians 3:20)

*LET US LOOK ONLY TO [KEEP OUR EYES ON] JESUS, THE ONE WHO BEGAN [PIONEER/FOUNDER OF; OR LEADER/PRINCE OF] OUR FAITH AND WHO MAKES IT PERFECT [COMPLETES IT]. HE SUFFERED DEATH ON [ENDURED] THE CROSS, ACCEPTING THE SHAME AS IF IT WERE NOTHING [DISREGARDING/DESPISING THE SHAME] BECAUSE OF THE JOY THAT GOD PUT BEFORE [LAY AHEAD FOR] HIM. AND NOW HE IS SITTING AT THE RIGHT SIDE [HAND] OF GOD'S THRONE [1:3; 13; Ps. 110:1].* (Hebrews 12:2)

The first thing we must do if we want to see true spiritual and physical prosperity is stop looking for a dramatic show, and start learning how to discern situations, people, and needs. We need to rise to meet those needs, rather than doing the same things all the time to try and get a rise out of others. We must stop paying so much attention to attention-seeking spirits and let some things die down on their own. We must gain a sense of composure, of calmness and spiritual presence, because that is when the Spirit has the best chance of speaking to us, working through us, and our reception to His presence in our midst.

The second thing we need to be willing to do is admit where we are failing people in areas of healing and deliverance. There are things we bill as normal or as a part of healing and deliverance that are not, in actuality, a part of deliverance or healing ministry. These include:

- **Soul ties:** Often promoted as part of purity culture, soul ties are supposedly spiritual connections that people have from prior relationships, especially if those relationships were sexual in nature. It's a sort of spiritual transference from one person to another by which it's believed those spirits carried by past lovers and significant others can impact or damage our lives now. Those ties can make it impossible to be in new relationships, to attract good relationships, and can make a total mockery of our lives, inducing poor health, spiritual distance, or issues with God.

There is no question that "familiar spirits" within us can seek out others with certain spirits or issues, and there is also no question that relationships can cause different feelings, issues, or damages within us, as people. There is nothing to suggest, however, that soul ties are a real thing that exist between people who are involved in a sexual relationship. There is also nothing to suggest that people are spiritually damaged every time a relationship ends, or that spirits transfer between people who are intimately involved. It's also relevant to say there is no mention, nor evidence, of soul ties existing in the Bible, and this is a relevant proof because people were far more superstitious in Biblical times.

There are many reasons why sexual relationships can be complicated and difficult, whether someone is married to someone or not, and whenever someone has been in a detrimental relationship, that person needs time to heal from the loss and the hurt as they go through the different stages that require them to reframe their entire relationship. The last thing someone needs is to think all the problems they have in their lives are due to a relationship that has now ended and start blaming someone else for their issues.

- **Generational curses:** If you ask a deliverance minister about issues or problems you might have, odds are good they will blame it on "generational curses." The way this theory runs is that the things our ancestors did, at some point in history, can cause "cursing," down to the present day. This theory is especially popular if it appears issues have been problems for multiple generations, such as alcoholism, drug abuse, incest, or poverty.

  To understand the concept of cursing, one must first understand the precept of blessing. The underlying definition of blessing is the intervention of God in one's life, on one's behalf, for one's benefit and protection. A curse, rather than being seen as something that was a punishment or a generational ailment, was the removal of God's hand of blessing in people's lives. When it occurred in perpetual generations, it was because it took that many generations for the defect, sinful ways, or issue to be rooted out of the patterns of influence and genetic materials.

Generational curses were not ever used to explain patterns of personal behavioral choices, bad decisions, or to excuse bad behaviors. People were still required to be accountable and atone for their own sins and turn their ways around. The concept of using a "generational curse" to explain family behavior, even if it was generational, was unheard of in Biblical times and equally at odds with spiritual warfare.

- **Inherited curses:** Whether it's a genetic disease or inherited traits, many of these things are now deemed as "curses," things that are inherited through the bloodline due to the sins of the ancestors. There are many who believe that whatever our ancestors did, we, too, will do, and because of whatever they might have done in their lives, we are inheriting those curses down to the present day.

  There is no evidence such a concept exists, or that multiple generations can inherit curses through disease, genetics, or inherited traits. There is likewise absolutely no evidence that genetic issues, traits, illnesses, or diseases are because of curses or transmitted because of curses.

- **Demonic bloodlines:** Akin to the issues of generational and inherited curses are those of the concept of demonism in one's bloodline, due to sin or some other issue of ancestral issues in the past. The difference between this concept and those of generational or inherited curses is that the issues are usually related to non-Christian activity (specifically witchcraft) as was practiced by one's ancestors. If you think about this one, it has a particular air of ridiculousness to it, because if you go far enough back in everyone's bloodline, there is witchcraft in all of them. Every person has a relative who either practiced witchcraft, engaged in superstitious behavior, cast a spell, sought out a witch for a problem, or believed someone had come against them with witchcraft because of the realities of our cultural ancestors. To say that we are now suffering because of something someone didn't know better about doing decades, centuries, or thousands of years ago, is absurd.

- **"Taking on the nature" of someone else:** This is not just a Christian belief; in fact, its origins are from the occult and New Age Movements. It is prevalent in different forms throughout religious circles. It is the belief that due to some practice, be it medical (such as a blood transfusion), spiritual, physical, or otherwise, one can adapt the nature of another person and cease to become who they are. For example, if one is sexually involved with a murderer, it is believed that a "murdering spirit" can change the nature of the other person, who was never a murderer to begin with. The belief is from old junk science, the belief that one's personality was dictated by singular forces or by a change in someone's physical being, and that morality, integrity, and character could be that easily influenced or changed.

Our spiritual deliverances – or our spiritual issues – or our general life issues, for that matter – are not as simple as one or two specific things that may exist somewhere in our familial lineage, especially given most of the same things exist in people's lineages, if one goes back far enough. All of us have something, all of us have our issues, and all of us have our battles with sin that require us to deal with ourselves, examine our own pasts and our own hurts, and come to a place where we are willing to grow and develop ourselves out of our positions of sin and into spiritual victory. We should all be willing to man up, as the expression goes, look at ourselves, and stop blaming everyone else and everything else for whatever is not going right with us spiritually.

These things are all proof that many people seek fame, but don't seek to do the real work of ministry that requires healing and time with others. Many are trying to make a name for themselves, they are trying to sound deep and discover causes for spiritual problems in the Body today, and instead, they are being messy and introducing false doctrines, panic, and spiritual error that is causing many to need healing and deliverance from things that otherwise may not be an issue in their lives.

## Witchcraft in today's church

Let us never be so naive as to believe witchcraft does not exist in the church. Witchcraft, as we have examined, is a part of life and being, in many different facets, throughout all cultures. The occult is not as distinct from the church as we might like to believe, as there are many churchgoers who also double as practicing witches and/or occultists. Sometimes the biggest offerings, the biggest churchgoers, and the biggest names in our congregations come from people who double-time as practitioners of magic, New Age principles, or who are active in the occult and occult rituals. There's a reason that much of occult symbolism and imagery comes from Christianity, and why many occultists used Christianity as their launching point for occult spirituality. The occult is a part of our reality, and while we do not have to accept its power, we do have to recognize it is very real and manifesting in many ways in our congregations.

This is not just about people who try to manipulate or exert power over others, although that is a part of witchcraft. We could talk extensively about that, but we need to pay attention to the way in which witchcraft has become commonplace in many churches, in its forms that are recognizable as exactly what they are. Numerology (playing different number games and assigning meanings to years based on vague assumptions of numerological significance) has become a regular tradition among televangelists, who do not even apply the numerological relevance properly. The concept of sending trinkets, charms, and amulets through the mail has all but become commonplace, as each item is believed to have some sort of relevance if one uses it, and then sends money. The church abounds with people who practice forms of mesmerism, hypnotism, spellcasting, among other things.

*SAY, 'THIS IS WHAT THE LORD GOD SAYS: HOW TERRIBLE IT WILL BE FOR [WOE TO THE] WOMEN WHO SEW MAGIC CHARMS [BANDS] ON THEIR WRISTS AND MAKE VEILS [OR HEADBANDS] OF EVERY LENGTH TO TRAP PEOPLE! YOU RUIN [ENTRAP; ENSNARE] THE LIVES [SOULS] OF MY PEOPLE BUT TRY TO [WILL YOU...?] SAVE YOUR OWN LIVES [SOULS]. FOR HANDFULS OF BARLEY AND PIECES [SCRAPS] OF BREAD, YOU HAVE DISHONORED [PROFANED; RITUALLY] ME AMONG MY PEOPLE. BY LYING TO MY PEOPLE, WHO LISTEN TO LIES, YOU HAVE KILLED PEOPLE [PUT TO DEATH SOULS] WHO SHOULD NOT DIE, AND YOU HAVE KEPT ALIVE THOSE WHO SHOULD NOT LIVE.*

"'SO THIS IS WHAT THE LORD GOD SAYS: I AM AGAINST YOUR MAGIC CHARMS [BANDS], BY WHICH YOU TRAP [ENSNARE; HUNT] PEOPLE [SOULS] AS IF THEY WERE BIRDS. I WILL TEAR THOSE CHARMS [THEM] OFF YOUR ARMS, AND I WILL FREE THOSE PEOPLE [SOULS] YOU HAVE TRAPPED [ENSNARE; HUNT] LIKE BIRDS. I WILL ALSO TEAR OFF YOUR VEILS [OR HEADBANDS] AND SAVE MY PEOPLE FROM YOUR HANDS. THEY WILL NO LONGER BE TRAPPED BY YOUR POWER [PREY IN YOUR HAND]. THEN YOU WILL KNOW THAT I AM THE LORD. BY YOUR LIES YOU HAVE CAUSED THOSE WHO DID RIGHT TO BE SAD [DISHEARTENED THE RIGHTEOUS], WHEN I DID NOT ·MAKE THEM SAD [GRIEVE THEM]. AND YOU HAVE ENCOURAGED THE WICKED NOT TO STOP BEING WICKED [TURN FROM THEIR WICKED WAYS], WHICH WOULD HAVE SAVED THEIR LIVES. SO YOU WILL NOT SEE FALSE VISIONS OR PROPHESY [PRACTICE DIVINATION] ANYMORE, AND I WILL SAVE MY PEOPLE FROM YOUR POWER [HANDS] SO YOU WILL KNOW THAT I AM THE LORD.'" (Ezekiel 17:18-23)

*I WISH YOU WOULD BE PATIENT WITH ME EVEN WHEN I AM A LITTLE FOOLISH [IN A LITTLE FOOLISHNESS], BUT YOU ARE ALREADY DOING THAT. [FOR] I AM JEALOUS OVER YOU WITH A JEALOUSY THAT COMES FROM GOD [OR GODLY JEALOUSY]. I PROMISED TO GIVE YOU TO CHRIST, AS YOUR ONLY HUSBAND. I WANT TO GIVE YOU AS HIS PURE BRIDE [VIRGIN]. BUT I AM AFRAID THAT YOUR MINDS WILL BE LED AWAY [OR CORRUPTED] FROM YOUR TRUE [SINCERE] AND PURE FOLLOWING OF CHRIST JUST AS EVE WAS TRICKED [DECEIVED] BY THE SNAKE [SERPENT] WITH HIS EVIL WAYS [CUNNING; CRAFTINESS; GEN. 3:1-6]. YOU ARE VERY PATIENT WITH [WILLINGLY PUT UP WITH; GLADLY TOLERATE] ANYONE WHO COMES TO YOU AND PREACHES A DIFFERENT JESUS FROM THE ONE WE PREACHED. YOU ARE VERY WILLING TO ACCEPT A SPIRIT THAT IS DIFFERENT FROM THE SPIRIT YOU RECEIVED, OR A GOSPEL THAT IS DIFFERENT FROM THE ONE YOU ACCEPTED [OR RECEIVED FROM US].*

*I DO NOT THINK THAT THOSE "GREAT [SUPER-] APOSTLES" ARE ANY BETTER THAN I AM. I MAY NOT BE A TRAINED SPEAKER, BUT I DO HAVE KNOWLEDGE. WE HAVE SHOWN THIS TO YOU CLEARLY IN EVERY WAY.*

*WAS IT WRONG [A SIN] FOR ME TO HUMBLE [LOWER] MYSELF AND HONOR [EXALT; LIFT UP] YOU BY PREACHING GOD'S GOOD NEWS [GOSPEL] TO YOU WITHOUT PAY? I ACCEPTED PAY FROM OTHER CHURCHES, TAKING THEIR MONEY ["ROBBING" THEM] SO I COULD SERVE YOU. IF I NEEDED SOMETHING WHEN I WAS WITH YOU, I DID NOT TROUBLE [BURDEN] ANY OF YOU. THE BROTHERS WHO CAME FROM MACEDONIA GAVE ME ALL THAT I NEEDED. I DID NOT ALLOW MYSELF TO DEPEND ON [BECOME A BURDEN TO] YOU IN ANY WAY, AND I WILL NEVER DEPEND ON YOU [KEEP DOING THIS]. NO ONE IN ACHAIA*

[SOUTHERN GREECE; 1:1] WILL STOP ME FROM BRAGGING [BOASTING] ABOUT THAT. I SAY THIS WITH THE TRUTH OF CHRIST IN ME [OR BY CHRIST'S TRUTH IN ME! A STRONG VOW OR OATH]. AND WHY DO I NOT DEPEND ON YOU [WHY]? DO YOU THINK IT IS BECAUSE I DO NOT LOVE YOU? GOD KNOWS THAT I LOVE YOU [GOD KNOWS!].

AND I WILL CONTINUE DOING WHAT I AM DOING NOW, BECAUSE I WANT TO STOP THOSE PEOPLE FROM HAVING A REASON TO BRAG [BOAST]. THEY WOULD LIKE [ARE LOOKING FOR AN OPPORTUNITY] TO SAY THAT THE WORK THEY BRAG [BOAST] ABOUT IS THE SAME AS [EQUAL TO] OURS. SUCH MEN ARE NOT TRUE APOSTLES [FALSE APOSTLES; PSEUDO-APOSTLES] BUT ARE WORKERS WHO LIE [DECEITFUL WORKERS]. THEY CHANGE THEMSELVES TO LOOK LIKE [...DISGUISING THEMSELVES AS; ...MASQUERADING AS] APOSTLES OF CHRIST. THIS DOES NOT SURPRISE US [AND NO WONDER, SINCE...]. EVEN SATAN CHANGES HIMSELF TO LOOK LIKE [DISGUISES HIMSELF AS; MASQUERADES AS] AN ·ANGEL [MESSENGER] OF LIGHT [TRYING TO FOOL PEOPLE INTO THINKING HE IS FROM GOD, WHO IS PURE LIGHT]. SO IT DOES NOT SURPRISE US IF SATAN'S SERVANTS ALSO MAKE THEMSELVES LOOK LIKE [MASQUERADE AS] SERVANTS WHO WORK FOR WHAT IS RIGHT [OF RIGHTEOUSNESS]. BUT IN THE END THEY WILL BE PUNISHED FOR WHAT THEY DO [THEIR END WILL MATCH THEIR DEEDS]. (2 Corinthians 11:1-15)

[FOR] MANY FALSE TEACHERS [DECEIVERS] ARE IN [HAVE GONE OUT INTO] THE WORLD NOW [MARK 13:5-6, 22] WHO DO NOT CONFESS THAT JESUS CHRIST CAME TO EARTH AS A HUMAN [IN THE FLESH]. ANYONE WHO DOES NOT CONFESS THIS IS A FALSE TEACHER [THE DECEIVER] AND AN ENEMY OF CHRIST [THE ANTICHRIST; ONE WHO RADICALLY OPPOSES CHRIST; 1 JOHN 2:18, 22; 4:3]. BE CAREFUL [WATCH] YOURSELVES THAT YOU DO NOT LOSE EVERYTHING YOU HAVE WORKED FOR, BUT THAT YOU RECEIVE YOUR FULL REWARD.

ANYONE WHO GOES BEYOND [RUNS AHEAD OF] CHRIST'S TEACHING AND DOES NOT CONTINUE TO FOLLOW ONLY HIS TEACHING [ABIDE/REMAIN IN IT] DOES NOT HAVE GOD. BUT WHOEVER CONTINUES TO FOLLOW [ABIDES/REMAINS IN] THE TEACHING OF CHRIST [THE TEACHING] HAS BOTH THE FATHER AND THE SON. IF SOMEONE COMES TO YOU AND DOES NOT BRING THIS TEACHING, DO NOT GREET [WELCOME] THAT PERSON OR ACCEPT [RECEIVE] THEM INTO YOUR HOUSE. IF YOU WELCOME SUCH A PERSON, YOU SHARE [PARTICIPATE] IN THE EVIL WORK. (2 John 7-11)

We need to pay careful attention to those who work and labor among us. There are many who need healing and deliverance, and will simply not submit themselves to the process, right in our midst. Not everyone operates by the Spirit of God, no matter what they might claim. There are those who might seem super-spiritual and ready to help, at any time, who might come against us in the spiritual realm. There is no reason for panic or alarm, and no reason to look at everyone with suspicion, but it is very real that we must be discerning and attentive to the leading of the Spirit when it comes to who – and what – we let things do for us.

## **What are we selling?**

If you've ever watched a deliverance minister, you will probably note a certain method and style. Deliverance (and often healing ministers, too) are quick to sell you anything and everything that you feel is lacking in your life. If it's wrong, they can fix it. If you've got anything that keeps you from fitting in, from being like everyone else, the deliverance minister will take care of it. Anything you want to change, anything you want to make you fit in better, anything you want to make adjust to more of a surface appearance as being like everyone else, the deliverance minister can "cure."

*People in church*

When it comes to deliverance ministry, the major sell is "normal," not "healing." The promise of the deliverance minister is to help someone who, in some way, does not fit in, to get along like the others in church, pushing conformity. In other words, the agenda for deliverance is often not freedom, helping people to accept who they are in Christ, overcome obstacles, or even find healing – it's to make them the same as everyone else.

The purpose of deliverance and healing should never, ever be to push a conformity agenda within those who are most in need of healing and deliverance in one's life. Healing and deliverance should not be a weapon used to make people feel more like outcasts, more unwelcome, more like there is something wrong with them, more alienated from God, and more like they are never going to get where they need to be. Behind healing and deliverance should be the peace and wholeness of God, something that offers completion, purpose, and an embrace of God's love in a way they would not find otherwise.

When we walk in the ministry of healing and deliverance, it should reflect just that: healing.

*The Lord hears good people when they [they] cry out to Him,*
  *and He saves them from all their troubles [distress].*
*The Lord is close to the brokenhearted,*
  *and He saves those whose spirits have been crushed.*
(Psalm 34:17-18)

*The Lord helps [supports] those who have been defeated [fallen]*
  *and takes care of [lifts up] those who are in trouble [bowed down].*
(Psalm 145:14)

*After Jesus called the crowd to Him, He said, "Listen and understand what I am saying [try to understand]. It is not what people put into their mouths [goes into the mouth] that makes them unclean [pollutes/defiles the person]. It is what comes out of their mouths that makes them unclean [pollutes/defiles the person]."*

*Then His followers [disciples] came to Him and asked, "Do you know that the Pharisees are angry [offended; shocked] because of what you said?"*

*Jesus answered, "Every plant that my Father in heaven has not planted Himself will be pulled up by the roots. Stay away from the Pharisees [leave/ignore them]; they are blind leaders [guides]. And if a blind person leads [guides] a blind person, both will fall into a ditch [pit; hole]."*

*Peter said, "Explain the example [parable] to us."*

*Jesus said, "Do you still not understand [Are you still so dull/foolish]? Surely you know [Don't you know...?] that all the food that enters the mouth goes into the stomach and then goes out of the body [into the sewer/latrine]." But what people say with their mouths [the things that come out of the mouth] comes from the way they think [the heart]; these are the things that make people unclean [pollute/defiled a person]. [For] Out*

*OF THE MIND [HEART] COME EVIL THOUGHTS [INTENTIONS; IDEAS], MURDER, ADULTERY, SEXUAL SINS, STEALING, LYING [FALSE WITNESS/TESTIMONY], AND SPEAKING EVIL OF OTHERS [SLANDER; BLASPHEMY]. THESE THINGS MAKE PEOPLE UNCLEAN [POLLUTED; DEFILED]; EATING WITH UNWASHED HANDS DOES NOT MAKE THEM UNCLEAN [POLLUTED; DEFILED]."* (Matthew 15:10-20)

Any time we attempt to use deliverance and healing for the purpose of deception, to manipulate people, or to try and push an agenda, we are promoting a concept of witchcraft. The purpose of church is not to make everyone the same, but to offer to each one whatever is needed in Christ to help them to be whole, just as Christ would desire them to be. Instead of treating deliverance and healing ministry like they are nothing more than giant gimmicks, we need to focus on the work of deliverance and let the fruit therein speak for itself. Deliverance and healing are not about conformity, but about transformation in Christ. That may, or may not, look like whatever we perceive as "correct."

This also draws our attention to the intense need to transform ourselves through the work of healing and deliverance. As conduits of healing and or deliverance, we, too, should undergo a transformation. It should not just be about making other people better, but about adapting a better sense of healing and deliverance within ourselves, desiring to become better models of the love of God as we understand better what people go through in their lives. This is different from pity; it is compassion, something that rises within us that desires to do good for others and to watch God intervene and change their lives in a way we cannot materialize in and of ourselves.

## **The mess of modern Christian doctrine**

Honesty in the issues that arise for healing and deliverance ministry, particularly the way they are used in the church today, also gives rise to the reality of messy modern Christian doctrine that is often the perpetrator of hurt, offense, damage, and true need of healing in today's world. Christian understanding, tradition, and teaching are used any assortment of ways in our churches, and this has often led to a strong justification in fleshly, errored attitudes that cause people to need healing and deliverance. This may sound contradictory to what Christianity is supposed to be about, and it certainly is. Unfortunately, however, whether fleshly or not, it is often the center and front stage of where we are at in church today.

*A BROTHER WHO HAS BEEN INSULTED [OFFENDED] IS HARDER TO WIN BACK THAN A WALLED CITY,*
*AND ARGUMENTS SEPARATE PEOPLE LIKE THE BARRED GATES OF A PALACE.*
(Proverbs 18:19)

The topic of "church hurt" is often spoken of in hushed terms, something that church acknowledges exists, but we really wish it didn't. The reason for this is simple: church hurt, as a designation, has given the church a bad name, a bad rap, and caused an overall sense of bad press as we survey the scene of church. Abuses of all sorts exist in every religion, but those in church often get extensive media attention. Many have wondered, why is this?

"Church hurt" is a general term used to identify hurt, pain, offense, or damage one encounters from someone who was either a leader of, a part of, or claimed to be a part of a church group or a group that claims Christian association. It is a social term rather than a clinical one, which means there's no specific association, nor definition, to define it. Sometimes church hurt is over something very minor, something that someone else might not find to be that big a deal or make that big a fuss about. Other times, church hurt is something larger than life, a radically abusive or offensive experience that changes a person's entire view of themselves and their faith. When someone has been hurt by people in church, they often cite it as a reason why they are hesitant to join back into another church group, give up on God and faith all together, or to receive certain aspects of Christian doctrine. For this reason, no matter how spurious we may feel a claim to church hurt might be, we must take church hurt seriously.

Modern-day church is often a contrast in extremes, all of which take a highly imbalanced approach to spiritual matters and faith living. When we start falling off in either/or ditches, we find people are extremely quick to be offensive, thus people are also quick to be offended. Churches that thrive on emotionalism breed strong, impassioned emotions (both positive and negative alike), and that means people who are a part of those groups are going to respond with strong emotions, in kind. It also means we are quick to defend behavior that might otherwise be deemed unacceptable. In examining what we see in church, we should also examine ourselves, on the following issues:

- **Using Scripture to defend unseemly, hostile, petty, or "fleshly" behavior:** There are many who argue for the sake of truth and are quick to point out that Jesus called the Scribes, Pharisees, and leaders any assortment of names, and that for us to do the same is acceptable, as well. The problem with this theory and attitude is that none of us are Jesus, and things Jesus said to them are within all of us. For Jesus to execute judgment is His place, not ours, and knowing what was within the hearts of others, Jesus rightly called out whatever was within them. We can easily misjudge someone's thoughts or motives and we can easily be wrong in what we think about someone, based about our own fleshly understandings. There is a major difference between Jesus' righteous judgment and just calling out people with vulgarity and unkindness because we are in the flesh, caught up in a rush of our emotions. Using Scripture to justify this kind of behavior is a direct contradiction to the purpose and work of Scripture, and it distorts its purpose in the lives of others. Behaving badly is wrong, no matter what "name" or justification it may be done in.

- **Being overly obsessed with holiness:** No one is questioning the Biblical call to be holy, but the definition of "holy" is not what we define as "holiness" today. Most associate holiness with denominational rules that revolve around exterior appearances and behaviors, such as clothing, length of hair, make-up, or activities such as drinking, smoking, or dancing. The problem is that holiness is about separateness, used to identify the people of God as different in their character than those who are not believers. The identification originally marked the Israelites as a nation set apart, who would not engage in the idolatry and practices associated with idolatry of their surrounding neighbors. That is the same for us, today: our practices and our ways should reflect a different character, a different spirit, than those of others around us. This designation is different from the concept of secularism, which did not exist in Biblical times, and means that it is different than not listening to music, wearing make-up, how we define our attire, or dancing. Certainly, we should follow Biblical protocol at all times, but this is different from defining everything we may disagree with personally in culture as a standard rule across the board.

- **Implementing rules, regulations, or attitudes about matters that don't reflect Christian character:** Not every trendy, contemporary doctrine, teaching, or thought present in Christianity today is Biblical. Much of what is taught reflects cultural desires to appear trendy, contemporary, or some version of what worked for someone else, and now the hope is that it will work for this group over here, as well. We pass a lot of things off as Biblical that simply are not: politics, American values, our own opinions, Christian-themed movies and merchandise, and sometimes even Biblical footnotes with a particular cultural slant. These thoughts and attitudes reflect in the way we treat people, especially if they are culturally unaccepted or culturally different, and they have the ability to turn the Gospel into something exclusive to others.

- **Minding our own selves too much:** If you are so busy taking care of your family, yourself, your own needs, your own opinions (and forcing others to think you feel that way because you are a Christian) and your own pursuits or aspirations to be good to somebody else, you are going to inadvertently hurt someone else or cause their view of Christianity to change.

*THE SON OF MAN WILL SEND OUT HIS ANGELS, AND THEY WILL GATHER [REMOVE; WEED] OUT OF HIS KINGDOM ALL WHO [OR ALL THINGS THAT] CAUSE SIN [ARE STUMBLING BLOCKS] AND ALL WHO DO EVIL [BREAK GOD'S LAW].* (Matthew 13:41)

*FOR THAT REASON WE SHOULD [OR LET US] STOP JUDGING EACH OTHER. WE MUST MAKE UP OUR MINDS NOT TO DO ANYTHING THAT WILL MAKE ANOTHER CHRISTIAN SIN [PLACE A STUMBLING BLOCK OR OBSTACLE BEFORE A BROTHER OR SISTER].* (Romans 14:13)

*BROTHERS AND SISTERS, I ASK [URGE; ENCOURAGE] YOU TO LOOK OUT FOR THOSE WHO CAUSE DIVISIONS [DISSENSION] AND WHO UPSET OTHER PEOPLE'S FAITH [CREATE OBSTACLES/STUMBLING BLOCKS]. THEY [OR SUCH THINGS] ARE AGAINST THE TRUE TEACHING YOU LEARNED, SO STAY AWAY FROM THEM.* (Romans 16:17)

*WE TRY NOT TO BE A PROBLEM [CAUSE OFFENSE; PLACE AN OBSTACLE/STUMBLING BLOCK] FOR ANYONE IN ANY WAY, SO THAT NO ONE WILL FIND FAULT WITH OUR WORK [MINISTRY].* (2 Corinthians 6:3)

Before we do anything – be it tell people we have a healing gift, operate healing and deliverance, or take that step to make that sort of claim in our lives, we need to carefully examine and judge our own motives. There are many in healing and deliverance who have caught on to a trend, a fast-moving, fast-paced scene where healing and deliverance sound like a good choice, like something to garner attention or maybe even help someone else. We need to speak and act rightly and step up and make sure we are not deliberately seeking to offend others with our actions. As a rule, Christians have a reputation for being virulent, shoving their doctrine, values, beliefs, and opinions down the throats of others. If we are to be agents of healing, we must lay ourselves down; our tendencies to act in the flesh and try to do what we do out of a sense of being right; and accept that others do not have the same opinions we have. We must then learn to embrace the character of Christ, as much as we claim to like His teaching, and take that nature on ourselves as agents of healing and deliverance.

*Praying Savior, TIvadar Kosztka Csontvary (1853-1919)*

## **More than one way to heal or deliver**

It has already been mentioned that healing and deliverance doesn't just take place at the altar, in a church, during a time deliberately set aside for healing and deliverance. Healing takes place in hospital rooms, in prayer closets, in counseling sessions, in support group meetings, in small groups, and as individuals seek God for their change, right where they are.

[THEREFORE] SINCE WE HAVE A GREAT HIGH PRIEST [2:17-18], JESUS THE SON OF GOD, WHO HAS GONE INTO [ASCENDED TO; OR PASSED THROUGH] HEAVEN [OR THE HEAVENS], LET US HOLD ON [FIRMLY] TO THE FAITH WE HAVE [THE

*CONFESSION/PROFESSION; OF OUR FAITH]. FOR OUR HIGH PRIEST IS ABLE [FOR WE DO NOT HAVE A HIGH PRIEST WHO IS UNABLE] TO UNDERSTAND [SYMPATHIZE WITH] OUR WEAKNESSES. HE WAS TEMPTED IN EVERY WAY THAT WE ARE, BUT HE DID NOT SIN. LET US, THEN, FEEL VERY SURE THAT WE CAN COME BEFORE [CONFIDENTLY APPROACH] GOD'S THRONE WHERE THERE IS GRACE [OF GRACE; AS OPPOSED TO A THRONE OF JUDGMENT AND CONDEMNATION]. THERE WE CAN RECEIVE MERCY AND GRACE [FIND GRACE] TO HELP US WHEN WE NEED IT [AT THE RIGHT TIME].* (Hebrews 4:14-16)

Yes, God does heal during meetings. Offering prayer or altar calls for healing during church services or meetings, and offering specialized healing or deliverance events, are wonderful things to do. There is no discouragement in such things, and no attempt or desire to put such things down. The only time any situation involving healing and deliverance should be questioned or condemned is if it is false, done under false pretenses, or causing harm to others. Healing and deliverance can and do come out of meetings, and the expectation that such can and should happen therein is an important and powerful precept, something we should explore and delve into as believers.

The point of this is that the form of healing is not dependent on a specific format, especially one that we have established as the sole or only way to promote or facilitate healing or deliverance in one's life. We can get so comfortable with certain ways of doing things that we overlook the fact that maybe it isn't the way someone needs healing, or the way that healing will be most effective in someone else's life. Just because it is what we are used to does not mean it is what's needed. Some different methods of healing include:

- Counseling
- Altar side-counseling (taking someone in another room to continue the process started at the altar)
- Private prayer and devotion
- Private deliverance and healing
- Small group
- Christian-based hospice care
- Acceptance

## Can Christians be in need of healing or deliverance?

There's a great debate raging about whether or not a Christian can be possessed, or even in need of healing. Some believe it is impossible, and others believe it's not. There doesn't seem to be a lot of middle ground between the two. Those who think it is impossible for a believer to need healing or deliverance believe those who come forward and admit their need aren't really Christians, because if they were, they wouldn't have their need for healing or deliverance, as they exist.

*When Jesus went to Peter's house, He saw that Peter's mother-in-law was sick in bed [lying down] with a fever. Jesus touched her hand, and the fever left her. Then she stood up and began to serve [waiting on] Jesus.*

*That evening people brought to Jesus many who had demons [were demon-possessed]. Jesus spoke and the demons left them [drove/cast out the demons with a word/command], and he healed all the sick. He did these things to bring about [fulfill] what Isaiah the prophet had said:*

*"He took our suffering [sicknesses; weaknesses]*
  *and carried [bore; removed] our diseases [Is. 53:4]."*
(Matthew 8:14-17)

Whether or not we want to admit it, we live in a fallen world, and there is forever a part of our lives that needs the redemptive power of Christ. None of us are perfect, and none of us are living in a perfect state. We all still encounter temptations, fall into sin, and deal with issues. We don't do things perfectly, and any of us can fall and need restoration. Thinking that we exist in a perfected state is not only dangerous, but it will also cause us to refrain from seeking out assistance when we need restoration.

We also experience things that ail us because we live in this world. Sin may be the root cause, but it doesn't mean that every time we deal with or encounter something that is due to our own sin or because we've fallen into spiritual possession. Sometimes things happen because they happen, and we need healing and restoration as a source of refreshment and encouragement in our lives. To deny believers of this because of the embrace of a theological technicality or a spiritual outlook is not right, nor is it spiritually proper.

## The healing and deliverance of non-Christians – can it happen?

The last thing we will examine in this chapter is the question as to whether non-Christians can receive healing or deliverance. One of the biggest questions many pose is can a non-Christian be healed or receive healing from God in an "unsaved" state. It is of great theological debate and one that deserves examination, especially considering the issue above. If true Christians don't need healing and deliverance and non-Christians can't be healed or delivered, then who can receive healing? Who is it for, if it's not for Christians and non-Christians, because then that eliminates everyone, in the entire world?

If we look at examples of healing and deliverance in the Scriptures, the majority of incidents happened to non-Christian individuals:

WHEN JESUS ENTERED THE CITY OF CAPERNAUM, AN ARMY OFFICER [CENTURION] CAME TO HIM, BEGGING [PLEADING] FOR HELP. THE OFFICER SAID, "LORD, MY SERVANT IS AT HOME IN BED. HE CAN'T MOVE HIS BODY [IS PARALYZED] AND IS IN MUCH PAIN [SUFFERING TERRIBLY]."

JESUS SAID TO THE OFFICER, "I WILL GO AND HEAL HIM. [OR SHALL I GO AND HEAL HIM?]"

THE OFFICER ANSWERED, "LORD [OR SIR], I'M NOT WORTHY [DO NOT DESERVE] FOR YOU TO COME INTO MY HOUSE. YOU ONLY NEED TO ·COMMAND IT [SAY THE WORD], AND MY SERVANT WILL BE HEALED. [FOR] I, TOO, AM A MAN ·UNDER THE AUTHORITY OF OTHERS [L UNDER AUTHORITY], AND I HAVE SOLDIERS UNDER MY COMMAND. I TELL ONE SOLDIER, 'GO,' AND HE GOES. I TELL ANOTHER SOLDIER, 'COME,' AND HE COMES. I SAY TO MY ·SERVANT [SLAVE], 'DO THIS,' AND MY ·SERVANT [SLAVE] DOES IT."

WHEN JESUS HEARD THIS, HE WAS AMAZED. HE SAID TO THOSE WHO WERE FOLLOWING HIM, "I TELL YOU THE TRUTH, THIS IS THE GREATEST FAITH I HAVE FOUND [L I HAVEN'T FOUND SUCH FAITH], ·EVEN IN ISRAEL [OR IN ALL ISRAEL]. MANY PEOPLE WILL COME FROM THE EAST AND FROM THE WEST AND WILL ·SIT AND EAT [RECLINE; THE POSTURE FOR A BANQUET OR DINNER PARTY] WITH ABRAHAM, ISAAC, AND JACOB IN THE KINGDOM OF HEAVEN [THE MESSIANIC BANQUET, A METAPHOR FOR GOD'S RESTORATION OF CREATION; IS. 25:6–8]. BUT THOSE PEOPLE WHO SHOULD BE IN [THE HEIRS OF; OR THE SUBJECTS OF; THE SONS OF] THE KINGDOM WILL BE THROWN OUTSIDE INTO THE DARKNESS [INTO THE OUTER DARKNESS], WHERE PEOPLE WILL CRY AND

GRIND THEIR TEETH WITH PAIN [THERE WILL BE WEEPING AND GNASHING OF TEETH; METAPHORS FOR AGONY AND TORMENT]."

THEN JESUS SAID TO THE OFFICER [CENTURION], "GO HOME. YOUR SERVANT WILL BE HEALED JUST AS YOU BELIEVED HE WOULD [LET IT BE DONE FOR YOU JUST AS YOU HAVE BELIEVED]." AND HIS SERVANT WAS HEALED THAT SAME HOUR [EXACT TIME]. (MATTHEW 8:5-13)

JESUS ANSWERED, "GOD SENT ME [I WAS SENT] ONLY TO THE LOST SHEEP, THE PEOPLE [HOUSE] OF ISRAEL."

THEN THE WOMAN CAME TO JESUS AGAIN AND BOWED BEFORE HIM AND SAID, "LORD, HELP ME!"

JESUS ANSWERED, "IT IS NOT RIGHT TO TAKE THE CHILDREN'S BREAD AND GIVE [THROW] IT TO THE DOGS." ["CHILDREN" REFERS TO ISRAEL; "DOGS" TO THE GENTILES.]

THE WOMAN SAID, "YES, LORD, BUT EVEN THE DOGS EAT THE CRUMBS THAT FALL FROM THEIR MASTERS' TABLE."

THEN JESUS ANSWERED, "[O] WOMAN, YOU HAVE GREAT FAITH! I WILL DO WHAT YOU ASKED [LET IT BE DONE FOR YOU AS YOU WISH]." AND AT THAT MOMENT [FROM THAT HOUR] THE WOMAN'S DAUGHTER WAS HEALED. (Matthew 15:24-28)

ONE DAY PETER AND JOHN WENT TO THE TEMPLE AT THREE O'CLOCK [THE NINTH HOUR; TIME WAS RECKONED FROM DAWN, TRADITIONALLY SET AT 6 AM], THE TIME SET EACH DAY FOR THE AFTERNOON PRAYER SERVICE [THE HOUR OF PRAYER]. THERE, AT THE TEMPLE GATE CALLED BEAUTIFUL GATE [UNKNOWN LOCATION, PERHAPS ONE OF SEVERAL GATES BETWEEN VARIOUS COURTYARDS], WAS A MAN WHO HAD BEEN CRIPPLED [LAME] ALL HIS LIFE [FROM HIS MOTHER'S WOMB]. EVERY DAY HE WAS CARRIED TO [PEOPLE WOULD LAY HIM AT] THIS GATE TO BEG FOR MONEY [ALMS] FROM THE PEOPLE GOING INTO THE TEMPLE [THE TEMPLE COMPLEX; 2:46]. THE MAN SAW PETER AND JOHN GOING INTO THE TEMPLE [COURTS; 2:46] AND ASKED THEM FOR MONEY [ALMS; HELP]. PETER AND JOHN LOOKED STRAIGHT [INTENTLY] AT HIM AND SAID, "LOOK AT US!" THE MAN LOOKED AT [PAID ATTENTION TO] THEM, THINKING THEY WERE GOING TO GIVE HIM SOME MONEY [SOMETHING]. BUT PETER SAID, "I DON'T HAVE ANY SILVER OR GOLD, BUT I DO HAVE SOMETHING ELSE I CAN GIVE YOU [WHAT I DO

*HAVE, I GIVE TO YOU]. BY THE POWER [IN THE NAME] OF JESUS CHRIST FROM NAZARETH [OR THE NAZARENE], STAND UP AND WALK [LUKE 5:23]!" THEN PETER TOOK THE MAN'S RIGHT HAND AND LIFTED [RAISED] HIM UP. IMMEDIATELY THE MAN'S FEET AND ANKLES BECAME STRONG. HE JUMPED UP [LEAPED], STOOD ON HIS FEET, AND BEGAN TO WALK. HE WENT INTO THE TEMPLE [COURTS; 2:46] WITH THEM, WALKING AND JUMPING [LEAPING] AND PRAISING GOD [IS. 35:4-6]. ALL THE PEOPLE RECOGNIZED HIM AS THE CRIPPLED [LAME] MAN WHO ALWAYS SAT BY THE BEAUTIFUL GATE [3:2] BEGGING FOR MONEY [ALMS; HELP]. NOW THEY SAW THIS SAME MAN WALKING AND PRAISING GOD, AND THEY WERE AMAZED. THEY WONDERED HOW THIS COULD HAPPEN [OR ...AND STUNNED/ASTONISHED AT WHAT HAD HAPPENED].* (Acts 3:1-10)

*THE APOSTLES DID MANY SIGNS [MIRACLES] AND MIRACLES [WONDERS] AMONG THE PEOPLE. AND THEY WOULD ALL MEET TOGETHER ON SOLOMON'S PORCH [SEE 3:11]. NONE OF THE OTHERS DARED TO JOIN THEM, BUT [OR EVEN THOUGH] ALL THE PEOPLE RESPECTED [PRAISED; HIGHLY REGARDED] THEM. MORE AND MORE MEN AND WOMEN BELIEVED IN THE LORD AND WERE ADDED TO THE GROUP [CROWD; MULTITUDE] OF BELIEVERS. [AS A RESULT] THE PEOPLE PLACED THEIR SICK ON BEDS [COTS] AND MATS IN THE STREETS, HOPING THAT WHEN PETER PASSED BY AT LEAST HIS SHADOW MIGHT FALL ON [SOME OF] THEM. CROWDS CAME FROM ALL THE TOWNS AROUND JERUSALEM, BRINGING THEIR SICK AND THOSE WHO WERE BOTHERED [TORMENTED] BY EVIL [UNCLEAN; DEMONS WERE VIEWED AS "UNCLEAN" OR DEFILING SPIRIT-BEINGS] SPIRITS, AND ALL OF THEM WERE HEALED.* (ACTS 5:12-16)

*ONCE, WHILE WE WERE GOING TO THE PLACE FOR PRAYER, A SERVANT [SLAVE] GIRL MET US. SHE HAD A SPECIAL SPIRIT [SPIRIT/DEMON OF DIVINATION/PREDICTION; PYTHON SPIRIT; PYTHON WAS THE SERPENT GOD THAT GUARDED THE DELPHIC ORACLE; THE TERM CAME TO BE USED OF THE ABILITY TO PREDICT THE FUTURE] IN HER, AND SHE EARNED A LOT OF MONEY FOR HER OWNERS BY TELLING FORTUNES. THIS GIRL FOLLOWED PAUL AND US, SHOUTING, "THESE MEN ARE SERVANTS [SLAVES] OF THE MOST HIGH GOD. THEY ARE TELLING YOU HOW YOU CAN BE SAVED [THE WAY/PATH OF SALVATION]."*

*SHE KEPT THIS UP FOR MANY DAYS. THIS BOTHERED [ANNOYED; EXASPERATED] PAUL, SO HE TURNED AND SAID TO THE SPIRIT, "BY THE POWER [NAME] OF JESUS CHRIST, I COMMAND YOU TO COME OUT OF HER!" IMMEDIATELY, [THAT VERY HOUR] THE SPIRIT CAME OUT.* (Acts 16:16-18)

GOD USED PAUL TO DO [THROUGH THE HANDS OF PAUL DID] SOME VERY SPECIAL [EXTRAORDINARY] MIRACLES. SOME PEOPLE TOOK HANDKERCHIEFS [FACE CLOTHS] AND CLOTHES [WORK APRONS; OR HAND TOWELS] THAT PAUL HAD USED [THAT HAD TOUCHED PAUL; FROM HIS SKIN] AND PUT THEM ON THE SICK. WHEN THEY DID THIS, THE SICK WERE HEALED [THE DISEASES LEFT THEM] AND EVIL SPIRITS LEFT [CAME OUT OF] THEM. (Acts 19:11-12)

AFTER THE MEN [MANY] HAD GONE WITHOUT FOOD [OR LOST THEIR APPETITE] FOR A LONG TIME, PAUL STOOD UP BEFORE THEM AND SAID, "MEN, YOU SHOULD HAVE LISTENED TO ME [OBEYED ME; TAKEN MY ADVICE]. YOU SHOULD NOT HAVE SAILED FROM CRETE. THEN YOU WOULD NOT HAVE ALL THIS TROUBLE AND LOSS. BUT NOW I TELL [URGE; ADVISE] YOU TO CHEER UP [KEEP UP YOUR COURAGE] BECAUSE NONE OF YOU WILL DIE [BE LOST]. ONLY THE SHIP WILL BE LOST. LAST [THIS] NIGHT AN ANGEL CAME TO [STOOD BY] ME FROM THE GOD I BELONG TO AND WORSHIP. THE ANGEL SAID, 'PAUL, DO NOT BE AFRAID. YOU MUST STAND BEFORE CAESAR. AND GOD HAS PROMISED YOU THAT HE WILL SAVE THE LIVES OF [GRACIOUSLY GRANTED SAFETY TO] EVERYONE SAILING WITH YOU.' SO MEN, HAVE COURAGE. [FOR] I TRUST IN GOD THAT EVERYTHING WILL HAPPEN AS HIS ANGEL TOLD ME [I HAVE BEEN TOLD]. BUT WE WILL CRASH [RUN AGROUND] ON AN [SOME/A CERTAIN] ISLAND." (Acts 27:21-26)

On the other hand, Christians also received healing and deliverance:

SO ANANIAS WENT TO THE HOUSE OF JUDAS. HE LAID [PLACED] HIS HANDS ON SAUL AND SAID, "BROTHER SAUL, THE LORD JESUS SENT ME. HE IS THE ONE YOU SAW [WHO APPEARED TO YOU] ON THE ROAD ON YOUR WAY HERE. HE SENT ME SO THAT YOU CAN SEE AGAIN AND BE FILLED WITH THE HOLY SPIRIT." IMMEDIATELY, SOMETHING THAT LOOKED LIKE FISH SCALES [OR FLAKES] FELL FROM SAUL'S EYES, AND HE WAS ABLE TO SEE AGAIN! THEN SAUL GOT UP AND WAS BAPTIZED. AFTER HE ATE SOME FOOD, HIS STRENGTH RETURNED. (Acts 9:17-19)

THE NIGHT BEFORE HEROD WAS TO BRING HIM TO TRIAL [OUT; EITHER FOR TRIAL OR FOR EXECUTION], PETER WAS SLEEPING BETWEEN TWO SOLDIERS, BOUND WITH TWO CHAINS. OTHER SOLDIERS WERE GUARDING THE DOOR OF THE JAIL. SUDDENLY, AN ANGEL OF THE LORD STOOD THERE, AND A LIGHT SHINED IN THE CELL. THE ANGEL STRUCK [TAPPED; POKED] PETER ON THE SIDE AND WOKE HIM UP. "HURRY! GET UP!" THE ANGEL SAID. AND THE CHAINS FELL OFF PETER'S HANDS [WRISTS]. THEN THE ANGEL TOLD HIM, "GET DRESSED [OR PUT ON YOUR BELT] AND PUT ON YOUR SANDALS." AND PETER DID. THEN THE ANGEL SAID, "PUT ON YOUR COAT [WRAP YOUR

*COAT/CLOAK AROUND YOU] AND FOLLOW ME." SO PETER FOLLOWED HIM OUT, BUT HE DID NOT KNOW IF WHAT THE ANGEL WAS DOING WAS REAL; HE THOUGHT HE MIGHT BE SEEING A VISION. THEY WENT PAST THE FIRST AND SECOND GUARDS AND CAME TO THE IRON GATE THAT SEPARATED THEM FROM [LED TO] THE CITY. THE GATE OPENED BY ITSELF FOR THEM, AND THEY WENT THROUGH IT. WHEN THEY HAD WALKED DOWN ONE STREET, THE ANGEL SUDDENLY LEFT HIM.* (Acts 12:6-10)

*WHEN WE WERE SAFE ON LAND [REACHED SAFETY], WE LEARNED THAT THE ISLAND WAS CALLED MALTA [58 MILES SOUTHWEST OF SICILY]. THE PEOPLE WHO LIVED THERE [NATIVE PEOPLE; BARBARIANS; A TERM REFERRING TO NON-GREEK SPEAKERS] WERE VERY GOOD [KIND] TO US. BECAUSE IT WAS RAINING AND VERY COLD, THEY MADE A FIRE AND WELCOMED ALL OF US. PAUL GATHERED A PILE OF STICKS [BRUSHWOOD] AND WAS PUTTING THEM ON THE FIRE WHEN A POISONOUS SNAKE [VIPER] CAME OUT BECAUSE OF THE HEAT AND BIT [FASTENED ITSELF TO] HIM ON THE HAND. THE PEOPLE LIVING ON THE ISLAND [NATIVE PEOPLE; 28:2] SAW THE SNAKE [CREATURE; ANIMAL] HANGING FROM PAUL'S HAND AND SAID TO EACH OTHER, "THIS MAN MUST BE A MURDERER! HE DID NOT DIE IN [ESCAPED FROM] THE SEA, BUT JUSTICE [DIKĒ; PRONOUNCED DI-KÁY; THE GODDESS OF JUSTICE] DOES NOT WANT [HAS NOT ALLOWED] HIM TO LIVE." BUT PAUL SHOOK THE SNAKE [CREATURE; ANIMAL] OFF INTO THE FIRE AND WAS NOT HURT [SUFFERED NO HARM]. THE PEOPLE [THEY] THOUGHT THAT PAUL WOULD SWELL UP OR FALL DOWN DEAD. THEY WAITED AND WATCHED HIM FOR A LONG TIME, BUT NOTHING BAD [UNUSUAL] HAPPENED TO HIM. SO THEY CHANGED THEIR MINDS AND SAID, "HE IS A GOD!"* (Acts 28:1-9)

It's obvious from reading the Scriptures that God desires everyone to be healed and delivered, and that such is available as a testimony to all, that any might find Him.

## **Chapter 12 Assignment**

- Based on an experience you have either had with healing and deliverance yourself (as a minister or as a recipient) or one you have heard of or researched, construct an essay (5-8 sentences) on the importance of healing and deliverance in the lives of believers today.

*Offering support*

# - CHAPTER THIRTEEN -
## Ethics in Healing and Deliverance

*The Lord has told you, human [O man], what is good;*
*He has told you what He wants [the Lord requires] from you:*
*to do what is right to other people [just],*
*love being kind to others [mercy; lovingkindness],*
*and live humbly, obeying [walk humbly with] your God.*
(Micah 6:8)

It is truly unfortunate that we do not consider ethics to be a part of Christian ministry, especially when it comes to healing and deliverance. Ethics are foundational, professional codes of conduct observed in most professions, but seldom, if ever, observed within ministry. There was a time in history when Christian ministers were expected to uphold the conducts of their denominations and were quickly stripped of papers when they failed to line up with the established requirements. Now, it is not uncommon to see people who have issues with one organization jump to another, not disclosing the reasons why they had issues where they did, and continuing their issues all along, all the way through yet another organization.

As believers, we should embody ethical principles, no matter what our job description may be. As Christian ministers, ethics should extend to every area of our ministries, and such is essential if we are working in healing and deliverance. It's easy for us to see the many ways people cross boundaries, mistreat others, and become downright abusive when they do not operate by regulation, ethical principle, and respect for others.

Ethics are not things that are always naturally inborn; in fact, ethics often address areas of potential issue, conflict, and integrity we might not ever consider without an outside suggestion. When we abide by conducts of ethics, however, it enhances our ministries, the principles behind which help to keep our reputations solid and allow the Spirit of God to move freely through our work.

## The principles of Christian ethics

Ethics are standards of honesty, broken down and assessed by situations and circumstances, for every aspect of an individual's dealings with other human beings in an interactive sense. In other words, ethics are principles by which we live and interact with individuals when dealing in business, ministry, and other professional settings. Rather than believing Christians are not called to ethics, Jesus holds us to a far higher ethical standard than the world abides by.

*BUT IF YOU DON'T WANT [IT IS UNDESIRABLE/EVIL IN YOUR EYES] TO SERVE THE LORD, YOU MUST CHOOSE FOR YOURSELVES TODAY WHOM YOU WILL SERVE. YOU MAY SERVE THE GODS THAT YOUR ANCESTORS WORSHIPED WHEN THEY LIVED ON THE OTHER SIDE OF THE EUPHRATES RIVER [RIVER], OR YOU MAY SERVE THE GODS OF THE AMORITES WHO LIVED IN THIS LAND. AS FOR ME AND MY FAMILY [HOUSE], WE WILL SERVE THE LORD.* (Joshua 24:15)

*NO ONE CAN SERVE TWO MASTERS [LORDS]. THE PERSON WILL HATE ONE MASTER AND LOVE THE OTHER, OR WILL FOLLOW [BE DEVOTED/LOYAL TO] ONE MASTER AND REFUSE TO FOLLOW [DESPISE] THE OTHER. YOU CANNOT SERVE BOTH GOD AND WORLDLY RICHES [MONEY; MAMMON].* (Matthew 6:24)

*ONE OF THE TEACHERS OF THE LAW [SCRIBES] CAME AND HEARD JESUS ARGUING WITH THE SADDUCEES. SEEING THAT JESUS GAVE GOOD ANSWERS TO THEIR QUESTIONS, HE ASKED JESUS, "WHICH OF THE COMMANDS IS MOST IMPORTANT?"*

*JESUS ANSWERED, "THE MOST IMPORTANT COMMAND IS THIS: 'LISTEN, PEOPLE OF ISRAEL [HEAR, O ISRAEL]! THE LORD OUR GOD IS THE ONLY LORD [ONE LORD]. LOVE THE LORD YOUR GOD WITH ALL YOUR HEART, ALL YOUR SOUL, ALL YOUR MIND, AND ALL YOUR STRENGTH' [DEUT. 6:4-5; THESE ARE THE OPENING WORDS OF THE SHEMA, THE*

*PRAYER SAID BY PIOUS JEWS TWICE A DAY]. THE SECOND COMMAND IS THIS: 'LOVE YOUR NEIGHBOR AS YOU LOVE YOURSELF' [LEV. 19:18]. THERE ARE NO COMMANDS ·MORE IMPORTANT [GREATER] THAN THESE."*

*THE MAN ANSWERED, "THAT WAS A GOOD ANSWER [WELL SAID!], TEACHER. YOU WERE RIGHT WHEN YOU SAID GOD IS THE ONLY LORD [ONE] AND THERE IS NO OTHER GOD BESIDES HIM. ONE MUST LOVE GOD WITH ALL HIS HEART, ALL HIS MIND, AND ALL HIS STRENGTH. AND ONE MUST LOVE HIS NEIGHBOR AS HE LOVES HIMSELF. THESE COMMANDS ARE MORE IMPORTANT THAN ALL THE ANIMALS [BURNT OFFERINGS] AND SACRIFICES WE OFFER TO GOD [1 SAM. 15:22; HOS. 6:6; MIC. 6:6-8]."*

*WHEN JESUS SAW THAT THE MAN ANSWERED HIM WISELY [THOUGHTFULLY; WITH INSIGHT], JESUS SAID TO HIM, "YOU ARE CLOSE TO THE KINGDOM OF GOD." AND AFTER THAT, NO ONE WAS BRAVE ENOUGH [DARED] TO ASK JESUS ANY MORE QUESTIONS.* (Mark 12:28-24)

*LIVE IN PEACE [HARMONY] WITH EACH OTHER. DO NOT BE PROUD [ARROGANT; HAUGHTY], BUT MAKE FRIENDS WITH THOSE WHO SEEM UNIMPORTANT [ASSOCIATE WITH THE HUMBLE/THOSE OF LOW SOCIAL STATUS; OR BE WILLING TO DO LOWLY TASKS]. DO NOT THINK HOW SMART [WISE; SUPERIOR] YOU ARE.*

*IF SOMEONE DOES WRONG TO YOU, DO NOT PAY HIM BACK BY DOING WRONG TO HIM [REPAY NO ONE EVIL FOR EVIL]. TRY TO DO [OR CONSIDER CAREFULLY] WHAT EVERYONE THINKS IS RIGHT [OTHERS VIEW AS GOOD/HONORABLE; IS GOOD/NOBLE BEFORE ALL PEOPLE]. DO YOUR BEST TO [IF POSSIBLE, FROM YOUR PART,] LIVE IN PEACE WITH EVERYONE.* (Romans 12:16-18)

*BE FULL OF JOY [REJOICE] IN THE LORD ALWAYS. I WILL SAY AGAIN, BE FULL OF JOY [REJOICE].*

*LET EVERYONE SEE THAT YOU ARE GENTLE [KIND; CONSIDERATE; PATIENT]. THE LORD IS COMING SOON [OR CLOSE AT HAND; NEAR]. DO NOT WORRY [BE ANXIOUS] ABOUT ANYTHING, BUT PRAY AND ASK GOD FOR EVERYTHING YOU NEED [OR MAKE YOUR REQUESTS KNOWN TO GOD], ALWAYS GIVING THANKS. AND GOD'S PEACE, WHICH IS SO GREAT WE CANNOT UNDERSTAND IT [TRANSCENDS/SURPASSES ALL COMPREHENSION], WILL KEEP [GUARD] YOUR HEARTS AND MINDS IN CHRIST JESUS.*

*[FINALLY; IN CONCLUSION; OR NOW THEN] BROTHERS AND SISTERS, THINK ABOUT [FOCUS YOUR THOUGHTS ON; FILL YOUR MINDS WITH] THINGS THAT ARE TRUE AND HONORABLE AND RIGHT [JUST] AND PURE AND BEAUTIFUL [LOVELY] AND RESPECTED [COMMENDABLE]. IF THERE IS ANYTHING THAT IS GOOD [MORALLY EXCELLENT] AND WORTHY OF PRAISE, THINK ABOUT [FOCUS YOUR THOUGHTS ON; FILL YOUR MINDS WITH] THESE THINGS.* (Philippians 4:4-8)

*EACH OF YOU HAS RECEIVED A GIFT TO USE TO SERVE OTHERS. BE GOOD SERVANTS [STEWARDS; MANAGERS] OF GOD'S VARIOUS GIFTS OF GRACE [ROM. 5:15-16; 6:23].* (1 Peter 4:10)

In pointing out that we must be good stewards and cannot serve multiple masters, Jesus is telling us about honesty, the bottom line of ethics. As Christians, we cannot tell others of Christ or claim to be workers in the harvest of the Lord and then behave without honesty and ethics. Being a Christian means being honest and ethical in every situation. We are to be honest with our employers or employees, honest with those we minister to and reach out to with the Gospel, honest in all our business and work dealings, and most importantly, honest with ourselves and our God as to which master we are serving.

Christian ethics demand that we abide by such honest principles despite what anyone else may be doing. It is often difficult and tempting to look at leaders who seem to get away with anything and everything, and think that they aren't following ethical precepts, so your ministry shouldn't, either. As servants living in the house and Kingdom of God, under His leadership, we cannot turn aside and try to live by the household regulations of other masters. Our households, businesses, and practices should always point to and reflect the precepts of our God. As we consider the needs of others and the comfort of others through ethics, we can remain truthful and objective and find a place of living in peace with other people. We may not like what everyone else does or agree with it, we can still have respect and regard for them as human beings created in the image of God. Ethics force us to live in such a way that considers the best interests of others as well as ourselves. The basic principles of general Christian ethics include:

- **Honesty:** The word "honesty" refers to a characteristic entitling reverence, respect, dignity, majesty, and sanctity. The honest life is a pure and honorable existence, noteworthy by its excellent character. In ethics, we are honest with God, honest with ourselves, and honest with others through living by ethical standards in all we do. Living by standards of honesty creates a real Christian person in a real and living Kingdom who serves a real and true God. Ethics provides honest things for all people, not just a select few.

- **Equality:** Many Christians are comfortable only with other Christians who look like, sound like, and act just like them. They don't consider those who are somehow different from them to be valid believers. They refuse to pray for others, receive others, or care about what others go through, often believing the hardships of those who are different are somehow deserved. Ethical Christians pray for all, whether someone is the same as them, or not; in their afflictions, suffering, difficulties, and situations; in thanksgiving for all God has done and we ask God to bless those who have blessed us, whether they are believers or not. An ethical Christian can reach out and work with anyone, whether they the same or not, and able to interact with anyone in the world, as so led.

- **Divine principle:** We should never live in such a way that our lives are a distraction to the Gospel. Such creates a negative witness and makes sure others do not want to hear about the Gospel. Our work is participation in God's principles, and we are called to uphold divine principles in the things we set out to do. Even when it's difficult, we should never forget God in our work.

- **Respect:** We should extend courtesy to all people, no matter who they are. It is our position to honor personal integrity, grace, and dignity to the essence of the human person. It is our position to focus on those honest things that are praiseworthy: true, honest, just, pure, lovely, and of good report.

- **Love of God and neighbor:** The heart of ethics is love for God above all and love of neighbor as oneself. If we love God before all, we will have no idols, we will not be profane with God's Name, we will honor God, and we will honor others.

## Codes of professional ethics

The concept of professional ethics are often more direct than Christian ethics, because they aren't so much about reflecting a lifestyle of faith as they are about making sure the job gets done and everyone's boundaries are respected as they are completed. As ministers involved in healing and deliverance ministry, we have a job to get done, and boundaries to respect. Christian ethics provide us a base for a spiritual foundation to ethics, and professional ethics give us ideas as to how to complete those tasks in a professional setting. Specific rules for professional ethical codes vary by profession, but universal codes include:[1]

*Ethics*

- Striving for excellence
- Trustworthiness
- Courtesy and respect
- Honesty, openness and transparency
- Competent and continually improving
- Play by the rules
- Act honorably and with integrity
- Respect confidentiality
- Set a good example

## Legalities of healing and deliverance ministry

Laws as pertain to healing and deliverance ministry are often nonexistent in the United States, because ministry of any sort falls under the heading of the First Amendment. Any time a practice is challenged or taken to legal authorities, legal agencies, such as courts, are hesitant to get involved. There is also the issue that people, as a rule, attend churches, ministries, and willingly submit to the practices therein with their full legal consent. If someone desires to leave a ministry or church, or to refuse to submit to a practice, they have the legal right to do so, unless they are held against their will. No matter how controversial a practice may be or even detrimental, legalities are often hesitant to step in and assist. The only cases where the state or government is willing to get involved relates to the imposition of a practice deemed unsafe, dangerous, or unethical to a minor, who is considered legally incapable of giving consent to such a practice. Even in cases where jurisdictions come against the practices of the group, it usually falls on the parents' involvement with the organization, and the parents lose custody for willingly submitting their child to the care of the group (child endangerment or abuse). When the group is mentioned in action, it is often in situations where a child is notably harmed, such as physical or sexual assault and battery.

Worldwide, the situation involving religious legalities and abuses does vary, but prosecution for various religious-based offenses are often not pursued, sometimes at all. There are some nations that do attempt to regulate such matters, but they are often difficult to prosecute. When a church or ministry does something blatantly illegal or generally distasteful, the media often creates an atmosphere of negative public opinion, casting a light of disdain on such ministries.

*ALL OF YOU MUST YIELD [OBEY; SUBMIT; BE SUBJECT] TO THE GOVERNMENT RULERS [AUTHORITIES]. [BECAUSE; FOR] NO ONE RULES [THERE IS NO AUTHORITY] UNLESS GOD HAS GIVEN HIM THE POWER TO RULE [EXCEPT BY/THROUGH GOD], AND NO ONE RULES NOW WITHOUT THAT POWER FROM GOD [THOSE THAT EXIST ARE APPOINTED/ESTABLISHED BY GOD]. SO THOSE WHO ARE AGAINST THE GOVERNMENT [REBEL/RESIST THE AUTHORITY] ARE REALLY AGAINST [RESISTING; OPPOSING] WHAT GOD HAS COMMANDED [ORDAINED; INSTITUTED]. AND THEY WILL BRING PUNISHMENT [JUDGMENT] ON THEMSELVES. [FOR] THOSE WHO DO RIGHT [GOOD] DO NOT HAVE TO FEAR THE RULERS; ONLY THOSE WHO DO WRONG [EVIL] FEAR THEM. DO YOU WANT TO BE UNAFRAID OF THE RULERS [AUTHORITY]? THEN DO WHAT IS RIGHT [GOOD], AND THEY WILL PRAISE [COMMEND] YOU. THE RULER IS GOD'S SERVANT TO HELP YOU [FOR YOUR GOOD]. BUT IF YOU DO WRONG, THEN BE AFRAID. HE HAS THE POWER TO PUNISH [FOR HE DOES NOT BEAR THE SWORD IN VAIN]; HE IS GOD'S SERVANT TO PUNISH [AN AVENGER FOR (GOD'S) WRATH TO] THOSE WHO DO WRONG. SO YOU MUST YIELD [SUBMIT; BE SUBJECT] TO THE GOVERNMENT, NOT ONLY BECAUSE YOU MIGHT BE PUNISHED [OF WRATH], BUT BECAUSE YOU KNOW IT IS RIGHT [OF (YOUR) CONSCIENCE].* (Romans 13:1-5)

While many countries have differing laws as pertain to ministry regulation, there is one commonality healing and deliverance ministries have with all other forms of ministry, and that is the requirement to abide by the laws in place within one's nation of operation. This may sound obvious, but there are many who feel they can do whatever they desire from a legal perspective when it comes to ministry. Protection of the First Amendment (or any existing laws in place for religious worship in any country) do not eliminate the possibility for personal prosecution for breaking other existing legal regulations that are in place for the protection and benefit of their citizens. Being in ministry does not give us the right to abuse or mistreat others, and this becomes highly relevant when it comes to healing and deliverance ministry. The history of deliverance and healing ministry are riddled with unconventional methods that have been dehumanizing, demoralizing, abusive, and it is most disturbing that many of the individuals who engaged in such practices are heroes of the healing and deliverance movement. It is contrary to healing and deliverance to operate ministry like an outlaw, hurting and violating others. Thus, whether in ministry or not, it pays to live as a law-abiding citizen, to operate ministries within the values of good conduct and respect for others, and to consider the world of healing and deliverance ministry as a work of healing and deliverance, not abuse or mistreatment.

**Legal cautions**

Because healing and deliverance ministry are frequently unregulated, deliverance and healing ministers may use methods, treatments, or dispense advice that is outside of the bounds of good sense and legality. There are some things that, no matter how moved one might feel to say or do, should never be done:

- Never dispense medical or psychiatric advice without the proper education, training, credentials, and licensing. If you are not a medical doctor, psychiatrist, psychologist, or physician, do not, under any circumstances, dispense medical or mental health advice. This applies to things such as practice, alternative medical ideas, remedies, and medication.

- Healing and deliverance ministry should never be used in place of or as a substitution for medical advice.

- Deliverance and healing ministers should never advise people against seeking out medical attention for a situation deemed medically relevant or necessary.

- If an individual appears to be physically or mentally incapacitated, stop any such session immediately, and obtain the necessary medical assistance to aid in their issue.

- If an individual appears physically or mentally incapacitated from the beginning, including unable to give consent to any healing or deliverance method in any form, refrain from working with said individual.

- Never, under any circumstances, advise someone to stop taking prescribed medications or working prescribed therapies.

- Never, under any circumstances, involve yourself sexually with those you have served as an administrator of healing or deliverance.

- Do not engage in deliverance or healing sessions with minors, unaccompanied without a legal parent or guardian present.

## **Discrimination**

Discrimination is a legitimate problem in the church as a whole but becomes an additional issue when dealing in healing and deliverance ministry. As much as we like to talk in circles about judgment and try and make it acceptable, much of judgment – at least in a professional ethics capacity – applies under headings of discrimination. No matter what excuse we might come up for discrimination practices: adhering to the Bible, Biblical standards, upholding understandings of Biblical principles, or adhering to tradition, discrimination is wrong. Discrimination is wrong whether it is illegal or not, and whether we have so-called "rights" to hide behind in its defense.

This, however, does not mean it never happens. Often, healing and deliverance ministers come into the work with pretty heavy ideals about what requires and constitutes the need for healing and deliverance. Current events, preaching trends, commentaries by the so-called appointed experts of Christianity, and personal influences what a person deems as most relevant in healing and deliverance, and what they do not.

*DON'T JUDGE OTHERS, OR YOU WILL [SO THAT YOU WILL NOT] BE JUDGED. YOU WILL BE JUDGED IN THE SAME WAY THAT YOU JUDGE OTHERS, AND THE AMOUNT YOU GIVE TO OTHERS WILL BE GIVEN TO YOU [OR THE STANDARD YOU USE FOR OTHERS WILL BE THE STANDARD USED FOR YOU; WITH THE MEASURE YOU MEASURE, IT WILL BE MEASURED TO YOU].*

*A civil rights march in 1960s America*

*"WHY DO YOU NOTICE THE LITTLE PIECE OF DUST [SPECK; TINY SPLINTER] IN YOUR FRIEND'S [BROTHER'S (OR SISTER'S)] EYE, BUT YOU DON'T NOTICE [CONSIDER] THE BIG PIECE OF WOOD [LOG; PLANK; BEAM] IN YOUR OWN EYE? HOW CAN YOU SAY TO YOUR FRIEND [BROTHER], 'LET ME TAKE THAT LITTLE PIECE OF DUST [SPECK; SPLINTER] OUT OF YOUR EYE'? LOOK AT YOURSELF [BEHOLD]! YOU STILL HAVE THAT BIG PIECE OF WOOD [LOG; PLANK; BEAM] IN YOUR OWN EYE. YOU HYPOCRITE! FIRST, TAKE THE WOOD [LOG; PLANK; BEAM] OUT OF YOUR OWN EYE. THEN YOU WILL SEE CLEARLY TO TAKE THE DUST [SPECK; SPLINTER] OUT OF YOUR FRIEND'S [BROTHER'S] EYE.* (Matthew 7:1-5)

*IF YOU WANT GOOD FRUIT, YOU MUST MAKE THE TREE GOOD [GROW A GOOD/HEALTHY TREE]. IF YOUR TREE IS NOT GOOD [YOU GROW A BAD/UNHEALTHY TREE], IT WILL HAVE BAD FRUIT. A TREE IS KNOWN [IDENTIFIED; RECOGNIZED] BY THE KIND OF FRUIT IT PRODUCES. YOU SNAKES [BROOD/OFFSPRING OF VIPERS]! YOU ARE EVIL PEOPLE, SO HOW CAN YOU SAY ANYTHING GOOD? [FOR] THE MOUTH SPEAKS THE THINGS THAT ARE IN*

*[OVERFLOW FROM] THE HEART. GOOD PEOPLE HAVE GOOD THINGS IN THEIR HEARTS, AND SO THEY SAY GOOD THINGS [BRING FORTH GOOD THINGS FROM THE GOOD TREASURE/STOREHOUSE]. BUT EVIL PEOPLE HAVE EVIL IN THEIR HEARTS, SO THEY SAY EVIL THINGS [BRING FORTH EVIL THINGS FROM THE EVIL TREASURE/STOREHOUSE]. AND I TELL YOU THAT ON THE JUDGMENT DAY PEOPLE WILL BE RESPONSIBLE [GIVE AN ACCOUNTING; ANSWER] FOR EVERY CARELESS [IDLE; THOUGHTLESS; UNHELPFUL] THING [WORD] THEY HAVE SAID. THE WORDS YOU HAVE SAID WILL BE USED TO JUDGE YOU. SOME OF YOUR WORDS WILL PROVE YOU RIGHT, BUT SOME OF YOUR WORDS WILL PROVE YOU GUILTY [FOR BY YOUR WORDS YOU WILL BE ACQUITTED/JUSTIFIED, AND BY YOUR WORDS YOU WILL BE CONDEMNED]."* (Matthew 12:33-37)

*DON'T JUDGE OTHERS, AND YOU WILL NOT BE JUDGED. DON'T ACCUSE OTHERS OF BEING GUILTY [CONDEMN OTHERS], AND YOU WILL NOT BE ACCUSED OF BEING GUILTY [CONDEMNED]. FORGIVE [PARDON; RELEASE], AND YOU WILL BE FORGIVEN [PARDONED; RELEASED].* (Luke 6:37)

*[THEREFORE] IF YOU THINK YOU CAN JUDGE OTHERS, [O MAN,] YOU ARE WRONG [WITHOUT EXCUSE]. [FOR] WHEN YOU JUDGE THEM, YOU ARE REALLY JUDGING YOURSELF GUILTY, BECAUSE YOU [WHO ARE JUDGING] DO THE SAME THINGS THEY DO.* (Romans 2:1)

Being gifted with the gift of healing and deliverance does not mean one never has issues they have to work out in their own lives, nor does it mean the gift of healing does not operate within them absent of influences or ideas they already had before they started working or developing their spiritual gift in a greater way. There are also many, many things we say or imply in church that indicate overt judgment, which translates to discrimination. Nobody is more "in need of healing" than someone else. Someone is not more in need of healing because they identify as homosexual or bisexual, because they are a certain race, because they do not modify typical gender behavior, because they are a child of a single parent or divorced parents, because they were once a drug addict, they are poor, they don't fit in with the conventional church crowd, or they tend to not like or cater to traditional church whims. Using healing and deliverance for this means is nothing more than an attempt to bully people and use the concept of healing and deliverance for conformity means.

There's no question that people who fit into the categories may, indeed, have things in their lives they need to heal from, but that is different from assuming they need healing because of who they are or assuming the healing they need is related to who they are. These assumptions and attitudes are precisely where discrimination enters the picture. If we walk into a situation and start deciding what people need based on what we know or think we know about them, we aren't letting the Spirit speak to us about what they really need or seek in their lives. If we make healing about what we see on the surface, we will never be true healers because it's only about trying to change what one finds personally offensive or problematic.

Healing and deliverance should never be used to fuel a personal agenda, a personal vendetta, personal dislike, or personal discrimination against any group. Being in healing and deliverance ministry means being open to working with many types and groups of people and being willing to see them with spiritual eyes for the end goal of meeting the needs they have as are touched and helped through divine love. The needs may not be what we see or assume to be an issue on the surface, nor may they be what we feel is most necessary to fix about someone or something in their lives, but it is and will be whatever God deems most necessary in any one's life. Overcoming discrimination helps us better hear from God, listen to the needs people tell us they have, and hear what may be a true underlying need as a result of something else that is not easily identified because we are looking too hard easing our own discomfort with things we can easily identify or see.

## **Total quackery**

There are many questionable requirements many have as evidence of healing or deliverance. These include any method that may require the following:

- Vomiting or inducing vomiting
- Physical assaults, such as hitting, shoving, kicking, or punching
- Inducing mental torture or taunting
- Verbal abuse (including foul language)
- Emotional abuse
- Shaming or mocking
- Shocking the body with electric shock therapy
- Isolation camps
- Alternative therapies (attachment, hypnotherapy, etc.)

- Homemade healing remedies (enemas, poultices, herbal concoctions, etc.)

There is nothing that says such are indicative of healing or deliverance, and no evidence that anyone in the Bible engaged in such methods when it comes to operating the work of healing and deliverance. Engaging in such opens up an individual to the following:

- Termination of one's ministerial license and ordination credentials
- Disassociation from networks and ministry affiliations
- Investigation
- Loss of 501(c)(3) or other charitable status
- Legal prosecution
- Imprisonment

No minister has the right to claim a healing gift and engage in methods that are unsafe, unproven, and dehumanizing. It probably does not need to be mentioned, but such methods are also a total discredit to the concept of faith healing and our claim of its need in the world today.

*DO TO OTHERS WHAT [TREAT OTHERS AS] YOU WOULD WANT THEM TO DO TO [TREAT] YOU.* (Luke 6:31)

We don't talk about Jesus' advice to do unto others as we wish they would do unto us nearly enough. If you wouldn't want someone to do it to you, if it's something that wouldn't help you to heal, odds are good it's not something that is going to help someone else, either…so just don't do it.

## **The intense power of suggestion**

In the 1980s, tales of using children in Satanic rites and rituals through a day care center in California caused widespread panic. The children in the day care center supposedly reported sexual abuse, sexual encounters with animals, and other vile acts as part of occult and Satanic ritual while they were in the care of those who ran the day care center. People were afraid to leave their children in the care of others and a mass frantic panic ensued over something known as Satanic Ritual Abuse. Everyone was afraid their child may be caught up in something just as heinous and awful, and would be permanently damaged.

The problem with the widespread panic, the claims of Satanic Ritual Abuse, and the accusations of the children were that the entire situation turned out to be fake. The children were interrogated by investigators, counseled by psychologists and psychiatrists, and subjected to hours of repeated questioning that was all laced with suggestion and "memories" that never really happened. No physical, sexual, or satanic abuse ever occurred. There is now question as to whether Satanic Ritual Abuse ever existed anywhere. It was all clever suggestion that triggered something known as False Memory Syndrome. In cases of False Memory Syndrome, events were suggested to happen so frequently or powerfully to someone else that the individual genuinely believes that event really happened, and they think they are remembering it, when it is nothing more than suggestion.

Even though we might not see people engage in such obvious examples of implanting false memories, it is not all that uncommon to meet healing and deliverance ministers who use the power of suggestion to illicit something within a person that might not really even exist. For example, if a person finds out that as a young child, that person grew up without one of their parents, they may automatically say that person has an issue with "fatherlessness" or "motherlessness," and use this personal stance as a catalyst root for all sorts of issues a person may have. The catch is, just because someone grew up without a parent doesn't mean they necessarily have an issue with it, or that they still have an issue with it, or have not resolved that issue at an earlier point in time. This is an issue of a healing and deliverance minister taking on the nature of an untrained armchair psychologist, drawing on the ideas and thoughts purported by different sources they've heard throughout their lives, and suggesting an issue to be present without truly understanding and assessing whether that issue is one of note for that individual.

This is why people might feel better or seem to be better after a healing or deliverance situation initially, but their state of perceived healing or deliverance passes with time. Because someone was either shamed into accepting what was spoken over them or doesn't have the self-knowledge to reject those words, they take on whatever was spoken over them, which creates a feeling of guilt. This sense of guilt, which often feels like the person is at fault for whatever the issue is they've assigned to the individual, is unrealistic and imposed, and leads a person to feel like they must receive this message, because the assumption is it's coming from someone who hears from God, so it must be true. This is a form of spiritual abuse; it is using a perceived authority or concept of divine authority to try and intimidate someone else into receiving a word that changes their perception and concept of self. It might seem like one is "healed" or "delivered" because whatever was stirred up or promoted was declared gone or going away, but it never really existed in the first place. This is different from healing; what it is, however, is spiritual manipulation, and its own form of witchcraft.

*Now the snake [serpent] was the most clever [shrewd; cunning; crafty] of all the wild animals the Lord God had made. One day the snake said to the woman, "Did God really say that you must not eat fruit from any tree in the garden?"*

*The woman answered the snake [3:1], "We may eat fruit from the trees in the garden. But God told us, 'You must not eat fruit from the tree that is in the middle of the garden [the tree of the knowledge of good and evil]. You must not even touch it [Eve was adding to the divine command], or you will die.'"*

*But the snake [3:1] said to the woman, "You will [most certainly] not die. [For] God knows that if you eat the fruit from that tree [from it], [your eyes will be opened and] you will learn about [experience; know about] good and evil and you will be like God!"* (Genesis 3:1-5)

Healing and deliverance are supposed to be individual specific. This means the way it's approached may be different, in different circumstances, for different people. There is no one, singular, sweeping method that applies for every single person, because we are supposed to be tapping into the word of the Spirit and the leading of God to address whatever healing need is present. We may recognize that need through God's leading, we may be told what it is, or we may have no idea what specifically that need may be, but the tailor-made method is for the specific betterment of the need God recognizes at the baseline or cause of a problem or issue.

    Any minister who practices healing and deliverance needs the unique ability to discern God from themselves and their own thoughts, and how to exercise the gift of healing without using said gift to claim "healings" and "deliverances" that aren't either, at all. Suggestion can be very powerful, and standing in authority means it's often better not to say something without proof positive assurance you have heard from God in any situation.

## **Licensing and training**

Some argue that training and licensing shouldn't be necessary because such implies one doesn't have a "gift," but has, instead, learned the regiment of a system. This argument is used against any assortment of spiritually based subjects, but when put to the test, it does not hold up. Any individual can go to church, watch what ministers or others do, and decide they are a "minister" by studying the power of observation alone. Doing such is not as hard as you would think; it's actually quite common among groups that think gifts do not require training. Instead of being properly trained in the areas of ministry required for excellence and conduct, people mimic what they see and claim it is genuine, because it appears to look just like what someone else does.

It's true that a genuine gift comes from God, and no one can tell you how to operate a spiritual gift if you do not have it. If you can't heal, you won't be able to heal if you take a long-winded class on healing, or if you mimic the behavior you see around you. The gift comes from God, and one is either able to exercise it, or not, so there is no possible way that a good education can tell someone how to have a gift they don't have.

The role of education in any ministry setting is vital and essential, because we don't just need to have a gift; we need to know how to use that gift and the proper exercise of it. Anyone can have a gift and use it improperly, wrongly, or for wrong reasons.

*LEARNING [OPENING] YOUR WORDS GIVES WISDOM [ILLUMINATES; GIVES LIGHT] AND UNDERSTANDING FOR THE FOOLISH [IMMATURE; SIMPLEMINDED].* (Psalm 119:130)

*TEACH [GIVE TO] THE WISE, AND THEY WILL BECOME EVEN WISER; TEACH [INFORM] GOOD PEOPLE [THE RIGHTEOUS], AND THEY WILL LEARN EVEN MORE [ADD TO THEIR LEARNING].* (Proverbs 9:9)

*ANYONE WHO LOVES LEARNING [KNOWLEDGE] ACCEPTS [LOVES] CORRECTION [INSTRUCTION; DISCIPLINE], BUT A PERSON WHO HATES BEING CORRECTED IS STUPID.* (Proverbs 12:1)

*Those who get wisdom [acquire heart] do themselves a favor [love themselves], and those who love learning [guard understanding] will succeed.* (Proverbs 19:18)

*King Nebuchadnezzar wanted only young Israelite men [children] who had nothing wrong with them [no blemish; 2 Sam. 14:25; Song 4:4]. They were to be handsome [of good appearance] and well educated [skilled in all wisdom], capable of learning [knowing knowledge] and understanding, and able to serve [stand] in his palace [Gen. 41:33]. Ashpenaz was to teach them the language and writings [literature] of the Babylonians [Chaldeans; probably Akkadian and Aramaic; the literature would include myths and legends as well as divination texts].* (Daniel 1:4)

*How terrible for [Woe to] you, you experts on the law. You have taken away the key to learning about God [knowledge]. You yourselves would not learn [did not enter], and you stopped [hindered; prevented] others from learning [entering], too.* (Luke 11:52)

Any minister who practices healing and deliverance needs extensive training to discern the voice of God as opposed to one's own thoughts, biases, or ideals in a given situation. Healing and deliverance are ministries based in the breakthrough principle, although not quite in the way we are accustomed to talking about breakthrough. The idea of breakthrough in a spiritual sense is not about suddenly receiving money or things, but about making a divine contact, a breaking through between this realm and heaven, for which a person is able to make contact with God. Whenever we operate healing and deliverance work, we are providing that breakthrough so someone can reach out to and touch heaven for the spiritual contact that he or she is seeking.

Healing and deliverance ministers should also be trained in principles as relate to faith and healing, Scriptural teachings on faith and healing, proper execution of laying on of hands and prayer, various healing techniques, such as counseling and encouragement, legalities as relate to healing and deliverance work, ethics, and general ministerial and Scriptural principles. Healing and deliverance ministers should also receive training in general ministry principles, operations, and training much like that received by any minister.

## Confidentiality

It's hard to watch healing or deliverance ministry in action (especially when it is televised or advertised as almost a spectator sport) and take the claims of requiring confidentiality or maintaining confidentiality seriously. In an era where people's dirty laundry has a nasty way of winding up all over social media and trailing all through church gossip trails, it seems like maintaining confidentiality and integrity in one's ministry is something of the past. Often disguised as general advice for the "church" or one's audience, people's personal information has a way of finding itself in everyone's hands, subject to everyone's judgment, and most unfortunately, to everyone's scrutiny.

Cries about transparency, testimony, and honesty are slowly eroding the church of its long-held traditions of privacy and confidentiality, especially as we encourage everyone to put everything out there, subject to everyone's thoughts and judgments. While yes, it is important to testify and to be honest, there is a difference between expecting people to air out their issues for everyone's entertainment purposes. Where nothing is off limits in the world, we need to ensure certain things stay within the confines of a service or other quieter healing and deliverance sessions at all times.

*GOSSIPS CAN'T KEEP [GO/WALK AROUND REVEALING] SECRETS,*
*BUT A TRUSTWORTHY PERSON CAN [KEEPS A CONFIDENCE; COVERS UP A WORD].*
(Proverbs 11:13)

*WHOEVER FORGIVES SOMEONE'S SIN MAKES A FRIEND [ONE WHO SEEKS LOVE CONCEALS AN OFFENSE],*
*BUT GOSSIPING ABOUT THE SIN [REPEATING A THING] BREAKS UP FRIENDSHIPS.*
(Proverbs 17:9)

*IN SUCH TIMES THE WISE PERSON WILL KEEP QUIET,*
  *BECAUSE IT IS A BAD [EVIL] TIME.*
(Amos 5:13)

Confidentiality rules vary slightly, depending on the type of an event or healing or deliverance session.

- **Service:** When a healing and deliverance service is public (or done as part of a conference or public service), everyone can see what transpires as part of the event. By virtue of attendance and receiving an altar call or coming forward for healing, those who come forward give their consent to participate in the spiritual rite and any and acknowledge any and all information that may come forth from it may become public knowledge. This is different from having prior knowledge about someone and then airing it out during an event, however. Any private knowledge obtained prior to any session should not be disclosed in public, and if there is a question that such will interfere with your ability to operate as a minister in healing and deliverance for that individual, then it is better to decline a specific ministry operation in that service.

    With private information or issues discerned in the healing and deliverance process, it is best to be discreet, and refrain from announcing such things to the entire room. It is possible to minister to someone at the altar without a microphone and with discretion, not announcing everyone's private information to the entire room.

- **Concurrent or post-service (private) session:** Sometimes additional healing, deliverance, or attention is needed that extends beyond what is available during a public service. There should always be one or two ministers on hand, who are trustworthy and properly trained in healing and deliverance, who can handle a variety of situations that require private-session healing and deliverance while a service is going on, or after a service is over. It's not realistic to expect a public service to revolve around one or two people and their needs, especially if such becomes extensive and more than can be reasonably handled in a few minutes. If someone needs additional time, is causing disruption, or just needs more time and a service is either ongoing or over, someone else with a proper gift and training can have the time and ability to handle whatever matters remain unfinished.

- **Television, internet, live stream, or radio taping:** It is my personal belief and wise advice that taping a healing or deliverance session for media usage is a bad idea. It is an invasion of people's privacy and dignity, it turns healing and deliverance work into a media spectacle, and it causes many legal issues for those who use such footage in the future. For such to be legal, media release forms must be signed by every individual in attendance, allowing their likeness, issues, and sessions to be used for public media usage. There is also the question that someone may change their mind later on or claim they did not understand what they were signing, thus creating additional legal issues later. Beyond these legal complications, the same rules apply as for any public healing and deliverance service.

- **Testimonies:** The testimonies of others are not ours to give. If we do not have expressed written permission to give a testimony, we should never do so. It is possible to relate our own experiences in healing and deliverance ministry, but such should never engage in specific details, mention names, or expose privacy and dignity.

- **Any non-public session:** Non-public sessions are not services but are private sessions when an individual comes for healing, prayer, anointing, encouragement, counseling, or advice. In such instances, all that happens in said services is strictly confidential.

## Release forms

Release forms are a controversial aspect of healing and deliverance ministry, but a necessary one, nonetheless. Healing and deliverance can touch on some difficult areas, can require additional information, or can require additional contacts to preserve the safety and effectiveness of healing and deliverance ministry. Even though any minister should be able to flow in a gift of healing and deliverance without a background on someone's life history, having additional information, especially when in a long-term counseling or deliverance situation, can be very helpful to aid the process and to assess a person's mental, spiritual, emotional, and physical states. Sometimes a person may have medical or physical limitations, mental or emotional issues, or spiritual problems that may impede, hamper, or cause adjustment or alteration to the normal, or standard, process.

Release forms should be used:

- Any time minors are involved.
- When private healing or delivering sessions are done.
- Whenever privately counseling someone.
- Any time someone has a condition.
- If the individual is not a member of your church or ministry.

Requested information should include:

- Disclosure of health issues that may somehow relate to the effectiveness of the process.
- All prescribed medications one is on.
- All illegal drugs or mentally altering substances one has used within the past ninety days.
- Any relevant history that may impact the effectiveness of the process.

Required components of release forms:

- Clarification on name, contact information.
- Emergency contact.
- Sections for necessary requested information, as found above.
- Disclaimer section which releases the deliverance minister and their ministry from any and all liability in the instance of accidental injury, ineffectiveness, or other unforeseen issues.
- Clarification on the confidential nature of any and all sessions.

## **Mental illness and deliverance ministry**

There are those in healing and deliverance ministry who deny mental illness is a real thing. Many believe it is akin to possession and a sign that someone has a spiritual issue while denying the realities of mental illness and the toll it often takes on the families of those who suffer from some form of it. In not dealing with it as a viable thing, those who are mentally ill are told not to seek out mental health assistance from professionally trained people and are often left to masquerade in church as super deep, desirably spiritual, and hearing from God, when in fact, they are just experiencing the difficulties of mental breakdown in various forms. According to the US Department of Health and Human Services:[2]

- One in five American adults experienced a mental health issue in 2014.

- One in twenty-five Americans live with a serious mental illness, such as schizophrenia, bipolar disorder, or major depression.

*Early psychiatric treatment, Serefeddin Sabuncuoglu (15th century)*

- Suicide is the tenth leading cause of death in the United States, more than double the number of lives lost due to homicide.

- Half of all mental disorders show first signs before a person turns fourteen years old, and three quarters of mental health disorders begin before age 24.

- Only 3-5% of violent acts are attributed to people living with a serious mental illness.

- Mental health problems can be due to biological factors (genes, physical illness, injury, brain chemistry), life experiences or trauma, or family history of mental issues.

Mental health issues are treated through therapy and counseling, medicinal treatments if such are believed to be beneficial (not all mental health patients take medication), and adjustments within one's lifestyle that can help them to cope with day-to-day living and the stresses and triggers they may encounter.

*SO DON'T WORRY [FEAR], BECAUSE I AM WITH YOU.*
  *DON'T BE AFRAID [DISMAYED], BECAUSE I AM YOUR GOD.*

*I WILL MAKE YOU STRONG [STRENGTHEN YOU] AND WILL HELP YOU;*
 *I WILL SUPPORT [UPHOLD] YOU WITH MY RIGHT HAND THAT SAVES YOU [OR RIGHTEOUS RIGHT HAND; A SYMBOL OF POWER TO SAVE AND PROTECT; EX. 15:6; PS. 63:8].*
(Isaiah 41:10)

*BUT YOU WERE TAUGHT TO BE MADE NEW IN YOUR HEARTS [THE SPIRIT/ATTITUDE OF YOUR MINDS]...* (Ephesians 4:23)

*GIVE ALL YOUR WORRIES TO HIM [CAST ALL YOUR ANXIETY ON HIM], BECAUSE HE CARES ABOUT YOU.* (1 Peter 5:7)

If we recognize these statistics as authoritative, we already know someone who is mentally ill, whether they recognize it themselves. We have known them, loved them, and have never felt the slightest compulsion to tell them they are crazy, they are demonic, they are possessed, or that they aren't spiritual. In some instances, you might think they are more spiritual than you are!

Most Christian-trained counselors and ministers do not have the proper training to handle mental health issues. Mental illness requires professional, skilled individuals who know how to best handle the issues at hand and address those with mental health issues in a way that will address their problems and help them come to a place of understanding. The mental health community has done much, over the years, to promote understanding, identify symptoms, and acknowledge the issues and triggers mentally ill patients have. Without this training, a person who is mentally ill will not receive the important tools they need to function in their world and in society.

This does not mean that Christian ministers or counselors cannot help the mentally ill, however; it just means they cannot do it alone. A Christian minister or counselor, especially one who believes in healing and deliverance, can go a long way in helping a mentally ill individual with regular maintenance of their situation, encouragement, love, and the reminder that God loves them and they are not damaged or evil. The presence and work can provide a safe place for a mentally ill individual to expand their support system and promote regular healthy activities into their lives that encourage spirituality and spiritual understanding.

Christian ministers should never, under any circumstances, encourage, force, or persuade mental health patients to stop taking medications, meeting with mental health professionals, or somehow treated as subhuman, evil, or damaged. If a Christian minister does not have the proper training to handle a mental illness problem in a clinical setting, they should maintain a list of contacts, phone numbers, and available services for references, programs, and support groups to help such individuals find the care they need.

**Drug and alcohol addiction and deliverance ministry**

Drug and alcohol abuse are, like mental illness, very controversial topics within healing and deliverance circles. Many refuse to believe the validity of drug and alcohol abuse as diseases and believe instead that alcohol and drug abuse are symptoms of demonic possession, spiritual bondage, or any other assortment of perspectives that attempt to deconstruct the commonly held beliefs about addiction. The reality is that drug and alcohol abuse aren't so cut and dry as to just fall into one perspective, or another. Drug and alcohol abuse take the form of addiction, which is a medical condition with consequences and side effects on one's body. Addiction's impact on the body makes it not so easy to simply walk away from, and major health issues result from the impact on addiction within a person. Labeling drug and alcohol abuse as "addiction" or "disease" does not nullify anyone's responsibility for using and abusing drugs and alcohol and does not change the fact that someone started engaging in certain behaviors that ran beyond a point they could not control. The stark reality of the bondage of drug and alcohol abuse (because it is a form of bondage, as well) is that addicts cannot stop through sheer will power, because they want to be better parents or people, or because they think God Himself wants them to stop. Addiction's complications do not mean a person is without any abilities, but that they have become powerless to their addiction, because at some point in time, they opened themselves up to give it power. This is not in a condemning way or something to look down upon them; it simply means that because substance abuse starts with the compulsion to use, even in the face of all information that tells us using drugs and alcohol are bad for our bodies, or from using a substance in a medically prescribed context, there is a transference of power away from the individual to the substance, and then that substance begins to control their lives. As the science of addiction changes the way an individual perceives the world and their interactions with it, a person who deals with addiction also changes. They may no longer be the person they once were, may engage in behaviors that seem unlike them (stealing, neglect, abuse, abandonment, etc.), or may lose interest in things that were once very important to them.

*WINE AND BEER [STRONG DRINK; AN ALCOHOLIC BEVERAGE MADE FROM GRAIN] MAKE PEOPLE LOUD [MOCKERS] AND UNCONTROLLED [CAROUSERS; BRAWLERS]; IT IS NOT WISE TO GET DRUNK ON [BE LED ASTRAY BY] THEM.* (Proverbs 20:1)

*I AM ALLOWED TO DO ALL THINGS [ALL THINGS ARE LAWFUL/PERMISSIBLE FOR ME; PROBABLY A SLOGAN THE CORINTHIANS WERE USING; SEE ALSO 7:1; 8:1, 4; 10:23]," BUT NOT ALL THINGS ARE GOOD FOR ME TO DO [PROFITABLE; BENEFICIAL]. "I AM ALLOWED TO DO ALL THINGS [ALL THINGS ARE LAWFUL/PERMISSIBLE FOR ME]," BUT I WILL NOT LET ANYTHING MAKE ME ITS SLAVE.* (1 Corinthians 6:12)

*DO NOT BE DRUNK WITH WINE, WHICH WILL RUIN YOU [IS DEBAUCHERY/RECKLESS LIVING], BUT BE FILLED WITH THE SPIRIT. SPEAK [...SPEAKING] TO EACH OTHER WITH PSALMS, HYMNS, AND SPIRITUAL SONGS, SINGING AND MAKING MUSIC IN YOUR HEARTS TO THE LORD. ALWAYS GIVE [...ALWAYS GIVING] THANKS TO GOD THE FATHER FOR EVERYTHING, IN THE NAME OF OUR LORD JESUS CHRIST.* (Ephesians 5:18-20)

According to the National Institute of Drug Abuse:[3]

- In 2013, 6.5 million Americans aged twelve or older used prescription drugs nonmedically (include: pain relievers, tranquilizers, sedatives, and stimulants).

- 1.3 million Americans had used hallucinogens (LSD, ecstasy).

- Methamphetamine use had increased to 595,000 users, up from 353,000 users in 2010.

- More than half of new illicit drug users begin with marijuana, followed by prescription pain relievers, and inhalants.

- Alcohol abuse has declined (between 2002 and 2013), but still exists in about 17.3 million Americans.

- About 22.7 million Americans (almost nine percent) need treatment for a drug or alcohol abuse problem, but only about 2.5 million people (less than 1 percent) received treatment.

Let's never be naïve enough to assume that addicts do not come to church while they are using. On the contrary, there are many who experience their first substance abuse encounters behind a church building, while no one is watching during a youth event, or a preacher's kid brings weed, alcohol, pills, or cigarettes to a church sleepover. There are many addicted church leaders, those who are the quickest to get up in the pulpit and condemn addiction programs, and many who use drugs and alcohol to cover up depression, disillusion, or other negative feelings they may have about ministry. There are also many who suffer from other forms of addiction that we are not as quick to talk about in church settings: overeating, sexual addiction, hoarding, compulsive gambling or spending, prescription pills, compulsive exercise, or even attention. When discussing such issues, while treatment may vary for such addictions, the principles are the same: someone has given their power to a substance which now controls all their lives.

*William Faden (1759-1836) trading alcohol for furs in the early 1600s Canada. Indigenous people had no experience with recreational drinking, as did Europeans, and often traded away resources for liquor with dire consequences. The first rehab was organized in 1750, and is remarkably like Alcoholics Anonymous today.*

There is no question that church involvement is often very important and useful to addicts who are in recovery. For people to successfully recover from addiction, they need to have support, encouragement, and things to be involved in that promote healthy living and spiritual insight. Individuals with substance abuse must learn how to re-live life as sober individuals, without drugs and alcohol, regaining their power back one day at a time as they refuse to use the substances which have caused them harm. The reality is, however, that much like mental illness, many Christian ministers are ill equipped to assist in the sobriety of addicts and alcoholics. Christian ministers should never advise addicts and alcoholics to go at it alone and should encourage membership and support for twelve-step programs (such as Alcoholics Anonymous, Narcotics Anonymous, and Celebrate Recovery) to aid in the process of needed accountability, support, tools and encouragement to live lives of sobriety and good health for their remaining years.

## Abuse and deliverance ministry

Abuse of all forms is a topic most of us would rather keep under wraps and pretend does not exist. The realities of culture, however, is that abuse is a dominant and multifaceted force that healing and deliverance ministers will see in their work.

- Only about 30% of sexual assault cases are reported to authorities, and only about 16% of adult rapes are reported to law enforcement.[4]

- One in five girls and one in 20 boys is a victim of child sexual abuse.[5]

- One in five women and one in 71 men will be raped at some point in their lives.[6]

- Nearly one in ten women has been raped by an intimate partner.[7]

- 91% of victims of rape and sexual assault are women. In eight out of ten cases, the victim knew the rapist.[8]

- Annually, rape costs the United States more than any other crime ($127 billion). Additionally, health care is 16% higher for women who were sexually abused as children.[9]

- 34% of people who sexually abuse a child are family members, and 96% of people who sexually abuse children are male.[10]

- The average age for which girls become victims of prostitution is 12 to 14 years, and 11 to 13 years for boys.[11]

- On average, nearly 20 people per minute – almost one every second – are physically abused by an intimate partner in the United States.[12]

- One in three women and one in four men have been victims of some sort of physical violence by an intimate partner.[13]

- 19% of all domestic violence situations include a weapon. The presence of a gun in a domestic violence situation increases the risk of homicide by 500%.[14]

- One in 15 children are exposed to intimate partner violence each year, and 90% are eyewitnesses to the violence.[15]

The long-term impacts of living with rape, sexual assault, or domestic violence are complicated and intimate, as many individuals who experience one or all these things in their lifetime go on to experience shades of it in other relationships, as well. Such is especially true if it is first perpetrated in childhood. While repeating cycles and experiences is not the same for everyone and there is no situation that is exactly the same for everyone, odds are good that an individual who has been subjected to one form of intimate violence has either seen or experienced more than one.

*Sarai, Abram's wife, had no children, but she had a slave girl from Egypt named Hagar. Sarai said to Abram, "Look, the Lord has not allowed me to have [prevented/restrained me from having] children, so have sexual relations with [go to] my slave girl. If she has a child, maybe I can have my own family [reproduce; have a child; build] through her [taking a second wife or concubine was common for a childless couple at the time]."*

*Abram did what Sarai said. It was after he had lived ten years in Canaan that Sarai gave Hagar to her husband Abram as a wife [or concubine]. (Hagar was her slave girl from Egypt.)*

*Abram had sexual relations with [went in to] Hagar, and she became pregnant [conceived]. When Hagar learned she was pregnant [conceived], she began to treat [look on] her mistress Sarai badly [with contempt]. Then Sarai said to Abram, "This is your fault [may the wrong/violence done to me be on you]. I gave my slave girl to you [into your embrace; into your lap], and* when she became pregnant [conceived], she began to treat [look on] me badly [with contempt]. Let the Lord decide who is right—[judge between] you or me."

But Abram said to Sarai, "You are Hagar's mistress [Your slave girl is in your hand/power]. Do anything you want [what is good in your eyes] to her." Then Sarai was hard on [afflicted; abused] Hagar, and Hagar ran away [fled from her presence]. (Genesis 16:1-6)

[Sometime later; After this] David had a son named Absalom and a son named Amnon. Absalom had a beautiful sister named Tamar, and Amnon loved her. Tamar was a virgin. Amnon made himself sick just thinking about her [by his obsession/frustration with her], because he could not find any chance to be alone with her [it seemed impossible for him to do anything to her; it appeared he could never have her].

Amnon had a friend named Jonadab son of Shimeah, David's brother. Jonadab was a very clever [shrewd; crafty; wise] man. He asked Amnon, "Son of the king, why do you look so sad [depressed; dejected] day after day [morning after morning]? Tell me what's wrong!"

Amnon told him, "I love Tamar, the sister of my half-brother [brother] Absalom."

Jonadab said to Amnon, "Go to bed and act as if you are [pretend to be] sick. Then [When...] your father will come to see you. Tell him, 'Please let my sister Tamar come in and give me food to eat. Let her make the food in front of me so I can watch and eat it from her hand.'"

So Amnon went to bed and acted sick. When King David came in to see him, Amnon said to him, "Please let my sister Tamar come in. Let her make two of her special cakes [some special bread] for me while I watch. Then I will eat them from her hands."

David sent for Tamar in the palace, saying, "Go to your brother Amnon's house and make some food for him." So Tamar went to her brother Amnon's house, and he was in bed [lying down]. Tamar took some dough and pressed it together with her hands [kneaded it]. She made some special cakes [bread] while Amnon watched. Then she baked them. Next she took the pan and served him [dished/poured them out before him], but he refused to eat.

He said to his servants, "All of you, leave me alone [Everyone get out of here]!" So they all left him alone [got out]. Amnon said to Tamar, "Bring the food into the ·bedroom [inner room] so I may eat from your hand."

Tamar took the cakes [bread] she had made and brought them to her brother Amnon in the bedroom [inner room]. She went to him so he could eat from her hands, but Amnon grabbed her. He said, "Sister, come and have sexual relations [lie] with me."

Tamar said to him, "No, [my] brother! Don't force [violate; rape; humiliate] me! This should never be [isn't] done in Israel! Don't do this ·shameful [disgraceful; wicked; vile] thing! I could never [Where could I...?] get rid of my shame! And you will be like the shameful [one of the greatest] fools [scoundrels] in Israel! Please talk with the king, and he will let you marry [not refuse your marrying] me."

But Amnon refused to listen to her. He was stronger than she was, so he forced her to have sexual relations with him [raped/humiliated her and lay with her]. After that, Amnon hated Tamar [intensely; with a great hatred]. He hated her more than he had loved her before. Amnon said to her, "Get up and leave [out]!"

Tamar said to him, "No! Sending me away would be worse [a greater wrong] than what you've already done [to me]!"

But he refused to listen to her. He called his young servant [man] back in and said, "Get this woman out of here and away from me! Lock the door after [behind] her." So his servant led her out of the room and bolted the door after [behind] her.

Tamar was wearing a special robe with long sleeves, because the king's virgin daughters wore this kind of robe. Tamar put ashes on her head and tore her special robe [a sign of mourning or distress]. Putting her hand on her head [or with her face in her hands], she went away, crying loudly.

*ABSALOM, TAMAR'S BROTHER, SAID TO HER, "HAS AMNON, YOUR BROTHER, FORCED YOU TO HAVE SEXUAL RELATIONS WITH HIM [BEEN WITH YOU]? FOR NOW, SISTER, BE QUIET [KEEP SILENT]. HE IS YOUR HALF-BROTHER. DON'T LET THIS UPSET YOU SO MUCH [WORRY ABOUT THIS; TAKE THIS TO HEART]!" SO TAMAR LIVED IN HER BROTHER ABSALOM'S HOUSE AND WAS SAD AND LONELY [DESOLATE AND INCONSOLABLE].*

*WHEN KING DAVID HEARD THE NEWS, HE WAS VERY ANGRY. ABSALOM DID NOT SAY A WORD, GOOD OR BAD, TO AMNON. BUT HE HATED AMNON FOR DISGRACING [VIOLATING; RAPING; HUMILIATING] HIS SISTER TAMAR.* (2 Samuel 13:1-22)

Individuals who have lived with intimate violence may experience forms of Post Traumatic Stress Disorder (PTSD), flashbacks, cutting, drug abuse or addiction, intimacy issues, anxiety, and other things that are not as simple as just telling someone to "get over it" or hope that a few trips to the altar will transform their lives and make them feel better about themselves and what happened to them. While there are certainly stories where prayer and deliverance work has helped, it is not, in and of itself, sufficient to heal the type of life trauma that often comes along with intimate abuse, especially when such is done from someone who is callous, uncaring, and doesn't understand.

Christian ministers are, much like the other specifications we spoke of here, often untrained to handle the magnitude of therapy and therapeutic intervention it takes to help someone process this type of life trauma. Unlike the other areas, while this is often dealt with in a callous way, it is also often the advice of Christian ministers that a man or woman should "perform" throughout their lives in a normal way, adopting certain roles and attitudes that relate to gender, and downplaying hurt or the way that we impose gender roles, ideas about submission and other matters, may make someone who lived through these things to feel. This means ministers should all try to be careful about victim shaming through teaching, and very cautious about how we counsel people who come to us for pre-wedding, marital, or personal counseling.

There are many things a Christian minister can do to help a person in such a situation, beyond just prayer and even encouragement. A minister can do something unique in this situation (and, by extension, with any we have discussed), and that is help affirm the worth and dignity of the human being who sits before you that has been violated. Encouragement, listening, affirmation, encouragement in daily living, anti-anxiety exercises, positive living, and spiritual grounding are all a wonderful addition to the professional treatment a person who has experienced intimate abuse may seek.

## **Accepting our limitations**

The best way to avoid legal issues and ramifications with healing and deliverance ministry is to admit that as a minister, you cannot do everything. We've all heard the cheerleading about the bigness of our God, but we are not God, and God has not appointed any one of us to be all-encompassing in our ministries.

*BECAUSE GOD HAS GIVEN ME A SPECIAL GIFT [HIS GRACE], I HAVE SOMETHING TO SAY TO EVERYONE AMONG YOU. DO NOT THINK YOU ARE BETTER THAN YOU ARE. [INSTEAD] YOU MUST DECIDE WHAT YOU REALLY ARE [THINK SENSIBLY; THINK WITH SOBER DISCERNMENT] BY [BASED ON; IN ACCORDANCE WITH] THE AMOUNT OF FAITH GOD HAS GIVEN YOU. [FOR JUST AS] EACH ONE OF US HAS A [ONE] BODY WITH MANY PARTS, AND THESE PARTS ALL HAVE DIFFERENT USES [FUNCTIONS]. IN THE SAME WAY, WE ARE MANY, BUT IN CHRIST WE ARE ALL ONE BODY, AND EACH PART BELONGS TO ALL THE OTHER PARTS [MEMBERS]. WE ALL HAVE DIFFERENT GIFTS, EACH OF WHICH CAME BECAUSE OF THE GRACE GOD GAVE US.* (Romans 12:3-6)

No matter how anointed we may be with healing and deliverance, none of us are God, and we are not going to become God. We don't heal by our own power, and our opinions and perspectives on the issues we see in this work are not sufficient to help anyone improve. Many of the arguments and postures we take on medical science, the media, and our general attitudes about healing and deliverance are closing us off from ways we can help people and enhance their healing and deliverance process while exposing us to legal ramifications and lawsuits. It's easy to be indignant and believe the way we do things is always best, but such is not going to help anyone to heal and is going to make sure our ministries do not grow and transform the lives of others. Being prepared, making good judgments, maintaining lists of resources, and most importantly, recognizing we do not do this work alone and there are many ways people can come to a place of healing and deliverance is most important as we support all who come to us in this process of better living and spiritual identity.

## Chapter 13 Assignments

- Construct a presentation on the ethics of healing and deliverance ministry.
- In keeping with the examination of different social issues in our world today, select an issue and do the necessary research on what is required to handle that issue in healing and deliverance ministry today.

*The Possessed Boy at the Foot of Mount Tabor, James Tissot, 1836-1902*

## - CHAPTER FOURTEEN -
## Regulating Healing and Deliverance Ministry

BUT WE HAVE TURNED AWAY FROM [REJECTED; RENOUNCED] SECRET [UNDERHANDED] AND SHAMEFUL WAYS. WE USE NO TRICKERY [DO NOT WALK IN DECEPTION], AND WE DO NOT CHANGE [DISTORT] THE TEACHING [WORD] OF GOD. WE TEACH THE TRUTH PLAINLY [FULLY/OPENLY DISCLOSE THE TRUTH], SHOWING EVERYONE WHO WE ARE SO THAT THEY CAN KNOW IN THEIR HEARTS WHAT KIND OF PEOPLE WE ARE [COMMENDING OURSELVES TO EVERY PERSON'S CONSCIENCE] IN GOD'S SIGHT.
(2 CORINTHIANS 4:2)

If you are a leader's leader or work in a network of ministers, you will, most likely, encounter a healing and deliverance ministry at some point in time. The work may be exclusively related to healing and deliverance or it may be a facet of what they do, but you will, most likely, see someone claiming to operate in the work of healing and deliverance through ministry. No matter what capacity of healing and deliverance, the odds are also high they will need guidance, instruction, or supervision for whatever it is they are doing. This may sound strange, but regulating deliverance ministry is often one of the most important things a leader with oversight capacity must do. Gift or not, healing and deliverance ministry requires guidance, especially as challenging or unconventional cases cause questions and need focus as they handle long-term or difficult situations. No matter how gifted someone is, accountability, solid leadership, training, and insight are required to help keep deliverance and healing ministry honest, upfront, and effective.

If you are in healing and deliverance ministry yourself and accountable to another leader, there are also things you can do and should know to keep the work of the ministry functioning. Regulations do not just fall on supervisory positions but begin with those who operate a ministry and are ready and prepared for the task and work at hand. In this chapter, we will discuss different ways to regulate the work of healing and deliverance ministry, both from the end of those who operate it and their respective leaders. Because there are no specific secular regulations to oversee healing and deliverance ministry, it becomes the job of Kingdom leadership to put effective regulations in place to prevent abuses, misleading claims, dishonesty, and burnout in such work. As a leader in position to assist with or lead someone with a deliverance and healing ministry, the job is important, essential, and just as relevant as those who do healing and deliverance work themselves.

**Getting involved**

Healing and deliverance ministries are affirmative, pro-active works that require their ministers and leaders to step up and be counted from the very beginning. As gifted as someone may be, that doesn't substitute the call and need to be involved and active within the work. It's a nice idea that healing and deliverance ministry gifts will dazzle the itinerant church circuit and lead to many other preaching invites, but reality is, unfortunately, not quite that simple. There are multitudes of preachers who claim to have the ability to work healing and deliverance. Given the ministry circuits are far more competitive than they used to be as people have flooded into ministry over the past twenty years, we must acknowledge that this is another reason why just having a gift or an ability is simply not enough to make ministry work. If you feel called to healing and deliverance ministry, it is essential to seek God as to how to best operate such a work. It's also important to consider that the way God may call you to handle your healing and deliverance work may not look like the standard "healing and deliverance" ministries that go from town to town, record their successes on television, and cast out demons at the altar. Your work may be counseling, encouragement, holding anointing and prayer sessions, healing services, or something else. Knowing the work to which you have been called is vital to getting involved in such a ministry.

There are also lots of possibilities relating to involvement. You may partner with or work in connection with another ministry or team up for a community healing event. There may be a time when you are called to apprentice or study under another ministry that is already established with this specific type of ministry work. As has already been said, taking the right study and legal precautions is always a must. If this is the work you feel called to do, there are many steps and ways you can execute it.

*WHOEVER GIVES TO OTHERS WILL GET RICHER [OR BLESSES OTHERS WILL BE REFRESHED];*
  *THOSE WHO HELP [SATISFY] OTHERS WILL THEMSELVES BE HELPED [SATISFIED].* (Proverbs 11:25)

*[FOR] GOD IS FAIR [NOT UNJUST]; HE WILL NOT FORGET THE WORK YOU DID AND THE LOVE YOU SHOWED FOR HIM [IN HIS NAME] BY HELPING [SERVING] HIS PEOPLE [HOLY PEOPLE; SAINTS]. AND HE WILL REMEMBER THAT YOU ARE STILL HELPING [SERVING] THEM.* (Hebrews 6:10)

The best advice to follow is observe with caution before getting too eagerly involved, try different things if you are unsure of your exact niche, and spend time in prayer and devotion. Learning about healing and deliverance ministry, all the options that go along with it, and to expand and allow your gift to speak for itself. As human beings, we have hits and misses; and the way we learn how to discern God is through training, testing, and experience that brings us to a better understanding of how God moves in and through us.

## Letting leadership help

If your leader is in a position where they cover other leaders, they are, most likely, extremely busy. This probably isn't a fact you are unaware of, but whether aware of it, or not, it is your leader's job to help oversee the work you are doing and make sure it is done right, that you are edified and encouraged, and that the work takes on a character that develops spiritual fruit. What this means: don't be afraid to ask for help when you need it, and don't misinterpret your leader's attempts to train and offer assistance as a threat to the work. Just like you have your purpose in the body, so too does leadership have theirs, and if you reject their assistance, you are rejecting their gift that is here for you and the betterment of the church.

*AND CHRIST GAVE GIFTS TO PEOPLE—HE MADE SOME TO BE APOSTLES, SOME TO BE*

*PROPHETS, SOME TO GO AND TELL THE GOOD NEWS, AND SOME TO HAVE THE WORK OF CARING FOR AND TEACHING GOD'S PEOPLE [HE HIMSELF GAVE APOSTLES, PROPHETS, EVANGELISTS, PASTORS/SHEPHERDS, AND TEACHERS]. CHRIST GAVE THOSE GIFTS TO PREPARE [...TO EQUIP] GOD'S HOLY PEOPLE FOR THE WORK OF SERVING, TO MAKE THE BODY OF CHRIST STRONGER. THIS WORK MUST CONTINUE UNTIL WE ARE ALL JOINED TOGETHER IN THE SAME FAITH [OR ALL REACH UNITY IN THE FAITH] AND IN THE SAME KNOWLEDGE OF THE SON OF GOD. WE MUST BECOME LIKE A MATURE PERSON [OR THE PERFECT MAN; CHRIST], GROWING UNTIL WE BECOME LIKE CHRIST AND HAVE HIS PERFECTION [TO THE MEASURE OF THE STATURE OF CHRIST'S FULLNESS].* (Ephesians 4:11-13)

*REMEMBER YOUR LEADERS WHO TAUGHT [PROCLAIMED; SPOKE] GOD'S MESSAGE [WORD] TO YOU. REMEMBER [CONSIDER; REFLECT ON] HOW THEY LIVED AND DIED [OR THE OUTCOME/RESULT OF THEIR WAY OF LIFE], AND COPY [IMITATE] THEIR FAITH.* (Hebrews 13:7)

Your leadership should never be perceived as an enemy to the work and ministry you operate. If that is how you perceive your leader, then it's time to rethink who your leader is, but that is an issue for another place and time. Each leader regulates and handles spiritual covering a little differently, and that means the specific rigors and level of monitoring or involvement may vary, depending on where your leader is, how far away they are from you, and what they expect from your ministry. A leader who understands the rigors and demands of such ministry should always be considered an ally, not just someone who can issue you papers or put you in their conference events from time to time. Good leaders provide a place of safe spiritual refuge, one where you can receive spiritual refreshing, even if it's just in the form of a message on social media or a phone call every so often. Leadership should offer counsel, be someone you can talk to, and be someone that you find the instruction and strength to continue in this work when it becomes difficult to handle and inspiring when things are going great. Our leadership helps keep deliverance ministry honest, on the up-and-up, and encouraged.

Don't use the pace of your leader's ministry work or the magnitude of it as an excuse to avoid communicating with your leader. Communication with a leader is vital for any ministry but becomes especially relevant in healing and deliverance ministry. The issues that relate to people's healing and deliverance are often complex, and some of what you see as a deliverance and healing minister may be trying, emotionally taxing, and spiritually draining. Also, don't use your own ministry pace as an excuse to avoid the directives and instructions of your leader. If there is one thing that is universal in ministry, it is being busy. You never want to get so far ahead of where you need to be that you lose sight of what you are doing and why you are doing it. Connection to leadership is vital when handling such a ministry, and it makes doing the work much easier and much more effective.

## If there's a suspect of something amiss

As we discussed in the last chapter, deliverance and healing ministries must be regulated and maintained by Kingdom leaders who are willing to take the time and investment in monitoring their work. That means every deliverance and healing ministry in existence should be covered by another leader who knows the people who run it, is familiar with the general scope of the work, and can account and verify the work that is done through this ministry. Renegade healing and deliverance ministries should be treated with both caution and suspect. Good leadership helps us to do what we need to get done, and we should never, ever resist good leadership in our lives. When we have right leadership working with us, it gives us an added layer of protection of integrity, reputation, and defense when people make accusations against our work or come at us in ways that make what we do seem suspect. This is especially true when dealing with matters that pertain to healing and deliverance. As a controversial ministry work to begin with, it is even more important that good leadership lends credibility to the acceptable service.

*SO WHEN YOU OFFER YOUR GIFT TO GOD [PRESENT YOUR OFFERING/SACRIFICE] AT THE ALTAR, AND YOU REMEMBER THAT YOUR BROTHER OR SISTER HAS SOMETHING AGAINST YOU, LEAVE YOUR GIFT [OFFERING; SACRIFICE] THERE AT THE ALTAR. GO AND MAKE PEACE [BE RECONCILED] WITH THAT PERSON [FIRST], AND THEN COME AND OFFER YOUR GIFT [PRESENT YOUR OFFERING/SACRIFICE].*

*"IF YOUR ENEMY [OPPONENT; ADVERSARY; ACCUSER] IS TAKING YOU TO COURT, BECOME FRIENDS [REACH AGREEMENT; SETTLE MATTERS] QUICKLY, BEFORE YOU GO [ON THE WAY] TO COURT. OTHERWISE, YOUR ENEMY [OPPONENT; ADVERSARY; ACCUSER] MIGHT TURN YOU OVER TO THE JUDGE, AND THE JUDGE MIGHT GIVE YOU TO THE GUARD*

*[OFFICER; WARDEN] TO PUT [THROW] YOU IN JAIL [PRISON]. I TELL YOU THE TRUTH, YOU WILL NOT [NEVER; CERTAINLY NOT] LEAVE THERE UNTIL YOU HAVE PAID EVERYTHING YOU OWE [THE LAST PENNY; GREEK: THE LAST QUADRANS; A SMALL COPPER COIN OF VERY LOW VALUE].* (Matthew 5:23-26)

*WHEN YOU HAVE SOMETHING AGAINST [A LEGAL DISPUTE WITH; A GRIEVANCE AGAINST] ANOTHER CHRISTIAN, HOW CAN YOU BRING YOURSELF [DARE] TO GO BEFORE JUDGES WHO ARE NOT RIGHT WITH GOD [OR THE PAGAN COURTS; THE UNRIGHTEOUS] INSTEAD OF BEFORE GOD'S PEOPLE [THE SAINTS]? SURELY [DON'T...?] YOU KNOW THAT GOD'S PEOPLE [THE SAINTS] WILL JUDGE THE WORLD. SO IF YOU ARE TO JUDGE THE WORLD, ARE YOU NOT ABLE TO JUDGE SMALL [TRIVIAL; THE SMALLEST OF] CASES AS WELL? YOU [DON'T YOU...?] KNOW THAT WE WILL JUDGE ANGELS, SO SURELY WE CAN JUDGE THE ORDINARY THINGS OF [OR MATTERS PERTAINING TO] THIS LIFE. IF YOU HAVE ORDINARY CASES [CASES/LEGAL DISPUTES OF THIS LIFE] THAT MUST BE JUDGED, ARE YOU GOING TO APPOINT PEOPLE AS JUDGES WHO MEAN NOTHING TO THE CHURCH? [WILL YOU APPOINT JUDGES WITH NO STANDING IN/WHOSE LIFESTYLE IS REJECTED BY THE CHURCH?; OR GO AHEAD AND APPOINT THE LEAST MEMBERS OF THE CHURCH TO JUDGE THEM! IN THE LATTER INTERPRETATION, PAUL SPEAKS SARCASTICALLY.] I SAY THIS TO SHAME YOU. SURELY THERE IS SOMEONE [IS THERE NO ONE...?] AMONG YOU WISE ENOUGH TO JUDGE A COMPLAINT [DISPUTE; CONFLICT] BETWEEN BELIEVERS [A BROTHER]. BUT NOW ONE BELIEVER [BROTHER] GOES TO COURT AGAINST ANOTHER BELIEVER [BROTHER]—AND YOU DO THIS IN FRONT OF UNBELIEVERS!* (1 Corinthians 6:1-6)

If there is genuine concern about what goes on in a healing and deliverance situation, the matter should be taken to your leader immediately, who then should, in turn, speak with you about whatever is going on in your ministry. They may also suggest a meeting with whoever is making the accusations and may mediate or investigate the situation further. If matters go beyond the immediate level of spirituality into legality, the proper authorities should be brought in to investigate. In all situations like this, it is your leader's job to get to the bottom of why such accusations are made, and what should be done to rectify or handle the matter. As some issues with healing and deliverance ministry may be serious, your leader may address them in different ways, may discuss the matter, consult with someone in an organization or their leader, or handle the accusation legally or spiritually.

## Spiritual imperialism

The issue of spiritual imperialism is foundationally difficult for many, but most relevant when we start discussing matters of healing and deliverance, particularly the posture and regulation we must take as applies to it. Spiritual imperialism is the use of religion, religious experience, or religious belief to try and influence a nation, people, or a group with some other ulterior motive. The agenda behind spiritual imperialism is often political, with the end goal to change the thinking or ideals of a nation or group of people. Whether spiritual imperialism is nothing more than control or about political ties, colonization, or imperialism in a political sense, spiritual imperialism is seen within healing and deliverance ministry. It's not uncommon to see deliverance ministers decide selectively who needs healing and deliverance, making it only accessible or available to those who they feel should receive it. They use their understanding of spiritual beliefs to justify bigotry and outright refuse to offer healing to certain groups of people.

*Curing a Possessed Woman, Limbourg Brothers (1385-1416)*

THE LORD SAYS, "ALL YOU WHO ARE THIRSTY, COME AND DRINK [TO THE WATERS; JOHN 7:37].
THOSE OF YOU WHO DO NOT HAVE MONEY, COME, BUY AND EAT [PROV. 9:5]!
COME BUY WINE AND MILK
  WITHOUT MONEY AND WITHOUT COST.
WHY SPEND YOUR MONEY ON SOMETHING THAT IS NOT REAL FOOD [BREAD]?
  WHY WORK FOR SOMETHING THAT DOESN'T REALLY SATISFY YOU?
LISTEN CLOSELY TO ME, AND YOU WILL EAT WHAT IS GOOD;
  YOUR SOUL WILL ENJOY [DELIGHT IN] THE RICH FOOD THAT SATISFIES [FAT].

*COME TO ME AND LISTEN [EXTEND YOUR EAR];*
  *LISTEN TO ME SO YOU MAY LIVE.*
*I WILL MAKE AN AGREEMENT WITH YOU THAT WILL LAST FOREVER [EVERLASTING COVENANT/TREATY WITH YOU].*
  *I WILL GIVE YOU THE BLESSINGS [COVENANT LOVE; LOYALTY; LOVINGKINDNESS; SURE MERCIES] I PROMISED TO DAVID [2 SAM. 7:11-14; PS. 89:33-35; ACTS 13:34].*
*[LOOK; BEHOLD] I MADE DAVID A WITNESS OF MY POWER FOR ALL [TO THE] NATIONS,*
  *A RULER AND COMMANDER OF MANY NATIONS.*
*[LOOK; BEHOLD] YOU WILL CALL FOR NATIONS THAT YOU DON'T YET KNOW.*
  *AND THESE NATIONS THAT DO NOT KNOW YOU WILL RUN TO YOU*
*BECAUSE OF THE LORD YOUR GOD,*
  *BECAUSE OF THE HOLY ONE OF ISRAEL [1:4] WHO HONORS [HAS GLORIFIED] YOU."*
*SO YOU SHOULD LOOK FOR [SEEK] THE LORD BEFORE IT IS TOO LATE [WHILE HE MAY BE FOUND];*
  *YOU SHOULD CALL TO HIM WHILE HE IS NEAR.*
(Isaiah 55:1-6)

*BECAUSE GOD HAS GIVEN ME A SPECIAL GIFT [HIS GRACE], I HAVE SOMETHING TO SAY TO EVERYONE AMONG YOU. DO NOT THINK YOU ARE BETTER THAN YOU ARE. [INSTEAD] YOU MUST DECIDE WHAT YOU REALLY ARE [THINK SENSIBLY; THINK WITH SOBER DISCERNMENT] BY [BASED ON; IN ACCORDANCE WITH] THE AMOUNT OF FAITH GOD HAS GIVEN YOU.* (Romans 12:3)

Healing and deliverance are important facets of the Kingdom of God that should be available to anyone, and anyone who comes with a sincere heart should be received with the warmth and sincerity of a true believer in Christ. The use of any sort of spiritual belief to try and make someone feel hated, like God does not love them, that they are unimportant to God, or to make people feel worse about their situation than they already do. Rather, the true minister of God who is interested in healing and deliverance makes themselves available, as needed, for the work of healing, however it comes. Religion is not used as an obstacle, but as a catalyst to do good and change lives.

## **Possession**

The question of healing and deliverance ministry can't be answered without discussing it in the safe context of regulation and identity. It might seem like something that is out of place for this stage of the book, but the reality is that not everything labeled as "possession" often is. There are also those who question whether spiritual possession is a legitimate thing, and that means accusations of it or claims of it should be regulated.

The definition of possession is when something is owned or controlled by another force. For example, we call the things we own, "possessions." This indicates they are not independent in themselves, but owned by someone else – in this case, you. The concept of spiritual possession is that an individual has become owned by something else: an evil spirit or demon, that has come to reside in them and is now controlling their lives, movements, thoughts, feelings, actions, and attitudes.

If we use the concept of possession in its truest definition, there are many ways someone can be "possessed" that have nothing to do with spirituality, at least as we understand it this side of heaven. We can be possessed with ideas and concepts we've learned, we can be possessed with ambition and drive, or we can be possessed with possessions, with completing certain facets of life or certain feelings we have about something. Though these are seldom talked about, we can be quick to dismiss as something else or ignore all together. They can be just as destructive, however, as being possessed by a spirit.

The concept of being possessed has been taken seriously throughout history, sometimes too much so. People were so insanely afraid of demons, ghosts, spirits, and forces they could not see, they would allow the idea of possession to drive them crazy, as well. They became possessed with the idea of spiritual possession, and this led many people into bad places. Today, we tend to treat the idea of possession as a joke, as something to be made light with, something we almost talk about in passing. If someone doesn't do what we think they should or we don't like them in some way, we might quickly label them as "possessed." This is the extreme opposite of taking such matters too seriously and can be just as bad and detrimental as taking everything too seriously. There are many things that can influence a person's behavior, ideas, thoughts, and attitudes that have nothing to do with demonic possession, and such should always be an option when it comes to claims that someone is spiritually influenced by an outside force.

*THE NEWS [FAME] ABOUT JESUS SPREAD ALL OVER [OR AS FAR AS] SYRIA, AND PEOPLE BROUGHT ALL THE SICK TO HIM. THEY WERE SUFFERING FROM DIFFERENT KINDS OF DISEASES. SOME WERE IN GREAT PAIN, SOME HAD DEMONS [WERE DEMON-POSSESSED],*

*SOME WERE EPILEPTICS, AND SOME WERE PARALYZED. JESUS HEALED ALL OF THEM.* (Matthew 4:24)

*THEN SOME PEOPLE BROUGHT TO JESUS A MAN WHO WAS BLIND AND COULD NOT TALK [MUTE], BECAUSE HE HAD A DEMON [WAS DEMON-POSSESSED/DEMONIZED]. JESUS HEALED THE MAN SO THAT HE COULD TALK AND SEE.*

*IN THE SYNAGOGUE A MAN WHO HAD WITHIN HIM AN EVIL SPIRIT [UNCLEAN SPIRIT; DEMONS WERE VIEWED AS "UNCLEAN" OR DEFILING SPIRIT-BEINGS] SHOUTED IN A LOUD VOICE, "JESUS OF NAZARETH! WHAT DO YOU WANT [HAVE TO DO] WITH US? DID YOU COME TO DESTROY US? I KNOW WHO YOU ARE—GOD'S HOLY ONE!"*

*JESUS COMMANDED [REPRIMANDED; REBUKED] THE EVIL SPIRIT, "BE QUIET! COME OUT OF THE MAN!" THE EVIL SPIRIT [DEMON] THREW THE MAN DOWN TO THE GROUND BEFORE ALL THE PEOPLE AND THEN LEFT THE MAN WITHOUT HURTING [INJURING] HIM.*

*[ALL] THE PEOPLE WERE AMAZED AND SAID TO EACH OTHER, "WHAT DOES THIS MEAN? [OR WHAT WORDS THESE ARE!] WITH AUTHORITY AND POWER HE COMMANDS [GIVES ORDERS TO] EVIL [DEFILING; UNCLEAN; V. 33] SPIRITS, AND THEY COME OUT."* (Matthew 12:22-24)

*WHEN JESUS GOT OUT OF THE BOAT, IMMEDIATELY A MAN WITH AN EVIL [DEFILING; UNCLEAN] SPIRIT CAME TO HIM FROM THE BURIAL CAVES [TOMBS; CEMETERY]. THIS MAN LIVED IN THE CAVES [TOMBS], AND NO ONE COULD TIE HIM UP [ANY MORE], NOT EVEN WITH A CHAIN. [FOR] MANY TIMES PEOPLE HAD USED [SHACKLES AND] CHAINS TO TIE THE MAN'S HANDS AND FEET, BUT HE ALWAYS BROKE THEM OFF [TORE APART THE CHAINS AND SMASHED THE SHACKLES]. NO ONE WAS STRONG ENOUGH TO CONTROL [SUBDUE] HIM. DAY AND NIGHT HE WOULD WANDER AROUND THE BURIAL CAVES [TOMBS] AND ON THE HILLS, SCREAMING AND CUTTING [BRUISING] HIMSELF WITH STONES... THEN JESUS ASKED HIM, "WHAT IS YOUR NAME?"*

*HE ANSWERED, "MY NAME IS LEGION [A LEGION WAS ABOUT 5,000 SOLDIERS IN THE ROMAN ARMY], BECAUSE WE ARE MANY SPIRITS." HE BEGGED JESUS AGAIN AND AGAIN NOT TO SEND THEM OUT OF THAT AREA [LAND; REGION].* (Mark 5:2-5,9-10)

The concept that someone can be influenced or overcome by spiritual forces is not alien, nor impossible. We are all influenced by something, and sometimes those influences are less than godly. It might not look like it does somewhere else or like it is stereotyped to look by Hollywood, but possession can be a very real and debilitating thing in someone's life. Identifying genuine possession by a spirit is a difficult task. Possession doesn't always play by normal rules, and there is no one standard list that seems to fit everyone's definition of what it means to be ruled by an evil spirit. Some people seem to be very cunning, some seem very wicked or violent, some seem to be very demure and quiet, and others still seem to be super-spiritual or like everything we would hope they should be. Thus, the measure of whether someone is possessed is not based on exterior signs or a list we can generate that will prove possession. Such lists certainly exist, but they don't prove much beyond a bunch of behaviors or characteristics that fit our exterior definitions of what it means to be evil or difficult. They do not deal with deeper levels of spiritual possession, or the different levels and ways people may be influenced by things infiltrating their lives.

The only true way someone can be clearly defined as possessed is through spiritual discernment. If someone has a true gifting ability to discern between spirits, a person who has the gift of discernment can identify what is really at work within someone's life and the effects of it therein. This means the operation of healing and deliverance ministry requires more than just the gift of being able to heal something that is obvious; it requires the gift of discernment, being able to identify what is behind matters and do so without randomly calling out everything that might be going on in someone's life. Discernment is a point of identity; while healing and deliverance offer the solution for the identifiable problem. By identifying the issue, healing and deliverance offers a tailor-made solution to the issue.

This general advice is often missing from healing and deliverance ministries today. Sometimes healing and deliverance are handled much like everything else: round 'em up, bring 'em up, load 'em out. We don't treat people like individuals, and most people who have a problem are often treated as if they are one. We hope the remedy will come through two or three minutes of an altar call, and when it doesn't, we tend to blame the person as not desiring deliverance or not wanting to be made well. These facts might be true, but the bigger picture, and bigger issue, is that sometimes we don't discern matters of deliverance and healing properly and we don't, therefore, address them correctly.

## Exorcism or "casting out"

Most people assume the way to do an exorcism, or "casting out," is to perform a long, drawn-out spiritual rite that involves taking authority over a demon possessing a person and then subjecting that demon, demanding it leave the person. There are different ways people might attempt to subdue a perceived demon, but most casting out or exorcism rites do vary greatly from each other. The one universal component is the laying on of hands and the demon demanded to leave the person in the Name of Jesus Christ, or in the Name of the Father, Son, and Holy Spirit. Additional facets may be the use of anointing oil, sacred music, prayer, and Scripture.

*WHEN THE TWO MEN WERE LEAVING, [LOOK; BEHOLD] SOME PEOPLE BROUGHT TO JESUS ANOTHER MAN WHO COULD NOT TALK BECAUSE HE HAD A DEMON IN HIM [A MUTE, DEMON-POSSESSED MAN]. AFTER JESUS FORCED THE DEMON TO LEAVE THE MAN [DROVE/CAST OUT THE DEMON], HE WAS ABLE [BEGAN] TO SPEAK. THE CROWD WAS AMAZED AND SAID, "WE HAVE NEVER SEEN ANYTHING LIKE THIS [NOTHING LIKE THIS HAS EVER BEEN SEEN/HAPPENED] IN ISRAEL.* (Matthew 9:32-33)

*JESUS COMMANDED [REPRIMANDED; REBUKED] THE DEMON AND IT CAME OUT OF HIM, AND THE BOY WAS HEALED FROM THAT TIME ON [MOMENT; HOUR].* (Matthew 17:18)

*[ALL] THE PEOPLE WERE AMAZED AND SAID TO EACH OTHER, "WHAT DOES THIS MEAN? [OR WHAT WORDS THESE ARE!] WITH AUTHORITY AND POWER HE COMMANDS [GIVES ORDERS TO] EVIL [DEFILING; UNCLEAN; V. 33] SPIRITS, AND THEY COME OUT."* (Luke 4:36)

*WHEN THE SEVENTY-TWO CAME BACK, THEY WERE VERY HAPPY [JOYFUL] AND SAID, "LORD, EVEN THE DEMONS OBEYED [SUBMIT TO] US WHEN WE USED YOUR NAME [IN YOUR NAME]!"* (Luke 10:17)

*SHE KEPT THIS UP FOR MANY DAYS. THIS BOTHERED [ANNOYED; EXASPERATED] PAUL, SO HE TURNED AND SAID TO THE SPIRIT, "BY THE POWER [NAME] OF JESUS CHRIST, I COMMAND YOU TO COME OUT OF HER!" IMMEDIATELY, [THAT VERY HOUR] THE SPIRIT CAME OUT.* (Acts 16:18)

If we have a general gift of healing, we don't need everyone's long, drawn-out history to complete an exorcism. Exorcisms shouldn't be big, dramatic, drawn-out battles between a perceived demon and the one casting the demon out. Authority should be firm; words spoken should be carefully guided and chosen; and no one should walk away from the experience injured, abused, or feeling worse than when they started.

## Public services

A public healing and deliverance service is any public service where healing and deliverance are either the theme of or an incorporation into the event itself. Since many services offer prayer, laying on of hands, belief for healing, or deliverance as part of their services, this means many services that are open to the general public take on the nature of healing and deliverance events. Healing and deliverance may not be the general theme of all the different events that they come up in, but they are a part of what happens, nonetheless, thus proving the importance of healing and deliverance.

There are different facets to a healing and deliverance section within any service, whether it is the whole focus of the event, or not. Healing and deliverance periods should be quieter, rather than loud and exuberant. They should focus on quiet, peaceful introspection and thoughts on the words spoken over any individual who desires them. It is a time for prayer, anointing with oil, laying on of hands, and listening to the needs of the people at the altar as they bring their issues before the Lord.

*A WICKED MESSENGER BRINGS NOTHING BUT TROUBLE [OR WILL FALL INTO EVIL], BUT A TRUSTWORTHY [RELIABLE] ONE [ENVOY] MAKES EVERYTHING RIGHT [BRINGS HEALING].* (Proverbs 13:17)

*A HAPPY HEART IS LIKE GOOD MEDICINE [BRINGS HEALING], BUT A BROKEN SPIRIT DRAINS YOUR STRENGTH [DRIES UP BONE].* (Proverbs 17:22)

*JESUS WENT EVERYWHERE IN GALILEE, TEACHING IN THE SYNAGOGUES, PREACHING THE GOOD NEWS ABOUT [GOSPEL OF] THE KINGDOM, AND HEALING ALL [OR EVERY KIND OF] THE PEOPLE'S DISEASES AND SICKNESSES.* (Matthew 4:23)

Ministers who operate healing and deliverance in such a manner need to poise themselves with a gentle and quiet spirit, not behaving in a loud or aggressive manner. The work of healing and deliverance should come from

God, and those who are present to witness the grace of God through healing and deliverance should understand it is the work of God, and not the individual who is the vessel God operates through. In any healing and deliverance service (especially those that are there for healing and deliverance), teaching on healing and deliverance should take center stage, and all should understand what they are seeking out, the results, the encouragement if things don't work out like you might hope, and ways to maintain health, healing, and deliverance in one's life.

## **Anointing and prayer**

The Scriptures indicate that the work of anointing the sick and offering prayer to those who desire it within a congregation is the responsibility of the elders of the church:

*Anointing of the sick, stained-glass window*

*ANYONE WHO IS SICK SHOULD CALL THE CHURCH'S ELDERS. THEY SHOULD PRAY FOR AND POUR OIL ON THE PERSON [ANOINT THAT PERSON WITH OLIVE OIL; ANOINTING PROBABLY INDICATES DEDICATING OR SETTING ASIDE THE PERSON TO GOD'S CARE; MARK 6:13] IN THE NAME OF THE LORD.* (James 5:14)

This doesn't mean someone else can't pray and anoint someone, but it does mean that those who are appointed to help a pastor or minister in the operation of their congregation should step up and make themselves available in such instances. Anointing of the sick and prayer should be done upon request, periodically through special services, and as part of any service where such is requested.

Anointing was associated with the balm and presence of the Holy Spirit as well as having a medicinal value and representation. When we consider the work of the Spirit, it moves much like the anointing oil used in anointing those who are sick: it moves by fluidity, it is a gold color, representing the highest of heaven and the most precious on earth, it is made with olives, pressed and crushed to release the anointing that comes forth from it, and it is used to heal and help those who find themselves in an ailing state. Anointing has the power to heal because by virtue of it, we bring forth the healing balm and presence of the Holy Spirit, the Comforter, the Healer.

## **Counseling**

All ministers should have training in counseling, even if it is just on a basic level. Counseling is a form of communication in which we allow those who come to us for counseling to seek out the answers and insights they need to discover on their own. Counseling is radically different from preaching or teaching in that when we preach or teach, we convey our thoughts and perceptions to those who hear us instead of bringing them to a place where they discover the needed and desired answers and insights on their own. Counseling is a personal, upfront attempt to give people suggestions and insights designed to bring about revelation and provide tools to help decision-making skills throughout life. It's not about what we, as ministers think, but as what the client thinks, and how they are able to develop healthy patterns of thought and behavior throughout their lives, even when the counselor or therapist is not in session.

Counseling must be kept confidential. The only time others are to be brought into a counseling session is in situations of group therapy, couple's counseling, or if a person has threatened to harm themselves, someone else, or an animal. When needing to consult on cases with other counselors, names should never be used, and clients should be consulted prior to bringing in any third parties.

In healing and deliverance, counseling is a long-term approach to an individual's experience. It's a situational plan, taking steps and applying those steps, one or two at a time, to help that individual handle the maintenance of spiritual healing and deliverance in their lives. Not everyone needs it, but many need to see ways they can apply healing and deliverance to their everyday lives. Specifics should be examined and encouraged, the client should be encouraged to share their thoughts, memories, experiences, and different things they are going through, and the counselor should be the first one to encourage progress and encouragement. Counseling should center on the unique needs of the individual, and the process should be seen as healing and therapeutic.

*WHERE NO COUNSEL IS, THE PEOPLE FALL: BUT IN THE MULTITUDE OF COUNSELLORS THERE IS SAFETY.* (Proverbs 11:14, KJV)

*FOOLS THINK THEY ARE DOING RIGHT [THE PATH OF FOOLS IS VIRTUOUS/RIGHT IN THEIR OWN EYES],*
*BUT THE WISE LISTEN TO ADVICE.*
(Proverbs 12:15)

*PEOPLE'S THOUGHTS [ADVICE; PURPOSE] CAN BE LIKE A DEEP WELL [WATERS],*
*BUT SOMEONE WITH UNDERSTANDING CAN FIND THE WISDOM THERE [DRAW IT OUT].*
(Proverbs 20:5)

It's a fair statement that not every minister is geared for counseling, and when it comes to healing and deliverance, not every minister is graced to handle the work of healing that counseling requires. If someone is in need of counseling and a minister is unable to provide that service, a minister should maintain a list of references on hand who are able to accommodate such a situation.

## **Giving word**

Giving a word of wisdom and a word of knowledge are part of the charismatic spiritual gifts, which are open to anyone in the church. Neither is limited to the work of healing and deliverance, but it is possible to deliver a word of knowledge or wisdom to someone about a condition, the cause of something, the circumstances surrounding it, or about the true way to healing and deliverance via such.

*IT IS THE SPIRIT THAT GIVES LIFE. THE FLESH DOESN'T GIVE LIFE [IS USELESS; COUNTS FOR NOTHING]. THE WORDS I TOLD YOU ARE SPIRIT, AND THEY GIVE LIFE [OR ARE FROM THE SPIRIT WHO GIVES LIFE].* (John 6:63)

*THIS IS WHAT THE SCRIPTURE SAYS [BUT WHAT DOES IT SAY?]: "THE WORD IS NEAR YOU;*

*IT IS IN YOUR MOUTH AND IN YOUR HEART [DEUT. 30:14; GOD'S SALVATION HAS BEEN BROUGHT NEAR THROUGH CHRIST AND IS RECEIVED BY FAITH]." THAT IS THE TEACHING [MESSAGE; WORD] OF FAITH THAT WE ARE TELLING [PREACH; PROCLAIM].* (Romans 10:8)

*DON'T SAY ANYTHING THAT WILL HURT OTHERS [LET ANY ROTTEN/UNHEALTHY WORD COME FROM YOUR MOUTH], BUT ONLY SAY WHAT IS HELPFUL [GOOD] TO MAKE OTHERS STRONGER [BUILD OTHERS UP] AND MEET [ACCORDING TO] THEIR NEEDS. THEN WHAT YOU SAY WILL DO GOOD [GIVE GRACE; BE A GIFT] TO THOSE WHO LISTEN TO YOU.* (Ephesians 4:29)

*WHEN YOU TALK, YOU SHOULD ALWAYS BE KIND [GRACIOUS] AND PLEASANT [WINSOME; ENGAGING; OR WHOLESOME; SEASONED WITH SALT] SO YOU WILL BE ABLE TO ANSWER EVERYONE IN THE WAY YOU SHOULD.* (Colossians 4:6)

In this particular book, we won't be looking at the specifications of what a word of wisdom or word of knowledge is (for more information on that, you can read *Ministry School Boot Camp: Training for Helps Ministry, Appointments, and Beyond* or *Manifestations of the Spirit: The Work of the Holy Spirit in the Church and in Your Life*), but for this particular situation, a word of wisdom or knowledge would provide insight and knowledge about a situation in a way that one cannot easily know anything about. Giving spiritual word is not giving one's own opinion, advice, or ideas, but conveying the word of God through the gift. This means that one who gives word must know when to speak and when to be silent, and what to convey through each word the Lord provides.

## **Encouragement/edification**

One of the most powerful forms of healing and deliverance can come in the form of encouragement and edification. Sometimes we downplay the relevance of a word spoken in the right time, for the right purposes, to the betterment and building up of another.

*AS IRON SHARPENS IRON,*
*SO PEOPLE CAN IMPROVE EACH OTHER [SHARPEN THEIR FRIENDS].*
(Proverbs 27:17)

*Two people are better than one,*
  *because they get more done by working together [a good return for their hard work/toil].*
*If one falls down,*
  *the other can help him [his colleague] up.*
*But it is bad [a pity] for the person who is alone and falls,*
  *because no one is there to help.*
*If two lie down together, they will be warm,*
  *but a person alone will not be warm.*
*An enemy [Someone] might defeat [overpower] one person,*
  *but two people together can defend themselves [stand up against them];*
*a rope that is woven of three strings is hard to break [a three-stranded cord does not quickly snap; having a friend is good, having more friends is better].*
(Ecclesiastes 4:9-12)

*I pray that the God Who gives hope will fill you with much [all] joy and peace while you trust [because you trust; through your faith] in Him. Then your hope will overflow by the power of the Holy Spirit.* (Romans 15:13)

*[Therefore,] Does your life in Christ give you strength? [If there is any encouragement in Christ...] Does His love comfort you? [...if any comfort from (His) love...] Do we share together in the Spirit? [...if any fellowship/sharing of the Spirit...] Do you have mercy and kindness? [...if any mercy/affection and kindness/compassion...] If so [...then], make me very happy [fulfill/complete my joy] by having the same thoughts [being like-minded/of one mind], sharing the same love, and having one mind [heart; soul] and purpose [goal; mind]. When you do things, do not let selfishness [rivalry; selfish ambition] or pride be your guide. Instead, be humble and give more honor [regard; value] to others than to yourselves. Do not be interested only in your own life [look out for your own interests], but be interested in the lives of others [look out for others' interests].* (Philippians 2:1-4)

*So encourage each other and give each other strength [build each other up], just as you are doing now.* (1 Thessalonians 5:11)

The spiritual gift of edification is more than just speaking clichés we hear frequently, repeating positive phrases, or trying to puff someone up. Genuine edification builds upon what's good and right within a person and even a situation and gives them that lift, that stirring, to continue to even greater things as they follow the right path in their lives. Encouragement acknowledges what's already great, and helps to promote what will be even better as time goes on.

Healing and deliverance is not just about the level of faith one has to be healed or delivered, it is also about how much faith and healing they have to remain that way. Encouragement and edification should not just take the form of encouraging people to pray, but also to live right, to take care of their physical bodies, to engage in spiritual practices to maintain well-being, to watch their attitudes, stress levels, and toxic thoughts, and to adopt an outlook that reflects the blessed perspective of the Kingdom.

## **Chapter 14 Assignments**

- Research a story of unethical practices in healing and deliverance and the solution to the issues present in that story as constructed through ethical precepts.
- Create a presentation on the different aspects of ethics you believe are most important to healing and deliverance ministry.

*A woman praying*

## - CHAPTER FIFTEEN -
## Helping Others Maintain Healing and Deliverance

By helping each other with your troubles [bearing each other's burdens],
you truly obey [accomplish; fulfill] the law of Christ.
(Galatians 6:2)

Throughout this book, we have looked at the complications of both the divine and the demonic, spirits, the occult, superstitions, spiritual warfare, and the ins and outs of healing and deliverance. As our final thought, we are going to consider the ways in which we can help people maintain healing and deliverance. When someone comes to us and experiences freedom, our job does not easily end; it often has additional steps and works that we can take to help people maintain their healing and deliverance. It is certainly the responsibility of the individual to maintain their own healing and deliverance in various ways, but as those who are a part of the healing process, our work doesn't begin and end at an altar call or a counseling session. We cannot control the behavior of other people, but we can certainly make sure we do not present ourselves and our work as a stumbling block to those who genuinely seek healing and deliverance and come out on the other side. As leaders, much of what we do is maintain those who we lead: we do our part to educate, to train, to teach, to disciple, to correct, and to encourage those who are under our care. In cases of healing and deliverance, this process is even more important: people need support. As agents of healing, we are a part of their support system that encourages them to stay the course and maintain the needed accountability to continue for God.

All of us need accountability; all of us need to help one another move forward; all of us need help to maintain the grounds and healing we have received in this life. Here we are going to learn about ways we can be of better support, ways we can help others as well as ourselves, and consider ways that things trip us up or make them more difficult than they need to be for ourselves and others.

**The mind in deliverance**

I've met many people who come to me, asking for healing or deliverance, with it in their minds that something specific is holding them bound, and they need freedom from it. Whether it's a wrong diagnosis from the doctor or something that doesn't even exist (such as the spirit of Jezebel or a spirit of intimidation), they believe they have that spirit, and they will not hear anything to the contrary. They believe they need to be delivered from that specific spirit, because that spirit is controlling their lives. Notably so, they may even manifest the characteristics of that imaginary spirit (or those people assign to it), it may damage things in their lives, and it may wreak havoc, no matter where they go.

This is an example of the power of the mind in deliverance. As we spoke in the last chapter about being careful as to what we say over people and the power of suggestion, people can quickly think they have things they don't because someone else suggested they have it or outright "spiritually diagnosed" them based on an assorted list of symptoms they endorse or believe. People speak it, they receive it, they embody it, and they start manifesting it, all because they received something that was spoken over them that wasn't even true.

*THE LORD SPOKE HIS WORD [WORD OF THE LORD CAME] TO ME, SAYING: "HUMAN [SON OF MAN; 2:1], PROPHESY AGAINST THE PROPHETS OF ISRAEL. SAY TO THOSE WHO MAKE UP THEIR OWN PROPHECIES [PROPHESY FROM THEIR HEARTS/IMAGINATION]... "NOW, HUMAN [SON OF MAN; 2:1], LOOK TOWARD THE WOMEN AMONG [DAUGHTERS OF] YOUR PEOPLE WHO MAKE UP THEIR OWN PROPHECIES [PROPHESY FROM THEIR OWN HEARTS/IMAGINATIONS]. PROPHESY AGAINST THEM."* (Ezekiel 13:1-2,17)

*[FOR] ALTHOUGH WE LIVE IN THE WORLD [WALK IN THE FLESH], WE DO NOT FIGHT [WAGE WAR] IN THE SAME WAY THE WORLD FIGHTS [ACCORDING TO THE FLESH]. WE*

*FIGHT WITH WEAPONS THAT ARE DIFFERENT FROM THOSE THE WORLD USES [NOT MERELY HUMAN WEAPONS; NOT OF THE FLESH]. OUR WEAPONS HAVE POWER FROM GOD THAT CAN DESTROY THE ENEMY'S STRONG PLACES [STRONGHOLDS; FORTRESSES]. WE DESTROY PEOPLE'S ARGUMENTS [HUMAN REASONING; SOPHISTRIES] AND EVERY PROUD THING [PRETENSION; EXALTED OPINION; HIGH THING] THAT RAISES ITSELF AGAINST THE KNOWLEDGE OF GOD. WE CAPTURE EVERY THOUGHT AND MAKE IT OBEY CHRIST.* (2 Corinthians 10:3-5)

Whether a spirit is real or not, whether a demon is real or not, whether a person's diagnosis is real or not, if someone thinks they have something, then they have it because they create it within their minds and they see the fruit of its manifestation in their lives. While it is imperative we strive for truth and accuracy in our ministries, we need to consider the fact that we may need to pray for people and deliver people from their own delusions in order to get to the place where they can receive real deliverance. Sometimes the stages of deliverance don't fall in an order that we are comfortable with, and we need to cast off the imaginations, vanities, and other ideas that cast themselves above God without even realizing they've done it.

## **Behavior modification with redemption and deliverance**

The discussion of healing and deliverance leads to the inevitable "remaining delivered" conversation. Some argue that for deliverance or healing to be legitimate, one can never get sick or have any symptoms of the issue, again. This is further complicated because some healings and deliverances require personal interest and involvement to maintain them, and then we have those who do not think a healing or deliverance is valid if it doesn't just require the person to walk away without any complications.

*Vegetables*

The issue of behavior modification is one we often dislike

in church, because it hits home at our personal issues, those we hope God will eradicate without our effort. We also deal with the question of heaven and hell, and many people fear for their salvation if they take steps to take care of themselves beyond just attending church. We fuss over things that aren't good for us on an eternal level, but the discussion needs to move beyond whether we will go to hell for those actions. There is great question in the Scriptures as to whether all things are allowed, but if they are truly beneficial – and it's not all about eternal benefit. We need to be willing to explore whether the things we do hurt our relationship with God, with others, and with ourselves, right now, because a lot of what we do might bring harm in the immediate rather than the eternal.

For example: we all have heard for years that smoking, drug use, and excessive drinking are all bad for us. Sedentary lifestyles aren't good for us. Being uneducated and ignorant isn't good for us. Living emotionally, out of control, is not good for us. Being chronically negative and exposed to people who are negative aren't good for us. Not getting enough sleep is not good for us. Not eating right is not good for us. Yet, somehow, some way, we all keep going on, plowing forward, with all the bad habits we've acquired, killing us all along the way.

*"I AM ALLOWED TO DO ALL THINGS [ALL THINGS ARE LAWFUL/PERMISSIBLE FOR ME; PROBABLY A SLOGAN THE CORINTHIANS WERE USING; SEE ALSO 7:1; 8:1, 4; 10:23]," BUT NOT ALL THINGS ARE GOOD FOR ME TO DO [PROFITABLE; BENEFICIAL]. "I AM ALLOWED TO DO ALL THINGS [ALL THINGS ARE LAWFUL/PERMISSIBLE FOR ME]," BUT I WILL NOT LET ANYTHING MAKE ME ITS SLAVE.* (1 Corinthians 6:12)

*"WE ARE ALLOWED TO DO ALL THINGS [ALL THINGS ARE LAWFUL/PERMISSIBLE]," BUT NOT ALL THINGS ARE GOOD FOR US TO DO [PROFITABLE; BENEFICIAL]. "WE ARE ALLOWED TO DO ALL THINGS [ALL THINGS ARE LAWFUL/PERMISSIBLE]," BUT NOT ALL THINGS HELP OTHERS GROW STRONGER [BUILD UP; THE QUOTATIONS WERE PROBABLY SLOGANS THE CORINTHIANS USED; 6:12, 13; 7:1; 8:1, 4]. DO NOT LOOK OUT ONLY FOR YOURSELVES. LOOK OUT FOR THE GOOD OF OTHERS.* (1 Corinthians 10:23)

All of us can benefit from changing our behavior, but it is especially relevant for those who have received some form of healing or deliverance (which should also be all of us, at some point or another). To maintain where we are, maintain our physical, spiritual, mental, and emotional status, we need to adopt change. If we are in our physical bodies, we are subject to new, additional, recurrent, or different problems because our bodies, minds, and emotions change throughout our lifetimes. The best way to maintain a good change is to make changes that bring us to a new place, one where even more healing, deliverance, and recovery can take place.

## **Promoting better spiritual and physical health**

As ministers, we have the responsibility to lead our congregations and ministries in pursuit of better spiritual and physical health. It may sound strange to comment on better spiritual health, but the reality is many of our churches reflect the sick, unhappy, biased mindsets that are keeping them down and ill. If all we teach on is certain sin, all we do is scream in people's faces, and even if we go to the other extreme to avoid such teaching all together, we aren't giving people the ability to come to a place of better spiritual health, where they are able to understand and interpret their spiritual relationship and make the changes they need to, therein.

Sometimes ministers think their only realm of encouragement should be on a spiritual level. It's true that, as ministers, the souls of people are a major focus and concern, but we should be concerned about the whole of people we minister to and work with. That is the essence of healing and deliverance in and of itself: caring about the whole of a person, rather than breaking people off into compartments and only caring about what happens to one part of them. Most spiritual leaders may not know the ins and outs of physical health, but they can certainly partner and work with individuals who do, who can help promote a holistic approach to individuals who seek greater spiritual insight in their lives.

*I WILL BRING BACK YOUR HEALTH*
  *AND HEAL YOUR INJURIES," SAYS THE LORD,*
*"BECAUSE OTHER PEOPLE FORCED YOU AWAY [THEY CALLED YOU 'DRIVEN OUT'/'AN OUTCAST'].*
  *THEY SAID ABOUT YOU, 'NO ONE CARES ABOUT [SEEKS] JERUSALEM [ZION; THE LOCATION OF THE TEMPLE]!'"* (Jeremiah 30:17)

*YOU SHOULD [DON'T YOU...?] KNOW THAT YOUR BODY IS A TEMPLE FOR THE HOLY SPIRIT WHO IS IN YOU AND WAS GIVEN TO YOU BY GOD. SO YOU DO NOT BELONG TO YOURSELVES, BECAUSE YOU WERE BOUGHT BY GOD [BOUGHT] FOR A PRICE. SO HONOR GOD WITH YOUR BODIES.* (1 Corinthians 6:19-20)

*EAT ANY MEAT THAT IS SOLD IN THE MEAT MARKET. DO NOT ASK QUESTIONS ABOUT IT [FOR CONSCIENCE'S SAKE]. YOU MAY EAT IT, "BECAUSE THE EARTH BELONGS TO THE LORD, AND EVERYTHING IN IT [ITS FULLNESS/ABUNDANCE/BOUNTY; PS. 24:1; 50:12; 89:11]."*

*THOSE WHO ARE NOT BELIEVERS MAY INVITE YOU TO EAT WITH THEM. IF YOU WANT TO GO, EAT ANYTHING THAT IS PUT BEFORE YOU. DO NOT ASK QUESTIONS ABOUT IT [FOR CONSCIENCE'S SAKE]. BUT IF ANYONE SAYS TO YOU, "THAT FOOD WAS OFFERED TO IDOLS," DO NOT EAT IT. DO NOT EAT IT BECAUSE OF THAT PERSON WHO TOLD YOU AND BECAUSE EATING IT MIGHT BE THOUGHT TO BE WRONG [FOR CONSCIENCE'S SAKE]. I DON'T MEAN YOU THINK IT IS WRONG [YOUR CONSCIENCE], BUT THE OTHER PERSON MIGHT [THE CONSCIENCE OF THE OTHER PERSON]. BUT WHY, YOU ASK, [OR FOR WHY] SHOULD MY FREEDOM BE JUDGED BY SOMEONE ELSE'S CONSCIENCE? IF I EAT THE MEAL WITH THANKFULNESS, WHY AM I CRITICIZED BECAUSE OF SOMETHING FOR WHICH I THANK GOD?*

*THE ANSWER IS [OR THEREFORE; IN SUMMARY], IF YOU EAT OR DRINK, OR IF YOU DO ANYTHING, DO IT ALL FOR THE GLORY OF GOD. NEVER DO ANYTHING THAT MIGHT HURT OTHERS—JEWS, GREEKS, OR GOD'S CHURCH—JUST AS I, ALSO, TRY TO PLEASE EVERYBODY IN EVERY WAY. I AM NOT TRYING TO DO WHAT IS GOOD [ADVANTAGEOUS] FOR ME BUT WHAT IS GOOD [ADVANTAGEOUS] FOR MOST PEOPLE SO THEY CAN BE SAVED.* (1 Corinthians 10:25-33)

Our people cannot be made well if they are not treated whole, entire, and not in part. There are many ways we can incorporate healthier attitudes into our spiritual lessons and teachings, including:

- A look at principles of health
- Nutrition and fitness classes
- Self-care
- Prayer walks
- Participating in community events as a church
- Holding the occasional service outside
- Street evangelism
- Encouraging members to play with their children outside
- Public health education on diseases, such as diabetes
- Prayer for health

- New spiritual classes and sermons, on topics and passages never studied before
- Promote healthier potluck or church dinners
- Incorporate physical activity and healthy eating into special interest ministry events
- Offer HIV/STI testing at the church
- When holding night services, make a point to dismiss at a reasonable hour
- Make sure services do not interfere with mealtimes

**Rejoice with those who rejoice, mourn with those who mourn**

The Scriptures give us a very important piece of wisdom we tend to overlook:

*YOUR LOVE MUST BE REAL [SINCERE; UNHYPOCRITICAL]. HATE [ABHOR; DESPISE] WHAT IS EVIL, AND HOLD ON [CLING] TO WHAT IS GOOD. LOVE [BE DEVOTED TO] EACH OTHER LIKE BROTHERS AND SISTERS [WITH FAMILY/BROTHERLY AFFECTION]. GIVE EACH OTHER MORE HONOR THAN YOU WANT FOR YOURSELVES [OR OUTDO ONE ANOTHER IN SHOWING HONOR; OR BE EAGER TO SHOW HONOR TO ONE ANOTHER]. DO NOT BE LAZY BUT WORK HARD [LACKING IN ZEAL], SERVING THE LORD WITH ALL YOUR HEART [A FERVENT/EAGER/ENTHUSIASTIC SPIRIT]. BE JOYFUL BECAUSE YOU HAVE HOPE [REJOICE IN HOPE]. BE PATIENT [ENDURE] WHEN TROUBLE COMES [IN SUFFERING/TRIBULATION], AND PRAY AT ALL TIMES [FAITHFULLY; WITH PERSISTENCE/PERSEVERANCE]. SHARE WITH GOD'S PEOPLE [THE SAINTS] WHO NEED HELP. BRING STRANGERS IN NEED INTO YOUR HOMES [PURSUE/BE EAGER TO SHOW HOSPITALITY].*

*WISH GOOD FOR [BLESS] THOSE WHO HARM [PERSECUTE] YOU; WISH THEM WELL [BLESS] AND DO NOT CURSE THEM. BE HAPPY [REJOICE] WITH THOSE WHO ARE HAPPY [REJOICE], AND BE SAD [WEEP] WITH THOSE WHO ARE SAD [WEEP]. LIVE IN PEACE [HARMONY] WITH EACH OTHER. DO NOT BE PROUD [ARROGANT; HAUGHTY], BUT MAKE FRIENDS WITH THOSE WHO SEEM UNIMPORTANT [ASSOCIATE WITH THE HUMBLE/THOSE OF LOW SOCIAL STATUS; OR BE WILLING TO DO LOWLY TASKS]. DO NOT THINK HOW SMART [WISE; SUPERIOR] YOU ARE.* (Romans 12:9-16)

The work of the church is not just about Gospel proclamation; it is also about Gospel living. We could tell every soul on this planet about Jesus

Christ, but if we do not take care of the church we have and make sure the infrastructure is in place to receive those people, we are never going to leave an impact in this world. Discipling people is more than just getting them saved and then preaching to them a few hours per week. Discipling individuals is a life-long commitment we make to see the Gospel through in each person we lead and supporting all members of the church as we go through and do the work we have been called to do. It's about more than just doing what we think of as minister tasks; it's about being a good human being and genuinely caring about what happens to others. If someone is afflicted, genuinely afflicted, we should care and do what we can to see them through; if someone mourns, we should understand what they are going through and comfort them through it; and if someone is happy, we should be happy for and with them. the Scripture's words are not just about the ends of salvation in terms of our choices, but also about what it looks like to live saved, to interact as a people who have been rescued and transformed from one thing to something else, and to how we should treat others around us.

As believers – not just leaders, but believers – we should be sincere in our love of others; shun evil; cling to good. Our devotion to one another should be evident to others. Being a Christian should be about our ability to do good to others, to become a family of faith instead of just families who come to something once a week. Our lives should change, our very being should change, and that means it should reflect in how we treat each other.

All of us in church should rejoice when someone is healed or delivered and we should all stand with those who encounter hard times. Instead of encouraging people to return to old ways and bad behaviors, we should stand with everyone who is in recovery, who is in remission, who has overcome something that brought them down, and encourage things that will help them to stay healed, delivered, and on the right walk for their spiritual lives.

## **What if it's not what we are looking for it to be?**

Sometimes people don't get "healed" or "delivered" in the way they'd hoped or in the way we hope they would. We love the altar calls where people walk away with a visible transformation: crutches are gone, getting out of wheelchairs, people who are visibly different than they used to be…all these things stir audiences, they make them believe healing and deliverance are real, and that it somehow makes us all feel better about our own faith, almost as a restorative property. We like the idea of things happening instantly, of not having to wait things out and we like the moments of instant deliverance. God certainly can – and does – operate by "suddenlies," but many more of us than not have to discipline ourselves to walk out the difficulties of our lives unto a place of victory. Our difficult times teach us things, they teach us things about ourselves, and there is, as we have discussed earlier, more than one way to find healing or deliverance from something. Just because it doesn't happen the way we want it to doesn't mean someone isn't coming into a place of healing and deliverance, and it certainly doesn't mean that someone didn't receive healing and deliverance in a different way.

Just because something doesn't manifest like we hoped it would doesn't mean people have a lack of faith, are doing something wrong, or aren't measuring up. What it does mean is that we are called that much more to stand with people through difficult things that don't have easy answers.

*WHEN AN EVIL [DEFILING; UNCLEAN] SPIRIT COMES OUT OF A PERSON, IT TRAVELS THROUGH DRY [WATERLESS; ARID] PLACES, LOOKING FOR A PLACE TO REST, BUT IT DOESN'T FIND IT. SO THE SPIRIT SAYS, "I WILL GO BACK TO THE HOUSE [THE PERSON] I LEFT." WHEN THE SPIRIT COMES BACK, IT FINDS THE HOUSE STILL EMPTY, SWEPT CLEAN, AND MADE NEAT [PUT IN ORDER; FIXED UP]. THEN THE EVIL SPIRIT GOES OUT AND BRINGS SEVEN OTHER SPIRITS EVEN MORE EVIL [WICKED] THAN IT IS, AND THEY GO IN AND LIVE THERE. SO THE PERSON HAS EVEN MORE TROUBLE THAN BEFORE [THE LAST STATE OF THAT PERSON IS WORSE THAN THE FIRST]. IT IS THE SAME WAY [SO IT WILL BE] WITH THE EVIL PEOPLE WHO LIVE TODAY [THIS EVIL GENERATION].* (Matthew 12:43-45)

The Scripture's commands to us are not just to be there for people when the going is good, but when it is hard, as well. This includes when healing and deliverance is not exactly how we might hope it to be, as well as when people deal with various temptations and issues that question the validity of one's deliverance. It is possible for spirits to re-attach themselves to people in their lives; it is possible for more spirits to return, and it is possible for them to be diverse or different from those that came before. The open door for this to enter in is clearly the lack of support that frequently results from deliverance. Everything can be made nice and tidy, and the door left flung wide open for spirits to return because we are constantly negative, telling people they aren't doing the right thing, telling them they are not healed and delivered, and ushering temptations such as family issues, sharing or offering things that aren't good, or making suggestions that there is something wrong with them for reaching a place of acceptance and maintenance all lead to people's downfall.

The Bible's advice to us in many different forms reminds us that we are not an island, and we don't sin by ourselves. The person who does the action is the one who gets caught, but that person didn't get there by themselves. There was a whole lot of dares, calling someone "chicken," doing everything but pulling the metaphorical trigger, and then running to avoid consequences. It should be our very desire to make sure we aren't this type of person, one who leads other people into sin and into places that hamper progress. As part of our spiritual transformation, we should reflect our change in how we help others.

## **Lead us not into temptation...**

*Exercise*

Temptation is one of those things that, no matter how much we might like it to vanish, never goes away. There will forever be things that challenge us and cause us to feel void, powerless, and like we'll never be able to withstand the pressure. Temptation finds us in the most unsuspecting places: a family event, our jobs, something that causes stress, or through the suggestion of someone who we'd never suspect. We find temptation when we are tired, stressed, hungry, or frustrated. It comes when we think too much of ourselves, and when we don't think enough. It might come through something familiar, or something else that seems or is new. No matter how you spin it, temptation is temptation is temptation.

STAY AWAKE [KEEP WATCH] AND PRAY FOR STRENGTH AGAINST TEMPTATION [OR NOT TO FAIL THE TEST]. THE SPIRIT WANTS TO DO WHAT IS RIGHT [IS WILLING], BUT THE BODY [OR HUMAN NATURE; THE FLESH] IS WEAK. (Matthew 26:41)

*But the worries of this life [world; age], the temptation [deceitfulness; seduction] of wealth, and many other evil desires [desires for other things] keep the teaching from growing and producing fruit in their lives [come in and choke the word, making it unfruitful].* (Mark 4:19)

*The seed that fell on rock is like those who hear God's teaching and accept [receive] it gladly [with joy], but they don't allow the teaching to go deep into their lives [have no root]. They believe for a while, but when trouble [a time of temptation/testing] comes, they give up [fall away; depart].* (Luke 8:13)

*Forgive us for our sins, because [as] we forgive everyone who has done wrong to us [sins against us; is indebted to us; sin is pictured as a debt owed]. And do not cause us to be tempted [or do not subject us to testing; lead us not into temptation].* (Luke 11:4)

*Jesus said to His followers [disciples], "Things that cause people to sin [Stumbling blocks; Causes of sin; Temptations] will happen [are inevitable; it is impossible for them not to come], but how terrible for [woe to] the person who causes them to happen!* (Luke 17:1)

*The only temptation [or trials] that has come to you is that which everyone has [(common to) human life]. But you can trust God [God is faithful], Who will not permit you to be tempted more than you can stand. But when you are tempted, He will also give you a way to escape so that you will be able to stand [endure] it.* (1 Corinthians 10:13)

*Those who want to become rich bring temptation to themselves [fall into temptation] and are caught in a trap. They want [desire] many foolish and harmful things that ruin and destroy people [plunge people into ruin and destruction].* (1 Timothy 6:9)

There are many different things we identify as "sin" that we do not talk about in church, because they aren't crowd-pleasers. The reason they aren't crowd-pleasers is simple: they are all behaviors that are a part of what we've come to understand as "church culture." Step back and think about some of them for a few minutes: the huge, massive, unhealthy church dinners where people overeat. Bake sales laden with those pies and cakes you just have to take home. The over-emphasis on marriage and getting married, pushing and encouraging singles to date and hook up, even if we don't think they should go as far as they do. Promoting sedentary lifestyles that are void of exercise. Discouraging education. All these things can fall into several categories the Bible clearly identifies as sin: gluttony, contention, meddling, judgment, laziness, and foolishness. We don't think of them that way, however, because it would mean we would challenge churches far beyond the boundaries where they are comfortable and people would never return.

Inadvertently, by picking and choosing what we want to promote because they please crowds, we are causing people to fall into all sorts of temptations and into all sorts of unhealthy, destructive patterns that are causing them to be sick and in bondage. The average churchgoer wants a miracle, not to hear that they must stop eating so much or stop trolling for a mate or go to school, because we've been told "God is going to do it!" for ages. But what does that mean? If someone has Type 2 diabetes related to obesity and they get healed from it but fail to adopt better choices for their eating and exercise, they will wind up with another problem, if not Type 2 Diabetes, all over again. It's not that they weren't delivered from their ailment, it's that they weren't delivered from the issues within themselves that need to change. The culture of church didn't extend change beyond the altar, and in hoping God would change everything in an instant, temptation crept back in and took over.

Yes, that alcoholic can't just have "one drink." Yes, that drug addict can't have just "one joint." Yes, that person with diabetes can't just have "one cupcake." Yes, that person who needs to lose weight or maintain good health can't skip the gym that "one time." We need to understand and encourage in their behavior modifications and be more willing and understanding to find new ways to be social with people that don't involve vices and temptations. As a church, we need to think of new ways to interact, ways that encourage and uplift in fellowship, and that do not lead us into tempting places that cause us trouble in the long-term.

## **Standing in the way of healing and deliverance**

No one likes facing the idea they might be standing in the way of healing and deliverance, but such does happen. All the things we have discussed about church life are all a part of the negative ways churches, without even thinking about it, often enhance and encourage people to remain sick and bound. We are creatures of habit, and being in church does not change that if we do not change ourselves.

Sometimes people do not see healing and deliverance because the church leadership is not equipped, nor trained, for empowerment. The angry, vicious, in-your-face-preacher is a part of the type of the Christian landscape. We think nice, quiet ministers are permissive, while fire-and-brimstone preachers are the "real deal." Anger, hostility, aggression, frustration, annoyance, berating, and even abuse are all a part of the traditional Christian preacher, someone who comes along and handles the work of ministry in a manner that is considered purposeful to instill a sense of sin and a fear of God.

The problem is that the methods we've used to promote fear and awareness of sin have never worked; they just promote fear and guilt. People still go on sinning, people still go on avoiding God, and we've contrived an endless number of loopholes and ways around the things we do to keep doing them and avoid the wrath of the preacher. The methods used have never produced the fruit unto repentance, because they have become a caricature of themselves, something that is considered "normal" and purposeful when it is not.

It has not helped that old school church training teaches us to be the best students of our leaders, willing and ready to do anything they ask. There's nothing wrong with teaching obedience and respect for leaders, but there is something wrong when we are seeking to obey our leaders more than we seek to obey God because we have never learned to hear His voice. If our belief is that God expects us to obey authority but not obey Him, we have a sincere – and serious – problem.

*JESUS CALLED THEM TOGETHER AND SAID, "YOU KNOW THAT THE RULERS OF OTHER NATIONS [THE GENTILES] LOVE TO SHOW THEIR POWER [LORD IT] OVER THE PEOPLE, AND THEIR IMPORTANT LEADERS [HIGH OFFICIALS; GREAT ONES] LOVE TO USE [EXERT] THEIR AUTHORITY [OVER THEM]. BUT IT SHOULD NOT BE [MUST NOT BE; IS NOT TO BE] THAT WAY AMONG YOU. [INSTEAD, BUT] WHOEVER WANTS TO BECOME GREAT AMONG YOU MUST SERVE THE REST OF YOU LIKE A SERVANT [BE YOUR SERVANT]. WHOEVER WANTS TO BECOME THE FIRST AMONG YOU MUST SERVE ALL OF YOU LIKE A SLAVE [BE YOUR SLAVE]. IN THE SAME WAY, THE SON OF MAN DID NOT COME TO BE SERVED. HE CAME TO SERVE OTHERS AND TO GIVE HIS LIFE AS A RANSOM FOR MANY PEOPLE [IS. 53:12; JOHN 11:49-50]."* (Mark 10:42-45)

*OBEY [OR HAVE CONFIDENCE IN] YOUR LEADERS AND ACT UNDER [OR SUBMIT TO] THEIR AUTHORITY. [FOR; BECAUSE] THEY ARE WATCHING OVER YOU, BECAUSE THEY ARE RESPONSIBLE [WILL GIVE AN ACCOUNT (TO GOD)] FOR YOUR SOULS [OR YOU]. OBEY THEM [DO THIS; ACT THIS WAY] SO THAT THEY WILL DO THIS WORK WITH JOY, NOT SADNESS [OR COMPLAINT; GROANING], FOR THAT WOULD BE OF NO BENEFIT [ADVANTAGE; HELP] TO YOU.* (Hebrews 13:17)

We should love our leaders; they should remind us of the love of God and of our need to connect with and work with Him. It should never be our leader's voice void of God, telling us what to do and guiding us in His place. No Christian should hear their leader's voice more than they hear God's, and no leader's voice should overtake the voice of God. If we desire healing and deliverance, we must learn how to follow God's leading, because it becomes relevant in each stage of the walk for healing and deliverance, and then the place of maintenance later. If we are not spiritually healthy, we will not be physically healthy, and if we are not able to hear from God, we are not spiritually developed.

## **Misusing healing and deliverance**

Victim shaming is a dark and unfortunate aspect of the world in which we live. Victim shaming occurs when a victim of a crime, an offense, or a situation is blamed for somehow causing it themselves. For example, rape victims are often blamed for incidents of rape because of their clothing, because they were out at a certain hour, because they knew the perpetrator, or because they went out on a date with them. These things do not change the fact that rapists rape out of a sense of power and control, not because they are lured by clothing, someone was out at a certain time, or who they know or date, but somehow, some way, in culture, we give the message that rapists are not accountable for their behavior – it was the victim's fault. Victim shaming is not exclusive to rape and is found in virtually any other setting where things happen to people that seem unfair or they "fall victim" to things. Whether it's cancer, infertility, loss of a child, a death in the family, HIV, other illness, physical malady, or general problems, people are quick to somehow make the person who experiences these things the cause of the problem, rather than trying to lift them up unto a solution.

The result is an entire church full of people who feel the need to act healed or delivered in the name of avoiding shaming victims. Victims are not encouraged to be angry or upset and are often accused of unforgiveness or bitterness if they display hurt or anger over what happened to them. The goal is they are to act "normal" and promote all the normal "churchy" things, pretending that nothing ever happened to them, and putting on the brave front that everything is, in all situations, all right.

The problem is that everything is not all right, such a person is not healed, and the issues will only be manifested in other ways if they are shamed as a victim. There are two very well-known female television preachers who both share from their extensive backgrounds that include rape, sexual abuse, physical abuse, and emotional abuse. A large part of their ministry personas lies in offering techniques and teaching for healing from abuse and shame, and both also talk a great deal about self-esteem. The question comes as their physical appearances tell a different story than what they claim with their mouths. While they may claim to "like themselves" and "accept the healing" that is theirs, they are both well over fifty years of age and have had extensive cosmetic surgery, so much so it has changed the look and shape of their faces and facial features. They wear large amounts of make-up and dress in styles and outfits that really don't suit the bodies of women their age. They claim to be healed, but the need to look a certain way, to appear a certain way on the surface, tells me that they are having issues within, issues that drive for perfection and having others accept them, so much so they are willing to alter their bodies and their appearance. They are still having the remnants of abuse, of living lives where they were mistreated, but now they are following the dictates of someone else as to who they should be and what they should look like.

I have often said I would have far more regard for their ministries if they would just say, "I was abused and I am angry about it" or "I am abused and I still feel ashamed, like I am not good enough." These two statements would go a lot further to help victims of abuse speak up, remove the stigma of being abused, and to help empower victims to embrace how they feel about what has happened to them than to just go on and claim their healing is acting and living like nothing ever happened to them. We need to do more than just feel better; we need to be better.

*BUT IF A MAN MEETS AN ENGAGED GIRL OUT IN THE COUNTRY [FIELD] AND FORCES HER TO HAVE SEXUAL RELATIONS WITH HIM [SEIZES HER AND LIES WITH HER], ONLY THE MAN WHO HAD SEXUAL RELATIONS [LAY] WITH HER MUST BE PUT TO DEATH. DON'T DO ANYTHING TO THE GIRL, BECAUSE SHE HAS NOT DONE A SIN WORTHY OF DEATH. THIS IS*

*LIKE THE PERSON WHO ATTACKS [RISES UP] AND MURDERS A NEIGHBOR; THE MAN FOUND THE ENGAGED GIRL IN THE COUNTRY [FIELD] AND SHE SCREAMED [YELLED FOR HELP], BUT NO ONE WAS THERE TO SAVE [RESCUE] HER.* (Deuteronomy 22:25-27)

*Reflection*

*AFTER THE LORD HAD SAID THESE THINGS TO JOB, HE SAID TO ELIPHAZ THE TEMANITE, "I AM ANGRY WITH [MY ANGER BURNS AGAINST] YOU AND YOUR TWO FRIENDS, BECAUSE YOU HAVE NOT SAID WHAT IS RIGHT [CORRECT] ABOUT ME, AS MY SERVANT JOB DID. NOW TAKE SEVEN BULLS AND SEVEN MALE SHEEP, AND GO TO MY SERVANT JOB, AND OFFER A BURNT OFFERING [LEV. 1:1-7] FOR YOURSELVES [FOR ATONEMENT]. MY SERVANT JOB WILL PRAY [INTERCEDE] FOR YOU, AND I WILL LISTEN TO [ACCEPT] HIS PRAYER. THEN I WILL NOT PUNISH YOU FOR BEING FOOLISH [TREAT YOU ACCORDING TO YOUR FOOLISHNESS]. YOU HAVE NOT SAID WHAT IS RIGHT [CORRECT] ABOUT ME, AS MY SERVANT JOB DID."* (Job 42:7-8)

Healing and deliverance are not platforms for victim shaming or to make people feel worse about things that have already happened to them. Victims need to be empowered with their voice; they need to be heard; they need to feel a place of restoration, where what has happened may never be right with that person, but that life can be great with other people and new opportunities galore. There is life after abuse; there is life after victimization; and the point is that the life that comes forth after is different, is more and transformative than it was before.

## Creating conscientious ministry

The last thing we will examine in this book is how to create a more conscientious ministry. We discussed earlier in this chapter about the way that ministers have actually been taught the opposite of conscientious work; they have been taught to be angry, belligerent, and indifferent to the problems and issues that may sit in people present in the pews or seats of a service or meeting. The only goal of the hostile preacher is guilt and fear, and they do not consider if their words do more harm than good, or cause people to never return. The goal of the typical minister is not creating healing and deliverance but being the cause of it! They might not think of it in this way, but the stark reality is the church, as it has been for generations and many times is now, is not a conduit for healing, but one for ignorant, paranoid, offense.

Conscientious ministry is the opposite of what we just discussed. It calls on the minister to be aware of the things that exist and are experienced in this world and take those things into consideration as well as those who may have been hurt by them. We may not consider ministry to be a cause of defense when it comes to the evils and ills of this world, but church should be the first line of defense. We should offer people refuge, the answer, the respite to the cares of the world and the hurts therein. Church is supposed to be the one place where we can come and lay our burdens down, picking up something that empowers us to go back out into the world and try it again, no matter how difficult things may have been for us in the past.

*MY GUILT HAS OVERWHELMED ME [PASSED OVER MY HEAD];*
  *LIKE A LOAD [BURDEN] IT WEIGHS ME DOWN [IS TOO HEAVY FOR ME].*
(Psalm 38:4)

*PRAISE [BLESSED BE] THE LORD, GOD OUR SAVIOR [VICTOR],*
  *WHO HELPS US [BEARS OUR BURDENS] EVERY DAY. SELAH [INTERLUDE]*
*OUR GOD IS A GOD WHO SAVES US [GIVES US VICTORY];*
  *THE LORD GOD SAVES US [BRINGS US OUT] FROM DEATH.*
(Psalm 68:18-20)

*I TOOK THE LOAD OFF [REMOVED THE BURDEN FROM] THEIR SHOULDERS;*
  *I LET THEM PUT DOWN THEIR BASKETS [THEIR HANDS WERE REMOVED FROM THE BASKETS].*
(Psalm 81:6)

*"COME TO ME, ALL OF YOU WHO ARE TIRED [WEARY] AND HAVE HEAVY LOADS [OVERBURDENED; HEAVY-LADEN] AND I WILL GIVE YOU REST. ACCEPT MY TEACHINGS [TAKE MY YOKE UPON YOU] AND LEARN FROM ME, BECAUSE I AM GENTLE AND HUMBLE*

*IN SPIRIT [HEART], AND YOU WILL FIND REST FOR YOUR LIVES [SOULS; JER. 6:16]. THE BURDEN THAT I ASK YOU TO ACCEPT [...BECAUSE MY YOKE] IS EASY; THE LOAD I GIVE YOU TO CARRY [AND MY BURDEN] IS LIGHT."* (Matthew 11:28-30)

*...TO SPEAK NO EVIL ABOUT ANYONE [SLANDER NO ONE], TO LIVE IN PEACE [AVOID FIGHTING], AND TO BE GENTLE AND POLITE [CONSIDERATE; COURTEOUS] TO ALL PEOPLE.* (Titus 3:2)

*BUT THE WISDOM THAT COMES FROM GOD [ABOVE; 3:15] IS FIRST OF ALL PURE, THEN PEACEFUL [PEACE-LOVING], GENTLE [PATIENT; CONSIDERATE], AND EASY TO PLEASE [OR WILLING TO YIELD; OR OPEN TO REASON]. THIS WISDOM IS ALWAYS READY TO HELP THOSE WHO ARE TROUBLED AND TO DO GOOD FOR OTHERS [FULL OF MERCY AND GOOD FRUITS]. IT IS ALWAYS FAIR [IMPARTIAL] AND HONEST [SINCERE; UNHYPOCRITICAL]. PEOPLE WHO WORK FOR PEACE IN A PEACEFUL WAY PLANT A GOOD CROP OF RIGHT LIVING [OR PEACEMAKERS WHO SOW WITH PEACE WILL HARVEST A CROP OF JUSTICE/RIGHTEOUSNESS; GAL. 5:22-23].* (James 3:17-18)

Conscientious ministry drags leadership into the twenty-first century and thinks extensively about the way in which we proclaim the Gospel and whether we are saying or using things that "sound Biblical" but do not consider the way our presentation sounds in the ear of someone who is world-weary and finding themselves hurt by the world. Some examples include:

- Rape, sexual assault, domestic violence, and women in general who have been mistreated by men having to hear about things such as "Eve's sin," submission, pleasing men, obeying men, or men as head of the household or priests in their homes.

- Individuals who have been victims of childhood abuse having to hear about honoring their parents or guardians without any context to the statement, whatsoever.

- Someone who is out of work or homeless hearing rhetoric that they are lazy or unwilling to work and should not receive government assistance in their time of need.

- Single parents hearing that they have somehow damaged their children and their children will be a problem forever, no matter how hard they try.

- Someone who has recently lost their parents or who doesn't have a traditional family structure having to deal with holiday messages about family, mothers, fathers, or extended family.

- Lesbian, gay, bisexual, transgender, and queer individuals having to hear derogatory remarks about sexual orientation or gender identity, spoken of as if God hates them and there is no place or right for them in the church.

- Parents, spouses, friends, and family members who know someone who was killed or brutalized by police or other authority figures, having to hear about authority and submitting to civil authorities.

- Someone who has been hurt at church or abused by a leader having to hear about leadership in a harsh and unrelenting way and told to obey a leader unconditionally.

- Someone who is divorced hearing about how "God hates divorce" and things that suggest divorced people will never make it into heaven.

- An infertile couple having to hear that they are unable to have children due to a "curse" or sin on their lives.

*Spiritual beauty and freedom from the Spirit*

- Someone with anxiety disorders having to hear that fear is a "sin" and that they can just stop being afraid with enough faith.

There are a multitude of problems in our world that don't' seem to have easy solutions or remedies. They seem to go on and on, from generation to generation, and generation after generation, we don't consider the deep hurts and feelings these people may experience. We go on and preach on through politics, through the perspectives we have about these things, and through our own personal hurts and lenses, those that don't want to deal with the problems of the world. The problems of the world, however, are exactly why we are here. Jesus does not pull us out of this world because He desires us to remain here and do His work and do it aware of the world around us and how we can best offer the solution, the remedy to whatever its. A spiritual leader may not be a lobbyist or take on causes from a secular perspective, but we should never, ever act like these things don't happen and should never promote teaching that is part of the problem.

If we understand God to be the great "I AM," that means God is with us now, attentive to our issues and pains, just as much as He was in those days. Hiding behind the Bible to hope that something will be different or non-existent isn't forcing us to understand the Bible in our day and time in a way that speaks to the issues and sensitivities that we, as people, have today. Healing and deliverance are foundational to our faith, not by an ancient standard that we cannot apply, but in a way that is relatable and helpful to our day and time.

Every minister of the Gospel has the responsibility to bring God to our day and time, prove that He is living and active, and that He is just as real as He was earlier in history. One of the biggest arguments many have against God is that He doesn't seem relevant or present today; but that argument isn't because people aren't looking for Him. They are coming to us, they are looking for signs that God is real and cares about them, right now. Healing and deliverance is one of the most powerful signs that God transcends time because He dwells outside of it, and that He does, indeed, love us, right now, with all we face in this world.

This is where healing and deliverance begins: it begins when each of us make the decision to minister, live, speak, and function life. We learn from the life of the past; we celebrate the power of testimony; we embrace history; and we live in it now, recognizing what's right in front of us. We embody change. We let God's healing and deliverance change us. We let the love of God make us aware of the need to reach out to others. Gifts are great, abilities are strong, but being a living testimony is the best evidence we have that God is still real and here, right now.

Let God heal your hurts, your biases, your fears, your areas where you are bound and captive by someone else, so you can be that agent who helps someone else get free. Take that first step to practice what you preach, and transform your own life, today.

## **Chapter 15 Assignments**

- List some specific steps you can take through your own ministry work to help people heal in specific areas.
- Looking over the concept of conscientious ministry, write an essay (5-8 sentences) on ways you can incorporate different aspects of awareness into your ministry work, to reach and impact new demographics.

# - REFERENCES -

Chapter 1 References

[1] "Kabbalistic Angelic Hierarchy." http://www.esoteric-school.org/esoteric-encyclopedia/51-angelic-hierarchy.html. Accessed April 4, 2017.
[2] Hopler, Whitney. "Chayot HaKodesh Angels." https://www.thoughtco.com/chayot-ha-kodesh-angels-123902 Accessed April 4, 2017.
[3] Hopler, Whitney. "Ophanim Angels." https://www.thoughtco.com/what-are-ophanim-angels-123917. Accessed April 4, 2017.
[4] Hopler, Whitney. "Angel Types In Judaism." https://www.thoughtco.com/angel-types-in-judaism-123835. Accessed April 4, 2017.
[5] Ibid.
[6] Ibid.
[7] Ibid.
[8] Ibid.
[9] Ibid.
[10] Ibid.
[11] "Kabbalistic Angelic Hierarchy." http://www.esoteric-school.org/esoteric-encyclopedia/51-angelic-hierarchy.html. Accessed April 4, 2017.
[12] "Nine Choirs Of Angels, The." http://www.catholic.org/saints/angels/angelchoir.php. Accessed April 4, 2017.
[13] Ibid.
[14] Ibid.
[15] Ibid.
[16] Ibid.
[17] Ibid.
[18] Ibid.
[19] Ibid.

[20] Ibid.
[21] The Book of Jubilees 1:26. http://www.pseudepigrapha.com/jubilees/1.htm. Accessed April 4, 2017.
[22] The Book of Jubilees 2:1. http://www.pseudepigrapha.com/jubilees/2.htm. Accessed April 4. 2017.
[23] 1 Enoch 60:9-23. http://www.pseudepigrapha.com/pseudepigrapha/1enoch_all.html#RL_Ch60. Accessed April 4, 2017.
[24] Ibid.
[25] Column 10:9-16. http://www.bibliotecapleyades.net/sitchin/guerradioses/guerradioses02a.htm. Accessed April 4, 2017.
[26] "Book of Tobit." https://en.wikipedia.org/wiki/Book_of_Tobit. Accessed April 5, 2017.
[27] "Assumption of Moses." https://en.wikipedia.org/wiki/Assumption_of_Moses. Accessed April 5, 2017.
[28] "Assumption of Moses Also Known As The Testament Of Moses, The, Chapter 10." http://wesley.nnu.edu/index.php?id=2124. Accessed April 5, 2017.
[29] Apocalypse of Abraham, The. https://en.wikipedia.org/wiki/Apocalypse_of_Abraham. Accessed April 5, 2017.
[30] The Apocalypse of Abraham 10:1-4. Accessed April 5, 2017. http://www.pseudepigrapha.com/pseudepigrapha/Apocalypse_of_Abraham.html
[31] The Apocalypse of Abraham 11:1-3. Accessed April 5, 2017. http://www.pseudepigrapha.com/pseudepigrapha/Apocalypse_of_Abraham.html
[32] The Apocalypse of Abraham 13:1-6. Accessed April 5, 2017. http://www.pseudepigrapha.com/pseudepigrapha/Apocalypse_of_Abraham.html
[33] The Apocalypse of Abraham 15:1-2. Accessed April 5, 2017. http://www.pseudepigrapha.com/pseudepigrapha/Apocalypse_of_Abraham.html. Accessed April 5, 2017.
[34] The Apocalypse of Zephaniah 3:1, 5-9. http://web.archive.org/web/20100330084339/http://userpages.burgoyne.com/bdespain/progress/progzeph.htm. Accessed April 5, 2017.
[35] The Apocalypse of Zephaniah 4:1-7. http://web.archive.org/web/20100330084339/http://userpages.burgoyne.com/bdespain/progress/progzeph.htm. Accessed April 5, 2017.
[36] The Apocalypse of Zephaniah 9:1-3. http://web.archive.org/web/20100330084339/http://userpages.burgoyne.com/bdespain/progress/progzeph.htm. Accessed April 5, 2017.
[37] The Apocalypse of Zephaniah 12:1-8. http://web.archive.org/web/20100330084339/http://userpages.burgoyne.com/bdespain/progress/progzeph.htm. Accessed April 5, 2017.
[38] 2 Baruch 6:1-8:2. http://www.pseudepigrapha.com/pseudepigrapha/2Baruch.html. Accessed April 5, 2017.
[39] 3 Baruch 12:1-17:4. http://www.pseudepigrapha.com/pseudepigrapha/3Baruch.html. Accessed April 5, 2017.
[40] Gospel of Bartholomew 3:6-7. http://gnosis.org/library/gosbart.htm. Accessed April 9, 2017.
[41] Gospel of Bartholomew 4:28-35. http://gnosis.org/library/gosbart.htm. Accessed April 9, 2017.
[42] The Epistle of the Apostles 13-14. http://www.interfaith.org/christianity/apocrypha-epistle-apostles/. Accessed April 9, 2017.
[43] Sibylline Oracles 2:280-300. http://www.interfaith.org/christianity/apocrypha-pseudo-sibylline-oracles-2/. Accessed April 9, 2017.
[44] Sibylline Oracles 3:1-4. http://www.interfaith.org/christianity/apocrypha-pseudo-sibylline-oracles-3/. Accessed April 9, 2017.
[45] The Apocalypse of Paul 8-10. http://www.interfaith.org/christianity/apocrypha-apocalypse-of-paul-1/. Accessed April 9, 2017.
[46] The Apocalypse of Paul 8-10. http://www.interfaith.org/christianity/apocrypha-apocalypse-of-

paul-1/. Accessed April 9, 2017.
[47]The Shepherd of Hermas Mandate 11 4[47]:6-[49]:3. http://www.interfaith.org/christianity/apocrypha-shepherd-of-hermas/. Accessed April 9. 2017.
[48]Shepherd of Hermas Parable 5 5[58]:1-5[58]3. http://www.interfaith.org/christianity/apocrypha-shepherd-of-hermas/. Accessed April 9. 2017.
[49]The Apocryphal Revelation of Saint John the Theologian. http://www.interfaith.org/christianity/apocrypha-revelation-of-john/. Accessed April 9, 2017.

Chapter 2 References

[1]2 Enoch 29:3-4. http://www.pseudepigrapha.com/pseudepigrapha/enochs2.htm#Ch29. Accessed April 6, 2017.
[2]2 Enoch 31:4-5. http://www.pseudepigrapha.com/pseudepigrapha/enochs2.htm#Ch29. Accessed April 6, 2017.
[3]1 Enoch 22:1-14. http://www.sacred-texts.com/bib/boe/boe025.htm. Accessed April 6, 2017.
[4]Apocalypse of Zephaniah 11:1-6. http://web.archive.org/web/20100330084339/http://userpages.burgoyne.com/bdespain/progress/progzeph.htm#Sc). Accessed April 7, 2017.
[5]1 Enoch 21:1-10. http://www.sacred-texts.com/bib/boe/boe024.htm. Accessed April 7, 2017.
[6]The Apocalypse of Peter, Verses 20-33. http://www.earlychristianwritings.com/text/apocalypsepeter-roberts.html) Accessed April 8, 2017.
[7]"Hell." https://en.wikipedia.org/wiki/Hell. Accessed April 9, 2017.
[8]"The Hierarchy and Orders of Demons." http://www.angelfire.com/empire/serpentis666/Orders.html. Accessed April 9, 2017.
[9]Ibid.
[10]Ibid.
[11]"Lower Orders of Demons." http://www.angelfire.com/empire/serpentis666/Lesser_Demons.html. Accessed April 9, 2017.
[12]"Hierarchy of Demons." http://www.hierarchystructure.com/hierarchy-of-demons/. Accessed April 7, 2017.
[13]Ibid.
[14]Ibid.
[15]"Classification of Demons." https://en.wikipedia.org/wiki/Classification_of_demons. Accessed April 7, 2017.
[16]Ibid.
[17]Ibid.
[18]Ibid.
[19]Ibid.
[20]Ibid.
[21]Ibid.
[22]Ibid.
[23]"Lilith." https://encyclopediasatanica.wordpress.com/2013/08/12/references-to-demons-in-the-apocryphal-texts/. Accessed April 7, 2017.
[24]The Book Of Jubilees 10:1-3. http://www.pseudepigrapha.com/jubilees/10.htm. Accessed April 7, 2017.
[25]The Book of Jubilees 10:8-11. http://www.pseudepigrapha.com/jubilees/10.htm. Accessed April 7, 2017.
[26]The Book of Jubilees 11:10-11. http://www.pseudepigrapha.com/jubilees/11.htm. Accessed April 7, 2017.
[27]The Book of Jubilees 17:16. http://www.pseudepigrapha.com/jubilees/17.htm. Accessed April 7, 2017.

[28] The Book of Jubilees 48:1-2. http://www.pseudepigrapha.com/jubilees/48.htm, Accessed April 7, 2017.
[29] The Book of Jubilees 48:15-16. http://www.pseudepigrapha.com/jubilees/48.htm. Accessed April 7, 2017.
[30] The Book of Jubilees 1:19. http://www.pseudepigrapha.com/jubilees/1.htm. Accessed April 7, 2017.
[31] 1 Enoch 15:1-11. http://www.sacred-texts.com/bib/boe/boe018.htm. Accessed April 7, 2017.
[32] 1 Enoch 8:1-9. http://book-ofenoch.com/chapter-8/. Accessed April 7, 2017.
[33] 1 Enoch 9:5-14. http://book-ofenoch.com/chapter-9/. Accessed April 7, 2017.
[34] 1 Enoch 10:3-9. http://book-ofenoch.com/chapter-10/. Accessed April 8, 2017.
[35] 3 Enoch 5, Introduction. https://archive.org/stream/HebrewBookOfEnochenoch3/BookOfEnoch3_djvu.txt. Accessed April 8, 2017.
[36] The Apocalypse of Abraham 13:1-7. http://www.pseudepigrapha.com/pseudepigrapha/Apocalypse_of_Abraham.html. Accessed April 8, 2017.
[37] The Apocalypse of Abraham 14:1-4. http://www.pseudepigrapha.com/pseudepigrapha/Apocalypse_of_Abraham.html. Accessed April 8, 2017.
[38] The Curses of Belial, Column 2:1-11. https://www.bibliotecapleyades.net/scrolls_deadsea/uncovered/uncovered07.htm, Accessed April 8, 2017.
[39] Song of The Sage, 4Q510-511. http://www.scoop.it/t/consumption/p/2888157752/2012/10/05/the-dead-sea-scrolls-revised-edition-songs-of-sages-lilith. Accessed April 8, 2017.
[40] The War Scroll Column 1:1,5-7. http://www.bibliotecapleyades.net/sitchin/guerradioses/guerradioses02a.htm. Accessed April 8, 2017.
[41] Ibid, Column 15:13-17.
[42] Ibid, Column 18:3.
[43] The Damascus Document 6:7-12. http://www.pseudepigrapha.com/pseudepigrapha/zadokite.html. Accessed April 8, 2017.
[44] The War With the Sons of Light with the Sons of Darkness Column 13:9-12. http://www.bibliotecapleyades.net/sitchin/guerradioses/guerradioses02a.htm. Accessed April 9, 2017.
[45] The War With the Sons of Light with the Sons of Darkness Column 16:11-14. http://www.bibliotecapleyades.net/sitchin/guerradioses/guerradioses02a.htm. Accessed April 9, 2017.
[46] The Damascus Document 2:4-7. http://www.pseudepigrapha.com/pseudepigrapha/zadokite.html. Accessed April 9, 2017.
[47] Gospel of Bartholomew 1:8-18. http://gnosis.org/library/gosbart.htm. Accessed April 9, 2017.
[48] Gospel of Bartholomew 4:10-19. Ibid.
[49] Gospel of Bartholomew 4:51-57. Ibid.
[50] Shepherd of Hermas Mandate 6 2:[36]4-2[36]10. http://www.interfaith.org/christianity/apocrypha-shepherd-of-hermas/. Accessed April 9, 2017.
[51] The Shepherd of Hermas, Mandate 7, 1[37]:1-1[37]4. http://www.interfaith.org/christianity/apocrypha-shepherd-of-hermas/. Accessed April 9, 2017.
[52] Sibylline Oracles 2:195-210. http://www.interfaith.org/christianity/apocrypha-pseudo-sibylline-oracles-2/. Accessed April 9, 2017.
[53] The Apocalypse of Paul. http://www.interfaith.org/christianity/apocrypha-apocalypse-of-paul-1/. Accessed April 9, 2017.
[54] The Acts of Andrew. http://www.interfaith.org/christianity/apocrypha-acts-of-andrew/. Accessed April 9, 2017.

[55] The Martyrdom of Bartholomew. http://www.interfaith.org/christianity/apocrypha-martyrdom-of-bartholomew/. Accessed April 9, 2017.
[56] The Gospel of Nicodemus 18:1-14. http://www.interfaith.org/christianity/apocrypha-nicodemus/. Accessed April 9, 2017.

Chapter 3 References

[1] *Strong's Exhaustive Concordance of the Bible*, #5315
[2] Ibid., #5590
[3] Ibid., #7308
[4] Ibid., #4151
[5] Ibid., #8163
[6] Ibid., #7700
[7] 1 Enoch 15:1-11. http://www.sacred-texts.com/bib/boe/boe018.htm. Accessed April 12, 2017.
[8] 1 Enoch 20:1-7. http://book-ofenoch.com/chapter-20/. Accessed April 11, 2017
[9] Marino, Lee Ann B. *Introduction To Missions*. Chapter 10: "Detecting Spiritual Strongholds And Spiritual Pitfalls In Missions." Cary, North Carolina: Apostolic University Press, 2017. Page 228-229.
[10] The Book of Jubilees 10:3. http://www.pseudepigrapha.com/jubilees/10.htm Accessed April 16, 2017.
[11] The Book of Jubilees 10:8-9. Ibid.
[12] The Apocryphal Revelation of Saint John The Theologian. http://www.interfaith.org/christianity/apocrypha-revelation-of-john/. Accessed April 14, 2017.
[13] "Boogeyman." https://en.wikipedia.org/wiki/Bogeyman. Accessed June 22, 2017.
[14] "Cambion." https://en.wikipedia.org/wiki/Cambion. Accessed April 14, 2017.
[15] "Classification of Demons." https://en.wikipedia.org/wiki/Classification_of_demons. Accessed April 14, 2017.
[16] "Drude." https://en.wikipedia.org/wiki/Drude. Accessed April 14, 2017.
[17] "Dwarf." https://en.wikipedia.org/wiki/Dwarf_(mythology). Accessed April 14, 2017.
[18] "Elf." https://en.wikipedia.org/wiki/Elf. Accessed April 14, 2017.
[19] "Fairy." https://en.wikipedia.org/wiki/Fairy. Accessed April 14, 2017.
[20] "Pixie." https://en.wikipedia.org/wiki/Pixie. Accessed April 14, 2017.
[21] "Ghost." https://en.wikipedia.org/wiki/Ghost. Accessed April 14, 2017.
[22] "Ghoul." https://en.wikipedia.org/wiki/Ghoul. Accessed April 14. 2017.
[23] "Gnome." https://en.wikipedia.org/wiki/Gnome. Accessed April 14, 2017.
[24] "Goblin." https://en.wikipedia.org/wiki/Goblin. Accessed April 14, 2017.
[25] "Gremlin." https://en.wikipedia.org/wiki/Gremlin. Accessed April 14, 2017.
[26] "Imp." https://en.wikipedia.org/wiki/Imp, Accessed April 14, 2017.
[27] "Incubus." https://en.wikipedia.org/wiki/Incubus. Accessed April 14, 2017.
[28] "Succubus." https://en.wikipedia.org/wiki/Succubus. Accessed April 14, 2017.
[29] "Revenant." https://en.wikipedia.org/wiki/Revenant. Accessed April 14, 2017.
[30] "Sprite." https://en.wikipedia.org/wiki/Sprite_(entity). Accessed April 15, 2017.
[31] "Troll." https://en.wikipedia.org/wiki/Troll. Accessed April 15, 2017.
[32] "Vampire." https://en.wikipedia.org/wiki/Vampire. Accessed April 15, 2017.
[33] "Werewolf." https://en.wikipedia.org/wiki/Werewolf. Accessed April 15, 2017.
[34] "Zombie." https://en.wikipedia.org/wiki/Zombie. Accessed April 15, 2017.

Chapter 4 References

[1] "Ahriman." http://www.deliriumsrealm.com/ahriman/. Accessed April 25, 2017.
[2] "Zoroastrian Beliefs." http://www.religionfacts.com/zoroastrianism/beliefs. Accessed April 25, 2017.

[3] "Daeva." https://en.wikipedia.org/wiki/Daeva. Accessed April 26, 2017.
[4] "Hinduism." https://en.wikipedia.org/wiki/Hinduism. Accessed April 26, 2017.
[5] "Demons." http://www.freebsd.nfo.sk/hinduism/demons.htm. Accessed April 26, 2017.
[6] "Buddhism." https://en.wikipedia.org/wiki/Buddhism. Accessed April 27, 2017.
[7] Crawford, Benna. "Do Buddhists Believe in Demons?" http://peopleof.oureverydaylife.com/buddhists-believe-demons-5744.html. Accessed April 27, 2017.
[8] Carter, Julie. "Demons in Buddhism." http://national-paranormal-society.org/demons-in-buddhism/. Accessed April 27, 2017.
[9] "Islam." https://en.wikipedia.org/wiki/Islam. Accessed April 27, 2017.
[10] "Imam." https://en.wikipedia.org/wiki/Iman_(concept)#The_six_articles_of_the_Islamic_faith. Accessed April 27, 2017.
[11] "Belief In Angels." http://www.islamicstudiesresources.com/uploads/1/9/8/1/19819855/belief-in-angels_aminormemoir.pdf. Accessed April 27, 2017.
[12] Huda. "Angels in Islam." https://www.thoughtco.com/angels-in-islam-2004030. Accessed April 27, 2017.
[13] Green, John. "Demons in the Muslim Culture." http://peopleof.oureverydaylife.com/demons-muslim-culture-7056.html. Accessed April 27, 2017.
[14] Kuruvilla, Carol. "5 Things People Believe About Demons, Exorcisms And The Spirit World." http://www.huffingtonpost.com/2014/10/30/demons-exorcism-spirit-world_n_6064260.html. Accessed April 27, 2017.
[15] "Indigenous Religions." http://www.encyclopedia.com/religion/encyclopedias-almanacs-transcripts-and-maps/indigenous-religions. Accessed April 27, 2017.
[16] "Gnostic World View, The: A Brief Summary Of Gnosticism." http://www.gnosis.org/gnintro.htm. Accessed April 28, 2017.
[17] "Archon (Gnosticism)." https://en.wikipedia.org/wiki/Archon_(Gnosticism). Accessed April 28, 2017.
[18] "Do Mormons Believe in Demons?" http://www.allaboutmormons.com/Questions/mormons_demons_20_born_raised_ENG_223.php. Accessed April 29, 2017.
[19] Zimmerman, Ray. "Evil Spirits, Angels, Psychic Powers, and Aliens." http://bahaiteachings.org/evil-spirits-angels-psychic-powers-and-aliens. Accessed April 29, 2017.
[20] "Mythology of the Ancient World." http://www.ancient-mythology.com/. Accessed April 29, 2017.
[21] "Ancient Mesopotamian Religion." https://en.wikipedia.org/wiki/Ancient_Mesopotamian_religion. Accessed April 29, 2017.
[22] "Finnish Mythology." https://en.wikipedia.org/wiki/Finnish_mythology. Accessed April 29, 2017.
[23] "Hungarian Mythology." https://en.wikipedia.org/wiki/Hungarian_mythology. Accessed April 29, 2017.
[24] "List of Slavic Mythological Figures." https://en.wikipedia.org/wiki/List_of_Slavic_mythological_figures. Accessed April 29, 2017.
[25] "Category: Egyptian Demons." https://en.wikipedia.org/wiki/Category:Egyptian_demons Accessed August 22, 2025.
[26] "Category: Irish Demons." https://en.wikipedia.org/wiki/Category:Irish_demons. Accessed August 22, 2025.
[27] "List of Greek Mythological Creatures." https://en.wikipedia.org/wiki/List_of_Greek_mythological_creatures. Accessed August 22, 2025.
[28] "Norse Demons." https://en.wikipedia.org/wiki/Category:Norse_demons. Accessed August 22, 2025.
[29] "Manes." https://en.wikipedia.org/wiki/Manes. Accessed August 22, 2025.
[30] "Yokai." https://en.wikipedia.org/wiki/Y%C5%8Dkai. Accessed August 22, 2025.
"Xibalba." https://en.wikipedia.org/wiki/Xibalba. Accessed August 22, 2025.

Chapter 5 References

[1] "Theosophy." https://www.britannica.com/topic/theosophy . Accessed May 4, 2017.
[2] "Divination, Magic & Occultic Activity In The Bible."http://www.religioustolerance.org/divin_bibl.htm. Accessed May 17, 2017.
[3] "Key of Solomon, The." https://en.wikipedia.org/wiki/Key_of_Solomon. Accessed May 17, 2017.
[4] "Lesser Key of Solomon, The." https://en.wikipedia.org/wiki/Lesser_Key_of_Solomon. Accessed May 17, 2017.
[5] "Hermetic Occult Books." http://www.occult-mysteries.org/hermetic-occult-books.html. Accessed May 17, 2017.
[6] "Tibetan Book of the Dead, The." https://www.summum.us/mummification/tbotd/. Accessed Mary 17, 2017.
[7] "Hermetic Occult Books." http://www.occult-mysteries.org/hermetic-occult-books.html. Accessed May 17, 2017.
[8] "La Clef De La Magie Noire." https://archive.org/details/LaClefDeLaMagieNoire. Accessed May 17, 2017.
[9] Ryan, Charles J. "What Is Theosophy: A General View For Inquirers." http://www.theosociety.org/pasadena/gdpmanu/ryan-wh/wit-hp.htm. Accessed May 5, 2015.
[10] "Thelema." http://thelemapedia.org/index.php/Thelema. Accessed May 5, 2017.
[11] "Kabbalah." https://en.wikipedia.org/wiki/Kabbalah. Accessed May 5, 2017.
[12] Pinson, DovBer. "What is Kabbalah: A Basic Introduction to The Kabbalah." http://www.chabad.org/library/article_cdo/aid/170308/jewish/What-is-Kabbalah.htm. Accessed May 5, 2017.
[13] "Sufism." https://www.britannica.com/topic/Sufism. Accessed May 6, 2017.
[14] "Tantra." https://en.wikipedia.org/wiki/Tantra. Accessed May 6, 2017.
[15] "Monasticism." https://orthodoxwiki.org/Monasticism. Accessed May 6, 2017.
[16] "New Thought." https://www.britannica.com/event/New-Thought. Accessed May 10, 2017.
[17] "Writings of Emanuel Swedenborg, The." http://newchristianbiblestudy.org/swedenborg/. Accessed May 10, 2017.
[18] "New Church, The." https://en.wikipedia.org/wiki/The_New_Church. Accessed May 10, 2017.
[19] "Freemasonry." http://www.newworldencyclopedia.org/entry/Freemasonry. Accessed May 10, 2017.
[20] "Prince Hall Freemasonry." https://en.wikipedia.org/wiki/Prince_Hall_Freemasonry. Accessed May 10, 2017.
[21] "History Of The Shriners." http://www.beashrinernow.com/About/Shriners/History. Accessed May 11, 2017.
[22] "Shriners." https://en.wikipedia.org/wiki/Shriners. Accessed May 11, 2017.
[23] "Order of the Eastern Star." https://en.wikipedia.org/wiki/Order_of_the_Eastern_Star. Accessed May 11, 2017.
[24] "Order of the Amaranth." http://amaranth.org/. Accessed May 11, 2017.
[25] "Order of Amarante." https://en.wikipedia.org/wiki/Amaranten_order. Accessed May 11, 2017.
[26] "White Shrine of Jerusalem." https://supremeshrine.org/. Accessed May 11, 2017.
[27] "Templars." https://www.britannica.com/topic/Templars. Accessed May 11, 2017.
[28] "Templar Spirituality." http://www.knightstemplarorder.org/templar-spirituality/. Accessed May 11, 2017.
[29] "What Is The S.O.O.B.?" http://www.knightstemplar.org/soob/membership.html. Accessed May 11, 2017.
[30] "Who We Are and What We Do." http://www.daughtersofthenile.com/about_who.htm. Accessed May 11, 2017.
[31] "Job's Daughters International." https://en.wikipedia.org/wiki/Job%27s_Daughters_International. Accessed May 11, 2017.

[32] "International Order of the Rainbow For Girls." https://en.wikipedia.org/wiki/International_Order_of_the_Rainbow_for_Girls. Accessed May 11, 2017.
[33] "What Is Rosicrucianism All About?" http://www.straightdope.com/columns/read/2225/what-is-rosicrucianism-all-about. Accessed May 11, 2017.
[34] "Rosicrucianism." https://en.wikipedia.org/wiki/Rosicrucianism. Accessed May 11, 2017.
[35] "Skull and Bones." https://en.wikipedia.org/wiki/Skull_and_Bones. Accessed May 11, 2017.
[36] "Orange Order." https://en.wikipedia.org/wiki/Orange_Order. Accessed May 11, 2017.
[37] "Damon and Pythias." https://en.wikipedia.org/wiki/Damon_and_Pythias. Accessed May 11, 2017.
[38] "Knights of Pythias." https://en.wikipedia.org/wiki/Knights_of_Pythias. Accessed May 11, 2017.
[39] "Independent Order of Odd Fellows." https://en.wikipedia.org/wiki/Independent_Order_of_Odd_Fellows. Accessed May 15, 2017.
[40] "Knights of Columbus." https://en.wikipedia.org/wiki/Knights_of_Columbus. Accessed May 15, 2017.
[41] "B'nai B'rith." https://en.wikipedia.org/wiki/B%27nai_B%27rith. Accessed May 15, 2017.
[42] "Fraternities and Sororities." https://en.wikipedia.org/wiki/Fraternities_and_sororities. Accessed May 15, 2017.
[43] "Thelema." http://www.thelemapedia.org/index.php/Thelema. Accessed May 15, 2017.
[44] "Ordo Templi Orientis." http://www.thelemapedia.org/index.php/Ordo_Templi_Orientis. Accessed May 15, 2017.
[45] "Hermetic Order of the Golden Dawn." https://en.wikipedia.org/wiki/Hermetic_Order_of_the_Golden_Dawn. Accessed May 15, 2017.
[46] "Cipher Manuscripts." https://en.wikipedia.org/wiki/Cipher_Manuscripts. Accessed May 15, 2017.
[47] "16 Mind-Blowing Facts the Illuminati Don't Want You To Know." http://whatculture.com/history/16-mind-blowing-facts-the-illuminati-dont-want-you-to-know?page=5. Accessed May 16, 2017.
[48] "16 Mind-Blowing Facts the Illuminati Don't Want You To Know." http://whatculture.com/history/16-mind-blowing-facts-the-illuminati-dont-want-you-to-know?page=6. Accessed May 16, 2017.
[49] "Illuminati, The." https://en.wikipedia.org/wiki/Illuminati. Accessed May 16, 2017.
[50] LaVey, Anton. "Nine Satanic Statements, The." http://www.churchofsatan.com/nine-satanic-statements.php. Accessed May 17, 2017.
[51] LaVey, Anton. "Eleven Satanic Rules of the Earth." http://www.churchofsatan.com/eleven-rules-of-earth.php. Accessed May 17, 2017.
[52] LaVey, Anton. "Nine Satanic Sins, The." http://www.churchofsatan.com/nine-satanic-sins.php. Accessed May 17, 2017.
[53] "Black Mass." https://en.wikipedia.org/wiki/Black_Mass. Accessed May 17, 2017.
[54] "Church of Satan." https://en.wikipedia.org/wiki/Church_of_Satan. Accessed May 17, 2017.
[55] "Satanic Holidays." https://en.wikipedia.org/wiki/Satanic_holidays. Accessed May 17, 2017.
[56] Beyer, Catherine. "Occult Symbols." https://www.thoughtco.com/occult-symbols-4123013. Accessed May 17, 2017.
[57] Ibid.
[58] "Shem haMephorash: The Ineffable Name For God In Kabbalistic Traditions." http://www.deliriumsrealm.com/shem-hamephorash/. Accessed May 17, 2017.
[59] Beyer, Catherine. "Elias Levi's Baphomet: The Goat of Mendes." https://www.thoughtco.com/eliphas-levis-baphomet-goat-of-mendes-95993. Accessed May 17, 2017.
[60] "Frequently Confused Symbols: The Pentacle, Pentagram, & The Sigil of Baphomet." http://www.religioustolerance.org/wic_pent.htm. Accessed May 17, 2017.
[61] Beyer, Catherine. "Rosy Cross or Rose Cross, The." https://www.thoughtco.com/the-rosy-cross-or-rose-cross-95997. Accessed May 17, 2017.
[62] "Hamsa Hand Meaning – The Hand of God/Hand of Fatima, The."

https://www.jewishgiftplace.com/Hamsa-Hand-Symbology.html. Accessed May 17, 2017.
[63]"Eye of Horus." https://en.wikipedia.org/wiki/Eye_of_Horus. Accessed May 17, 2017.
[64]"Cross and Crown." https://en.wikipedia.org/wiki/Cross_and_Crown. Accessed May 17, 2017.
[65]"Square and Compass." http://www.masonic-lodge-of-education.com/square-and-compasses.html. Accessed May 17, 2017.
[66]Beyer, Catherine. "Occult Symbols." https://www.thoughtco.com/occult-symbols-4123013. Accessed May 17, 2017.
[67]Pelaia, Ariela. "What Is The Star Of David In Judaism?" https://www.thoughtco.com/star-of-david-2076778. Accessed May 17, 2017.

Chapter 6 References

[1] Enoch 8:1-8:2. http://www.sacred-texts.com/bib/boe/boe012.htm. Accessed July 2, 2017.
[2]"Divination, Magic, & Occultic Activity In The Bible." http://www.religioustolerance.org/divin_bibl.htm. Accessed May 18, 2017.
[3]Rhodes, John Philip. *Wicca Unveiled: The Complete Rituals of Modern Witchcraft*. Glastonbury, Great Britain: Speaking Tree Books, 2000. Pg. 99-103.
[4]Ibid.
[5]Ibid.
[6]Ibid.
[7]Ibid.
[8]Ibid.
[9]Ibid.
[10]Ibid.
[11]"Types of Magic." http://hiddenlegacy.ilona-andrews.com/types-of-magic/. Accessed May 21, 2017.
[12]"Ancestral Magic." http://spellencyclopedia.wikia.com/wiki/Ancestral_Magic. Accessed May 21, 2017.
[13]"Enochian Magic." https://en.wikipedia.org/wiki/Enochian_magic. Accessed May 21, 2017.
[14]Beyer, Catherine. "What is Chaos Magic?" https://www.thoughtco.com/chaos-magic-95940. Accessed May 21, 2017.
[15]"Circle Magic." http://spellencyclopedia.wikia.com/wiki/Circle_Magic. Accessed May 21, 2017.
[16]"Deity Magic." http://spellencyclopedia.wikia.com/wiki/Deity_Magic. Accessed May 21, 2017.
[17]"Renaissance Magic." https://en.wikipedia.org/wiki/Renaissance_magic. Accessed May 21, 2017.
[18]"White Magic." http://spellencyclopedia.wikia.com/wiki/White_Magic. Accessed May 21, 2017.
[19]"Black Magic." http://spellencyclopedia.wikia.com/wiki/Black_Magic. Accessed May 21, 2017.
[20]"Ceremonial Magic." https://en.wikipedia.org/wiki/Ceremonial_magic. Accessed May 21, 2017.
[21]"Traditional Magic." http://spellencyclopedia.wikia.com/wiki/Traditional_Magic. Accessed May 21, 2017.
[22]"Sex Magic." https://en.wikipedia.org/wiki/Sex_magic. Accessed May 21, 2017.
[23]"How To Write A Spell." http://www.wikihow.com/Write-a-Spell. Accessed May 22, 2017.
[24]"Wiccan Spells: Free Wiccan Magic Spells, Rituals, and Incantations." http://www.spelwerx.com/wiccan-spells.html. Accessed May 22, 2017.
[25]Ibid.
[26]Ibid.
[27]"Grimoire." http://www.sacred-texts.com/grim/index.htm. Accessed May 22, 2017.
[28]"Divination." http://www.mysticscripts.com/divination/. Accessed May 22, 2017.
[29]"Methods of Divination." https://en.wikipedia.org/wiki/Methods_of_divination. Accessed May 22, 2017.
[30]"Tarot." https://en.wikipedia.org/wiki/Tarot. Accessed May 22, 2017.
[31]"Scrying." https://en.wikipedia.org/wiki/Scrying. Accessed May 22, 2017.
[32]"I Ching." https://en.wikipedia.org/wiki/I_Ching. Accessed May 22, 2017.

[33] "Number Symbolism." https://www.britannica.com/topic/number-symbolism#toc248158. Accessed May 23, 2017.
[34] "Biblical Numerology." https://en.wikipedia.org/wiki/Biblical_numerology. Accessed May 23, 2017.
[35] "Gematria." https://en.wikipedia.org/wiki/Gematria. Accessed May 23, 2017.
[36] "Horoscope." https://en.wikipedia.org/wiki/Horoscope. Accessed May 23, 2017.
[37] "Sun Sign Astrology." https://en.wikipedia.org/wiki/Sun_sign_astrology. Accessed May 23, 2017.
[38] "Shamanism." https://en.wikipedia.org/wiki/Shamanism. Accessed May 23, 2017.
[39] "Necromancy." https://en.wikipedia.org/wiki/Necromancy. Accessed May 23, 2017.
[40] "Ouija." https://en.wikipedia.org/wiki/Ouija. Accessed May 23, 2017.
[41] "Psychic." https://en.wikipedia.org/wiki/Psychic. Accessed May 22, 2017.
[42] "Psychic Reading." https://en.wikipedia.org/wiki/Psychic_reading. Accessed May 22, 2017.

Chapter 7 References

[1] "Superstition." https://en.wikipedia.org/wiki/Superstition. Accessed May 24, 2017.
[2] "Amulet." https://en.wikipedia.org/wiki/Amulet. Accessed May 24, 2017.
[3] "Good Luck Charm." https://en.wikipedia.org/wiki/Good_luck_charm. Accessed May 24, 2017.
[4] "Talisman." https://en.wikipedia.org/wiki/Talisman. Accessed May 24, 2017.
[5] Tchi, Rodika. "What Is Feng Shui?" https://www.thespruce.com/what-is-feng-shui-1275060. Accessed May 24, 2017.
[6] Tchi, Rodika. "How Do I Take the Right Compass Reading?" https://www.thespruce.com/how-do-i-take-the-right-compass-reading-1274516. Accessed May 24, 2017.

[7] "Household Deity." https://en.wikipedia.org/wiki/Household_deity. Accessed May 25, 2017.
[8] Ibid.
[9] Radford, Benjamin. "Evil Eye, The: Meaning Of The Curse & Protection Against It." http://www.livescience.com/40633-evil-eye.html. Accessed May 24, 2017.
[10] "Evil Eye." https://en.wikipedia.org/wiki/Evil_eye. Accessed May 24, 2017.
[11] Grauschopf, Sandra. "13 Lucky Charms to Motivate and Inspire You." https://www.thebalance.com/lucky-charms-to-attract-good-luck-895277. Accessed May 25, 2017.
[12] "List of Lucky Symbols." https://en.wikipedia.org/wiki/List_of_lucky_symbols. Accessed May 25, 2017.
[13] Ibid.
[14] Grauschopf, Sandra. "13 Lucky Charms to Motivate and Inspire You." https://www.thebalance.com/lucky-charms-to-attract-good-luck-895277. Accessed May 25, 2017.
[15] "Little Barn Star History, A." http://www.metalbarnstars.com/MetalBarnStar.aspx. Accessed May 25, 2017.
[16] "Coins." http://goodlucksymbols.com/coins/. Accessed May 25, 2017.
[17] Grauschopf, Sandra. "13 Lucky Charms to Motivate and Inspire You." https://www.thebalance.com/lucky-charms-to-attract-good-luck-895277. Accessed May 25, 2017.
[18] "Horseshoe." https://en.wikipedia.org/wiki/Horseshoe. Accessed May 25, 2017.
[19] "List of Lucky Symbols." https://en.wikipedia.org/wiki/List_of_lucky_symbols. Accessed May 25, 2017.
[20] Ibid.
[21] Grauschopf, Sandra. "13 Lucky Charms to Motivate and Inspire You." https://www.thebalance.com/lucky-charms-to-attract-good-luck-895277. Accessed May 25, 2017.
[22] Ibid.
[23] Tchi, Rodika. "Jade Meaning – Ancient Strength And Serenity." https://www.thespruce.com/jade-meaning-ancient-strength-and-serenity-1274373. Accessed May 25, 2017.
[24] "Ladybug Symbolism." http://goodlucksymbols.com/ladybug-symbolism/. Accessed May 25, 2017.

[25] "Maneki-Neko." https://en.wikipedia.org/wiki/Maneki-neko. Accessed May 25, 2017.
[26] "Dead Lucky! What Germans Consider Lucky Charms." https://www.goethe.de/en/kul/mol/20395873.html. Accessed May 25, 2017.
[27] Grauschopf, Sandra. "13 Lucky Charms to Motivate and Inspire You." https://www.thebalance.com/lucky-charms-to-attract-good-luck-895277. Accessed May 25, 2017.
[28] Adams, Bryan. "Wishbone Tradition, The – The Lucky Break." http://www.aaepa.com/2010/11/wishbone-traditionthe-lucky-break/. Accessed May 25, 2017.
[29] "Sarimanok." https://en.wikipedia.org/wiki/Sarimanok. Accessed May 25, 2017.
[30] "Elephants." http://goodlucksymbols.com/elephants/. Accessed May 25, 2017.
[37] "Ladder Superstition." http://psychiclibrary.com/beyondBooks/ladder-superstition/. Accessed May 26, 2017.
[38] Dove, Laurie L. "Why Is It Bad Luck To Break A Mirror?" http://people.howstuffworks.com/why-is-it-bad-luck-to-break-mirror.htm. Accessed May 26, 2017.
[39] "Are There Dark Origins Behind Step On A Crack And Break Your Mother's Back?" http://www.smartalecksguide.com/2011/09/are-there-dark-origins-behind-step-on.html. Accessed May 26, 2017.
[40] "Shoes On A Table." https://en.wikipedia.org/wiki/Shoes_on_a_table. Accessed May 26, 2017.
[41] "Rule Of Three." https://en.wikipedia.org/wiki/Rule_of_three_(writing). Accessed May 26, 2017.
[42] "Why Is Giving A Clock As A gift Unlucky?" http://www.cantonese.sheik.co.uk/phorum/read.php?1,65310. Accessed May 26, 2017.
[43] "Why Shouldn't we Walk On People's Graves?" https://www.quora.com/Why-shouldnt-we-walk-on-peoples-graves. Accessed May 26, 2017.
[44] "Shadows, Portraits, And Reflection Superstitions." http://chestofbooks.com/fairy-tale/Kentucky-Superstitions/Shadows-Portraits-And-Reflection-Superstitions.html. Accessed May 26, 2017.
[45] "Why Is It Bad Luck To Spill Salt?" http://www.wisegeek.com/why-is-it-bad-luck-to-spill-salt.htm#didyouknowout. Accessed May 26, 2017.
[46] "Knife Myths: Giving Knives as a Gift is Bad Luck." https://www.knife-depot.com/blog/knife-myths-giving-knives-as-a-gift-is-bad-luck/. Accessed May 27, 2017.
[47] "Rat Superstitions: Various Superstitions About Rats." http://www.snopes.com/luck/superstition/rats.asp. Accessed May 27, 2017.
[48] "List of Unlucky Symbols." https://en.wikipedia.org/wiki/List_of_unlucky_symbols. Accessed May 27, 2017.
[49] King, Helen. "Menotoxin – When Menstruation Can Kill?" http://www.wondersandmarvels.com/2013/09/menotoxin-when-menstruation-can-kill.html. Accessed May 27, 2017.
[50] "List Of Unlucky Symbols." http://www.wikiwand.com/en/List_of_unlucky_symbols. Accessed May 27, 2017.
[51] "Why Do We Wish On Shooting Stars?" http://hasnulyakin.blogspot.com/2011/06/why-do-we-wish-on-shooting-stars.html. Accessed May 27, 2017.
[52] "Why Do People Thor Salt Over Shoulders?" http://people.howstuffworks.com/why-do-people-throw-salt-over-shoulders.htm
[53] "Why Do People Tell Actors To Break A Leg?" http://www.todayifoundout.com/index.php/2012/11/origin-of-the-phrase-break-a-leg/. Accessed May 27, 2017.

## Chapter 9 References

[1] "Dead Sea Scrolls." https://en.wikipedia.org/wiki/Dead_Sea_Scrolls. Accessed June 2, 2017.
[2] Ibid.
[3] "Legend." http://www.bibliotecapleyades.net/sitchin/guerradioses/guerradioses02a.htm. Accessed June 2, 2017.

[4]Column 1:1-20. Ibid.
[5]Column 2:1-14. Ibid.
[6]Column 2:15-3:11. Ibid.
[7]Column 3:13-4:1-20. Ibid.
[8]Column 5:1-6:6. Ibid.
[9]Column 6:8-20. Ibid.
[10]Column 7:1-7. Ibid.
[11]Column 7:9-8:9. Ibid.
[12]Column 8:10-20. Ibid.
[13]Column 10:1-8. Ibid.
[14]Column 10:8-12:19. Ibid.
[15]Column 12:20-15:3. Ibid.
[16]Column 15:4-18:9. Ibid.
[17]Column 18:10-19:14. Ibid.

Chapter 11 References

[1]"Healing Through The Ages." http://www.healthylifeessex.co.uk/pages/wellbeing/Healing-thro-the-ages.html Accessed June 16, 2017.
[2]Koenig, Harold G. "Medicine And Religion: Twin Healing Traditions." http://catholicexchange.com/medicine-and-religion-twin-healing-traditions. Accessed June 16, 2017.
[3]Ibid.
[4]Ibid.
[5]"Smith Wigglesworth." https://en.wikipedia.org/wiki/Smith_Wigglesworth. Accessed June 16, 2017.
[6]"John G. Lake." https://en.wikipedia.org/wiki/John_G._Lake. Accessed June 16, 2017.
[7]"Faith Healing Ministry of Aimee Semple McPherson." http://www.thegreaternews.com/blog/11/29/2013/faith-healing-ministry-of-aimee-semple-mcpherson. Accessed June 16, 2017.
[8]Barrett, Stephen. "Some Thoughts About Faith Healing." https://www.quackwatch.com/01QuackeryRelatedTopics/faith.html. Accessed June 16, 2017.
[9]Ibid.
[10]Ibid.
[11]Ibid.

Chapter 13 References

[1]Valente, Leandro. "10 Golden Rules TO Professional Ethics In The Workplace." https://www.linkedin.com/pulse/20140831053426-77080879-10-golden-rules-to-professional-ethics-in-the-workplace. Accessed June 23, 2017.
[2]"Mental Health Myths And Facts." https://www.mentalhealth.gov/basics/myths-facts/index.html. Accessed June 26, 2017.
[3]"Nationwide Trends." https://www.drugabuse.gov/publications/drugfacts/nationwide-trends. Accessed June 26, 2017.
"Facts And Statistics." https://www.nsopw.gov/en-US/Education/FactsStatistics?AspxAutoDetectCookieSupport=1. Accessed June 27, 2017.
[5]"Statistics About Sexual Violence." http://www.nsvrc.org/sites/default/files/publications_nsvrc_factsheet_media-packet_statistics-about-sexual-violence_0.pdf. Accessed June 27, 2017.
[6]Ibid.
[7]Ibid.

[8] Ibid.
[9] Ibid.
[10] Ibid.
[11] Ibid.
[12] "National Statistics." http://www.ncadv.org/learn-more/statistics. Accessed June 27, 2017.
[13] Ibid.
[14] Ibid.
[15] Ibid.

## - ABOUT THE AUTHOR -
### Dr. Lee Ann B. Marino, Ph.D., D.Min., D.D.

**Dr. Lee Ann B. Marino, Ph.D., D.Min., D.D.** (she/her) is "everyone's favorite theologian" leading Gen X, Millennials, and Gen Z with expertise in leadership training, queer and feminist theology, general religion, and apostolic theology. She has served in ministry since 1998 and was ordained as a pastor in 2002 and an apostle in 2010. She founded what is now Sanctuary Apostolic Fellowship Empowerment (SAFE) Ministries in 2004. Under her ministry heading Dr. Marino is founder and Overseer of Sanctuary International Fellowship Tabernacle (SIFT) (the original home of National Coming Out Sunday) and The Sanctuary Network, and Chancellor of Apostolic Covenant Theological Seminary (ACTS).

Affectionately nicknamed "the Spitfire," Dr. Marino has spent over two decades as an "apostle, preacher, and teacher" (2 Timothy 1:11), exercising her personal mandate to become "all things to all people" (1 Corinthians 9:22). Her embrace of spiritual issues (both technical and intimate) has found its home among both seekers and believers, those who desire spiritual answers to today's issues.

Dr. Marino has preached throughout the United States, Puerto Rico, and Europe in hundreds of religious services and experiences throughout the years. A history maker in her own right, she has spent over two decades in advocacy, education, and work for and within minority spiritual communities (including African American, Hispanic, and LGBTQ+). She has also served as the first woman on all-male synods, councils, and panels, as well as the first preacher or speaker welcomed of a different race, sexual orientation, or identity among diverse communities. Today, Dr. Marino's work extends to over 150 countries as she hosts the popular *Kingdom Now* podcast, which is in the top 20 percentile of all podcasts worldwide. She is also the author of over 35 books and the popular Patheos column, *Leadership on Fire*. To date, she has had five bestselling titles within their subject matter: *Understanding Demonology, Spiritual Warfare, Healing, and Deliverance: A Manual for the Christian Minister*; *Ministry School Boot Camp: Training for Helps Ministries, Appointments, and Beyond*; *Discovering Intimacy: A Journey Through the Song of Solomon*; *Fruit of the Vine: Study and Commentary on the Fruit of the Spirit*; and *Ministering to LGBTQ+ (and Those Who Love Them): A Primer for Queer Theology* (and its accompanying workbook).

As a public icon and social media influencer, Dr. Marino advocates healthy body image (curvy/full-figured), representation as a demisexual/aromantic, and albinism awareness as a model. Known to those she works with, she is a spiritual mom, teacher, leader, professor, confidant, and friend. She continues to transform, receiving new teaching, revelation, and insight in this thing we call "ministry." Through years of spiritual growth and maturity, Dr. Marino stands as herself, here to present what God has given to her for any who have an ear to hear.

For more information, visit her website at kingdompowernow.org.

www.ingramcontent.com/pod-product-compliance
Lightning Source LLC
Chambersburg PA
CBHW080721230426
43665CB00020B/2569